Hans Claude Hamilton

Complete chronological index to the pictorial history of England

From the earliest times down to 1815

Hans Claude Hamilton

Complete chronological index to the pictorial history of England
From the earliest times down to 1815

ISBN/EAN: 9783337204181

Printed in Europe, USA, Canada, Australia, Japan

Cover: Foto ©ninafisch / pixelio.de

More available books at **www.hansebooks.com**

COMPLETE
CHRONOLOGICAL INDEX

TO THE

PICTORIAL
HISTORY OF ENGLAND

STANDARD EDITION

FROM THE EARLIEST TIMES DOWN TO 1815

BASED ON THAT PREPARED BY H. C. HAMILTON, ESQ., OF STATE-PAPER OFFICE

W. & R. CHAMBERS
LONDON AND EDINBURGH
1860

CHRONOLOGICAL INDEX

TO THE

PICTORIAL HISTORY OF ENGLAND.

VOLUME I.

BOOK I.

B.C.		PAGE
55. (Aug. 26.)	Julius Cæsar lands in Britain; gains several battles, and returns the same year to Gaul,	27–30
54.	Julius Cæsar lands a second time in Britain; fights Cassivellaunus; forces the passage of the Thames; takes the capital of Cassivellaunus; appoints a yearly tribute, and again returns to Gaul,	

A.D.		
43.	Aulus Plautius lands in Britain; defeats Caractacus and Togodumnus, and compels some of the tribes to submit. Claudius arrives in Britain, receives the submission of some of the tribes, and returns to Rome after being in the island six months,	30, 39, 40
50.	Ostorius Scapula, propraetor, arrives in Britain; carries on the war nine years; erects forts and lines; defeats the Iceni; captures Caractacus, and sends him to Rome,	40–42
59–61.	Paulinus Suetonius takes Mona (Anglesey). Boadicea defeats the Romans, but is afterwards defeated by Suetonius, and poisons herself,	43, 44
	Agricola completes the conquest of South Britain, and reconquers Mona,	45
80, 81.	Agricola's wall; erects a chain of forts from Solway Firth to the Firths of Clyde and Forth,	45
82.	Agricola subdues the Novantæ, Selgovæ, and Damnii, and clears the south-west of Scotland,	45, 46
83.	Crosses the Firth of Forth and defeats the Caledonians,	46
84.	Again defeats them at the Grampians under Galgacus. Britain discovered to be an island. Agricola recalled to Rome by Domitian,	46, 47
120.	Hadrian arrives in Britain; raises a rampart between the Solway Firth and German Ocean,	47
138.	Lollius Urbicus drives the Caledonians beyond the Clyde and Forth, and there fixes the Roman frontier; erects a rampart on the line of Agricola's forts,	47
183.	The Caledonians lay waste the country between the lines of Agricola and the wall of Hadrian,	49

A.D.		PAGE
207.	Severus lands in South Britain; penetrates into Caledonia; builds a wall parallel with those of Agricola and Hadrian,	49, 50
211.	He marches against the Caledonians, but dies at Eboracum (York). Caracalla yields the ground between the Solway and Tyne and the Firths of Clyde and Forth to the Caledonians,	52
288.	Carausius defeats the Scandinavian and Saxon pirates; is made emperor of Britain, &c. Britain a naval power,	53
297.	He is murdered at Eboracum,	53
337.	The Emperor Constantine the Great dies,	53
367.	The Picts and Scots pillage Augusta (London), and make the inhabitants slaves,	54
382.	Maximus becomes emperor of Britain, Gaul, Spain, and Italy,	54
388.	He is defeated and put to death by the Emperor Theodosius the Great,	54
395.	Theodosius dies, bequeathing the empire of the West to his son Honorius, over whom he appoints Stilicho guardian,	54
403.	The Roman Empire dismembered; part of the troops recalled,	55
411.	Constantine elected emperor of Britain; dies,	55
420.	The Romans finally abandon Britain,	55
428.	Leogaire MacNeil, first Christian king of Ireland, began to reign (Book II.),	223
441.	The Roman party in Britain petition Ætius for aid,	57
449.	Vortigern calls in the aid of the Saxons under Hengist and Horsa, whom he places in the Isle of Thanet,	57, 58

BOOK II.

463.	Leogaire MacNeil, first Christian king of Ireland, dies,	223
	Hengist and Horsa drive out the Picts and Scots; Vortigern marries Rowena,	140, 141
	The Saxons fortify Thanet; Vortigern is deposed, and Vortimer elected king.	

A.D.		PAGE
	The Saxons massacre the Britons at Stonehenge; Hengist founds in Kent the first Saxon kingdom,	141, 142
470.	Riothamus, king of Cornwall and parts of Devonshire, embarks with 12,000 British to assist the Gauls,	142
477.	Ella, the Saxon, with his three sons, lands in Sussex; defeats the Britons, and founds the kingdom of the South Saxons,	142
510.	He dies, having been the first Bretwalda,	145
527–9.	Ercenwine takes possession of Essex, and founds the kingdom of the East Saxons,	142
547.	Ida, the Angle, lands at Flamborough Head, settles between the Tees and the Tyne, and founds the kingdom of Bernicia,	142
568.	Ceawlin, king of Wessex, begins to reign, Ethelbert, king of Kent, becomes Bretwalda,	145 145
617.	Redwald, king of East Anglia, becomes Bretwalda,	145
	The Angles of Bernicia and Deira united, and called Northumbriana,	142
625.	Edwin styled 'Rex Anglorum' (by the pope), becomes king of Northumbria, Penda, prince of Mercia, and Cadwallader, king of North Wales, defeat and slay Edwin,	146 147
634.	Oswald defeats and slays Cadwallader at Hexham. He is acknowledged Bretwalda,	147
642.	He is slain in battle by Penda, and is succeeded in his kingdom by Oswy,	148
647.	The Britons of Cornwall and Devonshire submit to the Anglo-Saxons,	143
652.	Penda ravages Northumberland; Oswy sues for peace; the families of Penda and Oswy intermarry,	148
654.	Penda is defeated and slain near York,	148
655.	Oswy conquers Mercia and assumes the title of Bretwalda,	148
656.	Wulfere made king of Mercia, and becomes Bretwalda of parts south of the Humber,	148
	The yellow plague rages over Britain,	148
670.	Oswy dies, and Egfrid his son succeeds,	149
685.	He is slain in a war with Brude, king of the Picts,	149
737.	Ethelbald, king of Mercia, rules the country south of the Humber, except Wales,	149
743.	Donald, the third king of Ireland, begins to reign, and continues king until 763,	223
748.	The Danes make their first incursion into Ireland,	223
757–794.	Offa, king of Mercia, makes conquest in Sussex, Kent, and Oxfordshire; takes part of Mercia; defeats the Welsh; exacts tribute from the Northumbrians; builds a palace at Tamworth; and defeats the Danes who invade England,	149, 150
791–830.	Constantine and Ungus, Pictish kings, reign in succession in Scotland,	217
795.	Offa the Terrible dies,	150
800.	Beortric, king of Wessex, is poisoned by his wife Eadburgha, who is expelled the kingdom, and the title of queen abolished,	150
	Egbert becomes king of Wessex, defeats the Mercians, and takes possession of their kingdom; establishes sub-kings of Kent and East Anglia,	150
815.	The Danes settle in Armagh,	223

A.D.		PAGE
825.	Egbert subdues Northumbria, and assumes the title of Bretwalda,	151
830.	Ungus, king of Scots, dies,	217
832.	The Danish pirates land, and ravage the Isle of Sheppey,	151
834.	Egbert defeats the Danes and Britons of Cornwall and Devon at Hengsdown Hill,	152
836.	Kenneth II., Pictish king of Scots, begins to reign,	217
	Egbert dies, and is buried at Winchester, Accession of Ethelwulf, who gives Kent, Sussex, and Essex, to Athelstane,	152 152
843.	Kenneth II. acknowledged king of the Picts and Scots,	217
845.	Turgesius, the Dane, proclaimed king of all Ireland,	223
851.	The Danes defeated at Okeley by Ethelwulf and Ethelbald. The Danes are again defeated at Wenbury in Devon,	152
853.	Ethelwulf goes to Rome; Alfred, his son, is anointed king by the pope. Ethelwulf marries Judith, daughter of the king of the Franks, and revives the title of queen,	152, 153
	He returns to England, and divides the kingdom with Ethelbald,	153
857.	Ethelwulf dies,	153
	Ethelbald succeeds, and marries his father's widow,	153
859.	He dies, and is succeeded by Ethelbert, Kenneth MacAlpin, king of Scots, dies at Fortevoit,	153 218
863.	Donald III., successor of Kenneth, dies, and is succeeded by Constantine II.,	218
866, 867.	Ethelbert dies, and is succeeded by Ethelred, who fights nine battles against the Danes,	153, 154
871.	Accession of Alfred the Great,	154
875.	The Danes, under Halfdon, settle in Northumbria,	157
876.	They invade Wessex, land in Dorsetshire, and take Wareham. Alfred beats them at sea, and they evacuate Wessex,	157
	A Saxon fleet destroys the Danish ships at the mouth of the Exe. Guthrun capitulates at Exeter, and gives hostages,	157
878.	Alfred is surprised at Chippenham by the Danes under Guthrun, and is obliged to flee. He takes refuge in Athelney,	158
	Alfred defeats the Danes; Guthrun embraces Christianity; and England is then divided between him and Alfred,	160
	Asser made bishop of Sherborn,	161
879.	Guthrun the Dane baptised. An army of Pagans land and winter at Fulham,	161
882.	Constantine II., king of Scots, is defeated and slain by the Danes,	219
	Alfred gains a naval victory over the Danes,	162
885.	He gains another naval victory,	162
886.	He rebuilds and fortifies London,	162
	The Danes besiege Paris during this and the two following years,	162
893.	Grig and Etha, kings of Scots, dethroned, and Donald IV. succeeds,	219
893–6.	The Danes invade England, and land at Romney Marsh. Another division under Hasting land at Milton. The Danes of England rise in their favour; Alfred defeats them at Farnham; he raises the siege of Exeter. Ethelred, earl of the Mercians, takes Hasting's wife and *his two sons* prisoners, whom	

CHRONOLOGICAL INDEX.

A.D.		PAGE
	Alfred liberates. The Danes are repeatedly routed,	162, 163
901.	Alfred dies at the age of fifty-three, and is buried at Winchester,	167
	Edward and Ethelwald dispute the succession; the latter flies to Danelagh, and becomes king of the Danes,	168
904.	Donald IV., king of Scots, killed in battle near Forteviot, and is succeeded by Constantine III.,	219
905.	Ethelwald is slain in battle by Edward,	168
911.	Edward gains a signal victory over the Danes,	168
912.	Ethelred dies, and leaves the care of Mercia to his widow Ethelfleda; she drives the Danes out of Derby and Leicester; compels many of the tribes to submit, and takes the wife of the Welsh king prisoner,	168
920.	Ethelfleda dies,	168
925.	Accession of Athelstane; reduces all Wales; compels the Welsh to pay tribute; and drives the Cornish out of Devon,	168
934.	North Britain called for the first time Scotland,	218
937.	Athelstane defeats Anlaf the Dane, and Constantine, king of Scots, at Brunnaburgh; assumes the title of King of the Anglo-Saxons,	168
940.	He dies, and is buried at Malmsbury,	170
	Anlaf again invades England; takes a great part; Edmund Atheling regains possession of it,	170
944.	Constantine III., king of Scots, becomes abbot of the Culdees of St Andrews, and Malcolm I. succeeds,	219
	Kenneth is murdered by Fenella at Fettercairn,	220
946.	Edmund Atheling expels Dunmail, king of Cumbria, and gives the country to the king of Scots; puts out the eyes of Dunmail's sons; is stabbed by Leof; dies, and is buried at Glastonbury,	170
	Accession of Edred. He obliges the Danes of England to pay a fine, and incorporates Northumbria with the rest of the kingdom; he dies,	170, 171
948.	The Danes of Ireland embrace Christianity,	223
953.	Malcolm I., king of Scots, is killed,	219
955.	Accession of Edwy; appoints Edgar subregulus of part of England; marries Elgiva; Dunstan insults him, and is banished. The Northumbrians and Mercians rise and declare Edgar king of England north of the Thames,	171, 172
956.	Dunstan returns. Elgiva cruelly treated and murdered,	172
958, 959.	Edwy dies, and is succeeded by Edgar. Dunstan made archbishop of Canterbury,	172
	Edgar is styled Emperor of Albion and King of England,	173
	He causes the extirpation of wolves,	173
961.	Indulf, king of Scots, killed at the battle of the Bauds,	219
964.	Edgar issues a new coinage. Athelwold marries Elfrida; he is murdered; Edgar marries the widow,	173
965.	Duff, king of Scots, is assassinated,	219
973.	Kenneth, king of Scots, defeats Dunwallon, king of Strathclyde, and incorporates his kingdom with the rest of Scotland,	218

A.D.		PAGE
975.	Edgar dies, and is buried at Glastonbury,	173
	Accession of Edward the Martyr,	174
978.	He is murdered near Corfe Castle by an attendant of Elfrida,	175
979.	Ethelred is crowned at Kingston by Dunstan,	175
981.	Southampton is plundered, and its inhabitants taken as slaves by Sweyn, a prince of Denmark, who afterwards takes Chester, London, and attacks many other places,	176
991.	The Danes ravage all between Ipswich and Maldon, and slay Earl Brithnoth,	176
992.	A large fleet is collected in London, but Alfric, the principal commander, goes over to the Danes; the eyes of Elfgar, his son, are put out by Ethelred,	176
993.	A Danish host land, and take Bamborough Castle by storm,	176
994.	Sweyn, king of Denmark, and Olave, king of Norway, ravage the south, and are bought off by the payment of 16,000 pounds of silver,	176
998.	Ethelred prepares a large fleet,	177
1001.	The Danes again land and ravage the whole country; they are paid £24,000 to depart. The Dane-geld becomes permanent,	177
1002.	Ethelred marries Emma, the Flower of Normandy, the sister of Duke Richard,	177
(Nov. 13.)	The Danes throughout England are massacred on the feast of St Brice. Gunhilda, sister of Sweyn, is murdered, Sweyn invades England; plunders Exeter, and ravages Wiltshire,	177, 178
1003.	Malcolm II. of Scotland defeats and slays Kenneth the Grim, at the battle of Monivaird,	221
	The Danes take, plunder, and burn Norwich, and destroy numerous other towns,	178
1004.	The Danes return to the Baltic,	178
1006.	Sweyn again ravages the kingdom, and is paid £36,000 to retire,	178
1008.	A large fleet is built and equipped, but rendered useless by the treachery of the commanders; Wulfnoth takes twenty, and ravages the south coast, and eighty are destroyed by a storm,	178, 179
1009-11.	The Danes, called 'Thurkill's Host,' land in England, and ravage the country; city of Canterbury taken, and the archbishop Alphege murdered,	179
	Thurkill accepts £48,000 and the cession of some counties, and enters the service of Ethelred,	179
	The Danes, under Sweyn, sail up the Humber, and devastate the country; many counties submit, and some of the thanes do homage to him. Ethelred retires to Normandy,	179, 180
1013.	Sweyn is declared 'Full King of England.' He dies suddenly at Gainsborough, and Ethelred returns, but Canute is declared king by his Danish followers,	180
1014.	Brien the Brave, king of Ireland, is killed by the Danes at the battle of Clontarf,	223
1016.	Ethelred dies, and Edmund Ironside is chosen king by the Saxons. England is again divided, Canute reigning over the north, and Edmund the south. Edmund dies suddenly,	180
1017.	Canute succeeds to the whole kingdom of England; murders all the Saxon princes he can, except Edmund and Edward, who are sent to Sweden; he	

A.D.		PAGE
	marries Emma, the widow of Ethelred; engages in foreign wars,	180, 181
1019.	Compels the Cumbrians and Scots to submit,	181
1020.	Eadulf cedes to Malcolm, king of Scots, part of his dominions, called Lodonia,	221
1030.	Canute goes on a pilgrimage to Rome; visits Denmark; and after two years' absence, returns to England,	182, 183
1033.	Malcolm II., king of Scots, dies, and is succeeded by Duncan,	221
1034.	Robert, Duke of Normandy, dies,	192
1035.	Canute dies, and is buried at Winchester, The Wittenagemote declare that the kingdom shall be divided between Harold and Hardicanute,	184
	Hardicanute remains in Denmark; Edward lands, but returns to Normandy,	185
	Harold is declared full king over all the island,	185
1039.	Duncan, king of Scots, is murdered by Macbeth, who succeeds to the throne,	221, 222
1040.	Harold dies, and is buried at Westminster. Hardicanute arrives in England, and is accepted as king,	185
1042.	He dies at a feast, and is buried at Winchester,	186
	Accession of Edward the Confessor,	186
	He marries Editha, the daughter of Earl Godwin,	187
1043.	The Danes, under king Magnus, threaten to invade England, but retire,	188
1044.	Sweyn, second son of Earl Godwin, violates an abbess, and is exiled; he becomes a pirate, and murders his cousin Beorn; he is pardoned, and restored to his government,	189
1051.	Earl Godwin is disgraced; he flies to Flanders; his sons, Harold and Leofwin, go to Ireland,	190, 191
	Edward seizes the jewels and money of his queen Editha, and confines her in the monastery of Wherwell; William, Duke of Normandy, visits England at the king's invitation,	191
1052.	Earl Godwin lands on the south coast; he and his sons, Harold and Leofwin, sail up the Thames, and stop at Southwark; the Normans and French are banished; the queen set at liberty; Wilnot, one of the sons, and Haco, a grandson, of the earl, are given as hostages, and sent to Normandy; Sweyn is banished, and goes on a pilgrimage to Jerusalem; the Saxon authority is rendered supreme,	192, 193
	Earl Godwin dies at Windsor, and is succeeded in his titles and possessions by Harold, his eldest son,	194
1054.	Siward, Earl of Northumbria, defeats Macbeth near Dunsinane,	222
1056.	Macduff and Malcolm defeat and slay (Dec. 5.) Macbeth,	222
1059.	The Earl Algar dies,	194
1063.	Harold, with his brother Tostig, overcome the Welsh, who decapitate their king, Griffith, and send his head to Harold; the Welsh give hostages, and engage to pay the ancient tribute,	195
	Edward the Outlaw arrives in London, dies soon after, and is buried in St Paul's,	195
1064.	Turlogh becomes king of Ireland,	229
1065.	Harold is wrecked on the French coast; is taken prisoner; ransomed by the	

A.D.		PAGE
	Duke of Normandy; Harold swears to aid William to get possession of the English crown after Edward's death,	197-199
	Tostig is expelled from Northumbria, and Morcar is appointed earl in his stead; he flies to Bruges,	200
(Nov. 30.)	Harold arrives in London,	201
1066.	Edward the Confessor dies, and is buried (Jan. 5.) at Westminster,	203
	Harold is proclaimed king; the foreign favourites are dismissed; Duke William demands by his ambassadors the fulfilment of Harold's oath; he refuses; the pope sanctions the invasion of England,	204-206
	Tostig ravages the Isle of Wight and the coast of Lincolnshire; sails up the Humber, but is beaten off; Hardrada, king of Norway, invades England, and with Tostig, defeats Earls Morcar and Edwin, and takes York; Harold fights and beats them at Stamford Bridge, and Hardrada and Tostig are slain,	208, 209
(Sept. 28.)	The Normans land at Bulverhithe, march to Hastings, and form a fortified camp,	210
(Oct. 14.)	The battle of Hastings; Harold is slain,	212-215

BOOK III.

1066.	William takes Dover Castle,	359
	Edgar Atheling is declared king,	360
	William marches to Southwark; ravages the country; Edgar surrenders the crown to him; a fort, afterwards the Tower of London, built by William,	361
	Coronation of William I., surnamed The Conqueror, in Westminster Abbey on Christmas-day,	361, 362
	William I. holds his court at Barking, where he receives Edgar Atheling,	362
1067.	William I. goes over to Normandy, leaving (March.) Odo in command,	364
	Insurrection in Kent; Dover Castle is attacked; Count Eustace of Boulogne comes over, but retires,	365
	Edric rises in Herefordshire; the sons of Harold invade England from Ireland; are repulsed; the English rise in several parts,	365
(Dec. 6.)	William I. embarks at Dieppe for England,	366
	Keeps his Christmas in London; the Saxon laws to be observed,	366
1068.	William I. besieges and takes Exeter, and builds a castle there; he is crowned with his queen Matilda at York, by Archbishop Aldred,	366
	Harold's sons again invade England; are defeated, and seek refuge in Denmark,	366, 367
	William I. extends his conquests to Devonshire, Somersetshire, Gloucestershire, and Oxford, and many fortified cities,	367
	Earls Edwin and Morcar raise the people in the north,	368
	William I. marches and gives them battle on the Ouse, and defeats them; he takes York, and builds a citadel,	369
	Aldred, archbishop of York, curses William,	369
	Edgar Atheling and his family flee to Scotland,	369, 534
	Several Norman followers of William I. abandon England,	370

CHRONOLOGICAL INDEX.

A.D.		PAGE
	He sends his queen back to Normandy,	370
1069.	William I. raises the siege of York, and erects a second castle. Robert de Comine attacks and takes Durham, but he and his followers are destroyed in the night,	370
1072.	William I. advances into Scotland; subdues Malcolm III., who meets and gives hostages to William, and does homage at Abernethy,	373, 534, 536
1078. (Aug.)	The Danes under Osbeorn invade England. They are joined by Edgar Atheling; they besiege York; the Normans burn the city and cathedral, and 3000 of them are destroyed,	371
	William I. retakes York, and Edgar flees again to Scotland,	372
	William I. lays waste Northumbria,	372
	The conquered country partitioned out to Normans,	374, 375
	Earls Edwin and Morcar are admitted to their estates,	375
	William I. founds a new castle at Chester,	375
	Hereward, 'England's Darling,' raises an insurrection. Edwin and Morcar flee from William; the former is killed, and Morcar joins Hereward; the English make a fortified camp in the Isle of Ely; William besieges them for three months; the monks of Ely betray the camp, but Hereward escapes; he afterwards takes the oath of allegiance to William,	376–378
	William I. takes with him an English army, and reduces Maine,	379
	Edgar Atheling goes to Rouen to William,	380
	Some of the Norman barons raise an insurrection at Norwich; William besieges Dol in Brittany unsuccessfully; he returns to England,	381, 382
	Earl Waltheof is executed near Winchester,	382
	The abbot of Croyland is accused of idolatry, and degraded,	382
1077-9.	Robert of Normandy, William's eldest son, claims that province; he is refused; he revolts, and attacks the castle of Rouen; retires to Le Perche; again demands Normandy; is again refused; he goes to the French court; ravages Normandy; William besieges him in the castle of Gerberoy; is wounded by Robert; he abandons the siege; Robert is reconciled to the king,	383, 384
1079.	Malcolm III. makes an inroad into Northumberland,	536
1080.	Robert is sent to command against the Scots, but effects nothing,	536
	Robert finally leaves the king,	384
	Liulf, having been robbed by Gilbert and other retainers of the bishop of Durham, raises an insurrection; Gilbert is put to death; the bishop and his retinue are slain,	384, 385
1082-5.	Odo, bishop of Bayeux, is sent by the king against the insurgents; lays waste the country; Odo aspires to the popedom, and leaves England,	385
	William I. arrests him at the Isle of Wight, and sends him prisoner to Normandy,	386
	Queen Matilda dies,	386
	The Danes again appear upon the coast, but return,	386
	Canute, king of Denmark, prepares, with Olaf, king of Norway, to invade England; but afterwards abandons his purpose,	386, 387
	The Dane-geld again laid on by the king,	387
	William I. encourages commerce,	387
	William and Henry, the king's sons, disagree,	387
	The king lays waste a circumference of ninety miles in Hampshire, to make a hunting-ground,	387
	He enacts the forest-laws,	388
1086.	The king assembles all his vassals at Salisbury, who again take the oath of allegiance, and do homage,	388
	The king then departs for the continent with his sons William and Henry,	388
(July.)	Turlogh, king of Ireland, dies at Kinkora,	458
1087. (July.)	William I. lays siege to Mantes; it is taken, and burned; he receives an injury by his horse stumbling; he is carried to Rouen; removes to the monastery of St Gervas; liberates state prisoners; bequeaths Normandy to Robert, and gives 5000 pounds' weight of silver to Henry,	389
(Sept. 9.)	Death of William the Conqueror,	389
	His body is carried to Caen, and is buried in St Stephen's Church,	390, 391
	Accession of William Rufus,	392
	He imprisons the English, liberated by his father,	392, 393
	The bishop of Bayeux raises an insurrection in England in favour of Robert of Normandy,	394
	The Normans are defeated at sea; Rufus calls the Saxons together; besieges Odo, the bishop, in Pevensey Castle; Pevensey and Rochester castles are surrendered to the king; Odo departs from England, and the insurrection is quelled,	394–6
1089.	Archbishop Lanfranc dies; Rufus seizes the revenues of Canterbury,	396
1090.	The Norman barons rebel against Robert, and take many of his castles; Henry assists Robert, and throws Conan, the leader of the rebellion, over the battlements of a high tower,	396, 397
1091. (Jan.)	Rufus lands in Normandy, at the head of an English army; a peace is concluded; Rufus and Robert attack Henry, and lay siege to Mount St Michael, which he evacuates, and retires into Brittany,	397, 398
	Rufus engages in a war with Malcolm III. of Scotland,	398, 536, 537
	Malcolm does homage; Edgar Atheling comes to England, and lives in the court of Rufus,	398
1093. (Nov. 13.)	Malcolm III. and his son Edward killed at the siege of Alnwick Castle,	399, 537
(Nov. 16.)	Queen Margaret, his wife, the sister of Edgar Atheling, dies,	399, 538
1094. (May.)	Donald Bain seizes the throne of Scotland,	538
	Duncan offers to swear fealty to Rufus; invades Scotland; drives Donald Bain from the throne, and becomes king,	538
1094, 1095.	The Welsh invade the English border; Rufus marches against them; goes into Wales, but retreats; orders the erection of forts along the frontier,	399
	Mowbray, Earl of Northumberland, enters into a conspiracy against Rufus, to place Stephen on the throne; the king besieges him in Bamborough Castle; he is taken prisoner; his wife delivers	

A.D.		PAGE
	up the castle; the conspirators are variously punished,	400
1094.	Ireland is divided between Murtach, son of King Turlogh and Donald Mac-Lochlin,	459
1095.	Donald Bain causes the assassination of Duncan, and again becomes king of Scotland,	538
	He expels all foreign settlers, and abolishes all innovations on the customs of the country,	538
1096.	Robert resigns Normandy to Rufus for a sum of money,	400
	He sails to take possession of it,	401
1097.	Edgar Atheling marches into Scotland,	538
1098.	Defeats Donald Bain, and places his nephew, Edgar, on the throne,	538
1099.	The town of Mans is delivered up to Rufus,	401
(July 15.)	Jerusalem is captured by the Crusaders,	407
1100.	Helie besieges Mans; Rufus instantly repairs to Barfleur; Mans is surrendered; Rufus is wounded; he ravages the country, and returns to England,	401
(May.)	Richard, son of Duke Robert, is killed by an arrow in the New Forest,	401
(Aug. 1.)	Rufus is slain by an arrow in the New Forest, shot by Sir Walter Tyrrell, who flees to Normandy,	403
	Rufus is buried in Winchester Cathedral,	403
(Aug. 5.)	Accession of Henry I.,	405
	Henry I. grants a charter of liberties; restores the rights of the church; and promises to restore the laws of Edward the Confessor,	405, 406
(Nov. 11.)	Henry I. marries Maud, daughter of Malcolm, king of Scots,	406, 407
	He expels the favourites of Rufus,	407
	Robert prepares to invade England,	408
	The English fleet desert to him; he lands at Portsmouth; peace is concluded, and Henry cedes all his castles in Normandy to Robert,	409
	Henry I. goes to war with some of his barons; siege of Arundel Castle; of Bridgenorth; it is captured; capitulation of Shrewsbury,	409
	Robert comes to England, and is made prisoner,	410
	Robert is liberated and returns to Normandy,	410
1102.	Sibylla, the wife of Robert, dies,	410
1106.	Henry I. invades Normandy; Robert is defeated and taken prisoner; and Normandy falls into possession of Henry,	410–412
	Edgar Atheling is taken prisoner; brought to England, and a pension is allowed him,	411
	Duke Robert is committed to prison for life; he attempts to escape; is blinded by order of Henry,	411
	Henry I. secures William, the infant son of Robert, and commits him to the custody of Helie de St Saen,	412
1107. (Jan. 8.)	Edgar, king of Scotland, dies, and is succeeded by Alexander I.,	538
	Cumberland is severed from the kingdom of Scotland,	539
1110.	Matilda, the daughter of Henry I., affianced to Henry V., emperor of Germany, and a tax laid on the country to pay the marriage-portion,	412
	The Welsh are defeated; and a colony of Flemings established at Haverfordwest,	412
	Henry I. obliges the barons and prelates	

A.D.		PAGE
	to swear fealty to his son William at Salisbury,	413
1118.	Maud the Good, queen of Henry I., dies,	413
	Henry is engaged in a war with his Norman barons,	413
	Baldwin, Earl of Flanders, dies of his wound,	413
	The Order of the Templars founded,	746
(Aug. 20.)	The Battle of Brenville fought between Henry I. and Louis, king of France,	413
1120.	Eadmer elected bishop of St Andrews, but is not consecrated,	539
(Nov. 25.)	Henry I. sets sail from Barfleur for England,	414
	The *Blanche-nef*, the ship in which Prince William embarked, is wrecked, and all perish,	415
	Henry I. marries Alice, daughter of Geoffrey, Duke of Louvain,	416
1121.	MacLochlin, king of all Ireland, dies,	459
1124.	The Emperor Henry V. dies,	416
	Robert, prior of Scone, is made bishop of St Andrews, and consecrated by the archbishop of York,	539
(April 27.)	Alexander I., king of Scotland, dies, and is succeeded by David, Earl of Cumberland,	539, 540
1126.	Matilda, the widow of the Emperor Henry V., and daughter of Henry I., is declared the next heir to the throne,	416
	Fulk, Earl of Anjou, renounces his government in favour of his son, Geoffrey Plantagenet,	417
1127.	Matilda is married to Geoffrey Plantagenet at Rouen,	417
	Henry I. causes his barons again to swear to support the succession of Matilda; David, king of Scots, is the first to do so,	540
1128. (July 27.)	William of Normandy, the son of Robert, dies,	417
	Matilda leaves her husband, and comes over to England; she returns,	418
1133. (March.)	Matilda is delivered of a son at Mans, afterwards Henry II. of England,	418
	Henry I. again causes his barons to swear to support the succession of Matilda and her children,	418
	In the two following years Geoffrey and William were born,	418
1135.	Robert of Normandy dies,	411
(Nov. 25.)	Henry I. is taken sick while in Normandy,	418
(Dec. 1.)	He dies, leaving all his territories to his daughter Matilda,	418
	Stephen arrives in London, and is acknowledged king by the citizens,	421
(Dec. 26.)	Stephen crowned at Westminster,	422
	He calls a meeting of the clergy and barons at Oxford, who swear to obey him so long as he preserves the church-discipline; the pope confirms his election as king,	422
	Stephen grants a chapter of liberties; he allows his barons to fortify their castles,	422
1136.	Stephen goes to Normandy, and is received as the lawful successor,	422
	David, king of Scotland, invades England in favour of Matilda; a peace is concluded,	423
(Feb.)	Henry, David's son, is created Earl of Huntingdon; David again invades England; a truce is made,	423, 540
	Turlogh O'Connor, king of Connaught, is acknowledged king of all Ireland,	459
	Robert, Earl of Gloucester, comes to	

CHRONOLOGICAL INDEX.

A.D.		PAGE
	England; swears fealty to Stephen; raises an Insurrection in favour of Matilda; is aided by the king of Scots; Norwich and other royal castles are taken; Stephen regains them,	423
	Eleanor, daughter of the Duke of Aquitaine, is married to Louis VII. of France,	439
1138.	David, king of Scots, invades England	
(March.)	a third time,	423, 541
(June 9.)	Defeats the English at Clitherow,	541
(Aug. 22.)	The Battle of the Standard is fought at Northallerton,	424–426, 541
1139.	Peace concluded at Durham between David, king of Scots, and Stephen; David made Earl of Northumberland,	541
	Matilda lands in England; Stephen surprises her in Arundel Castle; she is allowed to depart; the barons of the north and west join Matilda,	428
1140.	Dermond MacMurrogh, king of Leinster, seizes seventeen of his nobility, and puts out their eyes,	460
1141.	Robert, Earl of Gloucester, takes	
(Feb. 2.)	Stephen prisoner before Lincoln,	430
(Mar. 2.)	The bishop of Winchester abandons Stephen, and the following day gives his benediction to Matilda in Winchester cathedral; she assumes royal authority,	430
(April 7.)	Matilda convenes a meeting of churchmen, who ratify her accession,	430, 431
(April 9.)	The deputies from London object; the legate, Winchester, excommunicates the adherents of Stephen,	431
(June.)	Matilda enters London; insults the queen and the bishop of Winchester,	431
	Matilda is driven from London by Queen Maud, and retires to Oxford; she attempts to seize the bishop of Winchester; he fortifies his palace; Matilda enters the Castle of Winchester, and lays siege to the palace,	432
(Aug. 1.)	The bishop besieges Winchester Castle,	433
(Sept. 14.)	Matilda makes her escape from the castle, and reaches Devizes Castle; is carried as a corpse from that place to Gloucester,	433
(Nov. 1.)	Stephen is set at liberty, in exchange for Robert, Earl of Gloucester,	433
	Stephen is formally restored,	434
1142.	Stephen invests the citadel of Oxford, and fires the town after three months' siege,	434
(Dec. 20.)	Matilda escapes in the snow; is joined by the Earl of Gloucester, and her son Prince Henry, at Wallingford; Oxford Castle surrenders,	435
1143.	Stephen is defeated at Wilton by the Earl of Gloucester,	435
(Oct.)	Robert, Earl of Gloucester, dies of a fever,	435
	Matilda quits England,	435
	The churches in half the kingdom are closed,	435
1149.	Prince Henry, Matilda's son, lands in Scotland, and is met at Carlisle by King David, who knights him,	436–541
	David and his son Henry invade England, and advance to Lancaster,	541
	Thomas-à-Becket goes to Rome and obtains a prohibition against the anointing of Prince Eustace,	446
1150.	Prince Henry succeeds as Duke of Anjou,	436
	Stephen requires the archbishop of Canterbury to anoint Prince Eustace, his son, but he refuses,	435

A.D.		PAGE
1151.	Ireland is divided between two princes by Turlogh O'Connor, after the battle of Moinmor,	459
	Maud, the queen of Stephen, dies,	438
1152.	Eleanor, wife of Louis VII. of France, is divorced,	439
	Prince Henry marries her, and obtains Poicton, Guienne, and Aquitaine,	436–439
	He lands in England with an army; he is met by Stephen at Wallingford; a truce is agreed on,	437
	Prince Eustace dies,	437
(June 12.)	Henry, son of David, king of Scotland, dies,	541
1153.	David, king of Scotland, dies, and is	
(May 24.)	succeeded by his grandson, Malcolm IV.,	541, 542
	Prince Henry appointed successor to Stephen,	437
	MacMurrogh, king of Leinster, carries off Dervorgilla, the wife of Tiernan O'Ruarc,	460
(Oct. 25.)	King Stephen dies,	438
(Dec.)	Henry arrives in England, and enters Winchester,	440
(Dec. 19.)	Henry II. crowned with his queen in Westminster Abbey,	440
	He makes the barons, and bishops swear fealty to his two sons, William and Henry,	441
	The king summons a great council, and obtains their sanction to resume the castles granted by Stephen and Matilda,	441
	Eleven hundred of them are levelled,	442
	At the siege of Bridgenorth, Henry's life is saved by Hubert de St Clair,	442
	Geoffrey, Henry's younger brother, lays claim to the earldom of Anjou,	442
1156.	Henry II. does homage to Louis VII., for Normandy and other provinces,	442
	He reduces Anjou, and grants Goeffrey a pension,	443
	Turlogh O'Connor, king of Ireland, called O'Connor the Great, dies, and is succeeded by Murtogh O'Lochlin as supreme king,	459
	Thomas-à-Becket is made chancellor of England, preceptor to the prince, and warden of the Tower,	440
1157.	Henry II. invades Wales; he is defeated with great loss at Coleshill Forest; he cuts down forests; erects forts; the Welsh, after a few months, do homage and give hostages,	443
	Malcolm IV. of Scotland resigns at Chester his claim to territory north of the Tyne, and all his right to Cumberland, and all other possessions in England, except the earldom of Huntingdon,	542
	Geoffrey, Henry's younger brother, dies,	443
	Henry II. claims Nantes, and takes possession of that and several other places,	443
	Thomas-à-Becket goes as ambassador to Paris,	444
	Henry II. soon after goes there in person,	444
	He commutes the personal services of his vassals for a sum, and raises a large army,	444, 445
1159.	He embarks for Toulouse with Malcolm, king of Scotland, 'whom he knights in France,' & Becket, and others,	445, 542
	Malcolm returns to Scotland; his nobles attempt to seize him,	542
	Henry II. takes Cahors, and returns to Normandy,	445

A.D.		PAGE
	Peace is concluded between Henry II. and Louis,	446
1160.	Constance, queen of France, dies; Louis marries Adelais, niece of King Stephen; Prince Henry is married to Margaret, daughter of Louis; Louis exiles the Knights Templars,	446
1162.	Thomas-à-Becket made Primate of England,	449
1163.	The Welsh rise in arms, but are defeated,	451
	Becket excommunicates William de Eynsford, but at the command of Henry absolves him,	448
(July 1.)	Malcolm IV. of Scotland renews his homage to King Henry at Woodstock,	543
1164. (Jan. 25.)	Becket and the clergy sign a series of articles, rendering the clergy subject to the civil courts for felony, at Clarendon, in Wiltshire, called the Constitutions of Clarendon,	449
	Becket is cited before the council at Northampton,	449
	He is accused of magic; sentenced to imprisonment,	450
(Oct. 26.)	He leaves Northampton and flies to Gravelines,	450
	He is reinvested by the pope as archbishop,	451
	Henry II. banishes his relations and friends, and seizes his goods and possessions,	451
	Malcolm IV. defeats and slays Somerled, thane of Argyle, and his son,	543
(Dec. 9.)	Malcolm IV. dies at Jedburgh, and is succeeded by William the Lion,	543
1166.	Insurrection in Brittany. Henry reduces the country to submission; he keeps his court at Mount St Michael,	451, 452, 543
(Dec.)	Murtoch O'Lochlin, king of Ireland, is killed in battle, and is succeeded by Roderick O'Connor,	459
1167.	Henry II. orders a tax to be levied for the support of the war in the Holy Land,	452
(May.)	Becket excommunicates the supporters of the Constitutions of Clarendon; and several of the favourites of Henry,	452
	Dermond MacMurrogh, king of Leinster, acknowledges himself vassal to Henry at Aquitaine; engages with Richard de Clare, Earl of Pembroke, called Strongbow, Maurice Fitzgerald, and Robert Fitzstephen, for aid in his restoration,	461, 462
1169.	Dermond is defeated by Roderick and O'Ruarc, and accepts part of his former territory as O'Ruarc's vassal,	462
	Peace is concluded between the kings of England and France; Henry's sons do homage for their several fiefs, &c.; marriage is agreed between Prince Richard and Alice, a daughter of Louis,	452
(Dec. 1.)	Becket lands at Sandwich,	454
	Excommunicates Ranulf, Robert de Broc, and the rector of Harrow,	454
	The excommunicated bishops appeal to the king,	454, 455
1170.	An English and Irish army, under the command of Dermond MacMurrogh, besieges Wexford, which surrenders,	462
	MacMurrogh is acknowledged king of Leinster,	463
(June 14.)	Prince Henry is crowned, during his father's lifetime, by the archbishop of York; William, king of Scots, and David his son, do homage to the prince,	453–543

A.D.		PAGE
(July 22.)	Henry II. and Becket are reconciled,	453
(Sept.)	Strongbow embarks at Milford Haven with a large force, and lands near Waterford; the city is attacked and taken; Strongbow marries Eva, the daughter of MacMurrogh; Dublin is taken; Meath is overrun,	464
	The English slaves in Ireland set at liberty,	465
	The Danes invade Ireland; attack Dublin; but are defeated,	465
	Dermond MacMurrogh dies, and Strongbow assumes the title of King of Leinster, in right of his wife,	465
	Laurence, archbishop of Dublin, causes a confederacy of native princes, under the command of Roderick, to invest Dublin; Strongbow cuts his way through the army of Roderick, which he routes,	465, 466
	Strongbow surrenders Dublin and other forts to the king, and holds the remainder in subjection to the English crown,	466
	Becket is murdered in St Augustine's Church, Canterbury,	455, 456
1171. (Oct. 18.)	Henry II., attended by Strongbow and a large army, lands at Crook, near Waterford,	466
	Henry II. receives the submission of many princes and chieftains; and all Ireland, except Ulster, is subjugated,	467
1172. (April 17.)	Henry II. appoints Hugh de Lacy governor of Dublin, and departs,	467
(May.)	Henry II. is absolved from the murder of Becket by the pope's legates at Avranches,	459
	Prince Henry is again crowned; his consort Margaret, daughter of Louis of France, is crowned with him,	467
	Prince Henry demands the sovereignty of either England or Normandy,	468
	He flies to the French court,	468
	The Irish rise against the English,	546
1173. (March.)	Richard and Geoffrey, the king's other sons, go to the French court, and Queen Eleanor abandons her husband, but is retaken and imprisoned,	468
	Prince Henry is acknowledged sole king of England by Louis of France,	468
	Henry II. declares that England belongs to the jurisdiction of the pope,	469
(June.)	The war commences in Normandy, but the rebels and invaders are repulsed, and a meeting takes place between the kings of England and France; the Earl of Leicester insults Henry II.,	469
	Richard de Lacy repulses the Scots; burns Berwick,	470
	The Earl of Leicester taken prisoner by De Lacy,	470
1174.	Louis and Prince Henry again attack Normandy; Prince Richard leads the insurgents in Poictou and Aquitaine,	470
	Roger de Mowbray revolts in Yorkshire; the Scotch invade England; Hugh Bigod takes Norwich Castle,	470
(July 8.)	Henry II. returns to England, bringing as prisoners his own and Prince Henry's wife; does penance at the grave of Becket,	470
	He is scourged in the church,	471
(July 12.)	Ranulph de Glanville takes William the Lion prisoner, with sixty Scottish lords; William is sent to Falaise,	471, 472
	Henry II. subdues the revolt in England,	

CHRONOLOGICAL INDEX.

A. D.		PAGE
	and leads his army into Normandy, where he raises the siege of Rouen,	471–544
	Henry II. is reconciled to his children, and peace is restored,	471
(Dec.)	William the Lion is released, on doing homage to Henry II.,	472–544
	The king of Ireland does homage to Henry II.,	546
1177.	Henry II. arbitrates the dispute between	
(March.)	Alfonso, king of Castile, and Sancho, king of Navarre,	472
1181.	William is excommunicated for opposing the church, and Scotland laid under an interdict; Pope Alexander dies; Pope Lucius III. reverses the decree of his predecessor,	544
1183.	Prince Richard refuses to do homage to his brother, Henry, for the duchy of Aquitaine; war commences between them,	473
1183, 1184.	King Henry and Prince Geoffrey are at war with Prince Henry and Prince Richard; Prince Henry submits to his father; King Henry is nearly assassinated at Limoges,	474
(June 11.)	Prince Henry dies,	475
	Henry II. takes Limoges by assault; takes several castles; captures Bertrand de Born; pardons him,	475
	Prince Geoffrey is reconciled to his father; Queen Eleanor is released from captivity,	475
	Geoffrey demands the earldom of Anjou; is refused; flies to the French court; prepares for war,	475, 476
1186.	He is killed at a tournament,	476
	Is buried by Philip II., king of France; Prince Richard heads another revolt in Aquitaine; submits to his father, and swears obedience,	476
	William the Lion marries Ermengarde, daughter of Viscount Beaumont; Henry restores the Castle of Edinburgh to him,	544
1187.	Donald Bane or MacWilliam, grandson of King Duncan, invades Ross and Moray, but is repulsed,	544
(Sept.)	Jerusalem is retaken by the Mohammedans,	476
1188.	Henry II. and Philip agree to march to the Holy Land,	476
(Jan.)		
(Feb.)	Henry II. calls a council at Gidington, in Northamptonshire; money is raised; the Jews are persecuted; and more money raised for the Holy War,	476, 477
(Nov.)	Prince Richard does homage to King Philip for his father's continental territories,	477
	Philip and Richard take many of Henry's towns,	477
1189.	Henry II. sues for peace; a treaty is prepared,	478
(June.)		
(July 6.)	King Henry dies at Chinon,	479
	Queen Eleanor is liberated, and made regent,	482
	Richard returns to England, accompanied by Prince John,	482
(Sept. 2.)	Proclamation forbidding Jews to be present at the coronation,	484
(Sept. 3.)	Richard I. is crowned at Westminster,	483
	Massacre of the Jews in London,	484
	Richard I. raises money for the crusade,	485
	Releases William the Lion from his obligations to the crown of England,	472, 485–545
	He appoints a regency,	485
1190.	Tancred is crowned at Palermo king of Sicily,	490

A. D.		PAGE
(Feb.)	Richard I. exchanges oaths with Philip of France,	486
	The English and French armies are assembled at Vezelai, and march to Lyon; the English fleet reaches Messina,	486–488
(March 16.)	A great massacre of the Jews at York,	504
(Sept. 23.)	Richard I. arrives at Messina,	489
	Takes Messina,	490, 491
	He receives a large sum from Tancred; affiances his nephew, Prince Arthur, to an infant daughter of Tancred,	491, 492
	Meets Tancred; has disputes with Philip,	492, 493
(March 30.)	Philip sails for Acre,	493
	Berengaria, the daughter of the king of Navarre, arrives in Brindisi; and sails in the English fleet for Acre,	493, 494
	Prince John is acknowledged heir to the throne,	507
	Richard I. reduces the island of Cyprus, and levies tribute; sends the emperor to a castle at Tripoli; he marries Berengaria at Limasol; embarks for Acre,	494, 495
(June 8.)	Richard I. arrives at Acre; the siege of the castle proceeds; the kings of England and France quarrel,	495
1191. (June 12.)	Acre is surrendered,	496
	Philip quits Acre, and returns to France,	497
	The Crusaders massacre the hostages given at the capitulation of Acre,	497
(Aug. 22.)	Richard I. marches towards Jerusalem,	497
(Sept. 7.)	Defeats Saladin near Azotus, and takes possession of Jaffa,	498
(Oct. 9.)	Prince John is declared chief governor of England; Longchamp, the justiciary, is deposed; John obtains possession of the Tower,	507, 508
(Nov.)	Richard I. marches from Jaffa; retreats to Ascalon,	498
	Quarrel between the Duke of Austria and Richard,	499
	He negotiates for peace with Saladin,	500
	Gives Guy of Lusignan the island of Cyprus,	500
	Conrad of Montferrat, titular king of Jerusalem, is murdered at Tyre,	500
	Henry of Champagne takes possession of Tyre; marries the widow of Conrad; and is acknowledged king of Jerusalem,	500, 501
1192.	Saladin takes the town of Jaffa, all but the citadel; Richard retakes it; battle of Jaffa,	501
	Truce is made for three years between the Crusaders and Saladin; and the former go to Jerusalem as pilgrims,	501, 502
(Oct.)	Richard I. sails from Acre,	502
(Nov.)	He is driven on shore on the coast of Istria; captured by the Duke of Austria, and confined in the castle of Tiernsteign,	502, 503
	John does homage to King Philip for his brother's dominions on the continent,	509
	John takes Windsor and Wallingford Castles; demands the crown in London; is repulsed,	509
	Philip prepares to make war on Normandy; John is betrothed to Alice, the French king's sister; Philip is defeated in Normandy by the Earl of Leicester,	509
1193.	The Duke of Austria sells King Richard to the Emperor Henry; he is confined in the Tyrol,	504–509

A.D.		PAGE
	The emperor and the duke are excommunicated,	509
	Richard I. is brought before the diet of the empire,	510
(Sept. 22.)	Terms are agreed upon for the liberation of Richard; 70,000 marks are raised for the ransom,	510
1194. (Feb.)	Richard I. is liberated,	510
(March 13.)	He lands at Sandwich,	511
	Marches to London; Nottingham Castle surrenders,	511
(March 30.)	Holds a great council at Nottingham,	511
	He is again crowned, but at Winchester,	511
(May.)	Richard I. lands at Barfleur; John submits, and is forgiven; Philip is defeated in several engagements,	511
1195.	Hubert Walter is appointed grand justiciary,	512
	A great famine and plague in England,	512
1197.	The barons of Brittany and Aquitaine revolt; join the French king,	513
	Richard I. imprisons the bishop of Beauvais in Rouen Castle,	513
(Sept.)	The Emperor Henry dies at Messina,	513
1198.	Richard I. defeats Philip near Gisors,	513
1199. (April 6.)	Death of King Richard,	514
(May 27.)	John is crowned at Westminster,	515, 516
	The French king demands for Arthur of Brittany all John's continental possessions except Normandy,	516
	The troops of John ravage Brittany,	517
1200.	Peace concluded, and Arthur disinherited,	517
	John marries Isabella, the wife of the Count de la Marche,	517
(Nov. 22.)	William the Lion does homage to John at Lincoln,	545
1201.	Constance, mother of Arthur of Brittany, dies,	517
1202.	Arthur invests the town of Mirebeau; takes it; Queen Eleanor, widow of Henry II., defends the citadel; John marches to her relief,	518
(July 31.)	John obtains possession of the town, and takes Arthur, the Count de la Marche, and others, prisoners,	518
	Arthur is confined at Falaise, and afterwards in the Castle of Rouen,	518
1203. (April 3.)	Death of Arthur,	519, 520
	A general insurrection takes place in Brittany,	520
(Dec.)	John flies from Rouen to England,	521
1204.	Normandy is reannexed to the French dominions,	521
	Brittany, Anjou, Maine, Touraine, and Poictou acknowledge Philip,	521
1206.	John invades Brittany; takes Rochelle; burns Angers; lays siege to Nantes; peace made for two years,	521
1207.	John disputes with the pope the right of appointing bishops; he expels the monks of Canterbury; seizes their effects,	522
1208. (March 23.)	The kingdom is laid under an interdict,	522
1209.	John is excommunicated,	522
	He applies for aid to the Mahommedans of Spain,	523
1210. (June 6.)	John lands in Ireland; receives the homage of many chieftains; reduces some castles; establishes English laws; appoints that the same money shall be current in both countries,	523
1211.	The Jews are again persecuted; John leads an army into Wales; obtains tribute and carries away hostages,	523

A.D.		PAGE
1212.	The barons of England revolt,	523
1213.	John is deposed by the pope; Philip collects a large fleet for the invasion of England; John sends out ships; they destroy the principal part of the French fleet; he encamps on Barham Downs; the pope's legate arrives, and John submits,	524
(May 15.)	John swears fealty to the pope,	524
	John orders Peter the Hermit to be murdered,	524
	Great naval victory gained over the French at Damme,	525
	The barons refuse to embark in an expedition against France; John makes war on them,	526
(Aug. 25.)	Langton swears the barons at London to maintain the charter of Henry I.,	526
1214.	John again marches an army against the French,	526
(July 27.)	Battle of Bouvines,	526, 527
(Oct. 19.)	A truce is made between England and France,	527
(Oct. 20.)	John returns to England,	527
(Nov. 20).	The barons swear at St Edmundsbury, to assert their rights,	527
(Dec. 4.)	William the Lion, king of Scotland, dies at Stirling,	545, 546
(Dec. 10.)	Accession of Alexander II.,	546
1215. (Jan.)	The barons demand the great charter,	527
(Feb. 2.)	John swears to engage in the Holy War,	528
	The barons present the heads of their demands; they elect Robert Fitz-Walter their leader,	528
(May 24.)	They enter London; John agrees to their terms,	528
(June 15.)	Meeting at Runnymead; John grants the Great Charter (Magna Charta),	528, 529
	The barons are excommunicated by the pope; John ravages the country; the king of Scots assists the barons; John pursues him as far as Edinburgh, and devastates Haddington, Dunbar, and Berwick,	530
(Dec. 16.)	The barons are again excommunicated, and London laid under an interdict,	530, 531
	The English crown is offered to Louis, son of Philip, king of France, by the confederate barons,	531
1216.	The French army lands at Sandwich;	
(May 30.)	Louis takes Rochester Castle,	531
(June 2.)	He enters London, and the barons do homage and swear fealty to him in St Paul's Cathedral,	531
	Louis besieges Dover Castle; the barons besiege Windsor Castle,	531, 532
(July 16.)	Pope Innocent dies,	531
(Oct.)	John marches through Peterborough; his baggage and army are nearly swallowed up by the Wash at Fossdike; he repairs to Swinesbond Abbey,	532
(Oct. 15.)	John is seized with fever; he appoints his son Henry his successor; the barons with him swear fealty to the prince,	532, 533
(Oct. 18.)	King John dies,	533

BOOK IV

1216. (Oct. 18.)	Accession of Henry III.,	671
(Oct. 28.)	Henry III. does homage to the pope for England and Ireland,	671
	Louis raises the siege of Dover Castle,	672

CHRONOLOGICAL INDEX. 11

A.D.		PAGE
(Nov. 6.)	The Tower of London is given up to him,	672
(Nov. 11.)	Great council at Bristol; the Earl of Pembroke chosen Rector Regis et Regni; Magna Charta is revised,	671
1217.	The Earl of Pembroke besieges Mount Sorel Castle,	673
(May 20.)	The battle called the 'Fair of Lincoln' fought,	673
(June.)	Louis offers terms of accommodation,	673
(Aug. 23.)	French fleet sails from Calais,	673
(Aug. 24.)	Hubert de Burgh takes or destroys the whole,	673
(Sept. 11.)	Louis agrees to abandon his claim on England,	674
(Sept. 14.)	He sails for France,	674
(Oct. 4.)	New charter granted to the city of London,	674
(Dec. 1.)	Alexander II., king of Scots, surrenders to Henry III. the town of Carlisle, and does homage for his English possessions, Treaty of commerce concluded with Norway,	700
		674
	Magna Charta again confirmed,	674, 675
	The Charter of Forests is granted,	675
1219. (May.)	The Earl of Pembroke, the regent, dies, Hubert de Burgh and the bishop of Winchester are appointed regents,	675
	Pandulph is made legate,	675
1221. (June 25.)	Joanna, Henry III.'s sister, is married to Alexander II.,	675–700
1223.	Henry III. declared of age,	675
1225.	A parliament is summoned at Westminster; money is granted on condition of the ratification of the two charters,	675
1229.	War declared against France,	676
1230.	Henry III. embarks from England, and lands at St Malo in Brittany, Louis takes several towns belonging to Henry III.,	676
		676
(Oct.)	Henry III. returns to England,	676
	Parliament refuses fresh supplies,	676
1232.	Hubert de Burgh is disgraced; sent to the Tower; his lands are forfeited; he escapes into Wales,	677
1234.	Hubert de Burgh restored to his honours,	677
1236.	Henry III. marries Eleanor, daughter of the Count of Provence; her relations are all appointed to high places,	678
1237. (Sept.)	A conference is held at York to settle the claims of the kings of Scots and England,	700, 701
1238. (Mar. 4.)	Queen Joan of Scots dies at Canterbury,	701
	Simon de Montfort, Earl of Leicester, marries Eleanor, Countess-dowager of Pembroke, sister of King Henry III.,	681
1239. (May 15.)	Alexander II. marries Mary, daughter of Ingelram de Couci,	701
1241. (Sept. 4.)	Alexander, son of the king of Scots, is born at Roxburgh,	702
1242.	Henry III. confides the care of the northern border to the king of Scots, Henry III. sails from Portsmouth, and lands on the Garonne; Louis defeats him near Taillebourg; again at Saintes; Henry III. flies to Blaye; truce agreed upon,	701
		678
1244.	Parliament vote twenty shillings on every knight's fee for the marriage of the king's daughter; the Jews are persecuted and plundered,	678, 679
	Henry III. proclaims war against Scotland,	701
(Aug. 13.)	Peace concluded at Newcastle,	701
1248.	The parliament remonstrate with Henry III., and refuse supplies; Henry III. establishes a fair in Westminster,	679

A.D.		PAGE
	Alexander II., king of Scots, claims homage for the western islands from the Lord of Argyle,	702
1249. (July 8.)	Alexander II. dies at Kerarry,	702
(July 13.)	Alexander III. is crowned at Scone,	702
1251. (Dec. 26.)	Alexander III. is married at York to Margaret, daughter of Henry III.; he does homage for his English possessions,	703
1253. (May 3.)	Henry III. solemnly swears in Westminster Hall to observe the charters, and obtains money,	679
	Prince Edward marries Eleanor, daughter of Alfonso, king of Castile,	680
	Prince Edward is declared king of Sicily,	680
1255. (Sept. 20.)	Henry III. meets Alexander III. and his queen at Roxburgh; and a regency for Scotland is framed,	703
1256.	Richard, Earl of Cornwall, is elected king of the Romans; is crowned at Aix-la-Chapelle,	681
1257.	Alexander III. is seized by some nobles; and a new regency for Scotland is appointed,	703
1258.	A great scarcity in England,	681
(May 2.)	Parliament is assembled at Westminster; the barons appear armed,	681
(June 11.)	The parliament called the 'Mad Parliament' meet at Oxford; committee of government appointed, and three sessions appointed to be held yearly; the king takes oaths to observe these acts,	682
1259.	The king of the Romans returns to England,	683
1260.	The king and queen of Scotland come to London,	704
1261. (Feb. 2.)	Henry III. dismisses the committee of government; seizes the Tower and the Mint; Prince Edward joins the barons; the king publishes a dispensation from the pope, absolving him from his oaths taken at Oxford,	683
	The queen of Scots is delivered of a daughter, Margaret, at Windsor,	704
1263. (Mar.)	The Earl of Gloucester raises his retainers,	683
(April.)	The queen takes refuge in St Paul's, and Prince Edward at Windsor,	683
(July.)	The foreigners are banished, and peace restored,	684
(July.)	The Earl of Ross invades the Hebrides; the king of Norway arrives,	704
(Aug. 5.)	An annular eclipse seen at Ronaldsvoo,	704
(Oct. 2.)	The battle of Largs is fought,	704, 705
(Oct.)	Henry III. defeats the barons, and Prince Edward joins him,	684
1264. (Jan. 21.)	Alexander, son of Alexander III., is born at Jedburgh,	705
	Henry III. and the barons refer their differences to the arbitration of Louis IX. of France; the civil war again rages; the Jews are again massacred and plundered throughout England,	684
(May 14.)	Battle of Lowes; Henry III. and Prince Edward are taken prisoners; the truce of Lewes is concluded,	685
1265.	Parliament is called, in which, for the first time, representatives appear,	685, 686
	Prince Edward escapes; battle of Kenilworth,	686
(Aug. 4.)	The battle of Evesham; the Earl of Leicester is slain,	686, 687
	Parliament at Winchester; London deprived of its charter; dictum of Kenilworth,	687
	Battle of Alton,	688

A. D.	PAGE
1267. Parliament at Marlborough; the dictum of Kenilworth accepted,	688
1270. (July.) Prince Edward sails for the Holy Land,	688
1271. Henry d'Almaine, son of the king of the Romans, is murdered by Simon and Guy de Montfort,	688
Prince Edward lands at Acre; takes Nazareth; the Moslems are massacred; returns to Acre; is wounded by an assassin,	690
1272. (Nov. 16.) Henry III. dies at Westminster, and is buried in the abbey,	688
(Nov. 20.) Edward I. proclaimed by the barons at the New Temple, and a regency appointed,	688
1273. (Feb.) Edward I. goes to Paris, and does homage to Philip III. for the lands in France,	691
1274. (May.) He receives a challenge at Guienne from the Count de Chalons; the 'little war of Chalons' is fought,	691, 692
The trade with the Flemings is renewed,	692
(Aug. 2.) Edward I. lands at Dover,	692
(Aug. 19.) He is crowned with his queen at Westminster,	693
Alexander III., king of Scots, does homage to Edward I.,	705
Edward I. persecutes and plunders the Jews, hanging two hundred and eighty in London,	693
1275. Margaret, queen of Scotland, dies,	705
1277. Edward I. invades Wales,	697
(Nov. 10.) Llewellyn, Prince of Wales, cedes the greater part of the country to Edward I.; does homage for the remainder,	697
1278. The king of Scotland again does homage to Edward I. for his English possessions,	705
1281. The Princess Margaret of Scotland is married to Eric, king of Norway,	705
1282. (March.) Llewellyn takes several places; the English are defeated at Menai Strait,	697, 698
(Nov. 6.) Edward I. is defeated; Llewellyn is slain,	698
1283. Margaret, queen of Norway, dies,	705
1284. (Jan. 28.) Alexander, prince of Scotland, dies,	706
(Feb. 5.) The succession of Scotland is settled on the 'Maiden of Norway,'	706
1285. (Apr. 15.) Alexander III., king of Scotland, marries Joleta, daughter of the Count de Dreux,	706
1286. (Mar. 16.) He is killed,	706
(Apr. 11.) A regency appointed,	706
(Sept. 20.) The adherents of Robert Bruce meet,	706
1290. (July 18.) The Treaty of Bridgeham is concluded, securing the integrity of the kingdom of Scotland,	707
(Sept.) The Maiden of Norway dies,	707
The Jews are expelled the kingdom, and their property seized,	693
1291. (May 10.) The Scotch barons appear at Norham, and Edward I. claims to be lord paramount of Scotland,	707, 708
(June 2.) The several competitors for the crown of Scotland admit Edward I.'s title as lord paramount,	708
(June 11.) The regents of Scotland surrender the kingdom to Edward I.; the castles are delivered up,	708
(June 15.) Baliol and Bruce swear fealty to Edward I.,	709
(Aug. 3.) The commissioners meet at Berwick,	709
1292. (June 2.) The consideration adjourned for the opinion of parliament,	709, 710
(Oct. 15.) Baliol and Bruce attend the parliament at Berwick; parliament decide in favour of Baliol,	710
(Nov. 6 and 17.) Edward I. adjudges the kingdom of Scotland to Baliol,	710

A. D.	PAGE
(Nov. 30.) Baliol is crowned at Scone,	710
(Dec. 26.) He does homage to Edward I. for his kingdom at Newcastle,	710
Edward I. hangs the Welsh bards,	711
1292. Edmund, the king's brother, makes conquests in France; Dover and its priory are burned,	711, 712
1293. Baliol releases Edward I. from the Treaty of Bridgeham,	712
(Oct. 15.) Baliol appears before the parliament; three of his castles and towns are taken from him for contempt,	712, 713
1294. At a parliament at Scone, the English of the court are dismissed,	713
The English parliament is compelled to grant a tenth on lay property, and a half on the incomes of the clergy,	719
1295. (Oct. 23.) Treaty between Scotland and France,	713
Edward I. obtains a grant of a tenth from the clergy,	719
1296. (Mar.) A Scottish army invades Cumberland,	713
(Mar. 30.) Edward I. takes Berwick and massacres the inhabitants,	713
(Apr. 5.) Baliol renounces his allegiance to Edward I.,	713
(May 18.) Roxburgh Castle surrendered to Edward I.,	714
Edinburgh and Stirling taken,	714
(July.) The Coronation Stone is removed from Scone to Westminster,	714
(Aug. 28.) The Scotch do fealty to Edward I. at Berwick,	714
Edward I. outlaws the clergy and seizes their goods,	719
1297. Wallace heads a revolt and takes Scone,	715
(July 9.) Some of the adherents of Wallace submit,	716
(Sept. 4.) Wallace gains a victory; the castles of Edinburgh, Dunbar, Roxburgh, and Berwick surrender; he is made guardian of the kingdom,	717
Parliament, under Prince Edward, pass the statute 'De Tallagio non Concedendo,'	721
1298. (Jan.) An English army is collected at York,	718
Truce for two years between Edward I. and Philip,	721
(March.) Edward I. arrives in England,	718
(July 22.) The battle of Falkirk; Edward I. ravages Scotland,	718, 719
1299. (Mar.) Edward I. attempts to introduce a new clause into the charters,	722
The charters are reconfirmed,	722
(Sept.) Edward I. marries Margaret of France; the Prince of Wales is contracted to Isabella of France,	723
(Nov.) An army is collected at Berwick,	724
The pope claims Scotland,	724
1300. Edward I. devastates Annandale,	724
1301. Parliament denies the authority of the pope in temporal matters,	724
Edward I. marches against Scotland,	724
1302. Truce with the Scotch,	724
1303. (Feb. 24.) John de Segrave is defeated by the Scotch,	725
(May 20.) A treaty of commerce is concluded,	723-725
Edward I. goes to Scotland; receives the homage of many barons,	725
1304. He demands a tallage on all cities and boroughs,	722
(July 20.) Castle of Stirling surrenders,	726
Wallace is captured and brought to London,	726
Robert Bruce dies,	727
1305. (Aug. 23.) Wallace is executed as a traitor,	726
1306. (Feb. 10.) Robert Bruce the younger slays Comyn,	728
(Mar. 27.) He is crowned king of Scotland at Scone,	728
(May 22.) The Prince of Wales is knighted,	728

A.D.	PAGE
(June 19.) Battle of Methven; Bruce is defeated; he flies to Ireland,	729
Nigel Bruce surrenders Kildrummie, and is hanged at Berwick,	729
1307. (Feb.) Thomas and Alexander Bruce are captured; they are executed at Carlisle,	729, 730
(May 10.) Battle of Loudon Hill; Bruce defeats the Earl of Pembroke; defeats the Earl of Gloucester,	730
1307. (July 7.) Edward I. dies at Burgh-upon-Sands,	730
(July 8.) Edward II. is acknowledged king at Carlisle,	730
(Oct.) Gaveston is made Earl of Cornwall,	731
1308. (Jan. 25.) Edward II. marries Isabella of France at Boulogne,	732
(Feb.) Gaveston is expelled, but made governor of Ireland,	732
(May 22.) Bruce gains the battle of Inverary,	735
The Templars are seized throughout England and Ireland,	747
1309. Gaveston returns,	732
(Oct.) The Templars of England are tried and condemned, and the order suppressed,	747
1310. The barons meet at Westminster, and appoint a committee of ordainers,	733
(Sept.) Edward II. marches into Scotland,	735
1311. (July.) Bruce ravages as far as Durham,	735
(Aug.) Parliament recalls the grants made by Edward to Gaveston, who is banished; parliament to be holden once every year,	733
(Dec.) Gaveston again returns; his honours regranted,	733
1312. (May 19.) Gaveston surrenders at Scarborough to the Earl of Pembroke,	733
He is beheaded at Blacklow Hill,	734
1313. (Mar. 7.) Bruce takes Roxburgh Castle,	736
(Mar. 14.) Randolph takes Edinburgh Castle,	736
Bruce again ravages Cumberland,	736
(June 23.) Battle of Bannockburn; the English are driven out of Scotland,	736–738
1314. The Scotch ravage the north of England,	738
1315. Edward Bruce lands at Carrickfergus,	738
1316. (Jan. 26.) He gains victories over the English,	738
(May 2.) He is crowned king of Ireland at Carrickfergus,	738
Bruce arrives, and overruns the south of Ireland,	739
1317. (May.) The two Bruces return to Ulster,	739
1318. (Mar. 28.) Berwick is taken by the Scotch,	739
Bruce makes two invasions of England,	739
(Oct. 5.) Edward Bruce is defeated and killed at Fagher, and the Scots are expelled from Ireland,	739
1319. Edward II. marches an army into Scotland; the Scots invade England; ravage Yorkshire,	739
(Sept. 23.) The battle called the Chapter of Mitton fought,	739
1321. (Aug.) The Despensers are banished by parliament,	740
(Oct.) They return to England,	740
1322. The elder Despenser is created Earl of Winchester,	741
1323. (May 30.) A suspension of arms for thirteen years agreed upon between England and Scotland,	741
Roger Mortimer escapes from the Tower,	741
Charles IV., king of France, overruns some of Edward II.'s continental possessions,	742
1325. (Mar.) Queen Isabella goes on a mission to Paris; Guienne and Ponthieu are surrendered to France; the Prince of Wales goes to France; Mortimer repairs to Paris; the Prince of Wales is affianced to Philippa, daughter of the Count of Hainault,	742
(Sept. 24.) Isabella and the Prince of Wales land with a small army at Orwell; she is joined by the barons; Edward II. takes ship with Despenser, and is driven on the coast of Wales,	743
The elder Despenser is taken at Bristol, and executed as a traitor,	743
(Sept. 26.) The Prince of Wales declared guardian of the kingdom,	744
Edward II. and the younger Despenser are captured; Despenser is executed at Hereford as a traitor; the king is sent to Kenilworth Castle,	744
1327. (Jan. 8.) Edward II. is deposed, and the Prince of Wales proclaimed king,	744
(Jan. 13.) Edward III. presides in parliament,	744
(Jan. 20.) Edward II. resigns the crown,	744
(Feb. 3.) The Scotch make an inroad into England; march as far as York; Edward III. marches against them,	749
(Aug.) The English and Scotch forces, after skirmishes, severally retire,	749, 750
(Sept.) Edward II. is murdered at Berkeley Castle, and buried in the abbey at Gloucester,	746
Parliament grants the queen £20,000 a year,	748
(Dec.) Philippa of Hainault arrives in England,	751
1328. (Jan. 24.) Edward III. marries her at York,	751
The independence of Scotland recognised,	751
(July 22.) The Princess Joanna, Edward III.'s sister, is married to David, Prince of Scotland,	751
(Oct.) Mortimer is created Earl of March,	751
1329. Edward III. does homage to Philip VI. of France,	757
(June.) Robert Bruce, king of Scotland, dies at Cardross,	751
1330. Parliament meets at Winchester,	752
(June.) Edward the Black Prince is born at Woodstock,	753
(Sept.) A joust held in Cheapside by the king,	753
(Oct. 19.) Mortimer is dragged from Nottingham Castle by Edward III. and his followers,	754
(Nov. 26.) Parliament is assembled; Mortimer is impeached of murder and other crimes,	754,755
(Nov. 29.) He is hanged at the Elms, and Queen Isabella is committed to custody,	755
1331. Lord James Douglas is killed in Spain,	755
Edward III. again does homage to the king of France for his continental possessions,	757
1332. (Aug.) Edward Baliol, son of King John Baliol, invades Scotland, and gains a victory at Duplin Moor,	755
(Sept. 24.) He is crowned king of Scotland at Scone,	756
He renews his oaths of fealty to Edward III.,	756
(Dec. 16.) He is obliged to fly from Scotland,	756
1333. (May.) The English army invests Berwick,	756
(July 19.) Battle of Halidon Hill,	756
King David II. and his queen are removed to France; Edward Baliol is reinstated as king,	756
He is again driven across the Border,	756
1335. (Aug.) Edward III. marches with an army into Scotland; is joined by Baliol; returns to England,	756
1336. Edward III. twice again marches into Scotland,	756
1338. (July.) He grants trading-privileges to the Flemings and Brabanters,	758
Baliol is again expelled from Scotland,	759
1339. (Sept.) Edward III. marches with his army into France; is abandoned by his allies,	758
1340. (Feb.) Edward III. returns to England,	758, 759

A.D.	PAGE
(June 22.) He sails with a fleet for Sluys,	759
(June 24.) Destroys the French fleet; is joined by his allies; challenges the French king to single combat; returns to England,	759
1341. (May 14.) David II., king of Scots, and his queen return from France; Edward III. concludes a truce with him,	759
Philip VI. beheads Olivier de Clisson and twelve other knights without trial,	762
1345. The Earl of Dorby drives the French out of Guienne,	763
John van Arteveldt is murdered at Ghent,	763
1346. (July.) Edward III. lands at Cape la Hogue with an army of English, Welsh, and Irish; he takes several towns, and forces the passage of Blanche-Taque,	763, 764
(Aug. 26.) Battle of Crecy gained by the Black Prince,	765-767
(Aug. 31.) Edward III. begins the siege of Calais,	768
(Sept.) David II. of Scotland invades England; takes several places,	768
(Oct. 17.) Battle of Nevil's Cross,	768
David II. is taken prisoner and sent to London,	768
1347. (June 18.) The English drive the French from before Roche-Derrien; capture Charles de Blois, and send him prisoner to England,	768, 769
(Aug. 3.) Calais is surrendered to Edward III.,	769, 770
Margaret of Calais is born,	770
1348. The French attempt to recover Calais,	771
(Nov.) The plague ravages London,	771
1349. Edward III. gains a naval victory over the Spaniards,	771
1350. Philip VI., king of France, dies, and is succeeded by John I.,	771
1355. Edward III. opens the campaign in France; he ravages a great part of the country,	771
1356. (Jan. 20.) Purchases all Balliol's rights to the Scotch throne; he burns Haddington and Edinburgh, and wastes the country; 'the burnt Candlemas,'	772
(Sept. 19.) Battle of Poictiers; John I. and his son Philip are taken prisoners,	772, 773
1357. (Apr. 24.) The Black Prince, King John I., and Prince Philip enter London,	773
(Oct. 3.) The Scots ransom David II.,	774
1359. Edward III. goes to France with a great army,	775
A French fleet take and plunder the town of Winchelsea,	775
1360. (Mar. 31.) Edward III. encamps before Paris,	775
(April.) Marches to Brittany,	775
(May.) The peace of Bretigny concluded; Edward III. renounces his pretensions to the crown of France,	775
(Oct. 24.) The two kings swear to the treaty; King John I. is set at liberty, and Edward III. returns to England,	775
1362. Queen Joanna of Scotland dies,	774
1363. David II. proposes to the parliament of Scotland that the Earl of Cambridge should succeed to the crown,	774
Edward Balliol dies,	774
1364. The Duke of Anjou breaks his parole, and leaves Calais,	776
King John I. returns to England,	776
(April.) Dies at the Savoy Palace,	776
1366. Richard of Bourdeaux, son of the Black Prince, is born,	780
The Black Prince returns to Guienne,	777
Charles V. of France invades Aquitaine,	777
Edward III. reassumes his title of King of France,	778
1369. Queen Philippa dies,	779

A.D.	PAGE
The Black Prince besieges Limoges, and massacres the inhabitants,	778
1371. David II., king of Scotland, dies,	774
Accession of Robert II.,	774
1372. (June.) The English fleet, under the Earl of Pembroke, captured by the Spaniards near Rochelle,	778
1374. Truce concluded between England and France,	770
1376. Several of the ministers are removed and imprisoned,	779
(June 8.) The Black Prince dies,	779
He is buried in Canterbury Cathedral,	779
Prince Richard is acknowledged by parliament heir to the throne,	780
The Speaker of the Commons is arrested, and William of Wickham, bishop of Winchester, dismissed the court,	780
1377. The Duke of Lancaster supports Wycliffe, and causes a riot in London; the Savoy Palace is plundered,	780
(Feb.) General amnesty proclaimed,	780
(June 21.) Edward III. dies,	781
(June 22.) Accession of Richard II.,	782
(Aug.) The French and Spaniards plunder and waste the Isle of Wight, Hastings, and Rye,	782
1378. Cherbourg is taken by the English; fourteen of the Spanish ships are captured; the harbour of Brest is ceded to the English,	783
John Mercer takes all the English ships in the port of Scarborough; John Philpot recovers the ships, takes the Spanish fleet, and captures Mercer,	783
(Oct.) Parliament grants Richard II. a new aid,	783
Some parts of Kent and Essex refuse to pay a poll-tax,	785
The people of Fobbing drive away one of the commissioners,	785
The peasants drive away the Chief-justice of the Pleas, and behead the jurors sent to try the rioters,	785
Jack Straw raises an insurrection in Essex, Kent, Suffolk, and Norfolk,	785
A tax-gatherer killed by Wat Tyler,	785
1381. (June 11.) The rebels encamp at Blackheath,	785, 786
The rebels plunder several places, and enter London; the prisons are demolished, and murders are committed,	786
(June 14.) Richard II. meets the rebels at Mile End,	787
Wat Tyler is slain in Smithfield,	788
The rebellion is repressed, and a general pardon is granted,	788, 789
Philip van Artaveldt raises the siege of Ghent,	790
1382. (Nov.) Philip van Artaveldt is defeated at the battle of Roscbecque, and is slain,	790
1385. (May.) A French army lands in Scotland; an inroad is made into England; Richard II. defeats the French and Scots; burns Edinburgh, Perth, and other towns; Henry of Bolingbroke is made Earl of Derby, the Earls of Cambridge and Buckingham created Dukes of York and Gloucester; Pole created Earl of Suffolk; Robert de Vere created Duke of Ireland; Roger, Earl of March, declared successor to the crown,	791
(July.) The Duke of Lancaster invades Castile; gains many battles; his daughter is married to the heir of the king of Castile,	791
1386. The Earl of Suffolk is dismissed; the Duke of Gloucester is appointed head of a regency,	792

A.D.		PAGE
1387.	(Aug.) The commission of regency declared illegal,	792
(Nov. 17.)	The Duke of Gloucester enters London; 'appeals' the king's adherents of treason,	792
1388.	The 'wonderful parliament' confirm the impeachments,	792, 793
(Aug. 15.)	The Battle of Otterbourne (Chevy Chase),	793
1389. (May.)	Richard II. assumes the government,	793, 794
1390. (April 19.)	Robert II., king of Scots, dies, and is succeeded by Robert III.,	794
	Gloucester is reconciled; Lancaster is created Duke of Aquitaine for life,	794
1394.	Truce with France concluded for four years,	794
	Richard II. marches into Ireland,	794
1396. (Oct.)	Richard II. goes to France, and marries Isabella, daughter of Charles VI.,	794
1397. (July.)	Richard II. arrests Warwick, Arundel, and Gloucester,	794
(Sept.)	Arundel is impeached, and beheaded,	795

A.D.		PAGE
(Sept. 17.)	Thomas Arundel, archbishop of Canterbury, impeached of high treason; banished for life,	795
	Parliament grants Richard II. a subsidy on wool for life,	795
1398. (Dec.)	The Duke of Lancaster dies, and Richard II. seizes his estates,	796
1399. (May.)	Richard II. sails for Ireland,	797
(July.)	Bolingbroke, Duke of Hereford, who had been banished for a quarrel with Norfolk, lands at Ravenspur,	797
1399.	The Duke of York goes to St Albans; Hereford is received in London; he takes Bristol Castle; Richard II. lands at Milford Haven; flies to Conway; is captured,	797
	He escapes; is retaken; sent to the Tower,	798
(Sept. 30.)	Parliament meets; Richard II. renounces the crown; Hereford is acknowledged king,	798–800

VOLUME II.

BOOK V.

A.D.		PAGE
1399.	Henry IV. calls a parliament in six days,	4
(Oct. 1.)	A deputation wait upon Richard II. in the Tower to renounce fealty to him,	5
(Oct. 13.)	Henry IV. is crowned in Westminster Abbey,	5
(Oct. 23.)	The lords agree that Richard II. shall be privately removed to safe custody,	6
	He is removed to Leeds, and several other castles,	6
	Prince Henry is created Prince of Wales, Duke of Guienne, Lancaster, and Cornwall, and Earl of Chester,	6
	Edmund Mortimer and his brother are lodged in Windsor Castle,	6
	The Earl of Salisbury plots the restoration of Richard II.,	6
	A statute for burning heretics is passed,	22
1400. (Jan. 3.)	A tournament is held at Oxford, at which it is intended to assassinate Henry IV. and his sons,	6, 7
(Jan. 4.)	The conspirators surprise Windsor Castle; they raise different parts of the country, and proclaim Richard II.; they are all captured and killed,	7
	Richard II. is murdered at Pontefract Castle,	7
	Henry IV. collects an army; marches to Edinburgh; but is repulsed by the Duke of Rothsay,	9
	Owen Glendower heads an insurrection in Wales,	9, 10
1401. (Feb.)	Henry IV. goes into Wales against Glendower,	10
1402. (Feb.)	Sir Roger de Clarendon and others are executed as traitors for asserting Richard II. to be alive,	11
(March.)	The Duke of Rothsay is imprisoned, and murdered in Falkland Castle,	19–131
(June.)	A Scottish army enters England; is defeated at Nesbit Moor; Earl Douglas ravages England as far as Newcastle,	11–131
(Sept. 14.)	Battle of Homildon Hill; Douglas is captured,	11–131

A.D.		PAGE
	Glendower gains the battles of Vurnwye and Knyghton, and captures Sir Edmund Mortimer,	11
1403.	Insurrection of the Percies of Northumberland,	13
	Douglas is liberated; the right of the Earl of March first insisted on,	14
(July 21.)	Battle of Shrewsbury; Hotspur is killed,	14, 15
	The French ravage the coast; take Guernsey and Jersey, and attack and burn Plymouth,	15
1404.	Ward, a Scotchman, personates Richard II.; a plot is formed against Henry IV.; it is suppressed; Serle, the contriver of it, is hanged,	16
(Oct. 6.)	The 'Parliamentum indoctorum' held; Henry IV. wishes to alienate a portion of the church-property,	16
1405.	The Earl of March and his brother escape from Windsor Castle; they are retaken; the Duke of York is seized and his estates sequestrated,	16
	An insurrection again breaks out in the north,	17
	Prince John defeats the rebels,	17
	The archbishop of York, the Earl of Nottingham, and others, are captured at Shipton-on-the-Moor; they are beheaded at Pontefract,	17
	The Lords Hastings, Falconbridge, and others, tried, convicted, and executed for treason at Durham,	17
(March.)	The Prince of Wales defeats the Welsh at Grosmont; takes Lampeter Castle,	17
(March 30.)	Henry IV. captures the heir-apparent of Scotland, and sends him to Pevensey Castle,	19–131
	The Prince of Wales subdues South Wales,	18
1406. (April 4.)	Robert III., king of Scotland, dies at Rothsay Castle,	131
	James Earl of Carrick is declared king, and Albany regent,	131

A.D.		PAGE
	The French take sixty castles and fortresses in Guienne and Saintonge; Isabella, widow of Richard II., is married to the Count of Angoulême; the French endeavour to retake Calais,	19, 20
(Nov. 23.)	The Duke of Orleans is murdered in Paris,	20
1408.	The Earl of Northumberland and Lord Bardolph take several castles in Northumberland,	19
(Feb. 23.)	They are defeated and slain at Branham Moor,	19
(June.)	The Duke of Burgundy is expelled,	20
1409.	The quarrel of the Dukes of Burgundy and Orleans is arranged,	20, 21
1411.	Henry IV. sends a force to aid the Duke of Burgundy; his partisans enter Paris,	21
(July 24.)	The Earl of Mar defeats the Lord of the Isles at the Battle of Harlaw,	132
	The treaty of Lochgillip; the Lord of the Isles acknowledges himself a vassal of the Scottish crown,	132
1412.	Henry IV. is acknowledged lawful Duke of Acquitaine,	21
	The Duke of Clarence lands with an army in Normandy; he marches through France,	21, 22
1413. (March 21.)	Accession of Henry V.,	24
(April.)	The body of Richard II. is removed from the Friar's Church, Langly, and buried in Westminster Abbey; Henry V. releases the Earl of March,	25
	Sir John Oldcastle is accused of heresy,	25
	Is committed to the Tower; is sentenced to be burnt; escapes from the Tower; endeavours to take the king at Eltham Palace,	25
1414. (Jan. 7.)	Henry V. takes some of the Lollards in St Giles's Fields, and at Harengay Park,	25
(Jan. 13.)	The Lollards are hanged and burnt in St Giles's Fields,	26
	Others are captured, and many executed,	26
1415. (April 16.)	Henry V. announces to a council at Westminster his determination to invade France; appoints the Duke of Bedford regent,	28
	Henry V. sails from Southampton,	29
(Aug. 17.)	Besieges Harfleur,	29
(Sept. 22.)	It is surrendered to him; he passes through Normandy,	29
(Oct. 14.)	Attempts to pass the Somme at Pont St Remy; is several times repulsed,	30
(Oct. 25.)	The battle of Agincourt,	30–34
	Henry V. marches to Calais,	34
	The dauphin dies,	36
	Henry V. sails for England,	34
	Parliament grants him for life a subsidy on wool and leather,	34
	The French besiege Harfleur,	35
1416. (Aug. 15.)	The Duke of Bedford sails from Rye; he gains a victory over the French and Genoese fleets; raises the siege of Harfleur; returns to England,	35
1417.	The Dauphin dies at Compiegne,	37
(Aug.)	Henry V. lands at Tongue; conquers many places in Normandy; the French sue for peace,	38
	The Scotch invade England; the 'foul raid,'	38–132
	Sir John Oldcastle is captured; tried as a traitor before the House of Lords,	38
(Dec.)	He is hanged and burnt in St Giles's Fields,	38
1418.	Henry V. takes various towns,	39
(July.)	He completes the conquest of Lower Normandy,	39

A.D.		PAGE
(July 14.)	The queen of France and the Duke of Burgundy enter Paris,	42
1419. (Jan 16.)	Henry V. captures Rouen; completes the conquest of Normandy,	43
(May.)	The Duke of Burgundy and the dauphin join against the English,	44, 45
	The Duke of Burgundy is assassinated at Montereau,	46
(July 27.)	Henry V. takes Pontoise,	46
(April.)	The treaty of Troyes is executed,	47
(June 2.)	Henry V. is married to the Princess Catherine of France,	47
(June 4.)	He marches to Sens, which he reduces,	48
	Takes Montereau, Villeneuve-le-Roy, and Melun,	48
(Dec.)	Henry V. and King Charles enter Paris; the two queens enter Paris,	48
(Dec. 6.)	The treaty of Troyes is ratified,	48
1421. (Jan.)	Henry V. leaves Paris; returns to London,	48
	Catherine is crowned Queen of England,	48
(March.)	The Earl of Buchan is made Constable of France by the dauphin Charles,	49
	The English parliament ratify the treaty of Troyes,	49
	James I., king of Scotland, is released from Windsor Castle,	49
(June 12.)	The English and Scottish armies land at Calais; several victories are gained,	49
	James I., king of Scots, besieges Dreux,	49
(Aug. 20.)	Dreux capitulates,	49
(Oct.)	Henry V. besieges Meaux,	49
(Dec. 6.)	The queen is delivered of a son at Windsor,	50
	Jacqueline, Countess of Hainault, takes refuge in England,	57
1422. (May.)	Meaux is taken, and the Bastard of Vaurus hanged,	50
(May 21.)	Queen Catherine lands at Harfleur,	50
(June.)	Henry V. and Catherine keep their court at the palace of the Louvre,	50
(Aug. 31.)	Henry V. dies at Vincennes,	51
	The Duke of Gloucester is appointed protector,	52
	The Duke of Bedford is appointed regent of France,	53, 54
(Oct.)	Charles VI. of France dies,	54
	The dauphin is proclaimed by his party Charles VII.,	54
	He is crowned and anointed at Poictiers,	54
	The Duke of Bedford proclaims Henry VI. at Paris, and fealty is sworn to him as king of France,	54
	He gains a victory over the French and Scotch before Crevant,	54
	The English, under John de la Pole, are defeated at La Gravelle,	55
	The Count de Richemont deserts from the English,	56
1423.	The Earl of Douglas is created Duke of Touraine,	56
1424. (Feb. 24.)	James I., king of Scotland, marries Lady Joanna Beaufort,	132
	He is released from his imprisonment in England,	56
(April 5.)	He arrives in Scotland, and is crowned,	133
(May.)	The Duke of Bedford besieges and takes Ivry in Normandy,	56
	Edmund Mortimer, Earl of March, dies,	89
(Aug. 17.)	Battle of Verneuil,	56, 57
1425.	Gloucester returns to England; the Duke of Brittany abandons the English; he is defeated and forced to swear to the treaty of Troyes,	58
	Queen Catherine marries Owen Tudor,	80
1427. (April.)	James I. of Scotland executes several Highland chiefs,	133

CHRONOLOGICAL INDEX.

A.D.		PAGE
1428.	The Duke of Gloucester's marriage is declared void; he marries Eleanor Cobham,	59
(March 21.)	James I. of Scotland, arrests several great lords,	133
(May.)	They are executed,	133
(Oct. 12.)	The siege of Orleans is commenced by the Earl of Salisbury,	60
(Nov.)	The Earl of Salisbury is wounded, and dies,	61
1429. (Feb.)	The Battle of Herrings fought at Rouvrai,	61
	The Maid of Orleans is introduced to Charles VII. at Chinon,	62
	She carries succours into Orleans,	65
	She heads a sortie; the bastille of Saint Loup is carried; she attacks Tournelles; is wounded; (May 8) Tournelles is captured,	66, 67
	Suffolk is made prisoner,	68
	Troyes is surrendered to Charles VII.,	69
(July 15.)	He enters Rheims with the Maid of Orleans,	69
(July 17.)	He is anointed and crowned in the cathedral,	60
(Sept. 12.)	The army of Charles VII. attack Paris; they are repulsed; the Maid is wounded,	72
1430. (May 25.)	The Maid relieves Compiegne; she is captured by the troops of the Duke of Burgundy,	73, 74
	Henry VI. is crowned at Westminster,	77
1431.	The Maid is sent to Rouen; she is tried for heresy, and sentenced to perpetual imprisonment,	74, 75
(May 24.)	She abjures,	76
(May 30.)	She is burnt in the market-place,	76, 77
(Nov.)	Henry VI. is crowned in Notre Dame in Paris,	77
	Many of the Highland captives are put to death by James I., king of Scotland,	134
1435.	A treaty of peace is signed between the king of France and the Duke of Burgundy,	78
(April.)	Paris and other towns surrender to the French king,	79
	The Duke of York is appointed regent of France,	79
	The Earl of Shrewsbury reduces the revolted towns of Normandy; takes Pontoise,	79
	The Duke of Gloucester raises the siege of Calais,	80
	The Scotch besiege Roxburgh; James I. suddenly returns to Scotland,	134
1437.	The Duke of Burgundy is defeated before Crotoy,	80
	The Duke of York is recalled; the Earl of Warwick is appointed to command,	80
	James I. of Scotland is assassinated,	134
1439.	The Earl of Warwick dies; York is reappointed,	80
	The Earl of Shrewsbury recovers Harfleur,	80
	The plague and famine ravage England and France,	80
1441.	The Duchess of Gloucester is accused of treason and sorcery; is condemned to perpetual imprisonment,	83
	Roger Bolingbroke and Margery Jourdayn are executed,	83
1442.	The Earl of Shrewsbury relieves Pontoise,	83
1444.	Truce agreed on for two years,	83
1447. (Feb. 11.)	The Duke of Gloucester is arrested for treason,	83
(Feb. 28.)	He is found dead in bed,	83

A.D.		PAGE
1449.	James II. of Scotland marries Mary of Gueldres,	135
	Rouen is taken by the Count of Dunois,	85
(Nov. 4.)	The citadel surrenders,	85
	The power of the Livingstons is destroyed in Scotland,	134, 135
	The Duke of York suppresses an insurrection in Ireland,	89
1450. (Jan.)	The Duke of Suffolk is committed to the Tower,	86
(March 17.)	He is impeached; is banished by the king,	87
(May 5.)	He is beheaded in a boat in the Channel,	87
	The English are defeated at Fourmigni,	85
(Aug. 12.)	Cherbourg is besieged; surrenders to the French; the whole of Normandy is lost,	85
1451.	Various towns surrender to the French; Bourdeaux, Bayonne, and Fronsac capitulate,	85
	Jack Cade raises an insurrection in Kent,	88
(June 24.)	He defeats the royal troops at Sevenoaks,	88
(July 4.)	He beheads the Lord Say in Cheapside,	88
	Cade is slain by Alexander Iden,	89
(Aug.)	The Duke of York returns to England,	89
(Nov.)	It is proposed in parliament that he shall be declared heir to the throne,	90
1452. (Feb.)	The Earl of Douglas is assassinated at Stirling,	135
	York levies an army; he disbands it; is made prisoner, and sent to London,	90
1453.	Queen Margaret is delivered of a son; he is created Prince of Wales and Earl of Chester,	92
	The Earl of Shrewsbury gains many victories in France; he is slain; Bourdeaux is retaken; the English return,	91
1454. (Feb.)	The Duke of York opens parliament as lieutenant for Henry VI.; he is elected protector,	91, 92
	Henry VI. resumes his authority,	92
(May 22.)	The Duke of York takes St Albans, and captures Henry VI.; the Duke of Somerset and many other nobles are slain,	92
	York is again declared protector,	93
1456.	Henry VI. again resumes his authority,	93
(March 25.)	The Lancastrians and Yorkists are reconciled,	93
1459. (Sept.)	The Yorkists gain a great victory at Bloreheath,	94
(Oct. 13.)	Sir Andrew Trollop deserts to Henry VI.,	94
(Oct. 14.)	York breaks up his camp, and retreats to Ireland,	94
(Nov. 20.)	He and his adherents are attainted in parliament,	94
	The sailors of the fleet at Calais desert, and take their ships to the Earl of Warwick; he sails to Dublin,	94
1460. (June.)	Warwick lands in Kent; he enters London with the son of York,	94, 95
	Battle of Northampton; Henry VI. is taken prisoner,	95
(July.)	James II. of Scotland is killed at the siege of Roxburgh,	135
(Oct. 16.)	The Duke of York returns to London; he dethrones the crown,	95
(Oct. 23.)	It is agreed in the Upper House that Henry VI. shall continue king, and on his death York shall succeed,	95, 96
	Battle of Wakefield; York is slain,	96
1461.	The Earl of March succeeds his father as Duke of York,	96

A.D.	PAGE
(Feb. 1.) Battle of Mortimer's Cross; Owen Tudor is taken, and with others is beheaded,	96
Queen Margaret defeats the Earl of Warwick,	96, 97
(Feb. 17.) Battle of Barnet; second battle of St. Albans; Henry VI. is retaken by the queen,	97
(Feb. 25.) The Duke of York enters London,	97
He is proclaimed king,	98
(March 10.) The bishop of Exeter is made chancellor,	102
(March 28.) Battle of Towton; Henry VI., Queen Margaret, and the Prince of Wales fly to Scotland,	98, 99
(June 29.) Edward IV. is crowned at Westminster; his brothers, George and Richard, are created Dukes of Clarence and Gloucester,	99
Queen Margaret goes to France; she returns to England with a small army; takes Alnwick, Bamborough, and Dunstanburgh Castles; she is driven off by the Earl of Warwick,	100
(Dec.) Bamborough and Dunstanburgh surrender,	100
1463. (Jan.) Alnwick Castle capitulates to Warwick, Henry VI. is conveyed to Wales; Margaret goes to Flanders,	100
1464. (April 25.) Henry VI. is brought back to England; the Lancastrians again take the field; they are defeated at Hedgley Moor,	101
(May 1.) Edward IV. marries the widow of Sir John Gray,	101
(May 15.) Battle of Hexham,	101
1465. The Duke of Luxembourg comes to England to the coronation of his niece, Henry VI. seized at Waddington Hall, and lodged by Warwick in the Tower,	101
(May 25.) Elizabeth is carried through the streets of London,	101, 102
(May 26.) She is crowned at Westminster,	102
The queen's relatives are advanced,	102
1467. The Earl of Warwick goes to Normandy, to negotiate a marriage between the son of Louis XI. of France and the Princess Margaret,	103
Edward IV. marries his sister Margaret to the Duke of Burgundy,	103
1468. Warwick again appears at court,	103
1469. (July.) Insurrection in Yorkshire; Edward IV. advances against the insurgents; retreats to Nottingham Castle,	104
(July 26.) Battle of Edgecote; the Earl of Pembroke is slain; the father and brother of Queen Elizabeth are captured and beheaded at Northampton,	104
Warwick returns to England; Edward IV. is confined in Middleham Castle,	104
He is released; an amnesty is agreed on,	104
1470. (March 12.) The battle of Erpingham; Edward IV. defeats the Lancastrians; Warwick and Clarence take refuge in Normandy,	104, 105
(June.) Queen Margaret and Warwick meet at Amboise,	105
The Prince of Wales is married to Anne, the second daughter of Warwick,	105
(Sept. 13.) Warwick lands on the coast of Devonshire,	106
Edward IV. takes ship, and sails for Holland,	107
(Oct. 6.) Warwick releases Henry VI. from the Tower; Queen Elizabeth takes refuge in the Sanctuary at Westminster; is there delivered of a son,	107
1471. (March 16.) Edward IV. lands at Ravenspur;	

A.D.	PAGE
he swears not to attempt to gain the crown; he reaches London,	108
(April 30.) Second battle of Barnet; Warwick is slain; Henry VI. is again sent to the Tower; Queen Margaret and the Prince of Wales land at Plymouth,	108, 109
(May 4.) Battle of Tewkesbury; the queen and prince are taken prisoners; the prince is murdered,	109
(May 21.) Edward IV. enters London,	110
(May 22.) Henry VI. is found dead in the Tower,	110
1472. Prince Edward is created Prince of Wales, and acknowledged heir to the throne,	111
The Duke of Gloucester marries the widow of the Prince of Wales, slain at Tewkesbury,	111
1475. Edward IV. contracts an alliance with the Dukes of Brittany and Burgundy; he demands the crown of France of Louis XI.,	111
Edward IV. raises money by benevolences,	112
(June 22.) He lands at Calais with a great army,	112
(Aug. 29.) A treaty is concluded,	112, 113
1476. Clarence is committed to the Tower,	114
1478. (Jan. 16.) Parliament is summoned; Clarence is accused of witchcraft and other crimes,	114
(Feb. 7.) He is found guilty, and sentenced to death,	114
(Feb. 18.) He dies, or is killed in the Tower,	114
1480. The Duke of Gloucester commands the army in Scotland,	115
1482. The Duke of Albany, after escaping to France, returns; assumes the title of Alexander, King of Scotland; agrees to accept the crown as a gift from Edward IV.,	136
(June.) Treaty of Fotheringay is executed between Edward IV. and Albany; the Duke of Gloucester takes the town of Berwick; the Earl of Angus hangs the nobles of James III. at the bridge of Lauder; James is taken to Edinburgh,	115–136
(July.) Albany and Gloucester march to Edinburgh,	115
(Aug.) James III. is liberated; Albany is appointed lieutenant-general of the kingdom,	115–136
Louis XI. affiances the dauphin to the daughter of the Duchess of Burgundy,	116
1483. (April 9.) Edward IV. dies; is buried at Windsor,	116
Gloucester returns from Scotland; he collects the nobility and others at York; they swear fealty to Edward V.,	118
(April 22.) He arrives at Northampton; the Lord Richard Gray, Earl Rivers, and the Duke of Buckingham meet him,	118
(April 23.) He places Rivers, Gray, Sir Thomas Vaughan, and Sir Richard Hawse under arrest,	118
Queen Elizabeth takes sanctuary with the Duke of York and her daughters at Westminster,	118
(May.) Edward V. is conveyed to the Tower,	119
(May 22.) Gloucester is appointed protector,	119
(June 13.) Lord Hastings is arrested,	120
He is beheaded,	121
(June 14.) Rivers, Gray, Vaughan, and Hawse are beheaded,	121
(June 16.) The Duke of York is carried to the Tower,	121
Jane Shore does penance,	121
(July 6.) Gloucester is crowned king of England	

A.D.		PAGE
	as Richard III., with his wife, Anne, at Westminster,	124
	Edward V. and the Duke of York are murdered,	125-314
	The Earl of Richmond is invited into England,	125, 126
(Oct.)	Richard III. summons a meeting of his adherents at Leicester,	126
(Oct. 18.)	The insurrection in favour of Richmond breaks out; he is proclaimed king in Exeter and other places,	126
	The Duke of Buckingham is captured and beheaded,	127
(Nov. 11.)	Parliament recognises Richard's title; his son Edward is declared Prince of Wales,	127
1484.	The Prince of Wales dies suddenly at Middleham Castle,	127
1485.	Queen Anne dies,	128
(Aug. 7.)	Richmond lands at Milford Haven,	129
(Aug 22.)	Battle of Bosworth Field; Richard III. is slain,	129
	Henry VII. is crowned on the field of battle,	129
	Richard III. is buried at the Grey Friars in Leicester,	130

BOOK VI.

1485. (Aug. 27.)	Henry VII. enters London,	281
(Sept. 21.)	The sweating sickness breaks out in London,	282
(Oct. 28.)	Jasper, Earl of Pembroke, is made Duke of Bedford; Lord Stanley and Sir Edward Courtenay are made Earls of Derby and Devonshire,	282
(Oct. 30.)	Henry VII. is crowned at Westminster,	282
	The Yeomen of the Guard established,	283
(Nov. 7.)	Parliament meets; the king's title is admitted,	283
	Henry VII. dates his reign from the day before the battle of Bosworth,	283, 284
	The crown is settled upon Henry VII. and the heirs of his body,	284
	All grants from the crown since 34th Henry VI. are resumed; an act of grace is published by the king,	285
1486. (Jan. 18.)	Henry VII. marries Elizabeth of York; union of the Houses of York and Lancaster,	285
	Pope Innocent VIII. gives a dispensation for the marriage, acknowledging Henry's title,	285, 286
	Henry VII. goes to York and other towns,	287
(June.)	Treaty of peace with Scotland,	287
(Sept. 20.)	The queen is delivered of a son; he is named Arthur,	287
(Nov.)	Lambert Simnel, the pretended Earl of Warwick, appears in Dublin, with Simon, the priest of Oxford,	287
	Henry VII. proclaims a general pardon,	288
	The queen-dowager is committed prisoner to the monastery of Bermondsey,	288
	The Marquis of Dorset is sent to the Tower,	288
	The Earl of Warwick is paraded through the streets of London,	288
	John de la Pole, Earl of Lincoln, flies to Flanders,	289
(May.)	Lambert Simnel is crowned in Dublin as King Edward VI.,	289
1487.	Simnel, with the Earl of Lincoln and others, and an army of Germans and Irish, land at the pile of Foudray,	289, 290

A.D.		PAGE
(June 16.)	Battle of Stoke; the rebels are defeated; Simnel and Simon are taken; the Earl of Lincoln is slain,	290
(Nov. 20.)	The queen is crowned at Westminster,	291
1488.	James III. of Scotland is driven from Edinburgh,	302
(June 18.)	Battle of Cangler Moor; James III. is killed; is buried at Cambuskenneth Abbey,	302, 303
(June 26.)	James IV. is crowned at Scone,	303
(July 20.)	The English and Breton army under Sir Edward Woodville and the Duke of Orleans are defeated between Audouillé and St Aubin du Cormier; Woodville is slain; the duke is taken prisoner; several are executed,	294
(Aug.)	The Duke of Brittany signs the treaty of Verger,	295
1489.	Parliament grants £75,000 to carry on the war in Brittany; Lord Willoughby de Broke lands with a small army,	295
	Sir Andrew Wood beats the English in sea-fights off Dunbar and St Abbs,	303, 304
1490.	Maximilian, king of the Romans, marries Anne, Duchess of Brittany, by proxy,	296
1491. (Dec. 6.)	She is married at the Castle of Langeais, in Touraine, to Charles VIII. of France,	298
	Perkin Warbeck lands at Cork, and declares himself the Duke of York, son of Edward IV.,	299
1492.	Henry VII. proceeds to France; lays siege to Boulogne,	298
(Oct. 27.)	A council is held, and peace proposed with France,	299
(Nov.)	The treaty of Estaples is signed,	299
1495. (July 3.)	Warbeck lands at Deal; the people rise against him; his adherents are sent to London; he escapes to Flanders, the rebels are all executed,	301
1496. (Feb.)	Treaty of commerce signed between England and Flanders; Warbeck retreats to Scotland,	301-304
	Warbeck is married to Lady Catherine Gordon, daughter of the Earl of Huntly,	304, 305
	A treaty is concluded between James IV. and Warbeck,	305
	James IV. invades England with Warbeck and an army of Scots, Germans, and Flemings; they retire,	306
1497. (July.)	Warbeck and his wife sail from Scotland; he lands in Ireland, but retires,	307
(Sept.)	He lands at Whitsand Bay, Cornwall; assumes the title of Richard IV.,	307
(Sept. 17.)	He attacks Exeter; is repulsed; marches to Taunton Dean; he flies to the sanctuary at Beaulieu; Warbeck surrenders,	308, 309
1498. (June.)	Warbeck escapes; he is captured; he is placed in the stocks in various places; reads his confession; is recommitted to the Tower,	309
	Charles VIII. of France dies, and is succeeded by Louis XII.,	311
1499.	Ralph Wilford personates the Earl of Warwick; raises an insurrection with Patrick, an Augustine friar,	309
(March.)	Wilford is taken and executed; the friar is imprisoned for life,	309
(July.)	A plot is formed to liberate the Earl of Warwick and Warbeck,	309
(Nov. 16.)	Warbeck is tried for treason, and convicted,	310
(Nov. 23.)	He is executed at Tyburn,	310
(Nov. 24.)	The Earl of Warwick is beheaded for treason,	310

A.D.		PAGE
1500.	A plague rages in London,	310
	Henry VII. goes to Calais,	310
1501.	He sends an embassy to Scotland; James IV. asks the hand of Margaret, Henry VII.'s eldest daughter,	311
(Nov. 6.)	Arthur is married to Catherine of Arragon,	312
1502. (April.)	Arthur, Prince of Wales, dies at Ludlow,	312
1503.	Henry, Prince of Wales, is affianced to the widow of his brother Arthur,	312
(July.)	Margaret, queen of Scotland, proceeds from London,	312
(Aug. 7.)	She enters Edinburgh,	312
(Aug. 8.)	She is married,	312
1504.	Edmund de la Pole, Earl of Suffolk, flies to Burgundy,	314
1505.	Prince Henry is knighted; Henry VII. obtains £30,000 from parliament,	314
1506. (Jan.)	The Archduke Philip, and his wife, Joanna, queen of Castile, are driven by stress of weather into Weymouth,	314, 315
(Jan. 17.)	Henry VII. meets Philip on Elworth Green, near Windsor,	315
(April.)	Philip and Joanna are permitted to depart,	315
	Anne Boleyn is born,	363
1509. (April 21.)	Henry VII. dies at Richmond; is buried in his chapel at Westminster,	317
	Accession of Henry VIII.,	318
(June 3.)	He is married to Catherine of Arragon at Greenwich,	319
(June 24.)	He is crowned, with his queen Catherine, at Westminster,	318
1513.	He obtains supplies from parliament; prepares for a war with France; arms his northern towns,	321, 322
(April.)	The English fleet is defeated in the harbour of Brest; Sir Edward Howard, the lord-admiral, is slain,	322
(May.)	Henry VIII. sends the vanguard of his army to Calais; the Earl of Suffolk is beheaded; appoints the queen governor of the realm; he sails for France,	323
(June 30.)	He lands at Calais; marches to the siege of Terouenne; the Emperor Maximilian joins him; the battle of the Spurs,	323-325
(Aug.)	Terouenne surrenders,	325
(Aug. 22.)	James IV., king of Scotland, crosses the Borders; besieges Norham Castle; it surrenders; takes Wark and Ford Castles,	326
(Sept. 9.)	Battle of Flodden Field; James IV. is slain,	327-330
(Sept. 22.)	Henry VIII. enters Tournay in triumph,	326
(Oct. 22.)	He returns with his army to England,	326
	He creates the Earl of Surrey, Duke of Norfolk,	330
1514. (Aug. 7.)	The Princess Mary, sister of Henry VIII, is married by proxy to Louis XII. of France,	331
(Oct. 9.)	She departs for France, and is remarried,	331
	Anne Boleyn is appointed maid of honour to Mary,	331-363
1515. (Jan. 1.)	Louis XII. dies, and is succeeded by Francis I.,	332
(March.)	Queen Mary marries Charles Brandon, Duke of Suffolk,	332
	Wolsey is created a cardinal,	332
	He is made chancellor and legate,	334
(May 3.)	Queen Margaret of Scotland comes to England,	351
	The regent Albany suppresses an insurrection raised by the Earl of Arran; Home and his brother are executed,	351, 352

A.D.		PAGE
	Albany leaves Scotland; Queen Margaret returns to Scotland,	352
1516 to 1518.	Francis I. marches with an army for the recovery of Milan; the battle of Marignano; Milan surrenders; he returns to France,	334, 335
(Oct. 4.)	A treaty of alliance is ratified between Henry VIII. and Francis I.,	336
1519. (Jan.)	The Emperor Maximilian dies,	336
(March.)	Francis I. proposes himself as a candidate for the empire,	336
(May.)	Henry VIII. announces himself a candidate,	336
(June 28.)	The Archduke Charles, king of Spain, is elected emperor, under the title of Charles V.,	337
(May 31.)	Henry VIII., the queen, and his retinue embark for Calais to meet Francis I.,	338
(June 7.)	The two kings meet at the Field of Cloth of Gold,	340-343
1521. (April 16.)	The Duke of Buckingham is arrested for treason, and taken to the Tower,	344
(May 13.)	He is tried and condemned,	344
(May 14.)	Orders are issued by Wolsey for the seizure of heretical books,	345
(May 17.)	Buckingham is beheaded on Tower Hill,	345
(July 30.)	Wolsey is sent ambassador to mediate between the emperor and Francis I.	345
(Oct.)	A league is made by Henry VIII. with the pope and the emperor,	346
	Henry's defence of the seven sacraments is sent to Leo X., who confers on him the title of Defender of the Faith,	345
1522.	Francis I. seizes the 'goods of English merchants in his ports,	347, 348
(May 26.)	The emperor lands at Dover; a treaty is concluded between him and Henry VIII. for the invasion of France,	348
	Forced loans are raised in London,	348, 349
(Aug.)	The Earl of Surrey opens the campaign; returns to Calais,	349
	The Earl of Surrey with a great army destroys Merse and the abbey of Jedburgh,	429
1523.	Parliament is assembled; Sir Thomas More is chosen Speaker of the Commons; Wolsey demands in person in the House of Commons £800,000 for the recovery of France; a property-tax is agreed to,	354, 355
(Sept. 4.)	The Duke of Suffolk opens the campaign in France,	355
	He returns to Calais,	357
1524.	Bonnivet, the commander of the French army, overruns Piedmont and the Milanese,	353
	The emperor retakes all the conquests of the French; death of the Chevalier Bayard,	353
	Siege of Marseilles; it is raised; the plague at Milan; siege of Pavia,	358, 359
1525. (Feb. 24.)	Battle of Pavia; Francis I. is taken prisoner,	359
	Henry VIII. attempts to levy money by benevolences for the conquest of France; it is refused; an insurrection is raised; the benevolence is not insisted on,	359, 360
(June.)	Henry VIII. and Wolsey disagree concerning the suppression of some monasteries,	362
	Henry VIII. concludes an alliance, offensive and defensive, with France,	361
	Francis I. abdicates in favour of his son the dauphin,	361
	Queen Margaret obtains possession of King James V.,	430

CHRONOLOGICAL INDEX.

A.D.	PAGE
1526. (Jan. 14.) The Concord of Madrid is signed; Francis I. is set at liberty, and returns to France,	361
Moncada seizes Rome; plunders the Vatican; the pope takes refuge in the Castle of St Angelo,	362
(Sept. 21.) A treaty of peace is signed, and the Spaniards leave Rome,	362
(Dec.) The Spaniards again invade the Roman States,	362
1527. (May 5.) Rome is assaulted, taken, and sacked by the Spaniards; the Constable Bourbon is killed; the pope and some of the cardinals are besieged in the Castle of St Angelo,	363
Henry VIII.'s marriage with Catherine of Arragon questioned,	364
(Aug.) Henry VIII. writes a treatise upon the unlawfulness of his marriage with Catherine,	366
The pope authorises Wolsey and another cardinal to decide the question of divorce; grants a dispensation for Henry VIII.'s marriage with any other woman,	367
1528. Henry VIII. demands a decretal bull from the pope,	367
Wolsey and Cardinal Campeggio are authorised to determine the divorce,	368
(May.) The sweating sickness breaks out in London,	368
(July.) James V. of Scotland obtains his freedom; banishes Angus,	430
(Aug.) The plague rages in Italy,	368
(Sept.) The French army in Italy surrender to the Imperialists,	368
1529. (July.) Wolsey has two bills filed against him in the Court of King's Bench, for exercising the functions of pope's legate,	371
Sentence is pronounced against him in the Court of King's Bench,	372
1530. He receives a free pardon from Henry VIII.,	373
(Nov. 4.) He is arrested for high treason,	373
(Nov. 29.) He dies at Leicester Abbey, and is buried in the Lady's Chapel of the monastery,	374
The marriage of Henry VIII. is declared illegal by the universities of Oxford and Cambridge,	375, 376
The foreign universities differ,	376
1531. (March.) The pope publishes a breve, forbidding Henry VIII. to contract a second marriage under pain of excommunication,	376
Thomas Cromwell advises Henry VIII. to act on the opinion of the English universities, and to obtain the sanction of parliament,	377
He advises Henry VIII. to declare himself supreme head of the church,	377
The whole body of the clergy are involved in a præmunire for abetting Wolsey in acting as pope's legate,	377, 378
The convocation offer £100,000, and acknowledge Henry VIII. to be protector and only supreme head of the church and clergy of England, as far as may be by the law of Christ; they are pardoned,	378
Sir Thomas More, the chancellor, and some peers, attend in the House of Commons, and declare the king's proceedings touching his marriage,	378
(May.) Thomas Bilney is burnt in Smithfield as a heretic, for attempting to expose the errors of popery,	378

A.D.	PAGE
1532. The war with Scotland again breaks out on the Borders,	430
(May 16.) Sir Thomas More retires,	378
(June 4.) Sir Thomas Audley is appointed chancellor,	378
Parliament abolishes annates, or first-fruits,	378
Anne Boleyn goes with Henry VIII. to Calais; they meet Francis I. at Boulogne,	379
Elizabeth Barton, the Holy Maid of Kent, is arrested by order of Henry VIII.,	384
(Nov. 15.) The pope signs a breve, declaring Henry VIII. and Anne excommunicated unless they should separate,	378, 379
1533. (Jan. 4 or 25.) Henry VIII. is married to Anne Boleyn at Whitehall,	379, 380
Cranmer is made archbishop of Canterbury,	380
(March.) Appeals to Rome prohibited by parliament,	380
Queen Catherine declared by parliament to be only Princess-dowager of Wales,	380
(May 23.) Cranmer pronounces her marriage with Henry VIII. to be null and void,	381
(May 28.) Cranmer declares to the clergy the marriage of Henry VIII. and Anne Boleyn, and confirms the same,	381
(June 1.) Anne is crowned at Westminster by Cranmer,	381
(July 11.) The pope annuls the judgment of Cranmer, and publishes his bull of excommunication against Henry VIII. and Anne,	381
(Sept. 7.) Anne is delivered of a girl, the Princess Elizabeth,	383
1534. Parliament prohibits every kind of payment or appeal to the pope; confirms Henry VIII.'s title as supreme head of the church; vests in the king only the right of appointing to all bishoprics; of deciding in all ecclesiastical causes,	384
(March 23.) The Consistory of Rome decides on the validity of Henry VIII.'s marriage with Catherine; the pope gives sentence,	384
Parliament declares the marriage between Henry VIII. and Anne lawful; sets aside the Princess Mary as illegitimate; settles the succession on the issue of Anne; declares it to be high treason to question the second marriage,	384
(April 21.) The Maid of Kent and her abettors are attainted of high treason, and others of misprision of treason,	385
They are executed at Tyburn,	385
Fisher, bishop of Rochester, and Sir Thomas More, are committed to the Tower,	385, 386
(Nov.) Parliament imposes new oaths; annexes first-fruits and tenths to the crown; empowers Henry VIII. to punish heresies,	386
1535. (May 25.) Some Dutch Anabaptists are burnt for denying the actual presence in the Eucharist,	386
(June 18.) Other Catholics are executed for denying the supremacy,	386
(June 22.) Fisher, bishop of Rochester, is beheaded for the same offence,	386
(July 6.) More is also executed for the same,	389
(Aug. 30.) Pope Paul III. signs a bull against Henry VIII. citing him to appear at Rome; in default, declares him to have forfeited the crown, and his children by Anne incapable of inheriting,	389
Sir Thomas Cromwell is appointed	

A.D.		PAGE
	vicar-general of Henry VIII.; he proposes the suppression of some monasteries, convents, and abbeys,	390
	Henry VIII. issues a commission to inquire into the conduct of the religious houses,	390
1536. (Jan. 8.)	Queen Catherine dies at Kimbolton,	390
(Jan. 29.)	Anne Boleyn is delivered of a son stillborn,	390, 391
(May 2.)	Anne is arrested for treason, and committed to the Tower; Viscount Rochford her brother, Norris, Smeaton, Brereton, and Weston are committed also,	391
	Anne is examined before the privy council,	392
	Smeaton confesses his guilt,	392
(May 10.)	Bills of indictment are found against all but Lord Rochford,	392
(May 12.)	Norris, Weston, Brereton, and Smeaton are arraigned and convicted of treason and adultery,	392
(May 15.)	Anne and Lord Rochford are tried in the Tower, and condemned to death,	393
(May 17.)	Smeaton is hanged; the others are beheaded,	394
	Cranmer pronounces the marriage of Anne to have been always null and void,	395
(May 19.)	Anne is beheaded in the Tower,	393, 394
(May 20.)	Henry VIII. marries Jane Seymour,	394
(June.)	Parliament passes an act of succession, entailing the crown on Henry VIII.'s issue by Jane Seymour; with power to Henry to bequeath the crown by letters-patent or will,	395
	Wales is united to England, and governed by the same laws,	425
	The lesser monasteries are suppressed,	396
	Henry VIII. reduces the number of sacraments to three,	397
	An English translation of the Bible ordered to be printed,	397
(Oct.)	An insurrection breaks out in Lincolnshire; the Duke of Suffolk negotiates,	397
	Henry VIII. answers the articles of complaint,	398
	An insurrection breaks out in the northern counties,	398, 399
(Oct.)	Lords Darcy, Lumley, and others, and the archbishop of York, join the northern insurgents, who are called the Pilgrims of Grace; Robert Aske is appointed leader,	399
	The Duke of Suffolk treats with them,	399
	Reginald Pole is created a cardinal,	401
1537.	The insurgents endeavour to take various places; disperse; Aske, Darcy, and others are taken,	400, 401
	Martial law is proclaimed in the north, and many executions take place,	401
(May.)	James V. and his queen land at Leith,	431
	The Bible is published in English; the Bishop's Book,	424
(Oct. 12.)	Queen Jane Seymour is delivered of a son,	402
(Oct. 24.)	She dies; the prince is created Prince of Wales, Duke of Cornwall, and Earl of Chester; Edward Seymour is created Earl of Hereford,	402
	Some of the larger monasteries are suppressed, and the abbeys are seized by Henry VIII.	402
	Thomas à Becket is cited to appear at Westminster,	402, 403
1538.	The Protestant princes of Germany send over a deputation to convert Henry VIII. to the Protestant faith,	409
(Nov.)	Thomas à Becket is declared a rebel and a traitor,	406
	John Lambert is tried for heresy in denying the real presence; Henry VIII. presides as supreme head of the church; Lambert is condemned to be burnt; he is executed in Smithfield,	406, 407
1539. (April 26.)	Parliament passes bills of attainder against the Countess of Salisbury and others,	408
	They are all condemned to death by bill in parliament without trial,	409
(May 18.)	Six questions are proposed concerning the Eucharist and other matters for the consideration of parliament,	410
(May 20.)	Henry VIII. disputes in parliament upon them; they are adopted, and called the Six Articles or the Bloody Statute,	410
	Shaxton, bishop of Salisbury, and Latimer resign their sees,	410
(June 11.)	Thomas à Becket is tried and convicted of treason, rebellion, and contumacy; his bones to be burnt; the riches of his shrine to be forfeited to the crown,	403
(July 10.)	Sir Adrian Fortescue and Sir Thomas Dingley are beheaded,	409
	Queen Margaret dies,	430
(Aug.)	All the jewels and plate of the shrine of Becket are taken from Canterbury,	403
(Dec.)	Anne of Cleves arrives at Dover,	413
1540. (Jan. 5.)	She is married to Henry VIII.,	414
	The remaining monasteries and other religious houses are suppressed; their lands divided amongst courtiers and favourites,	404
	Cromwell is created Earl of Essex, &c.,	414
(Feb.)	Henry VIII. sends an embassy to James V. of Scotland, recommending the sequestration of the property of the monasteries,	431
(June 10.)	Cromwell is arrested for treason, and taken to the Tower,	415
(June 19.)	He is attainted as a traitor and a heretic,	415
(July 9.)	Henry VIII. is divorced from Anne of Cleves,	415
(July 16.)	She addresses Henry VIII. as her brother,	416
	Henry VIII. is married to Catherine Howard,	417
(July 28.)	Cromwell is beheaded on Tower Hill,	417
(Aug. 8.)	Catherine Howard is publicly acknowledged queen,	417
(Sept.)	Ireland is devastated by civil war,	428
1541. (May 27.)	The Countess of Salisbury is beheaded in the Tower,	409
	An attempt is made to revive the Pilgrimage of Grace,	417
(June 28.)	Lord Leonard Gray is beheaded for treason,	426
(Aug.)	Henry VIII. proceeds on a progress in the north,	417
	Catherine Howard is accused to Henry VIII.,	417
	The accomplices of Catherine are imprisoned for life for misprision of treason,	422, 423
1542.	Henry VIII. resolves to raise Ireland to the rank of a kingdom; creates several of the native chiefs peers; Ulliac de Burgh, Murrock O'Brien, and O'Neil are made Earls of Clanricarde, Thomond, and Tyrone,	428
	The chiefs do homage for their lands to Henry VIII., and hold them by military service; letters-patent are granted them for securing the possession of the lands,	428

A.D.		PAGE
(Feb. 11.)	Catherine is attainted by parliament with Lady Rochford,	423
(Feb. 13.)	They are both beheaded in the Tower,	423
(Aug.)	The English invade the Scottish border; they are defeated at Haddenrig,	433
(Oct.)	Henry VIII. claims the sovereignty of Scotland; the Duke of Norfolk marches with a powerful army; the Scotch are routed on Solway Moss; many of the Scottish nobility are carried prisoners to England,	433
(Dec. 14.)	James V. dies,	434
(Dec. 22.)	The Earl of Arran becomes regent of Scotland,	434
1543. (Feb.)	The English parliament restore the Princess Mary to her place in the succession,	438
(March.)	The treaty of Greenwich is executed by Henry VIII. and Angus, and others of the regency,	436
(Aug.)	It is ratified by the nobles,	436
	The ships of Scotch merchants are seized in the English ports, whither they were driven by stress of weather,	437
(July.)	Henry VIII. is married to Catherine Parr,	438
	Queen Mary of Scotland is crowned at Stirling,	437
	The Earl of Angus and his associates execute a bond at Douglas Castle to serve Henry VIII.,	437
	Angus and his confederates are accused of treason, the treaty of marriage is declared void,	437
	George Wishart goes to Scotland, and preaches against popery,	446
1544. (May 4.)	An English army land at Leith, which they plunder; the Scotch evacuate Edinburgh; the Earl of Hertford attacks the castle; is defeated; burns the town, and lays waste the country; he retreats from Leith, burns the shipping, and retreats to Berwick; the Catholics and Protestants coalesce against the English,	440
1545.	Lennox with a fleet takes the isles of Arran and Bute, and ravages the coast of Scotland,	440, 441
	Sir Ralph Evre lays waste the country about Jedburgh and Kyle,	441
	Battle of Ancrum Moor; the English are defeated; Sir Ralph Evre is slain,	441
(July 16.)	A French fleet cast anchor at St Helen's, in the Isle of Wight; the English fleet in Portsmouth harbour is prevented going out by Henry VIII.,	442
	The French fleet returns to Brest,	442
(Nov.)	Parliament grants Henry VIII. a subsidy and the disposal of all colleges, charities, and hospitals,	443
	George Wishart is seized; is tried as a heretic, and burnt at St Andrews,	446
(May 29.)	Cardinal Beaton is assassinated,	446, 447
(Sept.)	The Earl of Hertford again marches into Scotland; burns and destroys the villages; attacks the abbey of Kelso; murders the monks; plunders the abbeys of Melrose and Dryburgh; he retreats,	445
(Dec. 12.)	The Duke of Norfolk and the Earl of Surrey are sent to the Tower,	449
1546. (June 7.)	Treaty of Campes; Henry VIII. agrees to give up Boulogne on payment of money by Francis,	447
1547. (Jan. 13.)	The Earl of Surrey is arraigned for treason at Guildhall, for using the	

A.D.		PAGE
	royal arms of Edward the Confessor, quartered with his own; he is found guilty of an attempt upon the throne,	449
(Jan. 19.)	He is beheaded,	450
	The Duke of Norfolk makes a confession; a bill of attainder is brought in, which passes both Houses in six days,	451
(Jan. 27.)	The royal assent is given to the bill by commission; orders are sent to the Tower for his execution on the following morning,	451
(Jan. 28.)	Henry VIII. dies early in the morning,	451
	The Duke of Norfolk is respited,	451
(Jan. 31.)	The death of Henry VIII. is announced to parliament,	453
(Jan. 31.)	King Edward VI. enters London, and proceeds to the Tower,	454
(Feb. 1.)	Henry VIII's will is read, appointing sixteen executors to be governors of Edward VI. till he should be sixteen years of age; the Earl of Hertford is appointed sole governor by the others,	454, 455
(Feb. 16.)	Henry VIII. is buried at Windsor,	456
(Feb. 18.)	The chancellor, the Earl of Southampton, issues a commission under the great seal enabling the masters of the court to make decrees,	457
(Feb. 20.)	Edward VI. is crowned at Westminster, the ceremony being shortened,	457
(March.)	Somerset is appointed sole governor of the king, and protector of the kingdom,	457
(March 31.)	Francis I. dies at Rambouillet, and is succeeded by his son, Henry II.,	458
(June.)	Lord Seymour, the Duke of Somerset's brother, marries Queen Catherine Parr,	473
(July.)	John Knox, with other prisoners, is carried to France,	459
	The Castle of St Andrews is demolished,	459
	The protector marches with an army for the invasion of Scotland; Lord Clinton commands the fleet,	459
(Sept. 10.)	Battle of Pinkie, at Salt Preston; Black Saturday; the Scotch army is routed,	460–463
	The Scottish camp is plundered,	463, 464
	The fleet take the island of Inchcolm; the town of Kinghorn; plunder and ravage the coast,	464
(Sept. 17.)	Leith is set on fire,	464
(Sept. 18.)	The army marches back towards the Border,	464
(Sept. 21.)	The protector takes possession of Hume Castle,	465
(Sept. 29.)	The English army recross the Tweed,	465
	Visitors of each diocese are appointed; an English copy of the Bible is ordered to be deposited in every parish church; other regulations are made,	465
	Bonner and Gardiner are committed to the Fleet,	466
(Nov. 4.)	Parliament repeals the act of Henry VIII. giving proclamations the force of laws, and many other statutes of the late reign,	466, 467
	Abolishes the Congé d'élire; orders the sacrament to be delivered to the laity; vests all chantries, colleges, and free chapels in the king,	467
	It also passes an act for punishing of vagabonds, and the relief of poor and impotent persons,	467
	All images are ordered to be removed from churches and chapels; the rich shrines are forfeited to the crown; act of general pardon published,	468
	New order of the sacrament of the Lord's Supper proclaimed; the elevation	

A.D.	PAGE	A.D.	PAGE
of the Host forbidden; the service to be in English,	468	(Dec. 13.) Somerset confesses before Edward VI. and council,	492
Cranmer publishes catechism in English,	469	1550. (Jan. 2.) He is fined and deprived of his offices,	492
1549. (April.) Bishop Gardiner is committed to the Tower,	468	(Feb. 16.) He receives a royal pardon,	492
(June.) A treaty of marriage between Queen Mary and the dauphin is here ratified,	469	Warwick is made lord high admiral, and great master of the household,	492
The queen goes on board the French fleet at Dumbarton,	469	(April.) Ridley is made bishop of London,	493
(Aug. 13.) She reaches Brest; proceeds to St Germain-en-Laye, is contracted to the dauphin,	469	(April 10.) The Duke of Somerset is again sworn in of the privy council,	492
		(May 2.) Joan of Kent is burnt in Smithfield for heresy,	492
Lord. Clinton, the admiral, lands at several places in Scotland, but is repulsed,	470	(July.) John Hooper is nominated bishop of Gloucester,	493
Lord Grey makes an incursion as far as Teviotdale and Liddesdale,	470	(Aug.) A fleet is sent to sea, to prevent the escape of the Princess Mary,	494
(Sept. 30.) The queen-dowager, wife of Seymour, dies, after giving birth to a daughter,	470	(Dec.) Two of her chaplains are indicted for performing mass,	494
(Oct. 15.) The plague rages in London,	470	1551. (Jan.) John Hooper, bishop of Gloucester, is committed to the Fleet,	493
(Nov. 24.) Parliament meets; a bill introduced in the Commons permitting the marriage of the clergy,	470	(March 18.) The Princess Mary is brought before the council,	494
(Dec. 13.) It is passed and carried to the House of Lords,	471	(March 20.) The princess is allowed to follow Roman Catholic worship,	494
The English are driven out of Jedburgh; the Castles of Hume and Fernihurst are retaken; the Scotch, assisted by the French, gain other successes and ravage the English border,	488	(May.) An agreement for marriage between Edward and Elizabeth, the French king's daughter, is made,	495
		(July.) The sweating sickness rages in London,	495
		(Aug.) The chief officers of the household of the Princess Mary are committed to the Tower,	494
1549. (Jan. 19.) The Lord Admiral Seymour is committed to the Tower for high treason,	478	Mary refuses to relinquish mass,	494
(Feb. 9.) The bill allowing the marriage of the clergy is considered in the House of Lords,	471	(Sept.) Warwick is made warden of the Scottish marches,	495
		(Oct.) He is created Duke of Northumberland,	495
(Feb. 19.) The bill is read a third time, and passed,	471	(Oct. 16.) The Duke of Somerset is arrested for conspiracy and treason, and committed to the Tower,	495
An act is passed establishing the use of the reformed liturgy, and another touching abstinence from flesh in Lent, &c.,	471	(Dec. 1.) He is found guilty of felony only,	496, 497
		1552. (Jan. 22.) He is beheaded on Tower Hill,	497, 498
(Feb. 23.) The whole council proceed to the Tower, and exhibit articles of charge against the lord admiral,	479	(Jan. 23.) Parliament meets; acts are passed for the enforcing the use of the Book of Common Prayer; for amending the law of treason; for the relief of the poor; for legalising the marriage of priests; and for other purposes,	498
(Feb. 27.) A bill of attainder is passed against him in the House of Lords,	479	
(March 20.) He is beheaded on Tower Hill,	480	
(June.) An insurrection breaks out in various parts of England against the Reformation and the use of the reformed liturgy,	481–483	(Feb. 26.) Some of the accomplices of the Duke of Somerset are executed,	493
		(April.) Edward VI. is afflicted by small-pox and measles,	499
Siege of Exeter by the rebels,	483, 484	1553. (March 1.) Parliament meets; the bishopric of Durham is suppressed,	499
Lord Russell defeats the rebels at Fenington Bridge,	485	(April.) Durham is created into a county palatine,	499
Ket's insurrection in Norfolk; the Tree of Reformation,	485, 486	(May.) Lord Guilford Dudley is married to Lady Jane Grey,	500
The Marquis of Northampton marches against Ket; he is driven out of Norwich by the rebels; Lord Sheffield is killed; Northampton retreats to London,	487	(June 11.) Edward VI. requires the crown-lawyers to draw a will, entailing the crown on Lady Jane Grey,	500
		(July 6.) Edward VI. dies at Greenwich,	500
(Aug. 6.) Lord Russell and Lord Grey raise the siege of Exeter; the rebels of the west are executed,	485	(July 8.) The lord mayor of London, and others of the citizens, swear allegiance to Lady Jane Grey,	502
		(July 10.) Jane is proclaimed queen,	502
(Aug. 27.) The Earl of Warwick defeats the Norfolk rebels at Dussingdale; Ket and all the principal rebels are executed,	487	(July 12.) Queen Mary sends an order from Framlingham Castle for her proclamation at Norwich,	503
(Oct.) The lords meet in London to complain of the lord-protector; Edward VI. is hastened to Windsor,	490, 491	The Duke of Northumberland marches against Queen Mary,	503
		Ridley preaches at Paul's Cross in favour of Queen Jane,	503
(Oct. 12.) The council meet at Windsor,	491	(July 19.) The council declare for Mary,	503
(Oct. 14.) The protector is brought before them; articles of impeachment are exhibited against him, he is sent to the Tower,	491	(July 20.) The Duke of Northumberland proclaims Mary at Cambridge,	504
(Nov. 4.) Parliament again meets; passes laws against prophecies, and repeals the act relating to vagabonds,	492	(July 21.) Northumberland is arrested for treason; he is conveyed to the Tower; many of the nobility are also committed there,	504

CHRONOLOGICAL INDEX.

A.D.		PAGE
(July 30.)	The Lady Elizabeth rides through London to meet Mary,	504
(Aug. 3.)	Queen Mary enters London; proceeds to the Tower; the Duke of Norfolk, Gardiner, and others are liberated; Bonner and Tunstall are liberated from the Fleet,	505
(Aug. 9.)	A mass is performed in the Tower for the obsequies of Edward VI.; the same day he is buried in Westminster Abbey, according to the Protestant rites,	505
(Aug. 18.)	The Duke of Northumberland, the Earl of Warwick, and the Marquis of Northampton are arraigned for treason in Westminster Hall; they are all condemned,	505
(Aug. 20.)	A sermon is preached in favour of the mass at Paul's Cross,	506
(Aug. 22.)	Northumberland and two others are beheaded,	506
(Aug. 23.)	Gardiner is made chancellor; the mass is performed in St Paul's Church,	506
(Sept. 14.)	Cranmer is arrested, and sent to the Tower,	507
(Oct. 1.)	Mary is crowned at Westminster with the ancient formalities,	507, 508
(Oct. 6.)	Parliament assembles; mass is performed; the bishop of Lincoln, Taylor, refuses to kneel, and is thrown out of the House of Lords,	508
	The queen is declared legitimate; the law of treason restored; all the statutes of Edward VI. respecting religion, repealed,	508
	Gardiner assembles the Convocation; the Book of Common Prayer declared an abomination; they recommend the suppression of the reformed English catechism,	508, 509
(Nov. 13.)	Lady Jane Grey, her husband, and Lord Ambrose Dudley, with Cranmer, are tried and condemned for treason; they are sent back to the Tower; Cranmer is respited, but detained for heresy,	509, 510
(Dec. 21.)	The church-service begins to be performed in Latin throughout England,	510
	Mary issues an order that no one shall preach without a licence,	510
	Judge Hales remonstrates; is thrown into prison; he kills himself,	510
1554. (Jan.)	Robert Dudley, son of Northumberland, is condemned as a traitor,	511
	Sir Peter Carew raises an insurrection in Devonshire against the Spanish match,	512
	Sir Thomas Wyatt raises a rebellion in Kent against the same,	512
(Jan. 25.)	The Duke of Suffolk flies to Warwickshire, and raises the people there,	512
(Jan. 29.)	The Duke of Norfolk marches against Sir Thomas Wyatt; the London trained bands desert to Wyatt at Rochester Bridge; Wyatt marches to Southwark; retires to Kingston; marches to London; is met at Hyde Park by the royal forces; he surrenders, and is committed to the Tower,	512-514
	The Princess Elizabeth is examined before the council,	515
(Feb. 12.)	Lady Jane Grey and her husband are beheaded,	517, 518
(Feb. 23.)	The Duke of Suffolk is beheaded,	518
(March 15.)	The Princess Elizabeth is sent to the Tower,	515-517
	Cranmer, Ridley, and Latimer are removed from the Tower to Oxford,	524
(April 11.)	Sir Thomas Wyatt is beheaded,	518
(April 14.)	Cranmer, Ridley, and Latimer are questioned before the commissioners at Oxford,	525
(April 16.)	Cranmer argues before the Consistory,	525
(April 17.)	Ridley does the same,	525
(April 18.)	Latimer does the same,	525
(April 28.)	Cranmer, Ridley, and Latimer are condemned to be burnt,	525
	The Earl of Devon is sent to Fotheringay Castle,	519
(July 19.)	The Prince of Spain arrives in Southampton water,	519
(July 23.)	Mary meets him at Winchester,	520
(Aug.)	They are married there; go to Windsor; enter London,	520
(Oct. 26.)	Some of the jury who acquitted Sir Nicholas Throgmorton are committed to prison,	519
(Nov. 12.)	Parliament meets; Cardinal Pole gives absolution; the acts against heretics are revised,	520, 521
1555.	Mary sends an embassy to the pope to confirm the reconciliation of England with the Church,	522
	A commission of ecclesiastics sits for the trial of Protestants; John Rogers is tried; he is condemned to be burnt,	522, 523
(Feb. 9.)	Bishop Hooper is burnt at Gloucester,	523
	Dr Taylor is burnt at Hadleigh,	523
(Mar. 30.)	Bishop Ferrar is burnt at St David's,	523
(May 31.)	John Cardmaker is burnt in London,	524
(June.)	John Bradford is also burnt in London,	524
	Many others are burnt in various parts of England for heresy,	527
(Sept.)	Philip II. quits England for the continent,	526
(Oct. 16.)	Ridley and Latimer are burnt at Oxford,	525
(Nov. 12.)	Bishop Gardiner, the chancellor, dies, and is succeeded by Heath, archbishop of York,	526
1556.	Forced loans are contracted,	527
	Embargoes are laid on foreign goods,	527
	Cranmer, having been formally condemned by the pope, is sentenced to be degraded and burnt,	527
	He signs his recantation,	527
(Mar. 21.)	He is taken to St Mary's Church, Oxford, to make a public declaration; he refuses; is burnt near Baliol College,	528
(Mar. 22.)	Cardinal Pole is consecrated and installed archbishop of Canterbury,	528
(June 27.)	Thirteen persons are burnt at Stratford le Bow for heresy,	528
	Sir John Cheke is sent to the Tower; he recants his heretical opinions,	530
1557. (March.)	King Philip II. of Spain revisits England,	532
	Thomas Stafford and a few others land at Scarborough; attack and surprise the castle; they are made prisoners; and Stafford and others, one, a Frenchman, are sent to London and tortured in the Tower,	532
(May 28.)	Stafford is beheaded,	532
(May 29.)	Saunders is pardoned; the others are hanged,	532
(June 7.)	Mary declares war against France,	532
(July 6.)	Philip II. departs from England,	532
	The Earl of Pembroke and Lord Robert Dudley go to the Low Countries with an army in aid of Philip,	532
	The army of Philip II. gains a battle under the walls of St Quintin,	533
1558. (Jan. 1.)	The Duke of Guise commences the siege of Calais; it is assaulted and taken in a few days,	533-535

A.D.		PAGE
(April 24.)	Mary, queen of Scots, is married to Francis, the eldest son of Henry II. of France,	536
	Parliament grants money for the recovery of Calais; the lord high admiral, Lord Clinton, sails to join Philip II. with an English fleet,	536
	The English and Flemish fleets take Conquet, and several other small places,	536, 537
	The battle of Gravelines; the French are defeated,	537
(Sept.)	Mary falls ill of the cold and hot fever,	537
(Nov. 17.)	She dies at St James's,	537
	Cardinal Pole dies the same day,	538
	Queen Elizabeth's accession is acknowledged by both Houses of Parliament; she is proclaimed,	539
(Nov. 18.)	Sir William Cecil is appointed secretary of state,	539
(Nov. 23.)	Queen Elizabeth removes from Hatfield; proceeds to the Charter House,	539
(Nov. 28.)	She enters London and proceeds to the Tower,	539
(Dec. 13.)	The body of Queen Mary is buried in Westminster Abbey with Roman Catholic ceremonials,	541
(Dec. 25.)	Mass is performed in the great closet; Queen Elizabeth retires after the reading of the gospel,	541
1559. (Jan. 13.)	Sir Henry Carey is created Lord Hunsdon,	541
(Jan. 14.)	Queen Elizabeth goes to Westminster,	541
(Jan. 15.)	She is crowned by the bishop of Carlisle in the ancient manner,	542
(Jan. 25.)	She meets the parliament; they restore the first-fruits and tenths to the crown; they declare the queen supreme head of the church; the laws of Edward VI. relating to religion are restored; the Book of Common Prayer re-established,	543
	Parliament exhorts Queen Elizabeth to marry; she declares her intention to live and die a virgin queen,	544
	Philip II. offers his hand in marriage,	544
(May 10.)	The queen-regent of Scotland summons the reformed clergy to Stirling,	547
(May 11.)	John Knox preaches against Catholicism,	548
	The queen-regent enters into a treaty with the reformers,	548
	The Acts of Supremacy and Uniformity are strictly enforced, and the Protestant religion established throughout England,	545
	John Knox and the Scottish reformers form themselves into the Congregation of the Lord,	548, 549
(July 10.)	Henry II. of France dies; is succeeded by Francis II., the husband of Mary, queen of Scots,	549
	A French army lands at Leith,	549
	The French fortify Leith,	555
	The titles of King and Queen of France, England, and Scotland, are assumed by Francis II. and Mary,	555
	The abbeys of Paisley, Kilwinning, and Dunfermline are suppressed,	556
(Nov. 6.)	The Lords of the Congregation attack Leith; they are defeated at Restalrig; they evacuate Edinburgh and fly to Stirling; the queen-regent re-enters Edinburgh,	559
1560. (Feb. 27.)	Elizabeth concludes a treaty at Berwick with the Lords of the Congregation,	559
(March.)	An English fleet appears in the Firth of Forth,	559

A.D.		PAGE
	The queen-regent takes refuge in Edinburgh Castle; the French army march to Leith,	560
	The English fleet blockade the port of Leith; the army and the Scotch attack the town by land,	560
(June 10.)	The queen-regent dies in Edinburgh Castle,	561
(July 7.)	The treaty of Edinburgh; Leith is surrendered to the Lords of the Congregation and the English,	561
	A separate peace is concluded between England and France, recognising Elizabeth's right to the crown of England, and agreeing that Mary shall not use the arms of England,	562
(Aug. 1.)	The Scotch parliament declare that the authority of the Roman Church is a usurpation; pass a declaration of faith renouncing the tenets and dogmas of that church, and disowning the authority of the pope,	563
	Queen Mary refuses to assent to the statutes passed against the Roman Catholic religion,	563
(Dec. 5.)	Francis II. of France dies, and is succeeded by Charles IX.; Mary retires from court, and resides at Rheims,	563
1561. (Aug.)	Queen Mary embarks at Calais,	565
(Aug. 19.)	She arrives at Leith; proceeds to Holyrood,	565
	John Knox has an interview with her,	565, 566
	Mary removes to Stirling; issues proclamations banishing the monks and friars,	566
	The Presbyterian clergy preach against the mass, dancing, and other amusements,	566
	Queen Mary's chapel is broken into, and the altar defiled; two offenders are indicted,	568
	John Knox writes to the Presbyterians to come armed to Edinburgh and release the prisoners; he is cited before the council; he defies them, and is discharged,	568
	Elizabeth pays off crown-debts; regulates the coinage; increases the naval force,	568
	Arthur and Edmund Pole are tried for high treason; they confess; are condemned; Elizabeth grants them a pardon,	569
1562.	Elizabeth sends an army under Sir Edward Poynings to take possession of Havre, and to aid the Protestants of France; Rouen is besieged and captured by the French,	570
	The Huguenots under Condé and Coligni are defeated at Dreux,	571
	The Earl of Arran is sent prisoner to Edinburgh Castle; Lord James Stuart, the half-brother of Queen Mary, is made Earl of Marr,	574
	Queen Mary proceeds on a royal progress to the north,	574
	Inverness Castle holds out against her; it is taken; the governor is put to death,	574
	Lord James Stuart is appointed Earl of Murray instead of Earl of Marr,	574
(Oct. 28.)	A battle is fought at Corrichie by Murray, against the Earl of Huntly, who is beaten,	575
	Huntly is killed; his son, Sir John Gordon, is captured and beheaded,	575
	Philip II. introduces the Inquisition into the Netherlands,	620
	Elizabeth proposes Lord Robert Dudley as a husband for Queen Mary,	575

CHRONOLOGICAL INDEX. 27

A.D.		PAGE
1563.	Persons are punished for conjuring and other offences,	572
(Feb. 24.)	The Duke of Guise is assassinated; peace is agreed on between the Huguenots and Roman Catholics,	572
(July 28.)	Havre is surrendered to the French,	573
(Sept.)	The plague rages in London,	574
(Sept. 29.)	Lord Robert Dudley is created Earl of Leicester,	575
1565.	Henry, Lord Darnley, son of the Earl of Lennox, sails for Scotland,	579
(Feb. 16.)	He visits Queen Mary at Wemyss Castle; Elizabeth remonstrates against the marriage with Darnley,	580
	The Earl of Murray joins Knox against Queen Mary; the assembly of the kirk demand that the queen shall conform to the Protestant faith, and abolish the Romish worship throughout Scotland,	581
(July 28.)	Darnley is married to Mary and proclaimed king,	581
	Murray, Chatelherault, Argyle, Glencairn, and Rothes, take up arms,	581
	Mary takes the field; the lords retreat into England; 'the round-about raid,'	581, 582
	Murray and the abbot of Kilwinning proceed to London; the French and Spanish ambassadors remonstrate against the encouragement of the Scottish rebellion,	582
	Mary calls her parliament together; attaints Murray and others,	583
	Mary and Darnley quarrel,	584
1566.	Darnley signs a bond to certain lords for the murder of Rizzio,	586
(Mar. 9.)	Rizzio is murdered by Ruthven and other conspirators,	596, 587
(Mar. 10.)	Murray and other banished lords return, Mary is reconciled to Murray,	587
	The Prince of Orange joins a confederacy against the Inquisition in the Netherlands,	588
(June 19.)	Mary is delivered of a son,	588
	Elizabeth declares to parliament that she will marry,	590
	Elizabeth remits part of the supplies voted by parliament,	591
(Dec.)	A determination is come to, to divorce Mary from Darnley,	594
	Darnley falls sick of the small-pox,	595
1567. (Jan. 14.)	Queen Mary arrives with the prince in Edinburgh,	595
(Jan. 25.)	She is reconciled to Darnley at Glasgow, Darnley is lodged at Kirk-a-Field,	595
(Feb. 10.)	Darnley is murdered,	595, 596
(Feb. 12.)	A reward is offered for the discovery of the murderers,	596
(Feb. 16.)	The Earl of Bothwell and others are accused,	596
(Mar. 21.)	Bothwell gets possession of Edinburgh Castle,	596
(April 9.)	Murray retires to France,	597
(April 12.)	Bothwell is arraigned for the murder of Darnley, and is acquitted,	597
	An act is passed renouncing the authority of Rome, and establishing the Protestant religion,	597
	Bothwell proposes to marry Mary; it is agreed to by many lords and others,	598
	Bothwell captures Mary at Foulbrigs, and takes her to Dunbar Castle,	598
(April 29.)	He takes Mary back to Edinburgh Castle,	598
(May 7.)	Applies for a divorce from his wife, which is granted,	599
	Bothwell is created Duke of Orkney,	599

A.D.		PAGE
(May 15.)	He is married to Queen Mary,	599
(June 6.)	Morton and other lords attempt to seize Mary and Bothwell; they escape to Dunbar,	600
	The confederate lords assume the powers of government,	600
(June 14.)	Mary marches against them; issues a proclamation; sleeps at Seton,	600
(June 15.)	Mary advances to Carberry Hill; she surrenders to the confederate lords; Bothwell departs for Dunbar,	601
	Mary is carried to Edinburgh; and from thence to Lochleven Castle,	602
	Bothwell flies to Norway; is thrown into the Castle of Malmoe,	602
	Captain Blackadder and others are tried and executed for the murder of Darnley,	603
(July 24.)	Mary resigns the crown to her son,	604
(July 20.)	Murray is appointed regent,	604
(Aug. 22.)	He is proclaimed regent; obtains possession of Edinburgh Castle,	605
(Sept. 30.)	Obtains possession of the Castle of Dunbar,	605, 606
	Raises Morton to high honours,	606
(Dec. 15.)	Murray assembles a parliament; the acts against popery are revived; the deposition of Mary and the appointment of the regent are confirmed, and Mary declared guilty of the murder of Darnley,	606
1568. (Mar. 25.)	Mary attempts to escape from Lochleven Castle,	606
(May 2.)	She escapes, and is carried to Hamilton; an army is assembled for her defence,	606, 607
	The regent marches against her,	607
(May 14.)	Battle of Langside; Mary's forces are defeated; she flies to Dundrennan Abbey,	607
(May 16.)	She passes to Workington, in Cumberland,	607
	Elizabeth refuses to see Mary till she is cleared of the murder of Darnley,	608
	Ulster is vested in the English crown, and is colonised by the English,	651
(July 16.)	Mary is carried to Bolton Castle,	611
1569. (Feb. 3.)	Mary is placed in Tutbury Castle,	618
	The Duke of Norfolk proposes to marry Queen Mary,	624
	Norfolk is invited to court,	626
(Oct. 2.)	He is arrested at St Albans,	626
(Oct. 9.)	He is committed to the Tower,	626
	An insurrection breaks out in York, Durham, and Northumberland; Dr Nicolas Morton arrives in England as apostolical penitentiary,	628
	Queen Mary is removed to Coventry,	629
(Nov. 16.)	The insurgents march to Durham; burn the Bible and Common Prayer Book, and celebrate mass in the cathedral; they retreat to Raby Castle; attack, and take Barnard Castle,	629
	They retreat towards the Borders,	630
1570. (Jan.)	Elizabeth issues a proclamation of pardon, She also issues a 'Declaration of the queen's proceedings since her reign,'	630
(Jan. 22.)	The Regent Murray is shot at Linlithgow, Chatelherault, Argyle, and Huntly assume the government of Scotland, as lieutenants of Queen Mary,	632
(April.)	Elizabeth sends two armies into Scotland; they ravage for a week, and then return,	632
(April 26.)	The armies again enter Scotland; take Hume and False Castles,	632
(May.)	A conspiracy is entered into in Norfolk; the conspirators are seized, tried, and executed,	633

A.D.		PAGE
1571.	The Earl of Lennox is made regent of Scotland; he seizes the Castle of Dumbarton,	645
	He hangs the archbishop of St Andrews at Stirling, without trial,	645
	The regent Lennox is shot, and the Earl of Marr is nominated regent,	646
(April.)	Bailly, a servant of Mary, queen of Scots, is seized at Dover, returning from the Duke of Alva; he is sent to the Tower and tortured,	637
(Aug. 4.)	The Duke of Norfolk is removed to one of his town houses,	638
(Sept. 7.)	He is again committed to the Tower,	638
	His servants are put to the torture,	638, 639
1572. (Jan. 14.)	The Earl of Shrewsbury, the keeper of Queen Mary, is nominated lord high steward for the trial of the Duke of Norfolk,	640
(Jan. 16.)	The duke is tried for treason and convicted,	640-642
(June 2.)	The Duke of Norfolk is beheaded on Tower Hill,	644
	Parliament declare the Queen of Scots incapable of succeeding to the English crown,	644
(July.)	The Earl of Northumberland is beheaded without trial,	645
(Aug. 22.)	The Admiral Coligni is attempted to be assassinated in the streets of Paris,	646
(Aug. 23.)	The massacre of St Bartholomew,	646, 647
	The Huguenots take the field in France,	648
(Oct. 28.)	The regent Marr dies at Stirling,	648
(Nov. 24.)	The Earl of Morton is chosen regent,	648
1573. (June 9.)	Maitland dies,	649
(Aug. 3.)	Kirkaldy is hanged and quartered as a traitor,	649
	Elizabeth sends secret aid to the Huguenots, and a fleet, to attempt the relief of Rochelle,	649
1574. (May.)	Charles IX. of France dies, and is succeeded by the Duke of Anjou, king of Poland, as Henry III.,	649
1576.	A treaty is concluded, by which the Huguenots are to exercise their religion,	649
	Henry III. heads the Catholic league to protect the church from the Protestants,	649
	Bothwell dies at the Castle of Malmoe,	652
1577. (Feb.)	Henry III. annuls the privileges granted to the Huguenots; they take up arms,	649
	Elizabeth concludes a treaty offensive and defensive with the Orange party,	649
1578.	A convention of Scotch nobility insist that James VI. shall undertake the government; the regent Morton retires to Lochleven Castle; he obtains possession of James's person, and resumes his authority,	652
	Esmé Stuart, Lord of Aubigny, arrives from France; is created Duke of Lennox; Morton is sent to prison,	652, 653
	Morton is executed by 'the maiden,'	653
	James VI. assumes the government,	653
	The Earl of Gowrie takes James VI., and keeps him prisoner at the Castle of Ruthven,	654
	James VI. resumes the government,	654
1580.	A great rising takes place in Ireland; the rebels are defeated, and the Italian soldiers put to the sword; Ulster and Connaught are reduced to obedience,	652
	Alençon, now Duke of Anjou, arrives at Greenwich as a suitor to Queen Elizabeth,	650
	He returns; Elizabeth submits the question of her marriage to the council,	650

A.D.		PAGE
1581.	An embassy arrives from Catherine de Medici; Elizabeth agrees to the marriage with the Duke of Anjou in six weeks,	650
	Anjou is elected king of the Netherlands; Elizabeth sends him supplies; he raises the siege of Cambray, and gains other successes; he returns to England,	650
	Anjou returns to the Netherlands, Elizabeth refusing to marry,	651
1583.	The Earl of Desmond is killed; his head is sent to Elizabeth; it is placed on London Bridge,	652
	Several papists are tortured and executed, charged with conspiracy against the government,	652
1584.	The Throckmorton plot; Francis Throckmorton is put on the rack; he is executed at Tyburn,	655
	The Jesuits, seminary priests, and English priests are ordered to quit the kingdom in forty days on pain of treason,	655
1585. (Feb.)	Elizabeth sends a large army into the Netherlands under the command of Leicester; he is made governor-general of the Low Countries; he attacks Zutphen; is defeated; Sir Philip Sidney is killed,	656
1586.	Babington's conspiracy to assassinate Elizabeth is discovered; he is taken with many of his adherents; they are tortured,	657
(Sept. 20.)	Some are executed in Lincoln's Inn Fields,	657
	Elizabeth issues a commission for the trial of Queen Mary,	658
	Mary is removed to Fotheringay Castle,	658
(Oct. 11.)	Thirty-six English commissioners arrive at the castle; they announce to Mary that she is to be tried for being accessory to Babington's conspiracy, and other treasons,	658
(Oct. 25.)	Mary is pronounced guilty of treason, and sentenced to death,	662
(Nov. 12.)	Both Houses address the queen, imploring her to order the execution of Mary,	662
1587. (Feb. 1.)	Elizabeth signs the warrant for her execution,	666
(Feb. 8.)	Queen Mary is beheaded in the great hall of the castle,	669-671
(Feb. 14.)	Davison, the secretary, is committed to the Tower; he is fined £10,000,	671
	Sir Robert Carey is sent to make excuses to James VI. for the execution of Mary,	671
(April 19.)	Sir Francis Drake sails into Cadiz roads, and destroys thirty ships,	672
	He takes or destroys 100 Spanish vessels; captures a large ship in the Tagus; performs other brilliant exploits,	672
(Nov.)	Elizabeth summons a great council of war; Sir Walter Raleigh advises that the expected invasion of the Spaniards be met at sea; vast preparations are made; a great camp is formed at Tilbury Fort; the queen reviews the troops at Tilbury Fort,	672-674
1588. (July 20.)	The invincible armada arrives in the Channel,	675
	The battle commences, and is continued several days, from the 20th to the 26th of July; the Duke of Medina Sidonia sails for Spain; many of his ships are wrecked at the Orkneys and on the coast of Norway; some of the Spaniards	

A.D.		PAGE
	are made prisoners in Scotland; others are taken in Ireland, and are put to death,	675–678
(Sept.)	The Duke of Medina arrives with the wreck of the armada at Santander,	678
(Sept. 4.)	The Earl of Leicester dies,	678
1589.	Elizabeth fits out a large fleet under Drake, which sails against Spain; he proclaims Don Antonio king of Portugal; the fleet do great damage on the Portuguese coast; the army gain several victories; the expedition returns to England with great loss,	678, 679
1590.	Essex marries the widow of Sir Philip Sidney,	679
1593.	Henry IV. of France becomes a Roman Catholic,	679
1595.	Drake and Sir John Hawkins die,	680
1596.	A fleet sails under the lord admiral to attack the Spanish coast,	680
(June.)	The fleet sails into the Bay of Cadiz; a sea-fight is gained by the English; Cadiz is taken,	680
1597.	Essex is made master of the ordinance,	680
(July.)	A large fleet is fitted out to attack the coast of Spain; Essex captures three Spanish ships; he returns; is received by the queen with displeasure,	680, 681
	Essex is made hereditary earl-marshal,	681
1598. (June.)	Elizabeth quarrels with Essex; he leaves the court,	681
(Aug. 4.)	Lord Burleigh dies,	681

A.D.		PAGE
	The Edict of Nantes is published,	682
	Valentine Thomas accuses James VI. of hiring him to assassinate the queen,	682
	An insurrection breaks out in Ireland, headed by the Earl of Tyrone; he defeats the English at Blackwater,	682
1599. (Mar.)	The Earl of Essex is appointed to command in Ireland; he leaves London with a large army; he effects nothing,	683
(Sept.)	He is called before the council,	684
	He is delivered into free custody,	684
1600.	The Gowrie Conspiracy; the Ruthvens attempt to assassinate James VI.	690, 691
1601.	Essex encourages papists at his house, and corresponds with James VI. about the succession,	684, 685
(Feb. 8.)	Essex, the Earls of Southampton and Rutland, and others attempt an insurrection in London; he is captured, and with Southampton sent to the Tower,	686, 687
(Feb. 25.)	Essex is executed privately in the Tower,	689
(Oct)	Elizabeth agrees to revoke patents for monopolies,	692, 693
(Dec. 24.)	Lord Mountjoy, deputy of Ireland, attacks the Spaniards in Ireland; he captures them,	693
1602.	The Earl of Tyrone surrenders to Mountjoy,	693
1603. (Mar. 21.)	Elizabeth is confined to her bed,	693, 694
(Mar. 22.)	She names James VI. of Scotland as her successor,	694
(Mar. 24.)	She dies,	694

VOLUME III.

BOOK VII.

A.D.		PAGE
1603.	James VI. is proclaimed in the city of London,	3
(Mar. 26.)	Sir Robert Carey arrives in Edinburgh,	2
(Mar. 30.)	Sir Charles Percy and Thomas Somerset arrive from the council to announce to James VI. his accession to the throne,	2
(April.)	Queen Elizabeth is buried at Westminster,	4
	Sir Robert Cecil meets James VI. at York,	4
	James VI. knights a vast number of persons on his journey,	5
(May 7.)	He arrives at the Charter House; issues a proclamation suspending all monopolies till examined; that royal protections shall cease, and that the oppressions of purveyors to the court be put down,	5
	He creates four earls and nine barons,	4
	A conspiracy is formed for seizing James VI. and forcing him to change his ministers, and to grant toleration; the 'Bye Plot' and the 'Main Plot;' Raleigh, Cobham, Grey of Wilton, and others are engaged,	7, 8
(July 25.)	James VI. is crowned at Westminster,	6
	Sir Walter Raleigh and Lord Cobham are committed to the Tower,	9
	The plague rages in London,	6
(Aug. 10.)	General fast every Wednesday during the plague,	7
	Treaty with Henry IV. of France,	7
(Nov. 15.)	The commoners in the 'Bye Plot' are tried and convicted at Winchester,	9

A.D.		PAGE
	Sir Walter Raleigh is tried for the 'Main,'	9–11
	He is found guilty of treason and condemned,	12
	Grey and Cobham are tried by a commission of peers; they are both condemned for treason,	12, 13
(Dec.)	Cobham, Grey, and Raleigh are sent to the Tower during James VI.'s pleasure,	14
1604. (Jan. 14–16.)	James VI. holds a meeting of the bishops and puritans at Hampton Court, acting as moderator; James VI. decides in favour of the bishops,	16, 17
	Whitgift dies; Bancroft is made archbishop of Canterbury,	17
	The non-conforming clergy are persecuted and driven from their livings,	17
	The papists are also persecuted,	17, 18
(March.)	Commissioners abrogate all hostile laws between England and Scotland,	35
	Parliament remonstrates against purveyance and monopolies; wardship and other abuses; tonnage and poundage is granted,	19
	Robert Catesby forms the Gunpowder Plot,	20, 21
	Guido Fawkes is brought to England by Winter,	21
	The conspirators meet and take the oath,	21
(Nov.)	The gunpowder conspirators proceed in their work of mining under the Houses of Parliament,	22, 23

A.D.	PAGE
1605. (May.) A cellar is hired under the Parliament House, and powder carried there,	23
(Sept.) Parliament is prorogued to the 5th of November,	24
Sir Everard Digby, Ambrose Rookwood, and Francis Tresham join the conspiracy,	24
(Oct. 26.) Lord Mounteagle receives a letter warning him to stay away from parliament,	25
He carries it to Secretary Cecil,	25
(Oct. 31.) James VI. comes from Royston; he reads the letter,	26
(Nov. 4.) The Lord Chamberlain Suffolk and Lord Mounteagle discover Fawkes,	27
(Nov. 6.) He is carried to the Tower,	27
(Nov. 10.) Fawkes on this and preceding days is tortured; he declares his associates,	27
Catesby, Winter, John and Christopher Wright, and Percy are killed,	28
1606. (Jan. 15.) A proclamation is issued against three Jesuits, Garnet, Greenway, and Gerard,	29
(Jan. 21.) Parliament meets; passes severe laws against the papists,	32
(Jan. 27.) Digby, the two Winters, Rookwood, Grant, Fawkes, Keyes, and Bates are tried; Digby pleads guilty; the rest are convicted; all are condemned to death as traitors,	29, 30
(Jan. 29, 30.) They are executed in St Paul's Churchyard,	30
Garnet, the Jesuit, is taken; his two servants, Owen and Chambers, and Oldcorn, a Jesuit, are also captured; all but Garnet are tortured; Owen kills himself,	30
Oldcorn and others are tried and executed at Worcester,	31
(May 3.) Garnet is executed,	32
(June.) The Earl of Northumberland is tried in the Star-Chamber, for seeking to be head of the papists and a promoter of toleration; he is sentenced to pay a fine of £30,000, to be deprived of his offices, and imprisoned for life,	32
(July.) Christian IV., king of Denmark, visits England,	33
(Nov. 18.) Parliament meets; Sir Christopher Pigot is expelled the House of Commons and committed to the Tower; Parliament refuses to naturalise the Scots born before the accession of James VI.; the king interferes with the liberties of the House of Commons,	34, 35
An ecclesiastical convention summoned by royal authority in Scotland, appoint moderators of the presbyteries and the bishops to be *ex officio* moderators of provincial synods,	65
1608. The Earl of Dorset dies; Cecil, now Earl of Salisbury, is appointed treasurer,	39
1609. A duty is laid on Corinth raisins; Bates, a Turkey merchant, resists payment; the barons of the Exchequer decide that the king has a right to levy taxes without the consent of parliament,	40
1610. (Feb. 14.) Parliament meets; Cecil asks the Lords for supplies; the Commons declare the decision of the Exchequer illegal; James VI. calls both Houses before him at Whitehall; the Commons insist upon the right of parliament to levy taxes,	40, 41
An arrangement of marriage between the	

A.D.	PAGE
Lady Arabella Stuart and William Seymour is discovered; they are summoned before the privy council; they are forbidden to marry without the king's leave,	46
(July.) Their marriage is detected; Lady Arabella is sent to the Tower; Seymour escapes to France,	46, 47
James VI. erects the High Commission Courts in Scotland; one at St Andrews, another at Glasgow,	65
The two Houses confer upon Dr Cowell's book on Prerogative; he is sent to prison, and his book suppressed by proclamation,	41
They agree to grant £200,000 a year revenue, upon James VI. giving up the right of wardship, purveyance, and other privileges,	43
(May 14.) Henry IV. of France is assassinated; is succeeded by Louis XIII.,	48
1611. Dr George Abbot is made archbishop of Canterbury,	45
(March.) Robert Carr is created Viscount Rochester,	49
1612. (May 24.) Robert Cecil, Earl of Salisbury, dies,	45
Carr is made lord chamberlain,	49
(Oct. 16.) The Count Palatine Frederic V. arrives in England to marry the Princess Elizabeth,	51
(Oct. 24.) Henry, Prince of Wales, falls sick,	51
(Nov. 6.) He dies,	52
(Dec.) The Princess Elizabeth is affianced to the palatine,	52
1613. (Feb. 14.) They are married,	52
(Sept. 25.) The marriage of the Earl and Countess of Essex is declared null and void,	54
(Nov. 4.) Carr is created Earl of Somerset,	54
(Dec. 26.) Somerset and the countess are married at Whitehall,	54
1614. (April 5.) Parliament is assembled; the Commons demand a conference with the Lords on the right of the king to tax the subject; the Lords demand the opinion of the judges; the judges, headed by Coke, chief-justice, refuse to give an opinion; the Lords decline the conference,	55
James VI. demands supplies; the Commons refuse without a redress of grievances,	56
(June 7.) Parliament (the 'Addle Parliament') is dissolved,	56
(June 15.) The Earl of Northampton dies; George Villiers appears at court; is made cupbearer to James VI,	57
1615. (Mar.) Sir Walter Raleigh is released from the Tower,	73
(April 25.) George Villiers is knighted,	53
James VI. grants a pardon to Somerset for all treasons and felonies; Ellesmere, the chancellor, refuses to put the great seal to it,	58
Somerset is arrested by warrant from the lord chief-justice; is committed to the Tower,	58
(Sept. 27.) The Lady Arabella Stuart dies mad in the Tower,	47
1616. (May 24.) The Countess of Somerset is arraigned; pleads guilty; is condemned to death,	61
(May 25.) Somerset is brought to trial; is declared guilty,	61, 62
Sir Edward Coke is disgraced; Montague is made chief-justice,	62, 63

CHRONOLOGICAL INDEX. 31

A.D.	PAGE
(Nov.) Lord Ellesmere is created Viscount Brackley,	63
1617. (Jan. 5.) Villiers is created Earl of Buckingham,	63
Francis Bacon is made lord-keeper,	63
(Mar. 28.) Sir Walter Raleigh sails for the recovery of Guiana,	74
(June.) James VI. arrives in Edinburgh,	66
An act is prepared to declare that whatever should be determined by the king, with the advice of the bishops and clergy, relating to ecclesiastical affairs, shall be law; the clergy remonstrate,	66
James VI. insists upon five articles at the meeting of St Andrews; the same are referred to a general meeting of the kirk; James returns to England,	66
On his way back he publishes his *Book of Sports*, and appoints its reading in the churches,	67
Bacon, who had fallen into disgrace, and quarrelled with Coke during James VI.'s absence, is received into favour,	68, 69
Coke is restored to the council-table,	70
(Nov. 13.) Raleigh and his companions recover the land of Guiana,	74
1618. (Jan. 4.) Bacon is made lord-chancellor,	70
(June.) Sir Walter Raleigh anchors at Plymouth; he is arrested; is carried to London; attempts to escape; is lodged in the Tower,	75, 76
(July.) Chancellor Bacon is created Baron Verulam,	70
(Oct. 28.) Raleigh is taken by habeas corpus to the Court of King's Bench to receive judgment for the treason committed in 1603; 'execution is granted,'	77, 78
(Oct. 29.) He is taken from the Gate-house and beheaded in Old Palace Yard,	78, 79
1621. (Jan. 27.) Bacon is created Viscount St Albans,	82
(Jan. 30.) Parliament meets; James VI. asks supplies for the war in the Palatinate,	81
(Feb. 15.) The Commons vote the supplies; they attack the monopolists; they commit Sir Francis Mitchell to the Tower; the lords adjudge him and his partner, Sir Giles Mompesson, to be degraded, fined, and imprisoned,	82
Yelverton is fined and imprisoned for life,	82
Bacon is impeached for corruption,	82
(April 24.) He confesses,	82, 83
(May 3.) The House of Lords deliver judgment; he is fined £40,000, and committed to the Tower during James VI.'s pleasure,	83
James VI. abolishes thirty-six of the monopolies and patents,	85
The Earls of Oxford and Southampton, Selden, and others, are committed by James VI. to prison without trial,	86
(Dec. 18.) The Commons enter a protestation of liberties on their journals,	87
James VI. expunges it,	88
1622. (Jan.) He commits Coke and Sir Robert Phillips to the Tower; Selden, Pym, and Mallery to other prisons,	88
1623. (Feb. 17.) The Prince of Wales and Buckingham proceed to Spain,	91
James VI. releases all the seminary priests and Jesuits from the London prisons,	91
The Prince of Wales is received at Madrid by the royal family of Spain,	93, 94
The Infanta Donna Maria adopts the style of Princess of England,	98
(Oct.) The prince refuses to marry the Infanta,	100

A.D.	PAGE
1624. (Feb. 19.) The Houses of Parliament assemble; James VI. asks for supplies for a Spanish war; supplies are voted to be applied by a parliamentary committee; strict orders are issued against all Catholics,	101, 102
The Earl of Middlesex is impeached; condemned by the Lords to pay a fine of £5000, and be imprisoned during pleasure,	103
Troops are raised and sent for the recovery of the Palatinate,	105, 106
1625. An embassy is sent to France to negotiate a marriage between the Princess Henrietta Maria and the Prince of Wales,	106
(Mar. 27.) James VI. dies,	108
Accession of King Charles I.,	108
The plague rages throughout London,	108
(May 1.) Henrietta Maria is married by proxy at Paris,	109
(June 8.) Charles I. meets her at Dover,	109
(June 10.) Parliament meets; Charles I. asks for supplies; the Commons grant a sum, and the duties of tonnage and poundage for one year; the Lords reject the latter part of the bill,	110, 111
Charles I. raises troops for the Palatinate by warrants of his own authority,	111
(July.) Ships are chartered in Charles I.'s name; they refuse to go against the Huguenots; the troops desert,	112
(Aug.) Parliament meets at Oxford; the Commons consider the various grievances; complain of the conduct of Buckingham,	112
(Aug. 12.) Charles I. suddenly dissolves parliament,	113
Writs are issued for loans to the king; tonnage and poundage are levied, though the bill did not pass; other means are devised for levying money to make war on Spain,	113
A large army and fleet are collected; the Dutch contribute sixteen ships; the expedition sails to the coast of Spain; fails; returns to Plymouth,	113, 114
Buckingham goes to Holland; pawns the crown jewels and plate,	114
Charles I. arbitrarily appoints seven members of the House of Commons to be sheriffs,	117
1626. The king agrees to submit to a secret committee the abuses of the state,	119
(May 10.) Sir John Eliot and Sir Dudley Digges are sent to the Tower,	121
The Commons refuse to proceed to business; the two members are released,	121
Charles I. commands the university of Cambridge to elect Buckingham chancellor,	121
(June 1.) He is elected by a majority of three,	122
(June 8.) Buckingham answers the impeachment of the Commons; pleads a pardon of the king,	122
A warrant is issued under the great seal for levying impost and export duties; forced loans are directed; ships are commanded to be furnished by the ports; troops are levied by lords-lieutenant,	123
Sir John Eliot and Hampden, and Sir Thomas Wentworth, are imprisoned for refusing to contribute to the loan,	123
The clergy preach in favour of the loan, and against parliaments,	123, 124
1627. (May.) Troops and ships are raised to aid	

A.D.		PAGE
	Rochelle; the Duke of Buckingham is appointed to command,	127
(July 11.)	The expedition lands; takes St Martin, and performs other unimportant operations,	128
1628.	Charles I. appoints commissioners to collect war-money; the commission is revoked; he orders duties to be levied on merchandise; the judges declare it illegal; the orders are revoked,	130
(Mar. 17.)	Parliament meets; some of the refusers are released,	130
(May 8.)	The Commons resolve that Charles I. has no right to commit without authority of law; that the habeas corpus writs cannot be denied; that forced loans are illegal,	131
(June 7.)	Charles I. gives his assent to the 'Petition of Right,'	134
(June 12.)	The Commons grant supplies; vote a remonstrance against Buckingham,	135
(Aug. 23.)	Buckingham is stabbed by Felton,	136
1629.	Sir Thomas Wentworth is created Baron and Viscount Wentworth,	145
(Jan. 20.)	Parliament meets; the Commons take into consideration the invasion of the 'Petition of Right,'	139
(Feb. 2.)	The Commons present to Charles I. their apology for delaying tonnage and poundage,	140
(Feb. 3.)	Charles I. commands them to proceed with the bill,	140
(Feb. 25.)	The Commons present a report, entitled 'Heads of Articles agreed upon, and to be insisted on by the House,' directed against Laud and Arminianism,	141
	Charles I. adjourns the House,	141
(Mar. 2.)	The House meets; is again adjourned by Charles I.,	141
	The House denies Charles I.'s right to adjourn them; they remonstrate; the Commons hold the speaker in the chair; they pass a resolution; adjourn themselves to the 10th,	141, 142
	Charles I. commits seven members to the Tower,	142
	They are cited before the Star Chamber and fined,	142, 143
(Nov.)	Sir John Eliot, Hollis, and Valentine are fined and imprisoned during Charles I.'s pleasure by the Court of King's Bench for words spoken in parliament,	144
1630. (May.)	The queen gives birth to a son,	151
	Charles I. revives several of the feudal customs; the monopolies are increased; the lands of former forests are seized, and other proceedings taken to raise money,	150, 151
	Many of the Puritans emigrate to America,	152
1632. (Nov. 27.)	Sir John Eliot dies in the Tower,	212
1633.	Charles I. pays a visit to Scotland,	156
	Wentworth is made lord deputy of Ireland,	168
	He calls a parliament; exacts implicit obedience to Charles I.; erects a court similar to the Star-Chamber,	169-171
(June.)	A Scottish parliament is summoned; it votes supplies,	156
(Aug. 6.)	Laud is made archbishop of Canterbury,	157
(Oct. 18.)	Charles I. issues a proclamation enforcing James VI.'s Book of Sports,	161
1634.	Grotius publishes his book Mare Liberum,	174
	Prynne is prosecuted in the Star-Chamber for writing Histrio Mastix; is fined	

A.D.		PAGE
	£10,000; is branded, his ears cut off, and his nose slit,	152-155
(June.)	Williams, the late lord-keeper, is fined £10,000 by the Star-Chamber, and imprisoned in the Tower during pleasure; and £8000 by the High Commission Court for writing the Holy Table,	163-165
	Laud has the power of licensing all printed books,	165, 166
1635.	Selden publishes his book Mare Clausum,	174
	The queen is delivered of a daughter,	173
	Writs for ship-money are sent into the inland counties,	176
1636.	The Dutch give £30,000 a year for liberty to fish,	174
1637. (June.)	Prynne, Dr Bastwick, and Burton are prosecuted in the Star-Chamber for libels on the church; are fined £5000 each; branded, and otherwise mutilated; sent to solitary imprisonment,	166
(July 23.)	The Book of Services for the Church of Scotland is read in St Giles's Kirk, Edinburgh, by the bishop of Edinburgh; a riot takes place; the bishop is attacked,	182, 183
	The council, by order of Charles I., issue a decree banishing the clergy who refuse to read the Book of Common Prayer,	184
(Nov. 6.)	The question of ship-money in the case of Hampden is argued before the whole judges of England,	179, 180
1638. (Feb. 19.)	The Scotch Presbyterians having demanded the removal of the Liturgy, the Book of Canons, and the abolition of the High Commission Court, Lord Traquair issues a proclamation against meetings on pain of treason,	186
	Lords Hume and Lindsay issue a counter-proclamation,	186
(Mar. 1.)	The Presbyterians hold a meeting at St Giles's Kirk, of which they take possession; they swear to the Covenant,	187
(June 12.)	Judgment is given in favour of Charles I. by a majority of the judges in the case of Hampden,	181
(Sept. 22.)	The Liturgy, the High Commission Court, and other grievances in Scotland are abolished by Charles I.'s proclamation at Edinburgh,	193
(Oct.)	The Covenanters demand a warrant for citing the Scotch bishops as criminals before the General Assembly at Glasgow,	195
(Nov.)	The bishops deny the jurisdiction of the assembly,	195
	The assembly proceed; excommunicate the bishops, and abolish Episcopacy throughout Scotland,	199
1639. (Feb. 15.)	Charles I. writes to the nobility and gentry commanding them to raise troops and meet him at York on the 1st of April,	200
	The queen issues a circular to the Catholics, calling upon them to aid in the Scottish war,	201
(Mar.)	General Leslie takes Edinburgh Castle for the Covenanters; other strong places are taken,	203
	Leslie and Montrose defeat the Marquis of Huntly, and take him to Edinburgh,	203
(April.)	The royal army encamps near Berwick,	204
(May 30.)	Leslie, with the Scottish army, advances across the Border, and takes up a position within a mile of Charles I.,	204
(June 24.)	Both armies are disbanded; Charles I. takes up his quarters at Berwick,	205

CHRONOLOGICAL INDEX. 33

A.D.		PAGE
(Aug.)	Edinburgh, and twenty other castles, are given up by the Covenanters in pursuance of the treaty,	207
(Aug. 20.)	The Scottish parliament meets; is prorogued,	207
	Lord Loudon is sent to London by the Covenanters; is seized and sent to the Tower for writing a letter signed 'Au Roi,'	207
	Wentworth is made lord-lieutenant of Ireland,	209
1640. (Jan. 12.)	He is created Earl of Strafford; returns to Ireland; calls a parliament,	209
(Mar. 17.)	The Irish parliament grants large supplies,	209
(April 13.)	The English parliament assembles,	210
	The first petition is presented to the House of Commons against ship-money, monopolies, the Star-Chamber, the High Commission Court, and other grievances,	212
	Both Houses are summoned before the king; he allows the Commons to enter into their grievances after they vote supplies, and declares that he never intended to make ship-money an annual revenue,	213
(April 30.)	The House of Commons resolves itself into a grand committee on ship-money; the Lords demand an immediate conference; the Commons refuse,	215
(May 2.)	Charles I. sends a message hastening the supplies,	215
	The Commons reply that they will resume the question on the morrow,	216
	The Commons meet; are summoned to the bar of the Lords by the Usher of the Black Rod; they attend without the speaker; Charles I. dissolves the parliament,	216, 217
	Writs of ship-money are issued and enforced; money is arbitrarily raised in various ways,	218
(May 11.)	The palace of Lambeth is attacked by a mob,	218, 219
(June 2.)	The Scottish parliament meets; puts forth manifestoes; levies a tax on rent; and otherwise prepares for the war and provides for the government,	219
(Aug.)	Leslie, the general of the Army of the Covenant, crosses the Tweed,	220
(Aug. 28.)	Rout of the royal forces at Newburn,	221
(Aug. 29.)	The royalists evacuate Newcastle; retreat to Northallerton,	222
Sept.)	Charles I. negotiates with the Scotch; twelve English peers petition the king to call a parliament; 10,000 of the Londoners petition to the same effect,	223
(Sept. 24.)	A great council of peers assembles at York by Charles I.'s summons,	224
(Oct. 16.)	An agreement is come to between the English and Scotch commissioners for the maintenance of the Scotch army for a time,	226
(Nov. 3.)	Charles I. opens the long parliament,	226
	Lenthall is chosen speaker of the Commons,	226
	Strafford is impeached by the Commons, and sent to the Tower,	230, 231
(Dec. 18.)	Laud is impeached by the Commons for high treason; he is committed to custody by the House of Lords,	229
1641. (Feb.)	Parliament votes money for the payment of the Scotch army,	234
(Mar. 11.)	The Commons resolve that the clergy shall not be magistrates or judges in any civil court,	234

A.D.		PAGE
(April 21.)	A bill of attainder against Strafford passes the Commons,	240
(May.)	The attainder of Strafford is passed in the Lords,	242
(May 10.)	The royal assent is given to the bill,	244
(May 11.)	Charles I. writes to the House of Lords in favour of Strafford,	244
(May 12.)	Strafford is beheaded on Tower Hill,	245
(June 22.)	The Commons grant tonnage and poundage, and vote six subsidies; pass bills imposing a poll-tax for paying the army, and for abolishing the Star-Chamber and High Commission Court,	247
(July 2 and 5.)	Charles I. gives his assent to them,	247
(Aug. 4.)	Thirteen bishops are impeached by the Commons,	248
	General Leslie is created Earl of Leven,	252
(Oct.)	An insurrection breaks out in Ireland; the Protestants are massacred,	252-254
(Oct. 31.)	The English House of Commons vote supplies in aid of the government of Ireland,	255
(Nov. 20.)	The parliament insist on their right to have a guard during their deliberations,	255
(Nov. 22.)	The Commons carry, by a majority, their 'remonstrance of the state of the kingdom,'	256
(Dec. 1.)	It is presented to Charles I.,	257
(Dec. 3.)	Charles I. makes a speech to both Houses,	257
(Dec. 15.)	The Commons, by a majority, vote the printing of 'the remonstrance,'	258
(Dec. 27.)	Some riots take place round the Houses of parliament,	260
	The thirteen bishops who had been impeached, having taken their places, remonstrate to Charles I. against all acts done in their absence,	261
(Dec. 31.)	The Commons send an address to Charles I. praying for a guard; they procure arms in the House,	262
1642. (Jan.)	Lord Kimbolton, Hollis, Haslerig, Pym, Hampden, and Strode are accused of treason before the Lords; a serjeant-at-arms demands the five who are members of the House of Commons,	262, 263
	Charles I. appears in person to the House of Commons, demands them, makes a speech, and retires; the House adjourns,	263, 264
	Charles I. issues a proclamation, charging Kimbolton and the five members with treason,	265
	The committee of the House of Commons declare the same, and all the late acts to be breaches of privilege,	266
	Parliament makes various rules for putting the country in a posture of defence,	267
	The Scottish commissioners offer to mediate between Charles I. and the parliament,	268
(Jan. 20.)	Charles I. desires both Houses to state all the grievances of the kingdom,	268
	Petitions are presented from London and other places, complaining of the delay in putting down the insurrection in Ireland,	269
	A conference, managed by Pym, takes place,	269, 270
	His speech is ordered by the Commons to be printed,	270
(Feb.)	Both Houses pass the Militia Bill,	274
	The Houses resolve to put the kingdom in a state of defence; issue orders; the militia ordinance is read, and the Commons state their declaration of fears,	275

A.D.		PAGE
(Mar. 7.)	Charles I. removes to Newmarket; refuses his assent to the militia ordinance,	275, 276
(Mar. 19.)	Charles I. arrives at York; organises a government there,	277, 278
	Hull is taken possession of for the parliament,	278
(April)	Messages pass between Charles I. and parliament,	280, 281
(May.)	He summons a county meeting at York; a small force is collected,	283
	The Scotch council mediate between Charles I. and the English parliament; they remonstrate against the king going to Ireland,	284
	Several members of both Houses go to Charles I. at York,	284
	Lord-keeper Littleton sends the great seal to Charles I.; he goes to York,	287
	Hyde joins Charles I. at the same place,	287, 288
(June.)	The fleet submit to the command of the Earl of Warwick as admiral for the parliament,	290
(July 12.)	The Earl of Essex is appointed captain-general of the army, and the Earl of Bedford general of the horse for the parliament,	290
	The parliament send a commission to Charles I. at Beverley, praying him to dismiss his garrisons,	292
	Charles I.'s forces endeavour to surprise Hull,	293
	He issues a proclamation for all persons capable of bearing arms to meet him at Nottingham,	293
(Aug. 25.)	Charles I. erects his standard on Nottingham Castle,	293
(Oct. 23.)	Battle of Edgehill,	297, 298
	Charles I. proceeds to Oxford; marches to Reading, which is evacuated,	298, 299
(Nov.)	Prince Rupert attacks Brentford; is repulsed; the royal army retreats to Oxford,	299, 300
1643. (Mar.)	Essex takes Reading,	301
	Waller and others are detected in a conspiracy to deliver the leaders of the parliament to Charles I.; two are executed; Waller and others are committed to the Tower,	302
(June 18.)	Battle of Chalgrove Field; Hampden is mortally wounded,	303, 304
(July.)	Cromwell gains a battle at Grantham,	305
	The royalists take Gainsborough and Lincoln,	305
	Charles L's troops defeat Sir William Waller at Devizes,	305
	The national synod for settling the government and form of worship of the Church of England meet at Westminster,	311
	Prince Rupert takes Bristol,	306
(Sept. 20.)	Battle of Newbury; the Earl of Falkland is killed,	307, 308
	The Solemn League and Covenant of England and Scotland is ordered to be taken,	309
1644. (Mar. 12.)	Laud is tried in the House of Lords,	325
(April.)	Charles I. retreats from Oxford to Worcester,	314
(July 2.)	Battle of Marston Moor,	315
(July 15.)	York is surrendered to the parliamentarians,	315
(Aug.)	The parliamentary troops of the west are beset; the cavalry escape; the foot surrender,	317, 318
	Charles I. marches from Cornwall into Devonshire; marches towards Oxford; second battle of Newbury; the king retreats to Oxford,	318, 319
(Oct.)	The Independents, with Cromwell, quarrel with the aristocracy,	319, 320
1645. (Jan. 10.)	Laud is beheaded,	326
	The Commons remodel the army, and appoint Fairfax general-in-chief,	322, 323
(Feb. 2.)	Montrose defeats the Covenanters,	338
	He gains several other battles,	338–340
(April 7.)	Sir Thomas Fairfax takes the command of the parliamentary army at Windsor,	324
(June 14.)	Battle of Naseby,	332-334
(July 2.)	Montrose gains the battle of Alford,	340
(Aug. 19.)	He takes Glasgow; Edinburgh surrenders,	340
(Sept. 11.)	Prince Rupert surrenders Bristol,	341
(Sept. 23.)	Battle of Rowton Heath,	341
	Battle of Philiphaugh; Montrose is defeated,	341
(Nov.)	Charles I. again negotiates with parliament,	345
1646. (April 27.)	He escapes from Oxford,	350
	He throws himself upon the protection of the Scotch army,	352
(July 23.)	The parliament send their final propositions to Charles I. at Newcastle,	358
	He refuses the conditions offered,	359
(Sept.)	The Scottish army agree to give up Charles I. to the parliamentarians for a sum of money,	360, 361
1647. (Jan. 30.)	Charles I. is delivered up at Newcastle,	362
(Feb.)	The Presbyterians in parliament endeavour to depress the Independents,	364–366
(May 25.)	The army refuse to disband without payment, &c.,	366
(June 3.)	A force from the Independents, headed by Joyce, remove Charles I. to Childerley,	367, 368
	Cromwell joins the army; they pledge themselves not to disband without redress of grievances,	368
	Cromwell, Fairfax, Ireton, and other leaders confer with Charles I.,	368
(June 10.)	The army marches towards London,	369
(Aug. 6.)	Fairfax appears in parliament; is thanked; made commander of all the forces in England and Wales, and constable of the Tower,	370
	The officers of the army draw up their 'Proposals for the settlement of the kingdom;' they are refused by Charles I.,	370, 371
(Nov. 10.)	Charles I. escapes from Hampton Court to the Isle of Wight,	374–378
(Dec. 14.)	Parliament sends four propositions for Charles I. to sign and agree to a personal interview,	379
(Dec. 24.)	He refuses to sign them,	379
(Dec. 28.)	He privately signs a treaty with the Scots,	379
1648. (Jan. 9.)	The army declare in favour of the parliament,	380, 381
(April 9.)	An insurrection in London in favour of Charles I.,	381
	The same in other places,	381
(April 24.)	The Presbyterians in parliament carry a vote in favour of King, Lords, and Commons,	382
	The insurrection is put down by Cromwell and Ireton,	382
	A Scotch army crosses the Borders; it is defeated by Cromwell at Preston,	382
(Aug. 27.)	Colchester is surrendered to Fairfax,	383
(Sept. 18.)	Fifteen commissioners are sent to enter into a treaty with Charles I. at Newport, Isle of Wight,	384

CHRONOLOGICAL INDEX.

A. D.
(Oct. 21.) Ingoldby's regiment declare Charles I. a traitor, ... 385
The army present a remonstrance to the two Houses, demanding that the office of king shall be elective, . . 386
(Nov. 30.) Charles I. is removed from Carisbrook Castle to Hurst Castle, . . 386
(Dec. 6.) Cromwell arrives in London, . . 387
(Dec. 6.) Colonel Pride and Colonel Rich with troops surround the House; Cromwell is thanked by the House, . 387, 388
(Dec. 8.) The 'Rump' consists of only fifty members, all Independents; a solemn fast is kept, ... 388
(Dec. 17-23.) Charles I. is removed from Hurst to Windsor, ... 388, 389
1649. (Jan. 6.) The ordinance for the trial of Charles I. passes, . . . 389
(Jan. 8.) The same is proclaimed, . . 389
(Jan. 19.) Charles I. is brought before the High Court of Justice, . . . 390
(Jan. 22.) He refuses to plead, . . 391, 392
(Jan. 25.) Commissioners from the Scotch parliament protest against the proceedings, 393
(Jan. 27.) Charles I. is condemned, . . 393-395
(Jan. 30.) He is beheaded, . . 396, 397
(Feb. 1.) The Commons vote for proceeding against some of the royalists, . . . 398
(Feb. 6.) They vote the abolition of the House of Lords, ... 399
(Feb. 7.) The office of king abolished, . 399
Charles II. is proclaimed, in Scotland, by the parliament; in Ireland, by the Marquis of Ormond, . . . 401
An insurrection breaks out in Ireland, 401
(Mar. 9.) Hamilton, Holland, and Capel are beheaded in Palace Yard, . . 400
(Aug. 15.) Cromwell goes to Ireland; suppresses the rebellion by the end of May 1650, 401
1650. Montrose proceeds to Scotland with a foreign force in favour of Charles II., 402
(May.) He is defeated at Invercarron; is hanged at Edinburgh, ... 402
(June.) Charles II. lands at the Frith of Cromarty; he takes the covenant, . . 402
(June 29.) Cromwell marches into Scotland, . 403
(Aug. 31.) The battle of Dunbar, . . 403, 404
1651. (Aug. 6.) Charles II. marches into England, 404
(Sept. 3.) Battle of Worcester, . . 405
The union and incorporation of Scotland and Ireland with England, . . 406
1652. (May 19.) Van Tromp sails up the Channel with a Dutch fleet; is brought to action by Blake, ... 406
(Sept. 28.) Blake beats the Dutch under De Ruyter and De Witt off Plymouth, . . 407
(Nov. 29.) Van Tromp gains a victory over Blake in the Downs, . . . 407
1653. (Feb. 18.) Blake fights Van Tromp for this and two succeeding days, and gains a victory, ... 407
(April 20.) Cromwell dissolves the Long Parliament, ... 410, 411
(July 31.) Blake defeats the Dutch fleet; Van Tromp is killed, . . . 415
(Dec.) Cromwell appointed Lord Protector, with a council, ... 413
1654. (July.) The Scotch refuse to acknowledge the Commonwealth, . . . 416
General Monk quells the insurrection there, ... 416
1656. (Jan.) A plot is formed for the restoration of Charles II., ... 410
Major Wildman is seized, with 'A declaration of the free and well-affected people of England now in arms against the tyrant Oliver Cromwell, Esq.,' 419
(Mar. 11.) The conspirators seize Salisbury; they are routed at South Molton, . . 419
The insurrection in other parts is quelled, ... 419
Cromwell divides England and Wales into eleven districts, and places over each a major-general, . . . 420
Jamaica is taken by the English under Vice-admiral Penn and General Venables; Blake checks the Barbary pirates in the Mediterranean; the Protector negotiates in favour of the Waldenses, ... 420
Treaty of alliance between England and France against Spain; Blake gains several victories, . . . 420
1657. (Feb. 23 to Mar. 26.) Cromwell is desired by parliament to assume the title of King, ... 421
(April 4.) He refuses the title of King, . 421
Major-general Harrison and other fifth-monarchy men are sent to the Tower, 421
(June.) Blake dies as he enters Plymouth Sound, ... 424, 425
Charles II. offers to marry Cromwell's daughter, ... 425
1658. (Jan. 20.) Parliament again meets; sixty peers summoned by writ take their seats in the Upper House, . 425, 426
(Feb. 4.) Cromwell dissolves the parliament, 426
A tract called *Killing no Murder* is circulated, ... 427
Cromwell suppresses another conspiracy for the Restoration; beheads Dr Hewit and Sir Henry Slingsby, . . 427
The English gain victories in the Low Countries, ... 427
(Aug.) The Protector's daughter, Lady Claypole, dies, ... 427
(Sept. 2.) He declares his son Richard his successor, 427
(Sept. 3.) The Protector dies, . . 427
Richard Cromwell is declared Lord Protector, ... 427
1659. (Jan. 27.) Parliament meets; the Commons and the 'Other House' pass an act of recognition of Richard Cromwell's title, 429
The Commons agree to transact business with the 'Other House,' . . 429
(May 6.) Lambert, Fleetwood, and others issue a declaration calling together the 'Long Parliament' or the 'Rump,' . . 430
Richard Cromwell signs his demission in form, ... 430
Fleetwood, in the name of the army, proffers allegiance to the 'Rump;' General Monk, from Scotland concurs for the army in the new revolution, 430
(June 22.) Henry Cromwell, lord-lieutenant of Ireland, for himself and the army, submits to parliament, . . 430
(July 4.) Parliament passes a bill exempting Richard Cromwell from all arrests for debt, ... 430
(Oct. 14.) The officers of the army declare Fleetwood commander-in-chief, . 431
(Oct. 29.) General Monk marches from Scotland; takes possession of Berwick, . 432
Lambert is appointed by the council of officers to command the army of the North, ... 432
(Dec. 22.) The soldiery about London insist on the sitting of parliament, . . *429
(Dec. 26.) Lenthall and the old parliament, the 'Rump,' resume, . . . *429

A.D.	PAGE
1660. (Jan.) Monk advances; Fairfax meets him at York, and agrees to the restoration of Charles II.,	*430
(April 25.) The new parliament meets; the peers are restored, and take their places,	*430
(May 1.) Letters from Charles II. are read in the council of state,	*431
They are sent to the Houses of Parliament,	*431
The navy declare for Charles II.,	*432
(May 8.) Charles II. is proclaimed at the gate of Westminster Hall,	*432

BOOK VIII.

1660. (May 29.) Charles II. enters London; makes Monk a Knight of the Garter and a privy-councillor; is addressed by both Houses of Parliament,	662
Measures are taken by parliament for the prosecution of the regicides; a bill of indemnity is passed excepting many persons: tonnage and poundage are granted to the king for life,	665, 666
Milton is committed to the custody of the serjeant-at-arms,	666
(July 7.) Monk is created Duke of Albemarle,	664
(July 9.) The Commons vote that the settlement of religion shall be left to the king,	667
Charles II. touches for the king's evil,	664
(Oct. 9.) The trial of the regicides takes place,	670–676
(Oct. 13, 15.) Ten of them are executed,	676, 677
(Dec. 8.) Oliver Cromwell, Bradshaw, and Ireton, are attainted,	678
1661. (Jan. 6.) Vennor, a fifth-monarchy man, raises a riot in London,	679
(Jan. 9.) The riot is suppressed; many rioters are killed; others are taken,	679
(Jan. 30.) The bodies of Cromwell, Bradshaw, and Ireton are disinterred, hanged, and otherwise misused,	678
The bodies of Cromwell's mother-in-law and daughter, of Dorislaus, May, Pym, Blake, and others, are exhumed and thrown into a pit in St Margaret's Churchyard,	678
The Marquis of Argyle, head of the Covenanters, is lured to Whitehall; he is sent to the Tower,	680
General Middleton is created Earl of Middleton, general of the army, and king's commissioner for holding Parliament; the Earl of Lauderdale is made secretary of state in Scotland,	681
The Marquis of Argyle is executed,	682
Sharp is made archbishop of St Andrew's,	683
Other bishops are consecrated by the archbishop of Canterbury and sent to their sees in Scotland,	683
All persons are required to take the oaths of allegiance and supremacy; the Earl of Cassilis, and Leighton, bishop of Dunblane, refuse,	683
(May 8.) The English parliament meets; the 'Pension Parliament;' the Solemn League and Covenant is ordered to be burnt by the hangman; an oath of 'non-resistance' established,	684
The bishops are restored to their seats in the House of Lords; a 'conformity act' is passed; a hearth and chimney tax is granted to the king for ever,	684, 685
(June 2.) Sir Henry Vane is tried in the Court of King's Bench; he is convicted of treason,	687–689
(June 14.) He is beheaded on Tower Hill,	689
Lambert pleads guilty to a charge of treason, and is imprisoned for life,	690
1662. The Act of Uniformity is enforced; upwards of two thousand ministers are thrust out of their livings,	691
Dunkirk is sold to the French,	692
1664. (Mar. 16.) Parliament reassembles; repeals the Triennial Act; passes the Conventicle Act,	693, 694
The Scotch parliament passes a similar act,	694
Archbishop Sharp puts it in force against the Presbyterians,	694
War is declared against the Dutch,	695
1665. The plague ravages London,	695
(June 3.) The Duke of York gains a victory over the Dutch fleet off Lowestoffe; Admiral Opdam is killed,	695, 696
The Earl of Sandwich attacks a Dutch fleet at Berghen, in Norway; is repulsed,	696
(Oct.) Parliament at Oxford passes the 'Five Mile Act,'	696
1666. (Feb.) The plague in London disappears,	697
(June 1–4.) Great battle between the English and Dutch fleets off the coast of Dunkirk, under Monk and Prince Rupert, and the Dutch admiral De Ruyter,	698
(July.) They again fight De Ruyter, and drive him into the Texel,	698
(Sept. 2.) The great fire of London commences near London Bridge,	699
(Nov. 13.) An insurrection of the Covenanters breaks out in the west of Scotland,	701
(Nov. 28.) The Covenanters are defeated on the Pentland Hills; many are hanged; others are tortured by order of Archbishop Sharp,	701
1667. (June.) De Ruyter destroys Sheerness, and a great quantity of English shipping,	701, 702
(Aug.) Treaty of Breda concluded; peace made between England, France, and Holland,	702
The Lord-chancellor Clarendon is desired to resign the great seal,	702
The great seal is taken from him, and given to Bridgman,	703
(Nov. 12.) Clarendon is impeached by the Commons; the Lords refuse to commit him,	703
He escapes to France; a bill for banishing him for life passes both Houses,	703
The 'Cabal' engross the powers of the government,	703
1668. The 'Triple Alliance' is formed between England, Holland, and Sweden,	706
(Oct.) James Mitchell fires at Archbishop Sharp; wounds the bishop of Orkney,	713
1670. (May 22.) Secret treaty with France; the 'Dover Treaty,'	707
Colonel Blood attempts to hang the Duke of Ormond,	708
(Oct.) Parliament votes an extraordinary supply for the navy; Sir John Coventry makes remarks in the House of Commons on Charles II.'s amours,	707
He is set upon by some of the Guards, who cut off his nose,	707, 708
1671. Colonel Blood attempts to steal the regalia from the Tower,	708, 709
1672. (Jan. 2.) Charles II., by the advice of the Cabal ministry, shuts up the Exchequer,	709
(May 28.) De Ruyter attacks the English and French fleets at Solebay; the Earl of Sandwich is killed,	710

CHRONOLOGICAL INDEX. 37

A.D.	PAGE
1673. Lauderdale publishes a pardon for all offences against the Scotch Conventicle Act,	713
(Feb.) Parliament meets; the Test Act is passed,	711
1674. (Jan. 7.) Charles II. declares in parliament that he has no secret treaty with France,	711
(Feb.) Mitchell is executed for firing at Archbishop Sharp,	729
1675. (April 13.) The session of parliament opens; the Commons demand the recall of the English under the Duke of Monmouth,	712
The Lords pass a bill imposing an oath that it is unlawful on any pretence to take up arms against the king and for the security of the Protestant religion; the Commons refuse it; parliament is prorogued,	712, 713
1676. War is general in the Low Countries, in Spain, Sicily, on the Upper and Lower Rhine, in Sweden, and in the German Provinces; in the Mediterranean, the Ocean, and the Baltic,	713
Louis XIV. gives Charles II. £100,000, and engages to send over troops; Charles II. writes and signs a treaty with Louis,	714
1677. (Feb. 5.) Parliament meets; Buckingham, Salisbury, Wharton, and Shaftesbury are committed to the Tower,	714
(May.) The Prince of Orange marries Mary, daughter of the Duke of York,	715
1678. Parliament votes money for ships, and an army of 30,000 men for a war with France,	715
Charles II. agrees to break with the states-general for a sum of money,	716
(Aug. 12.) Kirby informs Charles II. of a plot to assassinate him,	717
The plot is sworn to before Sir Edmondbury Godfrey,	718
(Sept. 28.) Titus Oates is summoned before the council; declares the popish plot,	718, 719
(Oct. 18.) Sir Edmondbury Godfrey is found murdered,	720
His body is buried, being attended by seventy-two Protestant divines in full canonicals,	721
(Oct. 21.) Parliament reassembles; Oates is called before both Houses; they commit the Catholic Lords, Stafford, Powis, Petre, Arundel, and Bellasis, to the Tower, and various persons to other prisons; grant Oates a pension,	721
(Nov. 28.) Oates accuses the queen of high-treason at the bar of the House of Commons,	723
The five lords in the Tower are impeached,	723
Mr Montague, the English ambassador at Paris, returns to England without leave,	725
He is returned to the House of Commons as member for Northampton,	726
His papers are seized; the house remonstrates; he produces other papers to the Commons criminating Danby; the latter is impeached; the Lords refuse to commit him to the Tower,	726
1679. (Mar. 6.) Parliament meets; Charles II. informs the two Houses he has granted a pardon to Danby, but dismissed him; he absconds,	728
(April 10.) Danby surrenders, and is sent to the Tower,	728
A new council of thirty is formed; Shaftesbury is at the head,	728

A.D.	PAGE
Charles II. recommends to the parliament the prosecution of the parties engaged in the popish plot; the disbanding of the army, and providing a fleet,	729
The Commons pass a bill of exclusion of the Duke of York,	729
The Habeas Corpus Act is passed,	729
(May 3.) Archbishop Sharp is put to death by Balfour and other Covenanters at Magus Muir,	730
(May 29.) The Covenanters burn the acts of parliament hostile to the kirk, and affix a declaration upon the market-cross of Rutherglen,	730
Defeat Graham of Claverhouse; take Glasgow; the Duke of Monmouth routs them at Bothwell Bridge,	730
Shaftesbury is dismissed,	731
1680. (Oct. 21.) The session of parliament opens; Dangerfield accuses the Duke of York of instigating him to murder Charles II.,	732
(Nov.) Lord Stafford is tried before the Peers; he is condemned; Charles II. alters the sentence to beheading; the Commons and sheriffs question his authority,	732
(Dec. 29.) Lord Stafford is beheaded,	733
1681. Charles II. refuses to sanction the Exclusion Bill,	733
(Jan.) The Commons vote that no supplies be granted without the Exclusion Bill,	733
(Mar. 21.) Parliament meets; the Bill of Exclusion is still insisted on,	733
Shaftesbury is committed to the Tower,	734
The Prince of Orange visits England,	735
Cameron and other Covenanters are defeated,	735
(July 27.) Donald Cargill and other Covenanters are executed for treason,	735
The Duke of York, as king's commissioner, opens the Scotch parliament; proposes a test to be taken by all, to maintain the supremacy of the king, and for passive obedience; Fletcher of Saltoun opposes and modifies the oath,	736
The duke calls upon Argyle to take the test; he does, but adds an explanation,	736
Argyle is committed to Edinburgh Castle for treason,	736
(Dec. 12.) He is condemned,	736
He escapes from the Tolbooth,	737
Violent measures are enacted against the Covenanters and Cameronians,	738
The Duke of Monmouth returns,	738
He is arrested; is admitted to bail,	739
The Rye House Plot is concerted,	740
(Nov.) Shaftesbury retires to Holland,	740
George, son of the Elector of Hanover, visits England,	759
1683. (June 12.) Keyling informs Lord Dartmouth of the Rye House Plot,	741-744
Lord Russell is apprehended and committed to the Tower,	745
Lord Grey is committed, but escapes to Holland,	745
(July 9.) Lord Howard is apprehended; he confesses,	746
Algernon Sidney, the Earl of Essex, and Hampden are committed to the Tower,	746
The Earl of Essex commits suicide in the Tower,	747
(July 13.) Lord Russell is tried and convicted,	747, 748
The Earl of Bedford offers £100,000 to save his son's life; Russell petitions Charles II.; writes a letter to the Duke of York,	748, 749

A.D.		PAGE
(July 21.)	Lord Russell is beheaded in Lincoln's Inn Fields,	749
(Sept. 7.)	Algernon Sidney is brought to trial in the Court of King's Bench,	751–753
(Oct. 25.)	The Duke of Monmouth has an audience of Charles II.,	754
(Nov. 25.)	Monmouth surrenders; confesses before Charles II. and the Duke of York,	754
(Dec. 8.)	Sidney is beheaded on Tower Hill,	754
	Monmouth receives a pardon; denies his confession; readmits it; flies to Holland,	755
	The English settlement at Tangier is abandoned,	760
1684.	The Covenanters and Cameronians are imprisoned at the Bass Rock, Dumbarton Castle, and other places,	757
	Sir Samuel Barnadiston is condemned for libel, and fined £10,000,	758
	Danby, Arundel, Powis, and Bellasis are released from the Tower,	758
	The Duke of York, notwithstanding the 'Test Act,' is again admitted to the privy council,	758
	Titus Oates is condemned in £100,000 damages under the act *De Scandalis Magnatum*, for a libel on the Duke of York,	758
1685. (Feb. 6.)	Charles II. dies,	762
	Accession of James II.; he immediately calls the council and addresses them, promising to support the government in church and state,	763
	He is proclaimed,	763
	He retains the late government,	764
	He publicly attends mass in state,	764
	He orders the publication of the fact of the late king having died a Roman Catholic,	764
	A proclamation is issued for levying the Excise and other duties without authority of parliament,	765
	All papists and dissenters are discharged from prison by royal warrant,	765
(April 23.)	James II. and the queen are crowned by Sancroft, archbishop of Canterbury,	765
(May 7.)	Titus Oates is tried for perjury; is convicted, fined, whipped, and put in the pillory,	766
	The Earl of Argyle lands in Scotland; declares he comes to re-establish the Covenant; he is routed by Lord Dumbarton near Glasgow,	768
(June 20.)	Argyle is captured and taken to Edinburgh Castle,	769
(June 14.)	The Duke of Monmouth lands at Lyme, declaring he comes to secure the Protestant religion, and to deliver the country from the tyranny of James, Duke of York,	770
(June 30.)	Argyle is beheaded,	768
(July 5.)	Battle of Sedgemoor,	774
(July 8.)	The Duke of Monmouth is captured,	775
	He is committed to the Tower,	776
	A bill of attainder passes both Houses,	768–776
(July 14.)	He writes to James II. for a respite; it is refused,	776
(July 15.)	He is beheaded on Tower Hill,	778
(Sept.)	Jeffreys is made lord chancellor,	780
	At Dorchester two hundred and thirty-nine rebels are executed,	781
	Many are sent as slaves to the West Indies; some are sold to courtiers for the same purpose,	781
(Sept. 30.)	Jeffreys returns to court, and is thanked by James II.,	782
	Lords Brandon, Delamere, and Stamford are proceeded against for high treason,	782

A.D.		PAGE
(Nov. 9.)	Both Houses address James II. to discharge all officers who refuse to take the Protestant test,	783
1686.	James II. issues letters mandatory to the English bishops, forbidding the clergy to preach on controversial points, and establishing an ecclesiastical commission,	784
	Compton, bishop of London, is suspended,	785
	Fifteen thousand soldiers are encamped on Hounslow Heath; Samuel Johnson, a clergyman, is fined, put in the pillory, and whipped,	785
1687.	James II. issues a declaration of liberty of conscience,	786
	Pechell, the vice-chancellor of Cambridge, is suspended by the Ecclesiastical Commission Court,	785
	The fellows of Magdalene College refuse to elect a papist their master,	786
	James II. cites the fellows before him at Oxford,	786
(July 3.)	The pope's nuncio is publicly introduced at court,	787
(Oct. 20.)	Parker is appointed master of Magdalene College by the commission, and Howe, elected by the fellows, displaced,	786
1688. (April 27.)	James II. publishes a new declaration of indulgence, and commands the clergy to read it in the churches,	788
(May 18.)	Several of the bishops petition the king against the declaration,	788
(May 20.)	The first day of reading the declaration only seven clergymen comply,	789
(June 8.)	The bishops who signed the petition are summoned before the council; they are committed to the Tower,	789
	Orders are issued for inserting the name of the Prince of Wales in the Common Prayer Book,	792
(May 30.)	The bishops are acquitted,	791
	Several noblemen go to the Prince of Orange,	792
	A correspondence is opened with him,	793
	The Prince of Orange collects large land and naval forces,	796
(Oct.)	The prince is baptised according to the Romish rites,	795
	James II. calls a great council; the archbishop of Canterbury, the Marquis of Halifax, and Lords Clarendon and Nottingham refuse to sit at the board with papists,	795
(Nov. 5.)	The Prince of Orange lands at Torbay; marches to Exeter,	797
	James II. goes to the camp at Hounslow; several of his officers desert,	798
(Nov. 16.)	James II. calls a council of war at Whitehall; the Prince of Wales is sent to Portsmouth,	798
(Nov. 19.)	Churchill and the Duke of Grafton desert to the Prince of Orange,	798
	The Princess Anne proceeds to the camp of the Prince of Orange,	798, 799
	The queen and Prince of Wales go to Calais,	799
	James II. quits London; is seized at the Isle of Sheppey, and sent to Faversham,	799
	Jeffreys is maltreated at Wapping; is committed to the Tower,	800
	A provisional council is formed; the Prince of Orange is invited to London; James II. returns to London; invites the Prince to a conference at Whitehall, which is refused,	800
(Dec. 23.)	James II. embarks in the Medway,	801
(Dec. 24.)	He reaches a fishing-smack hired for his use,	801
(Dec. 25.)	Lands at Ambleteuse,	801

VOLUME IV.

BOOK IX.

A.D.		PAGE
1688. (Dec. 25.)	The House of Lords request the Prince of Orange to take upon himself the administration of affairs, and to issue writs for a convention,	2
(Dec. 26.)	The members of the House of Commons of Charles II., the aldermen and common council of London, do the like,	2
1689. (Jan. 28.)	The Commons vote that James II. has abdicated,	4
(Jan. 31.)	The Lords vote that the throne is vacant,	4
(Feb.)	William and Mary are proclaimed king and queen,	5
(Feb. 13.)	King William III. makes his first speech from the throne,	9
(Mar. 1.)	A new oath of allegiance is framed and tendered; the archbishop of Canterbury and seven bishops refuse the oath; four hundred of the clergy do the like; 'nonjurors,'	9, 10
	The Commons suspend the Habeas Corpus Act,	10
	The hearth-tax is abolished,	10
	The attainders of Lord Russell and Algernon Sidney are reversed,	11
(Mar. 12.)	James II. lands at Kinsale; proceeds to various places; is acknowledged by the Catholics,	12
(April.)	The Scottish Convention of Estates resolve that James II. has forfeited the crown,	8
	The crown is offered to William and Mary by the deputies from the Scottish Convention,	8
	Naval action between Admiral Herbert and the French fleet,	12
	James II. forms a council of government in Dublin; he issues various proclamations; summons a parliament to meet in Dublin on the 7th of May,	13
	He commences the siege of Londonderry,	17
(May 7.)	The Irish parliament meets; the Act of Settlement, by which the English and Scotch Protestants hold their lands in Ireland, is repealed,	13
	Attaints the adherents of the Prince of Orange, and votes supplies, and passes an act for liberty of conscience,	14
	Lord Dundee raises an insurrection in Scotland in favour of James II.; battle of Killikrankie; Dundee is killed,	15
	William III. relieves Londonderry; the siege is raised,	17
(Aug. 13.)	Marshal Schomberg lands at Carrickfergus with a large army,	18
	He takes Belfast, Carrickfergus, Neury, and Dundalk,	23
(Nov. 16.)	The Bill of Rights and the Land-tax Act are passed,	19
1690. (Feb.)	The Duke of Berwick attacks Schomberg at Belturbet, but is repulsed,	23
(Mar.)	The Whigs, in the Lords introduce the Abjuration Bill, by which all persons in employment are to take an oath abjuring James II. and his title to the crown,	21
	The bill is thrown out by the Tories in the Commons,	22
(June 14.)	William III. lands at Belfast,	23
(June 16.)	James II. marches from Dublin,	24
(July 1.)	Battle of the Boyne; William III. passes the river,	25, 26
	Marshal Schomberg is killed,	26
	James II. embarks for France,	26
(July 3.)	William III. enters Dublin,	26
(Aug. 9.)	He commences the siege of Limerick,	26
(Aug. 30.)	He raises the siege and returns to England,	26
(Sept. 21.)	The Earl of Marlborough lands at Cork; he and the Duke of Wirtemburg besiege Cork and Kinsale; both are taken; the Duke of Grafton is killed,	28
(Oct.)	The Earl of Marlborough returns to England; the Duke of Berwick goes to France,	28
(Dec. 20.)	The Commons vote four millions for the support of the army and the fleet,	29
	Episcopacy is abolished in Scotland,	44
1691. (Jan. 6.)	William III. proceeds to the Hague,	30
(Jan. 26.)	He enters the Hague; the confederate princes meet him,	30
(Mar.)	The French besiege Mons,	32
(April 20.)	The town and garrison capitulate to the French,	32
	William III. returns to England; Tillotson is made archbishop of Canterbury, and the sees of the nonjuring bishops are filled up,	32
(May 1.)	William III. leaves London for Holland,	32
(May 2.)	Sails from Harwich; various military operations,	32, 33
(June 19.)	General Ginckel captures Athlone,	33
(July 12.)	Battle of Aghrim; the Irish and French are defeated,	33, 34
(Aug. 26.)	General Ginckel lays siege to Limerick,	34
(Sept.)	William III. returns to England,	33
	A proclamation is issued by the Scotch government, offering a pardon to all who take the oaths to the new government before the 1st of January 1692,	45
(Oct. 1.)	Limerick surrenders; a treaty is executed; and an end put to the Irish war,	34
	Ginckel is created Baron Aghrim and Earl of Athlone,	34
(Oct. 22.)	William III. meets parliament; supplies are voted for carrying on the war, and for increasing the army and navy,	35
1692.	A poll-tax is passed,	35
(Feb. 13.)	The massacre of Glencoe,	46
(Mar. 5.)	William III. embarks for the continent,	36
(May 5.)	The Earl of Marlborough is committed to the Tower,	37
(May 21, 22.)	Battle of La Hogue,	38, 39
(June 16.)	The Earl of Marlborough is released,	39
(June 30.)	Namur surrenders to the French,	36
	William III. attacks Mons; battle of Steinkirk; he is defeated,	36, 37
	De Grandval is shot for a plot to assassinate William III.,	37
(Oct. 19.)	William III. returns to London,	39
(Nov.)	He dismisses Admiral Russell,	40
(Dec.)	A bill for triennial parliaments, providing for annual sessions, and elections every three years passes both Houses; William III. refuses the royal assent,	40, 41
1693 (April.)	William III. again joins the allied army,	41

A.D.	PAGE
(June 17.) The Smyrna fleet is attacked; the French beat the English and Dutch fleets,	42, 43
(July 29.) William III. fights the battle of Landen; he is defeated,	41
Heidelberg is taken by the French,	41
(Nov.) William III. establishes a Whig government,	47
(Nov. 7.) Lord Falkland is removed, and Admiral Russell placed at the head of the Admiralty,	48
1694. (Feb.) Admiral Wheeler's fleet in the Mediterranean is destroyed by a tempest,	48
(April.) William III. joins the army, the military operations are continued,	49
(June 7.) Lord Berkeley with a fleet appears off Brest; the army lands under General Tollemache; they are wholly defeated; Tollemache is killed,	48, 49
Lord Berkeley bombards and destroys Dieppe and Havre de Grace,	49
Admiral Russell sails to the Mediterranean with an English and Dutch fleet; clears it of the French; relieves Barcelona; blockades Toulon; and gains other successes,	49
(Nov. 12.) The Triennial Bill passes both Houses,	49
(Dec. 22.) The royal assent is given to the Triennial Bill,	49
Dr Tennison is made archbishop of Canterbury,	50
(Dec. 28.) Queen Mary dies,	50
William III. is reconciled to the Princess Anne,	50
1695. (May 12.) William III. again embarks for the allied army,	53
The Earl of Breadalbane is sent to Edinburgh Castle by the Scottish parliament for the massacre of Glencoe,	47
A bill passes the Scottish parliament for colonising the Isthmus of Darien,	51
The Irish parliament pass many acts against the papists; they are rendered incapable of being guardians; the law of inheritance for papists is altered, and they are rendered incapable of holding land for more than thirty-one years; the Romish rites are forbidden, and priests are banished. (These acts were passed between 1692 and 1705,)	52
(Sept. 5.) Namur capitulates,	55
Lord Berkeley bombards Dunkirque, Calais, and St Malo, and destroys the town of Grandeval,	55
William III. makes a progress to the north,	56
(Nov.) An act is passed regulating trials in cases of treason; and one regulating the expenses of elections,	57
The Commons petition against the extensive grants made by William III. to the Earl of Portland; the king recalls them, and makes others,	58
1696. The Commons carry a motion for an act to create a Board of Trade; William III. takes offence at it,	59
(Feb. 11.) Captain Fisher discloses to the Earl of Portland a plot to assassinate William III.,	61
(Feb. 14.) Prendergast gives further information,	61
(Feb. 24.) William III. declares the discovery of the plot to parliament; a proclamation is issued against the conspirators,	61
(Mar.) Admiral Russell bombards Calais,	65
(Mar. 11.) Charnock, King, and Keys are tried and convicted of high treason at the Old Bailey,	63

A.D.	PAGE
(Mar. 18.) They are executed at Tyburn,	63
Sir John Friend, Sir William Perkins, Rookwood, Lowick, and Cranburn, are also tried, convicted, and executed,	64
Parliament suspends the Habeas Corpus Act; vote the banishment of all papists from London and Westminster, and propose a Protestant association for the defence of William III.,	64
(Oct.) William III. returns to England,	65
1697. (Jan.) The Earl of Monmouth is sent to the Tower,	67
(April 16.) Parliament is prorogued,	67
William III. creates Admiral Russell Earl of Orford; Somers, Lord Somers, Baron of Evesham, and lord-chancellor, and makes Sunderland lord-chamberlain; he appoints a council of regency, and goes to the continent,	68
(Sept. 20.) The Treaty of Ryswick is signed,	70
(Nov. 16.) William III. enters London,	71
(Dec. 3.) Parliament meets; William III. proposes keeping up a land-force; the Commons pass a resolution for disbanding the army raised since 1680; Sunderland retires; parliament votes a revenue of £700,000 a year to William III. for life,	71
1698. (July 26.) Paterson sails from Leith Roads with 1200 men for Darien,	82
(Nov.) They reach Darien, establish New St Andrews and New Edinburgh,	82
(Dec.) A bill is passed for disbanding the army, except 7000 in England, and 1200 in Ireland, natural born subjects; they send a bill up to the Lords,	77
1699. (Feb.) The Earl of Orford resigns his places,	80
The Darien expedition,	81–84
The colonists are reduced to great necessity; the remainder re-embark for Scotland,	82, 83
Captain Campbell and a new set of adventurers arrive; they attack the Spaniards at Subucantee; rout them; the Spaniards besiege them in New St Andrews; they capitulate; he returns to Scotland with the few remaining of his followers,	83
(Sept.) The Scottish company remonstrate upon the conduct pursued in regard to Paterson and his followers,	84
(Nov.) The Commons receive the report of the commissioners for taking the account of the Irish forfeited estates,	86, 87
1700. Lady Orkney's grant is brought into question,	87, 88
Sir Richard Leving is committed to the Tower,	83
(Feb. 6.) The Commons pass the Resumption Bill, and tack to it a money bill; the Lords amend it; the Commons reject the amendments; the Lords pass the bill,	88, 89
(April 11.) William III. gives his assent, and prorogues parliament,	89
Lord Somers is removed; Sir Nathan Wright is made lord-keeper,	90
(July.) Sir George Rooke, with the English and Dutch fleets, drives the Danish fleet into Copenhagen,	92
(July 30.) The Duke of Gloucester, son of the Princess Anne, dies,	96
1701. (Feb.) William III. recommends a settlement of the succession,	96, 97
Parliament votes large supplies for the army, navy, and garrisons,	100
The Commons resolve to impeach the	

HISTORY OF ENGLAND. 41

A.D.		PAGE
	Earl of Portland for negotiating the partition treaties; Lords Somers, Halifax, and Orford are also impeached for having advised the signing of them,	104, 105
	The Kentish Petition is presented,	106
	All the petitioners are sent to the Gate House,	106
(May 10.)	The impeachment of Lord Somers is carried up to the House of Lords,	109
(May 24.)	He sends his answer,	109
	He is acquitted,	112
	Orford is acquitted; the Lords dismiss the charges against Portland and Halifax,	112
(June.)	William III. embarks for Holland,	112
(Sept. 7.)	The second Grand Alliance is signed at the Hague,	113
(Sept. 16.)	James II. dies at St Germain,	114
(Nov. 4.)	William III. returns from Holland,	117
1702. (Jan. 2.)	A bill of attainder passes the Commons against James II.'s son,	121
(Feb. 21.)	William III. fractures his collar-bone,	121
(Feb. 26.)	He sends a message to parliament, recommending a union between England and Scotland,	121, 122
(Mar. 8.)	William III. dies,	123
	Accession of Queen Anne,	125
(Mar. 11.)	The Earl of Marlborough is made Knight of the Garter,	126
(Mar. 12.)	He is appointed captain-general of the English forces at home and abroad,	126
	He is made master of the ordnance,	126
	The Tories come into power,	127
(Mar. 28.)	Marlborough is sent ambassador to the Hague; is appointed to the chief command of the allied armies; returns to England,	128
(May 4.)	War is declared against France,	129
(May 12.)	Marlborough departs for Holland; begins military operations,	129, 130
(Aug.)	Rooke and Ormond destroy the Spanish galleons, and capture several ships with great wealth,	131
(Oct. 29.)	Liege, with its garrison, surrenders to Marlborough,	130
	Marlborough is captured on a canal, but liberated,	130
(Dec. 14.)	He is created a duke,	133
	Queen Anne gives him £5000 a year during her life,	133
1703. (Mar. 9.)	Marshal Villars reduces the town of Kehl,	136
(May 15.)	Cologne capitulates to the allies,	137
	The allies carry on various military operations,	137, 138
(Oct. 31.)	The Duke of Marlborough returns to England,	139
	The king of Spain (the Archduke Charles) arrives in England,	139
(Nov. 9.)	Parliament meets; Queen Anne announces the intention to recover the monarchy of Spain from the House of Bourbon, and restore it to that of Austria,	139
	Supplies are voted; the army and navy increased,	139, 140
1704. (Jan. 19.)	The Duke of Marlborough arrives at the Hague,	148
(Jan. 29.)	A union between England and Scotland is proposed,	142
(Feb. 4.)	Queen Anne, who has revived the Order of the Thistle, gives a green ribbon to the Duke of Argyle,	146
	Harley is made Secretary of State,	145
	The bill for recruiting the army passes for a year,	145

A.D.		PAGE
(Feb. 24.)	Marlborough returns to England,	149
(April.)	He rejoins the allied army,	149
(July 2.)	The battle of Schellenberg or Donawert,	152
	The Scottish parliament pass a bill called the Scottish Security Bill, for regulating the succession to the Scottish throne, and for disbanding the army; Queen Anne gives her assent,	147, 148
(July 23.)	Admiral Rooke takes Gibraltar,	150
(Aug. 13.)	Battle of Blenheim,	155–158
(Aug. 13, 15.)	Sea-fight off Malaga between the English and Dutch fleets under Rooke, and the French fleet under the command of the Count of Toulouse,	160
1705. (Feb. 17.)	Queen Anne grants the manor and honour of Woodstock to the Duke of Marlborough; the Commons grant money to pay off the incumbrances; the queen orders the erection of Blenheim House,	161
(Feb.)	Admiral Rooke is dismissed, and Sir Clondesley Shovel appointed to the command of the fleet,	162
(April.)	Marlborough again joins the allies; retakes Huy; the campaign closes in May,	163
	The war is carried on in Spain,	164
	The Earl of Peterborough gains many battles,	164, 165
(Oct.)	The new parliament meets; the Whigs have a majority in the House of Commons,	165
1706. (April.)	Marlborough again leaves England,	168
(May 23.)	Battle of Ramilies,	169
	Prince Eugene beats the French between the Doria and the Stura,	170
	The siege of Barcelona is raised by Peterborough,	170
(June 24.)	Galway takes Madrid,	171
1707. (Jan. 18.)	The Treaty of Union is passed by the Scottish parliament,	174
(Mar. 4.)	The act of Union receives the royal assent,	178
(Mar. 25.)	The last Scottish parliament rises,	177
(April 24.)	The last separate English parliament rises,	180
(April 28.)	The Duke of Marlborough and Charles XII. of Sweden, meet,	181
(Oct. 23.)	The first parliament of Great Britain meets,	190
(Dec. 23.)	Both Houses address Queen Anne to continue war till the whole of the Spanish territories are restored to the House of Austria,	191
1708.	Marlborough and Godolphin absent themselves from the Council,	195
	Harley is dismissed,	196
(Mar.)	Queen Anne announces to parliament an intention in Scotland to reinstate the Stuarts,	196
	The Duke of Hamilton and twenty-one other Scottish lords and gentlemen are arrested,	196
	Troops are marched into Scotland; Sir George Byng is sent with a fleet to Dunkirk, where the Pretender is ready to embark for Scotland,	196
	He captures the *Salisbury*, one of the French ships, with Lord Griffin, two sons of Lord Middleton, and some Irish officers, with five French companies on board,	197
	The Pretender returns to France,	198
(May.)	The French take Ghent, Ypres, and invest Oudenarde,	200
(July 11.)	Battle of Oudenarde,	200
(Sept.)	Admiral Leake conquers the island of Sardinia,	201

A.D.		PAGE
(Sept. 30.)	The fortress of St Philip, in Port Mahon, is taken by General Stanhope and Admiral Leake; the island of Minorca is taken by the English,	201
(Oct. 22.)	Lille is taken by Marlborough and Prince Eugene,	200
(Dec. 1.)	The citadel of Lille surrenders,	200
	Ghent, Bruges, and other places are retaken or surrender,	200
1709.	The House of Lords resolves that no peer of Great Britain, whether English or Scotch, having a seat, shall vote for representative peers for Scotland,	211
	The Commons exclude the eldest sons of Scottish peers from seats in the House of Commons,	211
(July 7.)	Prince Eugene and Marlborough besiege Tournay,	215
(July 30.)	Tournay surrenders,	215
(Sept. 12.)	Battle of Malplaquet,	216
(Nov. 5.)	Dr Sacheverell preaches a virulent sermon in St Paul's,	217
(Dec. 15.)	He is ordered to be impeached by the Commons for publishing his sermon; he is taken into custody,	218
1710. (Jan. 13.)	The impeachment is carried up to the Lords,	218
(Feb. 27.)	His trial takes place,	218-222
	Riots in London,	221
(Mar. 20.)	Sacheverell is found guilty of high crimes and misdemeanours,	222
(Mar. 23.)	He is sentenced not to preach for three years, and his sermons ordered to be burnt by the hangman,	222
	Illuminations in London and Westminster in consequence, and bonfires in the streets,	223
	The Whigs are dismissed from office, and are succeeded by the Tories,	225, 226
(April.)	Douay is besieged and taken by Marlborough and Eugene,	227
(July 27.)	Stanhope defeats King Philip near Almanara,	228
(Aug. 19.)	He is again defeated by Stanhope and Starenberg, near Saragoza; Saragoza surrenders,	228
(Sept. 21.)	Stanhope takes possession of Madrid,	228
(Sept. 28.)	King Charles enters Madrid,	228
(Dec. 9.)	Stanhope is defeated, and taken prisoner by the Duke of Vendôme,	228
(Dec. 10.)	Starenberg retreats before Vendôme,	228
1711.	A bill is brought into parliament requiring property qualifications for members of the Commons,	230
	Harley is created Earl of Oxford, and Earl Mortimer,	232
(June.)	An attempt is made by the English to conquer Canada,	237
(Dec. 21.)	Marlborough is charged in the Commons with misappropriating public money,	239
	He is dismissed from his employment by Queen Anne,	240
1712. (Jan.)	Robert Walpole is committed to the Tower, and expelled the House of Commons for corruption,	241
(Nov. 5.)	The king of Spain, Philip, signs his renunciation of the French succession,	250
(Nov. 15.)	The Duke of Hamilton and Lord Mohun fight a duel, and both are killed,	251
	The Duke of Marlborough retires to Brussels,	252
1713. (April 9.)	The session of parliament is opened; Queen Anne announces that the Treaty of Peace of Utrecht is signed,	253
(June 14.)	A motion for leave to bring in a bill for dissolving the Union between England and Scotland is lost in the Lords,	257
(Aug.)	Intrigues are entered into for the restoration of the Stuarts,	260-262
1714. (Feb. 16.)	The new parliament assembles,	262
(Mar. 2.)	Queen Anne delivers the speech from the throne; complains of the statement that the Hanoverian succession is in danger,	262-263
	The House of Commons vote that The Crisis, written by Mr Richard Steele, is a scandalous libel, and expel him the House,	264
	Lord Wharton moves in the Lords that the Protestant succession is in no danger; it is lost,	264
(April 12.)	A writ is demanded for summoning the Electoral Prince of Hanover, as Duke of Cambridge, to parliament,	265-268
(May 30.)	Queen Anne writes to the Electoral Prince,	272
	The Electress Sophia of Hanover dies,	273
(June 11.)	The Electoral Prince replies to Queen Anne's letter,	275
(June 23.)	A proclamation is issued for the apprehension of the Pretender,	276
(Aug. 1.)	Queen Anne dies,	280
	Accession of George I.; he is immediately proclaimed; the Duke of Marlborough arrives the same evening at Dover; the Houses of Lords and Commons sit,	281-284
	The Lords-Justices appointed by the Regency Act meet and appoint Addison secretary,	284
	The Duke of Marlborough is met on his entry into London by 200 gentlemen on horseback, and a long train of carriages; he proceeds to the House of Lords and takes the oaths to King George I.,	284
	George I. is proclaimed in Dublin,	284
	A reward of £100,000 is offered for the apprehension of the Pretender if he shall land,	285
(Sept. 18.)	George I. and his son Prince George land at Greenwich,	285, 286
	Marlborough is appointed commander-in-chief; the other offices are filled by Whigs,	286
1715. (Mar.)	George I. appears in person in parliament; his speech is read by Lord Cowper, the chancellor; he promises to make the constitution in church and state the rule of his government,	287
(June 9.)	Walpole impeaches Lord Bolingbroke of high crimes and misdemeanours,	288
(June 21.)	General Stanhope impeaches the Duke of Ormond,	288
	The Duke of Ormond flies to France,	289
(July.)	Riots in various places against the Hanoverians, Whigs, and dissenters,	290
	Bolingbroke and Ormond intrigue in France for the restoration of the Stuarts,	291
(Sept. 1.)	The Earl of Mar erects the standard of the Pretender at Brae Mar,	292
(Sept. 9.)	He issues a declaration calling on the people to arm, and assumes the title of Lieutenant-general of King James,	292
	The Earl of Hume and others are apprehended and sent to Edinburgh Castle,	292
	Troops are sent into Scotland; the Duke of Argyll is sent as commander-in-chief, and the Earl of Sutherland raises his clans for George I.,	292
	Mr Forster raises a rebellion in Northumberland,	292

CHRONOLOGICAL INDEX. 43

A.D.		PAGE
(Oct.)	The Earl of Derwentwater joins Forster,	293
(Oct. 12.)	Lord Kenmure proclaims the Pretender at Moffat,	293
	Kenmure joins Forster near Rothbury; they march to Kelso,	293
(Nov. 2.)	Mackintosh and Forster arrive at Penrith; they advance to Preston,	296
	General Wills marches against them; they lay down their arms; Lords Derwentwater, Widdrington, Kenmure, and other lords are taken; Mackintosh, Forster, and other gentlemen are also captured; the insurrection in England is suppressed,	297
(Nov. 13.)	Battle of Dunblane; the insurgents are routed,	297–299
(Dec. 22.)	The Pretender lands at Peterhead,	301
	He goes to Fetteresso; is joined by Mar and other Jacobites,	301
1716. (Jan. 6.)	He makes his public entry into Dundee,	302
(Jan. 9.)	Parliament reassembles; the rebel lords are impeached,	303
(Jan. 16.)	The Pretender holds a council at Perth,	304
(Jan. 19.)	The rebel lords are brought before the Peers in Westminster Hall; all but Winton plead guilty; are condemned,	303
(Jan. 24.)	The Duke of Argyll and General Cadogan advance and survey the roads leading to Perth,	304
(Jan. 31.)	The Pretender evacuates Perth and proceeds to Dundee,	305
(Feb. 3.)	Argyll follows him; the rebels retreat to Montrose,	305
(Feb. 4.)	The Pretender sails for France,	305
	The Earls of Carnwath and Widdrington are respited; Lord Nairn is saved,	308
(Feb. 23.)	The Earl of Nithsdale escapes from the Tower in his wife's clothes,	308
(Feb. 24.)	The Earls of Derwentwater and Kenmure are beheaded on Tower Hill,	308, 309
(Mar. 15.)	Lord Winton is condemned for treason, and sent back to the Tower,	309
(April.)	Forster, Mackintosh, and others, are convicted with twenty others for high treason; some escape; others are executed,	309
(June.)	George I. goes to Hanover,	311
	Negotiations take place for the 'French Treaty,' concerning the destruction of Dunkirk and matters relating to the north of Europe, and a scheme of the Swedes to invade England and restore the Stuarts,	311–314
	The French treaty is signed at the Hague,	317
(Dec.)	George I. returns to England,	317
	The treaty is signed at the Hague for Holland, and becomes 'The Triple Alliance,'	317
1717. (April.)	A change takes place in the ministry; the 'German ministry' is formed,	319
(June 24.)	The Earl of Oxford is tried before the Lords in Westminster Hall for high treason; he is acquitted,	319, 320
	The Earl of Carnwath, and Lords Widdrington and Nairn are discharged from the Tower,	320
(Aug.)	The Quadruple Alliance,	325
(Nov.)	The Spaniards conquer Sardinia,	322
1718. (Mar.)	A large naval armament is prepared at Portsmouth,	324
(June 4.)	The fleet sails under Sir George Byng for the Mediterranean,	325
(Aug. 11.)	Battle off Cape Passaro,	326, 327

A.D.		PAGE
1719. (May.)	George I. appoints a council of regency, and goes to Hanover,	332
(June 18.)	Fuenterabia surrenders to the French,	335
(Aug. 2.)	The Duke of Berwick besieges and takes St Sebastian,	335
(Aug. 17.)	The citadel of St Sebastian surrenders,	335
1720. (April 7.)	The South-sea Company Bill is passed,	350–352
(May.)	George I. is reconciled to the Prince of Wales,	352
(June.)	The South-sea Company's funds rise from 130 to 300,	352
(Aug.)	The South-sea stock rises to above 1000 per cent,	353
(Sept.)	The South-sea stock falls below 300,	353
	The South-sea scheme bursts; a general panic prevails,	353, 354
(Nov.)	The South-sea stock falls to 135,	354
(Dec. 12.)	The South-sea directors are ordered to lay their accounts before parliament,	354–355
(Dec. 21.)	Walpole brings in a bill to transfer part of the South-sea stock into the Bank, and part into the East India Company's stock,	355
1721.	Walpole's bill is passed,	355
(Feb. 16.)	The Secret Committee of the Commons present their report on the South-sea scheme,	355, 356
	The property of the directors is confiscated,	356
(April 2.)	Walpole is made first lord of the Treasury,	356
	He introduces a new bill for remedying the mischief of the South-sea scheme,	357
(June 13.)	A treaty of peace is signed between Great Britain and Spain,	357
(July 10.)	Walpole's new bill receives the royal assent,	357
1722. (May.)	Walpole receives intelligence of a new plot to restore the Pretender; several arrests take place; a camp is formed in Hyde Park, and other precautions taken,	360
(June 16.)	The Duke of Marlborough dies,	359
(Aug. 24.)	Bishop Atterbury is arrested and sent to the Tower,	360
1723.	Mr Layer is tried, convicted, and executed, for enlisting troops for the Pretender,	361
	A bill of banishment and deprivation passes the Commons against Bishop Atterbury,	361
(May 6.)	He is brought to the bar of the House of Lords; the bill is passed, and receives the royal assent,	361, 362
(June.)	Bolingbroke is pardoned, and returns to England; proposes to Walpole a coalition with the Tories; returns to France,	362, 363
1724. (April.)	Wood's coinage in Ireland creates disturbances; Dean Swift publishes *Drapier's Letters*,	364
	The printer is indicted; the grand jury ignore the bill,	365
	A riot takes place in Glasgow against the malt tax: nine persons are shot by the military; Captain Bushell is tried and convicted, but pardoned,	365
(Nov.)	Lord Bolingbroke is restored to his seat in parliament,	366
1725. (Jan.)	Peter the Great, czar of Russia, dies,	368
(Sept. 3.)	A treaty is signed at Hanover between Great Britain, France, and Prussia; Denmark and Holland accede soon after,	368
1726. (Jan. 20.)	Parliament meets; the treaty of Hanover is approved by a large majority,	369

A.D.		PAGE
(May.)	Sir Charles Wager blockades the Russian ports; Admiral Hosier goes on an expedition to the West Indies, and Sir John Jennings to the coast of Spain,	369
1727. (Jan.)	Palm, the Russian ambassador, presents a memorial to George I.; he is ordered to quit the kingdom; the British resident at Vienna is recalled,	370
(May 31.)	Preliminaries of peace are signed between England, France, Holland, and Russia,	371
(June 11.)	George I. dies on the road to Osnaburgh, Accession of George II.,	372, 372
(July 3.)	Walpole proposes a civil list of £830,000 a year should be settled on George II. for life,	377
(July 9.)	The same is agreed to, and £100,000 a year is settled on the queen for life,	377
1729.	Frederick, Prince of Wales, comes from Hanover,	380
(Feb. 26.)	The House of Commons resolves that it is a breach of privilege to publish their debates in a newspaper,	381
(May.)	The Spaniards erect the lines of San Roque,	381
(Nov. 9.)	The treaty of Seville is concluded,	381
1730. (Feb.)	The East India Company's charter is prolonged to 1766,	382
1731.	A bill passes for all pleadings and processes in courts of law to be in English,	383
(May 31.)	The Duke of Wharton dies at the convent of Poblet,	379
	Atterbury dies in Paris,	378
1734. (Feb. 14.)	The Prince of Orange is married to the princess-royal at St James's,	387
(Mar. 13.)	A bill is brought into the House of Commons for the repeal of the Septennial Act,	388
	It is debated and thrown out,	388-391
1735. (Jan.)	Parliament meets; an increase of the army and navy is voted, and a subsidy is voted to Denmark,	393
	The Prince of Wales marries Augusta, Princess of Saxe-Gotha,	399
	Bolingbroke goes to the continent,	393
	Sir John Norris with a fleet is sent to the Tagus,	394
1736. (Jan.)	Parliament meets; passes an act for laying a heavy duty on gin and other spirits,	395
(Mar.)	A bill to repeal the Test Act is thrown out by the Commons, and one for the relief of the Quakers by the Lords,	395
(May.)	A riot takes place in Edinburgh; Captain Porteous and his soldiers fire on the mob and kill several,	396, 397
	Captain Porteous is tried and convicted of murder,	396, 397
	He is respited,	396
(Sept. 7.)	A riotous mob attack the Tolbooth, and hang Captain Porteous,	397
1737. (July.)	The Prince of Wales and his family are dismissed from St James's Palace,	401
1739. (Oct. 19.)	War is proclaimed against Spain,	411
	The Jacobites assemble in Edinburgh to draw up a bond of association, &c.,	411
(Nov. 15.)	Parliament again meets; an act is passed giving all the prize-money taken to the seamen engaged in the capture,	411, 412
1740. (Feb. 21.)	An address is agreed to in the Commons to George II., that no treaty be entered into with Spain without having an acknowledgment of the right of English vessels to navigate the American seas without search,	412
	More than four millions of supplies are voted,	413
(Mar.)	Admiral Vernon captures Porto Bello,	413

A.D.		PAGE
(May.)	Anson is sent to the coasts of Chili and Peru,	414-416
(Dec.)	A Jacobite association is entered into at Edinburgh by some noblemen and gentlemen,	443
1741. (Feb.)	Sandys moves an address for the removal of Walpole; the motion is rejected,	416-421
	Lord Carteret makes a similar motion in the House of Lords, which is also rejected,	421
(Mar.)	Anson's store-ship, the *Wager*, is wrecked at Cape Horn,	446
(April 10.)	Battle of Molwitz,	423
(April 13.)	A subsidy of £300,000 is voted for the queen of Hungary,	422
(May.)	Carthagena is unsuccessfully attacked by the English,	426, 427
	Cuba is attacked with no better success,	428
(June.)	Anson arrives at Juan Fernandez,	446
(Dec.)	Walpole consents to the omission of a paragraph relating to the Spanish war in the address,	428
	He is defeated in the appointment of Chairman of Committee,	429
1742.	Drummond of Balhaldy arrives in Edinburgh, and meets 'the concert of gentlemen for managing the king's affairs in Scotland,' with news of aid from the French in the invasion of England,	443
	George II. offers the Prince of Wales an additional £50,000 a year to his income; he refuses so long as Walpole is in power,	429
(Jan. 21.)	Pulteney makes a motion against Walpole; it is lost on a division,	430
(Jan. 28.)	Walpole is defeated on the Chippenham election petition by a majority of one, and finally of sixteen,	430
(Feb. 1.)	He tenders his resignation to George II.,	430, 431
(Feb. 3.)	The Houses adjourn,	431
(Feb. 9.)	Walpole is created Earl of Orford,	431
(Feb. 11.)	He formally resigns all his places,	431
	Wilmington is made first lord of the Treasury,	432
(Mar. 9.)	Lord Limerick moves in the House of Commons for a secret committee to inquire into Walpole's administration; it is negatived,	434
(Mar. 23.)	He renews the motion, limited to ten years; it is carried,	434
	The secret committee bring up their report,	435
(July.)	Pulteney is created Earl of Bath,	433
	The war is carried on in Italy by the Spaniards,	436
	Battle off St Christopher's; the Spanish ships are beaten,	436
	The Spaniards attack the colony of Georgia, but are defeated by Oglethorpe,	437
(Nov.)	Anson reaches the Bay of Canton,	447
1743.	The Cardinal Fleury dies,	438
(Jan.)	Lord Bolingbroke returns to England,	439
	The act called the 'Gin Act,' passed in 1731, is repealed,	438
	Six millions of supplies are voted,	438
(April.)	Wilmington, first lord of the Treasury, dies; is succeeded by Pelham,	441
(June 20.)	Anson captures a Spanish galleon at Manilla,	447
(June 27.)	Battle of Dettingen; the Duke of Cumberland is wounded,	439, 440
(Dec. 23.)	The old Pretender signs a proclamation at Albano, to be published on his son's landing in England, and a commission	

CHRONOLOGICAL INDEX. 45

A.D.		PAGE
	appointing him his regent and *alter ego*,	444
1744. (Jan. 9.)	Prince Charles, the young Pretender, leaves Rome,	444
	The quadruple alliance between England, Holland, Austria, and Saxony,	450
(Feb. 18.)	George II. announces to the Houses the preparation for an invasion by the young Pretender,	442
	The Habeas Corpus Act is suspended for two months,	443
	The sons of the Pretender are attainted if they attempt to land; other precautions are taken,	443
	Supplies to the amount of ten millions are voted,	443
(June 15.)	Anson arrives at Spithead,	447
	Troops are raised and ships are equipped,	446
	War is declared between England and France,	446
(July 4.)	The treasure taken by Anson is carried in procession from Portsmouth to the Tower,	447
1745. (Mar. 18.)	Robert Walpole, Earl of Orford, dies,	450
(May 11.)	Battle of Fontenoy,	451, 452
	Tournay, Ghent, Bruges, Dendermond, and Oudenarde surrender to the French; Ostend is also captured,	452
(June 3.)	Battle of Hohen Friedberg,	453
(July 2.)	The young Pretender embarks at Nantes,	454
(July 15-25.)	Sails on board the *Doutelle*, in company with the *Elizabeth*; they are engaged by the *Lion*, an English ship; the young Pretender lands in Scotland with seven noblemen and gentlemen; 'The seven men of Moidart,'	454-456
(Aug. 6.)	The council of regency offer a reward for the apprehension of Charles Edward,	459
(Aug. 19.)	The young Pretender raises the royal standard, and publishes his father's proclamation,	458
(Sept. 4.)	Charles Edward enters Perth,	461
(Sept. 12.)	He crosses the ford of Frew,	463
(Sept. 16.)	He enters Edinburgh; his father is proclaimed,	466
(Sept. 19.)	Cope marches from Dunbar,	467
	Battle of Prestonpans; the royal army is routed,	469, 470
	Colonel Gardiner is killed,	471
	Dutch, Danish, and English troops, under the Duke of Cumberland, arrive from Flanders,	477, 478
(Oct.)	Several Highland gentlemen join the young Pretender at Edinburgh,	479
(Oct. 9, 10.)	He issues various proclamations,	481
(Oct. 18.)	Parliament assembles; the Habeas Corpus Act is suspended; new soldiers are put upon the footing of the old army; many regiments are ordered to be raised,	476, 477
(Nov. 1.)	Charles Edward appoints Lord Strathallan to command in Scotland, and marches south,	482
(Nov. 8.)	Crosses the Esk, and occupies Reddings in Cumberland,	483
(Nov. 10.)	Summons the city of Carlisle; lays siege to it,	483
(Nov. 15.)	The town and castle surrender,	483
(Nov. 17.)	Charles Edward enters Carlisle,	484
(Nov. 22.)	He arrives at Penrith,	485
(Nov. 27.)	The rebel army reaches Preston,	485
(Nov. 28.)	It reaches Wigan; part enters Manchester,	485
	The royal army lies at Newcastle under Wade, and at Lichfield under the Duke of Cumberland,	486

A.D.		PAGE
(Dec. 1.)	The rebel army crosses the Mersey near Stockport,	486
	Enters Macclesfield; Captain Weir is taken,	487
(Dec. 4.)	Charles Edward enters Derby,	487
	The old Pretender is proclaimed,	488
(Dec. 5.)	A council of war is held,	488
(Dec. 6.)	The rebel army commences its retreat,	488
	The royal army advances after it,	488
	The young Pretender precipitately retreats,	489
(Dec. 10.)	Leaves Manchester,	489
(Dec. 13.)	Arrives at Lancaster,	489
	Lord John Drummond, with the advanced guard, is set upon by the people between Penrith and Kendal,	489
(Dec. 16.)	The rebel army lies at Shapp,	489
(Dec. 17.)	The Duke of Cumberland and General Oglethorpe advance to Kendal,	490
(Dec. 19.)	The rebels re-enter Carlisle,	491
(Dec. 20.)	Cross the Esk and re-enter Scotland,	491
1746. (Jan. 17.)	Battle of Falkirk,	494-498
(Jan. 30.)	The Duke of Cumberland arrives at Edinburgh,	499
(Feb.)	The Pelham administration is displaced and restored,	502, 503
(Feb. 26.)	The Duke of Cumberland arrives at Aberdeen,	503
(Mar. 25.)	A ship with money for the Pretender is driven on shore by an English ship on the coast of Sutherland and taken,	505
(April 17.)	Battle of Culloden,	509-511
(May.)	Flora Macdonald secures the young Pretender's flight as far as Mugstote,	516
	Flora Macdonald is captured and sent to London,	517
	Escapes of the young Pretender,	515-520
	The Earl of Derwentwater is beheaded,	520
(Aug. 18.)	Balmerino and Kilmarnock are beheaded,	522
(Sept. 20.)	The Pretender embarks at Lochnanuagh,	520
(Sept. 29.)	Reaches Morlaix in Brittany,	520
1747. (April 9.)	Lord Lovat is beheaded,	525
	Flora Macdonald is released,	525
	The House of Lords bring the printers of the *Gentleman's* and *London Magazines* to their bar for breach of privilege, in printing the proceedings of Lord Lovat's trial,	526
(July.)	Bergen-op-Zoom is taken by the French, Marshal Belleisle's brother is defeated and killed at Exilles,	527
	Admiral Anson defeats the French fleet off Cape Finisterre; Admiral Hawke off Belleisle captures six ships, and Commodore Fox takes forty French ships richly laden from the West Indies,	527
	The younger son of the old Pretender is made a cardinal,	532
	A congress is proposed and agreed upon at Aix-la-Chapelle,	528
(Nov. 10.)	A new parliament assembles; the Commons vote thirteen millions of supplies; Lord Chesterfield recommends schools and villages to civilise the Highlands,	528
(Dec. 10.)	Duncan Forbes dies,	515
(Dec. 11.)	The young Pretender is forcibly expelled from France,	532
1748. (Mar. 11.)	The congress of Aix-la-Chapelle commences,	528
(Oct.)	The treaty of Aix-la-Chapelle is concluded,	530
1749.	A clause is introduced into the Mutiny Bill for subjecting officers on half-pay to martial law, and for enforcing an oath of secrecy upon all members of courts-martial,	532

A.D.		PAGE
1750. (April.)	A British colony is established in Nova Scotia,	533
	A settlement is commenced by the English and Scotch on the Mosquito coast in the Gulf of Mexico,	533
1751. (Mar. 20.)	The Prince of Wales dies,	537
	Prince George is created Prince of Wales,	539
(May 8.)	The Regency Bill passes both Houses,	539
(Dec. 15.)	Bolingbroke dies of cancer of the heart,	540
	In the course of this year the Gregorian calendar is adopted,	541
1752. (Jan. 7.)	Parliament meets; the treaty with Saxony, made by George II., is debated in both Houses,	541-543
(Jan. 28.)	A bill passes both Houses annexing to the crown the estates forfeited in Scotland by the late rebellion, and making provision out of the rents for establishing colonies and trade, and industry, in the Highlands,	543
(Mar.)	A bill is passed consolidating the several classes of annuities into five stocks,	544
(Nov.)	Disputes occur in the establishment of the Princess-dowager of Wales,	544-546
1753.	A bill for naturalising foreign Jews passes,	548, 549
	Parliament votes £20,000 to Mr Harrison for his improvement in chronometers; an act is passed for the purchase of the Harleian manuscripts and Montague House,	551
(Nov. 15.)	Parliament reassembles; the Duke of Newcastle moves to repeal the Jews Naturalisation Bill; a similar motion is made in the Commons; the bill is repealed,	551, 552
1754. (Mar. 6.)	Mr Pelham dies suddenly; the Duke of Newcastle is appointed first lord of the Treasury,	552
(May.)	The French make encroachments in Canada; the Indians attack and compel Major Washington to capitulate at a fort on the Ohio,	553
1755. (Mar.)	A million is voted for the defence of our American possessions; Admiral Boscawen is sent with a fleet to the Gulf of St Lawrence,	553
	Captain Howe and Captain Andrews take two French ships of the line,	554
(July.)	Sir Edward Hawke starts with a fleet on a cruise,	554
(Oct.)	Admiral Byng sails with a large fleet,	554
	Many important operations take place in Canada, and other parts of North America,	554
(Nov. 20.)	Mr Fox is made secretary of state,	556
1756.	Large votes pass for the army, navy, and supplies; 8000 Hanoverian and Hessian troops are allowed to be brought into England,	557
(May 18.)	Admiral Byng approaches Minorca,	558
(May 19.)	An action is fought with the French, in which Admiral West is engaged, but Byng is not,	558, 559
	The French fleet supplies the army besieging Minorca, and returns to Toulon,	559
	Admiral Byng returns to Gibraltar without attempting the relief of Fort St Philip,	559
(July.)	General Blakeney surrenders the fort,	559
	Admiral Hawke supersedes Byng, who is placed under arrest, and sent to Portsmouth,	559
	He is put in custody at Greenwich Hospital,	559

A.D.		PAGE
	Calcutta is taken by Sujah-u-Dowlah; the black-hole,	571
(Oct.)	Mr Fox resigns,	559
	Pitt is made secretary of state,	560
1757.	Lord Clive retakes Calcutta, and gains great victories in the East Indies,	571
	Admiral Byng is removed to Portsmouth and tried by a court-martial, and condemned to be shot,	562
Mar. 14.)	He is shot,	565
	Sir Edward Hawke is sent with a fleet to attempt the capture of Rochefort,	569
(Sept. 7.)	The Duke of Cumberland is defeated; the Convention of Closter-Seven,	569
(Sept. 23.)	Captain Howe takes the Isle of Aix,	569
(Oct. 3.)	The whole expedition returns,	560
	The Duke of Cumberland returns to England; resigns his commands,	571, 572
(Dec. 1.)	Parliament meets; a subsidy is voted for the king of Prussia,	572, 573
(Dec. 5.)	Battle of Lissa,	570
1758. (June 1.)	A large fleet sails for the French coast,	573
(Aug. 8.)	The English take Cherbourg,	574
(Sept.)	The French destroy a part of General Bligh's army at St Cas,	574
	Various military and naval operations in America, India, and the West Indies,	575
(Nov. 23.)	Parliament reassembles; twelve millions of supplies are voted,	576
1759.	Several engagements take place between the English and French fleets,	578
(July 31.)	Battle of Minden,	582
(Aug. 18.)	Admiral Boscawen gains a victory over the French fleet off Cape Lagos,	578
(Sept. 12.)	Battle on the heights of Abraham; Wolfe is killed,	581
(Sept. 17.)	Surrender of Quebec,	581
(Nov. 20.)	Sir Edward Hawke gains a victory over the French fleet in Quiberon Bay,	578
	Colonel Coote conquers Arcot,	581, 582
1760. (Feb.)	Thurot takes Carrickfergus, which he plunders; he puts to sea; is attacked and killed, and his three ships taken,	579
(April.)	The French, under M. Levi, lay siege to Quebec,	586
(May 9.)	Lord Colville raises the siege,	586
(Sept. 8.)	Vaudreuil capitulates, and the Canadas are won,	586
	The English, under Prince Ferdinand, defeat the French at Warburg,	587
(Oct. 25.)	King George II. dies suddenly,	587, 583
(Oct. 25.)	Accession of George III.,	795
(Oct. 31.)	A proclamation is made for the encouragement of piety and virtue, and for preventing and punishing vice, profaneness, and immorality,	795
	The name of the Duke of Cumberland is struck out of the Liturgy by order of George III. in council,	796
(Nov. 18.)	George III. meets parliament; he asks its cheerful and powerful assistance to prosecute the war for the Protestant interest,	796
1761.	The civil list is fixed at the clear annual sum of £800,000,	797
	Nineteen millions are voted for prosecuting the war,	797, 798
	£200,000 are voted to our colonies in America as compensation,	798
(April.)	An expedition under Keppel, with troops under General Hodgson, take Belleisle,	802
	Pondicherry surrenders at discretion early in the year to Colonel Coote,	802
	Dominica is reduced by Lord Rollo and Sir James Douglas,	802

CHRONOLOGICAL INDEX. 47

A.D.	PAGE
(July 15, 16.) The French, under Broglie and the Prince of Soubise, are defeated at Hohenewer by the combined army of English and Hanoverians under Prince Ferdinand,	800
Prince Albert Henry of Brunswick is killed,	801
The war continues in Germany with various success,	800–802
Negotiations are entered into with France,	802–804
The Family Compact is signed at Versailles,	804
(Sept. 22.) Prince Charles Edward is present in disguise at crowning of George III.,	806
(Oct. 6.) Mr Pitt resigns the seals of secretary of state,	804
A pension of £3000 a year is settled on Mr Pitt for three lives, and a peerage is conferred on his wife, Lady Hester, and her issue,	805
(Dec. 25.) Lord Bristol, ambassador at Madrid, returns,	806
The Spanish government order all English ships in their ports to be detained,	806
1762. (Feb.) Martinique is reduced by General Monckton and Admiral Rodney; Grenada, the Grenadines, St Lucia, St Vincent, and Tobago also surrender,	810
France and Spain commence war on Portugal,	811
The House of Commons vote £1,000,000, to enable George III. to assist the Portuguese,	811
Eight thousand British troops, commanded by Lord Tyrawley, the Earl of Loudon, General Townsend, Lord George Lennox, and Brigadiers Crawford and Burgoyne, land in Portugal,	811
Lord Tyrawley retires in disgust,	811
Burgoyne carries Valencia d'Alcantara by a coup-de-main,	811
Colonel Lee surprises the Spaniards, and routs them with terrible slaughter,	812
The Spaniards retreat from Portugal,	812
The Hermione, a Spanish register-ship, is captured off Cape St Vincent by two English frigates,	812
(Mar. 5.) An expedition against the Havanna sails from Portsmouth under General Lord Albemarle and Admiral Pococke,	809
(April.) Lord Bute becomes prime minister,	813
(May 5.) Alliance between Prussia and Russia; 20,000 Russians are put at the disposition of Frederick,	813
(June 4.) The expedition against the Havanna arrives there,	809
(July.) The allied armies, under Prince Ferdinand and the Marquis of Granby, reduce Cassel and expel the French from Hesse,	815
(Aug. 13.) The city of Havanna capitulates,	809
(Sept.) Negotiations for peace are opened between England and France,	815
(Oct. 6.) Manilla is carried by storm by Colonel William Draper,	809
(Nov. 3.) Preliminaries of peace are signed at Fontainebleau,	815
Canada and all its dependencies are ceded to Britain; also Tobago, Dominique, St Vincent, and the Grenadas, &c.,	815, 816
Spain cedes the Floridas and all the countries east and south-east of the Mississippi to Great Britain,	816
(Nov. 25.) Parliament assembles; the preliminaries of peace are laid before it; and after a	

A.D.	PAGE
stormy opposition, the definitive treaty is signed, and commercial communications are opened with France,	816
1763. (Feb. 15.) Treaty of Hubertsburg; termination of the Seven Years' War,	817
(April 8.) Bute resigns, also Sir Francis Dashwood, chancellor of the Exchequer, and Fox, paymaster of the forces,	818
Dashwood and Fox are created peers—the former as Baron le Despencer, the latter as Baron Holland,	818, 819
Mr George Grenville is made premier and chancellor of the Exchequer,	819
(May 1.) Mr Wilkes is arrested, brought before Lord Halifax, and sent to the Tower,	820
(May 3.) He is removed by writ of habeas corpus, and brought before the court at Westminster Hall,	820
(May 6.) Mr Wilkes is discharged,	820
(Dec.) Parliament votes £80,000 as a portion for the Princess Augusta, George III.'s eldest sister, about to be married to the Duke of Brunswick,	824
Wilkes brings actions against the two secretaries of state, Lords Egremont and Halifax, and Robert Wood, Esq., late under-secretary; a verdict is given against Wood, with £1000 damages to Wilkes,	824
General warrants are declared unconstitutional, illegal, and absolutely void; the Court of King's Bench afterwards affirms this,	824, 825
In the summer and autumn of this year the North American Indians fall on Pennsylvania, Maryland, and Virginia, plundering, burning, and destroying; they surprise several British forts in Canada, and massacre the garrisons; Sir William Johnston detaches the Indians of the Six Nations from the confederacy, and induces them to join the British against the other Indians; the savages at last submit to conditions,	827, 828
1764. (Jan. 19.) Parliament meets; the Wilkes war continues, and little else occupies its attention,	825
Benjamin Franklin comes to London with instructions to oppose the Stamp Act, and every other act that might be proposed in parliament to tax the people of America,	823
1765. Parliament meets; George III. in his speech recommends the carrying out of Grenville's scheme, and enforcing obedience in the colonies,	829
Fifty-five resolutions are agreed to by the Commons, and incorporated into an act, laying nearly the same stamp duties on the American colonies as are payable at this time in England,	830
(Mar. 22.) The Stamp Act receives the royal assent,	830
Wilkes is outlawed,	830
Illness of George III.,	830, 831
The Regency Bill is passed,	831, 832
(May 15.) It receives the royal assent,	832
(May 15.) A serious riot by the Spitalfield silk-weavers; the Guards, horse and foot, are called out and quell it,	832
(July 15.) The Marquis of Rockingham is made premier,	833
Chief-justice Pratt is created Lord Camden,	834
(Oct.) The Duke of Cumberland dies,	834
Great dissatisfaction in America respecting	

A. D.		PAGE
	the Stamp Act; riots occur in various places,	834
	Nine out of thirteen of the colonies send delegates to meet at New York, where various resolutions are adopted,	834
(Dec. 17.)	Parliament meets and is prorogued,	834
1766. (Jan. 14.)	Parliament meets; it debates on American affairs,	834–837
	The Stamp Act is repealed in the Commons,	838
(Mar.)	It passes the Lords, and receives the royal assent,	839
(April 25.)	The Commons resolves that general warrants are illegal, and if executed on any member of this House, a breach of privilege,	839
(April 29.)	The Commons pass a bill to restrain the issuing of warrants for seizing any one's papers except under certain regulations; the Lords throw it out,	839
	An act passes restraining the importation of foreign silks,	839
(June.)	Parliament is prorogued,	839
(July 10 or 12.)	Mr Pitt receives George III.'s personal commands to form a new administration,	839
(July 29.)	Mr Pitt is created Earl of Chatham,	840
(Aug. 2.)	The members of the new cabinet are announced in the *Gazette*,	841
	Dreadful animosities are excited between the Americans and the English soldiery,	842
	The Earl of Northumberland is created a duke,	843
(Nov. 11.)	Parliament meets,	843
	An embargo is laid upon wheat and wheat-flour going out of the kingdom, by George III. in council; parliament debates thereon,	843, 844
	Changes take place in the cabinet,	845
1767.	The land-tax is reduced to three shillings in the pound,	847
	A committee of inquiry is appointed by the Commons for examining into the state of the East India Company,	847
	The charter of the East India Company is renewed; their territorial rights fully admitted; and nearly all their demands granted, binding the company to pay £400,000 per annum to government in half-yearly payments,	848
(May.)	A bill is brought in for regulating the qualification of voters in trading companies,	849
	A bill is passed for restraining and limiting the making of dividends by the East India Company,	849
	Petitions, remonstrances, and bitter complaints from the American colonies against a new Mutiny Act,	849
	During this session annuities of £8000 each are settled on George III.'s brothers, the Dukes of York, Gloucester, and Cumberland,	850
	A trifling addition is made to the half-pay of lieutenants in the navy,	850
(Nov.)	An act is passed to extend the prohibition against exportation, and to encourage the importation of grain,	852
	Lord North becomes chancellor of the Exchequer,	852
	Other changes take place in the ministry; the Duke of Grafton's administration,	852, 853
1768.	An act is passed restricting the East India Company's dividends to 10 per cent.,	853
(Feb. 15.)	The Assembly of Massachusetts address	

A. D.		PAGE
	a circular-letter to all the other colonies, inviting them to combine in taking measures to defeat the obnoxious Stamp Act,	867
(Mar. 4.)	Wilkes sends a supplicating letter to George III.; no notice is taken of it,	853
	Wilkes is returned for the county of Middlesex by a large majority,	853, 854
(April 20.)	Wilkes declares himself ready to submit to the laws of his country, but is allowed to depart at perfect liberty,	854
(April—May.)	Riots take place on account of Wilkes,	854, 855
	The officers and men employed during the late riots are thanked in George III.'s name by Lord Barrington, the secretary at war,	855
	Riots and disturbances take place among the coal-heavers, sailors, and watermen,	855
(June 6.)	Wilkes is tried in the Court of King's Bench; the outlawry is reversed, and he is sentenced to pay a fine of £500, and be imprisoned ten calendar months,	855
	Serious riots take place at Boston,	868
(Aug.)	The merchants and traders of Boston agree not to import or send for certain goods from Great Britain from the 1st of January 1769 to the 1st of January 1770, until the act imposing the duties shall be absolutely repealed,	868
	The merchants of Connecticut and New York make similar agreements,	869
(Sept.)	The merchants of Salem do the same,	869
(Sept. 12.)	The Bostonians resolve to protect their chartered privileges, &c.,	868
	The ships of war come to an anchor off Boston, with guns shotted, and their broadsides covering the town,	869
(Oct. 1.)	Colonel Dalrymple lands the 27th and 14th regiments, with a train of artillery,	860
	Lord Chatham resigns office,	856
(Nov. 8.)	Parliament meets; the speech from the throne denounces the 'rebellious spirit' which prevailed in Massachusetts Bay,	858, 859
(Nov. 14.)	The Wilkes war recommences,	859
	A petition is presented claiming redress and liberty, as a member of parliament, for Mr Wilkes; it is agreed that he shall have liberty to attend the House to support the allegations of his petition, and be allowed the assistance of counsel,	859
(Nov. 23.)	An inquiry is moved for into the melancholy occurrences in St George's Fields; it is negatived,	859
1769. (Jan.)	A petition from the people of Boston, America, is contemptuously rejected in the Commons, and measures of rigour are urged by majorities in both Houses,	863
(Jan. 23.)	It is moved that Mr Wilkes is entitled to the privilege of parliament, to be discharged from imprisonment,	859, 860
(Jan. 31.)	Wilkes appears as a prisoner at the bar of the House of Commons,	860
(Feb. 3.)	He is expelled the House,	860
(Feb. 16.)	Wilkes is re-elected for Middlesex,	861
(Feb. 17.)	The House vote him incapable of sitting in this present parliament,	861
(Mar. 14.)	A petition or remonstrance from the people of New York, denying the right of parliament to tax them in any way, is refused to be received,	866
(Mar. 16.)	Wilkes is again returned for Middlesex,	862
(Mar. 17.)	The House declare the return null and void,	862
(April 13.)	Wilkes is re-elected for Middlesex,	862
(April 15.)	Luttrell is declared by the House member for Middlesex,	862

CHRONOLOGICAL INDEX.

A.D.		PAGE
	Parliament votes £513,511 to George III. to discharge his debts,	866
	The East India Company's charter is prolonged for five years, and they are allowed to increase their dividend to 12½ per cent.,	866
(May 9.)	George III. prorogues parliament, and is grossly insulted by the mob,	866
	The Virginian House of Burgesses vote a series of strong resolutions, and an address to George III.,	869
	The House of Representatives at Boston remonstrate with the governor, and request the removal of ships and troops; the governor denies having authority over the ships and troops,	870
	Subscriptions are made to pay Wilkes's fines, and to provide for his subsistence at the expiry of his imprisonment,	871
	The Irish parliament passes a bill for increasing the military establishment of that country,	873
1770. (Mar. 5.)	A serious riot takes place in Boston;	

A.D.		PAGE
	the soldiers fire on the mob, three are killed and five dangerously wounded,	893, 894
(Mar. 14.)	Lord Mayor Beckford, with 220 common councilmen, liverymen, and city officers present an address, remonstrance, and petition to George III. at St James's, praying that he will instantly dissolve parliament, and remove for ever all evil ministers and advisers,	884, 885
(Mar. 31.)	The Middlesex remonstrance is presented to George III.,	886
(April.)	Leave is given to bring in a bill repealing all the American taxes except the duty on tea,	888, 889
(May 23.)	Beckford the lord mayor, and the aldermen, present an address to George III., complaining of his majesty's answer to their former one,	890, 891
(June 21.)	Beckford dies,	891
(Oct.)	The Boston and Philadelphia merchants agree to import everything but tea,	894, 895
(Nov. 13.)	Parliament meets; Mr Grenville dies,	897

VOLUME V.

BOOK X.

A.D.		PAGE
1770. (Nov.)	The Commons are turned out of the House of Lords,	2
1771. (Mar.)	Whitham, a messenger of the House of Commons, takes Millar, a printer, into custody, but is himself carried before the lord mayor (Crosby) and Aldermen Wilkes and Oliver, who commit him to the Compter, but accept of bail,	8
(Mar. 18.)	The lord mayor is ordered to attend in his place in the House,	8
(Mar. 19.)	The lord mayor goes down to the House attended by an immense mob,	8
	The House of Commons command Wilkes's attendance at the bar; he refuses to attend unless in his seat as member for Middlesex,	9
(Mar. 25.)	The House of Commons resolve, 'That to release a person taken by virtue of the speaker's warrant, to apprehend a messenger of the House for executing his warrant, and to hold the messenger to bail for such pretended assault, are all breaches of privilege,'	10
(Mar. 26.)	Alderman Oliver is committed to the Tower,	10
(Mar. 27.)	Lord Mayor Crosby is committed to the Tower; the mob drag him in triumph to the Mansion House,	10, 11
(Mar. 28.)	The common council of the city unanimously pass a vote of thanks to such members of the House of Commons as had supported the lord mayor and his colleagues, and maintained the rights and privileges of the city,	11
(May.)	Lord Mayor Crosby and Alderman Oliver are released from the Tower,	11
(June.)	Wilkes and Bull are elected sheriffs,	15
1772. (Jan.)	A revolution takes place at Stockholm, organised by Gustavus III.,	26, 27
(Jan. 29.)	An increase of the navy is agreed to,	17

A.D.		PAGE
(Feb. 5.)	The land-tax for the year is fixed at three shillings in the pound,	17
(June 24.)	Wilkes, Crosby, and Oliver receive silver cups, in commemoration of their courageous and successful efforts in behalf of the printers and the freedom of the press,	23
(Aug. 2.)	The Treaty of the Partition of Poland is signed at St Petersburg,	40
	Some people of Rhode Island insult the British flag, board, capture, and burn the British man-of-war, the *Gaspee* schooner,	49, 50
(Nov.)	A bill is introduced to prevent the East India Company from sending out certain supervisors to settle matters in India,	43
1773.	The bill is carried in both Houses,	44
(Feb.)	A bill for the relief of Protestant Dissenters passes the Commons, but is rejected by the Lords,	46, 47
(Mar. 9.)	A loan of £1,400,000 is granted to the East India Company,	44
	The Company are allowed to export tea to America without paying export duty,	44
	A series of protests, commenced at Boston, runs through all the colonies upon Lord North's attempt to take the payment of the colonial judges out of the hands of the Houses of Assembly,	48
	The House of Assembly at Boston draw up a petition and remonstrance to George III., charging the governor, Mr Hutchinson, with betraying his trust and slandering the people under his government, &c., and praying for his instant removal, together with that of Mr Oliver, the lieutenant-governor,	49
(Nov. 30.)	The Bostonians refuse to allow tea to be	

A.D.		PAGE
	landed or put into store, and a strong guard, completely armed, which is regularly relieved night and day, is set to prevent it,	50
(Dec. 16.)	A Boston mob board the tea-ships, hoist out the chests, and discharge their contents into the sea, destroying many thousand pounds' worth of property,	51
1774. (Jan. 29.)	Benjamin Franklin, with Mr Dunning as counsel, appears before the privy council to speak to the Bostonian petition for the removal of the governor and lieutenant-governor,	52
	The petition is dismissed as 'groundless, scandalous, and voxatious,'	54
(Feb. 1.)	Franklin is dismissed from his place of postmaster-general of America,	54
	Four of the judges acquaint the House of Assembly that they had received their salary as granted by the Colonial Assembly; that they had not taken any part of the grant offered by the crown, and were determined to persevere in that line of conduct,	75
(Mar.)	The Assembly resolve to continue Franklin their agent in England; Governor Hutchinson refuses to ratify his appointment, or sanction their act for paying his salary,	76
(Mar. 31.)	The Boston Port Bill receives the royal assent,	54
(May 13.)	General Gage, the new governor, lands at Boston,	76
(May 14.)	A meeting takes place at Boston, which resolves to stop all importation from and export to Great Britain, and every part of the West Indies, till the Port Bill be repealed,	76
(May 24.)	The Virginia Assembly pass a resolution appointing a day of fasting, humiliation, prayer, &c., to turn the hearts of king and parliament to moderation and justice,	77
(June.)	The men of Salem enter into an association, and call it 'the solemn league and covenant,'	79
	General Gage fortifies Boston Neck, and removes to head-quarters the gunpowder and military stores from Charlestown, Cambridge, and other places,	80
	The people rise in arms and threaten to attack the troops,	80
(Oct.)	The Assembly of Massachusetts adjourn to Cambridge; appoint a Committee of Safety to take measures for the defence of the province; collectors of public money are appointed, powder-mills erected, and manufactories of arms established,	84
	The Committee of Safety call out the militia,	84
	Emissaries sent to Rhode Island, New Hampshire, and Connecticut, to request them to prepare their respective quotas, so as to make up an army of 20,000 men,	85
(Nov.)	The navy is reduced by 4000 seamen,	88
(Dec.)	The people of Rhode Island seize upon forty pieces of cannon belonging to the crown, and carry them off into the country,	85
	In New Hampshire a number of armed men seize Fort William, and carry off the ordnance, gunpowder, and military stores,	85
	Nearly everywhere orders are passed for	

A.D.		PAGE
	buying arms and ammunition at the public expense or by subscription, and for training the militia; mills are erected for making gunpowder, and manufactories for making arms, &c.,	85
1775. (Jan. 20.)	Lord Chatham moves an address to George III. in the House of Lords, for the removal of the troops from Boston, and for doing justice to the Americans; it is lost,	90-93
(Jan. 27, 29.)	Meetings take place between Lord Chatham and Franklin upon American affairs,	93
(Feb. 2.)	The Commons vote an address of thanks to George III. for communicating the papers upon American affairs,	97
	Lord North, in introducing the motion, intimates that a large military force is to be sent to America,	97
(Feb. 7.)	A conference is held between the two Houses on the address to the king, and, after a stormy debate in the Lords, it is agreed to,	97, 98
(Feb. 20.)	Lord North introduces his famous conciliatory motion; it is adopted by a large majority,	100, 101
(Mar. 21.)	The bill for cutting off the trade of New England passes the Lords,	99
(Mar. 22.)	Mr Burke produces his plan for America, comprised in thirteen resolutions; it is rejected,	102-104
(Mar. 30.)	The bill for cutting off the trade of New England, &c., receives the royal assent,	100
(April 18, 19.)	General Gage detaches the light infantry and grenadiers of his army, under Lieutenant-colonel Smith and Major Pitcairn, to Concord, to destroy a depôt of military stores,	106
	They are attacked by the Americans at Lexington; the Americans receive a check, and the troops proceed to Concord,	107
	The troops destroy the military stores, but on their return are set upon by the Americans, who drive them before them to Lexington, where they are saved by Lord Percy with a detachment of foot, marines, and two pieces of artillery, and retreat to Boston,	107, 108
	Twenty thousand Americans under Ward, Pribble, Heath, Prescot, and Thomas blockade Boston; they fix their head-quarters at Cambridge,	108
	They are joined by a strong detachment of troops from Connecticut under General Putnam,	108
(May 5.)	Obedience refused to General Gage,	109
	They strengthen their lines with sixteen field-pieces, four small brass guns, a few large iron guns taken out of merchant-vessels, and two or three mortars and howitzers,	109
	Fort Ticonderoga is taken by Ethan Allen and a small body of volunteers; he obtains possession of upwards of a hundred iron cannon, fifty swivels, two mortars, ten tons of musket-balls, and various other materials of war,	112, 113
	He reduces the Fort of Crown Point; surprises Skenesborough, and takes all there prisoners,	113
	Benedict Arnold captures a small British sloop-of-war at St John's, on Lake Champlain,	113
	Generals Howe, Burgoyne, and Clinton arrive at Boston, and are followed by	

CHRONOLOGICAL INDEX.

A.D.		PAGE
1775.	several regiments from Ireland, raising the force to nearly 10,000 men,	109
	Several skirmishes take place, in which the English are defeated,	110
(June 8.)	The Provincial Congress of Massachusetts resolve that the compact between the crown of Great Britain and that colony is dissolved by the violation of its charter,	110
	They recommend the people to proceed to the establishment of a new government,	110
	They proceed to assume in other matters all the powers of an independent and supreme government,	110
(June 16.)	The blockading army of Americans fortify Bunker's Hill,	110
(June 17.)	The *Lively* ship of war cannonades them,	110
	General Gage opens a battery upon them from Copp's Hill, in Boston,	111
	2000 troops are carried across the river to oppose the Americans,	111
	Battle of Bunker's Hill,	111, 112
(July.)	The Continental Congress despatch 3000 men under Generals Schuyler and Montgomery to Crown Point and Lake Champlain; they are attacked by a strong party of Indians, and forced to retreat to the Isle Aux Noix,	114
	The congress at Philadelphia form a plan of confederation and perpetual union, called the United Colonies of North America, and agree to thirteen articles,	120–122
	Colonel George Washington is chosen commander-in-chief,	122
	Washington arrives at head-quarters at Cambridge; forms a staff of officers, collects engineers, and establishes discipline and military subordination,	127, 128
	He contracts his line, and completely blockades the British troops by land,	128
	Wilkes presents a violent address and remonstrance to George III., for the dismissal of ministers and on American affairs, from the livery of London,	129
	Tryon, the governor of New York, notifies that orders had been given to the commanders of the king's ships, that if troops should be raised, fortifications erected, or the king's stores taken, they must consider the place in a state of rebellion, and act accordingly,	123
	A body of New Yorkers, in attempting to remove and carry off the cannon at the battery, are fired on by the *Asia* man-of-war, and three men are wounded,	123
	They seize and destroy two of the *Asia's* boats,	123
(Sept.)	General Montgomery is joined by 700 Indians of the Five Nations, whose services had been refused by General Carleton, governor of Canada,	114
	Ethan Allen, in attempting to take Montreal, is taken prisoner by Major Campbell of the 20th Regiment,	114, 115
(Oct.)	General Gage is recalled,	128
	The town of Falmouth, in Massachusetts, is bombarded by Captain Mowat in the *Canceaux*, and reduced to ruins,	128
	The American privateers scour the Mexican Gulf, seize the transports from the West Indies with provisions, and the store-ships with arms, ammunition, and other materials of war,	128
	Some of them sail to the coast of Africa,	

A.D.		PAGE
1775.	and buy or seize gunpowder from the British forts, before they are informed of the events on the American continent,	129
	They land on the island of Bermuda, surprise the magazines, and carry off all the powder,	129
	Congress assume the style of 'The Thirteen United Colonies,'	129
	They establish a post-office, and elect Benjamin Franklin postmaster-general,	129
(Nov. 1.)	A resolution is passed in both Houses, 'That bringing into any part of the dominions of Great Britain the electoral troops of his majesty, or any other foreign troops, without the previous consent of parliament, is dangerous and unconstitutional,'	136
(Nov. 3.)	Fort Chamblée, after a shameful defence, surrenders to a detachment sent by General Montgomery,	115
	General Montgomery besieges Fort St John, which surrenders unconditionally, with upwards of 500 regulars and 100 Canadian volunteers,	115
(Nov. 13.)	The land-tax is raised to four shillings in the pound,	142
	Montgomery enters Montreal without opposition,	115
	Arnold arrives at Point Levi, opposite Quebec,	116
(Nov. 14.)	He summons Quebec, but his flags are fired on, and he retires to Point Aux Trembles, and is there joined by General Montgomery,	116, 117
(Nov. 16.)	Mr Burke makes his famous motion for leave to bring in a bill 'for composing the present troubles and quieting the minds of his majesty's subjects in America;' it is rejected,	142
(Nov. 20.)	A bill is brought in for absolutely prohibiting all commercial intercourse with America, 'and for repealing, 'as useless 'and inapplicable, the Boston Port Bill, and restraining acts passed last session; it passes the Commons,	142, 143
	Lord Dunmore proclaims freedom to the slaves in Virginia who shall repair to his standard, and bear arms for George III.,	119
(Dec.)	Captain Fordyce attacks the Americans, but is defeated and killed,	120
(Dec. 20.)	The Americans open a battery within 700 yards of Quebec, but without effect; they retire,	117
(Dec. 21.)	The bill for prohibiting commercial intercourse with America, &c., passes the Lords,	143
(Dec. 31.)	General Montgomery, his aid-de-camp, and others, are killed on their advance upon Quebec,	118
	Arnold is wounded, and retires; Morgan and 340 Americans surrender,	118
	The Americans carry their approaches within half a mile of the British works on Bunker's Hill,	154
1776. (Jan.)	Lord Harcourt, the lord-lieutenant, proposes to the Irish House of Commons to send 4000 men out of the kingdom, and to receive 4000 Protestant foreign troops, without expense to Ireland; they assent to the first part of the proposition, but absolutely refuse the second,	144
(Feb.)	Colonel Macleod, in attempting to reach	

A.D.		PAGE
1776.	Wilmington, is decoyed into a swamp, foiled, and beaten; Macleod and the Highlanders are made prisoners,	157
(Mar. 2-4.)	The Americans bombard and cannonade Boston and the British lines,	155
(Mar. 4.)	General Thomas, with 2000 men, takes possession of the heights of Dorchester without opposition,	155
(Mar. 4.)	The report of the committee on the German treaties is received by the House of Commons,	145
(Mar. 4.)	The Duke of Richmond in the Lords moves an address to countermand the march of foreign troops, and to suspend hostilities altogether; it is negatived,	145, 146
(Mar. 5.)	General Thomas opens a cannonade on the town of Boston, and the ships of war; they are obliged to shift their anchorage; he digs trenches, and raises other works,	155
(Mar. 10, 11.)	Howe evacuates Boston,	155
(Mar. 11.)	The Commons vote £845,165 for the extraordinary army expenses of last year,	146
(Mar. 17.)	Howe's squadron weighs anchor and sails away,	155
	Washington sends his army by divisions into the provinces of New York,	156
(April 1.)	Arnold issues a proclamation making the paper-money of congress current in Canada,	152
(April 14.)	The whole American army is collected in the neighbourhood of New York,	156
	The congress pass a vote of thanks to Washington and his army for their wise and spirited conduct in the siege and acquisition of Boston, and direct a gold medal to be struck in commemoration,	156
(April 15, 19.)	The Duchess of Kingston is found guilty of bigamy,	148-150
(May 3.)	Lord Cornwallis arrives on the coast of North Carolina,	157
	General Clinton arrives at Cape Fear, and takes the chief command,	157
(May 5.)	General Thomas resolves to retreat from Quebec,	151
(May 6.)	Three English ships of war force their way through the ice to Quebec, and land two companies of the 29th Regiment, about 100 marines, and a few sailors,	151
	The Americans begin to fly without waiting to receive a shot,	151
	General Carleton sallies out, takes all their artillery and stores, nearly all their sick, and about 100 loiterers,	151
	General Thomas dies,	152
	Wilkes moves for leave to bring in a bill for reforming parliament; it is negatived without a division,	147
(May 15.)	The convention of Virginia instruct their delegates at congress to propose to that body an immediate declaration of independence,	160
	Carleton, being reinforced by more troops from England, repairs to Three Rivers, midway between Quebec and Montreal,	152
	The Americans are reinforced, and General Sullivan takes the command,	152
	General Sullivan sends General Thompson and Colonel St Clair to make a night-attack on the English position,	152, 153
	Their retreat to their boats is cut off by General Fraser in front, and General Nesbit in the rear; they are repulsed,	153

A.D.		PAGE
1776.	The mass of the Americans, led by Colonel Allen, on the following day cross the bridge and regain their boats,	153
	Sir Guy Carleton pursues them by water,	153
	General Burgoyne proceeds up the Sorel after Sullivan,	153
	Chamblée is abandoned and burnt by the Americans,	153
	They set fire to St John's, and retreat up the river; their whole army in a state of total insubordination,	153
	Burgoyne follows them closely, and takes possession of the posts evacuated by them,	153
	Sullivan and Arnold throw themselves on the Isle Aux Noix, where many of their men perish from fever,	153
	Canada is entirely freed from American arms,	153
	Energetic efforts are made for the recovery of Ticonderoga and the dominion of Lakes Champlain and St George,	153
	Clinton constructs two batteries on Long Island,	157
(June 7.)	Richard Henry Lee moves in congress a Declaration of Independence,	161
(June 10.)	Jefferson is appointed to make the draught,	161
(June 28.)	The declaration is reported to congress,	161
(June 28.)	The American fort (Sullivan's Island) bombarded in vain,	157, 158
	General Clinton with the troops sets sail to join General Howe,	159
(June 29.)	General Howe and the English army arrive at Sandy Hook,	162
	Howe is joined by Tryon,	165
	Washington throws up strong intrenchments at New York and on Long Island, and sinks vessels in various parts of the channel,	165
	Washington's army consists of more than 30,000 men, but a fourth are unfit for service from sickness,	165
	General Howe, with 9000 men, takes possession of Staten Island without opposition,	165
	During the summer it is discovered that many of the American privateers are French ships with a few Americans on board, and that France and Spain allow them to sell their prizes in their ports,	177
(July.)	Lord Howe sends a flag ashore with circular letters, acquainting the Americans with his powers, civil and military; declarations granting pardons, &c.,	165
(July 4.)	The Declaration of Independence is approved of by twelve of the thirteen states; New York alone unassenting,	161
(July 9.)	The province of New York assents to the Declaration,	162
(Aug. 22.)	General Howe puts his army in motion, and General Clinton, with 4000 men, lands in Gravesend Bay, Long Island, without opposition,	166
	Clinton's division is followed by the rest of the army,	166
	Washington reinforces Sullivan,	166, 167
	General Putnam supersedes Sullivan,	167
(Aug. 26, 27.)	Lord Howe defeats the Americans,	167, 168
(Aug. 28.)	The English break ground before one of the redoubts; in the meantime the Americans are ferried over the East River to New York,	168
(Aug. 29.)	Washington in the night-retreats,	168
	Two English frigates ascend the Hudson, and cut off communication by water	

CHRONOLOGICAL INDEX. 53

A.D. 1776.		PAGE
	between Washington's army and the remains of the army of Canada on Lake Champlain,	168
(Sept. 12.)	Washington evacuates New York,	169
	The British take possession of New York,	169
	Sir Henry Clinton lands at Kipp's Bay, three miles above New York, and defeats Washington,	169
	General Howe encamps in face of Washington's lines, covered on either flank by the British ships,	170
	Desertion from the American army becomes frequent,	170
	Congress vote an increase of pay and bounty-money, with other advantages,	170
(Sept. 20.)	A dreadful fire breaks out in New York; nearly a third of the city is reduced to ruins,	169
	Congress give the command of the squadron on Lake Champlain to Arnold,	174
(Oct. 12.)	The British flotilla engage Arnold below Crown Point,	175
(Oct. 12.)	General Howe lands at Frog's Neck,	171
(Oct. 22.)	Washington falls back to the edge of White Plains, and intrenches himself on the other side of the Bronx river,	172
(Oct. 31.)	Washington evacuates his lines; sets fire to all the houses in White Plains; crosses the Croton to North Castle; and takes up a most advantageous position,	172
(Nov. 8.)	Forty-five thousand seamen are voted, £3,205,505 for the expenses of the navy, and £500,000 to discharge the debts of the navy,	181
	Four thousand pounds are voted for Greenwich Hospital,	181
(Nov. 15.)	Lord Howe takes Fort Washington,	173
(Nov. 16.)	The Commons vote £3,000,000 for the army,	181, 182
(Nov. 18.)	Lord Cornwallis drives the Americans from Fort Lee,	173
	Cornwallis penetrates to the remotest parts of East and West Jersey,	173
	Sir Peter Parker takes Rhode Island,	173
(Dec. 7.)	A fire breaks out in his majesty's dockyard at Portsmouth; it is got under,	183
	During the recess of parliament, the public mind is dreadfully agitated by the attempts of an incendiary to burn all the shipping in the docks and all the arsenals,	182
(Dec. 20.)	Congress assemble at Baltimore,	175
	They greatly enlarge Washington's military powers, and authorise him to raise sixteen additional regiments,	175
	They vote a loan of 8,000,000 dollars, and make more paper-money,	175
	Agents are appointed to all the principal courts of Europe, to solicit their friendship for the newly-formed independent states,	176
	Petitions are signed by a great number of the inhabitants of New York, Long Island, and several other places, acknowledging the constitutional supremacy of Great Britain, and praying to be received into the king's peace and protection,	176
	Most of the towns of the two Jerseys send deputies for the same purpose to the commissioners,	176
	Several of the leading men of Philadelphia and Pennsylvania go over to the commissioners, Lord Howe and General Howe, at New York,	176
(No date.)	The management of affairs with the	

A.D. 1776.		PAGE
	Indians is withdrawn by the British, and the red men are allowed to adopt their own course with the back settlements,	176
	The Creeks and Cherokees ravage the back territories of Virginia and the Carolinas,	176
	The Creeks sue for a peace with the colonists, and the Cherokees are driven off with prodigious slaughter by the Carolina militia,	176
(Dec. 26.)	Washington crosses the Delaware and surprises Rhalle,	190, 191
(Dec. 31.)	Washington recrosses the Delaware and takes post at Trenton,	191
	Franklin arrives in Paris, to induce the French government to declare itself openly, and contract an alliance, offensive and defensive, with the United States,	197
1777. (Jan. 1.)	Lord Cornwallis concentrates his troops at Princetown,	191
	Washington resolves to fly by night,	191
	Lord Cornwallis pursues the Americans,	192
(Jan. 15.)	A machine and combustible materials are discovered in the hemp-room at Portsmouth,	183
	A reward is offered to one John the Painter to surrender himself for examination,	183
	Fires break out in various places; six or seven warehouses are consumed on the quay at Bristol,	183
	John the Painter is examined by members of the privy council,	183
	He is entrapped into a confession, and implicates Silas Deane, the agent of congress to France,	183, 184
	A bill is passed to enable the Admiralty to grant letters of marque, or 'letters of permission' and reprisal against the Americans,	185
(Jan. 25.)	Washington overruns East and West Jersey; becomes master of the coast opposite Staten Island; seizes Newark, Elizabeth Town, and Woodbridge, and fixes his head-quarters at Morris Town,	192
	Washington erects forts, mills, and magazines, and receives 20,000 stands of arms from France and 1000 barrels of gunpowder,	193
(Feb. 7.)	A bill is brought in to enable George III. to secure and detain persons charged with or suspected of the crime of high treason committed in America or on the high seas, or of piracy,	185
	It passes both Houses,	186
	John the Painter is executed,	184
(April 9.)	A grant is made of £618,340 to enable George III. to pay his debts, and £100,000 a year over and above the sum already fixed (£800,000 a year) for the better support of his majesty's household,	186, 187
	The British set fire to Danbury, and burn the stores,	193
	They encounter General Arnold intrenched, and defeat him,	193
	They defeat General Wooster also,	194
(May 7.)	The speaker, Sir Fletcher Norton, in presenting the bill for paying George III.'s debts at the bar of the House of Lords, reminds his majesty that the grant is *unusual, great beyond example, great beyond his majesty's highest expense;* but that the Commons had done so in a well-grounded confidence	

A.D. 1777.		PAGE
	that his majesty would apply *wisely* what they had granted liberally,	187
	The speaker receives the thanks of the House,	187
(May 9.)	The courtiers in the House arraign the conduct of the speaker in his speech to George III.; a long debate ensues, which ends in another vote of thanks to the speaker, carried *nem. con.*,	187, 188
(May 15.)	The common council of London resolve that the speech of the Hon. Sir Fletcher Norton shall be entered on the journals of their court, and the freedom of the city be conferred on him, to be presented in a gold box worth £50,	188
(May 30.)	Lord Chatham moves an address to George III. for the immediate cessation of hostilities with America; it is negatived,	188-190
(June.)	Washington takes up a strong position at Middle Brook,	195
	Howe crosses into the Jerseys,	195
(June 16.)	Burgoyne sets out to attack Ticonderoga,	202
(June 19.)	By a pretended precipitate retreat Howe induces Washington to leave his strong position, but by his slowness of execution Washington escapes,	195
(June 26.)	Washington retreats from Quibble Town,	195
	Lord Cornwallis routs Washington's advanced guard,	195
	Lord Cornwallis pursues them to Westfield,	195
(June 28.)	Howe concentrates his army at Amboy, and on the following day passes over to Staten Island, leaving Washington master of the Jerseys,	195
(July 2, 3.)	Works are thrown up for investing Ticonderoga,	202
(July 5.)	The Americans evacuate Ticonderoga,	202
(July 5.)	Howe embarks the mass of his army,	196
	Burgoyne gains possession of Skenesborough,	203
(July 10.)	Colonel Barton surprises General Prescot in bed, and threatens to hang him if Howe shoots Lee,	195
	Congress reward Barton with an elegant sword,	195
	Fraser defeats Colonel Warner,	203
	St Clair retreats to Manchester, and thence to Fort Edward,	203
(July 23.)	Howe sails from Sandy Hook,	196
	General Schuyler, the American commander-in-chief in the north, fixes his head-quarters at Fort Edward, on the left bank of the Hudson, and calls in St Clair and Long with the wreck of the army,	203
	He breaks up the roads and bridges, blocks up creeks and rivers, and sweeps the country bare of live-stock and all kinds of provisions,	203
	He implores congress for reinforcements; calls up the militia and backwoodsmen of New England and New York, and collects a numerous though motley force,	203
(July 30.)	Burgoyne reaches the Hudson near Fort Edward; Schuyler retires across the river at his approach,	204
	Howe reaches the Capes of Delaware,	196
(July 31.)	Congress give the rank and commission of major-general to the Marquis de Lafayette,	197
(Aug.)	British defeated in their attempt to take Bennington,	205, 206
	St Leger receives news that Arnold is advancing,	206

A.D. 1777.		PAGE
	He raises the siege of Fort Stanwix, and retreats, leaving behind him his artillery and stores, and his tents standing,	206
(Aug. 28.)	Howe proceeds up the Delaware, and lands his troops at Elk Head,	196
(Sept. 11.)	Howe and Cornwallis defeat the Americans at the forks of Brandywine,	196
	The Marquis de Lafayette fights on the side of the Americans,	196
	Howe takes possession of Wilmington, where he lodges his sick and wounded,	196
	General Gates, in supreme command of the Army of the North, is joined by Arnold,	206
(Sept. 27.)	Lord Cornwallis takes possession of Philadelphia,	198
	Lord Howe causes three batteries to be erected on the side of the river,	198
	Two American frigates, gun-boats, and row-galleys open a terrible fire on the batteries and town,	198, 199
(Oct.)	The Indians desert Burgoyne; his provisions become short,	207
	Gates is joined by General Lincoln,	207
	He detaches a body of New England militia to surprise Ticonderoga,	207
	They take a sloop and boats with provisions for Burgoyne; they also take possession of Mount Hope and Mount Defiance, and begin to attack Ticonderoga, but are repulsed,	207
	Burgoyne puts his men on half rations; his forage is exhausted, and his horses perishing from want; the red men desert, whole tribes at a time; the soldiers lose heart,	208
(Oct. 7.)	Burgoyne attempts to dislodge Gates; he is defeated,	208
	The American Colonel Brooks gains and keeps ground within the line of Burgoyne's intrenchments,	208
(Oct. 8.)	Lord Howe, with the mass of the British fleet, ascends the Delaware as far as the town of Newcastle,	199
	Fort Clinton is taken by Clinton,	212, 213
(Oct. 9.)	Burgoyne ascends the river to Saratoga, leaving his sick and wounded in hospital,	209
	Gates behaves with much humanity to the sick prisoners,	209
(Oct. 13.)	Burgoyne calls a council of war, which resolves to capitulate,	210
(Oct. 14.)	A cessation of arms is agreed on with Burgoyne,	211
	On the intelligence of Burgoyne's surrender, Fort George and Ticonderoga are evacuated,	211
(Nov. 17.)	Cornwallis takes Red Bank,	200
	Washington is reinforced by 4000 men,	200
(Dec. 2.)	The Duke of Richmond moves in the House of Lords for a committee to inquire into the state of the nation,	219, 220
	Fox makes a similar motion in the Commons,	220
	The number of seamen fixed for the ensuing year is 60,000, and that of the troops to be employed in America alone, 55,000,	223
(Dec. 6.)	A strong body of the Army of the North are driven from Edge Hill by Cornwallis,	200
	Washington takes up his winter-quarters at Valley Forge,	201
1778. (Jan.)	Liverpool, Manchester, Glasgow, and Edinburgh raise regiments at their	

CHRONOLOGICAL INDEX.

A.D. 1778.		PAGE
	own expense; and several independent companies are raised in Wales without cost or charge to the government,	224
	Many of the maritime towns arm ships to cruise in the Channel against American privateers, and Frenchmen under American colours,	224
	Washington issues a proclamation requiring the farmers within seventy miles of Valley Forge to thresh out one half of their grain by the 1st February, and the rest by the 1st March, under the penalty of having the whole seized as straw,	245
	Washington recommends congress to impress men for the army; they agree to it,	246
	Many of the impressed men desert to the British,	246
	The American army is in want of almost all necessaries, and a putrid fever breaks out in the camp,	246
(Mar.)	Lieutenant-colonel Mawhood partly routs a body of American militia,	248
	The expedition against Canada is given up,	247
	Lafayette returns to Albany, and, as general of the district, administers to the population a new form of oath devised by congress,	247
	Baron Steuben, a Prussian officer, joins the American service, to teach the raw troops of the republic the Prussian field-service,	247
	Steuben is made inspector-general of the American army,	248
(Mar. 17.)	Lord North informs the House of Commons that the French king, Louis XVI., had concluded a treaty of amity and commerce with George III.'s revolted subjects in North America, and that the British ambassador in Paris had been ordered home,	231
(Mar. 18.)	Louis XVI. issues an edict to seize all British ships in the ports of France,	242
(Mar. 27.)	Government lays an embargo on all French ships in British ports,	242
(April 7.)	The Duke of Richmond moves an address to George III., recapitulating the expense, loss, and misconduct of the war, and entreating his majesty to dismiss his ministers, and withdraw his forces by sea and land from America; it is negatived,	235–239
	Lord Chatham appears for 'the last time' in the House of Lords, and after a long speech is removed in a swoon,	236
	An American brigade under General Lacy is nearly surrounded at Crooked Billet by Lieutenant-colonel Abercrombie and Major Simcoe,	250
	Lacy loses all his baggage and stores,	250
(May 6.)	Burke draws the attention of the House to the great capabilities of Ireland,	233
	A bill repealing certain penalties and disabilities of the Irish Roman Catholics passes both Houses,	233
(May 7.)	An expedition by sea and land is made to destroy all the American shipping in the upper part of the Delaware between Philadelphia and Trenton,	250
	Forty-four American vessels are burnt,	250
(May 11.)	Lord Chatham dies,	236
(May 20.)	Howe detaches Generals Grant and Clinton with 5000 men against Lafayette, who outmanœuvres them, and rejoins Washington,	250

A.D. 1778.		PAGE
(May 24.)	Sir William Howe takes his departure, and Sir Henry Clinton assumes the chief command,	252
(May 26.)	A motion is made in the Commons for a select committee to consider the transactions of the northern army, the convention of Saratoga, and the means by which the general obtained his release,	234
	Burgoyne supports the motion, and justifies his conduct,	234
(June.)	Count D'Estaing sails from Toulon with a squadron for North America,	243
	He is pursued by Admiral Byron; Byron's squadron is scattered and crippled between the West Indies and the Banks of Newfoundland,	243
(June 6.)	Lord Carlisle, Governor Johnstone, and Mr Eden, the new commissioners, arrive at Philadelphia, but fail to effect any settlement of affairs,	252
(June 17.)	La Licorne, French frigate, strikes to the America, one of Admiral Keppel's fleet,	242
	The Arethusa engages the Belle Poule, which is towed ashore by French boats,	242
(June 17.)	Philadelphia is evacuated by the British,	253
	The American army enter Philadelphia as the British leave it,	253
	The Americans cross the Delaware, and pursue the British,	253
(June 28.)	The battle of Monmouth,	254, 255
(June 30.)	The French fleet arrives off Sandy Hook,	256
	Lord Howe with his fleet sails round to Sandy Hook,	256
	A thousand volunteers from the transports join Lord Howe,	256
(July.)	The Lively, 20-gun frigate, is taken in the midst of the French fleet, in a fog,	242
(July 27.)	Keppel engages the French fleet off Ushant,	243
	The troops of congress under Colonel Zebulon Butler, and the militia under Colonel Dennison, are attacked and massacred by the Indians,	261
	The Indians retire on the approach of a force sent against them by Washington,	261, 262
	Washington makes reprisals on the Indians,	262
(Aug. 8.)	D'Estaing prepares to land at Newport,	256
	The crews of four British frigates are landed, and the vessels set fire to,	256
(Aug. 9.)	Howe heaves in sight with the British fleet,	256
(Aug. 10.)	Sullivan begins the siege of Newport,	256
(Aug. 12.)	The Languedoc, D'Estaing's flag-ship, is dismasted, and the other French ships left in an unmanageable state,	257
(Aug. 13.)	The Renown attacks the Languedoc, and Commodore Hotham, in the Preston, falls in with the Tonnant; both these French ships narrowly escape,	257
	Sullivan raises the siege of Newport,	258
(Aug. 23.)	Keppel puts to sea; our privateers and cruisers capture a vast number of French trading-vessels,	243
(Aug. 29.)	Sir Robert Pigott engages Sullivan,	258
(Sept.)	Riots take place at Charlestown, in South Carolina, between Yankee and French seamen,	258
	Clinton, after relieving Rhode Island, returns to New York,	258
(Sept. 7.)	The Marquis de Bouillé, governor-general of Martinique, lands with 2000 men on Dominica, while the frigates and privateers attack by sea,	263

A.D.		PAGE
1778. (Sept.)	Lieutenant-governor Stewart capitulates,	263
	Howe gives the command of the squadron at New York to Rear-admiral Gambier, He goes to Rhode Island, and resigns the command of the American station to Vice-admiral Byron,	262
		262
	Howe leaves for England,	262
(Sept. 19.)	Clinton transmits to congress an extract of his instructions from the secretary of state,	268
	General Grey commits great havoc at Buzzard Bay, and on the island of Martha's Vineyard,	258
	He makes a successful incursion into New Jersey,	258
	A force of 3500 men under Lieutenant-colonel Campbell, convoyed by a squadron under Sir Peter Parker, is despatched to Savannah, the capital of Georgia,	258
	They encounter and defeat the Americans,	259
	The town of Savannah captured,	259
	The great majority of the inhabitants take the oath of allegiance to King George III.,	259
(Oct. 3.)	The royal commissioners issue a last manifesto and proclamation to the inhabitants of the colonies of every rank and denomination,	269
	Part of Byron's force is driven off the coast by a hurricane; D'Estaing puts to sea from Boston, to undertake operations in the West Indies,	262, 263
	Before leaving, he urges the French Canadians to take up arms against the English,	263
	Commodore Hotham sails from Sandy Hook, to escort Major-general Grant with 5000 men to protect the West India Islands,	263
	Congress enact that the circulation of the manifesto of the royal commissioners shall be considered seditious,	269, 270
(Nov.)	The royal commissioners close their commission,	270
	An amendment in the Commons, that George III.'s speech only asserted a *falsehood*, is negatived,	271
(Dec. 2.)	The sea-fight off Ushant is brought under debate,	271
	Palliser presents specific charges against Keppel; the Admiralty order a court-martial,	272
	Twelve admirals subscribe a memorial to George III., lamenting the injury done to Keppel, and to the service at large, by ordering the court-martial,	272
	Temple Luttrell moves an address for the trial of Palliser,	272
(Dec. 13.)	Major-general Grant, accompanied by the joint-squadrons of Hotham and Barrington, lands at the Grand Cul de Sac in the island of St Lucie,	263
	Brigadier-general Medows lands, and drives the French before him,	263
	Brigadier-general Prescott also lands, and secures the whole of the bay,	263
	D'Estaing arrives with a large fleet,	264
(Dec. 15.)	D'Estaing's fleet is beaten,	264
(Dec. 17.)	He nevertheless lands, and directs his whole force against Medows,	264
(Dec. 17.)	The French are foiled,	265
	The Chevalier de Micoud capitulates,	265
	The Marquis de Lafayette leaves for France,	265
1779. (Jan. 6.)	Vice-admiral Byron, with nine sail	

A.D.		PAGE
1779.	of the line, joins Rear-admiral Barrington at St Lucie,	280
	D'Estaing takes refuge in Martinique, where he is joined by the Marquis de Vaudreuil,	280
	The French take Senegal, and fortify it,	280
	The English under Sir Edward Hughes take Goree,	280
(Jan. 7.)	Admiral Keppel's trial commences at Portsmouth before five admirals and eight captains,	272
	The American general, Ashe, crosses the Savannah, and enters Augusta,	282
	General Prevost totally routs and disperses his force,	282
	An anti-popery riot takes place in Edinburgh,	305
(Feb. 11.)	Admiral Keppel is acquitted by the court-martial,	272
	On the news of his acquittal, the cities of London and Westminster illuminate for two successive nights,	272
(Feb. 11.)	Riots take place in London in consequence,	272, 273
(Feb. 12.)	Admiral Keppel receives the freedom of the city,	273
	Both Houses of Parliament pass votes of thanks to Keppel,	273
	Palliser demands a court-martial on himself,	273
(Mar.)	Sir Hugh Palliser is tried; the trial lasts twenty-one days; he is acquitted,	273
	Fox moves, 'That at the commencement of hostilities with France, the state of the navy was unequal to what the House and the nation were led to expect,' &c.; it is lost,	273, 274
	A few days after, Fox moves that the omission to reinforce Lord Howe in America before the month of June, and not sending a fleet to the Mediterranean, are gross instances of misconduct and neglect; he is again outvoted,	274
(April 19.)	Fox moves for the dismissal of Lord Sandwich from his majesty's presence and councils for ever; it is rejected,	274
	Lord Bristol makes a similar motion in the Lords, which is negatived,	274
	Keppel, Sir Robert Harland, Captain Leveson Gower, and some other officers of distinction resign,	274
	General Lincoln crosses the river to Augusta, then descends the opposite bank to the capital of Georgia,	282
(April 28.)	General Prevost, to oblige Lincoln to return, crosses the river into South Carolina with nearly the whole British army,	282
	Lincoln hurries down the southern bank to capture the town of Savannah,	282
	Prevost changes his plan, and marches for Charlestown, the capital of South Carolina,	282, 283
	Charlestown is put into a state of defence on the land-side,	283
(May 1.)	A fruitless attempt is made on the island of Jersey by the French,	280
	A large army is collected by Spain before negotiations terminate at St Roque, Algesiras, and Campo, near Gibraltar,	279
(May 10.)	Collier's squadron enters Elizabeth River, and lands a British force,	283
(May 11.)	The Marquis of Rockingham moves for the production of all such documents relative to the trade of Ireland as	

CHRONOLOGICAL INDEX. 57

A.D.		PAGE
1779.	will enable parliament to pursue effectual measures for promoting the wealth and comfort of both kingdoms,	276
	Lord Gower, president of the council, pledges himself that a proper plan for arranging the affairs of Ireland shall be prepared and laid before parliament, at the opening of the next session,	276
	General Prevost appears before Charlestown, and summons it to surrender,	283
(May 12.)	The British army withdraws through the night,	283
(May 13.)	The treaty of Teschen is signed,	240
	General Matthews devastates Norfolk and Gosport,	284
	The Americans burn a great many more of their vessels in Chesapeake Bay,	284
	In Portsmouth the British burn eight ships of war on the stocks,	284
(June 3.)	D'Orvilliers sails from Brest with thirty French sail of the line for the Spanish coast; he is joined in Cadiz Bay by thirty Spanish sail of the line, and at Ferrol by eight more,	279
	The English garrison of St Vincent capitulates,	280
	D'Estaing takes Grenada,	280, 281
	Collier and Matthews, accompanied by Clinton, proceed up the Hudson, to drive back Washington's people,	284
	The Americans fly without firing a shot,	284
	General Francis Maclean establishes a post to check the incursions of the Massachusetts men into Nova Scotia, &c.,	285
	The executive government of Massachusetts offer unusual bounty-money to all the men who will engage in an expedition against Maclean,	285
	An expedition is fitted out,	285
(June 16.)	Lord North informs the House that the Spanish ambassador had quitted London, after delivering a hostile manifesto to the secretary of state,	276
(June 17.)	A royal message and the Spanish manifesto are introduced,	276
	Both Houses are unanimous in their indignation against Spain and in the determination of supporting with spirit the war against the whole House of Bourbon,	276
(June 20.)	Prevost is unsuccessfully attacked at John's Island by Lincoln,	283
(June 21.)	Lord North proposes in the Commons that the number of the militia shall be doubled, and that individuals shall be enabled to raise loyal corps to assist in the defence of the kingdom,	277
	A bill to this effect passes the Commons,	277
	The Lords reject the clause 'enabling the king to double the militia,'	277
	The Indemnity Bill passes,	277
	The American squadron are repulsed in their attempts to enter the harbour of Penobscot,	285
(June 29.)	The committee on the conduct of the American war is dissolved without coming to any resolution on the business,	275
(July 5.)	Byron fights the French fleet off Grenada,	280, 281
	D'Estaing sails to the coast of Georgia and Carolina,	281
	Byron sails for St Christopher,	281
	Sir George Collier arrives in Penobscot Bay; the Americans abandon their ships and fly into the woods,	285, 286

A.D.		PAGE
1779.	Collier is superseded by Admiral Arbuthnot from England,	286
	Clinton withdraws the troops from Rhode Island,	286
	Tryon lands and takes possession of Newhaven, which he destroys,	284
	Tryon reduces Fairfield to ashes; also Norwalk and Greenfield,	284
(July 9.)	A proclamation is issued (in England) charging all officers, civil and military, in case of an invasion, to cause all horses, oxen, and cattle, and provisions to be driven from the sea-coast to places of security,	278
	Don Bernardo Galvez, governor of Louisiana, recognises the independence of the United States, and makes an irruption into the British colony of West Florida,	290
	The governor of Yucatan commences hostilities against the British settlers and logwood cutters in the Bay of Honduras,	291
	Dalling, governor of Jamaica, sends a small party of Irish volunteers under Captain Dalrymple to the Mosquito shore; they check the insolence of the Spaniards,	291
	They take a galleon with quicksilver worth 3,000,000 of piastres,	291
	Washington despatches General Wayne with a considerable force to fall upon the garrison of Stoney Point at night,	284, 285
	The English garrison are taken by surprise, and surrender,	285
	The garrison of Stoney Point evacuate on the approach of Clinton,	285
(Aug. 15.)	The French and Spanish fleets appear off Plymouth; several French frigates anchor in Cawsand Bay, and capture a number of coasting vessels,	280
(Aug. 16.)	The *Ardent*, Captain Boteler, falls in with the enemy's fleet, mistaking it for British, and is captured in sight of Plymouth,	280
	Sullivan wastes the lands of the Mohawks,	288
(Sept. 1.)	Admiral Hardy outmanoeuvres the combined fleet, and anchors at Spithead,	280
	The coast is covered with troops, militia and volunteers,	280
	A fatal sickness breaks out in the combined fleet,	280
	Great numbers of Spanish ships are captured,	280
	The Spaniards before Gibraltar make no impression,	280
	The French fleet appears off the mouth of the Savannah river,	286
	They surprise some English vessels,	286
	General Prevost fortifies Savannah,	286
	Captain Henry lends his ship's guns to be mounted on the batteries, and his sailors to work them; his marines are incorporated with the grenadiers of a regiment in garrison,	286, 287
(Sept. 13.)	D'Estaing summons General Prevost to surrender,	287
	Colonel Maitland throws himself into the town with 800 veterans, and Prevost informs his opponent that the place will be defended to the last extremity,	287
(Sept. 15.)	John Paul or Paul Jones appears off Ryemouth,	292
(Sept. 16.)	He enters the Firth of Forth, but next day a violent gale comes on, which drives him out the Firth,	292

A. D.	PAGE
1779. (Sept. 16.) General Lincoln, with the South Carolina army, arrives before Savannah,	287
(Sept. 23.) Paul Jones fights and captures two English ships,	292
The French government publicly thanks Paul Jones, and Louis XVI. confers on him the Order of Merit; congress also send him a vote of thanks, and give him the command of a new ship, *The America*,	293
The Indians retaliate on the provincial settlements,	289
Sullivan retires in disgust from the service,	289
(Oct. 6.) An action takes place off Ushant between the British and French fleets,	293
The East India Company build, at their own expense, three fine 74 gun-ships, and present them to government; they also offer bounty-money for raising 6000 seamen,	293
The French court issues an order to all its naval commanders not to molest or interrupt on any account Captain Cook, engaged on his third and last voyage of discovery and survey,	293
The siege of Savannah is raised,	287
Lincoln is deserted by the militia,	288
Changes take place in the cabinet,	293
(Nov. 25.) Parliament assembles; stormy debates take place on the addresses, which are carried, as also on the state of Ireland,	294–296
(Dec. 13.) Lord North brings forth his scheme of relief to Ireland,	296
Meetings are called and petitions framed in various counties for obtaining a reduction of expenditure and taxation, and also a reform in parliament,	298
A committee of 61 members is formed to carry on correspondence, and to prepare a plan of association in the City of York,	298
Clinton sails for Charlestown, in South Carolina,	317
The ships encounter a long and terrible storm; some of the transports are taken by the enemy, others are lost, and all are more or less damaged,	317
1780. (Jan.) Count Beyland, the Dutch commander, refuses to let Commodore Fielding search his merchant vessels, and fires on the boats sent off to search them,	316
An engagement ensues, and Beyland strikes his colours,	316
He is given to understand that he may hoist his colours and proceed on his voyage, the English having seized seven of the merchant vessels laden with warlike or naval stores,	316
Beyland hoists his flag, but declares that he cannot proceed without the seven captured vessels, and sails into Spithead, and anchors close to Fielding's squadron,	316
The Dutch remonstrate with the British cabinet,	316
They are told they cannot expect the benefits of friendship and alliance when they refuse England the assistance they are bound to give, but assist her enemies with naval stores,	316
(Jan. 8.) Sir George Rodney captures a rich Spanish convoy,	313
(Jan. 16.) Rodney gains a victory over a Spanish fleet off Cape St Vincent,	313
(Jan. and Feb.) Secret negotiations take place with the court of Spain,	334–336

A. D.	PAGE
1780. (Feb.) Rodney, after relieving Gibraltar, and sending supplies to Port Mahon, sails for the West Indies with part of the fleet,	314
A Spanish fleet, under Admirals Cordova and Gaston, capture the East and West India fleet under a weak escort off the Azores,	314
The convoy of two English ships of war escape; sixty sail are carried into Cadiz harbour with 1800 soldiers on board, and stores and merchandise estimated at £2,000,000,	314
(Feb. 11.) Burke introduces his plan of economical reform,	299
(Feb. 14.) Colonel Barré gives notice of a motion for more extensive reform than Mr Burke's,	300
Washington's distresses, and the loss of credit of congress, continue to increase,	323
Russia, Prussia, and other neutral powers call for an immediate concert among the nations on account of the affair with Beyland; Catherine of Russia issues a manifesto; the Armed Neutrality,	317
(Mar. 2.) Sir Guy Carleton and five others are appointed commissioners of accounts,	300
(Mar. 14.) Fort Mobile, in Florida, surrenders to Don Bernardo de Galves,	319
(Mar. 27.) Rodney reaches St Lucie, and joins Admiral Hyde Parker,	325
(Mar. 29.) Clinton's army lands on Charlestown Neck,	317
(April.) Whipple, the American commander, retires to Sullivan island, and afterwards to Charlestown,	318
Clinton detaches Colonel Tarleton to cut off Lincoln's horse,	318
(April 6.) A great public meeting is held at Westminster, with the advice and concurrence of the corresponding committees, to give weight to the county petitions; Mr Fox in the chair,	302
Mr Dunning's famous resolution, 'That the influence of the crown has increased, is increasing, and ought to be diminished,' passes with an amendment,	302
Mr Thomas Pitt moves, that it is the duty of the House to provide, as far as may be, an immediate and official redress of the grievances complained of in the petitions presented to the House from the different counties, cities, and towns of the kingdom; it is carried without a division,	303
(April 14.) Tarleton scatters Lincoln's horse,	318
Earl Cornwallis scours the country beyond the river, and cuts off all supplies from Lincoln, and all hopes of retreat,	318
(April 17.) Rodney defeats the French fleet,	325
(April 20.) Rodney cuts off the French fleet from Martinique; they take refuge at Guadaloupe,	326
(May 12.) Lincoln capitulates,	318
General Leslie's division takes possession of Charlestown,	319
(May 21.) The French fleet get into Fort Royal,	326
The French and Spanish fleets join,	326
A terrible sickness breaks out in the Spanish fleet, which extends to the French,	326
(May 25.) Two Connecticut regiments parade under arms, declaring they will either return home, or obtain subsistence at the point of the bayonet,	324

CHRONOLOGICAL INDEX. 59

A.D.		PAGE
1780.	Eighty-five Christian corresponding societies, affiliated to that of Edinburgh, are formed in different parts of the country; they choose Lord George Gordon president,	305, 306
	Tarleton scatters the troops of Buford,	319
(June 1, 4.)	Clinton and Arbuthnot issue proclamations for restoring peace,	320
(June 2.)	Lord George Gordon, accompanied by a mob of from 60,000 to 100,000, proceeds from St George's Fields to the House of Commons to present a petition against popery,	306, 307
	No-popery riots in London,	307
(June 3.)	Lord Bathurst moves an address to his Majesty George III., for prosecuting the authors, abettors, and instruments of the outrages committed,	308
(June 4.)	A popish chapel and several houses occupied by Catholics are destroyed by the mob in London,	308
(June 5.)	The privy council offer a reward of £500 for the discovery of the destroyers of the Bavarian and Sardinian chapels,	308
(June 5.)	Clinton returns to New York, leaving Cornwallis with 4000 men behind him,	320
(June 6.)	Riots continue in London for several days,	308–312
(June 10.)	Lord George Gordon is committed to the Tower for high treason,	312
	Burke moves five resolutions in favour of freedom of conscience, and in reprobation of the late disgraceful excesses; they are all agreed to,	313
	A bill passes the Commons to prevent papists from teaching or taking upon themselves the education or government of the children of Protestants,	313
	A premature insurrection of the royalists takes place in North Carolina,	320
(June 23.)	Clinton defeats General Greene,	324
(June 25.)	Clinton withdraws from the Jerseys, and returns to New York,	324
	The Marquis de Lafayette arrives at Washington's camp,	324
(July.)	Rodney sails for New York,	326
(July 13.)	The French fleet arrives at Rhode Island,	324
	Washington receives a commission from Louis XVI. as a Lieutenant-general of France,	324
	Admiral Graves arrives at Sandy Hook,	325
	The French fleet is blockaded in Newport harbour,	325
	Rochambeau fortifies himself on Rhode Island,	325
(Aug. 15.)	Cornwallis and Rawdon advance to meet Gates, and the advanced-guards fire on each other,	321
(Aug. 16.)	The American militia fly at the first charge,	321
	Tarleton defeats Colonel Sumter,	322
(Sept. 8.)	Cornwallis marches into the back parts of North Carolina; Colonel Ferguson advances to the frontiers of Virginia; Tarleton pursues an intermediate course,	322
	General Benedict Arnold opens a secret correspondence with Clinton,	326, 327
	Congress adopt two principles: 1st, That the army shall be engaged for the whole war; 2d, That the officers shall have half-pay for life,	332
(Sept. 24.)	Major André is taken prisoner,	328
(Sept. 25.)	Arnold escapes to the *Vulture* sloop of war,	328, 329
	Ferguson is defeated and killed,	322

A.D.		PAGE
1780.	Cornwallis commences a disastrous retreat upon South Carolina,	322
(Oct. 2.)	Major André is hanged,	330
(Oct. 29.)	Cornwallis takes up a position between Camden and Ninety-six,	322
	Tarleton drives back Marion, and defeats Sumter,	322
	General Gates is superseded by General Greene,	322
(Nov. 10.)	Sir Joseph Yorke presents his memorial to the States-general,	333
(Nov. 13.)	Ninety-one thousand men, including marines, are voted for the navy,	336
(Dec. 4.)	The minutes of the trial and sentence of the court-martial on Palliser are ordered to be laid before the House of Commons,	337
(Dec. 6.)	Parliament adjourns,	337
(Dec. 12.)	Sir Joseph Yorke presents another memorial to the States-general,	333
(Dec. 20.)	A royal manifesto is issued, declaring that Great Britain had issued letters of marque and reprisal against the Dutch, and justifying her conduct,	333–337
	Sir Joseph Yorke is recalled from the Hague,	334
(Dec. 29.)	The Dutch ambassador at the British Court, Count Welderen, demands his passports,	334
1781. (Jan. 1.)	A general revolt breaks out in Washington's line; the Pennsylvania line parade under arms, and declare they will march to the seat of congress, and either obtain redress or serve no longer,	342
	General Arnold appears in Hampton Road, on the Chesapeak, with 1200 men, to carry devastation into Virginia,	344
	Arnold lands at Westover, twenty-five miles from Richmond,	344
	Jefferson, the governor of the state, flies,	344
	Arnold encamps at Four Mile Creek, twelve miles below Richmond,	344, 345
	He enters Richmond, which is evacuated,	345
	Colonel Simcoe destroys a cannon-foundry and other buildings at Westham,	345
	Arnold burns Richmond,	345
	Congress raise three months' pay and some clothes, and forward them to the troops,	344
	Lieutenant-colonel Laurens is despatched to France for assistance; Thomas Payne goes with him,	344
	Lord George Gordon is tried for high treason, and acquitted on the ground of insanity,	313
	The French capture the capital of the Isle of Jersey,	341
	A hurricane damages the Spanish fleet in the Gulf of Mexico,	364
	Tarleton is defeated,	346
(Feb. 1.)	Lord Cornwallis scatters the North Carolina militia,	346
	Commodore de Tilley captures the *Romulus*,	345
	Greene retires into Virginia,	347
	Lee surprises a body of North Carolina royalists,	347
	Rodney, and a land force under General Vaghan, capture the valuable Dutch island of St Eustatius,	364
	Rodney detaches two ships of the line and a frigate; they capture a fleet of thirty Dutch West Indiamen and a ship of the line,	364
	Vaughan keeps the Dutch colours flying,	

HISTORY OF ENGLAND.

A.D.		PAGE
1781.	and decoys into the harbour a considerable number of Dutch, French, and American vessels, traders and privateers,	364
	The Islands of St Martin and Saba are also captured, and the Dutch settlements on the rivers Demarara and Essequibo in Guiana,	364
(Feb. 26.)	The Hon. William Pitt makes his first speech in the House of Commons, in opposition,	338
(Mar. 6.)	A personal conference is held at Newport, Rhode Island, between Washington, Rochambeau, Destouches, and other officers, to concert measures for capturing Arnold,	345
	It is resolved to embark part of Rochambeau's army under the Count de Viominil, and to risk the whole of the French fleet to escort it,	345, 346
(Mar. 8.)	The French fleet sails from Rhode Island,	346
	The battle of Guilford,	348, 349
	Greene retreats, almost all his militia leaving him for their homes,	349
(Mar. 16.)	Admiral Arbuthnot comes up with the French fleet off Cape Henry, and brings Destouches to action; after fighting for an hour, the French sheer off,	346
(Mar. 18.)	Cornwallis retires by easy marches to Cross Creek; Greene pursues him,	350
	Cornwallis retreats to Wilmington,	350
(Mar. 26.)	General Arnold superseded,	346
	The defence of Virginia is committed to Lafayette,	346
(April 2.)	The petition from the delegates of the county associations is presented to the House of Commons,	340
	Admiral Darby relieves Gibraltar,	342
(April 20.)	General Phillips takes Williamsburg,	346
	He takes York Town,	346
(April 23.)	The British at Fort Watson, on the Santee River, capitulate,	359
	Petersburg taken, and all the ships burnt,	346
	Phillipe and Arnold burn the tobacco, several mills, a rope-yard, stores, and shipping at Warwick and elsewhere,	346
(May 9.)	The Spaniards get possession of the whole of Florida,	364
(May 20.)	Cornwallis reaches Petersburg,	351
(May 21.)	Greene besieges Ninety-six,	360
(May 28.)	Lord Beauchamp brings in a bill to amend the Marriage Act, which passes both Houses,	340
(June.)	Tarleton captures and destroys at Charlottesville 1000 new firelocks, upwards of 400 barrels of powder, some hogsheads of tobacco, and some clothing for the army,	352
	Simcoe, by a stratagem, makes Baron Steuben suppose that the whole British army are advancing,	352
	Steuben retreats in disorder; Simcoe destroys the stores at the Point of Fork,	352
	Lafayette is joined by a numerous body of backwoodsmen,	352
(June 8.)	Colonel Lee arrives at Greene's camp, and marches the British prisoners captured at Augusta with a British standard reversed before the garrison,	360
	Commodore Johnstone captures a Dutch East Indiaman, with £40,000 in specie, and stores and provisions for Ceylon,	365
	Some of Rawdon's horse are surprised and captured by Colonel Lee,	361

A.D.		PAGE
1781. (July 4.)	Cornwallis sends part of his army across to Portsmouth,	353
	Cornwallis defeats Lafayette and Wayne,	353
	Lee is defeated by Colonel Coates at Monk's Corner,	361
	Lord Rawdon embarks for Europe,	361
	The Island of Tobago capitulates to the French,	365
(July 21.)	Commodore Johnstone captures four Dutch East Indiamen,	365
(Aug. 1.)	Cornwallis takes possession of York Town on York River, and proceeds to fortify it,	352
(Aug. 4.)	Colonel Hayne, who had sworn allegiance to King George III., having been taken in arms against the British, is hanged at Charlestown,	362
	A sea-fight takes place off Dogger Bank between English and Dutch,	367
	Sir Hyde Parker resigns the command in the North Sea,	367
	Sir Peter Parker is appointed to a squadron of frigates to blockade the Dutch ports,	367, 368
(Aug. 19.)	The French and Spanish troops under the Duke de Crillon land at Minorca, and occupy all the posts round Port Mahon; General Murray retires into Fort St Philip,	366
	The Duke de Crillon impudently offers General Murray £100,000, and rank and employment in the French or Spanish service, if he will surrender the fort to him,	366
	The combined Spanish and French fleets cruise in the Channel,	367
(Aug. 20.)	Portsmouth (America) is evacuated,	353
(Aug. 22.)	Cornwallis's force is concentrated at York and Gloucester,	353
(Aug. 30.)	Count de Grasse, with a new French fleet, arrives at the Chesapeak,	353
	Negapatnam, Pedang, and other places chiefly Dutch, surrender to the British,	365
(Sept. 5.)	Admiral Graves sights the French fleet within the Capes of Virginia; a partial action takes place; night separates the fleets,	354
(Sept. 6.)	Arnold lands at New London, in Connecticut, with a strong force,	355
	Fort Griswold taken by the British; great destruction of property,	355
	Washington holds a council of war on board De Grasse's ship, and measures are concerted for reducing Lord Cornwallis in York Town, with all possible speed,	355
	The battle of Eutaw,	363
(Sept. 10.)	Colonel Stuart retreats; he is pursued a short way by Greene,	364
	Congress order a gold medal to be struck in honour of Greene,	364
(Sept. 10.)	De Grasse bears away for the Chesapeak, and takes up his old anchorage within the Capes, where he finds M. de Barras with the Rhode Island squadron,	354
	Graves, after reconnoitring the French fleet, returns to New York,	354
	The whole power of the Americans and their allies is directed against York Town,	354
	Washington intrusts the defence of the Hudson to General Heath, and takes the chief command at the Chesapeak,	354
(Sept. 28.)	The combined army of Americans and French encamp two miles from Cornwallis's outer works,	356

CHRONOLOGICAL INDEX. 61

A.D. 1781.		PAGE
	Cornwallis concentrates his army within the works close round the village or town,	356
(Oct. 9.)	Batteries opened on Cornwallis,	368
(Oct. 14.)	Two redoubts are stormed and taken at York Town,	357
	Cornwallis's situation becomes desperate,	357
(Oct. 16.)	Lieutenant-colonel Abercrombie makes a sortie,	357
(Oct. 17.)	Cornwallis can scarcely shew a mounted gun on the side of the attack; his shells are nearly expended, and sickness breaks out in his camp,	357
(Oct. 19.)	He capitulates,	358
	Congress vote thanks to Washington, Rochambeau, De Grasse, and the officers of the allied army generally, and the corps of artillery and engineers particularly, &c.,	359
(Oct. 19.)	The British fleet under Graves, with Clinton, and 7000 troops on board, sails from Sandy Hook,	359
(Nov.)	De Grasse with the French fleet sails for the West Indies,	359
(Nov. 25.)	News of Lord Cornwallis's surrender reaches England,	359
(Nov. 26.)	General Elliot sallies out of Gibraltar, and destroys the Spanish works,	386
	Rear-admiral Kempenfelt sails to intercept the French merchant vessels sailing from Brest, under the escort of the Count de Guichen,	368
(Dec. 5.)	A hundred thousand men are voted for the navy,	370
	The House of Commons are occupied by discussions on the American war,	370, 371
(Dec. 12.)	Kempenfelt captures twenty sail of large transports and merchant vessels,	368
1782. (Jan.)	Fox moves for an inquiry into the causes of the ill success of the naval forces; it is agreed to,	372, 373
(Feb. 5.)	Minorca capitulates,	372
(Feb.)	Many of the French and Spanish troops shed tears as the garrison passes; the Duke de Crillon behaves with great honour and humanity,	372
	Hood dispossesses the French fleet of their anchorage,	381
	St Christopher's surrenders to Bouillé, which is followed by the surrender of Nevis and Montserrat,	381
	In the House of Lords an inquiry is agreed to into the causes of Lord Cornwallis's surrender, and the production of copies of all correspondence between ministers and Sir Henry Clinton,	373
	Lord George Germaine resigns, and is created Viscount Sackville,	373
	Welbore Ellis succeeds Lord George Germaine as secretary of state,	374
(Feb. 19.)	Rodney arrives at Barbadoes, and joins Hood,	381
	Rodney runs with the whole British fleet to St Lucie, and throws out frigates to watch the French in Martinique,	381
(Feb. 22.)	General Conway moves an address to King George III., imploring his majesty to listen to the advice of his Commons that the war with America may no longer be pursued,	374
(Feb. 27.)	General Conway's motion to stop hostilities with America is carried by a majority of nineteen,	274, 275
(Mar. 5.)	The attorney-general introduces his plan of a truce with America, which is agreed to without a division,	375

A.D. 1782.		PAGE
(Mar. 20.)	The ministry resign,	376
(Mar. 21.)	The Marquis of Rockingham is made premier,	376
	Admiral Keppel is created a viscount, and made first lord of the Admiralty; Dunning is created Baron Ashburton,	377
(April.)	The bill for excluding contractors from the House of Commons passes both Houses,	378
(April 12.)	Admiral Rodney completely defeats De Grasse,	382
(April 19.)	Hood captures, in the Mona Passage, between Hispaniola and Porto Rico, two ships of the line and two large frigates,	382
(April 20, 21.)	Barrington captures two French ships of the line, ten large transports, and a schooner, containing a great quantity of ordnance, ammunition, &c.,	383
	The combined fleets of France and Spain capture eighteen sail of British merchantmen and transports,	385
(May 3.)	The bill for excluding revenue-officers from voting for a member of parliament passes both Houses,	378
(May 5.)	The Dutch, with nine sail of the line, creep out of the Texel, to escort a convoy of their own, and cut off the British Baltic fleet,	385
	Lord Howe sails from Spithead, with twelve sail of the line, and the Dutch run back to the Texel; Howe blockades the Texel,	385
	Wilkes, by a large majority, gets the resolution of the 17th February 1769, and the proceedings founded on it, expunged from the journals of the House,	378
	A bill is passed for regulating the office of paymaster of the forces,	379
	Rodney is created a baron, and is voted an additional pension of £2000 a year,	382, 383
	Sir Samuel Hood is created a baron in the peerage of Ireland,	383
(June 28.)	Howe, Barrington, and Kempenfelt sail westward,	385
	Lord Shelburne is made premier, and William Pitt chancellor of the Exchequer,	380
(Aug. 13.)	General Greene complains of the condition of his army,	384
	Various latitudes, in summer and autumn of this year, are vexed by storms and hurricanes,	385
(Sept. 13.)	Siege of Gibraltar continues,	387
	Reverses of the besiegers,	388, 389
(Oct. 11.)	The British fleet under Lord Howe passes the Straits of Gibraltar,	389
	The Spanish fleet is anchored between Algeciras and the Orange Grove,	389
(Oct. 14.)	Lord Howe relieves Gibraltar,	389
(Oct. 19.)	Howe is closely followed by the combined fleets of France and Spain,	389, 390
(Oct. 20.)	A trifling action ensues,	390
	The French army, which had served against Cornwallis, after being collected and marched to Boston, is shipped to the West Indies, to defend their own sugar islands,	385
	British settlements in Hudson's Bay destroyed by the French; the Spaniards capture the Bahama Islands,	385
	The British capture some Spanish forts on the Mosquito shore, and take from the Dutch all their forts on the African coast, except Cape Town and a few places in its neighbourhood, &c.,	385

HISTORY OF ENGLAND.

A.D.		PAGE
1782. (Nov. 14.)	Howe, with the remainder of his fleet, anchors at St Helen's,	390
(Dec. 5.)	Parliament meets; the speech from the throne announces that his majesty had offered to declare the American colonies free and independent states,	391
1783. (Jan. 20.)	The preliminaries of peace are signed at Paris,	392, 393
(Jan. 24.)	The preliminaries of peace are laid before parliament; a coalition takes place between Fox and Lord North, who attack ministers with the utmost violence,	393
(Feb. 21.)	Lord John Cavendish moves a series of resolutions condemning the recent treaty, which are carried,	394
	Negotiations about forming a new ministry continue between George III. and the coalition,	394, 395
(April 2.)	George III. surrenders to the coalition, and the Duke of Portland becomes first lord of the Treasury,	395
(June 17.)	A petition is presented to parliament by the Quakers for the total abolition of the slave-trade,	396
(Sept. 2.)	Preliminary articles of peace with the Dutch are signed at Paris,	396
(Sept. 3.)	The definitive treaties with France, Spain, and America are signed at Paris,	396
(Nov.)	Fox's India Bill is rejected by the Lords,	398
(Dec. 19.)	The coalition cabinet is dismissed,	399
	Pitt is appointed first lord of the Treasury and chancellor of the Exchequer,	399
1784. (Jan. 12.)	Fox moves the resumption of the debate on the state of the nation, which is carried by a majority of thirty-nine,	400
(Jan. 23.)	The New India Bill of Pitt is thrown out,	401
	Fox obtains leave to bring in a new India Bill of his own,	401
(Feb.)	Efforts are made by Fox and his friends to have the defeated ministers removed, but the king takes part with them,	401, 402
(Mar.)	Fox repeats his efforts,	403
	The Mutiny Bill and the supplies are voted,	403
(June 21.)	Pitt carries several measures for stopping smuggling,	404
(June 30.)	A bill for the restoration of the Scottish estates forfeited in 1745 is passed,	404
1785. (Jan.)	Mr Pitt introduces the plan for commercial relief to Ireland in the House of Commons,	587
	The House resolves to examine the merchants and manufacturers at its own bar,	587, 588
(April 18.)	Pitt introduces a bill for reform in the representation of the people; it is thrown out,	588
	During this session a tax is imposed upon female servants, and an additional tax on male servants,	589
1786. (Mar.)	Mutiny Bill altered,	595
(May 15.)	Pitt's new Sinking Fund, or scheme for discharging the National Debt by compound interest,	595-597
(May 22.)	A bill passes both Houses for transferring certain duties on wines from the Customs to the Excise,	597
(June.)	A bill passes for appointing commissioners to inquire into the state and condition of the woods and forests and land-revenues belonging to the crown,	597
	During this session Warren Hastings,	

A.D.		PAGE
1786.	late governor-general of India, is impeached,	598
(Aug. 2.)	Attempted assassination of George III.,	648
	The Prince of Wales goes to Windsor, and is received by the queen, but the king will not see him,	652
	The new king of Prussia, Frederick William II., and the court of Versailles interfere as mediators between the Prince of Orange and the democratic party,	653, 654
(Sept. 29.)	A treaty of commerce and navigation is signed with France,	655, 656
(Dec.)	The French minister at the Hague breaks off negotiations in an abrupt manner, and sets off for Paris,	654
	Baron Goertz, the Prussian minister, is recalled,	654
	The authority of the Prince of Orange as stadtholder confirmed,	654
	Disturbances in the towns of Hattem and Elburg,	654, 655
	The Prince of Orange suspended by the states from all his military functions,	655
1787. (Jan. 1.)	The emperor of Austria, Joseph II., annihilates what was left of the old municipal liberty, &c., in Belgium,	682
	Joseph II. suppresses all the theological colleges in Belgium,	683
	A bill for the relief of insolvent debtors passes the Commons, but is thrown out in the Lords,	669
(Feb. 1, 2.)	Burke proceeds with his impeachment of Hastings,	672-676
(Feb. 12.)	The House of Commons debate upon the French treaty of commerce and navigation of Sept. 29, 1786,	657-662
(Feb. 22.)	The Assembly of Notables meet at Versailles,	740
(Feb. 26.)	Pitt's bill for consolidating the various duties upon articles of the Customs and Excise passes,	664
(Mar. 8.)	The treaty of commerce and navigation with France is approved of by both Houses,	662
(April.)	The states of Brabant take cognizance of the oppressions of their Austrian emperor, and refuse the customary subsidies until their grievances shall be redressed, &c.,	684
	The states of Flanders and Hainault do the same,	684
(April 26.)	A bill passes to authorise the commissioners of the Treasury to let out to farm the duties on post-horses,	669
(April 30.)	Fox denies *in toto* the marriage of the Prince of Wales with Mrs Fitzherbert,	666
(May 3.)	Pitt has an interview with the prince at Carleton House,	666
(May 24.)	The House of Commons vote the payment of the Prince of Wales's debts,	668
(May 25.)	The Assembly of Notables are dissolved by Louis XVI.,	740
	The Flemings still distrust their emperor, and enrol themselves as a volunteer militia,	684
(June.)	The Princess of Orange is insulted by a party of armed burghers,	676
	She applies to her brother, Frederick William II. of Prussia,	677
(July 10.)	The king of Prussia transmits a strong memorial to the states of Holland,	677
	The states of Holland reply, by another memorial, very unsatisfactory,	677
	The Emperor Joseph II. demands that the states of the Netherlands send deputies to Vienna,	685

CHRONOLOGICAL INDEX. 63

A.D.	PAGE
1787. (Aug. 6.) A *lit de justice* is held at Versailles, and the edicts are registered by royal command amid the silence of the parliament,	740
(Aug. 7.) The parliament of Paris protests,	740, 741
All the provincial parliaments join in sympathy with that of Paris; troubles break out in various parts of France,	741
(Aug. 15.) The deputies from Flanders are admitted to an audience of Joseph II. at Vienna, where he insists that all things in the provinces shall be put on the previous footing; the states are indignant,	685
Frederick William II. of Prussia sends another memorial to the states of Holland, insisting upon very humiliating terms,	678
Prussian troops are collected, under the Duke of Brunswick, on the frontiers of the United Provinces,	678
The Prince of Orange captures the towns of Wick and Harderwick,	678
The province of Zealand declares for the stadtholder,	678
The Dutch democrats declare it a high crime and misdemeanour to wear the Orange colours, and hang two men in the streets for doing so, &c.,	679
(Sept.) Louis XVI. recalls the parliament to Paris, and promises to withdraw the obnoxious land-tax and stamp-duty, lately imposed,	741
(Sept. 13.) The Duke of Brunswick enters Guelderland with 30,000 men,	679
(Sept. 17.) He takes Gorcum; the Dutch now abandon town after town, and mount the Orange cockade,	679
Nieuport, Schoonhoven, Dort, Leyden, Haarlem, and Rotterdam, all surrender without firing a gun,	680
The people of the Hague rise upon the republican volunteers, and drive them out of the town, or make them prisoners	680
Disturbances arise in Brussels,	685
Joseph II.'s declaration is published that the fundamental laws of the Belgian provinces shall be preserved entire, according to the tenor of the Joyous Entry,	686
(Oct. 10.) Amsterdam capitulates to the Duke of Brunswick,	681
Riots take place in the city,	681
The stadtholder is reinstated,	682
(Nov. 19.) Louis XVI. appears suddenly at the Palais de Justice, and compels the registration of a new edict for enormous loans,	741
(Dec. 5.) The Hessian subsidy of £36,003 for the year 1788 is agreed to,	687
(Dec. 10.) Grants are passed for the augmentation of the army, and for erecting fortifications in the West Indies,	687, 688
1788. (Jan. 31.) Charles Stuart, the Pretender, dies at Rome, and is buried with royal honours,	720
(Feb. 13.) The trial of Warren Hastings commences,	693, 694
(Mar. 14.) Pitt's declaratory bill for India passes,	690
A clause is introduced into the Mutiny Act, to incorporate with the army a newly raised corps of military artificers,	690
(April 28.) Sir Elijah Impey acquitted by the House of Commons,	693
(July 11.) A bill passes for the better regulation of the slave ships,	691
George III. prorogues parliament,	694, 695
Lafayette organises the Breton Club in	

A.D.	PAGE
1788. Paris; the troops begin to sympathise with the people; the Duc d'Orleans disseminates money, and encourages inflammatory speeches,	741
The tax-payers become refractory, and a drought, succeeded by a terrific hail-storm, destroys the crops, producing intense misery among the starving people,	741
(Aug. 24.) Necker becomes prime minister of France,	741
(Nov. 5.) George III. is afflicted with madness,	295
(Dec.) He is removed from Windsor to Kew, and placed more immediately under the charge of the Rev. Dr Willis,	697
(Dec. 12.) A debate ensues on the right of the Prince of Wales to the regency,	698
(Dec. 16.) The House of Commons resolves itself into a committee on the state of the nation; Pitt proposes three resolutions; they are all carried,	699-701
During this year disturbances take place in the Austrian Netherlands,	732-736
Many of the nobility and gentry seek temporary shelter in France and Holland,	735
1789. (Jan. 2.) William Wyndham Grenville is elected speaker on the death of Cornwall,	703
The Prince of Wales is appointed regent during his father's illness,	704
Intrigues, cabals, and difficulties take place in Sweden by the nobles against the king, Gustavus III.,	29
The states of Brabant refuse to vote any subsidies whatsoever; the Emperor Joseph II. recalls his oath to observe the terms of the Joyous Entry,	736
He arrests and banishes many persons, and intimates his intention of establishing, by military force, absolute government in the Netherlands,	736
Nearly all the nobility, gentry, clergy, manufacturers, merchants, burghers, and substantial farmers openly declare against Joseph II.,	736
(Feb.) Pitt's Regency Bill is read a first time,	708
(Feb. 9.) George III. is reported much better,	710
(Feb. 10.) The Emperor Joseph II. issues a formal declaration of war against the Ottoman Porte,	721
(Feb. 11.) The Irish parliament requests the Prince of Wales to take upon himself the government of the kingdom, as Prince Regent of Ireland, during the continuance of George III.'s indisposition,	713
(Feb. 12.) The Regency Bill passes the Commons, limiting the restriction on the making of peers to three years; it is sent up to the Lords,	712
(Feb. 19.) Lord Chancellor Thurlow announces that George III. has been for some time in a state of convalescence,	712
He moves that their lordships do not proceed with the Regency Bill; the motion is carried,	712
George III. is pronounced perfectly free from his complaint,	713, 714
(Mar.) An illumination takes place in London,	716
(Mar. 18.) £218,000 are granted for the extraordinaries of the Ordnance,	716
Pitt procures and guarantees a strict neutrality from Denmark to Sweden,	731
(April 2.) The shop-tax is repealed, and the additional tax and restrictions on hawkers and pedlers is abolished,	716

A.D.		PAGE
1789. (April 23.)	Is observed as a day of public thanksgiving for the recovery of George III.,	716, 717
(April 27.)	A disturbance takes place in Paris,	742
(May 4.)	The states-general of France assemble to the number of 1139; they, Louis XVI., and court, go in solemn procession to a religious service,	742
	Mobs enter the hall, converse with the deputies, scoff and insult the nobles and clergy; the deputies make violent speeches at their clubs in the evening,	743
	Bailly, the president of the Tiers Etat, in presenting an address to Louis XVI., studiously avoids all show of respect,	743
	Hostilities recommence in Finland between the Swedes and Russians, and several bloody actions take place,	731
(June.)	Gustavus III. assumes the command of his army, and gains a victory over the Russians,	732
	The Russians besiege Oczakoff,	722
(June 10.)	Pitt opens the budget,	717
(June 12.)	The Tiers Etat send a message to Louis XVI., the noblesse, and the clergy, that they are about to form themselves into a working assembly for legislative purposes, and inviting co-operation,	743
	No official assent is given, but some of the order of clergy take their seats among the deputies of the Tiers Etat,	743
(June 16.)	The Tiers Etat give themselves the name of the National Assembly,	743
(June 17.)	The Abbé Sieyes announces that the National Assembly represent the nation; they vote by acclamation various resolutions touching the price of corn, the misery of the people, &c., and that no taxes shall be valid without their assent,	743, 744
(June 24.)	One hundred and forty-eight priests or clergy, headed by Talleyrand, the archbishop of Vienne, and the bishop of Chartres join the deputies,	744
	Differences between the Tiers Etat and Louis XVI. grow more serious,	744
(June 26.)	The streets are rent with furious cries against the queen, the Comte d'Artois, the archbishop of Paris, and all unfavourable to the National Assembly,	744
	The clergy join them in a body,	744
	Orleans and a minority of peers also join them, and are received with tumultuous acclamations,	745
(June 27.)	The remainder of the nobles join the Tiers Etat,	745
	Great excitement prevails throughout France,	745
(July 1.)	Louis XVI. pardons the soldiers at the instigation of the Paris mob,	745
	The Duc de Broglie, head of the army, assembles 50,000 troops in Paris and Versailles, and on the road communicating with the two,	745
	Necker resigns, or is dismissed,	745
(July 12.)	Camille Desmoulins harangues the mob in the courtyard of the Palais Royal,	745
	The Parisian mob grows more riotous,	745
	Members of the French guard join them; Paris is wholly in their power,	745
	The National Assembly address Louis XVI. to withdraw the troops from Paris,	746
(July 14.)	The Bastille is stormed,	746
	The mob hang or maltreat many of the Swiss and invalid soldiers, while the	

A.D.		PAGE
1789.	Châtelet, and other prisons, become the scenes of renewed disorders,	746, 747
	The National Assembly send deputation after deputation to Louis XVI. to withdraw the troops from Paris, &c.,	747
(July 15.)	Louis XVI. orders all the troops to quit the capital, &c.,	747
	The excitement extends to Lyons, Caen, Rouen, and many other towns where the people rise,	747
	The Marshal de Broglie resigns, and quits France, narrowly escaping massacre; the Comte d'Artois, the Prince de Condé, Prince Polignac, and a host of nobles and high ecclesiastics also expatriate themselves,	747
(July 16.)	The Tobacco Bill passes the Commons,	718
	Louis XVI. sanctions the appointments of Bailly and Lafayette; expresses approval of all that has been done; puts on a tricolor cockade, and returns to Versailles,	747
	Many terrible massacres and scenes of violence occur during the remaining days of July; Necker is recalled,	747, 748
(July 26.)	Swedes defeated at sea by the Russians and Danes,	732
	Gustavus III. continues victorious by land,	732
(Aug. 4.)	In the National Assembly many of the higher orders voluntarily renounce pensions and privileges; a long list of reforms is agreed to, and extravagant fraternisation ensues,	748
(Aug. 5.)	Tithes are done away with,	748, 749
	The populace name Louis XVI. Monsieur Veto,	749
(Aug. 11.)	The Tobacco Bill passes the Lords,	718
(Aug. 25.)	The Russians again defeat the Swedes at sea,	732
(Sept. 14.)	Duke d'Arembrerg and others constitute a legal assembly of the states,	736
	They remonstrate with Joseph II.,	736
	Necker proposes, and the Assembly accept, that every French subject shall give to the state an extraordinary contribution of a fourth of his yearly income, to be paid at different times in three years, and to exempt the working-classes altogether,	750
	France suffers from famine,	750
(Sept. 22.)	The Austrians and Russians defeat the Turks at Martinitzi, in Wallachia,	728
(Oct. 1.)	A grand banquet is given at Versailles to the officers of the Flanders regiment; anti-popular songs are sung, &c.,	751
	Later in the evening the feast degenerates into an anti-democratic orgy,	751, 752
	The news, amplified, is carried to Paris; cries arise of Bread—bread! To Versailles—to Versailles! &c.,	752
	Stanislas Maillard, a National Guard, leads a mob of women to Versailles,	752, 753
	Louis XVI. manages to dismiss them with a few kind words, and promises of bread,	753
	Louis XVI. signs the document brought him by Mounier concerning the rights of man,	753
	Bailly and Lafayette arrive at Versailles with 30,000 National Guards, and about an equal number of the undisciplined mob,	753
	Lafayette urges Louis XVI. to come and reside in Paris,	753, 754
	The royal family return,	754

CHRONOLOGICAL INDEX.

A.D.		PAGE
1789.	The National Assembly renew their sittings,	755
	The Breton Club transfers its sittings to the hall of the convent of the Jacobins, and thence obtains the name of the Jacobin Club,	755
	The National Assembly review the financial state of the nation,	756
(Oct. 8.)	Belgrade, after a long siege, capitulates to the Austrians,	728
	Potemkin defeats the Turks at Tabac, near Bender,	728
	The Netherlands militia and volunteers drive Joseph II.'s garrisons out of Forts Lillo and Liefenshoeck,	736
	General Schröder retakes the forts, but is defeated at Turnhout,	736
(Nov. 2.)	The National Assembly confiscate all church property,	756
	Four hundred millions of assignats are put in circulation,	756
	The provincial parliaments are suppressed,	757
(Nov. 4.)	An association, called 'The Revolution Society,' meets in London to celebrate the memory of William III.,	757
	Many clubs are formed in England to encourage and disseminate liberal opinions; counter-societies also are formed,	757
	General Bender is defeated at Tirlemont by the Netherlanders,	737
	General Arberg is also routed; Louvain, Ghent, Bruges, Ostend, and other important cities proclaim their independence,	737
	Joseph II. tries to conciliate them,	737
(Nov. 20.)	The states of Flanders declare Joseph II. to have forfeited all right and title to the sovereignty,	737
	Dalton is forced to withdraw into Luxembourg,	738
	The Russians take Bender and several other important places between the Bog and the Dnieper,	728
(Dec. 17.)	The Russians take Oczakoff by storm,	723
(Dec. 31.)	The states of Brabant and Flanders enter into a league, offensive and defensive,	738
1790. (Jan.)	In the Netherlands, the Patriotic Assembly at Brussels becomes nearly as revolutionary as the Jacobin Club at Paris,	792, 793
(Jan. 12.)	The united Belgic States decree a strict censorship,	793
(Jan. 21.)	Parliament is opened by George III. in person,	757
	Fox draws down many animadversions by praising the conduct of the French army,	758
(Feb. 4.)	Louis XVI., king of France, makes a speech to the National Assembly,	781, 782
	An oath of loyalty and patriotism is everywhere taken,	782
(Feb. 9.)	Discussions take place in the Commons; Fox defending, and Burke condemning the French Revolution,	758
(Feb. 16.)	Hastings's trial recommences at Westminster Hall,	770
(Feb. 20.)	The Emperor Joseph II. dies, and is succeeded by Leopold II.,	774
(Mar. 2.)	Fox brings forward the subject of the repeal of the Test and Corporation Acts,	758, 759
(Mar. 4.)	A motion is made for leave to bring in a bill to amend the representation of the people in parliament; it is withdrawn,	759

A.D.		PAGE
1790.	The National Assembly discuss when their own powers are to cease,	782
	The Jacobin Club is in greater favour with the people than the National Assembly,	782, 783
	The Belgians quarrel among themselves; the democratic party gains the ascendency; Duke of Ursel ill used,	793
(Mar. 31.)	Dundas opens the Indian budget, announcing great increase of revenue, &c.,	760
(April 15.)	Pitt opens the budget for the year with congratulations on the prosperous state of the finances of the country,	760, 761
	The troops of the Emperor Leopold II. defeat the disorganised and ill-commanded Belgians wherever they meet them,	794
	The Emperor Leopold II. issues a memorial, solemnly pledging himself to observe every article of the Joyous Entry, and to restore the states to their original constitution,	794
	He puts an end to the causes of discontent in Hungary, and obtains from it both money and men,	794, 795
	War breaks out between England and Tippoo Saib, who despatches a secret message to France for assistance,	797
	Colonel Floyd obliged to retreat before the Mysore army,	707, 708
	The Bengal government raise two armies,	798
(May 11.)	Burke calls the attention of the House to the protracted continuance of Hastings's trial,	770, 771
(May 16.)	The British minister at Madrid lays a strong remonstrance before the court on the subject of Nootka Sound,	765
	Tippoo evacuates the Travancore country, and retreats to Seringapatam,	798
(June 4.)	An armistice is agreed upon between the Emperor Leopold II. and the Sultan,	775
	Treaty at Reichenbach,	775
(June 4.)	Charles IV. of Spain sends a declaration to all European courts on the subject of the 'unexpected' dispute between his court and that of Great Britain,	765, 766
(June 19.)	The Assembly decree that all hereditary titles shall be abolished, and all citizens shall take in future their family and patronymic names; no liveries shall be worn by servants or bear a coat-of-arms or escutcheon,	785
	The Champ de Mars is prepared for a national fête,	785, 786
(June 22.)	Lord Howe is appointed to the command of the British fleet,	768
	General Medows drives Tippoo Saib beyond the mountains,	798
	Abercrombie reduces nearly all the places held by the enemy on the Malabar coast; the Rajah of Travancore is re-established in his dominions,	798
(July 3.)	The Swedes are defeated by the Russians in the Bay of Viborg,	778
(July 9.)	The Swedes, in their turn, defeat the Russians with immense loss,	778
	The Empress Catherine II. sues for peace,	778
(July 12-14.)	The grand fête takes place; universal jubilation ensues,	786, 787
	Mirabeau has an interview with the queen,	788
(Aug. 14.)	A treaty is entered into at Warela between Russia and Sweden,	779
	The Duke of Orleans returns to France,	789
	The Marquis Bouillé is made commander of all the forces on the eastern frontier of France,	780

A.D.		PAGE
1790.	The Imperialists, under General Bender, are concentrated on the frontiers of Belgium; the Belgian Congress are refused assistance by other nations,	795
(Sept. 4.)	Necker resigns,	790
	Towards the end of the year, the Jacobin and Cordelier Clubs gain an obvious ascendency over the National Assembly,	790
	The Duke of Orleans introduces his son, the Duc de Chartres, to the Jacobin Club, and takes his turn as door-keeper,	791
(Oct.)	Religion is treated with more and more disrespect in France; irreligious clubs are formed,	791, 792
	Marat lashes the people to frenzy by his writings in the journal called *L'Ami du Peuple*,	792
	The Emperor Leopold II. satisfies the people of Belgium,	795
(Nov.)	General Bender crosses the Meuse, and advances on Brussels,	796
(Dec. 2.)	Brussels surrenders to the Austrians, and all the cities of Flanders and Brabant follow the example,	796
(Dec. 10.)	A convention is signed at the Hague between Austria, Great Britain, Holland, and Prussia, restoring all the old rights and privileges to Belgium,	796
	During the summer and autumn a savage and desultory war is carried on between the Russians and the Turks,	797
(Dec. 25.)	Ismael is assaulted and carried with dreadful slaughter,	779–801
1791. (Jan.)	The National Assembly decree that a civil oath, 'serment civique,' shall be taken by all the ecclesiastics yet remaining in France; Louis XVI. assents,	825, 826
	The priests are expelled from many municipalities,	826
	Another club, called the Société Fraternelle, is established,	827
	Only four bishops, of whom one is Talleyrand, another Loménie de Brienne, take the oath; the others, 132, are expelled from their dioceses,	827, 828
	The curés, professors in colleges, teachers in schools, and other functionaries, similarly expelled, amount to nearly 80,000,	828
	The Abbés Grégoire, Lindet, Gouttes, and Lamourette, become bishops of Blois, Evreux, Autun, and Lyons,	828
	The new bishops demand communion with the Holy See, recognising it as the centre of Catholic Unity,	828
	The new bishops and curés preach sermons laudatory of the revolution,	828
	The Assembly interdict appeals to the pope,	828
	After the extradition of the clergy, the pope in a formal document declares the 'serment civique' impious, &c.,	828
	Many of the new bishops and priests resign their offices, and abandon the country,	828
	Many insermenté priests continue to be upheld by the peasantry,	828
(Feb. 22.)	An émeute occurs among the women of Paris,	829
	The gaming-houses are suppressed,	830
	A large number of royalist nobles and gentlemen go singly to the Tuileries, and gain admission, fearing that the	

A.D.		PAGE
1791.	life of Louis XVI. is about to be menaced,	830
	The guard ignominiously eject them, and they are brutally treated by the mob,	830
	Marat accuses Lafayette and Bailly of being at the bottom of the whole affair,	830
(April 2.)	Mirabeau dies,	830, 831
(April 4.)	He has a solemn public funeral at the Church of St Geneviève,	831
	The Jacobin journals begin to denounce Louis XVI.; Danton ferociously declaims against him,	831
	Lafayette throws up the command of the National Guard, but withdraws his resignation,	831
	Robespierre rises rapidly into power in the Assembly,	831
(April 18.)	Mr Wilberforce moves for leave to bring in a bill to prevent the further importation of slaves into the British colonies in the West Indies; the motion is negatived,	815, 816
(May 6.)	The Quebec Bill is recommitted,	806–813
(May 16.)	Robespierre moves and carries a decree, that no member of the present legislature shall be eligible to the next,	831
	He attempts to obtain a decree for universal suffrage, but fails,	831
	He obtains a decree abolishing the punishment of death, except in cases which the legislature may declare to be high treason,	831
	Louis XVI. announces his intention to leave Paris,	833
(May 18.)	The Quebec Bill passes,	814
	Lord Cornwallis, after conquering Bangalore, carries the war into Mysore,	853
(May 15.)	Cornwallis defeats Tippoo at Arikera,	854
(May 24.)	Dundas lays before the House of Commons an account of the state of the finances of India,	819
(June 3.)	Sheridan moves no fewer than forty resolutions calculated to discredit the management of the finances; some are adopted or amended,	818, 819
(June 6.)	The libel case bill is thrown out by the Lords,	818
(June 10.)	'Church of St Geneviève converted into a pantheon,'	832
	On account of the scarcity of money, the Assembly order the church bells to be coined,	832
(June 20.)	Flight of Louis XVI.,	832
	The Assembly assume sovereign power,	832, 833
	The populace attack the Tuileries,	833
	Santerre, Danton, &c., excite the mob of Paris,	833
	The busts of Louis XVI. are destroyed; crowns, king, queen, dauphin, royal, Bourbon, &c., effaced from sign-boards, &c.,	833
	At midnight, Louis XVI. and royal family are stopped at Varennes by Drouet and the mayor of Varennes,	834
	The royal family are brought back to Paris, and are insulted,	835
	The Tuileries is guarded,	836
	During this week Marie Antoinette's hair becomes white from grief,	836
	In the clubs, Lafayette, Bailly, Barnave, and Lameth, are denounced as traitors to the nation,	836, 837
(July 5.)	Two hundred and seventy of the moderate members of the Assembly protest against the decrees launched at Louis XVI.,	837

CHRONOLOGICAL INDEX.

A.D.		PAGE
1791.	(July 14.) The apotheosis of Voltaire,	838
	(July 17.) The Jacobins and Cordeliers call a meeting of patriots to meet in the Champ de Mars, to sign a petition for the abolition of royalty,	837
	An immense concourse assembles in the Champ de Mars round the altar of the Federation,	837
	The populace demand the re-election of the Assembly and the deposition of Louis XVI.,	837
	Many arrests of violent republican journalists take place,	837
	(July 18.) The Assembly approve of the conduct of Bailly and Lafayette,	837
	(Aug.) The Assembly revise the constitution,	838
	Cornwallis takes Oussoor, Rajahcottah, Nundydroog, Savondroog, Ootradroog, and other hill-forts in his way,	854
	(Sept. 13.) Louis XVI. accepts the constitution *pur et simple*,	838
	(Sept. 29.) It is decreed that the clubs can have no political existence, &c.,	839
	Decrees are passed giving the rights of free citizens to Jews and negroes,	839
	(Sept. 30.) The National Assembly are dissolved,	839
	(Oct. 1.) The Legislative or Constituent Assembly commence their sittings in Paris,	840
	Lafayette resigns the command of the National Guard,	844
	Louis XVI. visits the Assembly, and expresses his pleasure at meeting them, &c.,	841
	(Oct. 20.) Severe decrees are passed against the emigrants,	843
	(Nov. 16.) Bailly resigns the mayoralty of Paris,	844
	Pétion is elected mayor; Manuel, procureur of the commune; and Danton, substitut-adjoint to the procureur,	844, 845
	(Nov. 19.) Louis XVI. refuses to sanction the harsh decree against the unsworn priests of La Vendée,	844
	(Nov. 29.) Severe decrees are passed against the priests, and a religious war inaugurated,	842
	A decree is passed that Louis XVI. shall declare war against the German princes,	846
	(Dec.) The Count de Narbonne, minister of war, states to the Assembly that Louis XVI. had commissioned him to assemble an army on the frontier, within a month, of 150,000 men,	846
	That Lafayette, Rochambeau, and Luckner would be appointed to command the three armies which it was to be divided into,	846
	The Legislative Assembly are divided into three parties—a Droit, a Centre, and a Gauche,	847
1792.	(Feb.) Cornwallis arrives at Seringapatam,	854
	(Feb. 6.) He defeats the Mysoreans,	854
	(Feb. 7.) Tippoo is driven into his fortress,	854, 855
	(Feb. 13.) Debates take place on Russo-Turkish affairs,	848
	(Feb. 17.) Resolutions are passed for a diminution or removal of various taxes,	849
	(Feb. 24.) Tippoo offers to submit to terms of capitulation,	855
	A bill passes for the establishment of five police-offices in the metropolis, and giving increased power to justices, magistrates, and constables,	850
	(Mar. 16.) Gustavus III. of Sweden is shot by Count Ankarström at a masked ball at Stockholm,	857
	(Mar. 19.) The arrangements with Tippoo are definitively signed; England acquires all	

A.D.		PAGE
1792.	Tippoo's territories on the coast of Malabar, &c.,	855
	The Emperor Leopold II. of Austria dies, and is succeeded by Francis II.,	856
	The French ministry is dismissed, and the Girondists enter office; it is called the 'sans-culotte ministry,'	858
	The Assembly rescind the decree for the abolition of capital punishments, and decide that the mode of decapitation shall be by the guillotine,	859
	Scenes of bloodshed are continual in Avignon, Provence, and Languedoc,	859
	Robespierre is called to account in the Jacobin Club, for having spoken of Almighty God watching over the salvation of the free French people,	859
	(April 2.) Mr Wilberforce carries a measure in the Commons against slavery,	849, 850
	(April 15.) The Fête of Liberty takes place in the Champ de Mars,	860
	(April 23.) Several resolutions regarding the slave-trade, and its total abolition in 1796, are carried in the Commons, but defeated in the Lords,	850
	(May.) Dumouriez sketches a plan of campaign,	860, 861
	Fox's libel bill passes into a law,	852
	General Dillon's division is put to flight near Tournay,	861
	(May 18.) The Empress Catherine II.'s manifesto against the new Polish constitution is made public, and on the same day 100,000 Russians and Cossacks cross the frontier,	856
	(May 30.) Louis XVI.'s guard is dissolved,	861
	(May 31.) Stanislaus Augustus II. of Poland applies for aid to Frederick William II. of Prussia,	857
	(June.) The Assembly award transportation or imprisonment to all priests who have refused to take the 'serment civique,'	862
	Louis XVI. refuses to sign either decree,	862
	(June 3.) Frederick William II. of Prussia sends an insulting letter to Stanislaus Augustus II., and announces that he shall not interfere to save Poland from Russia,	857
	(June 13.) Roland, Servan, and Clavières are dismissed; they appeal to the Assembly, who take up their cause as martyrs to patriotism,	862
	In spite of George III.'s proclamation, now editions of the *Rights of Man* are published, and political clubs and societies persevere in meeting and passing resolutions,	852
	(June 17.) Kosciuszko brilliantly repulses the Russians at Dubienka,	857
	(June 18.) The Poles repel an attack at Zielonce by a superior army,	857
	Stanislaus Augustus II. of Poland applies for an armistice, which is contemptuously refused,	857
	Lafayette denounces mob-rule to the Assembly from his camp at Maubenge,	862
	Louis XVI. is forced to stand on a table for four hours with a cap of liberty on his head, and to drink to liberty and the nation,	863
	(June 28.) Lafayette enters Paris suddenly; he goes to the Assembly; demands the punishment of the rioters of the 20th and the suppression of the Jacobin and Cordelier Clubs,	863
	The Assembly appoint a committee to consider his suggestions,	864
	(June 29.) Lafayette starts off to join the army,	864
	(July 2.) A theatrical reconciliation takes place	

A.D.		PAGE
1792.	between the different parties in the Assembly,	864
(July 10.)	The French ministry resign,	864
(July 11.)	The Assembly vote 'The country is in danger,'	864
	A bonfire is made, consisting of crowns, coronets, genealogy-books, parchment-titles of nobility, and other emblems of aristocratic institutions,	865
	The Duke of Brunswick, commanding the allies on the frontiers, fulminates a manifesto against the French republicans,	866
	The rage of the French nation at this document is indescribable,	866
	Armed bodies of men arrive from Marseilles, singing the Marseilless Hymn,	866
(July 23.)	Stanislaus Augustus II. of Poland signs the Act of Confederation of Targowica,	857
(Aug. 4.)	Pétion demands the dethronement of Louis XVI.,	867
	All the sections of Paris demand the dethronement of Louis XVI. but one,	867
(Aug. 9.)	Intercepted letters from the emigrant princes are read in the Assembly,	868
	Paris is greatly excited,	868
(Aug. 9, 10.)	The tocsin sounds; all over Paris armed bands appear in every section,	868
	Danton declares 'that the people must strike or be stricken,'	868
	Royalists and Feuillants flock to the Tuileries, to aid if possible their unfortunate sovereign,	869
	The mob commence to acts of murder,	869
	The royal family take refuge with the Assembly,	869, 870
	The Swiss defend the Tuileries,	870
	They are massacred,	870, 871
	The Assembly vote that the National Convention shall be elected by universal suffrage of all citizens of age,	872
	A new ministry is formed of three Girondists and three Jacobins,	872
	Pétion is re-elected mayor,	872
	Anacharsis Clootz, the 'orator of mankind,' makes an oration on the rights of man and the vices of kings,	872
	Louis XVI. and royal family are lodged in the tower of the Temple,	872
	The Princess de Lamballe is imprisoned in La Force,	873
(Aug. 17.)	The Assembly appoint a 'court to try the enemies of the people,'	873
	Le Nain, the sculptor, presents a bust of the elder Brutus to the Jacobin Club,	874
	The Assembly decree all bronze crucifixes and statues of saints to be melted down for casting into cannon, and the iron railings of churches and palaces to be converted into pikes, &c.,	874
	Lafayette imprisons three commissioners,	874
(Aug. 19.)	He is captured by the Austrians,	874
	Dumouriez is appointed commander-in-chief of the Army of the North,	875
(Aug. 22.)	The allies capture Longwy,	875
	The Assembly decree a levy of 30,000 new troops,	875
(Aug. 29.)	Danton proposes a scheme to excite the 'terror' of the royalists,	875, 876
(Sept. 1.)	A false report is circulated that Verdun had fallen by treachery,	876
	Armed citizens march for Verdun,	876
	On the 2d and four following days Paris is imbued with blood; the September massacres; the Princess de Lamballe is murdered,	876-880

A.D.		PAGE
1792. (Sept. 9.)	The allies force the passage at La Croix-aux-bois,	881
	Dumouriez regains his lost advantage,	881
	The Duke of Brunswick's force amounts to about 65,000 men, Dumouriez' about 75,000,	881
(Sept. 20.)	Brunswick attacks Kellermann at Valmy,	881
	The Dukes of Chartres and Montpensier, sons of the Duke of Orleans, are present as officers,	881
	Montesquiou captures the valuable fortress of Montmelian, near the Pass of Mont Cenis,	884
	The National Convention is divided into the Girondists, Mountain, and Plain, 884,	885
	Two Englishmen are chosen members— Thomas Payne and Dr Priestley,	885
	The Convention decree, amongst other things, *the abolition of royalty*,	885
(Sept. 23.)	General Anselme captures Nice,	884
	The citadel of Mont Albano, overhanging Nice, is captured,	884
	The French are checked at Saorgio,	884
	Admiral Truguet bombards Oneglia, and massacres the inhabitants for an alleged informality to a flag of truce,	884
(Sept. 30.)	General Custine takes the city of Spires,	883
	The Duke of Brunswick strikes his camp, and retreats towards the frontier,	882
(Oct. 5.)	Custine takes the city of Worms,	883
	Dumouriez goes to Paris, and is fêted,	882
	Saxe Teschen, Austrian general in the Netherlands, bombards Lille; Dumouriez compels him to retreat,	882
(Oct. 21.)	Custine takes Mayence,	883
(Oct. 27.)	He enters Frankfort,	883, 884
(Oct. 27.)	Dumouriez crosses into the Austrian Netherlands,	882
(Oct. 29.)	Louvet accuses Robespierre of various crimes, &c.,	886
(Nov. 5.)	Robespierre is acquitted,	886
	Robespierre, the 'incorruptible,' is received with enthusiasm by the Jacobin Club,	886, 887
(Nov. 5.)	The battle of Jemappe,	882
	Tournay, Courtrai, Menin, Bruges, Nienport, Ostend, successively open their gates to the French, and all Hainault and Flanders belong to the French,	882
	Saxe Teschen retreats to Brussels; Dumouriez follows him,	882
(Nov. 14.)	Brussels surrenders to Dumouriez,	882
	Dumouriez takes Mechlin, and orders the siege of Antwerp and Namur,	882
(Nov. 27.)	He defeats Saxe Teschen at Tirlemont; the Austrians are also defeated at Liege on the same day; Saxe Teschen finally retreats,	882, 883
	Antwerp, Liege, and Namur successively surrender,	883
(Dec. 2.)	Dumouriez is master of all the Austrian Netherlands, except the duchy of Luxembourg; Jacobin clubs are formed in Liege and Brussels,	883
	Danton and Lacroix, commissioners from Paris to Liege, plunder the country,	883
(Dec. 3.)	Robespierre recommends that Louis XVI. be put to death without any trial at all,	888
(Dec. 10.)	The Convention agree that Louis XVI. shall be brought to their bar to-morrow,	889
(Dec. 11.)	Trial of Louis XVI. commences,	889-901
(Dec. 12.)	Dumouriez goes into winter-quarters at Aix-la-Chapelle,	883
(Dec. 19.)	During the debate in the Commons on the Alien Bill, Burke's famous dagger-scene takes place,	900

CHRONOLOGICAL INDEX. 69

A.D.		PAGE
1792. (Dec. 28.)	Spain promises to remain neutral, on condition that the life of Louis XVI. shall be spared,	892
1793. (Jan. 1.)	Several addresses are presented to the Convention from the departments, demanding the immediate execution of Louis XVI.,	892
(Jan. 14.)	The Hall of the Convention is surrounded by an immense crowd, vociferating 'Death to the Tyrant,'	892
	Philippe Egalité, once Duc d'Orleans, votes with the majority against Louis XVI.,	893

A.D.		PAGE
1793. (Jan. 20.)	Louis XVI. has a last interview with his family,	895
(Jan. 21.)	The execution of Louis XVI.,	895–897
(Jan. 23.)	The Convention vindicate their conduct to the French people,	897
(Jan. 30.)	The execution of Louis XVI. is announced to the House of Commons, the dismissal of the French ambassador, and the determination of the government to increase the land and sea forces,	900
(Feb. 2.)	Both Houses sanction the policy of war against the government of France,	900

VOLUME VI.

BOOK X.

A.D.		PAGE
1793.	The East India Company's charter is renewed,	1
(Jan.)	Frederick William II. of Prussia seizes Thorn and Dantzic,	5
(Feb. 3.)	The Polish diet protest against the Prussian invasion,	5
(Feb. 17.)	Dumouriez takes Breda; Klundert and Gertruydenburg capitulate,	3
	Dumouriez fails before Williamstadt,	3
(Feb. 25.)	Frightful disorders take place in Paris,	11
(Feb. 28.)	General Miazinski is defeated,	3
(Mar.)	The Traitorous Correspondence Bill passes,	1
(Mar. 1.)	The French under Miazinski are again defeated,	3
(Mar. 8.)	The Prince of Saxe Coburg defeats the French,	3
(Mar. 9.)	A new Extraordinary Criminal Tribunal is established in Paris,	12
(Mar. 18.)	Dumouriez is defeated,	3
	General Miazinski is guillotined,	4
	The partition of Poland,	6
	Frederick William II. of Prussia invests Mayence,	6
	The civil war breaks out in La Vendée,	20
	The Vendéans obtain many successes,	21
(April 2.)	Dumouriez makes prisoners of the commissioners from the Convention,	4
	Dumouriez is formally deposed by the Convention,	4
	He escapes across the frontier,	4
(April 12.)	Marat is committed to the Abbaye,	13
(April 24.)	He is tried and acquitted,	13
(April 30.)	The House of Commons grant leave to issue five millions of Exchequer bills,	2
(May 8.)	Dampierre, the successor of Dumouriez, is defeated and killed,	5
(May 10.)	The Convention transfer their sittings to the Tuileries, now styled The Palais National,	13
(May 23.)	Lamarche, who succeeded Dampierre, is defeated,	5
	The allies besiege Valenciennes, blockade Condé, and confront Lamarche,	5
(May 29.)	A society called the Republican Union is formed under the management of Robespierre, Marat, Danton, Chaumette, and Pache,	13
(May 30.)	The command of the National Guards is given to Henriot,	14
	The Convention decree that the Girondists be impeached, &c.,	14

A.D.		PAGE
1793.	Madame Roland is arrested,	14
	The French, under Defiers, are defeated by the Spaniards,	7
(June 1.)	The Reign of Terror,	14
	Marat is placed at the head of the National Guard and the Paris force,	14
(June 8.)	The French are repulsed at Fort Raus by the Italian artillery,	7
(June 12.)	The French are again repulsed,	7
	The Duke of Montferrat drives the French out of Upper Savoy,	7
	Kellermann and the Savoyard republicans compel him to retreat over Mont Cenis and the Little St Bernard,	7
	Lyons is captured by the troops of the Convention,	8
(June 21.)	Parliament is prorogued,	3
(July 13.)	Marat is assassinated by Charlotte Corday,	15
(July 17.)	The French defeat the Spaniards,	7
(July 17.)	Charlotte Corday is guillotined,	15
	Lord Hood obtains possession of Marseilles,	9
	General Cartaux cantons his army around Toulon,	9
	General O'Hara takes the command of the troops at Toulon,	10
	General Dugommier is appointed to the command of the French army at Toulon, and Napoleon Bonaparte to the artillery,	10
(July 22.)	Mayence surrenders to the Prussians,	6
	Condé is captured by the Austrians,	6
	Valenciennes is captured by the English,	6
(Aug.)	The Duke of York besieges Dunkirk,	6
	Robespierre is appointed a member of the Committee of Public Safety,	16
(Aug. 10.)	The statues of Liberty, Nature, and the People are worshipped,	16
	General Custine is guillotined,	16
	The Vendéans defeat General Kleber,	21
(Sept. 11.)	Quesnoy is captured by the Prince of Coburg,	6
(Sept. 15.)	The French are defeated by the Austrians,	6
(Sept. 17.)	The terrible 'Loi des Suspects' is passed by the Convention,	16
	Carrier goes to Nantes; and during the last four months of the year puts to death 15,000 persons,	21
	Similar atrocities take place at Lyons, Arras, Orange, and Bordeaux,	21
	A reformation is made of the calendar; the year is divided into four equal parts; the Sabbath is abolished, &c.,	22
	Installation of atheism,	22

HISTORY OF ENGLAND.

A.D.		PAGE
1793. (Oct. 7.)	Lyons surrenders to Couthon,	19
(Oct. 14.)	Marie Antoinette is tried before the Revolutionary Tribunal, and found guilty,	17
(Oct. 15.)	General Jourdan compels the Prince of Coburg to recross the Sambre,	6
	Marie Antoinette is guillotined,	17
(Oct. 18.)	The king of Sardinia is defeated at Giletta,	8
	Captain Saumarez captures a large French frigate off Barfleur,	8, 9
	The British capture Tobago, St Pierre, and Miquelon, and take possession of the western or French portion of the island of St Domingo,	9
	All the enemy's posts in the East Indies are taken,	9
	The Duke of Brunswick drives back the French,	6
	The Prussians besiege Landau,	6
	The Austrians besiege Strasburg,	6
	The command of the French army is given to General Hoche,	6
	Hoche beats off Wurmser,	6
	He is defeated by the Prussians under Brunswick,	6
(Oct. 31.)	Twenty Girondists are guillotined,	18
(Nov. 6.)	Philippe Egalité, Duke of Orleans, is guillotined,	18
(Nov. 7.)	Gobel, bishop of Paris, heads a procession of atheists to the Convention,	22
(Nov. 9.)	Madame Roland is guillotined,	19
	Roland commits suicide on news of her death,	19
(Nov. 10.)	The Feast of Reason is celebrated,	22
	A republican sabbath is celebrated in Paris every tenth day,	22
(Nov. 11.)	The churches are desecrated,	22
(Nov. 30.)	The English meet with a severe repulse at Toulon,	10
	Many of the Girondists are captured, and executed in the provinces,	19
	Bailly, the illustrious astronomer, is guillotined,	19
(Dec.)	Hoche surprises the Austrians,	6
	The French recover Weissemburg, Landau,' and their former frontier line, besides the Palatinate, where Hoche fixes his winter-quarters,	6
(Dec. 17.)	The English are again repulsed at Toulon,	10
	Sir Sidney Smith burns the ships and explodes the magazines,	10
	The French army enter Toulon; murder and massacre the inhabitants; the guillotine is made permanent,	11
	Admiral Gell sends the Scipio, 74, into Genoa harbour, where it seizes the Modeste, French frigate,	11
	The pope and the grand-master of the Knights of Malta close their ports against the French,	11
	In November and December the Vendéans meet with severe reverses,	21
	Seditious clubs are formed in various parts of Great Britain. Thomas Muir, Esq., advocate, and the Rev. Thomas Fyshe Palmer, are condemned to transportation,	24–30
1794. (Jan. 6.)	Skirving, secretary of the 'British Convention,' is condemned to be transported for fourteen years,	30
(Jan. 13.)	Margarot, London delegate to the 'British Convention,' is condemned to fourteen years' transportation,	30
	An augmentation of 85,000 men is voted for the navy,	23

A.D.		PAGE
1794. (Feb. 2.)	£19,939,000 are voted for the war, and a loan of £11,000,000,	23
(Feb. 7.)	Lord Hood blockades Corsica,	40
(Mar. 13.)	The Convention arrest Hébert, Ronsin, Vincent, Chabot, Bazire, and others,	55
(Mar. 14.)	Chaumette, Clootz, and Gobel are arrested,	55
	They are tried, condemned, and nineteen are guillotined,	55
(Mar. 25.)	The island of Martinique is conquered by the English,	38
	Madalinski raises the standard of independence at Cracow,	64
	Kosciuszko is made dictator,	64
	He imposes a property tax,	64
(Mar. 30.)	Herault de Sechelles, Camille Desmoulins, Philippeaux, Lacroix, and Danton are seized,	55
(April 5.)	Danton and fourteen others are put to death,	56
(April 6.)	The French violate the Genoese neutrality,	51
	Kosciuszko defeats the Russians at Raclawicő,	64, 65
(April 17.)	The Polish garrison of Warsaw drive the Russians out of the city,	65
(April 23.)	The Lithuanians burst into insurrection at Wilna,	65
	The Piedmontese are defeated by the French,	52
	St Lucie, Guadaloupe, and dependencies capitulate to the English,	38
	The Duke of York quarrels with the Austrian commanders, and refuses to serve under Clairfait,	43
	Francis II. of Austria takes the command of the allies,	43
	Pichegru captures Courtrai and Menin,	43
	Jourdan drives the Austrians from their lines at Luxembourg,	44
(May 1.)	The Spaniards are defeated at Roussillon,	49
(May 2.)	A bill for the abolition of the slave-trade is thrown out by the Lords,	33
(May 10.)	Jourdan is defeated at Tournay,	44
	The Habeas Corpus Act is suspended,	32
	John Thelwall, Horne Tooke, and others are committed to the Tower, charged with high treason,	32
	General Dumas drives the Piedmontese to Susa,	52, 53
(May 21.)	Bastia capitulates,	41
	General Whyte captures Port-au-Prince,	38
	A French squadron lands 2000 troops; they are joined by negroes and mulattoes,	38
	The French royalists are plundered, burnt, and murdered by the republicans,	39
(May.)	Two French corvettes are taken by Lord Howe's fleet,	33
	The Austrians defeat the republicans on the Sambre,	44
	The Duke of York is defeated,	45
	Clairfait defeats Pichegru at Ypres,	45
	Pichegru defeats Clairfait,	45
	The Prince of Orange defeats Jourdan,	45
(June 1.)	'The Glorious First of June,' Lord Howe's victory,	34, 35
(June 5.)	Kosciuszko is defeated at Sszezekociny,	65
(June 8.)	Another Polish corps is almost annihilated at Chelm,	65
(June 8.)	The 'Fête à l'Etre Suprême' is held,	57
	During the next six weeks 'eleven hundred and eight' victims are guillotined in Paris,	57
(June 15.)	Cracow surrenders,	65
	The ancient crown of Corsica is offered to George III. of Great Britain, and	

CHRONOLOGICAL INDEX.

A.D.		PAGE
1794.	accepted; Sir Gilbert Elliott is made viceroy,	42
(June 26.)	Coburg is defeated by Jourdan,	45, 46
	The allies retreat upon Antwerp and Louvain; the towns of Bruges, Oudenarde, and Tournay open their gates to the French; Valenciennes, Condé, Quesnoy, and Landrecies capitulate,	46
	Pichegru and Jourdan form a junction; they defeat Coburg,	46
(July.)	An Austrian army crosses the frontiers into Little Poland,	66
	The Prussians and Russians besiege Warsaw,	66
(July 5.)	Ghent opens its gates to the republicans,	46
(July 9.)	The French enter Brussels in triumph,	46
(July 13.)	Bonaparte receives a commission from the Convention,	53
(July 23.)	The French enter Antwerp in triumph,	46
	Clairfait abandons Louvain and Liege,	46
	Beaulieu evacuates Namur,	46
	The English abandon Antwerp,	46
(July 27, Aug. 1, 3.)	The Prussians and Russians sustain severe losses,	66
(July 27.)	Robespierre and others are arrested,	59
(July 28.)	They are guillotined,	59
	Within forty-eight hours, eighty-one persons, chiefly supporters of Robespierre, are condemned and guillotined,	60
	Changes take place in the British cabinet,	68
(Aug. 10.)	Calvi capitulates; Nelson loses an eye,	42
(Aug. 12.)	Wilna is bombarded, and a strong Russian army enters it,	66
(Sept.)	The whole of Great Poland falls into the possession of the Poles,	66
(Sept. 22.)	The allies abandon their strong positions, and retire across the Bormida to Acqui,	53
(Sept. 29–Oct. 3.)	Clairfait is forced to retreat across the Rhine; Cologne, Bonn, Coblentz, Worms, and other towns submit to the republicans, leaving them masters of every place except Mayence,	43
(Sept.)	Venloo, on the Maes, is carried by a coup de main, and Bois-le-Duc surrenders to the French,	48
(Oct. 10.)	Kosciuszko is defeated at Macziowicé,	67
	Nimeguen is taken by the French,	48
	Maestricht surrenders to Kleber,	48
	The Spaniards are defeated,	49
(Nov. 4.)	Suvaroff takes Praga,	67
(Nov. 6.)	Warsaw capitulates to Suvaroff,	67
	The Third Partition of Poland,	68
	Stanislaus Augustus II., king of Poland, abdicates,	68
(Nov. 22.)	Tooke is acquitted,	69
	The Jacobin Club is suppressed by the Convention,	61
(Dec. 16.)	Carrier, Pinard, and Moreau Grandmaison are guillotined,	62
	Thomas Paine is released from prison by the Convention,	62
	The French royalists in Guadaloupe are massacred,	39
(Dec. 30.)	George III. announces to parliament the conclusion of a treaty of amity, commerce, and navigation with the United States of America,	72
(Dec. 30.)	General Dundas drives the French beyond the Waal,	79
1795. (Jan. 6.)	Pichegru crosses the Waal; the British retreat,	79
(Jan. 7.)	An augmentation of seamen and marines is agreed to,	73
(Jan. 11.)	Pichegru attacks Walmoden,	79
1795. (Jan. 19.)	The stadtholder and his son embark for England,	80
	Pichegru enters Amsterdam,	80
	Haarlem and Leyden declare for the French,	80
	The French gain possession of St Eustatius in the West Indies; the English troops in St Lucie are overpowered,	86
	The republican principles spread to Grenada, Dominica, and St Vincent,	86
	The Maroons of Jamaica prosecute a long and bloody war,	86
	The United Irishmen take themselves, and exact from their converts, a solemn oath to be faithful and secret,	124
(Jan. 30.)	The admiral of the Dutch squadron in Zealand hoists the French flag, and takes possession of Flushing and Middlebourg,	80
	The British parliament agree to a loan of four millions to Francis II. of Austria,	73
	Bergen-op-Zoom and other fortresses throw open their gates and fraternise with the French,	80
	The republican party reverse the sentences of the democrats of 1787; recall the exiles, and publish the Declaration of the Rights of Man,	80
	An embargo is laid upon all Dutch ships and goods in the ports of Great Britain, Ireland, and the colonies,	80
(Feb. 18.)	A treaty of defensive alliance is concluded and signed at St Petersburg between Great Britain and Russia,	83
	A treaty of pacification signed at Nantes between the Vendéans and the French republic,	90
(Mar. 2.)	Billaud Varennes, Collot d'Herbois, and Barrère are placed under arrest,	92
(Mar. 13, 14.)	Admiral Hotham engages the French fleet, which is compelled to 'haul off,'	84
	The remains of the Duke of York's army embark for England,	80
(Mar. 20.)	A struggle takes place in Paris between the Jeunesse Dorée and sans culottes,	92
(Mar. 22.)	Billaud Varennes, Collot d'Herbois, and Barrère are condemned to transportation for life,	92
	Pichegru routs the sans culottes,	92
(April 5.)	Frederick William II. of Prussia concludes a treaty with the French republic,	81
(April 8.)	The Princess Caroline of Brunswick is married to the Prince of Wales,	76
	The respectable class, headed by Logendre, Barras, and others, overthrow the Montagnards and mob, and drive them out of the Convention hall,	92
(May 29.)	A treaty of defensive alliance is concluded at Vienna, between Francis II. of Germany and Great Britain,	83
(June 8.)	The dauphin, Louis XVII., dies in the Temple,	93
	The French fleet is defeated by Admiral Bridport,	86
	A meeting is held in St George's Fields, to petition for annual parliaments and universal suffrage,	94
	The French Directory conclude a treaty with Wolfe Tone, Arthur O'Connor, and Lord Edward Fitzgerald, the leaders of the Irish revolutionists,	97
(July 3.)	The French royalists capture Fort Penthièvre,	91
	General Hoche overthrows the royalists of Brittany,	91

72   HISTORY OF ENGLAND.

A.D.		PAGE
1795. (July 7.)	The Austrian general Bender surrenders to the French,	86
(July 14.)	Vice-admiral Sir G. Keith Elphinstone and Major-general Craig take possession of Simon's Town, Cape of Good Hope,	81
(July 20.)	The republican prisoners betray Fort Penthièvre into the hands of General Hoche,	91
	A guerrilla warfare commences in Brittany against the republicans,	91
(July 22.)	Spain signs a treaty of peace at Basle with the French republic,	82
(Aug.)	Pichegru captures Dusseldorf, and occupies Manheim,	86
	General Jourdan joins Pichegru in the reduction of Mayence,	86
	Clairfait drives back Jourdan,	86, 87
	Clairfait throws a considerable part of his army into Mayence,	87
(Aug. 22.)	A new constitution, prepared by the Abbé Sièyes, is accepted by the Convention,	93
(Sept.)	Stofflet and Charette are taken and shot; the Vendéan and Breton insurgents put down; the British ships and troops are withdrawn,	91
	The Jeunesse Dorée organise,	91, 92
(Sept. 23.)	The town and castle of Cape Town surrender,	81
	By the end of the year, the British take possession of all the places held by the Dutch in the island of Ceylon, with Malacca, Cochin, Chinsura, Amboyna, and Banda,	81
(Oct. 4.)	Paris is again a scene of bloodshed,	93
(Oct. 5.)	Napoleon Bonaparte puts down the insurgents,	94
	The Directory is composed by Barras, Sièyes, Rewbell, Letourneur, and Réveillère-Lepeaux,	94
	Sièyes soon resigns, and is replaced by Carnot, who forms vast schemes for military conquest in Germany and Italy,	94
	The Directory publish an amnesty for political offences,	94
(Oct. 29.)	Clairfait drives the republicans from their fortified lines,	87
	Wurmser drives Pichegru within the walls of Manheim,	87
	Pichegru recrosses the Rhine, and effects a junction with Jourdan,	87
(Oct. 29.)	George III. is fired at opposite the Ordnance Office,	95
	On leaving the House of Lords, a stone is thrown at his carriage, and cries of 'Bread! Bread! and no Pitt! Peace! Peace!'	95
	Nelson destroys many vessels on the coast of Italy,	89
(Nov. 22.)	Manheim surrenders to Wurmser; the Austrians recover the whole of the Palatinate, and the country between the Rhine and the Moselle,	87
	An armistice is agreed upon between the Austrians and French,	87
	Massena defeats the Piedmontese and Austrians in Italy,	89
	They are saved by Nelson keeping open the Bocchetta Pass,	90
	The French take up their winter-quarters at Vado and Savona,	90
(Dec.)	During this year a democratic revolution is effected in Genoa,	97
1796. (Jan.)	Pichegru is superseded by Moreau,	104
	The Archduke Charles defeats one of Jourdan's divisions, and forces him	

A.D.		PAGE
1796.	to relinquish the siege of Ehrenbreitstein,	104
(Feb.)	Wolfe Tone goes to Paris as the representative of the Irish patriots; he is made a brigadier-general,	124
(Mar. 26.)	Bonaparte arrives at Nice to take the command of the Army of Italy,	106
	General Nichols recovers the island of Grenada from the French insurgents,	99
(April 11.)	Beaulieu defeats the French advanced-guard at Voltri, near Genoa,	106
	Bonaparte defeats D'Argenteau near Montenotte,	106
	Provern, with an Austrian division of 2000 men, lays down his arms,	106
(April 15.)	Wukassowich scatters the French army under Massena near Dego, but is forced to retire by General Laharpe and Bonaparte,	106
	Bonaparte drives Colli from Ceva; follows him to Mondovi; dislodges him, and pursues him beyond Cherasco; Colli retreats to Carignan, near Turin,	106
(May.)	In the course of the session two budgets are produced, and two new loans contracted, amounting together to £25,500,000,	97
(May 10.)	Bonaparte carries the bridge of Lodi,	106
(May 15.)	He makes a triumphal entrance into Milan,	106
	The French plunder Lombardy, Parma, Modena, &c.,	107
	Excesses of the French troops in Pavia,	107
	Bonaparte overruns Tuscany,	107
	In the course of the summer, Burke publishes the first two of his celebrated *Letters on a Regicide Peace*,	97
	The Directory issue a decree preventing the admission of English goods into any part of France and Belgium, the French dependencies, Holland, and the German states on the Rhine,	97
	General Abercrombie regains entire possession of St Lucie,	99
	General Whyte captures the Dutch settlements of Demerara, Berbice, and Essequibo,	99
(June.)	O'Connor enters France and concludes a treaty with General Hoche,	125
(June 18.)	Pope Pius VI. sues to the French for terms,	107
(June 23.)	Bonaparte grants an armistice,	107
	The cession of the provinces of Bologna and Ferrara, the citadel and port of Ancona, and the closing of the Papal ports to the English and their allies,	107
(June 24.)	Moreau takes the fortress of Kehl, and after a series of victories advances into the heart of Swabia,	105
	Jourdan takes Frankfort, Wurtzburg, and other towns,	105
(July.)	Moreau captures Ulm and Donawert,	105
	Bonaparte raises the blockade of Mantua; concentrates his forces, and crushes Quosnadowich,	107
(Aug. 3 and 5.)	He defeats Wurmser near Castiglione,	108
(Aug. 17.)	The Dutch squadron is captured in Saldanha Bay by Rear-admiral Elphinstone,	99
(Aug. 24.)	The Archduke Charles defeats Jourdan at Amberg,	105
(Sept. 3.)	He defeats him again severely at Wurtzburg,	105
(Sept. 4.)	Bonaparte defeats an Austrian division in the lower valley of the Tyrol, and enters the city of Trento,	108

A.D.	PAGE
1796. (Sept. 14.) Wurmser throws himself into Mantua,	108
(Sept. 16.) The Archduke Charles again defeats the French at Aschaffenburg,	105
(Sept. 25.) Moreau begins his famous retreat through the Black Forest,	105
(Oct.) Nelson, after blockading Leghorn, seizes Elba and the small island of Capraja,	100
Sir Gilbert Elliott alienates the affections of the Corsicans from the English,	100
(Oct. 2.) The Imperial general Latour is defeated at Biberach by Moreau,	105
(Oct. 8.) Genoa shuts her ports against British shipping,	99
Spain declares war against England,	99
The king of Naples concludes a peace with France,	99
(Oct. 16.) Vittor Amedeo, king of Sardinia, dies broken-hearted,	100
(Oct. 19.) The Spanish admiral proceeds to Corsica, and covers the landing of a French invading force from Leghorn,	99
(Oct. 20.) Windham, the secretary at war, announces that the whole military force of the country consists of 195,674 men,	109
(Oct. 20.) Corsica is evacuated by the British,	100, 101
The British evacuate Elba,	101
Rear-admiral Richery sails to Newfoundland; plunders and sets fire to the fishermen's huts, destroys their vessels and fishing-stages,	101
(Nov. 6.) Bonaparte is repulsed by Alvinzi at Le Nove, and retreats to Verona,	108
(Nov. 12.) Bonaparte is again repulsed by Alvinzi at Caldiero,	108
(Nov. 14.) The battle of Arcola,	108, 109
The Empress Catherine II. of Russia dies, and is succeeded by her son Paul I.,	138
(Dec.) Richery picks up a great many English merchant-vessels; escapes through the Channel fleet in a haze, and joins the Brest fleet,	101
(Dec. 17.) The Brest fleet, under Vice-admiral Morard de Galles, with 25,000 men on board under Hoche, sails from Brest,	101, 102
(Dec. 24.) Rear-admiral Bonvet enters Bantry Bay,	102
Admiral Bouvet leaves Bantry Bay for Brest; the French fleet is scattered; many taken, and others wrecked,	102
1797. (Jan. 14.) Alvinzi is defeated at Rivoli; General Provera surrenders; Wurmser in Mantua capitulates,	118
The French overrun the greater part of the Papal states,	118
(Feb. 9.) The directors of the Bank of England inform Pitt that, if they comply with his request to advance £1,500,000, they would be forced to shut their doors,	110
(Feb. 14.) Battle off Cape St Vincent,	116
The island of Trinidad reduced by the British,	117
(Feb. 20.) Some French troops land on the Welsh coast, near Fishguard; they surrender without firing a shot,	117
(Mar.) Bonaparte is joined by Bernadotte; the Archduke Charles retreats towards Vienna,	118
(April 7.) An armistice is agreed to,	118
Mutiny on board the Channel fleet,	111
Bonaparte signs the preliminaries of peace with Austria at Leoben,	118
(April 23.) The grievances of the seamen are, after some delay, promised to be redressed, and the mutiny ceases,	113
The navy is further increased,	111
The Austrians are defeated by Moreau,	117
(May 7.) Mutiny in the Channel fleet again breaks out; but after two days, redress is actually obtained, and it ceases,	113, 114
(May 20.) Mutiny breaks out at the Nore,	114
(May 24.) The government pardon is offered and rejected,	115
(May 26.) Mr Grey moves *for a sweeping reform in parliament,*	115
The mutineers behave with great insolence,	115
Bonaparte takes possession of Venice; Genoa is democratised and affiliated,	118, 119
Pichegru, Willot, General Ramel, and sixty other members of the legislature are arrested,	121
(June.) The buoys at the mouth of the Thames are taken up, batteries for firing red-hot shot erected along-shore, and a proclamation issued declaring the ships in a state of rebellion, &c.,	115
(June 4.) The mutinous fleet fire a royal salute in honour of George III.'s birthday,	115
Several of the ships desert the rebels,	115
(June 13.) The bloody flag has disappeared from every mast-head,	115
(June 14.) President Parker, the leader of the mutineers, is given up,	115, 116
(June 30.) Parker is hanged,	116
A few of the delegates are afterwards executed; some are flogged through the fleet, and others left under sentence in prison-ships,	116
(July.) Nelson makes an unfortunate attack on the island of Teneriffe; he loses his right arm,	117
(Sept.) Pichegru, Willot, Barbé-Marbois, Carnot, Bartholomy, and others, are transported for life to Cayenne,	121
The proprietors, editors, and writers of forty-two journals are condemned to deportation to French Guiana,	122
(Oct. 11.) Admiral Duncan attacks and defeats the Dutch fleet under Admiral de Winter,	116
(Oct. 17.) The definitive treaty of peace between France and Austria is signed at Campo Formio, near Udine,	119, 120
(Nov. 2.) Parliament meets; the addresses are voted; supplies voted to the amount of £25,000,000, and the assessed taxes trebled,	122
A congress to settle the affairs of Germany is held at Rastadt; Bonaparte goes as plenipotentiary,	120
The French agents at Rome receive urgent instructions to discredit all revealed religion, and particularly the Roman Catholic,	132
The Roman democrats insult the pope's guards, and even the pope himself,	132
The populace rise against the democrats,	132
(Dec. 28.) Three hundred democrats assemble at the Villa Medici, and are harangued by General Duphot, who hoists the tricolour,	132, 133
Joseph Bonaparte proposes pacific measures,	133
A combat takes place; General Duphot is mortally wounded,	133
Joseph Bonaparte flees to Florence, denouncing the pope as the assassin of Duphot,	133
1798. (Jan. 7.) The Vaudois beg assistance from the French republic to put down aristocracy and defend liberty,	129
The Swiss Federal Diet, perplexed and distracted, quit Aarau,	129

A.D.		PAGE
1798.	General Menard concentrates in the Pays de Vaud, and with the Swiss demagogues organises a provisional government at Lausanne,	129
	The Directory order Berthier to march instantly to Rome with a large body of troops,	133
	Loretto is sacked; Osimo is plundered and burnt,	133
(Feb. 10.)	Rome capitulates,	133
(Feb. 15.)	The Roman democrats proclaim the ancient republican form of government to be restored,	133
	The pope is confined in the Vatican,	133
	The Roman demagogues wreak their vengeance on their late superiors and masters; a reaction in the common people takes place,	133
	Assassinations become frequent,	133
(Feb. 20.)	The pope is seized and hurried into Tuscany,	134
	The French decree the separation of the Pays de Vaud from Bern, &c.,	129, 130
	General Brune arrives on the Swiss frontiers; the Bernese obtain a truce for fifteen days; Brune's army amounts to 40,000 or 45,000 men,	130
	A pressing letter is sent to the French Directory by the 'Irish Executive' urging immediate succour,	126
	Talleyrand assures them that an expedition is getting ready in the French ports, and would certainly sail in April,	126
(Mar. 2.)	Brune leads the main body of his army against Freyburg; many of the Swiss contingents withdraw, leaving less than 15,000 men to defend Bern,	130
(Mar. 5.)	Brune is driven back,	130
	General d'Erlach, who commanded part of the Swiss army, is defeated,	130
	Brune enters the city of the Fighting Bear,	130
	General Brune plunders Bern and Freyburg,	130
	The traders and manufacturers of Zurich and other towns are taxed, fined, and harried; compelled to admit French garrisons, &c.,	130
	The French form Switzerland into a republic,	131
	Aloys Reding, with 1200 Switzers, beats the French repeatedly,	131
	The king of Sardinia is forced to admit a French garrison into Turin, and all the other citadels he had hitherto retained,	134
	Some arrests are ordered in Dublin,	126
	Warrants are issued against several conspirators; MacNevin and Emmett are soon apprehended, and Sampson is seized at Carlisle and brought back to Dublin,	127
(April.)	The Alien Bill is revived, and the suspension of the Habeas Corpus Act renewed or prolonged,	122
	The Irish fly to arms in all parts of the country,	122
(May 19.)	Bonaparte sails from Toulon for the conquest of Egypt,	134
(May 23.)	Lord Edward Fitzgerald is surprised in bed,	127
(May 24.)	The Irish rebels make an abortive attempt on Naas, Carlow, and some other towns,	127
(May 25.)	An army of more than 14,000 pikemen,	

A.D.		PAGE
1798.	headed by Father John Murphy, march to Wexford, defeat part of the garrison, and kill all the prisoners they take,	127
(May 30.)	Wexford surrenders to the rebels; the Protestants who remain are barbarously used; the rebels take Enniscorthy, procure some artillery, and fortify Vinegar Hill,	127
	The rebels are driven back from New Ross,	127
	The best of the Catholics in the north express their abhorrence of the rising, and offer their services to government,	127
	Minorca surrenders to the British,	123
	The British troops are withdrawn from San Domingo,	128, 129
(June 5.)	Lord Edward Fitzgerald dies of his wounds,	127
(June 11.)	The French take Malta,	134
(June 21.)	Lord Lake defeats the rebels at Vinegar Hill, and retakes Wexford and Enniscorthy,	127
(June 30.)	The French land within three miles of Alexandria,	135
(July.)	The town of Alexandria is taken,	135
	Of the leading Irish conspirators only four are executed,	127
	The French commissioners order that every canton shall take a solemn oath to preserve for ever the new French constitution of the Helvetic Republic,	131
	The small mountain cantons refuse to perjure themselves,	131
	Schauenburg, with 15,000 men, marches against them,	131
	The battle of the Pyramids,	135
(July 23.)	Bonaparte enters Cairo, &c.,	135
(Aug.)	The battle of the Nile,	136, 137
	The sultan declares war against France,	137
	Three French frigates reach Killala, and throw on shore 900 troops of the line, commanded by General Humbert,	127, 128
	Humbert marches to Castlebar,	128
	He defeats General Lake at Castlebar,	128
	Humbert in turn is beaten by Lake,	128
(Sept. 8.)	The French lay down their arms, and become prisoners of war,	128
(Sept. 9.)	The Nidwalders' 1800 or 2000 men are defeated in a mountain-pass, after fighting from sunrise to sunset,	131
	The victors shew no mercy,	131
	The cattle are carried off by the French, houses and cottages are set on fire, fruit-trees cut down, &c.,	131
	The exactions of the Directory over the rest of Switzerland continue,	131, 132
	Nelson is created Baron Nelson of the Nile,	137
(Oct.)	Sir John Borlase Warren takes a portion of the French squadron sent to Ireland,	128
	Wolfe Tone is executed,	128
(Nov.)	The island of Gozo capitulates to a detachment of Nelson's squadron,	138
	The king of Naples, along with General Mack, enters the Roman States,	139
(Nov. 29.)	The king of Naples enters Rome in triumph,	139
(Dec.)	Mack's army is scattered by General Macdonald,	139
	The king of Naples flies from Rome, and Mack follows him,	139
(Dec. 21.)	The king of Naples and his family embark for Palermo,	139
	The lazzaroni of Naples fight the French desperately for three days,	139
1799. (Jan.)	Pitt's Income-tax Bill passes both Houses,	138

CHRONOLOGICAL INDEX. 75

A.D.		PAGE
1799. (Jan. 22.)	A royal message is delivered to both Houses, recommending the consideration of a union between England and Ireland,	138
(Jan. 23.)	Naples is converted into the Republica Parthenopen,	139
	The French seize upon the royal property, the estates of the church, and of the monastic orders; ransack the national museum for choice manuscripts, books, statues, and pictures,	139
	They appropriate the curiosities and works of antiquity discovered in Herculaneum and Pompeii,	139
	The fortress of Ehrenbreitstein capitulates to the French,	140
	Jourdan crosses the Rhine, and establishes himself in Suabia,	140
(Feb.)	Bonaparte quits Cairo, crosses the desert with 10,000 men, takes Gaza, storms Jaffa,	141
	He arrives before Acre, which is defended by the Pasha Djezzar, Colonel Phillippeaux, an emigrant royalist, and Sir Sidney Smith,	141
(Mar. 5.)	General Harris enters the Mysore territory, moving on Seringapatam, and reducing all the forts on his way,	144
	The Directory declare war against the Emperor Francis II.,	140
	Jourdan advances towards the Danube, and is defeated by the Archduke Charles in several engagements,	140
	The Austrian general Melas obliges the French to retire beyond the Mincio,	140
	Moreau takes the command of the French; he also is beaten,	140
(Mar. 27.)	Harris defeats Tippoo Sultaun,	144
	Tippoo retreats to Seringapatam,	144
(April 18.)	Suvaroff, with 50,000 Russians, joins Melas, and takes the command of both armies,	140
(April 27.)	Suvaroff gains the battle of Cassano; the citadels of Brescia and Peschiera surrender; Mantua is closely invested; Suvaroff enters Milan in triumph,	140
	Moreau retreats hastily towards Genoa,	140
	The Archduke Charles drives Jourdan across the Rhine,	140
	The Austrian generals, Bellegarde and Hotze, recover the Grison country, drive the French from the St Gothard, pour into Switzerland, and reduce Massena to act on the defensive,	140
(May 4.)	Seringapatam is stormed and captured; Tippoo falls,	144
(May 7.)	Macdonald commences a rapid march from Naples; traverses the Roman States and the whole of Tuscany; reaches the river Trebia, and is joined by Victor,	140
	He is crushed by Suvaroff,	140
	He flies to the Bocchetta Pass, and is joined by Moreau with reinforcements,	140
	Moreau is superseded by Joubert,	140
(May 21.)	The French raise the siege of Acre,	141
(June 14.)	Bonaparte re-enters Cairo,	141
(June and July.)	The Neapolitan kingdom is recovered from the French,	141
	A detachment of Nelson's squadron blockade Civita Vecchia; the French capitulate, as also the garrison of St Angelo,	141
(July.)	Bonaparte and his army march to Aboukir,	142
(July 21.)	A great battle is fought against the Turks,	142

A.D.		PAGE
1799. (Aug. 5.)	Richard Earl Howe dies,	114
	An army of 30,000 men assemble on the coast of Kent,	141
	Sir Ralph Abercromby lands at the Helder; the Texel is occupied by the British fleet; the Dutch fleet surrender, or hoist the Orange flag,	141
	General Brune is repulsed by Abercromby,	141
(Aug. 16.)	Joubert is beaten by Suvaroff behind Novi; Joubert is killed,	140
	The wreck of the French army fly towards the city of Genoa,	140
	Suvaroff strikes across the Alps into Switzerland, but has to retreat before Massena,	140, 141
	The French are again left absolute masters of Switzerland,	140
(Aug. 23.)	Bonaparte, leaving his army, and taking with him Murat, Lannes, Berthier, Marmont, and three savans, embarks at Alexandria for France in two small frigates,	142
	Pope Pius VI. dies at Valence, on the Rhone,	141
	A detachment of the army of General Melas recovers the whole of Tuscany,	141
(Oct. 9.)	Bonaparte lands in the Gulf of Frejus,	142
(Nov. 10.)	The Council of Five Hundred, in Paris, is cleared by Murat and a detachment of grenadiers with fixed bayonets,	143
	All the ardent republicans are proscribed; three provisional consuls are appointed —the Abbé Sièyes, Roger Ducos, and Napoleon Bonaparte,	143
(Dec. 24.)	'The Constitution of the year 8' is promulgated,	143
	The Abbé Sièyes and Roger Ducos become senators; Napoleon Bonaparte first consul; Cambacérès and Lebrun, second and third consuls,	143
1800. (Feb.)	The suspension of the Habeas Corpus Act is continued,	147
(April 25.)	Moreau crosses the Rhine, defeats the Austrians, and penetrates to Ulm,	151
(May 13.)	Bonaparte prepares to march from Lausanne with 36,000 men, and forty pieces of cannon, up the Great St Bernard,	149
	The left wing, under Moncey, is ordered to cross the Alps by the pass of St Gothard; 5000 men, under Turreau, at Mont Cenis; and 5000, under Chabran, the Little St Bernard,	149
(May 16.)	Bonaparte's vanguard, under Lannes, descends the Great St Bernard into the valley of Aosta,	149
(May 17.)	Lannes drives in a detachment of Austrians,	149
	Bonaparte drives the Austrian divisions before him, and is joined by Moncey, Chabran, and Turreau,	149
(May.)	Moreau crosses the Danube, overruns great part of Bavaria, and captures Munich,	151, 152
(June 2.)	Bonaparte enters Milan without opposition,	149, 150
(June 5.)	Massena surrenders Genoa,	150
	Melas concentrates at Alessandria on the Bormida,	150
	Bonaparte takes up a position at Marengo,	150
(June 14.)	The battle of Marengo,	150
(June 16.)	The Austrians give up Piedmont, the Genoese territory, and all Lombardy as far as the river Oglio,	151
	Bonaparte enters Milan like a consul and conqueror of ancient Rome,	151

A.D.		PAGE
1800. (July 3.)	Bonaparte makes a triumphal entry into Paris,	151
	Bonaparte orders Moreau to accede to a truce with the Austrians till the month of September,	152
	Bonaparte orders the French armies to be put in motion; the Army of Italy, under Brune, drives the Austrians beyond the Adige and Brenta, and advances to a few miles from Venice,	152
(Sept. 15.)	Malta surrenders to Major-general Pigot,	152, 153
	The Dutch island of Curaçoa surrenders to a small British force,	153
(Nov. 11.)	Parliament meets, and passes a number of acts, granting bounties on the importation of foreign corn, enjoining the baking of mixed and inferior flour, &c.,	153
(Dec. 2.)	The battle of Hohenlinden,	152
	The Emperor Francis II. is compelled to sue for a separate peace,	152
1801. (Jan.)	Many new titles are conferred on the Irish nobility; several of them are created peers of the United Kingdom,	154
(Jan. 22.)	The first Imperial Parliament is opened by commission; Mr Addington is re-elected speaker,	154
(Jan. 31.)	Mr Pitt writes a letter to George III. on Catholic emancipation,	155
(Feb. 1.)	George III. replies, stating his opposition to Catholic emancipation, but hoping Mr Pitt will keep his situation, &c.,	155, 156
(Feb. 2.)	George III. meets parliament; he states that a fresh storm is gathering in the north, and that the court of St Petersburg had already committed outrages against the ships, property, and persons of his subjects, &c.,	154
	He also states that a convention had been concluded between Russia and the courts of Copenhagen and Stockholm,	154
	Preparations are made for sending a British fleet into the Baltic,	155
(Feb. 3.)	Mr Pitt tenders his resignation,	156
(Feb. 5.)	George III. intrusts the formation of a new ministry to Mr Addington,	156
(Feb. 9.)	The treaty of Lunéville is signed between France and Austria,	152
(Feb. 18.)	The House resolves itself into a committee of supply; the sum required is £42,197,000; £25,500,000 is borrowed, and some new taxes imposed,	157
	£2,500,000 is borrowed for Ireland,	158
(Mar. 2.)	The British fleet anchors in Aboukir Bay, and lands troops on the 8th,	166
(Mar. 13.)	An indecisive action is fought by Sir Ralph Abercromby between Aboukir and Alexandria,	167
	The Addington administration is formed,	159
	The act for the suppression of rebellion and the suspension of the Habeas Corpus Act are continued, and an act for preventing seditious meetings is revived,	159
(Mar. 19.)	Fort Aboukir capitulates,	167
	The battle of Alexandria,	167, 168
(Mar. 24.)	The Emperor Paul I. of Russia is murdered,	163
(Mar. 28.)	Sir Ralph Abercromby dies,	168
(April 1.)	The British fleet anchors within two leagues of Copenhagen,	161
(April 2.)	The battle of Copenhagen,	161, 162
	A suspension of hostilities is agreed to for twenty-four hours,	162

A.D.		PAGE
1801. (April 7.)	Major-general Baird sails from Bombay with an Anglo-Indian army for Egypt,	169
(April 9.)	An armistice is concluded with the Danes for fourteen weeks,	162, 163
	Sir Hyde Parker demands an explicit declaration from Sweden, whether she will adhere to or abandon hostile measures with Great Britain,	163
(April 15.)	Intelligence is received in London of the success of the attack on Copenhagen, and the death of the Emperor Paul I.,	159
	Nelson is raised to a viscounty,	163
(April 22.)	Gustavus IV. of Sweden replies to Sir Hyde Parker, that he will not refuse to listen to equitable proposals made by deputies properly authorised by King George III. of Great Britain, to the united northern powers,	163
	The Emperor Alexander I. accepts the offer of England to settle the dispute by a convention,	163
	General Hutchinson, commanding the British army in Egypt, is reinforced by 3000 men; Rosetta and Fort Julien are taken,	169
	He cuts the embankments of the Aboukir lake, and insulates Alexandria; he drives the French (4000) from Ramanich, and proceeds up the Nile to Cairo,	169
	A Spanish army, under Godoy, the Prince of the Peace, invades Portugal,	169
(May 5.)	Sir Hyde Parker is recalled, and Nelson is appointed commander-in-chief,	164
(May 7.)	Nelson leaves a portion of his fleet at Carlscrona to watch the Swedish, and sails for Revel,	164
	He opens a communication with the Emperor Alexander I.,	164
	Nelson sails from Revel; meets the Russian admiral Tchitchagoff, despatched by Alexander I., to enter into friendly explanations,	164
(May 17.)	General Baird reaches Jeddah, and is joined by an English division from the Cape of Good Hope,	169
(June.)	Nelson is invited to St Petersburg,	164
(June 8.)	Baird reaches Kosseir, and commences landing his troops,	169
(June 17.)	A convention is signed at St Petersburg by Lord St Helens, in which all disputes are adjusted; Sweden and Denmark accede to the same terms,	164, 165
	Nelson returns to England,	164
(June 27.)	At Cairo, the French general, Belliard, capitulates,	169
	Portugal purchases peace (the treaty of Olivenza) by yielding some territory to Spain, and engaging to shut her ports against the English,	169
	Menou capitulates on the same terms as Belliard, and Egypt is cleared of the French,	169
	Bonaparte refuses to concur in the treaty of Olivenza, and sends a French army, 25,000 strong, through Spain to attack Portugal,	169
	The Portuguese apply for succour from England; £300,000 are sent to them and some ships,	169
	The French invest Almeida, and menace Lisbon and Oporto,	169
(July 6.)	Rear-admiral Sir James Saumarez unsuccessfully attacks a French squadron in Algesiras Bay,	170
(July 12.)	Saumarez renews the attack, and is victorious,	170

CHRONOLOGICAL INDEX. 77

A.D.		PAGE
1801. (Sept.)	Bonaparte concludes a concordat with the pope,	185
	A definitive treaty is concluded at Madrid; Bonaparte agreeing to withdraw his troops, and respect the independence and integrity of Portugal, &c.,	169
(Oct. 1.)	Preliminaries of peace are signed with France,	170
(Dec. 14.)	A great French fleet and land-army sails from Brest for the West Indies,	172
	Admiral Mitchell is despatched to watch their proceedings,	173
1802. (Jan. 11.)	Bonaparte enters Lyons in triumph, and meets a grand consulta from the Cisalpine Republic,	173
	Bonaparte is appointed president of the Cisalpine Republic for ten years, and to be re-eligible,	173
(Mar. 27.)	Peace at Amiens,	170–172
	A petition is presented from the city of London for the abolition of the Income-tax,	180
(April 5.)	The Income-tax is repealed,	180
	A new Militia Bill is carried through both Houses,	181
(May 19.)	The Legion of Honour is established in France with great pomp, and proclaimed a law of the state,	187
(Aug. 2.)	Bonaparte is proclaimed consul for life,	188
	During this year the French under Leclerc are engaged in a war with the negroes of St Domingo under Toussaint Louverture,	191
	Toussaint Louverture is taken prisoner, and sent to France in chains,	191, 192
	He is confined in the castle of Joux, in the coldest part of the Jura mountains; he is found dead in the winter of 1803,	192
(Sept. 2.)	Bonaparte annexes and incorporates the whole of Piedmont with France,	194
	A fresh army of French is marched into Switzerland,	194
(Oct.)	Bonaparte adds to his other titles that of 'Mediator of the Helvetic League,'	194
	He forces the federal government to agree to maintain a body of 16,000 men in his service; retains Geneva and the bishopric of Basle, separating from Berne the whole of the Valais, which country not long after is incorporated with France,	194
(Nov. 2.)	General Leclerc dies in St Domingo,	192
(Dec. 1.)	General Rochambeau evacuates Cape Français in St Domingo; the whole of the fleet or convoy, with troops, civilians, and planters who leave the island, are captured by the English,	192
1803. (Feb. 21.)	Colonel Despard and six others are executed,	198
	Jean Peltier, the journalist, is found guilty of publishing libels on Napoleon Bonaparte,	204–206
(Mar. 8.)	A royal message is delivered to parliament, which is received as the signal of approaching war by the country and all Europe,	198
(Mar. 11.)	Ten thousand additional seamen are voted,	199
(Mar. 13.)	Bonaparte insults the British ambassador,	209, 210
(May 12.)	Lord Whitworth leaves Paris for England, leaving Mr Talbot, secretary of the embassy, behind,	212
	Bonaparte gives orders that Mr Talbot shall be detained as a prisoner of war,	213

A.D.		PAGE
1803. (May 16.)	Andréossi, the French ambassador, takes his departure,	200
	About 200 French and Dutch vessels are detained or captured, containing property estimated at three millions sterling,	213
(May 22.)	Bonaparte issues a decree for the detention of all the English found in the territories of France,	213
	General Mortier conquers the electorate of Hanover,	213
(June 20.)	A bill passes both Houses, without a division, to levy an army of reserve, 50,000 strong, to be raised by ballot, their services to extend, during the war, to Great Britain, Ireland, and the Channel islands,	201
(June 22.)	The island of St Lucie is recaptured by Commodore Hood and General Grinfield,	217
	The colonies of Demerara, Essequibo, and Berbice are reduced in rapid succession,	217
	Ships and gunboats are cut out of Havre, St Vallory, and many other ports and roadsteads; the batteries of Dieppe are knocked to pieces, and many vessels burnt on the stocks,	217
	The town of Granville is bombarded and burned,	217
(June 30.)	The French garrison in Tobago capitulates,	217
	The islands of St Pierre and Miquelon, off Newfoundland, are taken by an English man-of-war,	217
(July.)	Mortier levies contributions on the electorate of Hanover,	213
	He also levies contributions on the Hanse Towns of Hamburg and Bremen, and closes the navigation of the Elbe and Weser against the English,	213, 214
	The mouths of the Elbe and Weser are blockaded by the English,	214
	Bonaparte organises an Irish Legion, and matures plots for an insurrection in Ireland,	214
(July 22.)	The levy *en masse* bill is passed,	202
(July 23.)	The rabble of Dublin and the peasantry collect in vast numbers in St James Street and its neighbourhood; pikes are distributed,	215
	Some murders take place during the day, but at night a hundred and fifty soldiers, headed by two subalterns, set the rabble to the rout,	216
	Emmett, Redmond, and Russel are taken; Dowdall and Allen escape from the island,	216
(Aug. 1.)	A new property and income tax is passed,	203
	The lord-lieutenant of Ireland is authorised to raise a loan of £1,000,000,	203
	The total amount of supplies granted for the year is £41,363,192,	203
	Holkar joins Scindiah and the Rajah of Berar,	218
	Wellesley takes Ahmednughur by escalade,	219
(Aug. 29.)	He enters Aurungabad; Scindiah and the Rajah of Berar rush with an immense army of cavalry into the Nizam's territory, and march upon Hyderabad,	219
(Aug. 29.)	The town of Coel opens its gates at Lake's approach,	220
(Sept. 4.)	Lake storms the fortress of Alli Ghur,	220
(Sept. 11.)	Lake drives Louis Bourquien beyond the Jumna,	221

A.D.		PAGE
1803. (Sept. 12.)	Delhi, together with the fort, are evacuated,	221
(Sept. 19.)	Emmett is executed; Redmond and two working-men are also executed,	216, 217
	The battle of Assaye,	219, 220
(Oct. 17.)	Lake takes Agra,	221
(Nov. 1.)	Lake defeats Scindiah at the village of Laswarree,	221
	Scindiah asks for and obtains a truce from General Wellesley; the Rajah of Berar still keeps the field,	222
	The power of Scindiah and the Mahratta confederacy is shattered before the end of the year,	222
(Nov. 22.)	The suspension of the Habeas Corpus Act is continued, and the prolongation of martial law in Ireland,	226
(Nov. 29.)	The battle of Argaum,	222
(Dec. 15.)	The fortress of Gawil-Ghur taken,	223
(Dec. 17.)	The Rajah of Berar signs the conditions of peace with Wellesley,	223
	Scindiah also agrees never to take into or retain in his service any Frenchman, or the subject of any other European or American power at war with the British government, &c.,	223
	During this year various other successes are obtained in India,	223, 224
	In the course of this year, 300,000 men are furnished by the volunteer associations, all well equipped for home defence,	225
	The Code Civil des Français (afterwards the Code Napoleon) is promulgated,	189
1804. (Feb.)	Wellesley crosses the Godavery, and puts down the independent freebooting parties,	224
(Feb. 14.)	It is publicly announced that George III. is seriously indisposed,	226
	Commodore Dance defeats a French fleet near the Straits of Malacca; Dance is afterwards knighted for this action, and receives other honours,	234
(Feb. 15.)	Moreau is arrested; Pichegru and Georges-Cadoudal are taken; about forty other persons are soon after taken, on a charge of conspiring to assassinate Bonaparte,	238
(Feb. 27.)	A decree of the senate suspends for two years the functions of the jury in cases of attempts against the person of Napoleon Bonaparte,	247
	It is announced that George III. is gradually advancing towards entire recovery,	226
(Mar. 7.)	Goree, on the coast of Africa, is lost, and won again by Captain Dixon of the Inconstant frigate,	233, 234
(Mar. 14.)	George III. is in such a state as to warrant the lords commissioners in giving the royal assent to several bills,	226
	The Duc d'Enghien seized on foreign territory,	239
(Mar. 21.)	He is tried upon six charges in the dead of the night, and murdered by shooting in the moat of Vincennes,	240–243
	The courts of Russia and Sweden remonstrate,	243
	Pichegru is found strangled in his bed in a cell of the Temple; it is pretended he committed suicide,	244
(April 10.)	The motion that Napoleon Bonaparte be proclaimed Emperor of the French is debated in the Tribunate, and carried with only one dissentient voice, that of Carnot,	249

A.D.		PAGE
1804. (May 8.)	Captain John Wesley Wright, who had landed Pichegru and his companions in the preceding autumn, is captured by the French,	245
(May 12.)	Pitt becomes premier, and a new administration is formed,	230, 231
(May 18.)	Pitt takes his seat as Chancellor of the Exchequer, having been returned by the university of Cambridge,	231
	Bonaparte accepts the imperial title; Cambacérès is made arch-chancellor of the empire, and Lebrun arch-treasurer,	250
(May 19.)	The Emperor Napoleon I. and empress hold a grand levée at the Tuileries; Napoleon I. issues a decree naming eighteen of his first generals marshals of France,	250
	Every brother and sister of Napoleon I. receive the title of Imperial Highness, and the grand dignitaries of the empire that of Serene Highness, &c.,	251
	The colony of Surinam is taken by Major-general Sir Charles Green and Commodore Hood,	233
(May 30.)	Wilberforce moves and carries a resolution, to bring in a bill for the total abolition of the slave-trade,	231
(June 2.)	Captain Wright is found one morning in his cell in the Temple with his throat cut from ear to ear,	245
(June 7.)	The Abolition of the Slave-trade Bill is read a second time, and carried,	231
(June 10.)	Sentence of death is passed upon Georges-Cadoudal, Bouvet de Lozier, Lajolais, Armand de Polignac, and sixteen others; Moreau, Jules de Polignac, and three others are condemned to two years' imprisonment,	248
	The rest of the prisoners are acquitted, but are thrown into prison by order of Bonaparte,	248
(June 23.)	All the gentlemen capitally convicted are reprieved, except Georges and Coster Saint Victor,	248
	It is proposed to Moreau to exchange his two years' imprisonment for banishment, which he accepts,	248
(June 29.)	Louis XVIII. addresses a protest against the usurpation of his throne to the sovereigns of Europe; Napoleon I. orders it to be published in the Moniteur,	251
(July.)	Wellesley, having broken up the army in the Deccan, returns to Seringapatam,	225
	The supplies voted this session amount to £53,609,574; to raise this money, recourse is had to new taxes and duties, to loans and annuities, and to three lotteries,	233
(Oct. 5.)	Captain Graham Moore captures a Spanish squadron,	235
(Oct. 25.)	Sir George Rumbold, British minister at Hamburg, is seized at his house at Grindel by a party of French soldiers, conveyed across the Elbe to Hanover, and thence to Paris,	252, 253
	He is afterwards liberated on his parole not to return to Hamburg,	255
(Nov. 13.)	Holkar is defeated by General Fraser; General Fraser is mortally wounded,	299
(Nov. 17.)	Lord Lake defeats the whole cavalry of Holkar at Furruckabad,	299
(Nov. 27.)	The Spanish court issue an order to make reprisals on English property,	236
	Napoleon I. is privately remarried by Cardinal Fesch at midnight,	252

CHRONOLOGICAL INDEX.

A.D.		PAGE
1804. (Dec.)	The Mahrattas evacuate the citadel of Deeg,	299
(Dec. 2.)	Napoleon I. is crowned at Notre Dame by the pope,	252
(Dec. 12.)	Charles IV., king of Spain, formally declares war against Great Britain,	236
1805. (Jan. 2.)	Napoleon I. addresses a letter to George III., under the title of Sir and Brother,	253
	A diplomatic note in answer is sent by Lord Mulgrave, foreign secretary, to Talleyrand,	254
(Jan. 3.)	The siege of Bhurtpore,	299–302
(Feb. 8.)	Leave is given to bring in a bill to continue the suspension of the Habeas Corpus Act in Ireland,	257
	The total supply voted for the year is £55,590,000,	258
(Feb. 10.)	The Abolition of Slavery Bill is read a first time,	258
(Feb. 28.)	It is thrown out,	259
(Mar. 17.)	Deputies from the Italian republic wait upon Napoleon I. at the Tuileries, and offer him the crown of Italy; he accepts,	268
	Napoleon I. appoints Prince Eugene Beauharnais viceroy of Italy,	268
	Major-general Wellesley, on the point of leaving the East for ever, is presented with an address of gratitude from the natives of Seringapatam, Hindus and Mussulmans,	225
(April 6.)	Charges of misapplication of money, connivance at peculation, &c., are brought against Lord Melville,	259
	Whitbread's resolutions to bring Lord Melville to justice are carried by the casting-vote of the speaker,	259
	Pitt informs the House that Lord Melville had resigned office,	259
	The House agrees that the resolutions of the 6th, concerning Lord Melville, be laid before his majesty George III.,	260
(April 11.)	A treaty is signed between England and Russia,	267
(April 21.)	Lord Lake marches from Bhurtpore in pursuit of Holkar and Scindiah,	302
	The Marquis Cornwallis arrives at Calcutta to succeed the Marquis Wellesley as governor-general,	302
(April 27.)	Sir Charles Middleton is created Baron Barham,	260
(April 30.)	He is made first lord of the Admiralty,	260
(May 6.)	Lord Melville's name is erased from the list of the privy council,	262
(May 7.)	Nelson runs through the straits of Gibraltar in pursuit of Villeneuve, the French admiral,	284
	Villeneuve reaches Martinique,	283
(May 16.)	Pitt names the commissioners for naval inquiry, and moves that they shall inquire into all abuses 'that *do* exist in the said department;' the motion is carried,	262–263
(May 26.)	Napoleon I. is crowned king of Italy at Milan, and institutes the Order of the Iron Crown,	268
(June 4.)	Nelson arrives at Barbadoes, from thence he sails for Tobago and Trinidad, Grenada and Antigua,	284
(June 7.)	Villeneuve captures a homeward-bound British convoy of fifteen merchantvessels, and sails for Europe; he burns the merchant-vessels to prevent their recapture,	284
	Napoleon I. opens the session of the Italian legislative body,	268

A.D.		PAGE
1805.	The Genoese pray to be united to the French empire,	268
(June 9.)	An imperial decree unites the Genoese or Ligurian Republic to France for ever,	268
	Napoleon I. transforms the ancient republic of Lucca into a principality, and gives it to his sister Eliza and her husband Baciocchi, to be held as a fief of the French empire,	269
(June 11.)	Lord Melville makes a speech in his own defence,	263–266
	Whitbread moves he be impeached of high crimes and misdemeanours,	266
(June 12.)	Whitbread's motion is negatived, and an amendment for a prosecution by the attorney-general carried,	266
(June 13.)	Nelson sails from Antigua for Europe in pursuit of Villeneuve,	284
(June 25.)	A motion is carried that Lord Melville be impeached,	267
(June 26.)	Whitbread impeaches Lord Melville,	267
(July.)	Some changes take place in the cabinet,	267
(July 17.)	Nelson arrives off Cape St Vincent, and sails for the straits of Gibraltar to take in provisions, &c.,	285
(July 22.)	Sir Robert Calder obtains a slight victory over the French fleet,	286
	The Marquis Cornwallis dies at Gazipoor, near Benares,	303
(Aug. 9.)	By a treaty signed at St Petersburg, Austria becomes a member of the league with England, Russia, and Sweden,	267
(Aug. 18.)	Nelson lands at Spithead,	286
(Aug. 28.)	The army of England becomes the army of Germany; 150,000 men march from Boulogne in five separate columns for the Rhine, under Marshals Soult, Davoust, Ney, Lannes, and Murat,	269
(Sept. 29.)	Nelson arrives off Cadiz (his birthday),	288
(Oct. 10.)	Battle of Wertingen; the Austrians are defeated,	272
(Oct. 12.)	Soult surprises and captures an entire Austrian division at Memmingen; Dupont repels an attack of the Archduke Ferdinand,	272
	Ney routes the Archduke Ferdinand at Elchingen, and at the bridges over the Danube at Guntzburg,	272
	Detached masses of troops surrender to the French without firing a shot,	273
(Oct. 19.)	Mack agrees to evacuate Ulm, and gives up his army and everything in the town next day,	273
	The battle of Trafalgar; death of Nelson,	290–296
	The use of the Spanish hospitals is offered by Solano, and the Spanish honour pledged for the care of the wounded men,	296, 297
	Napoleon I. reinstates the Elector Maximilian Joseph in Munich; leaves Munich, and marches on Vienna,	275
(Nov. 1.)	The Archduke Charles commences his retreat through the mountain-passes of Carinthia, reaches Laybach, and is joined by the Archduke John, driven out of the Tyrol by Ney,	277
(Nov. 4.)	Sir Richard Strachan captures the remnant of the French fleet which escaped at Trafalgar,	296
(Nov. 7.)	The Emperor Francis II. and his family flee from Vienna into Moravia,	275
(Nov. 13.)	The French take possession of Vienna,	276
(Nov. 22.)	Napoleon I. fixes his head-quarters at	

A.D.		PAGE
1805.	Brunn; the Emperors Francis II. and Alexander I. retreat to Olmutz,	277
(Nov. 23.)	A treaty is signed with Scindiah,	305
	Napoleon I. retreats to the plain of Austerlitz,	278
	Admiral Villeneuve is brought to England, and liberated on parole; he is allowed to return to France, where his name is soon added to the ambiguous list of suicides,	297
	Nelson is buried in St Paul's,	298
(Dec. 2.)	The battle of Austerlitz,	278, 279
(Dec. 4.)	The Emperor Francis II. of Austria has a personal interview with Napoleon I. in the French camp,	280
(Dec. 6.)	An armistice is signed by Marshal Berthier and Lichtenstein,	280
	Napoleon I. promises to assign to Prussia for ever the electorate of Hanover,	281
	The Emperor Alexander I. retires by regular day-marches to his own territories; Napoleon I. returns to Vienna,	281
(Dec. 10.)	Lord Lake plunges into the Punjab in pursuit of Holkar,	304
(Dec. 26.)	A definitive treaty is signed by the Emperor Francis II. at Presburg (the treaty of Presburg),	281
	The army under Gustavus IV., king of Sweden, is broken up,	282
	During this year, the Princess of Wales begins to be suspected of improper conduct,	318, 319
	A man called Lowten is engaged to collect evidence, and act as a spy,	318, 319
1806. (Jan. 7.)	The treaty between Lake and Holkar ratified,	304
	The Cape of Good Hope is recovered by Sir David Baird,	329
(Jan. 23.)	Pitt dies at Putney in his forty-seventh year,	306
	Napoleon I. proclaims that the Bourbon dynasty of Naples had ceased to reign; he orders General St Cyr to march upon Naples,	321
	More than 60,000 men are in full march upon Naples, to oppose which is a small disorganised Neapolitan army, with 3000 British and about 4000 Russians,	321
	The Russians embark for Corfu; the British fly to the banks of the Garigliano,	321
	King Ferdinand IV. of Naples embarks for Palermo,	321
	The British embark for Sicily,	321
	Napoleon I. makes a triumphal entry into Paris,	336
(Feb. 4.)	The Grenville ministry is formed (all the talents),	307, 308
(Feb. 6.)	Sir John Duckworth defeats the French squadron off St Domingo,	333
(Feb. 11.)	St Cyr crosses the frontiers of Naples; Queen Caroline with her daughters embark for Sicily,	321
	Admiral Lord Collingwood despatches Sir Sidney Smith with a small squadron, to give such aid and assistance as may be practicable,	321
(Feb. 14.)	A Frenchman waits upon Fox, and details a plan for the assassination of Napoleon I.; Fox detains him in custody,	300
	Fox, as foreign secretary, opens a correspondence with Talleyrand, attempting to bring about a peace,	309
(Feb. 15.)	Joseph Bonaparte enters Naples, and takes up his abode as king,	322

A.D.		PAGE
1806.	General Regnier subdues nearly all Calabria,	322
	Joseph Bonaparte establishes a government, or ministry; visits Calabria,	322
	The English gain possession of the island of Capri, which commands the Gulf of Naples,	323
	Prince William of Hesse-Philipstadt defends the fortress of Gaeta; Sir Sidney Smith throws succours into the place, lands English sailors, and inflicts several severe blows on Massena's forces,	323
	General Regnier captures the Maratea in Calabria,	323
	Amantea cannot be taken by the French; Roggio is retaken from them; the castle of Scylla, which had surrendered to the French, is invested; Regnier retreats towards Monteleone,	323
(Mar.)	Bonaparte creates his marshals dukes, &c.,	337
(Mar. 28.)	The supplies for the year are £48,916,000; among the proposed ways and means are a loan of £18,000,000 and war-taxes to the amount of £19,500,000,	314
	A duty of forty shillings a ton is imposed upon pig-iron; the income and property tax is raised to 10 per cent. on all property above £50 a year; lotteries are continued as a source of revenue,	314
	A free interchange of all kinds of grain is permitted between Great Britain and Ireland,	314
	A bill passes prohibiting, under strict penalties, the exportation of slaves from the British colonies after the 1st of January 1807,	315
(April.)	A bill is passed to prevent the employment of any fresh ships in the African slave-trade; the duration limited to two years,	315
(April 29.)	The trial of Lord Melville commences,	315, 316
	Sir John Borlase Warren captures Admiral Linois near Brest,	335
	Sir E. Pellew burns several Dutch vessels at Batavia, and carries off others as prizes,	335
(May.)	Lord Yarmouth arrives at Paris as plenipotentiary,	310–312
	Additional Force Bill is repealed,	313
(May 30.)	Windham's plan for limited service is introduced, and carried, and, by way of clause, inserted in the annual Mutiny Bill,	313
	Windham's plan for altering the military system passes, and similar benefits are voted to the navy,	313
	Collingwood is raised to the peerage,	314
	The thanks of parliament are also voted to Admiral Sir Richard Strachan, and to Admiral Sir John Duckworth,	314
(June 5.)	Napoleon I. proclaims his brother Louis king of Holland,	338
(June 12.)	Lord Melville is declared not guilty,	317
(June 27.)	Buenos Ayres capitulates,	329
(July 1.)	Sir John Stuart effects a landing in Naples near the town of Nicastro,	323
(July 4.)	The battle of Maida,	324–326
	Regnier retreats,	327
	Several detachments of the French are destroyed or surrender to the English,	327
	Regnier continues his retreat for Cassano in Upper Calabria, his soldiers committing every kind of atrocity,	327

CHRONOLOGICAL INDEX. 81

A.D.		PAGE
1806. (July 12.)	The commissioners on the Princess of Wales's conduct give in their report,	320
	Sir Sidney Smith sweeps the Italian coast, from the mouth of the Tiber to the Bay of Naples,	328
(July 20.)	The Prince of Hesse-Philipstadt is mortally wounded; the garrison of Gaeta capitulate,	328
	The Confederation of the Rhine separate themselves from the Germanic empire, and unite in a distinct confederation,	336
(Aug. 4.)	Regnier reaches Cassano, and is joined by Verdier,	327
(Aug. 10.)	The English at Buenos Ayres capitulate,	330
	Sir Home Popham blockades the Rio de la Plata, and proceeds to attack Monte Video, but cannot get near enough,	330
	Prince Jerome Bonaparte in the *Veteran*, 74, captures and burns six vessels of a homeward-bound convoy from Quebec,	334
(Aug. 11.)	The two fugitive generals (Regnier and Verdier) effect a junction with Massena,	327
	The daring partisan Piccioli raises nearly all the population of the Abruzzi, and Fra Diavolo scours the Terra di Lavoro and the garden plains behind Naples,	328
	Sir John Stuart's little army, reduced by malaria fevers, embarks for Sicily,	328
	Dessalines, the emperor of Hayti, is murdered by Christophe and Pétion; Christophe succeeds him; he issues a proclamation opening the ports of his dominions to neutral powers,	332, 333
	A bloody war ensues between Christophe and Pétion; Christophe remains undisputed master of the greater part of the country,	333
	Christophe proclaims himself king of Hayti under the title of Henry I.,	333
(Sept. 13.)	Fox dies,	349, 350
	Commodore Sir Samuel Hood captures four out of five large frigates that escape out of Rochefort,	335
	Lord Cochrane performs some daring exploits in the river Gironde,	335
(Oct. 8.)	Napoleon I.'s columns, having been collected about Bamberg, turn the Prussian left, gain possession of most of their magazines, and interpose between their main body and Berlin,	341
(Oct. 9.)	Frederick William III. of Prussia puts his army in motion,	340
(Oct. 14.)	The battles of Auerstadt and Jena,	341, 342
(Oct. 15.)	Marshal Möllendorf surrenders at Erfurt; General Kalkreuth, in attempting to cross the Harts mountains, is overtaken and routed,	342
	Bernadotte completely beats Prince Eugene of Wurtemberg,	342
(Oct. 18.)	Marshal Davoust takes possession of Leipsic,	343
(Oct. 25.)	Napoleon I. enters Berlin,	343
	He despatches Marshal Mortier to occupy the free-trading city of Hamburg, and to seize all British goods and property there,	344
	The Prince of Hohenlohe surrenders to Murat and Lannes,	345
	Blucher, being hemmed in by Soult, Murat, Lannes, and Bernadotte, throws himself into the town of Lubeck,	345
	Reinforcements having arrived from the Cape of Good Hope, Sir Home Popham lands a body of English troops at	

A.D.		PAGE
1806.	Maldonado, and the Spaniards are driven from the isle of Gorriti,	330
	During this year, General Miranda commences the war of independence in Spanish South America,	331, 332
	Napoleon I. makes General Dombrowski issue a proclamation to the Poles,	347
(Nov. 6.)	A battle takes place in the streets of Lubeck,	345
(Nov. 7.)	With tears in his eyes Blucher lays down his arms, and is sent prisoner to Hamburg,	345
	The Prussian fortresses of Spandau, Kustrin, Hameln, Nieuburg, and Magdeburg all surrender without attempting the least resistance,	346
	Frederick William III. of Prussia flees to the fortress of Königsburg on the Pregel,	346
(Nov. 16.)	Napoleon I. establishes his head-quarters at Posen,	347
(Nov. 21.)	He issues his well-known Berlin Decree against Great Britain and British manufactures, &c.,	344
	War breaks out between the Turks and Russians,	340
(Dec. 11.)	Napoleon I. enters Warsaw in triumph; he signs a most advantageous peace with the elector of Saxony, who is transformed into a king,	348
(Dec. 19.)	The new parliament assembles, and is opened by commission; the addresses are carried without a division,	350, 351
(Dec. 22.)	The papers relating to the late negotiations with Napoleon I. are presented to the House of Lords,	351
	The thanks of both Houses are voted to Major-general Sir John Stuart, and others,	351
(Dec. 26.)	Battle of Pultusk; the French retreat to Warsaw,	348
1807. (Jan. 1.)	The Dutch island of Curaçoa is captured,	383
	A bill for abolishing the slave-trade is read a first time, and printed,	355
(Jan. 18.)	An armament under Sir S. Auchmuty lands at Monte Video,	365
	The Spaniards make a sally, which is repelled with great slaughter,	365
	George III. sends a written message to the Princess of Wales, stating that he was satisfied there was no foundation for the charges of pregnancy and delivery, but that there was evidence of a deportment unbecoming her station,	320
	Mr Arbuthnot, British ambassador to the Porte, with his secretaries, attachés, dragomans, &c., go on board the *Endymion* frigate, and steal away from Constantinople,	370
	Arbuthnot joins Admiral Louis's squadron off Tenedos, and renews negotiations with the Porte through his dragoman, Berto-Pisani,	370, 371
(Jan. 25.)	The French suffer a reverse from the Russians,	389
(Feb. 2.)	Monte Video is taken by storm,	365
(Feb. 5.)	The bill for abolishing the slave-trade is read a second time,	355, 356
	It passes the Lords without a division, and is sent down to the Commons,	356
(Feb. 8.)	The battle of Eylau,	389–391
(Feb. 12.)	Napoleon I. proposes a suspension of hostilities and a separate peace, and to restore nearly all his dominions to Frederick William III. of Prussia,	391

A.D.		PAGE
1807.	Frederick William III. of Prussia refuses to accede to any peace in which Russia is not included,	391
(Feb. 19.)	Napoleon I. retreats to his old line on the Vistula,	391
	Beningsen advances, and occupies all the country evacuated by the enemy,	391
(Feb. 19.)	Duckworth's squadron engages a Turkish squadron above the castle of Abydos,	371, 372
	Alexander I. of Russia applies to the British government to negotiate a loan for him of six millions; the ministry decline; this gives mortal offence,	391
(Mar. 1.)	Sir John Duckworth bears up for the Dardanelles,	376
(Mar. 3.)	His fleet is injured in passing through the straits,	376, 377
	Duckworth sails for the mouths of the Nile,	377
(Mar. 16.)	The Slave-trade Bill, amended, is read a third time in the Commons,	356
	The amended Slave-trade Bill is carried back to the Lords,	356
(Mar. 20.)	Alexandria capitulates to Major-general M'Kenzie Fraser,	378
(Mar. 22.)	Sir John Duckworth's squadron arrives at Alexandria,	378
(Mar. 25.)	The Slave-trade Bill receives the royal assent,	357
(Mar. 25-31.)	The Duke of Portland becomes premier,	360-362
(Mar. 27.)	The British are defeated at Rosetta,	378
	The army in Alexandria are in a state of famine; Duckworth sails for England in the *Royal George*,	373
(April.)	The new ministry do all they can to excite a cry in the country against popery,	362, 363
(April 9.)	Brigadier-general Stewart and Colonel Oswald are detached to take Rosetta by regular siege,	379
(April 22.)	Colonel Macleod's detachment is completely cut off,	379
(April 23.)	Brigadier-general Stewart is driven from all his positions,	379
(May.)	The sultan declares war against England,	379
(May 27.)	The Prussian general Kalkreuth surrenders,	392
(May 31.)	Sultan Selim ceases to reign,	379-382
(June 14.)	The battle of Friedland,	393
	Beningsen retreats to Tilsit, where he is reinforced,	394
	Königsberg surrenders,	394
	A suspension of hostilities is agreed on between Napoleon I. and Alexander I. of Russia,	394
(June 22.)	The new parliament meets,	365
	The Irish Insurrection Bill passes,	365
(June 25.)	Napoleon I. and Alexander I. meet on a raft on the river Niemen, near Tilsit,	394
(June 26.)	The two emperors take up their residence in Tilsit,	394
(June 28.)	General Whitelocke lands nearly 8000 men thirty miles to the eastward of Buenos Ayres,	366
(July 1.)	The Russian admiral Siniavin defeats a Turkish squadron,	379
	The British attempt to storm Buenos Ayres; the Spaniards defend the city bravely,	367, 368
	General Craufurd surrenders to the Spaniards,	368
	Whitelocke agrees to withdraw,	368
	A treaty of peace is signed at Tilsit between France and Russia,	394, 395
1807. (July 9.)	A treaty of peace is signed at Tilsit between France and Prussia,	394, 395
	Napoleon I. arrives in Paris,	397
(July 26.)	Admiral Gambier, with a fleet and troops, sails for Denmark,	385
(Aug.)	The Crown Prince is asked to deliver up the Danish fleet; he refuses; Copenhagen put in a state of defence,	385
(Aug. 9.)	Talleyrand either voluntarily resigns or is dismissed from office,	413
(Aug. 12.)	The Crown Prince quits Copenhagen for Jutland,	385
(Aug. 17.)	The Danish gun-boats are driven into Copenhagen by the bomb-vessels,	386
(Aug. 18.)	Jerome Bonaparte made king of Westphalia,	397
	The French and their allies are beaten near Stralsund by Gustavus IV. of Sweden,	396
(Aug. 19.)	Gustavus IV. of Sweden evacuates Stralsund,	396
(Aug. 20.)	The Swedish army is landed on the island of Rugen, where fortifications and field-works are erected,	396
(Aug. 21.)	The island of Zealand is completely surrounded by the British ships,	386
(Aug. 22.)	General Fraser agrees to evacuate Egypt,	379
(Aug. 23.)	Lord Rosslyn's division is landed in Kioge Bay,	386
(Aug. 27.)	The Danish praams and gun-boats, &c., are driven away by the British with considerable loss,	386, 387
(Aug. 29.)	Sir Arthur Wellesley defeats the Danes at Kioge,	387
	The Danes in Copenhagen attempt several sorties,	387
(Sept. 1.)	Commodore Keats is detached to blockade Stralsund,	387
(Sept. 2-5.)	Copenhagen is bombarded,	387
(Sept. 4.)	Vice-admiral T. Macnamara Russell and Captain Lord Falkland capture the Danish island of Heligoland,	388
(Sept. 6.)	Copenhagen capitulates,	387
	The Swedish army in Rugen capitulate to the French,	396
(Sept. 17.)	The Danish fleet is taken away,	387, 388
(Sept. 23.)	The remains of General Fraser's army sail from Egypt for Sicily,	379
(Oct. 18.)	A French army, under Junot, commences its march through Spain for the frontiers of Portugal,	397
	Napoleon I. proclaims that the House of Braganza has ceased to reign in Europe,	397
	Denmark declares war against England,	388
(Oct. 27.)	A treaty is concluded at Fontainebleau between France and Spain,	397
(Nov. 4.)	The British government order reprisals to be granted against the ships, goods, and subjects of Denmark,	388
(Nov. 16.)	Napoleon I. quits Paris to visit Milan and Venice,	396
(Nov. 29.)	The prince regent of Portugal, his court, and an immense number of Portuguese nobility, &c.—in all, 18,000—sail for Brazil,	397
(Nov. 30.)	Junot and his army enter Lisbon,	397
	Sir Sidney Smith blockades the Tagus,	397
(Dec. 17.)	Napoleon I. issues his celebrated Milan decree,	398
	Napoleon I. informs the queen regent of Etruria, that she must resign Tuscany for the new kingdom of Northern Lusitania,	398
	Tuscany is occupied by French troops,	398
	The Danish West India islands of St	

CHRONOLOGICAL INDEX.

A.D.		PAGE
1807.	Thomas, St John's, and Santa Croce surrender to the British,	388
	A great many merchant-vessels, carrying the Danish flag, are captured,	388
1808. (Jan.)	French divisions march into Spain as friends, and seize St Sebastian, Pamplona, and Barcelona,	401
	Godoy orders the commanders of fortresses to receive the French as friends and allies,	401
(Feb.)	General Miollis enters Rome; the pope shuts himself up in the Quirinal Palace, which the French surround with their artillery,	398
(Mar. 13.)	Murat arrives at Burgos to take the command-in-chief in Spain,	403
(Mar. 18.)	General Whitelocke is condemned to be cashiered,	369
(Mar. 19.)	Charles IV. abdicates in favour of his son Ferdinand,	403, 404
(Mar. 23.)	Ferdinand VII. makes his entry into Madrid as king,	404
	Murat intimates that he cannot recognise the abdication without instructions from the Emperor Napoleon I.,	404
	He opens a correspondence with the queen and the prisoner Godoy,	404
	Charles IV. writes to Napoleon I., and declares that the abdication was forced upon him,	404
	The sword of Francis I. is presented by Ferdinand VII. to Murat, to be presented to the Emperor Napoleon I.,	404, 405
	A bill passes for regulating commercial intercourse with the United States,	399
	A clause is carried for insertion in the Mutiny Bill, to permit soldiers to enlist for life,	400
(April 2.)	Napoleon I. annexes the Marches or Adriatic provinces of the pope to his kingdom of Italy,	399
	General Savary is sent to Madrid, and reports unfavourably of Murat's conduct,	405
(April 8.)	General Castaños, commanding the army of Andalusia, applies to the English for aid,	415
(April 20.)	Ferdinand VII. arrives at Bayonne to visit Napoleon I.,	407
	Napoleon I. declares, 'that the interests of my house and of my empire demand that the Bourbons shall no longer reign in Spain,'	407, 408
	Don Carlos, in attempting to pass out of one of the gates of Bayonne, is forcibly stopped by a gendarme,	408
	Murat is ordered to take Godoy out of prison; he arrives at Bayonne, and is received by Napoleon I. as a bosom-friend,	409
(April 30.)	Charles IV., the queen, and Don Francesco de Paulo, their youngest son, and two or three grandees, arrive at Bayonne,	409
(May.)	Charles IV. protests that his abdication of the 19th March had proceeded from violence, and calls upon his son to restore him to the crown,	409
	Ferdinand VII. offers to do so with the sanction of the Cortes,	409
	Ferdinand VII. offers to resign the crown unconditionally, provided they are permitted to quit Bayonne and return to their own country and capital,	409
(May 5.)	Insurrection breaks out in every town of Spain, except those occupied by strong French garrisons,	414

A.D.		PAGE
1808.	The French issue manifestoes; the people spit upon and tear them; French agents are slaughtered,	415
	Charles IV. resigns all Spanish colonies and territories whatever, to his friend and faithful ally Napoleon I., emperor of the French, &c.,	410
(May 6.)	Ferdinand VII. signs a formal act restoring the crown to his father,	410
(May 10.)	Ferdinand VII. is forced to sign his second and final act of abdication,	410, 411
	The Spaniards in Junot's army desert in small parties, and afterwards a whole regiment,	430
	Junot plunders remorselessly at Lisbon, and Kellermann and his other generals closely follow his example,	430
	The Spanish general Bellesta disarms and arrests the French at Oporto,	430
	Bellesta marches to Coruña with his prisoners,	430
	The Portuguese governor of Oporto declares for the French, and puts down the popular insurrection,	430
	Junot disarms 4200 Spanish troops,	430
	The Portuguese rise in insurrection; a provisional junta is formed at Oporto,	431
	The junta of Oporto proclaim the prince, and declare war against the French,	431
	The town of Evora becomes the centre of the insurrection,	431, 432
	The inhabitants of Evora are massacred by the French,	432
	General Margaron executes similar vengeance at Leyria; equally atrocious scenes take place at Guarda, at Beja, and Villaviçosa,	432
	After plundering Evora, Elvas, and Portalegre, Loison marches to Abrantes, on his route to Lisbon,	432
(May 25.)	The inhabitants of Zaragoza and the peasantry fly to arms,	425
	Don José Palafox is made commander,	425
(May 31.)	Palafox formally declares war against the emperor of the French,	426
(June 8.)	The British government resolve to afford the loyal party in Spain the assistance of 10,000 men,	416
(June 10.)	Lord Collingwood goes through the straits to Cadiz, to take the command of the fleet assembled there,	416
	General Spencer arrives at Cadiz with 5000 men,	416
	Duhesme, commanding the French army in Catalonia, fails to take Gerona by storm,	428
	Duhesme is obliged to retreat upon Barcelona; he burns the towns and villages in passing,	428, 429
	Lord Collingwood concludes a treaty with the captain-general of the Balearic Isles, which renders the Spanish ships and troops available for the Catalans,	429
	The French army in Catalonia is reinforced,	429
	Duhesme is again unsuccessful before Gerona,	429
	Duhesme flies for Barcelona,	429
	Barcelona is blockaded by Lord Cochrane,	429
	Duhesme reaches Barcelona, flying before the Spanish general Caldagues,	429
(June 14.)	The Spaniards are defeated by the French near Valladolid,	418
	The town of Medina del Rio Seco is defended by the inhabitants and monks; many French soldiers are killed from under cover,	418

A.D. 1808.		PAGE
	Bessières liberates his prisoners, and is recalled to Madrid,	418
(June 16.)	General Lefebvre Desnouettes begins to invest Zaragoza,	426
	The town of Zaragoza is put in a state of defence,	426
	Verange, the Spanish general, is defeated,	426
	Palafox enters Zaragoza,	426
(June 17.)	Dupont begins to retreat,	418, 419
(June 18.)	Jaen is stormed by Dupont.	419
	Dupont is reinforced by General Vedel; he detaches General Cassagne against the Granadians,	419
	Cassagne beats the insurgents,	419
(June 23.)	Joseph issues a proclamation to his late Neapolitan subjects,	412
(June 28, 29.)	Marshal Moncey attacks Valencia,	429
(June 29.)	In the evening, Moncey relinquishes the attack, and begins a hasty retreat,	429
	He defeats completely the Spanish general, Serbelloni, in the open field,	429
	Tuscany is formally annexed to the French empire,	398
	The Junta of Seville declare peace with England,	417
	Castaños holds the French general, Dupont, in check,	417
(July 3.)	An atrocious butchery is committed at Cuença,	429, 430
	Insurgent bands gather round Moncey and Frère, cutting off their stragglers, and killing every Frenchman they can surprise,	430
	Marshal Moncey is recalled to Madrid, to protect his gracious Majesty King Joseph,	430
	The Maid of Zaragoza distinguishes herself	426
(July 7.)	Napoleon I. appoints Joseph to the throne of Spain and the Indies,	412
(July 12.)	Lieutenant-general Sir Arthur Wellesley sails from the Cove of Cork for the peninsula,	432
(July 15.)	Napoleon I. appoints Murat king of Naples and Sicily,	412
	Dupont is reinforced by General Gobert,	419
(July 19.)	The battle of Baylen; defeat of the French,	420
	Joseph makes his entry into Madrid,	415
	General Wellesley arrives at Coruña,	432, 433
(July 22.)	Dupont and Vedel surrender, with their whole army of 18,000 or 19,000 men, to Castaños,	421
	Some of the French prisoners are robbed and massacred,	421
	Joseph is proclaimed king at Madrid,	415
	The Supreme Junta of Spain and the Indies declare war against Joseph,	415
	All the French ships in Cadiz are seized, and the officers and crews made prisoners,	415
(July 30.)	General Wellesley anchors in Mondego Bay, and next day the troops are landed near the town of Figueira,	433
(Aug.)	Generals Castaños and Morla are welcomed with great honour and ceremony at Seville; the junta adopt Morla's opinion, and break the capitulation,	421, 422
(Aug. 3 or 4.)	The French open a tremendous battery on the quarter of Zaragoza called Santa Engracia,	427
	The storming columns rush into the very heart of the city,	427
	Fearful street-fighting takes place,	427
	One half of the town is in possession of the French,	427

A.D. 1808.		PAGE
(Aug. 5.)	Don Francisco Palafox enters the city with a reinforcement of 2000 or 3000 Spanish guards and Swiss veterans,	427
	General Spencer joins Wellesley from Cadiz,	433
(Aug. 7.)	Murderous street-fighting still takes place in Zaragoza,	427
(Aug. 14.)	The French raise the siege of Zaragoza,	428
	The English enter the town of Alcobaça,	434
(Aug. 16.)	Battle of Roliça; the French are worsted,	434, 435
	General Wellesley is superseded by Sir Harry Burrard,	435
(Aug. 21.)	Battle of Vimeiro; the British break and scatter the French,	436
(Aug. 22.)	Sir Hew Dalrymple supersedes Sir Harry Burrard,	436
(Aug. 23.)	Sir Hew Dalrymple advances from Vimeiro to Ramalhal, near Torres Vedras,	437
	Castaños enters Madrid,	425
(Aug. 26.)	Sir John Moore arrives in Maceira Bay, with 20,000 men,	438
(Aug. 30.)	Junot signs the Definitive Treaty,	438
(Aug. 31.)	Sir Hew Dalrymple ratifies the Convention at Torres Vedras, called the Convention of Cintra,	438, 439
	A separate convention is signed between Admirals Cotton and Siniavin,	439
(Sept.)	The forts on the Tagus are taken possession of by the British, and the port of Lisbon is opened to their shipping,	439
	A council of regency is appointed,	439
	Napoleon I. and the Emperor of Russia meet at Erfurt, and address a joint-letter to the king of England, inviting him to a speedy pacification,	444
(Oct. 4–18.)	The island of Capri, in the Gulf of Naples, is taken by Murat's troops,	493
	Sir John Moore's army, on account of the scantiness of subsistence in Portugal, is obliged to march by different routes,	442
(Oct. 13.)	Sir David Baird, with 10,000 men, anchors at Coruña,	442
	The French pour into Spain through the mountain-passes behind the Ebro,	443
(Oct. 27.)	Napoleon I. sets out from Paris to cross the Pyrenees,	445
(Oct. 31.)	General Blake is worsted by Lefebvre,	446
(Nov. 1.)	The French enter Bilbos,	446
(Nov. 5.)	Blake defeats a French division,	446
(Nov. 8.)	Napoleon I. arrives at his brother's head-quarters at Vitoria, and takes the entire direction of the campaign,	446
(Nov. 9.)	Blake's rear-guard is surprised and defeated with great loss; he flees to Reynosa, to secure a strong position,	446
	Blake flees to the port of Santander,	446
	The magazines at Reynosa fall into the hands of the French,	446
(Nov. 11.)	Sir John Moore crosses the boundary of Portugal, and arrives at Ciudad Rodrigo,	442
	Sir Hew Dalrymple, and Sir Harry Burrard are recalled,	440
(Nov. 14.)	Another revolution takes place at Constantinople,	501–503
	Sir John Moore orders Hope and Baird to hasten to Salamanca,	444
(Nov. 23.)	The battle of Tudela; the Spaniards are defeated,	446
(Nov. 28.)	Sir John Moore determines to lead back his troops to Lisbon,	448
(Nov. 30.)	Sir John Moore receives favourable news from Madrid,	449
	Napoleon I. carries the principal pass of Somosierra,	447

CHRONOLOGICAL INDEX.

A.D.		PAGE
1808. (Dec. 2.)	Bessières takes possession of the heights of Madrid; Napoleon I. arrives, and the town is summoned and attacked,	447
(Dec. 4.)	Madrid surrenders,	448
	Joseph Bonaparte enters Madrid at the tail of the French army,	448
(Dec. 5 or 6.)	Sir John Moore is joined by the ordnance from General Hope's division,	450
(Dec. 9.)	Colonel Graham brings news of the capitulation of Madrid,	451
(Dec. 20.)	The whole of the forces of Moore, Baird, and Hope unite at and near Mayorga, Napoleon I. suspends every other operation, and not fewer than 100,000 men are hurrying forward by four different routes to crush Moore,	452
(Dec. 26.)	The whole British army is safely behind the Esla,	453
	Moore rests two days at Benevente, where he is obliged to destroy most of his stores,	453
(Dec. 27.)	The court of inquiry on the Convention of Cintra, after several adjournments, exonerates all the generals,	440
(Dec. 29.)	The mass of the British army reach Astorga,	453
	Lord Paget scatters the French,	453, 454
1809. (Jan. 1.)	Napoleon I. takes possession of Astorga,	454
(Jan. 2.)	Napoleon I. intrusts the pursuit of Moore to Soult,	454
	Soult throws himself into Galicia, and his cavalry are soon close to the British rear; the roads are wretched with snow and rain,	454
	The British have almost no provisions; nothing but sour wine,	454
	Whenever the French come up, the British form in good order, and beat them off,	454
	General the Hon. Sir E. Paget repulses a greatly superior force before Lugo,	454
(Jan. 5.)	A treaty of peace is signed between the Ottoman Porte and England,	500
	The czar declares war anew, upon the pretext of the sultan's treaty with England,	503
(Jan. 13.)	Moore reaches Coruña,	455
	Canning signs a treaty of alliance with the Spanish insurgents,	461
(Jan. 16.)	The battle of Coruña,	455–457
(Jan. 17.)	The embarkation of the British army commences,	458
(Jan. 18.)	The rear-guard is embarked, and all sail for England,	458
(Jan. 27.)	Mr Wardle makes a motion for a committee of inquiry into the conduct of the Duke of York and Mrs Mary Anne Clarke, carrying on a traffic in commissions and promotions,	462, 463
	The inquiry occupies the attention of parliament for seven weeks,	463–466
(Feb.)	Votes of thanks are passed in both Houses to Sir Arthur Wellesley,	470
(Feb. 14.)	Zaragoza surrenders to the French,	470
	The Prince Regent of Portugal appoints General Beresford to the chief command of all his troops,	471
(Mar. 17.)	The Duke of York is pronounced guiltless of corruption, &c.,	466
(Mar. 21.)	The Duke of York tenders his resignation; it is accepted,	467
	The Duke of York is succeeded as commander-in-chief by Lieutenant-general Sir David Dundas,	467
1809.	During this session a bill passes to prevent the sale and brokerage of offices,	467, 468
	Francis II. of Austria declares war against France,	508
	Sir Arthur Wellesley accepts the chief command of the British forces in the Peninsula,	470
(Mar. 29.)	Soult takes possession of Oporto,	470
(April.)	The Tyrolese rise against the French, and choose Andrew Hofer as their generalissimo,	517, 518
(April 10.)	The Archduke Charles crosses the Inn, and occupies Bavaria; the Archduke John descends the Alps into Italy, driving the French and Italian troops of Eugene Beauharnais before him,	508
	In Poland the Archduke Ferdinand defeats Poniatowski, and marches as a conqueror into the city of Warsaw,	508
(April 12.)	Lord Cochrane, with fireships, and covered by Lord Gambier's frigates and small vessels, partially destroys the French ships in Basque Roads,	507
	Lord Cochrane, on his return to England, receives the red riband of the Bath,	508
(April 15.)	Sir Arthur Wellesley sails from Portsmouth,	470
(April 20.)	Napoleon I. defeats the Archduke Charles's advanced-guard at Abensberg,	508
(April 22.)	Sir Arthur Wellesley arrives at Lisbon and takes the command,	470, 471
(April 23.)	Napoleon I. takes the city of Ratisbon,	508
	Napoleon I. thoroughly defeats the Archduke Charles at Eckmuhl,	508
	The archduke retires into Bohemia,	508
(April 28.)	Sir Arthur Wellesley leaves Lisbon for Coimbra,	471
	Hofer defeats the Bavarian troops in the Valley of the Eisach,	518
	Poniatowski drives the Austrians out of Warsaw,	512
(May.)	Poniatowski defeats the Archduke Ferdinand in two battles,	512
	Eugene Beauharnais is defeated at Sacile by the Archduke John,	513
(May 4.)	A bill is introduced and afterwards passed to prevent the procuring or obtaining seats by corrupt practices, and for the prevention of bribery,	469
(May 9.)	Wellesley moves in the direction of Oporto,	471
(May 11.)	The passage of the Douro; the British charge the French through the streets of Oporto; Soult retreats in the utmost confusion,	471
	Soult changes his route for Salamonde and Montealegre,	473
	Napoleon I. enters Vienna in triumph,	508
(May 16.)	Wellesley overtakes Soult at Salamanca, and cuts up his rear-guard,	473
	Wellesley pursues the French to the frontiers of Spain, and then returns to Oporto,	473, 474
(May 17.)	Napoleon I. issues a decree uniting the remainder of the Roman States to the French empire,	514
(May 21, 22.)	The battle of Aspern,	509
	The loss of the French in killed and wounded is very great; Marshal Lannes, Duke of Montebello, Generals Espagne and Saint-Hilaire are killed,	509
	Alexander I. of Russia declares war against Austria; patriotic insurrections break out in all parts of Germany; Jerome, king of Westphalia, is compelled to fly from his capital, &c.,	509

A.D.		PAGE
1809.	Beauharnais worsts the Archduke John in a battle near Conegliano,	513
	Twenty thousand Tyrolese peasants take Innspruck,	518
	The Tyrolese surround and take 4000 or 5000 disciplined French troops; they also beat 3000 or 4000 Bavarian troops, and all the battalions and squadrons in succession,	518
(June.)	The king of Wurtemburg is nearly reduced to as sad straits as his brother-in-law, the king of Westphalia,	510
	Macdonald is beaten in two affairs in the mountains of Carniola,	513
(June 11.)	Sir John Stuart, with 15,000 British troops, embarks at Messina,	495
(June 13.)	The French abandon the greater part of their posts along the shore of Calabria Ulteriore,	495
	Arms and ammunition are landed and sent up the country for the use of the insurgents,	495
(June 14.)	The Archduke John is defeated at Raab by the French,	513
(June 15.)	Sir Francis Burdett makes a motion for a sweeping reform in parliament, and is outvoted,	469
(July 5.)	Napoleon I. establishes himself on the left bank of the Danube,	510
(July 6.)	The battle of Wagram; the Austrians are defeated,	510, 511
(July 6.)	Pope Pius VII. is seized,	514
	Napoleon I. takes up his residence in the imperial palace of Schönbrunn,	512
	Sir John Stuart returns to Sicily,	497
	The siege of Scylla is unsuccessful,	497
	The French garrison of Scylla soon after abandon it,	497
(July 20.)	Cuesta effects a junction with Wellesley at Oropesa,	474
(July 22.)	The combined armies of Wellesley and Cuesta attack Marshal Victor's outposts at Talavera, and drive them in,	475
(July 27, 28.)	The battle of Talavera; the French are defeated,	477, 478
	General Robert Craufurd joins Wellesley,	479
(Aug. 1 or 2.)	Flushing is invested by the British,	488
(Aug. 3.)	The British army set out for Oropesa, leaving Cuesta at Talavera to protect the hospitals,	480
	Wellesley retreats across the Tagus,	481
	Marshal Lefebvre is defeated by the Tyrolese; Innspruck is recovered, which Hofer enters, and acts as viceroy,	519
(Aug. 13.)	Flushing is bombarded,	488
(Aug. 15.)	General Monnet, commanding the garrison of Flushing, requests an armistice,	488
(Aug. 16.)	The capitulation is signed,	489
	Marshal Bernadotte arrives at Antwerp,	489
(Aug. 27.)	Chatham calls a council of war, which is of opinion that it is not advisable to undertake further operations,	489
(Aug. 30, 31.)	The French open a fire of guns and mortars from both banks of the river, and compel the ships to retire,	489
(Sept. 2.)	Wellesley's head-quarters are at Badajoz,	482
(Sept. 4.)	Sir Arthur Wellesley is raised to the peerage,	483
	Every part of Zealand is evacuated by the English, except the island of Walcheren,	489
	An irregular guerilla warfare goes on in Spain,	483
(Sept. 14.)	Chatham embarks for England,	489
	The Walcheren fever increases fearfully among the soldiery,	489–491

A.D.		PAGE
1809. (Sept. 21.)	A duel takes place between Lord Castlereagh and Mr Canning,	522
	The Duke of Portland resigns, and dies a few days after,	522
	An expedition sails from Messina against the islands of Corfu, Zante, and Cephalonia,	499, 500
	The Russians force the passes of the Balkan or Mount Hæmus, and advance on Constantinople,	503
(Oct. 1.)	The expedition from Messina anchors in the Bay of Zante,	500
(Oct. 2.)	The French commander capitulates,	500
	The islands of Zante, Cephalonia, Ithaca, and Cerigo are surrendered,	500
(Oct. 10.)	Lord Wellington arrives at Lisbon, and determines on the construction of the famous lines at Torres Vedras,	484
(Oct. 14.)	The treaty of Schönbrunn,	515
(Oct. 22.)	While the Russians are investing Silistria, they are attacked and defeated by the Turks,	503, 504
	A second action takes place; the Russians are again defeated,	504
(Oct. 25.)	A grand national jubilee takes place on George III. entering upon the fiftieth year of his reign,	562
(Nov. 26.)	The destruction of the piers and floodgates of Flushing begun; the arsenals and magazines are burned,	492
	Hofer gains one more victory in the vale of Passeyer; Speckbacher and other chiefs gain several more advantages,	519, 520
	The French, Bavarians, and Saxons get possession of the larger towns and villages in the Tyrol,	520
	Many of the insurgents are taken prisoners, and shot or hanged,	520
(Dec. 3.)	Napoleon I. returns triumphantly to Paris, and opens the session of the Corps Legislatif,	515
	Mr Perceval becomes prime-minister, and the administration is formed,	525
	The British army quits Spain,	486
	During this year the British take possession of the French West India colonies of Cayenne and Martinique, and part of Spanish San Domingo, also Senegal on the coast of Africa,	504
(Dec. 10.)	Gerona surrenders,	536
	Blake is twice defeated by Suchet,	536
	Soult is appointed chief of the staff and principal military adviser of King Joseph,	536
(Dec. 15.)	A grand *conseil de famille* is held at the palace of the Tuileries, where the divorce of Napoleon I. and Josephine is settled,	556, 557
	Josephine is left with the title of Empress-Queen, an annual revenue of 2,000,000 of francs, and the royal domain of Navarre,	557
1810. (Jan.)	Soult enters Seville in triumph,	536
	The Dutch settlement of Amboyna, with its dependent islands, is taken,	555
	Murat threatens Sicily with invasion,	555
	Hofer is betrayed by a priest called Doney,	520
(Feb.)	Hofer is condemned and shot,	520, 521
(Feb. 15.)	The siege of Cadiz,	538
	The whole of Andalusia is overrun by the French,	538
(Feb. 22.)	Lord Collingwood writes to the Admiralty for permission to return to England on account of bad health,	505
	Guadaloupe surrenders to the British,	555

CHRONOLOGICAL INDEX. 87

A.D.		PAGE
1810. (Mar. 3.)	Lord Collingwood resigns the command to Rear-admiral Martin,	505
(Mar. 7.)	He dies at sea,	506
(Mar. 11.)	Berthier, acting as proxy for Napoleon I., receives the hand of the Archduchess Maria Louisa at Schönbrunn,	558
(April 1.)	Napoleon I. and Maria Louisa come to St Cloud to be married ecclesiastically,	559
	The marriage is unpopular both in France and Austria,	559
	During the month of April, London is in a ferment on account of Sir Francis Burdett,	527–532
	The French enter Murcia, and force the Spaniards to retreat down to the eastern coast, and take shelter in Alicant; the whole population of Andalusia is in arms,	538
	A body of French left at Ronda is surprised and defeated by General Lacey and a detachment of Spanish troops,	538
	In Catalonia, O'Donnell completely foils Marshals Suchet, Augereau, and Macdonald in several of their enterprises,	538
	Ney, Kellermann, and Loison threaten the Portuguese frontier,	538
(May.)	Marshal Massena takes the command over the corps of Ney, Kellermann, Loison, Junot, and Drouet,	539
(June 1.)	Napoleon I. arrives in Paris,	560
	During Napoleon I.'s absence, Fouché opens a communication with Sir Francis Baring,	560
(June 3.)	Napoleon I., incensed at Fouché's conduct, dismisses him from office; Savary is installed in his place,	560
	Massena commences to invest Ciudad Rodrigo,	539
(June 21.)	Parliament is prorogued, and Burdett and Jones are liberated,	533, 534
	A vote of thanks and £2000 per annum are passed to Lord Wellington,	534
	Addresses to George III. are carried to induce other nations to co-operate in the abolition of the slave-trade,	534
	A scheme for parliamentary reform is rejected,	535
(June 29.)	After having had disputes with his brother Louis, king of Holland, Napoleon I. sends General Oudinot, who takes possession of Utrecht, and demands entrance into Amsterdam,	560, 561
(July 1.)	Louis signs an act of abdication in favour of his infant son, and a proclamation to the Dutch people,	561
(July 9.)	Napoleon I. issues a decree that 'Holland is re-united to France,'	561
	The Isle of Bourbon submits to the British,	555
(July 10.)	Ciudad Rodrigo capitulates, and the French enter it,	539
	The Dutch island of Banda and its dependencies are reduced by Captain Cole,	555
	By a decree of the Prince Regent of Portugal, Wellington is appointed commander-in-chief and marshal-general of the Portuguese army,	550
(Sept. 15.)	The great French army begins its march down the valley of the Mondego,	542
	Wellington takes up a strong position in front of Coimbra,	542
	General Cavaignac embarks at Reggio, and effects a landing about seven miles south of Messina; he is repulsed by Colonel G. Campbell with the greatest facility,	555

A.D.		PAGE
1810. (Sept. 24.)	The Spanish Cortes at Cadiz commence their proceedings, &c.,	553
	They appoint a new regency, and pass various decrees,	554
(Sept. 27.)	The battle of Busaco,	542–544
	The French are beaten at all points,	544
(Oct. 6.)	Wellington writes to the British minister at Lisbon, to tell the members of regency to mind their own business,	550, 551
(Oct. 7.)	Massena comes in sight of the lines of Torres Vedras,	546
(Oct. 8.)	The allied army enter the lines of Torres Vedras, which are daily strengthened,	548
	Massena reconnoitres the lines for some days,	548
	Wellington is reinforced from England and Gibraltar,	548
(Oct. 25.)	It is publicly announced that George III. is again attacked with the mental malady under which he had formerly laboured,	563
(Nov. 2.)	The Princess Amelia dies,	563
(Nov. 15.)	Massena begins a retrograde movement, and fixes his head-quarters at Torres Novas,	549
(Nov. 30.)	The Portuguese troops at Torres Vedras begin to desert,	551
	Wellington is obliged to provide the starving Spanish troops from his own stores,	551
	The French army in Portugal subsist only by plunder,	551
(Dec. 3.)	The French in the Mauritius capitulate,	555
	By the opening of 1811, France has not a ship on the Indian Ocean, or a strip of land in either of the Indies,	555
(Dec. 13.)	Friesland, Oldenburg, Bremen, all the line of coast to Hamburg, with all the country between Hamburg and Lubeck, are annexed to the French empire,	561
	During this year, Marshal Bernadotte is elected crown-prince of Sweden, with the throne in succession,	562
(Dec. 20.)	The House of Commons passes resolutions declaring the competency of both Houses of parliament to supply the deficiency of the executive power; the appointment of the Prince of Wales as regent, &c.,	564, 565
	The resolutions are taken to the Lords, and carried,	564, 565
(Dec. 30.)	Mr Perceval proposes the same restrictions and limitations on the powers of the regent as were passed in 1788; they are agreed to,	565
(Dec. 31.)	The French fail in their attempt to carry Tarifa by storm,	603
1811. (Jan. 1.)	A clause is added to the Regency Bill for allowing the regent to bestow the peerage upon deserving civilians, lawyers, &c.,	565
	The Portuguese regency claim the entire control and distribution of the English subsidy; Wellington insists that it should be under the control of the British ambassador,	575
	Whole brigades of Portuguese are frequently left without bread, and are left to be fed by the English commissariat, &c.,	576
(Jan. 22.)	Soult captures the fortress of Olivença,	576
(Feb.)	He receives orders to act in concert with Massena; a new French army of 70,000 men is formed in the north of Spain under Marshal Bessières,	576
(Feb. 19.)	Soult sits down to besiege Badajoz,	576
	Massena's army is demoralised,	576

A.D.		PAGE
1811. (Mar.)	The battle of Barrosa; the French are defeated,	581
	Admiral Keats dismantles all the sea-defences and batteries on the Bay of Cadiz, from Rota to Santa Maria, except Catalina,	581
(Mar. 11.)	Badajos surrenders,	579, 580
	Soult gives up the command to Mortier, and hastens to Seville,	580
	The French are repulsed at the bridge of Coimbra,	577
(Mar. 19.)	Wellington compels Massena to retreat, and to forsake his foraging-parties,	578
(Mar. 20.)	The Empress Maria Louisa is delivered of a son, who receives the titles of Prince of the French Empire and King of Rome,	590
	Every horror that can make war hideous attends Massena's retreat,	578
	Mortier captures Campo-Mayor,	581
(Mar. 25.)	On the appearance of Marshal Beresford, the French evacuate Campo-Mayor, and retreat to Badajoz, pursued all the way by the British cavalry,	582
	The king of Sweden transfers the whole royal authority to Bernadotte, the crown-prince,	589
	Bernadotte resolves to act as a Swede, and not as a French marshal,	589
(April 5.)	Beresford begins to cross the Guadiana,	582
(April 6.)	Massena crosses the Agueda into Spain; the termination of the third French invasion of Portugal,	579
(April 9-15.)	The British recover the fortress of Olivenza, and two or three important positions on the Valverde river,	582
(April 20.)	Wellington arrives at Beresford's camp, reconnoitres Badajoz, and orders immediate operations against it,	582
(May 2.)	Massena re-enters Portugal,	582
	Badajoz is invested,	584
	A Spanish army is collected in Estremadura to co-operate with Beresford; Castaños agrees to serve under him, and leave the entire command of the allies to him,	584
(May 5.)	The battle of Fuentes de Onoro; the French are defeated,	583
	Massena is recalled; Marshal Marmont succeeds him,	584
	Marshal Ney, Generals Junot and Loison repair to Paris, whither King Joseph had preceded them,	584
	Marmont continues the retreat, and retires to Salamanca, where he puts his army into cantonments,	584
(May 6.)	The report of the Bullion Committee is presented, and discussed for four nights,	572
(May 16.)	The battle of Albuera; defeat of the French,	585, 586
(May 25.)	The Duke of York is reappointed commander-in-chief; he establishes regimental schools on the Bell system,	571
(June 16.)	Napoleon I. opens the Corps Legislatif, where deputies from Holland, the United Provinces, Hanse Towns, Swiss, &c., assemble,	590, 591
	The pope refuses to fill up the vacant bishoprics; Napoleon I. assembles a French ecclesiastical council; they adopt a report which he himself had dictated,	591, 592
(June 28.)	Marshal Suchet takes Tarragona by storm,	589
	Marmont separates from Soult, and marches to Salamanca; Wellington makes a	

A.D.		PAGE
1811.	corresponding movement to the northward, leaving General Hill in the Alemtejo,	588
(July 24.)	Parliament is prorogued by commission,	574
(Aug.)	The islands of Java and Madura are reduced by a British and sepoy army from Madras,	590
(Oct. 25.)	Blake is defeated by Suchet, in the province of Valencia,	589
(Oct. 28.)	General Hill routs the French general, Girard, at Arroyo Molinos, in Spanish Estremadura,	588
(Dec.)	During this autumn and winter, the Russian czar, Alexander I., is traduced by the most atrocious calumnies published at Paris under the authority of Napoleon I.,	593
1812. (Jan.)	The city of Valencia capitulates,	589
(Jan. 16.)	The king of the Two Sicilies transfers all his rights and prerogatives to his son, Don Francisco,	620
	The command of the Sicilian troops is given to Lord William Bentinck,	620
	A constitution is framed on the plan of the British,	621, 622
(Jan. 19.)	Ciudad Rodrigo is stormed and carried,	601
	Napoleon I. sends Davoust to take possession of Swedish Pomerania and the Isle of Rugen,	636
(Feb. 19.)	The Marquis Wellesley resigns the foreign secretaryship, and is succeeded by Lord Castlereagh,	596
(Mar. 16.)	Wellington invests Badajoz,	602
	Soult collects all his disposable forces at Seville, to march to the relief of Badajoz; Marmont enters Portugal, and ravages the country east of Estrella,	602
	A treaty of alliance between Sweden and Russia is signed at St Petersburg,	640
	Napoleon I. pours troops into Prussia, Pomerania, and the Duchy of Warsaw,	636
(April 6, 7.)	Badajoz is stormed,	602
(April 9.)	Soult retreats to Seville,	603
(April 13.)	Wellington moves the main body of his army to the north; Marmont retreats to Salamanca,	603
	General Hill carries the strong forts erected by the French at Almaraz,	603
(April 14.)	At a secret sitting of congress, an embargo is laid upon all ships and vessels of the United States for ninety days, to lessen the number that would be at the mercy of England when war is declared,	630
(May.)	Napoleon I. directs Maret, Duke of Bassano, to propose negotiations with England on the basis of the uti possidetis,	636
	Lord Castlereagh replies that England's engagements with the Spanish cortes rendered the acknowledgment of Joseph impossible,	636
(May 9.)	Napoleon I. and the Empress set out from Paris for Dresden,	636
	The kings of Bavaria, Würtemburg, Saxony, and other tributary princes, meet Napoleon I. at Dresden, also the emperor and empress of Austria, and the king of Prussia,	636
	The king of Prussia, Frederick William III., having already placed 20,000 men at Napoleon I.'s disposal, Francis II. of Austria engages to furnish 30,000 men to act against Russian Poland,	636
(May 11.)	Mr Percival is shot in the lobby of the House of Commons by Bellingham,	597
(May 18.)	Bellingham is executed,	598

CHRONOLOGICAL INDEX. 89

A.D.		PAGE
1812. (May 28.)	The preliminaries of peace between Russia and Turkey are ratified at Bucharest,	640
	The fastest sailing ships, brigs, and schooners of the American merchant service are fitted out as privateers,	630
(June 2.)	Napoleon I. arrives at Thorn; his army consists of 270,000 French, 80,000 Germans of the Confederation of the Rhine, 30,000 Poles, 20,000 Italians, and 20,000 Prussians,	636
(June 8.)	Lord Liverpool is appointed first lord of the Treasury,	600
(June 24, 25.)	The grand army, in three columns, crosses the Niemen, and enters Lithuania without opposition,	636
	The Russian army, under Barclay de Tolli, evacuates Wilna, and retires towards the Dwina; another army 80,000 strong, under Prince Bagration, is stationed near the Dnieper,	636
(June 28.)	Napoleon I. enters Wilna,	636
	The French, Germans, and Poles maraud, plunder, and violate,	637
(July 16.)	The grand army leaves Wilna,	637
	In their march through Lithuania more than 100,000 men drop off from death, sickness, desertion, or through the surprises and captures of the Cossacks,	637
	Murat pursues the Russian rear-guard, and nearly every evening attacks it,	638
	Partial engagements take place at Mohileff and Witepsk; Barclay de Tolli continues his retreat on Smolensk,	638
	The Americans cross the Detroit frontier, and issue a proclamation calling on the oppressed citizens of Canada to throw off their allegiance, &c.,	632
(July 22.)	The battle of Salamanca; the French are defeated,	606, 607
	A treaty of peace and amity between Great Britain and Sweden is ratified,	640
	General Maitland lands at Port Mahon, in Minorca,	610
(July 31.)	Wellington marches against King Joseph Bonaparte,	607, 608
(Aug. 1.)	Maitland runs down the coast to Alicante,	610, 611
(Aug. 9.)	Wellington's head-quarters are at St Ildefonso; Joseph Bonaparte flies to the left bank of the Tagus,	608
(Aug. 10.)	Maitland's troops are landed at Alicante; Suchet withdraws,	611
	The American general, Hull, capitulates; the fort of Detroit, its ordnance, stores, and a fine American vessel in the harbour, become the prizes of the conquerors,	632
	The Americans fortify their Niagara frontier, and assemble an army on it,	632
(Aug. 12, 14.)	Wellington enters Madrid; the French surrender; great rejoicings,	608
	In consequence of the fall of Madrid, Soult raises the siege of Cadiz, abandons the whole of Western Andalusia, and concentrates in Granada,	608
	Soult's retreat is very disastrous,	608
	Seville taken by assault,	608
	Suchet having joined Joseph Bonaparte, Maitland retires into Alicante,	611
(Aug. 15.)	Napoleon I. crosses the Dnieper, and enters Russia proper with 180,000 men,	638
(Aug. 16.)	Barclay de Tolli evacuates Smolensk; the Russian rear-guard sets fire to the town; every town and village on the route is set fire to and deserted,	638

A.D.		PAGE
1812	Barclay de Tolli continues his retreat upon Moscow,	638
	On Hill's approach, Joseph Bonaparte abandons the line of the Tagus; Hill occupies Toledo, Ypez, and Aranjuez,	608
(Aug. 19.)	The *Guerrière* frigate, Captain James Richard Dacres (British), strikes to the American frigate *Constitution*,	633, 634
	A treaty of peace and amity between Great Britain and Russia is ratified; the Russian fleet is sent to winter in England,	640
(Sept. 1.)	Wellington marches to meet Clausel,	611
(Sept. 7.)	Wellington enters Valladolid,	611
(Sept. 7.)	Battle of Borodino,	638
(Sept. 14.)	The French enter Moscow; a fire breaks out in the evening, which is extinguished during the night,	638
(Sept. 15.)	Napoleon I. takes up his quarters in the Kremlin,	638
(Sept. 16.)	At night the fire breaks out again; Moscow is in flames in a dozen quarters at once; nothing can stop the conflagration; on the third day of its raging, Napoleon I. abandons the Kremlin,	638, 639
(Sept. 19.)	The rage of the fire abates; Napoleon I. remains among the ruins for five weeks; the French feed upon their salted horses,	639
	The allied army enters Burgos,	611
(Oct.)	General Maitland resigns his command at Alicante; General W. Clinton succeeds him,	615
	3000 Americans cross the Niagara opposite the village of Queenstown, and land on the Canadian shore; they are at first successful, but are afterwards defeated,	632, 633
(Oct. 19.)	The Grande Armée begins its retreat from Moscow 120,000 strong, pursued by the Hettman Platoff and his Cossacks; on reaching Viazma, on the Wop, it is reduced to 60,000 fighting-men,	639
(Oct. 21.)	Wellington raises the siege of the castle of Burgos,	612
(Oct. 25.)	The *Macedonian* frigate (British), after a severe struggle, strikes to the American frigate *United States* (55),	635
(Oct. 29.)	Wellington continues his retreat,	612, 613
(Nov. 3.)	Wellington is joined by Hill,	613
(Nov. 6.)	The Grande Armée is overtaken by the Russian winter; the men die like rotting sheep,	639
(Nov. 14.)	Napoleon I. leaves Smolensk with 40,000 men,	639
	On arriving at Orcsa, in Lithuania, he has only 12,000 men with arms in their hands, and his 40,000 horses are dwindled down to 3000,	639
	On approaching the Berezina, he is joined by a corps of reserve of 50,000 men; in effecting the passage of that river, one half of the army is lost, and scarcely a remnant of discipline is left,	639
	During the retreat from Burgos, the British soldiers suffer severely,	614
(Dec. 2.)	General Campbell takes the command at Alicante,	616
(Dec. 3.)	Napoleon I. arrives at Malodeszno and issues his famous Twenty-ninth bulletin, declaring that, except the Guards, he had no longer an army,	639
(Dec. 5.)	He takes leave of some of his generals, and commences a rapid flight towards France,	639
(Dec. 18.)	Napoleon I. arrives in Paris,	639

HISTORY OF ENGLAND.

A.D.		PAGE
1812. (Dec. 22.)	The Emperor Alexander I. concentrates his army at Wilna; it advances in two grand divisions,	662
(Dec. 29.)	The *Java* frigate (British) surrenders to the American, *Constitution*,	635
	The British sloop *Frolic* is captured by the American sloop *Wasp*,	635
	A few hours after the battle, the *Frolic* is recaptured, and the *Wasp* captured by the British *Poictiers*,	635
1813. (Jan.)	Marshal Soult is recalled to oppose the Russians in Germany,	641
	The army of Portugal is under the command of General Reille, with headquarters at Valladolid; the Army of the Centre, under Drouet, at Madrid; the Army of the South at Toledo,	641
	Generals Clausel and Foy have separate divisions in Aragon and Biscay, all under the command of King Joseph, assisted by Marshal Jourdan,	641
	The Spanish cortes make Wellington commander-in-chief,	641
(Jan. 22.)	Frederick William III. of Prussia proposes an armistice to Napoleon I.; it is rejected,	662, 663
	The Americans overrun the Michigan territory,	736
	General Harrison fortifies himself near the Miami river,	736
	Many warlike tribes of Indians join the English and Canadians,	736, 737
(Feb. 28.)	Prussia concludes a treaty of alliance, offensive and defensive, with Russia at Kalisch; the basis of the Sixth Coalition against France,	663
	The Russians blockade Dantzic,' and advance from the Vistula to the Oder; they are joined by the Prussian general, Bulow, and his veterans,	663
(Mar. 4.)	Berlin is evacuated by the French,	663
	Insurrections against the French break out simultaneously in all parts of Germany,	663
(Mar. 27.)	Dresden is evacuated by the French,	663
	The Cossacks sweep the French out of Pomerania and Mecklenburg,	663
	Beauharnais repulses the Russians,	663
(Mar. 30.)	Napoleon I. confers the regency on Maria Louisa,	662
(April.)	The allies advance and occupy Leipsig,	663
	Suchet takes the field in force,	658
(April 11.)	The Spaniards are defeated at Yecla,	658
(April 13.)	Suchet attacks Sir John Murray in the mountainous country of Castalla, but is repulsed,	658
(April 15.)	Napoleon I. quits St Cloud,	662
(April 16.)	He is at Mayence, inspects the troops, and has an interview with several of the German princes of the Confederation of the Rhine,	662
(May 1.)	Marshal Bessières is slain,	664
(May 2.)	Napoleon I. wins the battle of Lutzen,	663
(May 5.)	The Americans, at the batteries on the river Miami, are put to headlong flight by a bayonet-charge of British troops under Procter,	737
	The Canadian militia go home, the Indians to the Detroit frontier, and Colonel Procter is obliged to follow them,	737
	York, on Lake Ontario, in Upper Canada, is taken by the American general, Dearborn,	735
	Wellington commences active operations; the allied army enters Spain in three separate bodies,	641

A.D.		PAGE
1813. (May. 21.)	Napoleon I. forces the Russians and Prussians to retire from the field of Bautzen,	663, 664
(May 23.)	Napoleon I.'s favourite aide-de-camp, General Duroc, is killed,	664
(May 29.)	Sir George Prevost lands at Sackett's Harbour on Lake Ontario, but is compelled to retreat,	736
(June, beginning of.)	Napoleon I. enters Dresden; an armistice is agreed to,	664
(June 1.)	The fight between the English frigate *Shannon*, Captain Broke, and the American frigate *Chesapeake*, Captain Laurence, off Boston Harbour; the *Chesapeake*, after eleven minutes' firing, is boarded and taken,	733, 734
	King Joseph flies from Madrid, and the French army retire upon Burgos,	641
(June 5.)	The Americans are scattered by the British,	736
	General Dearborn evacuates all the Canadian bank of the Niagara,	736
(June 6, 7.)	Murray opens batteries on Tarragona, but, through fear of Suchet and Mathieu, determines on an immediate embarkation, and abandons his artillery,	659
(June 12.)	The French abandon Burgos, and retreat to the Ebro,	641
	Wellington drives them back upon Vittoria after an engagement at Osma,	641
(June 14.)	Great Britain becomes a party to the coalition or treaty with Russia and Prussia,	664
(June 17.)	Lord William Bentinck arrives from Sicily at Tarragona to take the command; Bentinck leads the disheartened forces back to Alicante,	660
	On reaching Alicante, Bentinck joins the Duque del Parque,	661
	Sir S. Beckwith captures the fortified camp of the Americans at Hampton in Virginia,	739
(June 21.)	The battle of Vittoria; defeat of the French,	642, 643
	General Clausel flies by the Central Pyrenees into France; General Foy falls back rapidly on Bayonne,	645
	Wellington advances with the main body of his army to occupy the passes of the Pyrenees,	645
(July.)	Suchet withdraws into Catalonia,	660
	Admiral Cockburn, on the coast of North Carolina, captures the islands, towns, and ports of Portsmouth and Ooracoke,	739
	The Spanish general O'Donnel reduces the Castle of Pancorbo,	646
(July 7.)	The last divisions of Joseph's army are driven from the valley of San Estevan, and obliged to retreat into France,	646
	Wellington becomes master of the passes of San Estevan, Donna Maria, Maya, and Roncesvalles,	646
	Soult succeeds Jourdan,	646, 647
(July 17.)	The convent and a redoubt are carried by assault,	647
	Soult makes a partial attack on Wellington's fourth division; he is foiled,	649
(July 28.)	Soult renews his attack; he is repulsed with great loss,	649
(July 30.)	The French begin the assault on Hill's front, and are repulsed; Picton and Dalhousie turn the two flanks, and drive the French out of Ostiz; the French give way at all points, and fly precipitately,	649

CHRONOLOGICAL INDEX. 91

A.D.		PAGE
1813.	Wellington pursues them as far as Olagns,	649
	Bentinck invests Tarragona,	660
(July 31.)	Soult's scattered forces are in full retreat into France, followed by the allies,	650
	Soult rallies his shattered divisions,	651
(Aug. 2.)	Wellington drives Clausel before him,	651
(Aug. 10.)	Austria joins the allies,	665
(Aug. 14.)	The American brig *Argus* is captured in the Irish Channel by the British brig *Pelican*,	734
	Suchet relieves the garrison of Tarragona, and retreats,	660
	Tarragona is made the rendezvous of the British fleet,	660
(Aug. 24, 25, 27.)	A series of battles is fought about Dresden, and Napoleon I. is successful,	665
	Vandamme is cut off and surrounded, and made prisoner at Culm, in Bohemia,	665
	Oudinot is beaten at Gross Beeren by Bernadotte,	665
	Moreau joins the allies,	666
(Aug. 26.)	Theodor Körner, the patriot and poet, the Tyrtæus of the German war, is killed on the Lower Elbe, in the midst of a band of German students,	666
(Aug. 27.)	General Moreau, in the battle near Dresden, has both his legs carried off by a cannon-ball,	666
	The Spaniards twice repulse the French on the heights on San Marcial,	652
	Another corps of French is defeated on another road to San Sebastian,	652
	San Sebastian assaulted and taken,	652
	Moreau dies,	666
(Sept. 4.)	The British brig *Boxer* is captured by the American brig *Enterprise*,	734
(Sept. 6.)	Ney is beaten at the battle of Dennewitz, near Berlin,	665
	Blucher routs the French on the Katzbach, in Silesia, and gains the name of 'Marshal Forwards,'	665
	Napoleon I.'s German auxiliaries begin to forsake him,	665
	He begins his retreat upon Leipzig,	665
(Sept. 8.)	Rey surrenders the Castle of San Sebastian,	655
(Sept. 10.)	A desperate action takes place between the Americans and the British on Lake Erie; the latter are defeated,	738
(Sept. 12, 13.)	Suchet defeats an advanced corps of Bentinck,	660
(Sept. 14.)	Suchet, in force, drives the whole of the allied army from Villa Franca,	660
	Bentinck is succeeded by General W. Clinton,	660
(Oct.)	Three American armies are put in motion for the Canada frontier,	738
(Oct. 16.)	The first battle of Leipzig; the French are repulsed,	665
(Oct. 18.)	The second battle of Leipzig; the French are routed,	666
(Oct. 19.)	The allies burst into Leipzig, and capture 25,000 of the French rear,	666
(Oct. 30.)	Napoleon I. fights his way through the Bavarians at Hanau,	666
(Oct. 31.)	Pamplona surrenders,	655
(Nov. 9.)	Napoleon I. reaches Paris,	666
(Nov. 10.)	Wellington's forces begin to descend into the valleys on the French side of the Pyrenees,	655
	The French are driven before the British divisions,	656
	The allies cross the Nivelle at St Pé; the French hastily abandon their works,	656
	Wellington's head-quarters are at St Jean de Luz, on the right bank of the Nivelle,	656

A.D.		PAGE
1813. (Nov. 14.)	The senators wait upon Napoleon I. at the Tuileries with an address of felicitation and congratulation,	667
	The Legislative Body appoint a committee to draw up a report on the state of the nation,	667
(Nov. 15.)	The people of Amsterdam rise in a body and hoist the Orange colours,	669
	The Prince of Orange is recalled,	669
	The Swedes overrun Holstein,	670
	The Swiss diet declares the absolute neutrality of the nineteen cantons,	670
	Murat sends an envoy to confer with Lord William Bentinck in Sicily,	691
	Murat sends a confidential agent to Vienna, to propose a truce in Italy, &c.,	691, 692
(Nov. and Dec.)	80,000 Frenchmen in Magdeburg, Stettin, Dantzic (Dec. 24), and other Prussian fortresses, surrender to the allies,	666
(Dec. 1.)	The Prince of Orange enters Amsterdam, and assumes the title of Sovereign Prince of the United Netherlands,	670
(Dec. 10.)	Soult attacks the British, but is twice repulsed,	657
(Dec. 13.)	Soult unsuccessfully attacks the British under Hill,	657
(Dec. 19.)	The Austrians are permitted to pass through Switzerland to France, &c.,	670
	Both Upper and Lower Canada are entirely freed from the presence of the American invaders,	739
	Prince Schwartzenberg invades Alsace; other Austrians follow,	684
(Dec. 29.)	Nine of the old Swiss cantons declare Napoleon I.'s mediation at an end; deputies meet at Zurich to establish a new federal act,	670, 671
1814. (Jan.)	The Russians cross the Rhine near Rastadt; the Cossacks spread far into France,	684
	Blucher defeats Marshals Marmont and Victor,	684
	The French abandon nearly all their fortresses on the left bank of the Rhine without a struggle; by the middle of the month, one-third of France is invaded,	684
(Jan. 8.)	Napoleon I. reorganises and increases the National Guard of Paris,	682
(Jan. 11.)	A treaty is concluded between Austria and Naples,	692
	Two divisions of the Neapolitan army are hurried forward to take possession of Rome and Ancona,	692
	All the French generals, and most of the French officers, desert from Murat and join Beauharnais,	692
	Darbou surrenders Ancona, and Miollis evacuates Sant' Angelo; other French garrisons capitulate,	692
	Lord William Bentinck, with his Anglo-Sicilian army, lands some troops in the suburbs of Leghorn, and cannonades the town,	692
(Jan. 22.)	Napoleon I. sends an order to Fontainebleau that the pope should leave the place next day, and return to Italy,	693
(Jan. 23.)	Napoleon I. receives the oaths of fidelity of the officers of the new Parisian Garde Nationale; he confers the regency on Maria Louisa,	683
(Jan. 25.)	Napoleon I. quits Paris for the army collecting in Champagne,	683
	The pope, on his journey through Italy,	

A.D. 1814.		PAGE
	is followed by a countless multitude; on the Nura, in Parma, he meets the van of the Neapolitan army; the soldiers quit their ranks, and fall on their knees before him, &c.,	693
	Murat instructs his general, Carascoa, to persuade the pope to remain in Parma or Piacenza for the present; he pursues his route to Cesena,	693
	The pope has an interview with Murat at Bologna, and goes to Cesena, where he remains till Napoleon I. goes to Elba,	693
(Jan. 27.)	Napoleon I. surprises and defeats a vanguard of the allies at St Dizier,	684
(Jan. 29.)	Napoleon I. falls upon Blucher near Brienne, and beats him,	684, 685
(Jan. 30.)	The battle is renewed at La Rothière; Blucher gives way; a Prussian division under General Yorck retakes St Dizier,	685
	Wittgenstein defeats the French cavalry,	685
(Feb. 1.)	The Prussians defeat the French at La Rothière,	685
	Napoleon I. retreats to Troyes, where he is joined by his old imperial guard,	685
(Feb. 5.)	Yorck takes the town of Chalons-sur-Marne,	685
	The congress of the allied powers commences its deliberations at Chatillon-sur-Seine,	684
(Feb. 6.)	Napoleon I. abandons the city of Troyes, and goes in pursuit of Blucher,	685
(Feb. 7.)	Schwartzenberg's van enters Troyes, where the white flag is hoisted,	685
(Feb. 10.)	Napoleon I. defeats Blucher at Champaubert,	685
(Feb. 11.)	Napoleon I. defeats Blucher at Montmirail; Schwartzenberg advances on Paris, taking Sens, Nogent, Montereau, and Pont-sur-Seine,	685
	Napoleon I. leaves Blucher, and posts after Schwartzenberg,	685
(Feb. 18.)	Napoleon I., having been joined by Victor and Oudinot, attacks and defeats the prince royal of Würtemburg at Montereau,	685
(Feb. 22.)	Napoleon I. again defeats Blucher,	685, 686
(Feb. 24.)	Napoleon I. obliges Schwartzenberg to retreat beyond Troyes,	686
	Napoleon I. cannot maintain himself at Troyes; Blucher drives Marshal Macdonald before him, and advances on Paris; and after several more battles, Napoleon I. leaves the road to Paris open to the allies,	686
(Feb. 27.)	The battle of Orthes,	676
	Louis XVIII. proclaimed at Bordeaux,	676
(Mar. 7.)	General Graham, in attempting to carry Bergen-op-Zoom, is repulsed,	690
(Mar. 12.)	The Duke d'Angoulême enters Bordeaux,	687
(Mar. 18.)	Wellington advances to Vic Bigorre; Soult retreats to some good positions at Tarbes,	677
(Mar. 22.)	Napoleon I. releases Ferdinand VII.,	677
(Mar. 24.)	Soult arrives at Toulouse,	677
(Mar. 28.)	The Prince of Orange assumes the royal title, and offers a new constitution to the Dutch nation, which is accepted at Amsterdam,	690
	Marshal Marmont is driven back under the walls of the city,	686
	The empress-regent flies from Paris to Blois,	686
	Paris capitulates,	686
(Mar. 31.)	Alexander I. of Russia and Frederick William III. of Prussia enter Paris,	

A.D. 1814.		PAGE
	and it is in the undisturbed possession of the allies,	686
	Napoleon I. shuts himself up in the palace of Fontainebleau,	686
	Alexander I. of Russia takes up his residence at the mansion of Talleyrand,	687
(April 1.)	Frederick William III. of Prussia, Prince Schwartzenberg, and others, meet at Talleyrand's house, and open conferences with him and Alexander I.,	687
	The senate declare that Napoleon I. had forfeited the throne and the right of inheritance in his family,	687
	A provisional government is formed, consisting of Talleyrand, Dalberg, Buernonville, and some others,	687
(April 3.)	All the members of the Corps Legislatif in Paris assent to the decree of the senate; the Court of Cassation also send in their adherence to the provisional government,	687
	Marshals Ney, Berthier, Lefebvre, Oudinot, Macdonald, and Bertrand wait upon Napoleon I., and recommend an immediate abdication,	687
	Napoleon I. signs an act of abdication, with a reservation in favour of the rights of his son and of the empress,	687
	The coalition refuses to accept it,	687
	Alexander I. proposes the island of Elba, with the retention of the imperial title, and a large annual allowance from France, &c.,	687
(April 9.)	Maria Louisa and her son quit Blois, and place themselves under the protection of the emperor of Austria,	689
	The provisional government and the senate draw up and publish the sketch of a constitution to be accepted by Louis XVIII.,	689
(April 10.)	The battle of Toulouse; the French are defeated,	678–680
	Soult retreats to Carcassonne,	680
	Napoleon I. signs a second act, in which he renounces unconditionally for himself and his heirs the thrones of France and Italy,	688
	The Count d'Artois arrives in the neighbourhood of Paris,	689
(April 12.)	A grand reception is given him in the capital,	689
	Wellington enters Toulouse, where the white flag of the Bourbons is flying,	680
	The people of Milan, reinforced by the people of Pavia and other towns, rise in a mass, break the statue of Napoleon, and murder his chief minister,	693
	Eugene Beauharnais concludes a convention with Marshal Bellegarde,	694
	Eugene Beauharnais retires to Munich,	694
(April 17.)	Soult acknowledges the provisional government,	680, 681
	Genoa capitulates to Lord William Bentinck,	694
	Marshal Bellegarde proclaims at Milan the restoration of the legitimate sovereignty of the emperor of Austria, Francis II.,	695
(April 19.)	Marshal Suchet concludes a convention similar to Soult,	681
(April 20.)	Napoleon I. takes an affectionate leave of his old guard,	688
(April 28.)	Napoleon I. embarks for Elba in the *Undaunted*, Captain Usher,	683
	The fort of Oswego taken from the Americans,	739

CHRONOLOGICAL INDEX.

A. D.		PAGE
1814. (May 2.)	The States-general of the United Provinces meet at the Hague, and take the oaths to the new constitution,	690
(May 3.)	Louis XVIII. makes his solemn entry into Paris,	689
(May 4.)	Napoleon I. arrives at Porto-Ferrajo, Ferdinand VII. of Spain issues a royal declaration at Valencia,	688
(May 11.)	General Eguia imprisons all the liberal members of the cortes he can find in Madrid,	696
(May 12.)	Ferdinand VII. enters Madrid, and is received with enthusiasm,	696
(May 20.)	The king of Sardinia enters Turin, and establishes his government on the old basis; Genoa is joined to the Sardinian dominions,	695
	Francis II. of Austria lays his hand upon Venice and other cities and states, as Brescia, Cremona, Guastalla, Parma, Piacenza, &c.,	695
	Murat returns hastily to Naples,	695
(May 24.)	The pope makes his solemn entrance into Rome, and restores the old ecclesiastical government,	695
	The Duke of Wellington arrives at Madrid to mediate between the infuriated parties,	696
(May 26.)	The Empress Josephine dies at Malmaison,	689
(May 30.)	The allied powers of Great Britain, Austria, Russia, and Prussia sign at Paris a treaty of peace and amity with France, and arrange the restoration of colonies, &c.,	689, 690
(June.)	France is evacuated by the foreign armies,	690
	Alexander I. of Russia and his sister, Frederick William III. of Prussia and his two sons, come to London to visit the Prince Regent; great festivities take place,	690
(June 14.)	The Duke of Wellington issues his farewell general orders to the army,	696
(June 28.)	The Duke of Wellington receives the thanks of the House of Lords,	697
(July 1.)	The Duke of Wellington receives the thanks of the House of Commons,	697
	The American general Ripley crosses Niagara, and advances into Canada,	739
(July 25.)	A battle is fought close to the cataract of Niagara,	739, 740
	Colonel Pilkington takes all the islands in the Bay of Passmaquoddy,	741
(Aug.)	The king of the Netherlands resigns all right to the Cape of Good Hope, getting back Demerara, Essequibo, Berbice, Java, Sumatra, &c.,	691
	The Duke of Wellington proceeds to Paris as ambassador to Louis XVIII.,	697
(Aug. 14.)	The Norwegian notables sign a convention with Bernadotte, who agrees to accept a very democratic constitution framed by the diet of Norway, &c.,	691
	Hanover is raised to the titular dignity of a kingdom,	691
	Admiral Sir Alexander Cochrane, having on board the land troops of Majorgeneral Ross, ascends the Patuxent river; the Americans set fire to Commodore Barney's flotilla,	740
	Major-general Ross and his troops reach Bladensberg, five miles from Washington,	740
	The British attack and defeat the Americans,	740

A. D.		PAGE
1814.	In the evening, the British enter Washington, and destroy the public buildings, arsenal, dockyard, &c.,	740
(Aug. 25.)	The British commence a leisurely retreat,	740
	Alexandria taken by the British,	740
(Sept.)	The British reduce the whole district of Maine, &c.,	741
(Sept. 11.)	Captain Downie attacks the Americans in Plattsburg Bay, and is killed; the British vessels strike their colours,	742
	Sir George Prevost orders the British army to retreat,	742
(Sept. 12.)	The city of Baltimore is unsuccessfully attacked,	741
(Oct. 20.)	The General Diet of Norway agrees to the union of Norway with Sweden,	691
(Dec. 23.)	The British troops attack New Orleans; they are repulsed,	743
(Dec. 24.)	A treaty of peace and amity is signed at Ghent between America and Great Britain,	747
1815. (Jan. 1.)	New Orleans attacked unsuccessfully by the British,	744
(Jan. 8.)	New Orleans again unsuccessfully attacked,	744, 745
	The Duke of Wellington repairs to the great congress of Vienna,	697
(Feb. 0.)	Parliament reassembles,	697
(Feb. 11.)	Fort Mobile is captured by General Lambert and Admiral Sir A. Cochrane,	746
(Feb. 26.)	Napoleon I. escapes from Elba,	699
(Mar. 1.)	Napoleon I. lands at Cannes, a short distance from Frejus, without opposition,	699
(Mar. 5.)	Near Grenoble, Napoleon I. is joined by a battalion of infantry, which had been sent to stop his march,	699, 700
(Mar. 7.)	The garrison and authorities of Grenoble renew their allegiance to him,	700
	The troops and populace of Lyons follow the example of Grenoble,	700
	Ney joins him with his whole force,	700
(Mar. 13.)	The ministers of the eight powers, assembled at Vienna, declare Napoleon I. an outlaw, &c.,	698
	Alexander I. of Russia and Francis II. of Austria, with the assembled plenipotentiaries and generals of all nations, call upon the Duke of Wellington to draw up a grand plan of military operations,	698
(Mar. 19.)	Napoleon I. sleeps at Fontainebleau; Louis XVIII. quits Paris for Lille,	700
	Napoleon I. arrives at the Tuileries,	701
(Mar. 22.)	Murat and his whole army are in motion,	728
(Mar. 23.)	Austria, Russia, Prussia, and Great Britain conclude the treaty of Vienna,	698
(Mar. 29.)	The Duke of Wellington leaves Vienna, to examine the military state of affairs in Belgium,	698
(April 4.)	The Duke of Wellington arrives in Brussels,	698
(April 6.)	A message is delivered to both Houses from the Prince Regent, that Napoleon I. had escaped from Elba, and that he had given orders for the immediate augmentation of the land and sea forces, &c.,	697
	The ministerial addresses to the Regent are carried in both Houses,	698
	The budget of the year is raised to nearly £90,000,000,	698
	Murat sustains a severe check at Occhiobello, on the Po, &c.,	728
	Murat retreats to the frontiers of Naples,	728

A.D.		PAGE
1815. (May 1-4.)	The Austrians and Neapolitans cross the frontiers nearly at the same time,	728
	Several strong fortresses and many walled towns capitulate upon summons to the Austrians, and hoist the Bourbon flag,	729
	The Neapolitan soldiers desert from Murat in shoals; Napoleon L's mother, his uncle Cardinal Fesch, and his sister Pauline fly from Naples to France; Murat's children are sent for safety to the fortress of Gaeta,	729
	The division of Murat's army in the fortified camp of Mignano fall into a panic and fly,	729
	Murat quits the remnant of his army, and travels incognito to Naples,	729
(May 20.)	The Neapolitan generals conclude a convention with the Austrians at Casa Lanza,	729
	Murat flies from Naples to the island of Ischia,	729
(May 22.)	Caroline Bonaparte, protected by English sailors and marines, embarks in the British man-of-war,	729
(May 23.)	The Austrians and Bourbon prince Leopold enter Naples in triumph,	729
	Murat sails in a small coasting vessel to the coast of France,	729, 730
(May 28 or 29.)	Murat enters the port of Frejus; he offers his services to France; they are refused,	730
(June 2.)	Napoleon I. is obliged, by his brother Lucien and the liberals, to proclaim a sort of constitution,	701
(June 4.)	Napoleon I., his great officers of state, marshals, generals, &c., take their oaths to the constitution at a grand celebration called a Champ de Mai, held in the Champ de Mars,	701
	The Chambers of Peers and Representatives meet, and their first act is to pronounce the dethronement of Napoleon I.,	701
(June 11.)	Napoleon I. quits Paris to open the campaign,	702
(June 14.)	He advances to the Belgian frontier with about 125,000 men,	702
	Wellington's force in the field amounts to 76,000 men,	702
	Blucher's head-quarters are at Namur; his force, with Bulow's corps, amounts to 80,000 men and 200 cannon,	702
(June 15.)	Napoleon I. crosses the Sambre, advances on Charleroi, and drives back the Prussian outposts,	703
	Napoleon I. establishes his head-quarters at Charleroi; Blucher concentrates the Prussian army upon Sombref, occupying the villages of St Amand and Ligny, in front of that position,	704
	Marshal Ney forces back on the farmhouse of Quatre Bras a brigade of the army of the Netherlands,	704
(June 16.)	Before sunrise Wellington's army are on the march,	704
	The Prince of Orange pushes back Ney's advanced-guard, and recovers some of the ground between Quatre Bras and Charleroi,	704
	The Duke of Wellington confers with Blucher at Bry,	704
	The battle of Ligny; Blucher defeated,	704
	The battle of Quatre Bras; Ney is beaten,	704
(June 17.)	Napoleon I. orders Grouchy to pursue Blucher,	704

A.D.		PAGE
1815.	The Duke of Wellington makes a retrograde movement upon Waterloo, and retires leisurely by Genappe,	705
	Napoleon I. forms a junction with Ney, and has 78,000 men in front of Waterloo,	705
(June 18.)	The battle of Waterloo,	706-708
	The French army is completely destroyed,	708
(June 19.)	Grouchy retreats on the frontiers of France,	709
(June 20.)	Napoleon I. carries the news of his defeat to Paris himself,	709
(June 21 or 22.)	The Chambers demand Napoleon I.'s abdication,	710
	Lucien Bonaparte harangues and pleads for Napoleon I. in vain,	710
(June 22.)	Napoleon I. signs an act of abdication in favour of his son, Napoleon II., and retires to Malmaison,	710
	The Chamber of Peers set up a provisional government; Fouché is named president,	711
(June 29.)	Five commissioners, sent by the provisional government at Paris, wait upon Wellington at Etrées, to negotiate a suspension of hostilities, &c.,	711
	Wellington will not consent to suspend hostilities as long as a soldier of the French army remains in Paris,	712
	Murat writes to Fouché for a passport, but, as before, gets no answer,	730
	He also writes to Louis XVIII., enclosing it to Fouché; after many adventures, he gets to Corsica, where some desperadoes gather round him,	730
(July 1.)	Wellington takes up a position a few miles from Paris, his right on the village of Richebourg, his left on the Forest of Bondy; Blucher crosses the Seine at St Germain,	711
(July 2.)	The Prussian army is at Plessis-Piquet, its left at St Cloud, and its reserve at Versailles,	711
	Some hard fighting takes place between the army of Napoleon II. and Blucher on the heights of St Cloud and Meudon, and in the village of Issy; the Prussian corps of General Zeithen surmounts every obstacle,	712
(July 3.)	The French attempt to recover the village of Issy, but are repulsed,	712
	The provisional government send out a flag of truce,	712
(July 6.)	Marshal Ney flies from Paris in disguise; Louis XVIII. is at St Denis,	712, 713
(July 7.)	The British and Prussian armies take possession of Paris,	713
(July 8.)	Louis XVIII. re-enters Paris, escorted by the National Guard,	713
(July 10.)	Napoleon I. sends Las Cases and Savary with a flag of truce to Captain Maitland of the *Bellerophon*, to negotiate a passage to England, &c.,	714
(July 15.)	Napoleon I. with his suite go on board the *Bellerophon*, saying to Captain Maitland: 'Sir, I come to claim the protection of your prince and your laws,'	714
(July 24.)	The *Bellerophon* enters Torbay,	714
(Aug. 19.)	Labédoyère is shot,	723
(Oct. 13.)	Murat is shot in his forty-fifth year,	731, 732
(Nov. 20.)	Treaties and conventions are signed at Paris by the allies and Louis XVIII.,	732
(Nov. 22.)	Lavalette, Napoleon I.'s director-general of the Post-office, is condemned to death,	725
(Dec. 7.)	Marshal Ney is shot in the public gardens of the Luxembourg Palace,	724

CHRONOLOGICAL INDEX TO VOL. VII.

HISTORY OF THE PEACE.

BOOK I.

1815.

	Page
Peace of Paris,	1
Holy Alliance,	2
Congress of Vienna,	2
Secret Treaty,	3
Paris in the Autumn of 1815,	4
Territorial Limits settled by Peace,	5

1816.

	Page
State of Parties,	6
Parliamentary Leaders,	7
Lord Chancellor Eldon,	7
Lord Liverpool and his Colleagues,	7
The Opposition,	7
Lord Castlereagh and his Colleagues,	8
The Opposition,	9
Fourth Session of Fifth Parliament,	10
Speech,	10
India—Pindarree War,	12
Civil List,	15
Marriage of the Princess Charlotte,	15
Agriculture,	16
Manufactures and Commerce,	20
Depression of Industry,	21
Currency,	22
Labour,	23
Coal Districts—Machine-breaking,	24
Private Benevolence,	25
Parliamentary Reform,	26
Writings of Cobbett,	28
Hampden Clubs,	29
Spenceans,	31
Address of the City,	32
Real Dangers,	33
Algiers,	33
Bombardment,	35
Progress of Social Improvement,	37
Criminal Laws,	37
Police,	39
Gaslight,	40
Mendicity and Vagrancy,	40
Law of Settlement,	41
Administration of Poor-laws,	41
Education,	44
Savings-banks,	45
Elgin Marbles,	46

1808–1816.

	Page
Spanish America,	47
Colonial Misgovernment,	47
General Miranda,	47
Mr Pitt,	47
The Addington Cabinet,	48
The Grenville Cabinet,	48
The Portland Cabinet,	48
The Perceval Cabinet,	48
Improvement of Brazil,	48
Difficulties of the Spanish Provincials,	49

	Page
Mexico,	49
New Grenada—Venezuela,	50
Earthquake at Caracas,	51
Rio de la Plata—Paraguay—Chili,	51
Position of Affairs in 1816,	52

1817.

	Page
Opening of Parliament,	52
Outrage on the Prince-regent,	52
Alarm,	52
Reports of Secret Committees,	53
March of the Blanketeers,	54
Derby Insurrection,	55
Prosecutions for Libel,	59
Hone's Trials,	60
Death of the Princess Charlotte,	63
Sinecures,	65
Roman Catholic Claims,	65
Parliamentary Reform,	65
India—Pindarree War,	65
Mahratta Wars,	71

1818.

	Page
Meeting of Parliament,	78
Prince-regent's Speech,	79
Address,	79
State of the Country,	80
Proceedings of Parliament,	81
Report of Secret Committees,	81
Bill of Indemnity,	83
Scotch Burgh Reform,	85
Bank Restriction Act,	87
Royal Marriages,	88
Slave-trade,	89
Alien Act,	89
Dissolution,	90
General Election,	91
Strike of Manchester Spinners,	92
Death of the Queen,	93
Death of Sir S. Romilly,	93
Congress of Aix-la-Chapelle,	93
State of the Country,	95
Revival of the Reform Agitation,	95

1819.

	Page
State of the Country,	96
Opening of Parliament,	96
Care of the King's Person,	97
Resumption of Cash-payments,	98
Financial Measures,	100
Prorogation,	102
Condition of the Government,	103
Continuance of Reform Agitation,	104
Condition of the People,	104
Novelties in the Reform Movement,	106
Drilling,	106
Manchester Meeting,	107
Conduct of the Manchester Magistrates,	110
Conduct of the Government,	111

	Page
General Excitement,	112
Session of Parliament,	113
Death of George III.,	113

BOOK II.

1820.

	Page
Revival of Sedition,	114
Cato-Street Conspiracy,	114
Alarms,	115
The King's Speech,	115
Spies and Informers,	116
Sedition in Scotland,	116
Trials of the Radicals,	116
The Demagogue,	116
Accession of George IV.,	118
Position of the Queen,	118
King's Marriage in 1795,	118
The Queen Abroad,	120
The Queen's Return,	120
King's Message,	121
Queen's Message,	121
Commission agreed to,	121
Lords' Report. Queen's Trial,	122
The Defence,	124
Abandonment of the Bill,	124
The Queen's Law-officers,	124
Prorogation,	124
The Queen goes to St Paul's,	124
Her Claim to be Crowned,	125
Her Death and Funeral,	125
Dissolution and New Parliament,	126
State of the Country,	126
Death of Grattan,	126
Education,	126
Capital Punishments,	127
Agricultural Distress,	128

1821.

	Page
Parliamentary Reform,	128
Catholic Claims,	131
Constitutional Association,	131
King's Visit to Ireland,	132
Coronation,	132
Death of Napoleon,	133
Coalition with the Grenville Party,	135

1822.

	Page
Retirement of Lord Sidmouth,	135
Mr Peel—Mr Canning,	136
Lord Wellesley in Ireland,	137
Motion in favour of Catholic Peers,	138
Peterborough Questions,	138
New Marriage Act,	139
Close of Session,	140
King's Visit to Scotland,	140
Death of Lord Londonderry,	140
Mr Canning, Foreign Secretary,	141

	Page		Page		Page
Lord Amherst goes to India,	141	Remarkable Seasons,	215	Prospects of Ireland,	266
Policy of Castlereagh,	141	Art and Literature,	217	Admission of Catholic Peers,	267
The Princes and Peoples of Europe,	142	Necrology,	217	Changes in the Cabinet,	268
Revolutions Abroad,	143	Politicians,	217	Parliamentary Reform—Lord Blandford,	268
Policy of Canning,	144	Men of Science,	218	Duel,	268
Congress of Verona,	146	Travellers,	219	Parliamentary Proceedings,	268
		Artists,	220	Relations with Portugal,	269
1823.		Authors,	221	King's Speech,	271
French Invasion of Spain,	146	Poets: Byron, Keats, Shelley,	221	Affairs of France,	271
Overthrow of Spanish Revolution,	148	Close of the Period,	223	Law of the Press,	272
South American Provinces,	148			Villèle's Resignation,	273
Appeal from Portugal,	150			Prince Polignac,	274
New Era of Conflict,	151	**BOOK III.**			
Deaths of Potentates,	151	**1827.**		**1830.**	
Affairs of Greece,	152				
Algiers—Ashantee War,	153	Opening of New Parliament,	224	Polignac Ministry,	274
Burmese War,	154	Death of the Duke of York,	225	Summons to the Chambers,	275
Oregon,	155	Grant to the Duke of Clarence,	227	Dissolution of the Chambers,	276
Aliens,	156	Illness of Lord Liverpool,	227	The Elections—Ministers' Memorial,	277
Changes in the Ministry,	157	Lord Liverpool and Mr Canning,	227	Issue of the Ordinances,	278
Mr Canning and Mr Huskisson,	158	Lord Liverpool as Minister,	228	Protest of the Journalists,	278
The Debt and Taxation,	161	The Corn Bill,	228	Destruction of the Press,	278
Commercial Policy,	163	Catholic Question,	229	Conference at the Tuileries,	279
Spitalfields and Navigation Acts,	165	New Administration,	229	Messages to and from the King,	279
Parliamentary Topics,	166	Mr Canning consulted,	230	Marshal Marmont,	280
Negro Slavery,	168	Mr Peel,	230	Second Conference,	281
Government Resolutions,	168	Resignation of Cabinet Ministers,	230	Retreat to St Cloud,	281
Circular and its Reception,	169	Mr Canning, Premier—New Cabinet,	231	Wanderings of the Royal Family,	282
Smith the Missionary,	170	Retirement of Lord Eldon,	231	Reception in England,	283
Close of the Session,	172	Enmity to Mr Canning,	232	Conduct of the Revolution,	283
		Business of Parliament,	233	Fate of the Ministers,	283
1824.		The Corn Bill,	233	Duke of Brunswick,	283
Prosperity,	172	Close of the Session,	234	Death of the Pope,	283
Repeal of the Spitalfields Acts,	174	Mr Canning's Health—His Death,	234	Russia and Turkey,	284
Artisan Restriction Laws,	174	Funeral and Honours,	234	Settlement of Greece,	284
Free Trade—Silk Duties,	175	Character of Mr Canning,	235	Distress in England,	285
Wool Duty,	177	Lord Goderich, Premier,	236	State of the King,	286
Reduction of Duties and Bounties,	178	His Colleagues,	236	Duke of Wellington,	286
Uniformity of Weights & Measures,	178	Affairs of Greece,	236	State of Parties,	286
Close of Session—Speculation,	178	Treaty of London,	238	Mr Peel,	286
Joint-stock Companies,	180	The Porte—The Egyptian Fleet,	238	Press Prosecutions,	287
		Battle of Navarino,	239	King's Speech—Reductions,	288
1825.		Ambassadors leave Constantinople,	230	Removal of Duties,	289
Collapse—Panic—Crash,	183	Greek Pirates,	239	East India Committee,	290
Issue of Small Notes and Coin,	184	Troubles in the Cabinet,	240	Removal of a Judge,	290
		Dissolution of the Ministry,	240	Welsh and Scotch Judicature,	290
1826.		Duke of Wellington, Premier,	241	Forgery,	290
King's Speech,	184			Jewish Disabilities,	290
Arrangement with Bank of England,	184	**1828.**		Parliamentary Reform,	291
Suppression of Small Notes,	184	The Wellington Cabinet,	241	Duke of Newcastle,	293
Scotch Banks,	186	King's Speech,	242	Illness of the King,	293
Branch and Joint-stock Banks,	186	The Porte,	242	His Death—his Life and Character,	294
Advances on Goods,	186	Finance Committee,	244	Character of the Reign,	294
Position of Ministers,	186	Repeal of Dissenters' Disabilities,	244	Achievements,	295
Suffering of the Period,	187	Dissensions in the Cabinet,	246	Desiderata,	296
Riots,	188	Mr Huskisson's Resignation,	248	State of Operatives,	296
Release of Bonded Corn,	189	Changes in the Administration,	248	Crimes and Punishments,	297–299
Opening the Ports,	189	Catholic Question,	248	Accidents,	300
Emigration—Colonial Office,	190	Clare Election,	249	Arts and Edifices,	301–304
Emigration Committee,	191	State of Ireland,	251	Hanwell Asylum,	304
Catholic Question reviewed,	191	Brunswick Clubs,	252	Drainage,	304
State of Opinion in 1824,	196	Forty-shilling Freeholders,	252	Railway,	304
Catholic Association,	197	The Viceroy—His Recall,	253	Reading for the Blind,	305
Catholic Deputation,	198	Aspect of the Question,	253	Scott's Novels,	305
Mr O'Connell,	199	Close of the Session of 1828,	254	Shakspeare Festival—Actors,	306
Progress of the Question,	202	Affairs of Portugal,	254	Irving,	306
Sir F. Burdett's Relief Bill,	202	Don Miguel in England,	254	Religious Parties,	307
Duke of York's Declaration,	202	His Usurpation,	254	Conversions of Catholics,	307
Bill lost,	203	Queen of Portugal in England,	256	Intolerance of Opinion,	307
Catholics and Dissenters,	203	Death of Lord Liverpool,	257	Dissenters' Marriages,	308
Aspect of the Question,	204			Press at Calcutta.—Stamp Duty,	309
Chancery Reform,	204	**1829.**		Protector of Slaves,	309
Government moves for Inquiry,	205	Difficulties in the Cabinet,	257	Treaty with Brazil,	309
Report of Commissioners,	206	The King,	257	Spring-guns,	309
Lord Eldon,	207	Mr Peel's Resignation of his Seat in Parliament,	258	Society for the Diffusion of Useful Knowledge,	310
Bill proposed,	207	King's Speech and the Address,	259	Necrology,	312
Jurors in India,	207	Catholic Relief Bill—Mr Peel,	259	Political Deaths,	312, 313
Finance,	207	The Duke of Wellington,	261	Travellers,	313
Close of Session and Dissolution,	208	Catholic Relief Bill passed,	262	Men of Business,	313–316
The Elections,	209	The King's Vacillation,	262	Artists,	316–318
Crimes and Punishments,	209	The Bill becomes Law,	264	Men of Letters,	318–321
Education,	211	Irish 'Forties,'	264	Philosophers,	321–324
Emigration,	213	Clare Election,	265	Philanthropists,	324, 325
Arts and Discovery,	213				

CHRONOLOGICAL INDEX.

BOOK IV.

1830.

	Page
William IV.,	326
King's Message—Regency Question,	327
Manners of the Commons,	327
Prorogation—Dissolution,	328
Sympathy with France,	328
Mr Brougham,	328
Yorkshire Election,	329
New House,	329
Death of Mr Huskisson,	329
O'Connell and the Viceroy,	330
Repeal of the Union,	330
Rick-burning,	333
Anxieties of Parties,	334
Opening of the Session,	334
The Duke's Declaration,	334
Alderman Key's Panic,	336
Change of Ministry,	337
The Grey Ministry,	337
Regency Bill,	338
Official Salaries,	339
State of Ireland—The Cholera,	339

1831.

	Page
Popular Discontents,	339
Prospect of Conflict,	339
Ministerial Declaration,	340
Reform Bill brought forward,	340
Reception of the Bill,	342
Debate—First Reading,	344
Second Reading,	345
Defeat of Ministers,	345
True Crisis,	345
The Palace,	346
The Lords—The Commons,	347
Prorogation—Dissolution,	348
General Election,	348
Popular Action—Riots,	349
New House,	350
Second Reform Bill—Committee,	350
Bill passes the Commons,	350
First Reading in the Lords—Debate,	350
Lord Grey—The Bishops,	351
The Bill lost—Prorogation,	352
Vote of Confidence,	352
Riots at Derby and Nottingham,	352
At Bristol,	353
Prevalence of Order,	355
National Political Union,	355
Metropolitan Union,	355
Question of a Creation of Peers,	356
The Waverers,	356
Gravity of the Time,	356
Proclamation against Political Unions,	356
The Cholera,	356
The Unknown Tongues,	357
Opening of the Session,	357
Third Reform Bill,	357

1832.

	Page
Final Passage through the Commons,	358
First Reading in the Lords,	358
Debate and Division,	358
Pressure from Without,	358
Meetings and Petitions,	358
Newhall Hill Meeting,	359
Defeat of Ministers,	360
Resignation of Ministers,	360
Address of the Commons,	360
Attempt to form a Cabinet,	361
Failure,	361
Agitation throughout the Country,	361
The Unions,	362
London Municipality,	362
Soldiery and Police,	362
Lord Grey recalled,	364
King's Appeal to the Peers,	364
Progress of the Bill,	364
Its Passage into Law,	364
Position of the House of Lords,	365

	Page
Substance of the Reform Bill,	365
What the Bill is and is not,	368
State of Public Interests,	369
The King—The Administration,	369
Aspects of the Time,	369
The Cholera—The Poor-law,	370
Swan River Settlement,	371
Slavery—Canada—India,	371
Irish Church—Tithes—Law Reform,	372
Education—Bank,	372
Municipal Reform,	372
Strength of the Government,	373
Weakness of the Government,	373
Civil List—Pensions—Regal Income,	374
Pauperism,	375
Confusion of Poverty with Pauperism,	375

1832-1834.

	Page
New Poor-law—its Principles,	376
Its Machinery,	377
Reception of the Measure,	377
Its Passage and Operation,	379
Factory Children,	379

1833.

	Page
Renewal of the Bank Charter,	380
India Company's Charter,	381
Negro Slavery,	383
Abolition Movements,	384
Negro Emancipation,	386
First of August 1834,	386

1831-1834.

	Page
Irish Church,	387
Prosecution of O'Connell,	388
Irish Outrage,	389
Royal Notice of Tithes,	390
First and Second Acts of 1832,	391
Act of 1833,	392
Tardy Truth about Tithes,	392
Proposed Act of 1834—Bill lost,	393
Irish Ecclesiastical Commission,	393
Irish Census—Reductions,	393
Appropriation Doctrine—Delays,	394
Appropriation refused,	395
Irish Church Temporalities Bill passes,	395
Official Changes,	395
Mr Ward's Critical Motion,	395
King's Declaration,	396
Commission of Inquiry,	397
Coercion Bill,	398
Negotiation with Mr O'Connell,	398
Mr Littleton's Explanation,	398
Resignation of Lord Althorp,	399
Of Lord Grey,	399
Lord Grey's Farewell,	399
His Political Character,	400
Religious Crisis,	401
The Tractarians,	402
The Evangelical Party,	403
Death of Wilberforce,	403
Of Hannah More,	404
Moderate Church Party,	404
Opening of Universities to Dissenters,	405
The Church in Danger,	405
Church Reform,	406
Lord Henley—Dr Arnold,	406
The Dissenters,	406
Government Circular,	407
Perplexities of Ministers,	407
Admission of Quakers to Parliament,	407
Continued Exclusion of Jews,	407
Deaths of Robert Hall—Rowland Hill—Charles Wesley—Adam Clarke—Rammohun Roy—Dr Doyle,	408, 409
Schism in the Scotch Church,	409
Irving,	409
St Simonism,	410

	Page
Proposed Ecclesiastical Commission,	410
Finance—First Budget,	411
Statements of 1832 and 1833,	412
Assessed Taxes Movement,	413
The House-tax,	413
Statement of 1834,	414
Westminster Election,	414
Malt-tax—Surplus of 1834,	414
The Corn-laws,	414
Total Reductions,	415
Poor-law for Ireland,	415
Registry of Deeds—The Ballot,	415
Military Flogging,	416
Impressment of Seamen,	416
Popular Discontents,	416
Trades Unions,	417
Dorsetshire Labourers,	417
Day of the Trades,	417
Changes in the Cabinet,	418
Late Intrigues,	418
Irish Tithes,	419
The Lord-chancellor,	419
Lord Durham,	419
The Grey Banquet,	419
Prospect of New Parties,	420
Dissolution of the Ministry,	420
Retirement of Lord Brougham,	420
Lord Lyndhurst succeeds,	420
Lord Brougham's Law Reforms,	420
Local Courts Bill,	421
Chancery Reform,	421
Retirement of Lord Spencer,	421

1830-1834.

	Page
Affairs of France,	422
The Duke of Orleans,	422
The Charter,	423
Louis Philippe accepts the Crown,	423
Disquiet,	424
Suicide of the Duke de Bourbon,	424
Disturbance in Paris,	424
Constitution of the Chambers,	424
Abolition of Hereditary Peerage,	425
Electoral Law—Parties,	425
Press Prosecutions,	425
Insurrections,	426
Fortification of Paris,	426
Characteristics of the Reign,	427
Death of Lafayette,	427
Separation of Belgium and Holland,	427
Prince Leopold King of Belgium,	428
Brunswick—Saxony—Hesse Cassel—Baden—Switzerland—Italy—Spain—Death of the King,	429
Don Carlos,	429
Portugal,	429
Death of Don Pedro,	429
Marriage of the Queen,	429
Her Widowhood,	429
Egypt and Turkey,	429
Poland—Revolt,	430
Defeat of the Poles,	430
Character of the Struggle,	430
Royalty in England,	431
The Coronation of William IV.,	431
The Princess Victoria,	431
Assault on the King,	431
Popular Ignorance,	432
Riots,	432
Anatomy Bill—Medical Education,	432
Criminal Trials,	433
Steam in the East,	434
Conveyance of Mails,	434
Diving to Wrecks,	434
The Drummond Light,	434
Polar Discovery,	435
Islington Cattle Market,	435
Peterborough Cathedral,	435
New London Bridge,	435
Education,	435
British Association Meetings,	435
Statistics of Suicide,	435
Duelling,	435
Loss of the *Rothsay Castle*,	436

HISTORY OF THE PEACE.

Entry	Page
Fire at the Dublin Custom-house,	436
Burning of Houses of Parliament,	436
Necrology,	437
Political Deaths,	437–439
Men of Science,	439
Seamen and Travellers,	439, 440
Actors,	441
Musicians,	441
Architects,	442
Antiquarians,	442
Artists,	442
Authors,	443
Philanthropists,	445

BOOK V.
1834–35.

Entry	Page
The three Parties,	447
The Duke's Offices,	447
Position of Sir R. Peel,	448
New Cabinet,	448
Dissolution of Parliament,	449
Tamworth Manifesto,	449
The New Parliament,	450
Temper of the Time,	450
Election of the Speaker,	451
King's Speech,	451
Debate on the Malt-tax,	452
Lord Londonderry's Appointment,	452
Dissenters' Marriages,	453
Ecclesiastical Commission,	454
Ministerial Defeats,	455
London University Charter,	455
Conflicts in Parliament,	455
Appropriation Question,	456
Resignation of the Cabinet,	457

1835–1839.

Entry	Page
Difficulties,	457
The Melbourne Administration,	458
Lord Melbourne,	458
Mr Charles Grant,	459
Lord John Russell,	459
Irish Administration,	460
Two Great Questions,	461
The Irish Church,	461
Appropriation Question,	461
Church Rates,	463
Surrender of the Appropriation Principle,	464
Second Great Question,	465
Municipal Reform,	465
Corporation Commission,	465
Rise and History of Municipal Institutions,	466
Report of Commissioners,	467
Existing State of Things,	467
Principle of the Case,	468
Defects of the Reform,	469
Substance of the Bill,	470
The Bill in the Commons,	471
In the Lords—it becomes Law,	471
Ecclesiastical Commissions,	472
Popular Ignorance,	472
Courtenay Delusion,	473
Results of the Delusion,	473
Non-residence Act,	474
Abolition of Sinecures,	474
Tithe Commutation Act,	474
Popular Education,	474
Lord Brougham's Scheme,	476
Ministerial Scheme,	476
Conduct of the Peers,	478
Peerage Reform,	479
Chartism—Radical Chartists,	481
Tory Chartists,	483
Hungering Chartists,	483
Factious Chartists,	483
Orangeism,	484
Duke of Cumberland,	485
Colonel Fairman,	485
Orange Peers,	486
Plot,	486

Entry	Page
Action of Orangeism—Detection,	488
Committee of Inquiry,	489
Mr Hume's Resolutions,	489
Address to the King,	489
Colonel Fairman's Contumacy,	489
Proposed Prosecution,	490
Death of Haywood,	490
Address to the King,	490
Dissolution of Orangeism,	490
Ireland from 1835–1840,	491
Various Theories,	491
Religious Rancour,	491
Distrust of Law,	491
Principle of Government,	491
Political Corruption,	491
Municipal Deterioration,	492
Uncertainty of Subsistence,	492
Fundamental Difficulty,	492
Insecurity of Title to Land,	492
Impartiality to Sects,	493
Ribbonmen and Orangemen,	493
Catholics in the Jury-box,	494
National Education,	494
Impartiality of Law,	495
Decrease of Crime,	496
The Viceroy's Clemency,	496
Thomas Drummond,	496
Reform of Constabulary,	498
Of Magistracy,	498
Prevention of Crime,	498
Repression of Crime,	498
Government by Functionaries or by Apostles,	498
The Queen—O'Connell,	499
Father Mathew,	500
Temperance Movement,	500
The Franchise and Registration,	502
Lord Stanley's Registration Bill,	502
The Government Bill,	503
Failure of both,	504
Political Education,	504
Municipal Reform,	505
The Measure,	506
Certainty of Maintenance,	508
O'Connell on the Poor-law,	508
Question of a Poor-law,	508
History of the Measure,	510
Its early Operation,	511
Resignation of Lord Normanby,	512
Whig Government of Ireland,	512

1835–1838.

Entry	Page
Church and State,	513
Church of Scotland,	513
Severance not Dissant,	513
Patronage,	513
Dissent,	514
Resort to Church Extension,	514
Commission of Inquiry,	514
Teinds—Bishops' Teinds,	515
Reports of Commission,	516
Election Struggles,	516
Impotence of the Church,	516
Government favours Church Extension,	516
Incompetence of Parliament and Ministers,	517

1835–1837.

Entry	Page
Agricultural Distress,	518
Committee of Inquiry,	518
Result—Finance,	518
Duties—Budget—Distress,	519
Joint-stock Banks,	520
Committee of Inquiry—Acts,	520
National Registration—Marriage,	521
Births and Deaths,	522
First Operation,	522
Imprisonment for Debt,	522
Counsel for Felons,	522
Coroners' Powers,	522
New Houses of Parliament,	524
Admission of Ladies to Debates,	525
Privilege of Parliament,	526

Entry	Page
Weakness of the Administration,	526
Illness of the King,	527
His Death,	528
Accession of Queen Victoria,	528
Severance of Hanover from England,	528
The Council,	528
William IV.,	529
His Funeral,	530
Queen Victoria,	530
Queen proclaimed,	531
Continuance of the Melbourne Ministry,	532
Party Discontents,	532
The Queen's Favour,	532
Radical Reform Party,	534

1835–1838.

Entry	Page
Portents in Europe—France,	535
The Representation,	535
Free-trade Inquiry,	536
Monster Trial,	536
Plots—Strasburg Insurrection,	537
Press Law,	538
Foreign Relations—Algeria,	539
Release of State Prisoners,	539
Marriage of the Duke of Orleans,	539
Of the Princess Marie,	539
Distress,	540
Dissolution of the Chamber,	540
Death of Talleyrand,	540
Spain—Queen Regent,	541
Queen Isabella—Carlist War,	541
British Legion,	541
Three young Queens,	542
Portugal,	542
The English in Portugal,	543
Portuguese Indigence,	543
Central Europe,	543
Zoll Verein,	543
Austrian Commercial Treaty,	544
Russia,	544
The Emperor at Warsaw,	545
Passage of the Dardanelles,	545
Circassia—Persia—Cracow,	545
Death of the Emperor of Austria,	545
Coronation of his Successor,	546
Hanover—Proceedings of the King,	546
Denmark,	546
Opening of a Constitution,	547
Sweden and Norway,	547
Holland and Belgium,	547
Young Germany,	547
Switzerland,	547
Prince Louis Napoleon,	548
Zillerthal Protestants,	548
Lutherans of Prussia,	548
Mixed Marriages,	548
The Pietists—Hungary,	548

1838–1841.

Entry	Page
Canada—Lord Durham,	549
Sketch of Canada as a British Colony,	550
The Assembly of the Council,	550
Stoppage of Official Salaries,	550
Canada Resolutions,	550
Rebellion—Gosford Commission,	551
Constitution of Lower Canada suspended,	551
Lord Durham's Offices—his Powers,	552
Executive Council,	552
State of the Canadas,	552
Speedy Improvements,	553
Scheme of Federal Union of Colonies,	553
Disposal of Prisoners,	554
Ordinance of the 28th of June,	554
Approval at Home,	554
Attacks by Opposition,	554
Lord Brougham's Declaratory Bill,	555
Ministers succumb,	555
Confused Result,	555
Disallowance of the Ordinance,	555
Retirement of Lord Glenelg,	555
Reception of the News in Canada,	555
Necessity of Resignation,	556

CHRONOLOGICAL INDEX.

	Page
The Prisoners,	556
Proclamation—Report,	556
Return of the Commission,	556
Incidents,	557
Lord Durham's Decline and Death,	557
His Character,	557
Mr Charles Buller,	558
Lord Sydenham (Mr C. Poulett Thomson),	558
Responsible Government,	558
Union of the Canadas,	558
Death of Lord Sydenham,	558
His Character,	559
Jamaica—The Planters,	559
Imperial Agents,	560
Lord Sligo—Sir Lionel Smith,	560
Proposed Suspension of the Constitution,	560
Weakness of Ministers,	560
Their Resignation,	560
Bedchamber Question,	561
Sir R. Peel summoned,	561
Household Appointments,	561
Restoration of the Whig Ministers,	562
Election of a Speaker,	562
New Jamaica Bill,	562
Official Changes,	562
Queen's Engagement,	562
Her Marriage,	563
Prince Albert's Annuity,	563
Dark Times,	564
Successive Harvests,	565
Grinding of Corn in Bond,	566
Discontents—Trade Unions,	566
Factory Question,	566
Chartism—National Convention,	567
National Petition,	568
John Frost—Riots,	568
Rising at Newport,	569
Origin of the Anti-corn-law League,	569
Delegates—The Ministers,	570
Motion for Inquiry refused,	570
Consequences,	570
Attacks on the Queen,	571
Dockyard Fires—Storms,	572
Repeal Agitation,	572
Troubles in the East,	572
Birth of the Princess Royal,	572

1837-1841.

	Page
Criminal Law Commission,	572
Restriction of the Punishment of Death,	573
Results of the Commission,	574
Infants' Custody Bill,	574
Lord Brougham on the Position of Wives,	574
Division in the Lords,	575
Bill of 1839 made Law,	575
Post-office System,	576
Rowland Hill—his Facts,	577
His Proposal,	578
History of the Movement,	578
The Reform made Law,	579
Immediate Results,	579
Further Results,	580
Privilege of Parliament,	580
State of the Case,	580
The Sheriffs—The House,	581
The Court of Queen's Bench,	581
Bill of Enactment,	582
Unsatisfactory Conclusion,	582
Imbecility of the Administration,	583
Queen's Speech,	583
Finance—Last Resort—The Budget,	583
Fixed Corn-duty proposed,	583
Defeat on the Sugar-duties,	583
Vote of Want of Confidence,	584
Dissolution of Parliament,	584

1835-1841.

	Page
The Queen at Guildhall,	584
The Coronation,	584
Her Marriage,	596

	Page
Birth of Heir to the Throne,	585
State of the People—Crime,	586
Times Testimonial,	586
Game Laws—Lord Suffield,	586
Opium-eating,	586
Church-building and Bishoprics,	587
Religious Intolerance,	587
Grace Darling,	587
Agricultural Associations,	588
India Cotton,	589
Niger Expedition,	589
President Steamer,	590
Royal Exchange burnt—Other Fires,	590
Balloons—Thames Conservancy,	590
The Eglinton Tournament,	590
Mummy Inquest—Trial of a Peer,	591
Suicides from the Monument,	591
India Mails,	591
Acarus Crossii,	592
Deaths,	592
Men of Science,	592, 593
Travellers,	593, 594
Court Personages,	594
Wealthy Personages,	595
Politicians,	595-597
Religious Philanthropists,	597
Musicians—Architects—Artists,	598
Actors,	599
Men of Letters—Orientalists,	600
Authors—light Literature,	601-603
Historians,	603
Philosophers,	603, 604

BOOK VI.
1841.

	Page
General Election,	605
New Parliament—Queen's Speech,	606
The Address amended,	607
Queen's Household changed,	607
Resignation of Ministers,	607
New Administration,	608
Lord Aberdeen,	608
Sir James Graham—Lord Stanley,	608
Lord Wharncliffe—Mr Gladstone,	608
First Nights in Parliament,	609
Prorogation—Policy of China,	610
State of China,	612
The Opium Question,	612
British Superintendents—Lord Napier,	612
Political Relations in Abeyance,	613
Opium Traffic prohibited,	613
Negligence at Home,	614
Crisis—War,	615
Chusan taken—Negotiation,	616
Warfare—Captain Elliot superseded,	617
Sir Henry Pottinger,	617
Capture of Ningpo,	617
Treaty of Peace,	617
Governor-general sent to China,	618
Opium Compensation,	618
Sir Henry Pottinger's Testimony,	618
India—Troubles,	619
North-west Frontier,	619
Fear of Russia,	619
Designs of Persia,	620
Rulers of Afghanistan,	620
British Agency at Cabool,	620
Herat—Explanations of Russia,	621
Lord Auckland's Declaration of War against Afghanistan,	621
Afghan Princes,	622
Scheme of Alliance,	623
Ameers of Sinde,	623
Invasion of Afghanistan,	623
The Bolan Pass—Ghuznee,	623
Settlement at Cabool—Khiva,	624
Troubles of the British,	624
Portents—The Punjaub,	625
Recall of Lord Auckland,	625
Lord Ellenborough,	625
The British at Cabool,	625

	Page
Rising at Cabool,	626
Murder of the Envoy,	626
Retreat of the British,	627
Lady Sale—General Sale,	627
Relief from India,	628
Murder of Shah Soojah,	628
Evacuation of Afghanistan,	628
Lord Ellenborough's Proclamation,	629
Recall of Lord Ellenborough,	629
Sir Henry Hardinge, Governor-general,	629
Sinde in 1842—Battle of Meanee,	629
Gwalior,	630
Wyburd, Stoddart, and Conolly,	630
Borneo—James Brooke,	631
Labuan ceded to Great Britain,	632

1842-1843.

	Page
Condition and Fate of Parties,	632
The Distress—Riots,	635
Rebecca and her Children,	637
Commission of Inquiry,	638
South Wales Turnpike Act,	638
The Court—Alarms,	638
Murder of Mr Drummond,	638
Opening of the Session of 1842,	639
Secession of the Duke of Buckingham,	639
The Queen's Speech,	639
The Corn Question,	640
The Ministerial Scheme,	640
Corn Bill of 1842,	640
Its Reception—Bill becomes Law,	641
Financial Statement,	641
Financial Scheme,	643
Income Tax—New Tariff,	643
Passage of the Bill,	646
Sugar Duties—Domestic View,	646
The Anti-Slavery View,	647
Poor-law Renewal Act,	647
Law of Literary Property,	647
Petitions for an Extension of Copyright,	648
Proposed Bills,	649
Copyright Law of 1842,	649
Election Compromises,	649
Mr Roebuck,	649
Stewardship of the Chiltern Hundreds,	650
Proceedings in the House,	650
Character of the Session,	650
Legislation for the Working-classes,	651
Lord Howick's Distress Motion,	652
Lord Ashley,	652
Mines and Collieries Act,	653
Government Factory Bill,	653
Education Clauses,	653
Education Clauses withdrawn,	655
Vacillation about the New Bill,	655
Decision against the Ten-hour Clause,	656
Debate on Colonisation,	656
Early-closing Movement,	656
Case of Governesses,	657
Improvement of Dwellings,	657

1841-1846.

	Page
Movements in Ireland,	657
O'Connell's Proceedings,	658
'Monster Meetings,'	659
Arbitration Courts,	659
Anti-rent Movement,	660
Irish Arms Act,	660
Clontarf Meeting,	661
Arrest of Repeal Leaders,	661
The Trials,	662
The Verdict—The Sentence,	663
Appeal to the Lords,	663
Judgment reversed,	663
Demonstrations,	664
O'Connell as a Landlord,	665
His Decline and Death,	665
Industrial Improvements,	666
Charitable Bequests Act,	666

HISTORY OF THE PEACE.

	Page
Penal Acts Repeal,	666
Viceroyalty discussed,	666
Endowment of Catholic Clergy,	667
Maynooth Grant,	667
New Colleges,	668
The Devon Commission,	668
Coercion Bill—Bill lost,	669
Threatenings of Famine,	669

1839-1844.

	Page
Church Patronage in Scotland,	669
The Veto Law,	670
The Auchterarder Case,	670
The Strathbogie Case,	670
Position of the Church Party,	672
Lord Aberdeen's Bill,	672
The General Assembly,	672
Its Memorial,	672
Reply of Government,	672
Quoad Sacra Ministers,	673
Petition of the Assembly—Failure,	673
Preparations for Secession,	673
The Secession,	673
Counter Proceedings,	674
Act of Separation,	674
Spirit of the Movement,	674
The Religious World in England,	674
Troubles in the Church,	675
Oxford,	675
Tractarian Secession,	676
Death of Dr Arnold,	677
Death of Sydney Smith,	677
Augmentation of Clergy,	678
Colonial Bishoprics,	678
Consolidation of Sees,	678
Struggles of Government and Church,	679
Dissenters' Chapels Bill,	680
Relief to Jews,	681

1842-1845.

	Page
Canada Corn Question,	681
Confusion of Parties,	682
Passage of the Bill,	682
Corn-law Debates,	682
Richard Cobden,	683
The League,	684
London Election,	686
Anecdotes,	687
League Registration,	687
Freehold Land Scheme,	687
The Game Laws,	688
Financial Statements of 1843, 1844,	691
Sugar-duties,	691
Mr Miles's Motion,	692
Crisis of Parties,	692
Reduction of the 3½ per Cents.,	693
Bank Act of 1844,	693
Railway Extension,	695
Railway Legislation,	696
Delivery of Plans,	697

	Page
Gauge Question,	697
Poor-law Amendments,	698
Post-office Espionage,	698
Alien Act,	699
Antagonism in Europe—Russia,	700
The Caucasus—Servia—Cracow,	701
Russian Jews,	701
The Czar and Pope Gregory XVI.,	702
Portugal and Spain,	702
Switzerland—Hanover—Sweden,	702
Turkey and Egypt,	703
Route to India,	704
France—War Spirit,	704
Right of Search,	705
Death of the Duke of Orleans,	706
Royal Visits,	706
Tahiti,	706
Spanish Question,	707
Death of the Duke D'Angoulême,	709
Boulogne Invasion,	709
Napoleon's Remains,	709
Algeria,	709
M. Guizot in 1842,	709
American Relations—The Frontier,	710
Right of Search,	710
'The Creole,'	711
'Repeal' Sympathy,	711
'Repudiation,'	711
Texas and Mexico,	711
Boundary Question,	711
Oregon Question,	712
India—Sikh Invasion,	713
The Sandwich Islands,	714
Van Diemen's Land,	715
South Australia—New Zealand,	715
Canada—Compensation Question,	717
Fires at Quebec—St John's—Hamburg—Smyrna—New York,	718

1845.

	Page
The Corn Question,	718
Mr Gladstone's Retirement,	719
Financial Statement,	719
Agricultural Interests—Portents,	721
Bad Weather—The Potato Rot,	722
The League—More Portents,	723
Lord John Russell's Letter,	724
Cabinet Councils,	724
Announcement of the *Times*,	724
Resignation of Ministers,	726
Negotiation with Lord John Russell,	726
Return of Sir Robert Peel to Power,	727
Death of Lord Wharncliffe,	727
Sir Robert Peel's Position,	727

1846.

	Page
Opening of the Session,	727
Further Remission of Duties,	727
The Revenue prosperous,	728
The Corn Duties,	728
Relief to Farmers—The Issue,	728

	Page
The Minister,	729
Nature of the Reform,	730
Dissolution of the League,	730
Irish Life Bill,	730
Resignation of Ministers,	730
The retiring Minister,	730

1841-1846.

	Page
Deaths.—Royal,	731
Of Statesmen and Warriors,	731, 732
Of Artists,	732-734
Men of Science,	734, 735
Literary Men,	735-739
Other Benefactors,	739, 740
Living Benefactors,	740
George Stephenson,	740
Barry,	740
Macready,	740
Turner,	740
Wordsworth,	740
Joanna Baillie,	741
Rogers,	741
Alfred Tennyson,	741
Wilson,	741
Jeffrey,	741
Thomas Macaulay,	741
Landor,	742
Hallam,	742
Carlyle,	742
Maria Edgeworth,	742
Bulwer,	742
Dickens,	743
Punch,	743
Herschel,	743
Faraday,	743

1815-1846.

	Page
National Advancement,	743
Electric Telegraph,	744
Sun-painting,	744
Lord Rosse's Telescope,	744
The Thames Tunnel,	744
British Scientific Association,	744
Geology,	745
Medicine,	745
Sanitary Improvement,	745
Agricultural Associations,	746
Prisons and Criminal Law,	746
Extinction of Slavery,	746
Education,	746
Popular Music,	747
Popular Art,	747
The Educator,	747
Methods of Charity,	747
Duelling,	747
Political Morality,	748
What remains,	748
The Labour Question,	748
Lists of Cabinet Ministers, from 1814 to 1846,	750-752
Index,	753-762

COMPLETE
GENERAL INDEX

TO THE

PICTORIAL

HISTORY OF ENGLAND

STANDARD EDITION

IN SEVEN VOLUMES

W. & R. CHAMBERS
LONDON AND EDINBURGH
1860

GENERAL INDEX

TO THE

PICTORIAL HISTORY OF ENGLAND.

	PAGE
ADARIS's embassy to Athens, i.	15
Abhaye prison, broken into by a Parisian mob, v.	745, 877
ABBÉ SIÈYES, a French ecclesiastic, v.	743, 745, 887
ABBOT, Dr George, iii. 45, 47, 51, 53, 117, 124, 130, 157, 433	
ABBOTT, Dr Robert, chaplain to James I., iii.	520
ABD-EL-KADER and the French, vii.	700
Abduction case of the Wakefields, vii.	298
ABERCROMBY, Mr, speaker of the House of Commons, vii.	451
———, Sir Ralph, a British general— iv. 575; vi. 141, 166, 168	
ABERDEEN, Lord; Portrait, vii.	517, 608-710
ABERGAVENNY, Lady, pleads for life of Mrs Lisle, iii.	780
ABERNETHY, John, death of, in 1831, vii.	440
Abjuration Bill, the, iv.	21
Aboukir, Battle of, fought July 25, 1799, vi.	142
Accession of Queen Victoria, vii.	528-533
ACHAIUS, king of the Scoti, i.	217
Acorns beaten down for swine, i.	277
Acre, siege of, 300,000 Christians perish at, i.	495, 496
——— by Bonaparte, vi.	141, 142
Acropolis, View of, vii.	237
Act for the Security of the Kingdom; quotations from— iv. 148	
ACTON, Sir Roger, a Lollard; executed, ii.	26
Actresses first appear on English stage in 17th century, iii.	897
Acts of parliament, vii.	89, 101, 113, 127, 128
———. See Parliament, ii., iii., iv., v., vi.	
ADAM, Robert, an eminent architect, vi.	863, 867, 868
ADAMS, John; Portrait of, v.	78
Addington cabinet, vii.	48
ADDINGTON, Mr, prime-minister, vi.	761
ADDISON, an eminent literary character, iv. 234, 324, 685, 745	
ADELAIDE, queen of William IV., vii.	531
ADELIA, affianced wife of Prince Richard, i.	477, 478
———, or ALICE, queen of Henry I., i.	416, 428
———, queen of Louis VII., i.	446
Adjutators, alias Agitators, instituted by Cromwell, iii.	366
ADRIAN IV., Pope, an Englishman, i.	442
ADY, Joseph, the notorious swindler, vii.	299
ÆLFRIC, his Saxon Homilies, i.	301
Afghan princes, vii.	622
Afghanistan, or Cabool; its importance, &c., vii.	619-631
African discoveries of Captain Clapperton, vii.	215
AGAR, Sir Anthony; slain in capture of Calais, ii.	534
AGATHA, the mother of Edgar Atheling, i.	360
AGGAS, Ralph, an eminent surveyor and engraver, iii.	577
Aghrim, battle of, fought July 12, 1691, iv.	83
Agincourt, or Azincourt, Battle of, &c., ii.	30-36, 233, 234
———, song on victory of; English part-music, iii.	564
AGRICOLA, Cnæus Julius, a Roman general, i.	44-47
Agricultural and commercial interests, approximation of, vii.	633
Agricultural chemistry, science of, vii.	746
——— distress in 1821 and 1835, vii.	128, 518
——— improvements in Ireland, vii.	666

	PAGE
Agricultural societies, institution of, vii.	588
Agriculture, i. 106, 276, 596, 599, 833, 840; vi. 811, 818, 820; vii. 16, 20, 666, 721	
———, illustration, ii.	188, 190, 803, 806
———, introduction of turnips, &c., v.	468
AGUILAR, Don Juan d', a Spanish general, ii.	693
Air-pump, invented by Otto von Guericke, iv.	728
AITKIN, James, alias John the Painter; executed, v.	182-184
Aix-la-Chapelle, Congress of, vii.	93-95
———, Treaty of,	iii. 706; iv. 530
AKBER KHAN, son of Dost Mohammed, vii.	625-628
ALAN, lord of Richmond, i.	406
———, of Galloway, commotions after his death, i.	700
Alarms, vii.	52, 115, 638
ALBAN, St, first British martyr, i.	74
ALBANO, Francisco, a Bolognese painter, iii.	569
ALBANY, Duke of, ii.	9, 11, 19, 38, 49, 131, 132
———, Duke of, Murdoch Stewart, ii.	131-133
———, Duke of, regent in 1515, ii.	350-354, 359, 361, 429
———, Duke of, second son of James II.— ii. 114, 115, 135, 136	
Albany, View of, v.	247
ALBEMARLE, Arnold Joost von Keppel, iv.	122, 245, 249
———, Christopher Monk, duke of, iii.	772
———, George Monk, duke of— iii. 430*-432, 664, 681, 698	
———, William de Mandeville, earl of, i.	483-485
ALBERIC, bishop of Ostia, i.	426
ALBERONI, Julius, a Spanish statesman, iv. 321-323, 332, 345	
ALBERT, Archduke, king of Spanish Netherlands, ii. 680, 685	
———, archbishop of York, rebuilds the cathedral, i.	310
———, D', king of Navarre, ii.	321
———, D', prince of Bearn, ii.	292, 294, 296
———, Henry d', king of Navarre, ii.	365
———, Jean d', constable of France, ii.	29, 31-33
———, Prince; Portrait, vii.	563, 585, 586
ALBINEY, William d', defends Rochester Castle, i.	530
Albinn, name for Scotland used by Gaels, i.	21
ALBINUS, Clodius, governor of Britain, i.	49
Albion, son of Neptune, i.	8
———, the early name of England, i.	21
Alcazar, Battle of; king of Portugal slain, ii.	651
Alchemy, doubts about its lawfulness, ii.	207
———, its influence on medical science, i.	844, 845
ALCUIN, Flaccus, a prelate of the 8th century, i.	307
ALDERIC, William of, an adherent of Count of Aumale, i.	400
ALDRED, an early English historian, i.	542
———, archbishop of York, i.	204, 360, 369
ALDRICH, Henry, dean of Christ Church, Oxford, iii.	562, 750
ALENÇON, Duke of; slain at battle of Agincourt, ii.	19, 21, 33
———, Duke of, a suitor of Queen Elizabeth, ii.	636, 649
———, Duke of; his address to Talbot, ii.	68
Aleppo, great earthquake at, vii.	215
ALESSI, Guiseppe, leader of an insurrection in Italy, iii.	395
ALEXANDER, archdeacon of Salisbury, i.	426, 429, 430
———— I., king of Scotland, i.	538, 539

ALEXANDER II., son of William the Lion, i. 530, 546, 700–702
——— III., son of Alexander II., i. . 702–707
——— III., Pope, i. 446
——— V., Pope, surnamed Philargi, ii. . 17
——— VI., Pope, nephew of Calixtus III., ii. 311–318
——— emperor of Russia—
  vi. 163, 394, 503, 504, 686, 690; vii. 1, 2, 94, 152
Alexandria, Battle of, fought March 21, 1801, vi. 166–168
ALFERE, ealderman of Mercia, i. . . 174–176
ALFORD, Edward, appointed sheriff by Charles I., iii. 117, 534
ALFRED, brother of Edward the Confessor, i. . 184–188
——— the Great, youngest son of Ethelwulf—
  i. 153–168, 246, 266, 305
ALFRIC, earl of Mercia, a traitor, i. . 176–178
ALGAR, son of Earl Leofric, i. . . . 194
Algeria, Colonel Pelissier's barbarity at, vii. . 709
Algiers, Bombardment of; View, vii. . . 33–37
———, last war with, vii. . . . 153
———, View of, vi. 747
ALOITHA, queen of Harold, king of England, i. . 209
Alicant; taken and retaken, iv. . . 171, 216
ALICE, Princess, sister of Philip II. of France, i. . 509
Alien Act, the, vii. . . . 89, 156, 157, 699
——— Bill, Lord Grenville introduces the, v. . 900
ALIVERDY, Khan, viceroy of the Great Mogul, v. 605
Aliwal, Battle of, vii. 714
ALLAN, the Breton, i. 374
ALLECTUS, a Briton, kills the Emperor Carausius, i. 53
ALLEN, archbishop of Dublin; murdered, ii. . 425
———, Ethan, an American revolutionist, v. 112–115, 153
———, Mr, quoted, i. . . . 533, 534, 537, 538, 580
———, William, death of, in 1843, vii. . . 739
Alliance, the Holy, vii. 2
ALLIDONE, Sir Richard, iii. . . . 791
ALMAINE, Henry d', son of Richard, king of Rome, i. 688
Almanza, Battle of, gained by Duke of Berwick, iv. 182
Almeida, View of, vi. 541
ALMERIO, Master of the English Templars, i. . 528
Almonry, the, at Westminster; View of Caxton's House, ii. 203
ALPHEGE, archbishop of Canterbury, i. . . 179
ALRED, archbishop of York, i. . . . 204
ALTHORP, Lord, chancellor of the exchequer; Portrait—
  vii. 338, 360–369, 394, 396–399, 407–421
Alton, Battle of, i. 688
Alum, letters-patent granted to dig for, &c., ii. . 811
ALVA, Duke, of Netherlands, ii. 321, 531, 621, 626, 639, 649
ALWIN, bishop of Winchester, i. . . 188
ALWYN, of East-Anglia, a powerful noble, i. . 174
ALZEVEDO, Dom Antonio d', a Portuguese ambassador—
  iv. 394
AMADEUS VIII., the retired duke of Savoy, ii. . 138, 139
Amboyna, one of the Molucca Islands, iii. . 105, 106
AMBROSIUS, Aurelius, head of a Roman party, i. . 57
Ameers of Sinde, the, vii. . . 623, 629, 630
America, abolition of slavery in, vii. . . 385–387
———, history of the United States, &c., vi. . 624–635
———, relations of England with, vii. . . 710
——— See also GEORGE III., v. 79, 80, 85, 107, 116, 150
  163, 202, 288, 463, 464, 583
———, Spanish, vii. 47–52
American militia and minute men at Lexington, View of, v. 107
American paper-credits, unsound system of, vii. 520, 521
——— presidents, vii. 710
Amersfoort, View of, v. 681
AMHERST, General; captures Cape Breton, iv. . 575
———, Lord, governor-general of India, vii. . 141
Amiens, Treaty of, vi. . . . 170, 636
Anabaptists, Lutherans, &c., burned by Henry VIII., ii. 386
ANAGNI, John of, cardinal and papal legate, i. . 478
Anatomy Bill; interesting incident, vii. . . 432
Ancrum Moor, on the Teviot, total defeat of English at, ii. 441
ANDERSON; his pamphlet on Goldsmiths' mysteries, iii. 549
Anderson's Place, Charles I. made prisoner here, iii. 360

ANDERTON, Henry, a celebrated painter, iii. . 882
ANDRÉ, Major John, a British officer; Portrait, v. 327, 330
———, St, a Marshal of France, ii. . . 495
Andredswold, the, or forest of Andreade, i. . 142, 162
ANDREWS, Dr Lancelot, bishop of Winchester—
  iii. 465, 607, 608
ANGELO, Michel, an illustrious painter, sculptor, &c. iii. 570
ANGERSTEIN, Mr, death of, in 1823, vii. . . 220
Angles, the, or Anglo-Saxons, i. . . 139, 142
ANGLESEY, Arthur Annesley, earl of, iii. . 670, 672
Anglesey, Island of, anciently called Mona, i. . 43, 61
ANGLESEY, Marquis of, viceroy of Ireland, recalled—
  vii. 253, 339
Anglo-Saxon king, his arms and accoutrements, i. . 156
——— language—
  i. 139, 140, 165–167, 182, 293–300, 611, 612
ANGOULEME, Charles, count of, son of Duke of Orleans—
  ii. 19–21
———, Duke of, invests Rochelle, iii. . . 135
ANGUIER, François, a sculptor of 17th century, iii. . 576
ANGUS, Archibald Douglas, earl of, ii. . 115, 304, 327
———, Earl of, marries Queen Margaret. ii. 349, 351, 352
ANJOU, Duke of, previously Alençon, ii. . . 649–651
———, Geoffrey Plantagenet, earl of, i. 417, 418, 434, 436
———, Henri, duke of, elected king of Poland, ii. . 649
Anjou, province of France, wars in, ii. . 48, 55, 80, 81, 86
———, René of, brother of Charles VII.'s queen, ii. 59, 81, 86
ANKARSTRÖM assassinates Gustavus Adolphus, v. . 857
Annates, or first-fruits paid to popes; abolished, ii. 378
ANNE BOLEYN, queen of Henry VIII., ii. . 331, 363–395
———; the Catholics' opinion of her marriage, iii. 96
———, czarina of Russia, iv. . . . 415
———, daughter of the Duke of Brittany, ii. 292, 295–298
———, Lady, wife of Prince Edward—
  ii. 105, 111, 124, 127, 128
——— of Bohemia, queen of Richard II., i. . 790
——— of Cleves, queen of Henry VIII., ii. 412–421, 507, 532
——— of Denmark, queen of James I—
  iii. 3–6, 11, 37, 73, 80, 623
———, Queen of England—
  iii. 760, 795, 798; iv. 19, 36, 125, 260 588, 679
ANNEBAUT, admiral of Francis I., ii. . . 442
ANNESE, Gennaro, raises a rebellion in Italy, iii. . 395
ANNIUS, or NANNI, his fabled history of England, i. . 8
Annuity, discussions on Prince Albert's, vii. . 563
ANSELM, abbot of Becco, i. . . 406, 550–552
———, chaplain to Richard I., i. . . 502
ANSON, Commodore; Portrait of, &c., iv. . 447, 573, 654
Antarctic discoveries of 1820–1826, vii. . . 215
Anti-Corn-Law delegates, procession of the, vii. . 640
——— League, origin of—
  vii. 569–571, 583, 639, 724–726
Anti-rent movement in Ireland, vii. . . 660
ANTONINUS, Pius, reign, and Portrait of, i. . 47, 48
ANTRIM, Earl of, taken prisoner by General Monro, iii. 310
Antwerp, city and commerce of, &c., ii. . 786, 793, 794
Apostles, government in Ireland by, vii. . 498–502
Appeals of arms and judicial encounters, ii. . 247
——— of treason abolished, ii. . . . 5
APPIUS, Colonel; his disgraceful conduct at Fontenoy, iv. 451
Appleby, Camden's description of its decayed state, iii. 656
Apprentices, description of, in 17th century, iii. . 634
Appropriation question, speeches and debates on, vii. 456–465
APULDORE, William, confessor of Richard II., i. . 787
Aqueduct over the river Irwell; View of, v. . 472
Aqueducts, vi. 826
AQUINAS, St Thomas, Henry VIII.'s favourite—
  ii. 333, 345, 366
Arbitration courts, scheme for establishing Irish, vii. 659, 660
ARBUTHNOT, Dr John, iv. 746
ARCHER, John, tortured on the rack, iii. . . 518
Archers; Illustration, ii. 260
Architecture, i. . 4, 167, 307–318, 614–633, 854–860;
  vi. 862–871, 890–896
———; Illustrations, ii. 222–233, 303, 601, 841–851
——— of 17th century, iii. . . . 567–577

GENERAL INDEX.

Architecture of the 18th century, iv., 685-700
———— of the 19th century, v. 526, 527
Arcole, Bridge of, Bonaparte's losses at the, vi. 108
Arcon, Chevalier d', a French engineer, v. 387-390
Arcot, royal palace at, v. 631
Arden, executed by Elizabeth as a traitor, ii. 654
Arden, or Arden, John, an English surgeon, i. 845
Arembero, Count d'; his embassy to James I., iii. 7, 9
Argyle, Earl of, takes up arms for James VI., ii. 652
———, Earl of; charged with treason, iii. 736, 737, 767, 768
———, Earl of; chief of the Covenanters— iii. 199, 251, 337-340, 680, 682
Arianism in Britain, i. 74
Aristotle, his supposed mention of Ireland, i. 14
Arkwright, the mechanist, vi. 840
————, Sir R., inventor of the spinning-frame— vii. 489-492
Armada, the Spanish; illustration of, &c., ii. 674-678
Armagnac, Bernard, count of, ii. 21, 26-28, 35-42
————, Count of, ii. 42-48
Armed Neutrality, the, 1780, v. 314
Armies, ancient British, i. 37
————, Standing, iv. 630-632
Arminius, James, leader of the Arminians, iii. 47
Armorica, peopled by the Cymry, i. 8
Armour, defensive, not used by the Britons, i. 36
————, suits of, banners, &c., i. 639, 640, 872-877; ii. 241, 857-870; iii. 625-627, 890
Armstrong, Archibald, the famous court-fool, iii. 94
————, John, a poet and physician, v. 502
————, John, of Gilnockie; hanged by James V., iii. 549
————, Sir T., a Rye-house conspirator, iii. 740, 755
Army, Orangeism in the, vii. 488
Arne, T. A., an eminent composer of music, v. 530
Arnold, an American revolutionist— v. 113, 117, 118, 174, 326-332, 351
————, Dr; Portrait, vii. 357, 369, 370, 402, 406, 677
Arran, Earl of, revolted in 1516, ii. 351-353
————, Earl of, son of Duke Chatelherault, ii. 552, 558, 574
————, James Hamilton, earl of, regent of Scotland— ii. 434-440, 536, 548, 556, 557, 581, 583, 604, 606, 614, 632
————, James Stuart, earl of, ii. 652-654
Arras, Congress of, ii. 78
Arthur, fable of his Round Table, i. 23
————, nephew of Richard I., i. 506, 507, 515-520
————, prince of Wales, ii. 287, 289, 310, 312
Articles, Thirty-nine; petition against, v. 18-20, 46, 47
Artisans, group of; illustration, i. 195
Artois, Count d', brother of Louis XVIII., vi. 639
————, Count d', uncle of Philip III. of France, i. 712
————, Robert of, brother-in-law of Philip of France, i. 758
Arts, the Fine, disquisitions on, i. 118, 289, 603, 842
————, the Fine. See Literature, Science, &c.— ii. 196-235, 813-854; iii. 560-616, 870-886; iv. 685-749; v. 499-532; vi. 850-905
———— and Manufactures, vi. 817-849
———— and Manufactures, Society for Encouragement of— iv. 681
————, improvement of the, by immigration of foreigners— vii. 747
Arun, the river, in Sussex, i. 103, 142
Arundel Castle, View of, i. 428, 429
Arundel, Edmund Fitzalan, earl of, i. 739
————, Henry Fitzalan, earl of, ii. 454
————, Philip Howard, earl of, ii. 654
————, Richard Fitzalan, earl of, i. 795
————, Thomas, archbishop of Canterbury— i. 795; ii. 14, 25; iii. 163
Ascham, Roger, tutor to Queen Elizabeth; Portrait, ii. 813
Ashantee wars, the, vii. 153
Ashburnham, J., a royalist, iii. 293, 352, 354, 369, 371, 376
Ashburton, Lord; his American mission, vii. 17, 712
Ashley, Lord; Portrait, vii. 566, 567, 652-656
————, Sir John, admiral of the Blue, iv. 38
Ashridge, Bucks, the work of James Wyatt, vi. 895

Ashton, chaplain to the Earl of Essex, ii. 698
Asia, map of, vii. 611
Aske, Robert, leader of insurgents in Yorkshire, ii. 399-401
Askew, Anne; burnt as a heretic in Smithfield, ii. 447, 448
Asoff-ul-Dowla, nabob of Oude, v. 627, 639-641
Aspern, Battle of, fought May 21 and 22, 1809, vi. 509
Asser, the monk, a friend of King Alfred— i. 158, 161, 165, 166
Assessed taxes movement of 1834, vii. 413
Assignats, French, of 1790, v. 756, 790
Assize, Grand, great importance of, i. 573
Astley, Sir Jacob, a royalist; his services, iii. 297, 316
————'s Amphitheatre burnt down, vii. 590
Aston, or Asheneden, Berkshire, signal victory at, i. 154
Astoria Library, purchased by Edinburgh Faculty of Advocates, vii. 214
Astronomical instrument, Celtic, found in Ireland— i. 122, 123
Astronomy, vi. 890
Athelney, Isle of, fastness of Alfred in 878, i. 153, 166
Athelstane, King, grandson of Alfred, i. 168-170, 297
Athelwold, a courtier of Edgar, i. 173
Athole, Earl of, takes up arms for James VI., ii. 652
————, Patrick, earl of, i. 701
Atomic Theory, the, vi. 890
Attainders, reversal of, in 1824 and 1826, vii. 216
Atterbury, Dr Francis, bishop of Rochester— iv. 257, 280, 359
Attorney-general, and king's solicitor; their offices, ii. 164
Attorneys, statute restricting number of, ii. 195
Attwood, Thomas, death of, in 1838, vii. 598
Auchterarder case, the, vii. 670
Auckland, Lord, formerly Mr William Eden, vi. 796
————, Lord, governor-general of India, vii. 619-625
Audner, or Osthere, a learned foreigner, i. 166
Audley, Lord, defeated at Bloreheath, Shropshire, ii. 94
————, Lord, joins the Cornish insurrection, ii. 306
————, Sir Thomas, becomes chancellor— ii. 378, 391, 393, 405
Augusta, princess of Saxe Gotha, iv. 399, 539
Augustine and forty monks arrive in England— i. 145, 230-233
Augustus, improvements in Britain by, i. 105
———— II., king of Poland, iv. 387
Aumale, Harcourt, count of, takes De la Pole prisoner, ii. 55, 56
Aurengzebe, Great Mogul, v. 599
Austerlitz, Battle of, fought December 2, 1805— vi. 278, 279
Austria, Archduke of, sends an ambassador to James I., iii. 7
Austria and England, commercial treaty between, vii. 544
Austria, Charles archduke of, vi. 118, 140, 276, 508-511
————, John archduke of; Portrait of, vi. 152, 511-514
————, Leopold, duke of, i. 499, 503, 504
————, Maria Louisa, archduchess of— vi. 556-559, 590, 686
Austria, Russian conference at, in 1844, vii. 701
Auverquerque, M., iv. 6, 123, 148, 151, 163, 169
Avebury, Druidical temple of, i. 68
Averna, City of, opens its gates to Count Daun, iv. 184
Avienus, Festus, his narrative of Carthaginian voyage, i. 14
Avignon, incorporated with France, v. 830
Avisa, wife of King John, i. 517
Avison, Charles; his Essay on Musical Expression, iv. 713
Avon, river, in Hampshire, i. 142
Avranches, Hugh d', surnamed the Wolf, i. 376, 385
Axe-heads, called Celts, of tin and copper, i. 104
Ayscue, Sir George, conquers Barbadians, iii. 549

Babbage's *Economy of Machinery and Manufactures*, quoted, vii. 434
Babington, Anthony; executed as a traitor, ii. 657
Bacon, John, an eminent sculptor; Portrait of, vi. 875, 876
————, Roger, the philosopher, i. 843

HISTORY OF ENGLAND.

	PAGE
BACON, Sir Francis; quoted, &c., ii. 288, 289, 291, 293, 298, 307, 312, 498, 542, 684, 686–688; iii. 4, 6, 19, 34, 63, 67, 68, 70, 82, 83, 610, 611	
———, Sir Nicholas, keeper of the seals, ii.	543
Baconian Philosophy, iv.	716
Badajoz, View of, vi.	579, 584, 602, 603
BADBY, a Lollard; denies transubstantiation; burnt, ii.	146
BAGNALL, Sir Henry; defeated and slain at Tyrone, ii.	682
BAGOT, Sir Charles, governor of Canada, vii.	717
Bahama Islands, captured by the Spaniards, v.	385
BAILLIE, Joanna, vii.	741
——— of Jerviswood; executed, iii.	746, 755
BAILLY, Charles, a servant of the queen of Scots, ii.	637, 638
———, mayor of Paris, v. 743, 744, 747, 784, 792, 825–845	
BAILY, the astronomer, death of, in 1844, vii.	735
BAIRD, Sir David, retakes the Cape of Good Hope, vi.	329
———, death of, in 1828, vii.	313
BAKER, a Romish priest; his attentions to Lord Lovat, iv.	525
BAKER, Major, joint-governor of Londonderry, iv.	16
———, Sir Richard; his *Kings of England*, iii.	615
BALCANQUEL, W., publicly rebuked by James VI., iii.	442
BALCARRAS, Earl of; his commission to Galloway, iii.	769
BALDWIN, a Jesuit, resident at Spanish Flanders, iii.	29
———, archbishop of Canterbury, i.	483
——— de Bethune, a priest, i.	502
BALFOUR, John, of Kinloch, kills Archbishop Sharp, iii.	736
———, Sir James, a conspirator in Darnley's murder, ii.	605
———, Sir Wm., lieutenant of the Tower, iii. 240, 259, 317	
BALIOL, Edward, king of Scotland, ii. 724, 755, 756, 759	
———, John, nearest relative of Alexander III.— i. 707–715, 724	
———, Joycelin, excommunicated by à Becket, i.	452
BALL, John, executed as a traitor, i.	789
BALLANTINE, bishop of Aberdeen, iii.	478, 484
BALLANTYNE, James, the printer; his death, vii.	445
Balloon-voyage of 480 miles in 17 hours, vii.	590
Ballot, objections against the, vii.	415, 416
Balls, v.	539
Baltic, arms and costume of tribes on shores of, i.	139
———, observations of early navigators on the, i.	166, 167
BALTIMORE, Lord, Charles I. grants Maryland to, iii.	549
Bamborough, View of the Rock and Castle, &c., i.	147, 176
BAMFORD, Samuel, secretary of a Hampden Club— vii. 29–32, 54–58, 95, 104, 106–110, 116, 117	
BAMPTON, Thomas de, commissioner of the pole-tax, i.	785
BANCROFT, Dr, of Canterbury, iii. 17, 41, 44, 45, 460, 463, 466	
Banditti, the Gloucestershire gang captured, vii.	209
BANIM, the Irish novelist, death of, vii.	736
Bank charter, renewal of the, in 1833, vii.	380, 381
——— of England, founded 1693, iv.	657
——— charter of 1844, vii.	693–695
———; Views of, &c.— iv. 110, 792–794, 806, 810, 814–817, 865, 892	
——— Scotland, and Bank Royal; when founded, iv.	659
——— Restriction Act, vii.	87
Banking system, joint-stock, vii.	520, 521
Bankruptcies, vi.	802, 806, 809, 813–816
BANKS, Mr; his complaint to government against the League, vii.	684
BANKS, Sir Joseph, death of, in 1820, vii.	217
———, Thomas, an eminent English sculptor, vi.	874, 875
BANNISTER, Jack, death of, vii.	599
Bannockburn, Battle of. See Robert Bruce, i.	736–738
BAR, Duke of, and other nobles who fell at Agincourt, ii.	33
Barbadoes, rising of the slaveholders in, vii.	170
BARBAULD, Mrs, death of, in 1825, vii.	220
BARBAZAN, an officer serving Armagnac, ii.	41, 48
BARBER, a Rye-house conspirator, iii.	741, 743
BARBOUR, John, a Scottish historian and poet, i.	735, 851
Barcelona fever; its effects on France, vii.	143, 144
——— taken by the Earl of Peterborough, iv.	164, 165
BARCLAY, John, author of two political romances, iii.	616
BARDOLF, lieutenant of Calais; slain, ii.	34
———, Lord, a participator in Percy's rebellions, ii.	17, 19
Bards of Celtic nations, i.	63–65

	PAGE
BARILLON, a minister of Louis XIV., iii. 716, 727, 761, 774	
Barking Church, Archbishop Laud buried at, iii.	326
———, William I. keeps his court here, i.	362
Barnet, first and second Battles of, ii.	97, 108
BARNWELL, P., counsels better government of Ireland, ii.	428
BARR, confederacy of, formed 1678, v.	32
BARRAS, a French revolutionist; Portrait of, vi.	58
BARRÉ, Isaac, v.	4, 21, 46, 51, 58, 71, 133, 300
———, Isaac; Portrait of, &c., iv.	830, 834, 862, 897
———, Luke de, a knight and a poet, i.	419
Barricades, French, vii.	273, 274, 279
Barrier Treaty of 1712, iv.	243
BARRINGTON, Lord, secretary at war, iv. 556; v.	239, 274
———, quoted, i.	577, 812, 814, 816, 820
———, Sir Jonah; his removal from the Irish Admiralty, vii.	290
BARROW, Dr, an eminent mathematician and divine— iii. 610, 802	
———, Dr Isaac, the mathematician and divine, iv.	729
Barrows, ancient and Roman British, i.	130, 131, 133
BARRY, James, a celebrated artist; Portrait of, v.	522
———, Mr, architect of the new Houses of Parliament; Portrait, vii.	523–525
Bartholomew Fair; illustrations, iv.	776, 777
BARTOLOZZI, Francesco, an eminent engraver, v.	521
BARTON, E., holy maid of Kent; executed at Tyburn— ii. 384, 385	
Basil, Council of, ii.	138
Basilica of St Paul at Rome, View of, after fire in 1823, i.	311
Basques and Bearnois take Bayonne from the English, ii.	85
Bass Rock, last spot in Scotland which held out for the Stuarts, iv.	16
Bass Rock, with the prisons of the Covenanters, iii.	757
BASSOMPIERRE, Marshal de, iii.	125, 127, 135
Bastia, in Corsica, View of, vi.	41
Bastille, attacks on the, by French Revolutionists, v. 746, 747	
BASTWICK, Dr, a Parliamentarian, iii.	166, 293
BATES, a Turkish merchant, resists a duty on currants, iii.	40
Bath, a fashionable watering-place, iv.	771
BATH, Chandos of Brittany, earl of, ii.	286
———, Henry Bourchier, earl of, iii.	292
———, John Granville, earl of, iii.	767
———, William Pulteney, earl of, iv.	245, 366, 399, 433
BATHURST, Earl, death of, in 1834, vii.	438
———, Henry, earl of, lord chancellor, v.	4, 423
———, Lord; opposes war preparations, iv.	370
Battle Abbey, founded by William I., View of, &c., i.	358, 359
BATTONI, Pompeo, an Italian painter of 18th century, iv.	839
BAVARIA, Elector of, besieges city of Brussels— iv. 151–158, 211	
———, Electoral Prince of, iv.	84
———, Louis of, recommends punishment of Luther— ii. 345	
———, Maximilian Joseph, elector of, v.	240
BAXTER, Richard; quoted, iii.	490, 668, 819
———; his death, iv.	733
BAYARD, a celebrated French commander, ii.	323, 325, 358
Bayeux Tapestry, detailed account of, i.	196–215
BAYNAM, Sir Edward, condemned for treason, ii.	689
Baynard's Castle, London; View of, ii.	122, 127
———; private supper at, iii.	57
Bayonet invented in reign of Charles II., iii.	891
Bayonne, city of, surrenders to Gaston de Foix, ii.	65
———, View of, vi.	677
BEAL; his portrait of Dr Edward Stillingfleet, iv.	589
BEALE, R., informs Mary Stuart of her sentence, ii. 663, 668	
Bear-baiting, iii.	642
———, garden, Southwark; Illustration, iii.	886
BEATON, Cardinal David, archbishop— ii. 431–436, 440, 446, 447	
———, James, archbishop of Glasgow, ii. 352, 353, 430, 431	
BEATOUN, archbishop of Glasgow, iii.	450
BEAUFORT, Henry, cardinal, ii. 52, 57, 58, 70, 71, 77–84, 150	
———, Joanna, queen of James I. of Scotland, ii.	132
BEAUFOY, Mr; his exertions for Dissenters, vi.	743, 749

GENERAL INDEX. 101

BEAUHARNAIS, Eugene de; Portrait of—
    vi. 510-514, 661, 663, 694
BEAUMONT, Francis, a dramatic writer, iii. . 595
————, French ambassador to Whitehall, iii. . 15
————, Sir George Howland, death of, in 1827, vii. 316
BEAUVAIS, Bishop of, a relative of Philip II., i. 513, 526
BECKET, Thomas à; his shrine broken open, ii. 402, 403
————, primate of England, i. 444-456, 552-555
————'s crown, View of, i. . . . 556
BECKFORD, Alderman; Portrait of—
    iv. 848, 864, 873, 884, 889-891
————, William, death of, in 1844, vii. . 736
BECKWITH endeavours to deliver up Hull to Charles I.—
    iii. 282
Bedchamber question, the, vii. . . . 561
BEDE, the Venerable, quoted—
    i. 18-23, 229, 234, 290, 291, 305
BEDFORD, Dr; his work on hereditary right, iv. . 270
————, Duke of; his death, vii. . . . 595
————, Duke of, son of Henry IV., ii. 17, 29, 35, 50, 52-79
————, Francis Russell, earl of, ii. . 589, 591
————, Jasper Tudor, duke of. See Pembroke, ii. 282
————, John Russell, duke of, iv. . 529, 815, 821
————, John Russell, earl of, ii. 402, 423, 469, 483, 485
————, William Russell, earl and duke of, iii. 62, 748
BEDINGFIELD, confessor to James II. when Duke of York, iii. 717
BEDINGFIELD, Sir Henry, constable of the Tower, ii. 519
BEDLOE, W.; depositions in murder of Sir E. Godfrey—
    iii. 721
BEDYLL, Dr Thomas, clerk of the council, ii. . 381
Beggars in Ireland; their reception of the poor-law, vii. 511
Behmenists, or disciples of Jacob Behmen, iii. . 813
BEHN, Mrs Aphra, the Astræa of Pope, iii. . 878
BELESME, Robert de, earl of Shrewsbury, i. 408-410
Belgæ, doubtful if a German or Celtic race, i. . 10, 27
Belgic colonies in South Britain, Celtic, i. . 11
Belgium and Holland, separation of, vii. . 423, 547
BELHAVEN, Lord; his speech against the Union, iv. 173
BELKNAPE, Sir Robert, chief-justice of Common Pleas, i. 735
BELL, Dr Andrew, death of, in 1831, vii. . . 446
————, Henry, death of, vii. . . . 440
————, Henry; his connection with steam-navigation—
    vi. 830, 831
————, Sir Charles, death of, in 1842, vii. . 734, 735
BELLARMINE, Cardinal, and the casuist Parsons, iii. 33, 95
BELLASIS, Henry, sent to the Fleet prison, iii. . 217
————, Lord; governor of Newark, iii. . 344, 354
Belleisle, taken by the English; illustration, iv. . 802
BELLIÈVRE, M. de, a French ambassador, iii. . 359
————; sent to intercede for Mary Stuart, iii. 664, 665
BELLINGHAM shoots Mr Percival, M.P., vi. . 597, 598
BELLIUS, Martinus, a fictitious name, iii. . 806
Bells, their introduction among the Anglo-Saxons, i. 316
Belsize House, View of, iv. . . . 774
BELZONI, the traveller, death of, in 1823, vii. . 219
Benares, View of, v. 626
BENBOWE, Admiral, dies of his wounds at Jamaica, iv. 145
Benedictine monks, institution of; Portrait of one—
    i. 559, 560
Benevolence, private, vii. . . . 25, 26
Benevolences, moneys raised for kings; abolished, ii. 300
BENNET, G., gives the name of Quakers to Fox's followers, iii. 809
BENNET, John; his set of madrigals, iii. . 563
————, Sir John; impeached for corruption, iii. 53, 82
BENTHAM, Jeremy, Portraits of, vi. . 784, 890
BENTINCK, Lord William, iv. 616-623, 658, 669, 692-694
BEORHTRIC, or BRIHTRIC, king of Wessex, i. . 160
BEORN, assassinated by Sweyn, his cousin, i. . 189, 193
BEOWULF and HROTHGAR, account of, i. . 300
BERENGARIA, daughter of king of Navarre, i. 493-495, 502
BERESFORD, Marshal, a brave British general—
    vi. 584-586, 607, 678, 679
Bergen-op-Zoom, View of, vi. . . . 81
Berkeley Castle, View of; Edward II. murdered here, i. 745

BERKELEY, Earl of; his game destroyed by Elizabeth, ii. 888
————, George, lord, a British admiral, iv. . 49, 55
————, Lord; demands a jury-trial, i. . . 755
————, Sir John, iii. . . . 369, 371, 376
————, Sir William, killed in an action with the Dutch, iii. 698
BERKLEY, Justice; impeached for treason, iii. . 180, 231
BERKSHIRE, Earl of, Charles I.'s letter to, iii. . 274
————, T. H., Viscount Andover, earl of, iii. 121, 122
Berlin, View of, vi. 343
Bermondsey, View of the old monastery of, ii. . 291
BERNADOTTE. See CHARLES XIII.
Bernicia, kingdom of, in Durham, i. . . 142
BERNINI, an architect and sculptor, iii. . 576
BEROLD, a butcher of Rouen, i. . . 415
BERRI, Duke of, uncle to Duke of Orleans, ii. 20, 21, 28, 31
BERTHA, wife of Ethelbert of Kent, i. . . 145
BERTHIER, a young French officer, v. . . 829
BERTRAM, Professor C., published a MS. by a Roman general, i. 76
BERWICK, James Fitz-James, duke of—
    iii. 801; iv. 23, 28, 59, 159, 182, 335, 336, 392
Berwick-upon-Tweed, taken by Henry IV., ii. 17, 115
BEST, Captain, obtains charter from Great Mogul, iii. 530
BETHAM, Sir W., antiquary, quoted, i. 9, 11, 15-17, 22, 122
Beverley, attributed cause of its flourishing condition, iii. 656
BEVERN, Prince of, mortally wounded at Schellenberg, iv. 153
BEWICK, an eminent wood-engraver, v. . 528
————, Thomas; his improvements on wood-engraving, vi. 880
BEZA, Theodore, a divine of great eminence, iii. 65, 806
Bible Society, British and Foreign; its revenues, vi. 765
————, translations of the, . i. 808; ii. 712-716, 789
Bicêtre, terrific scene at, v. . . . 879
BIDDLE, John, father of English Unitarians, iii. . 424
BIDLOO, a Dutchman, physician to William III., iv. 121
BIENFAIT, Richard de, justiciary of England, i. . 381
Billiards, iii. 641
BILNEY, a man of learning; burnt in Smithfield, ii. 378
BILSON, Thomas, bishop of Winchester, iii. . 54
BIND, Francis, an eminent sculptor, iv. . 706
BIRDE, Wm., a musician in reign of Edward VI., iii. 561, 563
BIRKBECK, Dr, originator of the Mechanics' Institutes—
    vii. 212, 213, 739
Birmingham, association for parliamentary reform in, vi. 292
————, Chartist turbulence at, vii. . . 568
————, formerly Bremicham, iii. . . 655
————, great reform meeting at, vii. . 359-364
Births and deaths at sea registered by captains, vii. 522
Bishops, petitioning; medal struck in honour of, iii. 788-791
BISSET, William, banished into England, i. . 701
BLACK, John, a Scottish preacher, iii. . . 17
————, Joseph, a celebrated chemist, iv. . 735
————, Joseph, a celebrated chemist, v. . 518
BLACKADDER, Captain, executed for the murder of Darnley, ii. 603
Blackburn, iii. 656
BLACKBURNE, Francis, an English divine, v. . 408, 409
Blackfriars Bridge, vi. . . . . .
BLACKHALL, Dr Offspring, elected to the see of Exeter, iv. 193
BLACKMORE, Sir Richard, a voluminous poet, iv. 747
BLACKSTONE, Sir Wm., a celebrated English lawyer, iv. 860
————, Sir William; quoted, iii. . 834, 843
————, Sir William, the English lawyer, v. . 438
BLACKWALL, styled the arch-priest; imprisoned, iii. 33
BLAKE, Admiral, iii. . . . 316, 414, 420, 424
BLAKENEY, General; his defence of Stirling Castle—
    iv. 493, 559
BLANCHARD, Laman, death of, vii. . . 736
BLANDFORD, Marquis of, vii. . . . 291
Blanketeers, march of the, vii. . . . 54
Blasphemy, prosecutions for, vii. . . 211
Bleaching, process of, vi. 843
Blenheim, Battle of; Blenheim House, iv. 155-158, 162, 696
BLITH, first points out advantages of growing clover, iii. 557
Blind, reading for the, vii. . . . 305

HISTORY OF ENGLAND.

BLINKHORNE, conspires to give up London to Charles I.— iii. 302
Blockade, Bonaparte's celebrated, vi. . . 811, 812
BLOIS, Charles de, claims the duchy of Brittany, i. 760, 769
——, Henry de, cardinal, abbot of Glastonbury, i. 615
——, Peter, traveller and author, i. 472, 480, 606, 606, 644
BLONDEAU, Peter, a French artist, iii. . . . 556
BLOOD, Colonel; his exploits, iii. . 708, 709, 770
Blood, Harvey discovers circulation of the, iv. . 718
BLOOMFIELD, Robert, the poet, death of, in 1823, vii. 221
BLOUNT, Sir Christopher, a catholic, ii. 684, 686, 688, 689
——, Sir Thomas, and others, executed, ii. . . 7
——, Sir Walter; slain at Shrewsbury, ii. . . 15
BLÜCHER, the eminent Prussian general—
 vi. 663, 665, 686, 704, 708
Blue-stocking Clubs, origin of, v. 543
BOADICEA, widow of King Prasutagus, i. . 43, 44
Board of Trade, William III. opposes remodelling, iv. 59
Bocland, i. 248
Body-snatching, vii. 211
BOETHIUS' De Consolatione Philosophiæ, i. 296, 301, 302
BOHADIN, the Arabian historian, quoted, i. . . 500
Bohemia, John de Luxemburg, king of, i. . . 768
BOHUN, Eleanor, duchess of Gloucester, ii. . . 232
Bolan Pass, disasters of the British at the, vii. . 623
BOLEYN, Mary, daughter of Sir Thomas Boleyn, ii. 364, 395
——, Sir Thomas, ii. . 363, 364, 368, 374-376
BOLINGBROKE, Henry St John, viscount, iv. 145, 196, 248,
 249, 236, 288, 291, 307, 362, 366, 439, 540, 626, 746
BOLINGBROKE, Roger, a learned astronomer, ii. . 83
BOLIVAR, captain-general of Venezuela and New
 Grenada, vii. 50, 51
Bombay Island; View of, v. 599
BONAPARTE, Jerome, king of Westphalia, vi. . 395
——, Joseph, king of Naples—
 vi. 321, 322, 412, 424, 608, 611-615, 641-643
——, Louis, king of Holland, vi. . 338, 560, 561
——, Lucien; Portrait of, vi. . . 187, 560
——, Napoleon Francis Charles Joseph, king of
 Rome, vi. 590
BONAPARTE, Napoleon, the Great, . v. 871, 875;
 vi. 8, 10, 51, 93, 105-108, 119, 135, 141-143, 150, 151,
 170-721; vii. 3-10, 48, 133, 709
Bond, grinding of corn held in, vii. . . . 556
BONIFACE VIII., Pope, i. 719, 724
BONNER, Edmund, bishop—
 ii. 382, 466, 493, 505, 524, 539, 715
BONNIVET, Admiral de; leads French across Alps, ii. 356, 358
Bonnymuir, Battle of, vii. 116
BONVILE, Lord; beheaded, ii. . . . 92, 97
BOOTH, Sir G., royalist insurrection headed by, iii. 431, 817
Boots, an instrument of torture; its inventor, iii. . 701
Bordeaux, city of, ii. 8, 85, 91
Borderers, iii. 848
BORN, Bertrand de, a bard as well as warrior, i. 471-475, 513
Borneo, island of, vii. 631, 632
Borodino, Battle of, fought 1812, vi. . . . 638
BOSCAWEN, a British admiral; his service in India, v. 601
——, Edward, a British admiral, iv. . 553, 578
——, Mr, advocates the printing of the votes of
 the House of Commons, iii. . . . 843
Bosham, Harold's journey to, i. . . . 197
BOSSUET, bishop of Meaux, iv. . . . 59
Boston, Map and Plan of, v. . . . 79, 80
—— Neck, View of, v. 91
—— Port bill, passed March 1774, v. . 54-77
——, View of, iv. 835
Bosworth Field, King Richard III. slain in this battle, ii. 129
Botanical garden, Oxford, founded by Earl of Danby, iv. 736
Bothwell Bridge, Battle of, iii. . . . 730, 827
BOTHWELL, J. H., earl of, ii. 552, 558, 556, 587, 593, 595-603
——, Ramsay, Lord, favourite of James III., ii. 304, 329
BOUCICAULT, Marshal, taken prisoner at Agincourt, ii. 33
BOUFFLERS, Marshal; his defence of Namur—
 iv. 33, 53, 55, 68, 69
BOUGHTON, Joan, the first English female martyr, ii. 698

BOUILLÉ, Marquis de, v. . 365, 788-790, 833-847
Boulogne, Henrys VII. and VIII. besiege, ii. . 298, 439
—— invasion, vii. 709
BOULOGNE, Raynaud, earl of, i. . . . 526
Boulogne, View of, vi. 235
BOULTON, the great engineer; Portrait of, &c., v. 475, 482
Boundary question between Great Britain and America—
 vii. 711
Bounties, reduction of duties on, vii. . . 178
BOURBON, Charles, duke of, ii. . 356, 358, 359, 363
——, Duke of, suicide of the, vii. . . 424
——, Duke of, at the congress of Arras, ii. . 78
——, Duke of; his manifestoes, &c., ii. 8, 21, 30, 33
——, James of, count of La Marche, ii. . . 18
——, John, duke of, i. 776
——, John, duke of, brother of the cardinal, ii. 112
——, Pierre de, lord of Beaujeu, ii. . 292, 293
——, the Cardinal of, brother of John, ii. . 112
BOURCHIER, Joan; burnt in reign of Edward VI., ii. 448, 492
BOURCHIER, Cardinal, archbishop of Canterbury—
 ii. 147, 282, 700
——, Sir John, ii. 286
BOURGES, Archbishop of, conference with Henry V., ii. 28
BOURNONVILLE, De, and other knights, executed, ii. 27
——, Duke of, minister of Philip V. of Spain—
 iv. 371
Bouvines, Battle of, i. 526
BOVES, Hugh de, head of a band of marauders, i. 530
BOWLES, Sir John, proposes a successor to William III.—
 iv. 110
BOWRING, Dr, dinner given to him at Manchester, vii. 570
Boxing, iv. 775
BOYCE, Wm., a musical composer of 18th century, iv. 561
BOYDELL, John, an English engraver, vi. 871-873, 878, 879
BOYLE, Hon. R.; his improvements on the air-pump, iv. 728
——, Mr Henry, secretary of state, iv. . . 196
Boyne, Battle of the, fought July 1, 1690, iv. . 24-26
BRABANT, Anthony, duke of; slain at Agincourt, ii. 32, 34, 57
——, Duke of, son of Anthony, ii. . . 59
——, John, duke of, brother of the preceding, ii. 57-59
BRACKENBURY, Sir Robert, governor of the Tower, ii. 125, 129
BRACKLEY, Thomas, viscount, lord-chancellor, iii. 56, 60, 63
BRADDOCK, Major-general; slain in battle with French—
 iv. 554
Bradford, iii. 655
BRADFORD, Francis Newport, earl of, iv. . . 127
BRADLEY, James, the philosopher; his discoveries, iv. 733
——, Mr, his gun improvements, vi. . 837, 838
BRADSHAW, a brewer, elected for Westminster, iii. 130, 390
BRAGANZA, Catherine of, queen of Charles II.—
 iii. 685, 686, 722
BRAMAH, Joseph, his famous locks, vi. . . 836
BRAMANTE, L. d'Urbino, an Italian architect, iii. 570
BRANDENBURG, Elector of; his war with Louis XIV., iii. 712
BRANDON, Sir William, standard-bearer of Richmond, ii. 129
BRANDRETH, leader of the Derby insurrection, vii. 56-59
BRANDT, Portrait of, v. 289
Branham Moor, Battle of, ii. . . . 19
BRAOUSE, William de, a nobleman, i. . . 522
Brazil, improvement of, vii. . . . 48
BREDALBANE, Lord; implicated in massacre of
 Glencoe, iv. 45-47
Broda, taken by the Spanish general Spinola, iii. 106, 431
BREMBER, Sir Nicholas, lord mayor of London, i. . 792
BRENTFORD, Patrick Ruthven, earl of, iii. . 207, 219
Bronville, Battle of, i. 413
BRERETON, William, gentleman of Privy-chamber, ii. 391-394
Brest, action off; Sir Edward Howard slain, ii. . 322
——, William III.'s attempts against, iv. . . 48
BRETEUIL, Eustace of, i. 414
——, W. de, treasurer to William Rufus, i. 402-405
Brotigny, Treaty of, ii. . . . 28, 35, 44, 80
Breton Club, organised by Lafayette, v. . . 741
Bretwalda, or Britwalda, an ancient title, i. . 144, 145
BREWSTER, Sir Francis; his Irish commission, iv. . 86
BRIANT, Alex, a seminary priest; confined in Tower, iii. 520

GENERAL INDEX. 103

Bribery at elections, vi. . . . 770
————, Mr Roebuck on, vii. . 649, 650
BRICE, St; on this festival, English massacre of Danes—
i. 177, 178
Bricks, known to the Anglo-Saxons, i. . . 315
Bridge-Street Gang, or Constitutional Association, vii. 132
Bridgeham, treaty of, i. . . . 707, 712
Bridgenorth, castle of, in Shropshire, i. . . 442
Bridges, erection of, in 18th century, v. 471; vi. 820-823
BRIDGEWATER, Duke of, his colliery tunnels, vi. . 827
————, John Egerton, earl of, iv. . . 80, 89
BRIDGMAN, Sir Orlando, iii. 517, 670, 672, 703-706, 844
Brigade, Irish, origin of the, 1691, iv. . . 34
BRIGGS, Henry, an English mathematician, iv. . 717
BRIGHT, Mr; Portrait, vii. . . . 689-691
Brighton, formerly Drightbelmsted, iii. . . 655
BRIHTRIC, brother of Edric, i. . . . 179
BRINDLEY, James, an eminent engineer, iv. . 680
————; Portrait of, v. 472, 473; vi. 818, 826
BRIOT, Nicholas, introduces coining by machinery, iii. 554, 578
BRISSAC, massacred by French mob in Sept. 1792, v. 361
BRISSOT, head of the Girondists, v. 11-14, 17, 18
————, Jean Pierre, v. . 837-847, 853-894
Bristol, Derby, and Nottingham riots, vii. . 352-354
BRISTOL, J. Digby, earl of, iii. 60, 93, 112, 119, 123, 130, 224
Bristol, slave-trade carried on at this town in 11th century, i. 270
Britain, early history of, &c., i. 1, 8, 11, 25-33, 118, 144
Britannia, figure of, modelled after Duchess of Richmond, iii. 868
Britannia, its derivation; earliest figure of, i. . 11, 48
BRITHNOTH, Earl, of Danish descent, i. . . 176
British Association; its first meeting in 1831, v. 435, 744
————, Colonies, North America, map of the chief, v. 116
————, India, north-west frontiers of, vii. . 619
————, Islands, original population and history, i. 1, 118
————, Legion and the Carlist war, vii. . . 541-543
BRITO, Gulielmus, quoted, i. . . . 641
————, Richard, one of the murderers of Becket, i. 455, 456
Britons, the, i. . 1-25, 27-57, 77, 91, 93, 98-142
BRITTANY, Conan le Petit, duke of, i. . 443, 444, 452
————, Francis II., duke of, ii. . 126, 292-295
————, John de Montfort, duke of, i. . . 784
————, John, duke of, ii. . 21, 32, 54, 56, 58
BRITTON'S opinion of 'peine forte et dure,' quoted, i. 814
BRITTON, a coalman; first part-music performance, iii. 885
BROC, Ranulf de; invectives against Becket, i. . 454
————, Robert de, excommunicated by Becket, i. . 454
BROKE, captain of the Shannon frigate, vi. . 733
————, Lord, Sir Robert Willoughby, ii. . . 286
————, Sir Richard, ravages the Scottish borders, ii. 441
BROMLEY, Sir Thomas, lord chief-justice—
ii. 500, 518, 659, 660
BROOKE, G., brother to Lord Cobham; beheaded, iii. 8, 9, 13
————, Lord, and Lord Say, leaders of an emigration scheme to New England, iii. . 182, 204, 218
BROOKE, Sir J., Rajah of Sarawak; Portrait, vii. 631, 632
BROTHERS, Richard, an insane fanatic, vi. . 757, 758
BROUGHAM, Lord; his sketches of eminent lawyers, &c.—
vi. 783-790; vii. 3, 9-11, 14-21, 44, 92, 121-127, 167,
212, 310, 327-329, 338, 373, 419-421, 476, 554, &c.
BROUNKER, Lord, first president of Royal Society—
iii. 696, 836; iv. 728
BROWN, George, archbishop of Dublin, ii. . 427, 428
————, Lancelot, a celebrated landscape gardener, vi. 865
————, Robert, founder of the Brownists, ii. . 745
BROWNE, Mr S., a member of House of Commons, iii. 325
————, Sir T., author of Religio Medici, iii. 578, 613
Brownists, soften down into Independents, ii. . 745
BROXLEY, abbot of, i. 509
BRUCE, David, son of the great Robert, i. . 751, 755-774
————, Edward, brother of the great King Robert, i. 737-739
————, James, minister of Kingsbarns, iii. . 184
————, Michael; his assistance to Lavalette, vi. 725, 727
————, Nigel, younger brother of Robert Bruce, i. 729
————, Robert de, a follower of the Conqueror, i. 375

BRUCE, Robert de, king of Scotland, i. 715, 716, 724, 727-751
————, lord of Annandale, i. 685, 707, 715, 727
————, Thomas and Alexander, i. . . 729, 730
BRUIN, Robert de, chief-justice of King's Bench, i. . 812
BRUMMELL, Beau, death of, vii. . . . 595
BRUNEL, Mr I. K., engineer of the Thames Tunnel—
vii. 300, 301
BRUNSWICK, Duke of; his deposition, vii. . 283
————, Duke of, gives final impulse to rabid republicanism in France, v. . 865, 866, 875
BRUNSWICK, Duke of, killed at Quatre Bras, vi. . 709
Brunswick, or Orange Clubs, vii. . . 251-254
BRUNSWICK, Prince Albert Henry of, mortally wounded, iv. 801
————, Prince Ferdinand of, iv. . . 582, 583
————, Prince Francis of, slain at Hochkirchen, iv. 575
Brunswick Theatre, fearful accident at, vii. . 300
BRUNSWICK WOLFENBÜTTEL, Duchess of, iv. . 556
Brussels, View of, vi. 702
BRUTUS and his Trojan colony, i. . . 8, 11
Brython, a colony from Llydaw, Bretagne, i. . 9
Bualth, Prince Llewellyn slain here, i. . . 693
BUCCLEUCH, Francis, Earl of, iii. . . 490
BUCHAN, Earl of, a brother of Robert III., ii. . 131
————, Earl of, son of the Regent Albany, ii. 48, 50, 56, 132
————, John Comyn, Earl of, i. . . 735
BUCHANAN, George, the poet and historian—
ii. 612, 813; iii. 38, 485
Buckhurst House; Plan of, ii. . . . 843
BUCKHURST, Lord, informs Mary Stuart of her sentence, ii. 663
BUCKINGHAM, Duke of; his secession from the Peel ministry, vii. 639
BUCKINGHAM, Edward Stafford, duke of, ii. 286, 323, 343-345
————, George Villiers, duke of, iii. 57, 53, 71, 82,
91, 98, 103, 109, 114-129, 133, 136, 137, 629
————, G. V., son and heir of the preceding—
iii. 700, 893
————, H. S., duke of—
ii. 118, 119, 122, 124, 126, 127, 343
————, Humphrey Stafford, duke of, ii. 88, 92, 95
————, John Sheffield, duke of, iv. . 104, 165
Buckingham Palace, by Inigo Jones, iii. . . 722
————, erection of, vii. . . . 302
Buckle manufacture, vi. . . . 639
Budgets, vii. . 87, 233, 269, 411, 519, 583
Buenos Ayres, View of, v. . . . 330
Building, progress of, in reign of Queen Elizabeth, ii. 889
BULL, Dr, first professor of music in Gresham College, iii. 562
BULLER, Mr Charles, Canadian secretary, vii. . 556-558
Bullion, iv. 658
————, Committee, vi. . . . 813, 814
BÜLOW, a Prussian general, vi. . . . 707
BULWER, the novelist, vii. . . . 742
Bunker's Hill; View of, &c., v. . . . 111
BUNYAN, J., author of Pilgrim's Progress; his Portrait, iii. 802
BURBAGE, James, a play-licence granted to, iii. . 583
BURCHILL, Dr Robert, a Greek and Hebrew scholar, iii. 72
BURDETT, Sir Francis; confined in the Tower, vi. 527-533
————, chairman of the London Hampden Club; Portrait, vii. 30, 31, 91, 102, 112, 202, 732, 752
BURDETT, Thomas, accused of practising magic, ii. . 114
BURGH, Hubert de, regent of England, i. . 520, 673-677
————, Ulliac de, created Earl of Clanricarde, ii. . 428
Burgos, View of, vi. 612
BURGOYNE, General, v. . . 109, 202, 211, 253
————, John, an English general, iv. . 811, 812
————'s attack on the American batteaux; illustration, v. 204
Burgundians, their code of written law, i. . 145
BURGUNDY, Charles the Rash, duke of, ii. 103, 105-108, 114
————, Duke of, grandson of Louis XIV., iv. 212, 246
————, Jean sans peur, ii. . . . 20, 27, 36-46
————, Margaret, Duchess of—
ii. 289, 290, 299, 300, 305, 313
BURGUNDY, Mary, Duchess of, ii. . 114-116, 297, 298
————, Philip, duke of, ii. . . . 7, 8, 17
————, Philip the Good, duke of, ii. 34, 47-60, 100-103

BURKE, Lord William, taken prisoner by the Scots, i. 738
BURKE, the orator and statesman— iv. 832, 834, 838, 859, 860, 887, 897; v. 56, 74, 102, 104, 180, 228, 299, 309, 379, 642-647, 672-676, 691-694, 757-759, 804-815, 821-824, 851-855, 898-901; vi. 97, 752
BURKE and HARE, the notorious murderers, vii. 297, 298
BURLEIGH, Sir W. C., lord—
    ii. 459, 539, 551, 639, 671, 680, 681, 750
BURLEY, Sir Simon, a friend of the Black Prince, i. 785, 793
BURLINGTON, Lord, his great influence on architecture, vi. 862
———, Richard Boyle, earl of, iv. . . . 700
Burmese war, the, vii. 154, 155
BURNES, Sir Alexander; his commercial mission to Cabool, vii. 620-626
BURNET, Dr, iv. 6, 46, 50, 52, 73, 97, 110, 590, 591, 610, 733, 739
———, Dr Gilbert, quoted, iii. 477, 562, 690, 720, 749, 802
BURNEY, Miss Fanny, death of, in 1840; Portrait, vii. 601
BURNS, Robert, the celebrated Scottish poet, ii. . 838
———, Portrait, vi. 858, 859
BURROUGH, Sir John, killed by a random shot, iii. . 128
BURTON, Henry, punished for writing seditious books, iii. 166
Burton Latimer, rectory of, in Northamptonshire, iii. 124
BURTON, Mr, quoted, iv. 81
———, R., author of *Anatomy of Melancholy*, iii. 614
Bury, iii. 656
BUSHELL, Captain, quells a malt-tax insurrection, iv. 865
BUSHER, Leonard; his tract on religious toleration, iii. 806
BUSHNELL, John, a sculptor of some eminence, iv. . 706
BUTE, John Stuart, earl of,
    iv. 557, 560, 795, 797, 798, 817, 818, 837
BUTLER, Charles, death of, in 1832, vii. . . 438
———, Colonel, uncle to Earl of Ormond, iii. . 270, 271
———, Edmund, justiciary of Ireland, i. . . 788
———, Lady Eleanor, death of, in 1829, vii. . . 321
———, Samuel, the witty author of *Hudibras*, iii. 874
BUTLERS, family of the, settled in Ireland, ii. . 289, 425
Buttons, manufacture of, vi. 838
BUXTON, Mr T. Powell; his strenuous opposition to slavery, vii. 384-387, 589
Bye Conspiracy, account of, &c., iii. . . 8, 9, 13
BYNG, Admiral John, iv. 554, 563-564
———, Rear-admiral Sir George, iv. 160, 196, 325, 326, 338-343
BYRON, Admiral, . . . iv. 328, 365; v. 243, 230
———, Lord, a poet of splendid genius, vi. . 883, 888
———, death of, in 1824, vii. . . . 221
———, Sir John, lieutenant of the Tower, iii. . 267, 310

Cabal Ministry; they form the Triple Alliance, iii. 705, 706
Cabinet-councils on the potato-crop, vii. . . 724
——— ministers, from 1841-1846, vii. . . 750
Cabochiens, faction of, butchers of Paris, ii. . 26-28, 36
Cabool or Afghanistan; its importance, &c., vii. 619-631
——— retreat of the British from, vii. . . 627
CABOT, or GABOTTO, John, a Venetian, ii. . . 776
———, Sebastian, second son of the preceding, ii. 776, 782
CABRAL, Pedro Alvarez de, discovers coast of Brazil, ii. 777
CABRERA, the Carlist leader, vii. . . . 541
CADE, Jack; his insurrection, ii. . . . 87-89
Caen Wood, Hampstead, View of, vi. . . . 867
Caer Bran, circular stone wall and fortress, i. . 100
——— Caradoc, British camp on hill in Shropshire, i. 41
——— Din, or Dinas, Welsh names for forts, i. . 99, 100
——— Morus, a circular intrenchment at Cellan, i. . 99
CAERMARTHEN, Marquis of, iv. 48
Caernarvon Castle, View of, i. 699
CÆSAR, C. Julius, i. . . . 25-37, 105, 135
———, Sir J., a commissioner in divorce of Earl of Essex, iii. 53
CÆSAR's narrative of his British expeditions; chief observations, &c., i. 27-36, 59-77, 99, 102, 104, 119, 125
CAJETANO, Cardinal, the pope's legate, ii. . . 707
Calais, town, harbour, and vicinity of, i. 27, 30, 768-770
Calais; View of, &c., ii. . 79, 80, 93, 94, 105, 533-535
CALAMY, chosen by Presbyterians, as their advocate—
    iii. 668, 819
Calcutta, factory of, an independent presidency, iv. 677
Calcutta stamp-duty, vii. 300
———; Views of, &c., v. . . . 606-628
CALDER, Sir Robert, severely reprimanded by court-martial, vi. 237
CALDERWOOD, David; quoted, iii. 60, 436, 439, 450, 470
Caledonia, the ancient name of North Britain, i. . 17, 23
Caledonian Canal, opened in 1822, vii. . . 213
Caledonians, the, i. 6, 9, 46-48
Calendar, the French Revolutionary, vi. . . 22
Calico-printing commenced in England—
    iii. 868; v. 495; vi. 843, 844
CALLCOTT, the painter, death of, vii. . . . 733
CALONNE, Charles-Alexandre de, v. . . . 740
Calvinists crown the palatine Frederick at Prague, iii. 80, 81
Camalodunum, taken by the Romans, i. . . 40, 43
Camberwell, fire of the old church at, vii. . . 590
Cambray, congress held here in 1721, iv. . . 357
Cambridge, King's College; illustrations—
    ii. 197, 198, 224, 376
——— observatory, vote for, vii. . . 214
CAMBRIDGE, Richard, earl of, ii. . . 6, 29, 89
Cambridge, University of, first institution of, i. 606; iii. 785
Camden, Battle of, fought August 1780, v. . 321, 322
CAMDEN, Charles Pratt, earl of—
    iv. 820, 824, 827, 834, 844, 875, 877, 888; v. 93, 105
———; his Portrait, &c., iii. . . . 560, 616, 656
———, Marquis of; his death, vii. . . . 595
——— questions account of Trojan population, i. 8, 11, 187
CAMELFORD, Thomas Pitt, earl of, v. . . . 18
Camera-obscura, invented by Baptista della Porta, iv. 713
CAMERON, a leader of the Covenanters, iii. . . 735
———, Dr Archibald, executed as a traitor, iv. 519, 551
———, Jenny, confined in Edinburgh Castle, iv. . 501
———, of Clunes, conceals the young Pretender, iv. 519
———, of Lochiel, a partisan of young Pretender, iv. 456
———, Richard, founder of the Macmillanites, iv. 620
Cameronians; their opposition to the Union, iv. 44, 173
CAMMOCK, Rear-admiral, iv. 328, 337
CAMPBELL, bishop of the Isles; excommunicated, iii. 434
———, Captain, of Finab, iv. 83, 300
———, Colin, a distinguished architect, iv. . . 700
———, Lord; Portrait, vii. . . . . 664, &c.
———, Thomas, a distinguished poet, vi. . . 887
———, the poet, death of, in 1844, vii. . . 737, 738
CAMPEGGIO, Cardinal, the pope's legate, ii. . 367-369, 371
Campos, Treaty of; its provisions, &c., ii. . . 447, 457
CAMPION, the Jesuit, executed, ii. . . . 654
———; tortured by order of Elizabeth, iii. 519
Campo Formio, Treaty of, concluded in 1797, vi. . 119
CAMVILLE, Richard de, i. 495
Canada, affairs of, vii. . . . 549-559, 717, 718
———, corn question, vii. 681, 682
Canadas, Lower and Upper, iv. . . . 579-581
Canadian rebel prisoners, disposal of the, vii. . 554-556
Canal, Duke of Bridgewater's, opened July 17, 1761—
    v. 472, 473
Canals, iv. 820, 826
———, origin of navigable, in England, iv. . . 681
CANNING, secretary for foreign affairs, vi. . 362, 522
———, the Right Hon. George; Portrait—
    vii. 10, 45, 83, 136-138, 140, 141, 144-236, 244
Cannon, descriptions of English and French, ii. 329, 330
——— specimen of ancient, i. 874
Canon Law; six books on, i. 803
Canterbury, Battles at, &c., i. 30-33, 77, 142, 309, 558, 615
CANTERBURY, Lord, death of, in 1845, vii. . . 731
Cantii, a British tribe settled in Kent, i. . 27-33, 77
Canton, attack of the British on, vii. . . 617
CANUTE, son of the king of Denmark, i. . 371, 386, 387
——— the Great, i. 179-184
CANYNGS, William, mayor of Bristol, ii. . . 176
CAPEL, Lord Arthur; beheaded, iii. . 212, 281, 400
Capital punishment, diminution of, vii. . . 127
——— punishments, 1820-1826, vii. . . 200-211
CARACALLA, son of Severus, i. 52, 53
Caracas, great earthquake at, in 1812, vii. . . 51

GENERAL INDEX. 105

	PAGE
CARACTACUS, a British general, i.	39-42
CARADOC, supposed British name of Caractacus, i.	41
CARAUSIUS, a famous British general, i.	53
Carberry Hill, surrender of Mary queen of Scots at—	ii. 600, 601
Cardiff Castle, View of, as it appeared in 1775, i.	411
CARDIGAN, Lord, trial of, vii.	591
CARDONEL, secretary to Duke of Marlborough, iv.	241
Cards, playing of, invented, ii.	258, 891
CAREW, Sir George, founders in action with Annebaut, ii.	442
———, Sir George, governor of Ireland, ii.	680, 684
———, Sir Peter, opposes marriage of Mary of England, ii.	512
CAREY, Dr, death of, in 1834, vii.	600
———, Sir R., announces death of Elizabeth to James VI., iii.	2
CAREY, Sir Robert, son of Lord Hunsdon, ii.	671
CARGILL, Donald, a fanatic preacher in Scotland, iii.	730, 735
Caribbee Isles; their conquerors, iv.	810
Carisbrooke Castle, Isle of Wight; View of, iii.	380
CARLETON, Sir Dudley, iii.	114, 118, 125, 136, 576
———, Sir Guy, governor of Canada; examination of, &c., v.	65, 66, 113, 114, 151, 300, 383
Carlisle Castle, View of, iv.	434
CARLISLE, James Hay, earl of, iii.	14, 37, 100, 540
———, Sir Anthony, death of, in 1840, vii.	593
Carlisle, View of, i.	398
Carlist war and the British Legion, vii.	541-543
CARLOS, Don; his conquests in Italy, iv.	391-394
Carlton House, View of, vii.	216
CARLYLE, Thomas; Portrait, vii.	481, 482, 742
Carmelites, massacre of 200 priests at the, v.	877
Carnac, a great Druidical temple in Brittany, i.	68
CARNAC, Major, arrives in India, 1763, v.	617
CARNARVON, Lord, his strange idea of the metallic currency, vii.	185
CARNE, Sir Edward, announces succession of Elizabeth, ii.	543
CAROLINA WILHELMINA, Queen—	iv. 374, 377, 381, 393, 402, 403
CAROLINE MATILDA, Queen of Christian VII. of Denmark,	iv. 829; v. 23-25
CAROLINE, Princess, third daughter of George II., iv.	578
———, queen of George IV.,	vi. 76; vii. 118-125
Carpenter's Hall, Philadelphia, View of, v.	82
Carpets, Brussels, made at Kidderminster in 1745, iv.	758
———, in 17th century, used for covering tables, iii.	619
CARR, John, an eminent architect, vi.	863
CARRIER, inventor of the mariages républicains—	vi. 21, 22, 61, 62
Carrighhill, subterranean chamber at, i.	97
CARRION, a celebrated nun of 17th century, iii.	98
CARTERET, John, Viscount, iv.	343, 365, 400, 448
Carthagena; View of the Bay, &c., iv.	426, 427
Carthaginians, their voyages to Britain and Ireland, i.	14
Carthusian monasteries, a number of monks hanged, ii.	386
Carthusians, when introduced into England, i.	559, 560
CARTWRIGHT, inventor of the first power-loom, vi.	842, 845
———, Major, vii.	30, 31
———, Thomas, bishop of Chester,	iii. 785; iv. 590
———, Thomas, of Cambridge, ii.	635
CARY, Dr H. F., death of, in 1844, vii.	737
Cashel, Psalter of, i.	303
Cashmere, scene in; illustration, vii.	622
Cash-payments, resumption of, vii.	98-100
———, suspension of, vi.	806, 807, 810, 813-817
CASIMIR, Duke, offers his hand to Queen Elizabeth—	ii. 575, 650
CASLON; his improvements in English printing-type, iv.	684
Cassano, Battle of, fought April 27, 1799, vi.	140
Cassiterides, or Scilly Islands, i.	93, 104
CASSIVELLAUNUS, chief of confederated Britons, i.	30-38
CASTAÑETA, commands a Spanish expedition to Sicily, iv.	325
Castello Branco, View of, vi.	549
CASTIGLIONE, Prince of, taken prisoner by Austrians, iv.	184

	PAGE
CASTLEHAVEN, Earl of; mention of Irish Rebellion—	iii. 254, 310
CASTLEMAINE, Lady, mistress of Charles II., iii.	685, 706
———, Roger Palmer, earl of, iii.	685, 784
CASTLEREAGH, Lord, secretary-at-war, vi.	302, 522
———, Portrait—	vii. 2-14, 97, 100, 121-123, 134, 140-142
Castles, construction of strong, in England, i.	615
CATALANI, Madame, the eminent vocalist, vi.	905
Cateau Cambresis, Peace of; its articles, ii.	547
CATESBY, a chief adviser of Richard III., ii.	128, 284
———, Robert, a Catholic gentleman, iii.	20-28
CATHCART, William Shaw, earl, vi.	365-388
CATHELINEAU, a leader of the Vendeans, vi.	20, 21
CATHERINE, empress of Russia, v.	805
——— of La Rochelle, an impostor, ii.	70, 73
——— of Medicis, niece of Clement VII., ii.	382
——— PARR, wife of Henry VIII.—	ii. 438, 439, 447, 473, 476
———, queen of France, ii.	28, 38, 44, 47-52, 80, 125
——— II., empress of Russia—	iv. 814, 815; v. 27-43, 316, 848, 849, 856, 857
———, wife of Arthur, prince of Wales,	ii. 312, 317
	319, 323, 330, 336, 364-367, 376, 380-383, 390
Catholic Association, vii.	197-202, 251-254, 259
——— clergy, endowment of, vii.	667
——— Committee, the, vi.	772, 773
——— Emancipation, Roman,	vi. 771-774;
	vii. 102, 131, 167, 191-204, 228, 248, 258-267
——— peers admitted to parliament, and take the oaths, vii.	267
Catholic Relief Bill of 1829, vii.	259-262
Catholics, conversions of, vii.	307
———, Roman, conspiracies against James I.—	iii. 8, 19, 22, 721
———, Roman; movements in their favour, vii.	753-774
CATINAT, Marshal, a French general, iv.	33, 68, 113
Cato-Street conspiracy, vii.	114, 115
Catterthuns, White and Black, two strong hill-forts, i.	99
CATUS, a Roman procurator, i.	43
Caucasus, desperation of Russian despotism in the, vii.	701
CAULIAC, Guy de, quoted, i.	845
Cavalry, British and Roman, i.	36, 38
CAVENDISH, Wolsey's biographer, ii.	365, 374, 377
CAW, king of Strathclyde, i.	217, 218, 289
CAXTON, Wm., first English printer, ii.	121, 202-204, 207, 209
CEAWLIN, king of Wessex, i.	145
CECIL, Sir Robert, iii.	3-12, 30, 32-34, 39, 41, 45
———, Sir R., son of Earl of Burghley, ii.	679, 681, 687, 692
CELESTINE III., Pope, i.	513
CELLIER, Mrs; Plan of Meal-tub Plot found in her house, ii.	732
Celts, warlike implements of the, i.	36
Central countries of Europe, state of the, vii.	543
CEOAL defeats the Danes at Wenbury, i.	152
CERDIC, founder of the kingdom of Wessex, i.	142
Ceremonies, Master of the, instituted by James I., iii.	7
CERUTTI, a member of the Legislative Assembly, v.	840
Ceylon, its villages compared to British, &c., i.	8, 9, 33, 34
———, taken from Dutch by Sir Edward Hughes, v.	631
CHADWICK, Mr; his sanitary improvements, vii.	745
Chain-shot, invention of, attributed to De Witt, iii.	698
Chalgrove Field, Battle of, iii.	304
CHALLONER; he is hanged near his own house, iii.	302
CHALMERS, Alexander, death of, vii.	600
———, Dr; Portrait, vii.	671-674
———, his derivation of Picts, i.	13
Chamber of Deputies, the French, in reign of Louis Philippe, vii.	540
CHAMBERLAIN, Dr, an obstetrical practitioner, iii.	792
Chamberlain, his office, i.	569
CHAMBERLAYNE, Robert, esquire to Henry V., his effigy, ii.	241
CHAMBERS, Richard, fined £2000, iii.	145
———, Sir Wm., an eminent architect, v. 526; vi. 865, 866
Chambers, subterranean, i.	97, 98
Champ de Mars, Fête of the Federation at; View, v.	585-587

CHAMPNEYS, Sir Thomas, mayor of London, ii. . 850
Chancellor, office of the, i. 569
Chancery, abuses in the Court of, vi. . . 790
———, account of the Court of, . i. 574, 818 ; ii. 761
——— Court, origin and properties of the, v. 428–432
——— reform, vii. 204–207
——— Bill of 1834, vii. 421
CHANTREY, Sir Francis, an eminent sculptor, vi. 901, 902
———, death of, in 1841 ; Portrait, vii. . 732, 733
CHAPMAN, George, a dramatic writer, iii. . . 592
Chapter-house, St Paul's, from an old print, iv. 609
Characteristics and achievements of the reign of
 George IV., vii. 294–296
CHARETTE, a leader of the Vendeans ; Portrait of, vi. 20
Chariots, British war ; their form, &c., i. . . 34–36
Charitable Bequests Act of 1844, vii. . . 666
Charity, improved methods in the practice of, vii. . 747
CHARLEMAGNE, the emperor, i. . . 150, 266
CHARLES EDWARD STUART—
 iv. 445, 454–511, 515–532, 806, 807 ; v. 720, 721
——— JOHN XIV., king of Sweden, v. . . 634
——— LOUIS, nephew of Charles I., iii. . 173, 174
——— the Bald, king of the Franks, i. . 152, 153
——— I., king of England—
  iii. 63, 90–100, 108–397, 432*, 551–553, 607
——— II., king of England, iii. 151, 383, 384, 395, 401, 404,
  405, 425, 431, 431*, 432*, 494, 662–762, 801, 868
——— II., king of Spain, iii. . . . 707, 711
——— III., king of Spain, iv. 139, 159, 803, 806 ; v. 278
——— IV., king of France, i. . . . 742, 757
——— IV., king of Spain, vi. . 48, 401–404, 411
——— V., the emperor, ii. . 315, 331, 336–338
  345–348, 356, 365, 367, 368, 389, 531, 541, 707
——— V., king of France, i. . 773–779, 783, 784
——— VI., emperor of Germany, iv. . . 414
——— VI., king of France, . i. 791, 792 ; ii. 7, 9, 13,
  17, 20–22, 26–34, 36–41, 47, 48, 54
——— VII., king of France, ii. . 37, 41–56, 59–80
——— VIII., king of France, ii. 292, 294, 297–299, 311
——— IX., king of France, ii. . . 563, 647, 649
——— X., king of France ; Portrait of, v. . 740, 744
———; his dethronement, &c.—
  vii. 271–283
——— XI., king of Sweden, iv. . . . 69
——— XII., king of Sweden, iv. . 181, 313, 329
——— XIII., Bernadotte, king of Sweden—
  vi. 589, 635, 640, 665, 670, 690, 691
Charlestown, America, View of, v. . . 296
CHARLETON, Charles, Lord Howard of, iii. . 238
———, Dr, impugns the opinion of Inigo Jones
 of Stonehenge being a Roman temple, iii. . 574
CHARLOTTA AUGUSTA, eldest daughter of George III., vi. 111
CHARLOTTE, Princess, marriage and death of the—
  vii. 15, 63–65
———, Queen, death of, vii. . . . 93, 97
———, SOPHIA, of Mecklenburg-Strelitz, iv. 799, 808
CHARNOCK ; he is executed as a traitor, iv. . 59, 63
Charter House, proclamations by James I. at the, &c.—
  iii. 5, 785
Charters ; Confirmation of the Great Charter, &c., i. 812, 813
Chartism and Radical Chartists, vii. . . 481
——— and torch-light meetings, &c., vii. . 567–569
Chartist intervention in Rebecca Riots, vii. . . 637
CHASTELAR, a crazed French poet, iii. . . 585
CHATEAUBRIAND, M., French minister of foreign affairs, vii.146
CHATEAUNEUF, L'Aubespine de, French ambassador—
  ii. 664, 671
Châtelet, Prison of the, pulled down in 1802, v. . 747
CHATHAM, William Pitt, Earl of, iv. . 403, 449, 554,
 555, 568, 570, 795, 805, 816, 820, 823, 833–840,
 850, 856, 857, 872, 874, 879–884, 887, 888, 890, 897 ;
 v. 12, 13, 22, 47, 57, 74, 89, 90, 94, 95, 147, 188, 215,
 218, 235–238.
CHAUCER, Geoffrey, i. 851
———, father of English poetry, ii. . . 52
Chaumont, Treaty of, concluded 1st March 1814, vii. 2

Cheapside; illustration of procession of Mary de'
 Medici, iii. 246
CHEETOO, a Pindaree chief, vii. . . . 66–70
CHEKE, Sir John, a Greek scholar, ii. . 453, 504, 530
Chemical manufactures, vi. 847
Chemistry, iv. 735
CHENEY, Sir John, a knight-banneret, ii. . . 282
———, Sir John, slain by Richard III. at Bosworth
 Field, ii. 129
Cherbourg, attacked by sea and land ; surrenders, ii. 85
CHESTER, Gherband, earl of, i. . . 375, 376
Chester, receives benefit of English laws, ii. . 425
CHESTERFIELD, Lord—
 iv. 374, 387, 428, 449, 526, 528, 541, 841, 846
Chevy Chase (Otterburne), Battle of, i. . . 793
CHEVNEY, Sir Thomas, privy-councillor, ii. . 454
CHEYTE SING, nabob of Benares, v. . . 625–640
CHICHELEY, archbishop of Canterbury, ii. 26, 146, 147
CHILD, Dr William, a musician of 17th century, iii. 566
———, Sir Josiah ; Portrait of, iii. . . 851, 853
CHILDE, Sir Richard, a wealthy trader, iv. . . 315
Chili, obtains its freedom in 1817, vii. . . 52
CHILLINGWORTH, William, an eminent divine, iii. . 610
Chiltern Hundreds, stewardship of the, vii. . 650
China and its peace-policy, vii. . . 610–619
Chinese, popular English notion of the, vii. . 612
———, treaty of peace with the, vii. . . 617
Chippenham, a strong town of the Saxons, i. . 158
Chivalry, declension and extinction of, ii. . 247, 249, 251
Cholera, Asiatic ; its spread in Europe in 1830—
  vii. 71, 339, 357, 369, 370
CHOLMONDELEY, George, Earl, iv. . 442, 449, 477
———, Hugh, Earl, iv. 253
Chorley, in Lancashire, burning of a cotton-mill at, vii. 296
CHRISTIAN IV., king of Denmark, iii. . . 33
Christian Knowledge, Society for Promoting, vi. 765
CHRISTIANA, second sister of Edgar Atheling, i. . 406
Christianity, introduction into Britain—
  i. 73, 74, 145, 231, 233
CHRISTIE, James, death of, in 1831, vii. . . 442
CHRISTINE, Madame, second daughter of Mary de'
 Medici, iii. 51, 63
Christmas festivities ; illustrations, ii. . 255, 892
Chroniclers, list of, in 13th and 14th centuries, i. 847
Chronometer, invented by Harrison about 1741—
  v. 497 ; vi. 839
CHRYSANTUS, lieutenant of Theodosius, i. . . 54
Chun Castle, Plan and description of, i. . 99, 100
Chunar, Treaty of, concluded in 1781, v. . 633, 641
Church, Orangeism in the, vii. . . . 488
——— extension and patronage in Scotland, vii. 514–517
——— of Scotland ; its conflicts with the state, vii. 513–518
——— patronage in Scotland, vii. . . 669–674
——— rates, the Dissenters refuse to pay, vii. . 463
Churches, increase in the building of new, vii. . 587
———, pagan temples turned into, i. . 232, 233
CHURCHILL, Captain, iii. . . . 738, 765
———, Charles, a poet and satirist, iv. 819 ; v. 502
———, George, iv. . . 127, 149, 155, 157
Chusan, conquest of the island of, vii. . . 616
CIBBER, Caius Gabriel, an eminent sculptor, iii. 883
CICERO, Marcus Tullius ; his epistles quoted, i. . 105
———, Quintus, serves under Cæsar in Britain, i. 105
Cider Bill, the, iv. 818, 839
Ciederholm, iv. 181
Cingalese village, i. 34
CIPRIANI, Giovanni Baptista, an eminent painter, v. 521
Circassians ; their noble battles with Russia, vi. . 545
Cistercians ; Illustration of a monk, i. . 559, 560
Ciudad Rodrigo ; View of the Fortress, vi. 540, 601
Civil and Military Transactions, . i. 25–58, 138–223,
  358–546, 671–800 ; iii. 2–432*, 662–801
Civil list, bill for better regulation of, vii. . 15, 374
Civilisation, progress of, i. . . 5, 6, 13, 34
CLANRANALD, mortally wounded at Dunblane, iv. . 298
CLANRICKARD, Earl of ; his death, iii. . . 170

GENERAL INDEX.

Clare election, vii. 249-251, 265
Clare, Robert Nugent, Viscount, iv. . 846
———, Roger, earl of, i. . . . 448
Clarence, George, duke of, ii. . . 99, 101, 104-115
———, Isabella, duchess of, ii. . 104, 105, 111, 114
———, T. Plantagenet, duke of, ii. 15, 21, 22, 33, 44, 48, 49
Clarendon, Constitutions of, i. . . 449, 555-557
Clarendon, Earl of; declaims against Hanoverian troops, iv. 489
Clarendon, Edward Hyde, earl of, iii. 44, 90, 115, 136, 158, 178, 204, 205, 217, 219, 220, 256, 285, 287, 480, 490, 524, 653, 663, 686, 690, 693, 697, 702-705, 829, 834
Clarendon, Henry Hyde, earl of, iv. . . 4
Clarendon House, from a print of the period, iii. . 704
Clarendon, Sir Roger, natural son of the Black Prince, ii. 11
Clarges, Dr, M.P., iii. *431
Clarke, Adam, death of, in 1834, vii. . . 408
———, Dr E. D., the traveller, death of, in 1822, vii. 219
———, Dr John, a Baptist, iii. . . . 807
———, Dr Samuel, a celebrated divine, v. . 408, 410
———, Dr Samuel; Portrait of, iv. . . 615, 616
Clarkson, Thomas, death of, in 1846, vii. . 730
Clas Merddin, a name of Britain, i. . . 8
Claude, Queen, wife of Francis I., ii. . . 332, 364
Claudian the poet, quoted, i. . . . 19
Claudius, the Emperor, i. . . . 39-43
Claydon, a currier, and others burnt for Lollardism, ii. 147
Claypole, Lady, Cromwell's daughter, iii. . 425
Clement, Jacques, assassinates Henri III. of France, ii. 672
———, one of the judges of Charles I.; executed, iii. 664, 676
——— VII., Giulio dei Medici, Pope—
ii. 357, 362-371, 381-384
——— XIV., Pope; Portrait of, v. . . 417
Clementina, Princess; her escape from Inspruck, iv. 332, 335
Clerambault; he is drowned in the Danube, iv. . 157
Clergy, augmentation of, vii. . . . 678
Clerk, John, bishop of Bath and Wells, ii. . 383
Clermont, counsellor of Charles, dauphin of France, i. 774
———, Count of, ii. 19
———, Duke of, iv. 570
Cléry, valet of Louis XVI., v. 871, 873, 879, 889, 894, 895
Cleveland, Duchess of, mistress of Charles II., iii. 725, 762
Clever, a schoolmaster, attempts an insurrection, ii. 531
Cleverly; his illustration of defeat of Dutch fleet, iii. 415
Cleves, Duke of, prince of Protestant Confederacy, ii. 412, 416
Clifford, John, Lord, ii. . . . 93, 96
———, Sir Robert, secret agent of Henry VII., ii. 300, 301
———, Thomas, Lord, a supporter of the red rose, ii. 92
———, Thomas, lord-treasurer, iii. . . 711
Clinton, Edward, Lord, ii. . . 459, 464
———, General Sir Henry, v. 109, 112, 157, 317, 383
Clive, Robert, Lord; Portrait of, &c., v. . 601-623
Clocks and watches, vi. 839
Clontarf, monster meeting at, vii. . . 661
Clootz, Jean Baptist, a Prussian baron, v. . 785, 872
Cloister Seven, Convention of, signed September 1757, iv. 569
Cloth-market, Leeds; illustration of, iii. . 529
Clotworthy, Sir John, iii. . . 237, 254, 326, 369
Clover introduced from the Netherlands, ii. . 806
Clubs, Political, iii. 894
Clutterbuck, one of the lords of the Treasury, iv. 422
Coaches, iii. 863
———; illustrations, iv. 762
———, introduction of, ii. . . . 887
Coal districts, condition of the, vii. . . 24
———gas, first used for illuminating streets and buildings in 1792, vi. . . . 832
Coal; its use increases as woods diminish, ii. . 191, 806
———mining, extension and improvement in, v. . 478
———tar, origin of the manufacture of, about 1779, v. 484
Coalition ministry, 1782, v. . . . 303
Cobbet, Lieutenant-colonel, a Parliamentary officer—
iii. 386, 391
Cobbett, William; Portrait, vii. 21, 27-29, 60, 96, 209, 595
Conden, Richard; Portrait, vii. 570, 639, 683-688, 692-730
Cobham, Eleanor, duchess of Gloucester, ii. . 59, 83
Cobham, Lord; concerned in Main and Rye Plots, iii. 5-15
———, Lord, Sir John Oldcastle, ii. . 25, 38, 147
———, Richard Temple, Lord, iv. . . 336
Cochrane, a favourite of James III., ii. . . 136
———, Colonel; arrested, iii. . . . 251
———, Lord, a British admiral, vii. 30, 31, 33, 237
———, Sir Alex., an English admiral, vi. 388, 507, 740
———, Sir J., a Rye-house Plot conspirator, iii. 768, 769
Cockayne, Alderman; obtains patent for dyeing cloths, iii. 536
Cockburn, Sir George, conveys Napoleon to St Helena, vi. 717
Cock-fighting, a favourite amusement, ii. . . 891
Codrington, Sir Edward, a British admiral, vii. 238-240
Coehorn, a celebrated engineer, iv. . . 53, 137
Coercion Bill, the Irish, vii. . . 398, 399, 418, 669
Cœur, Jacques, a French merchant, ii. . 177, 178
Coffee; its introduction into England by Edwards, iii. 548
Coifi, high-priest of the Anglo-Saxon paganism, i. . 235
Coimbra, View of, vi. 543
Coinage in the reign of George III., v. 467; vi. 817, 880
Coiner at work, i. 594
Coining, vi. 817, 838
——— machinery at Soho operating in 1783, v. 484
———, process of; illustration, ii. . . 796
Coins and Medals, ancient British, i. 4, 26, 53, 110-112, 125, 150-152, 167, 180, 271, 837, 838
Coins; illustrations of, &c., ii. . 184, 185, 305, 797-803
——— of early Norman kings, i. . . 594, 595
Coke, Earl of Leicester, death of, vii. . . 739
———, Mr, solicitor-general at trial of Charles I., iii. 390, 676
———, Roger, quoted, iii. . . . 318, 357
———, Sir Edward, the eminent lawyer, ii. . 686, 767
———, Sir John, secretary of state, iii. . . 146
Colchester Castle, remains of, from an original drawing, iii. 383
Colebrook Dale; View of Iron Bridge, v. . 481
Colechurch, Peter of, architect, i. . . 615
Coleman; letters relative to Popish plot, iii. 523, 719, 723, 724
Coleridge, an English poet, vi. . 858, 883, 885
———, Henry Nelson, nephew of the poet, vi. . 737
———, S. T., death of, in 1834; Portrait—
vii. 445, 446, 576
Colet, Dean, founder of St Paul's school, ii. . 815
Coligni, Admiral, the Huguenot leader, ii. 570, 573, 646, 647
College, Stephen, a joiner, executed as a traitor, iii. 734
Colleges, &c.; illustration, ii. . . . 814, 815
———, grant for institution of Irish, vii. . . 668
Collier, Jeremy, a nonjuring clergyman, iv. . 64
Collieries, vi. 832
Collingwood, Admiral; Portrait of, v. 285, 295, 506
Collins, William, a distinguished poet, v. . 502
Colonial bishoprics, institution of, vii. . . 678
——— misgovernment, vii. . . . 47
Colonisation, debate on systematic, vii. . . 656
Colonna, a powerful Roman family, ii. 357, 358, 362
Coloredo, Count, governor of Milan, iv. . 342
Columba, St, born in Donegal, i. . 228, 229, 244, 290
Columbanus, St, preacher of Christianity, i. . 289, 290
Columbus, discovery of America by, ii. . 775, 776
Combe, Dr Andrew, vii. 745
Combination laws, committee's report on the, vii. 174
Comine, Robert de, i. 370
Comines, the historian, ii. 111, 112, 126, 128, 209, 292
Comius, a steady adherent of Cæsar, i. . 26-33
Commerce and manufactures, vii. . 20, 21
———, French council of, founded 1700, iv. . 662
———, general prosperity of, iii. . . 851
——— in fifteenth century, ii. . . 170-175
———, regulations respecting, &c., i. . 824-836
Commercial and agricultural interests, approximation of, vii. 633
Commercial League of Germany, formation of the, vii. 543
——— policy of 1823, vii. . . . 163-165
——— treaties, vi. . . . 796, 805, 806
Commission, special, on Rebecca riots, vii. . 637
Common Prayer-book substituted for Mass-book, ii. 731, 732
Commons, House of. (See Parliament.) i., ii., iv., v., vi.

	PAGE
Commons, remarkable scene in the House of, vii.	347, 348
———, rights of, in Anglo-Saxon times, i.	351
———; their manners in 1830, vii.	327
Commonwealth, iii. . 226–234, 241–432, 429*–432*,	565
COMNENA, Anna, quoted, i.	640
Company, the African, founded 1672, iii.	866
Compiegne, besieged; Joan of Arc made prisoner, ii.	73, 74
COMPTON, Henry, bishop of London, iii. 785, 795, 798; iv.	257
COMYN, John, stabbed by Bruce, &c., i. . 685,	724–728
CONAN, a powerful burgess, i.	396
Conciergerie, Paris, View of the, vi. . . .	16, 17
CONCINI, Marshal d'Ancre, murdered by Vitry, iii.	63
CONDÉ, Prince of, chief of Huguenots—	
ii. 570, 571, 573, 621,	626
CONDORCET, John, Marquis de—	
v. 825, 837–847, 885, 893; vi.	19
Conduit erected in Leadenhall Street, 1665, iii.	805
Confession, Auricular, ii.	397
CONFLANS, John de, killed by Stephen Marcel, i.	774
———, M., commander of the Brest fleet, iv.	578
Conformity Bill, passed 1661, iii. . . 685, 690,	823
———, the Occasional, iv. . 132, 140,	239
CONGLETON, Lord. See Sir Henry Parnell, vii.	
CONGREVE, a dramatic writer, iv.	748
CONINGSBY, Lord, present at battle of the Boyne, iv.	24
Connaught, claimed by Charles I., iii.	170
CONOLLY, Captain, fate of, vii. . . . 630,	631
CONRAD, marquis of Montferrat, i. . . .	496–500
Conscience, anecdote of remarkable case of, vii.	687
Consolidated Fund, vi.	791
Constable of England, office of the, i.	558
CONSTABLE, Sir William, iii.	323
Constance, Council of; its enactments as to synods, ii.	138
CONSTANCE, of Castile, wife of Louis VII., i. . 444,	446
CONSTANTINE, an associate of William Tyndal, ii.	712
———, brother of the Emperor of Russia, vii.	143
———, king of the Picts, i.	217
———, namesake of the great emperor, i.	55
———, the Great, Profile of, i.	53
———, II., king of Scotland, i. . . 218,	219
———, III., assumed the cowl, i.	219
———, IV., slain in battle, i.	220
Constantinople, View of, vi.	380
CONSTANTIUS, Chlorus, a Roman emperor, i.	53
Constitution, Government, and Laws, . i. 76, 82, 84, 246, 562, 809; ii. 155–169, 750–770; iii. 495–526, 828–850; iv. 626–653; v. 423–441; vi.	775–794
Constitutional Association, formation of the, vii.	132
——————— Legislation, vi.	774–779
Constitutional Queries, the, v.	534
CONTADES, Marshal, defeated at battle of Minden, iv.	582
CONTERIE, a leader of the Vendeans, vi.	
CONTI, Prince de, a candidate for crown of Poland, iv. 68,	448
Conventicle Act passed March 16, 1664, iii.	694
Convention, the Scottish; their decisions, iv.	7, 8
CUNVERSANO, William, count of, i.	408
Convocations of Clergy, vii.	608–617
CONWAY, General, iv. . 826, 833–836, 850, 860, 865,	876
——————— ; Portrait of, &c., v.	133
CONYERS, Mr, M.P., iv.	106
———, Sir John, iii.	259
COOK, Captain, a musician of 17th century, iii.	684
———, George, an engraver, death of, vii.	442
———, Shadrach, a nonjuring clergyman, iv.	64
———, Sir Anthony, a preceptor of Edward VI., ii.	453
———; Sir Thomas, M.P., iv.	51
———, Wm., publisher of first English newspaper, iii.	615
Cookery of the 17th century, iii.	639
COOPER, Alderman, forced to proclaim young Pretender, iv.	438
COOPER, Samuel, a miniature painter, iii. . 423,	560
———, Sir Astley P., death of, in 1841, vii.	593
COOTE, Sir Eyre, commander of Fort St George, v. 630,	632
———, defeats the French, iv. . . 581,	802
COPE, Sir J., commander-in-chief for Scotland—	
iv. 458–460,	525

	PAGE
COPE, Sir Walter, Earl of Salisbury's dying speech to, iii.	45
Copenhagen, Battle of, fought April 2, 1801, vi.	161–163
———, bombarded by the English fleet, vi.	385, 388
COPLEY, Anthony; banished, iii.	8, 9, 15
Copper, iv.	684
——— coinage first appeared in 1613, iii.	554
———, exportation of, prohibited, ii.	811
———, manufactures, vi.	837
COPPOCK, Thomas, created bishop of Carlisle, iv.	488, 492
Copyright law of 1842, Lord Mahon's amendments on, vii.	640
Coracles, British, delineation of these light boats, i.	56
CORBET, Colonel, executed as a regicide, iii.	690
CORBETT, high-bailiff of the city of Westminster, v.	584
CORBOIL, William, archbishop of Canterbury, i.	422
CORDAY, Charlotte, assassinates Marat, vi.	15
Cordeliers, Club of, instituted 1790, v. . . 783,	790
CORITON, M.P., summoned before the privy-council, iii.	142
Corn, a fixed duty proposed on, vii.	583
——— Bill, vii. . . 228, 233, 246, 640,	641
——— duties, debates on the, vii.	728–730
——— in bond, grinding of, vii.	566
———, its importation, vi.	816, 818
——— law debates, vii.	682–688
———, law permitting exportation of, iv.	663
———-laws, vii. . . . 415,	713
———, letting out bonded, vii.	189
CORNWALL, Captain, death of, iv.	446
Cornwall, insurrection in, ii.	306–308
———, its independence, &c., i. . . 142,	152
———, the Constantine Tolman, a large stone, i.	101
CORNWALL, Richard, earl of, i. . 675, 680, 683,	688
CORNWALLIS, Lord, governor-general of India—	
v. 822,	853–855
———, Marquis of; Portrait, &c., v. 173, 321,	351–359
———, Sir C., English ambassador at Madrid, iii.	30
———, Sir Thomas, one of Mary's councillors, ii.	515
Coronation-chair in Westminster Abbey, i.	219
——— oath, vii.	104
——— of George IV., vii.	132
——— of Queen Victoria, vii.	585
Corporation commission appointed on municipal reform, vii.	465–467
Corraniad, the, from Pwyll Settle, on the Humber, i.	9
CORREGGIO, Antonio Allegri da, the painter, iii.	567
Corrichie, Battle of, gained by the Earl of Murray, ii.	575
Corsica annexes itself to Great Britain, vi.	39
———, right of sovereignty given to France, iv.	857
Corunna, View of, vi.	456
COSENS, master of St Peter's, Westminster, iii. . 139,	229
COSPATRIC, governor of Northumberland, i. . 372, 375,	379
COSSIM ALI MEER, nabob of Bengal, v.	617–619
Costume, i. 92, 104, 144, 156, 159, 174, 636, 637, 866–872; vi. 76, 911–917,	920–923
——— in 15th and 16th centuries, ii.	856–861
——— in 17th century, iii.	888–890
——— of 17th century; illustrations, iv.	750–757
——— of 18th century, v.	570–573
COTES, Roger, a mathematician, iv.	731
COTTINGTON, Francis, Lord, iii. . . 91, 153, 162,	247
Cotton, attention given to growth of Indian, vii.	589
——— manufacture; its importance in 18th century, v.	488–492
Cotton manufactures, vi.	840–843
COTTON, Mr, a Boston clergyman, iii.	807
———, Sir John Hynde, iv.	449
———, Sir Robert, iii. . . 53, 112,	391
Cotton-spinners, strike of the Manchester, vii.	92
Country, political condition and prospects of the—	
vii. 80, 81, 95, 96,	126
COURCY, Dame de, intimates to Charles Richard II.'s death, ii.	7
COURCY, Robert de, slain in battle, i.	443
Court-a-street Chapel, View of, ii.	712
COURTEN, Sir W., founds a colony in Barbadoes, iii. 536,	541
COURTENAY delusion, vii.	473
———, William, bishop of London, i.	780

GENERAL INDEX. 109

Courtship, iv. 760-762
Courts-martial; origin of their introduction, iv. . 11
COUTANCE, Geoffrey of, i. 394
Covenant, the National, iii. . 186, 309, 701
Covenanters. See also Leslie, iii. . 701, 729, 730, 735
Covent Garden Theatre; View of, vii. . . 302
Coventry Act, passed 1670, iii. . . . 708
COVENTRY, Sir John; maimed by the king's guards, iii. 707, 708
——, Sir Thomas, the lord-keeper, iii. . 117, 144, 175
Coventry weavers, vii. 176, 177
COVERDALE, Miles, bishop of Exeter, ii. . 405, 509, 713
COWELL, Dr, a high churchman, iii. . . . 41
COWLEY, Abraham, a poet of great merit, iii. 578, 604, 874
COWPER, William, a distinguished poet, vi. . 849-851
——, William, earl, iv. . . 165, 287, 324
Cox, Dr, preceptor of Edward VI.; Burnet's account of, ii. 458
COXE, Archdeacon, memoirs of, iv. . . 32
CRABBE, George, death of, in 1832, vii. . . 445
——, Rev. George, a distinguished poet, vi. 849, 863, 887
CRABTREE, William, an astronomer, iv. . . 717
Cracow, Russian despotism in, vii. . . 545, 701
Cradle of James I.; illustration, iii. . . 622
CRADOC, Sir Matthew, marries widow of Perkin Warbeck, ii. 310
CRAGGS, James; his death by small-pox, iv. . 280, 356
CRAIG, the colleague of Knox, ii. . . . 599
CRANFIELD, Lionel, earl of Middlesex, iii. 71, 86, 101, 103
CRANMER, T., archbishop, ii. 375-377, 380, 381, 390, 395, 405-407, 410, 417, 438, 448, 451, 454, 465-468, 479, 493, 507, 509, 525, 527, 528, 696, 728, 735
CRANSTOUN, Colonel; killed at battle of Malplaquet, iv. 216
CRAVEN, Lord; his mission to Holland, iii. . 174
——, William, earl of; petitions for extra seamen, iv. 884
CRAWFORD, Earl of, agrees to seize Earl of Argyle, iii. 250, 251
CRAWLEY, Justice, argues in favour of ship-money, iii. 180
Crecy, Battle of, gained by the Black Prince, i. . 765-768
Creole, affair of the, vii. 711
Crescent, Bath, View of the, vi. . . . 864
Crespi, Treaty of, ratified by Charles V. and Francis I., ii. 439
CRESSET, secretary to the Princess Dowager, iv. . 539
CRESSY, Mr, Cranmer the family tutor of, ii. . 374, 375
Crevant, victory of English over French and Scots at, ii. 54
Crevelt, Battle of, fought 1758, iv. . . . 575
CREW, Sir John, committed to the Tower, iii. . 217
——, Sir Randolph, chief-justice of the King's Bench, iii. 128
——, Sir Thomas; his commission to Ireland, iii. 55, 57, 88
CREWE, Nathaniel, bishop of Durham, . iii. 785; iv. 580
CRICHTON, laird of Brunston, ii. . . . 445, 446
——, Lord Sanquhar, executed in reign of James I., iii. 38
CRICHTON, Sir William, chancellor of James I., ii. 134, 135
CRILLON, Duke de, takes island of Minorca, v. . 366, 372
Crime, vii. 297-299, 498, 586
—— in Ireland, decrease of, vii. . . . 496
—— in 19th century, vi. 935
Criminal laws, vii. 37-40, 101, 209-211, 233, 572-574, 746
—— or penal legislation, vi. . . . 782-790
—— trials; interesting cases of 1830-1834, vii. . 433
Criminals conducted to prison and death; illustrations, ii. 169
CRISPIN, William, count of Evreux, i. . . 413
CROFT, Elizabeth, pretends to be a 'spirit in the wall,' ii. 519
CROFTS, Sir William, iii. 302
CROKE, Justice; his Portrait, iii. . . 181, 829
CROMPTON, Samuel, inventor of the mule-jenny, v. . 492
CROMWELL, Henry, second son of Oliver, iii. . 416, 679
——, Lord, a Yorkist, killed at Barnet, ii. . 109
——, Oliver, lord-protector, iii. 140, 182, 212, 201, 319-321, 331, 332, 335, 366, 378, 408-427, 432*, 556
CROMWELL, Richard, lord-protector, iii. 427,428,430;432*,666
——, Thos., earl of Essex, son of a blacksmith, ii. 377, 378,383-386,390,396,399,403,405,407,409-417,750,850
Cronborg Castle; View of, v. . . . 24
CROSBY, a Jacobite spy, committed to prison, iv. . 59
——, Lord-mayor, committed to the Tower, v. . 10, 11

Crosby-place, Bishopsgate, the residence of Gloucester, ii. 119
Crossii acarus, discovery of the, vii. . . 502
CROWLE, reprimanded at bar of House of Commons, iv. 535
Crown-lands, grants of, by William I. and successors, ii. 165
——, inalienable in England and Wales, iv. . 645
CROY, Sire de, at the battle of Agincourt, ii. . 33
Croydon, this monastery burnt, with 900 volumes, i. 610
Croyland, Abbey of, founded by king of Mercia, i. 310, 377
Crusades against Zisca and Hussites; also the Turks, ii. 150
——, general passion for, i. . . 400, 401
Cudgel-playing, single-stick, and quarter-staff, ii. . 261
CUDWORTH, Dr Ralph, iii. . . 578, 610, 880
CUFFE, secretary to the Earl of Essex, ii. . 684, 685, 689
CUGNOT, a Frenchman, his steam-carriage, vi. . 825
CUJAVIA, Bishop of, proclaims king of Poland, iv. 68
Culdees, of Scotland, opposed to St Augustine, &c., i. 229, 244
CULEN, king of Scotland, i. . . . 219, 220
CULLEY, an improver of live-stock, vi. . . 818
Cullinden or Drummossie Moor; View of, &c., iv. 506-511
CULLUM, Sir T., extracts from, about husbandry, i. 838, 839
Cultivation, or farming, among Anglo-Saxons, i. 276, *et seq.*
CUMBERLAND, Duke of; Portrait, vii. 328, 468, 485, &c.
——, Henry Frederic, duke of, v. . 21, 93, 145
——, Richard, a dramatic writer, v. . . 335
——, Wm. Augustus, duke of—
iv. 499, 513, 569, 572, 796
CUNNINGHAM, Allan, death of, in 1842, vii. . 732
——, bishop of Aberdeen, iii. . . . 445
Currants, introduced from Zante, ii. . . 806, 882
Currency, vii. 22, 23
CURSON, Sir Robert, ii. 313, 314
CURWEN, Dr, preaches before the king at Greenwich—
ii. 381, 382
——, Mr; his plan for abolishing poor-rates, vii. 42, 43
CUSACKE, Sir Thomas, advises on affairs of Ireland, ii. 428
CUSTINE, a French revolutionary general, v. . 883
Custom-house, as it appeared before the great fire, iii. 527
Customs duties, vi. 792, 797
Custrin or Zorndorf, Battle of, iv. . . . 575
CUTHBERT, St, i. 158, 159, 290
Cutlery, vi. 836
CUTTS, Lord, leads the English to capture of Namur, iv. 55
Cymry, the, i. . . . 8, 22, 23, 216, 219
CYVELIOCH, Owen, leader of clans of Powisland, i. 451

DACRE, Leonard, espouses the cause of Mary Stuart, ii. 631
——, Lord, at Flodden, ii. . 328, 329, 350, 353, 354
——, Randall of; his intrigues in Scotland, ii. . 305
D'ADDA, the pope's minister, iii. . . 785, 787
DAGWORTH, Sir Thomas, an English general, i. . 768
DAHL, Michael, a Swedish painter, iv. . . 702
D'AIGUILLON, Duke, iv. 574
DALBIER, Colonel, iii. 202, 324
DALE, Mr David, his cotton-works, vi. . . 841
Dalkeith, Castle of, surrendered to Covenanters, &c., iii. 203
Dalriada, a district of north-east of Ireland, i. 18, 217-222
DALRYMPLE, Sir David, lord-advocate, is disgraced, iv. 238
——, Sir Hew, vi. 437-441
——, Sir John, privy to massacre of Glencoe, iv. 8, 44
DALTON announces the atomic theory, vi. . . 890
——, Dr, death of, in 1844, vii. . . . 735
DALZIEL; his cruelty to the Covenanters, iii. . 701
DAMER, the Hon. Mrs, death of, in 1828, vii. . 316
Damfront, citizens appoint Prince Henry governor of, i. 398
DAMPIER, Wm., a celebrated English navigator, iv. 405, 654
DANBY, T. Osborne, earl of, iii. 696, 711, 712, 717, 720-729
Danelagh, or Dane-law, i. . . 157-168, 176, 371
Danes, the, a Scandinavian race, i. . . . 138
DANGERFIELD, discovers Meal-tub Plot, &c., iii. 732, 766, 776
D'ANGOULÈME, Duke, death of, vii. . . 709
DANIEL, Samuel; his History of England, iii. . 600, 614
Danish warriors; their arms, costume, &c., i. 151-156
DANTON, a French revolutionist; Portrait of, vi. 4
——, George James, the French revolutionist—
v. 750, 783, 787, 792, 831, 845-847, 867-896
DANVERS, Sir Charles; beheaded, ii. . . 689

	PAGE
Darcy, Lord, a leader of the 'Pilgrims of Grace,' ii.	399-401
Darent Church, heads of windows at, i.	316
Darien Company, established 1699, iv.	81-84, 90, 91
Darling, Grace; Portrait, vii.	587, 588
Darmstadt, prince of Hesse, iv.	160, 164, 165
Darnley, Lord H. S., king—	
ii.	578-581, 534, 585, 588, 592, 595
———, Lord, James Stuart, at battle of Crevant, ii.	54, 55
Dartmouth, George Legge, Lord, iii.	741, 760
———, William Legge, Lord, iv.	225
———, William Legge, earl of; Portrait, v.	67
Darwin, Dr Erasmus, a physician and poet—	
iii. 601; vi.	851-853
Dashwood, Sir James, iv.	552
Das Minas, Marquis, takes several places in Castile, iv.	150
Daubeney, Giles, Lord, ii.	286, 306, 308
———, William; beheaded, ii.	300
Daun, Count, iv.	184, 340
D'Avaux accompanies King James to Ireland, iv.	11
Davenant, Dr Charles; his Portrait, iii.	657, 851
———, Sir William, iii.	359, 599, 897
David, prince of North Wales, i.	697-699
———, son of Malcolm III., i. 423, 425, 426, 538, 540, 541	
———, the painter, designs the Car of Liberty, v.	860
Davidson, the African traveller, death of, vii.	593
Davies, Lady; fancied she had the spirit of Daniel	
in her, iii.	157
Davies, Mary, a mistress of Charles II., iii.	706
———, Sir John, attorney-general of James I., iii. 40, 602	
———, Sir John, condemned for treason; pardoned, ii.	689
Davis, John, a navigator of the 16th century, ii.	790
———, Sir John, vii.	618
Davison, fined for defrauding the government, vi.	354, 355
———, J., a Presbyterian minister of 16th century—	
iii.	445, 448
———, William, secretary, ii.	649, 666, 667, 671
Davy, Sir Humphry, vi.	833, 800
———, Sir Humphry; Portrait, vii.	211, 322-324
Dawe, George, the painter, death of, in 1829, vii.	316
Dawes, Sir Wm., consecrated to bishopric of Chester, iv.	193
Dawson, Mr; his views of the Catholic Association, vii.	251
Day, George, bishop of Chichester, ii.	493
———, John; receives a price-current patent, iii.	544
Day of the Trades; its result, vii.	417
Dead, prayer for the; for parents and family, &c., ii. 397, 716	
Dean, General, killed in a battle with Van Tromp, iii.	414
Deane, Silas; Portrait of, v.	230
Death, losses by—	
vii. 151, 217-223, 312-325, 437-446, 592-603, 731-740	
Death, punishment of, vii.	167, 163, 573
De Broglie, a French marshal, iv.	424, 439, 441
Debt and taxation, vii.	161-163
———, bill of 1836 for abolishing imprisonment for, vii.	522
———, National, history of the, iv.	651-653
De Castries, M., a French commander, iv.	587
Decker, T., a dramatic writer of 17th century, iii. 593, 594	
Declaration of the Duke of Wellington on parlia-	
mentary reform, vii.	335
Declaratory Bill of Lord Brougham, vii.	554
Deeds, registry of, in 1834, vii.	415
Deering, Sir Edward, iii.	227, 310, 491
Defoe, Daniel, an eminent political writer—	
iv. 108, 173, 747, 748	
Defrobani, supposed to be Tabrobane, or Ceylon, i.	9
De hæretico comburendo, writ, abolished, iii.	714
Deira, kingdom of, founded about 550, i.	142
Deities, Gaulish, i.	69
De la Clue, M., commander of the Toulon fleet, iv.	578
Delaval, Sir Ralph, vice-admiral of the Red, iv.	37, 38
Delawar, Charles West, Lord, iii.	367
D'Elbœuf, Marquis, ii.	554, 560
Delhi, View of, vi.	216, 304
Dell, secretary to Archbishop Laud, iii.	506
Della Cruscan school, writers of, vi.	853-855
Delorges, Marshal; invests Heidelberg, iv.	41, 42, 49
———, French ambassador, iii.	765

	PAGE
Delvin, Lord; arrested by the House of Commons, iii.	270
Demerara, rising of the slaves in, vii.	170, 171
———, View of, vi.	233
Denbigh, William Fielding, earl of, iii.	71
Dendy, Serjeant, proclaims the trial of Charles L, iii.	389
Denham, Baron; his order against church-ales, &c.—	
iii.	160, 603
Denman, Chief-justice, questions authority of House	
of Commons, justifying a case of libel, &c.—	
vii.	526, 575, 580-582
Denmark and Jutland, early population of, i.	140
Denmark, George, prince of, iii.	760, 798
———, George, prince of; Portrait of, &c.—	
iv.	128, 134, 202
Denmark, King of, solicits hand of Queen Elizabeth, ii.	562
———, liberality of the King of, vii.	546
Denny, Sir Anthony, an executor of Henry VIII.—	
ii.	451, 454
Deputies, dissolution of the French Chamber of, vii.	273
Derby, Charles Stanley, earl of, iii.	431
Derby, insurrection, vii.	55-59
Derby, James Stanley, earl of, iii.	292, 405
———, Lord Stanley, earl of. See Stanley, ii.	282
Derby, Nottingham, and Bristol riots, vii.	352, 353
Derbyshire, lead-mines worked by Romans in, i.	117
Dereham, Francis; executed as a traitor, ii.	417, 420
Dermond Mac Murrogh, king of Leinster, i. 429, 460-465	
De Ruyter, a Dutch admiral, iii. 407, 698, 701, 711, 714	
Derwentwater, James Ratcliff, 3d and last earl of, iv.	300
Desborough, Cromwell's brother-in-law, iii.	422, 432
Deseze, one of the counsel of Louis XVI., v.	891, 894
Desmond, Earl of, assassinated by Kelly of Moriarty, ii.	652
———, Earl of, rebels against Henry VIII., ii.	340
———, George Fielding, earl of, iii.	71
Desmoulins, Benoit Camille, a French revolutionist—	
v. 745, 750, 783, 737, 792, 862-896	
Despard, an officer in the English army; tried and	
executed for high treason; Portrait of, vi.	196-193
Despencer, Hugh, a favourite of Edward II., i.	740-744
———, Lord le; beheaded by people of Bristol, ii.	5-7
———, Sir F. Dashwood, lord, iv.	534, 563, 585, 818, 820
Des Roches, Peter, regent of England, i.	675-677
D'Estrées, a French admiral, iii.	710
Dettingen, Battle of, fought June 16, 1743, iv.	440
Devizes, Castle of, i.	427, 433
———, Chartist riot at, vii.	568
Devon Commission, the, vii.	668
Devon, Earl of; beheaded after battle of Edgecote, ii.	104
———, E. C., earl of; committed to the Tower, ii.	282, 313
———, Edward Courtenay, earl of—	
ii.	505, 510, 515, 519, 521
———, Henry Courtenay, earl of; beheaded—	
ii.	408, 505, 510
———, Thomas Courtenay, earl of; beheaded, ii.	02, 09
Devonport, iii.	655
Devonshire, Duchess of; her death, in 1824, vii.	220
———, Georgiana, duchess of; Portrait, v.	714
———, William Cavendish, duke of, iv.	65, 67
———, William Cavendish, earl of, iii.	288
D'Ewes, Sir S., an English antiquary and statesman, iii.	155
Dewint, an excellent painter in water-colours, vi.	898
De Witt, John, a Dutch statesman, iii. 208, 407, 698,	710
Dibdin, Charles, a celebrated poet and composer, vi.	852
Dickens, Charles; Portrait, vii.	742, 743
Diepenbeck, a pupil of Rubens, iii.	569
Dieppe, View of, vi.	216
Digby, Lord George, iii. 216, 227, 240, 267, 272, 341, 342	
———, Sir Everard; executed as a traitor, iii.	24, 27-30
———, Sir Kenelm, a Catholic gentleman, iii. 218, 424, 568	
Diggss, Leonard, a mathematician, &c., iv.	715
———, Sir Dudley, iii. 55, 88, 120, 121, 132, 145, 536	
———, Thomas; his tract on Parallaxes, iv.	715
Dillon, Lord, iii.	310
Dingham, Mrs, imports the art of making starch, ii.	884
Diodorus Siculus, quoted, i.	15
Dionysius Periegetes, gives names to England and Ireland, i.	21

GENERAL INDEX. 111

Disruption in Church of Scotland; signing of seceders—
vii. 674
Dissenters and Catholics, enmity between the, vii. . 203
——— Chapels Bill, vii. . . . 680, 681
——— disabilities, repeal of, &c.—
vii. 244–246, 654, 674–684
———, Episcopalian, iii. 787
———, Fox moves for repeal of old laws against, v. 852
———, marriages, Lord John Russell's measure
for, vii. 308, 453
Dissenters, opening of universities to, vii. . 405, 406
———, the, vi. . . . 748, 768–770
———, the Church of Scotland and the, vii. 513, 514
Distress of the people during terrible winter of
1836–37, vii. 519
Dives, Sir Lewis, iii. 271
Diving-bell, the, iii. 869
——— to wrecks in 1832, vii. 434
Divitiacus, prince of the Ædui, i. . . 65
Dobson, William, a pupil of Vandyke, iii. . . 569
Dockyard fires, vii. 572
Dodd, Mr George, the engineer; his death, in 1827, vii. 316
———, his remarkable steam-voyage, vi. . 831, 832
Dodington, George Bubb, iv. . . 399, 797, 813, 814
Dodwell, Henry, a conjuror, iv. . . 32, 614
D'Oisel, a French general, ii. . . . 559–561
Doleman, Colonel, iii. 407
Dollond, John, invented the achromatic telescope, iv. 733
Domesday-book, contents of, &c., i. . 391, 578–580
Dominica, Island of; View of Roseau, iv. . 802, 803
Dominican friars; illustration of, &c., i. . 803, 804
Donald; his accusation against Marquis of Hamilton
iii. 150
——— III, king of Scotland, i. . . . 218
——— IV., king of Scotland, i. . . . 219
——— VI. (Bane), king of Scotland, i. . . 538
Don Carlos, vii. 708
——— Miguel; Portrait, vii. . . 254–256, 271
——— Pedro, emperor of Brazil, vii. . . 152
Donne, Dr John, a poet, and dean of St Paul's, iii. 603
Donnington Castle; illustration, iii. . . 307
Donop, Count, mortally wounded at Mud Bank, v. 199
Donoughmore, the round tower of, i. . . 13
Doppino, Dr, Protestant bishop of Meath, iv. . 14
Donisiacs, Dr; he is assassinated, iii. . 390, 402
Dorset, Edward Sackville, earl of, iii. . 83, 137, 155
———, Lionel Cranfield, earl of, iv. . . 203
———, T. Gray, marquis of, a general of Henry VIII., ii. 321
———, Thomas Gray, marquis of, son of Elizabeth
Woodville, ii. 113, 118, 119, 126, 127, 283, 286, 288, 291
Dorset, Thomas Sackville, earl of, iii. . . 39, 581
Dorsetshire labourers, transportation of the, vii. . 417
Dort, Synod of; its judgment against Conrad Vorstius, iii. 48
Douay, capitulates to Marlborough, iv. . 227, 249
Douglas, Archibald, earl of; slain at Verneuil, ii. 56, 132
———, Archibald, concerned in murder of Darnley, ii. 653
———, Catherine, tries to save James I. of Scotland, ii. 134
———, Earl, commander at battle of Chevy Chase, i. 793
———, Earl; wounded at Homildon Hill, ii. 11, 13–15, 49
———, Gawin, bishop of Dunkeld; his poetry, ii. 352, 353
———, General, iv. 25
———, George, stabs David Rizzio, ii. . . 586
———, James, ninth earl of, ii. . . . 135
———, John, rector of University of St Andrews, iii. 436
———, Lord James, i. . 730, 736–741, 749–751, 755
———, Robert, chaplain to the Earl of Leven, iii. 316
———, sheriff of Teviotdale, iii. . . . 222
———, Sir Archibald, regent of Scotland, i. . 756
———, Sir Robert, falls at battle of Steinkirk, iv. . 37
———, Sir Wm., first noble who joined Wallace, i. 715, 716
———, William, poniarded by James II., ii. . 135
———, W.; seized by Crichton, and executed, ii. 134, 135
———, W., procures Mary's escape from Lochleven, ii. 606
Doun, Lord, dies of wounds received in battle, iv. 587
Dover Castle, Henry VIII. and Charles V. at, ii. 338, 339, 781
Dover, Henry Carey, earl of, iii. . . . 288

Dover; View of Port and Castle, &c., i. . 26, 27, 189, 190
Dower, English Law of, vi. 786
Dowland, John, a celebrated musician, vi. . . 563
Downes, John, a commissioner on trial of Charles I. iii. 393
Downie, Captain, killed in harbour of Plattsburg, vi. 742
Downing, a military chaplain; his detestable conduct, iii. 690
Downton, Captain, of the East India Company, iii. 530
Drainage, great improvements in 1830, vii. . 304
Drake, Sir F., a conspirator in the Rye-house Plot, iii. 740
———, Sir Francis, ii. 656, 672, 673, 676–678, 680, 789, 790
Drama, the, ... iii. 579–599; vi. 860
———, illustrations, ii. . . . 877–880
Dramatic representations, parliamentary committee
on, vii. 441
Dramatists of the 18th century, v. . . 499–506
Draper, Colonel William; his capture, iv. . 809
Drayton, Michael, a voluminous poet, iii. . 586, 600
Dreux, Battle of, ii. 571
Dreux Brezé, marries a relative of William I., i. . 374
Drilling of Radicals, vii. 106
Dring, R.; his residence the first Quaker meeting-
house, iii. 810
Drogheda, Lord; his Irish commission, iv. . 86, 88
Drouet, Jean Baptist; capture of Louis XVI., v. 834, 836
Drought and harvest of 1826, vii. . . . 209
Druids, i. . . 25, 26, 43, 59–61, 64, 83, 101, 119–123
Drummond, James, a partisan of the young Pretender, iv. 461
———, Mr Edward, shot in the street, vii. . 638
——— of Bochaldy, a Jacobite, iv. . . 443
———, T., inventor of Drummond light—
vii. 434, 496–498
———, William, a graceful poet, iii. . •. 602
Drury, a priest; executed, iii. . . . 33
———, Sir Drew, a fanatical Puritan, ii. . 658
———, Sir William, destroys houses of the Hamiltons, ii. 632
Dryden, John, the poet, iii. . 424, 784, 870, 876, 877
———, John, review of his works, iv. . . 737
Du Dartas, translated by Joshua Sylvester, iii. . 585, 601
Dubicska, Battle of, fought 17th July 1792, v. . 857
Dublin Custom-house, fire at the, vii. . . 436
———, police and constabulary force of, vii. . 498
———, View of, in reign of Charles I., iii. . 253
Dubois, Abbé, minister of state to Duke of Orleans—
iv. 312, 363
Duckworth, Sir John, vi. . . . 371–379
Dudley, Earl, death of, in 1833, vii. . 236, 438
———, John, Viscount Lisle, ii. . . 442, 454, 455
———, Lord Edward, abandons the Castle of Ham, ii. 535
———, Lord Guildford, ii. . 499, 509, 510, 517, 518
———, Sir Andrew, captures a Scotch man-of-war, ii. 458
Duel between the Duke of Wellington and Lord
Winchilsea, vii. 268
Duelling, iv. 766
———, check given to practice of, vii. . . 436, 747
———; its relation to ancient chivalrous combats, ii. 869
Duels of the 17th century, iii. . . 621–626, 893
Dufay, keeper of the king's garden at Paris, iv. . 734
Duff, succeeded Indulf on the Scottish throne, i. . 219
Dugald Stewart's Monument, Calton Hill, Edinburgh;
View of, iv. 320
Dugdale, one of the witnesses against Lord Strafford, iii. 732
Du Gusselin, constable of France, i. . . 779, 783
Duke or Dux, a Roman military dignity, i. . 90, 882
Dumont, plans the assassination of William III., iv. 37
Dumouriez, General; Portrait of, v. . . 858–896
Dunbar, archbishop of Glasgow, iii. . . 644
Dunbar Castle; View of the ruins, . i. 714; iii. 404
Dunbar, Earl of, iii. 65, 466
———, William, an early Scottish poet, ii. . 838
Dunbarton Castle, in hands of the Covenanters, iii. 203
Dundarton, Lord, routs Earl of Argyle near Glasgow, iii. 768
Dunblane, battle of, fought November 13, 1715, iv. 299
Duncan, illegitimate son of Malcolm III., i. . 538
———, Viscount, victor of Camperdown, vi. . 116, 117
Duncombe, Sir Sanders; his sedan-chair patent, iii. . 544
Dundas, Mr Robert, lord advocate, vi. . . 756

HISTORY OF ENGLAND.

Dunfermline Abbey, View of, i. . . . 752
DUNFERMLINE, Earl of, iii. 205
DUNGARVON, Lord, iii. 277
Dunkirk, View of, iii. 692
DUNMORE, Lord, governor of Virginia, v. . 119, 120, 159
DUNNE, Sir D., a commissioner in divorce of Earl of Essex, iii. 53
DUNOIS, Count of; his generalship and valour— ii. 62, 66, 71, 85
DUNSTABLE, John of, inventor of figurate harmony, iii. 561
DUNSTAN, St, abbot of Glastonbury, i. . 170–176, 240–244
Duntocher Bridge, on the line of Graham's Dike, i. . 48
DUPLEIX, Joseph, governor of Pondicherry, v. . 600–605
Duplin-moor, victory gained here by Edward Baliol, i. 775
Du QUESNE, a French general, iii. . . . 710
Durham Cathedral, View of the nave of, i. . 621
DURHAM, Lord; Portrait, vii. 340, 346, 347, 419, 420, 549–557
Durham, the bishopric of, suppressed, &c., ii. . 499
————, View of, &c., i. 372, 373
DURIE, John, a minister of Edinburgh, iii. . 64, 438, 441
DUROC, General, favourite aide-de-camp of Napoleon, vi. 664
DURST, a victorious Pictish king, i. . . . 216
DURY, General, slain at St Cas, iv. . . . 574
Dutch sluice-breakers attacking a dike; Illustration, v. 680
Duties, remission of, on several articles of tariff, vii. 289, 727
DUVENNSEEDE, Baron de Wassenaer, vii. . . 270
Dwellings of the poor, projects for improving the, vii. 657
Dyeing, improvements in the art of, vi. . . 843, 844
————, regulations concerning, ii. . . . 809

EADBALD, king of Kent, marries his father's widow— i. 145, 233
EADBURGHA, daughter of the king of Mercia, i. . 150
EADMER, bishop of St Andrews, in Scotland, i. . 530
EANRED, king of Northumbria, i. . . . 151
EARLE, Mr, one of the secretaries to English parliament, iii. 320
EARLE, Sir Walter; reports a new gunpowder plot— iii. 242, 264
Earl's Barton; View of the church, i. . . 315
Early-closing movement, vii. 656
Earthenware, improvements in, iv. . . . 684
Earthquakes, storms, eclipses, &c., of 1820–1826, vii. 215
East-Anglia, kingdom of, i. . . . 142, 150
————, fearful portents in the, vii. . . 572
———— India Company, . iii. 547, 548, 860; iv. 847, 866; v. 20, 43, 458–461, 464; vi. 800, 801, 804, 810, 816, 834
East India Company, Parliamentary committee to inquire into charter of, vii. 290
East India Company, the United, v. . . . 600
———————— House, Leadenhall Street; View of, vii. . 289
————, steam in the, vii. 434
Easterlings, the; their character, ii. . . . 107
Eaton Hall, Cheshire; View of, vi. . . . 896
EMOLT, Duke of, iv. 392
Ecclesiastical Commission, established by James II., iii. 784
———————— of 1835, vii. . . 454, 472
Ecclesiasticus, Book of, and the *Apocrypha*, discussed, iii. 16
EDEN, Sir Frederick; quoted, iii. . . 659, 660
EDERA, Father, a Jesuit of great credit at court of Vienna, iv. 69
EDGAR ATHELING, grandson of Edmund Ironside— i. 181, 360–362, 369–372, 379, 380, 398, 411
————, King, brother of King Edwy, i. . 171–174
————, son of Malcolm III., i. . . 538
EDGECOMBE, Captain; his expedition to Minorca, iv. 558
Edgcote, Battle of, ii. 104
EDGCUMBE, Richard, created baron Edgcumbe, iv. . 434
Edge Hill, Battle of, iii. 297
EDGEWORTH DE FIRMONT, Louis XVI.'s confessor, v. 895
————, Miss, vii. 742
EDITHA, daughter of King Edgar, i. . . 175
EDILFRID, king of Northumbria, i. . 145, 146, 233, 234
Edinburgh in 1689; political rancour and treachery of, iv. 44
————, Treaty of; Illustrations, ii. 561, 562, 588, 648
————, View of, vii. 725

Edinburgh; Views of St Giles's, Old Tron Church, and Market Cross, iii. 182–184, 682
EDITHA, daughter of Earl Godwin, i. 187, 191, 193, 203, 366
EDMONDS, Sir T., an intriguing diplomatist, iii. 15, 52, 140
EDMUND ATHELING, succeeds his brother Athelstane, i. 170
————, brother of Edmund L., i. . . . 711
————, King, surnamed Ironside, i. . 180, 181, 195
————, second son of Henry III., i. . . 680
EDNOTH, an English nobleman, i. . . . 365
EDRED, brother of Edmund the Atheling, i. . . 170
EDRIC, a man of talent, a favourite of Ethelred, i. 178, 179
————, surnamed the Forester, i. . . 362, 365, 375
Education, ... iii. 632; iv. 761–765; vii. 126, 211, 372, 435, 504, 653–655, 746
————, national, vii. 44, 45
————, popular, vii. 474–477
EDWARD ATHELING, son of Edmund Ironside, i. . 195
———— PLANTAGENET, prince of Wales, ii. . 127
————, son of Henry VI., ii. . 92, 95–97, 105, 106, 109
————, the Black Prince, i. . . . 753, 765–780
————, the Confessor, i. . . . 180, 184, 203
————, the Elder, king of Wessex, i. . . 168
————, the Martyr, i. 174, 175
———— I., king of England, i. . . 680–730, 781, 837
———— II., king of England, i. . 723, 726, 730–746, 837
———— III., king of England, i. . . 742–781, 837
———— IV., king of England— ii. 90, 94–117, 121, 165, 243, 244
———— V., king of England, ii. . 116–126, 130, 313, 314
———— VI., ii. 436, 452–500, 695, 729–734, 764, 800, 822
EDWARDS, a merchant, introduces coffee into England, iii. 548
————, Richard, a dramatic writer of 16th century, iii. 584
————, T., a commissioner in divorce of Earl of Essex, iii. 53
EDWARDS, the informer, vii. . . . 114–116
EDWIN, king of Northumbria, i. . 146, 147, 234, 235
————, son of Algar, i. . 208, 360, 361, 368, 369, 375, 376
EDWY, king of the Anglo-Saxons, i. . . 171, 172
EFFINGHAM, Thomas Howard, earl of, v. . . 105
EGBERT, archbishop of York, i. . . . 266, 307
————, king of Wessex, i. . . . 150, 152
EGERTON, Lord-keeper, a partisan of James I., iii. 3, 5, 463
EGLANTINE, Fabre d', an orator in the Cordelier Club, v. 783
Eglinton tournament, the grand, vii. . . . 590
EGMONT, Count of; assaulted by a mob, ii. . . 519
————, Lord, supposed author of *Constitutional Queries*, iv. 534
EGREMONT, Charles Wyndham, earl of, iv. . . 820
————, Sir John, joins the northern insurgents, ii. 296
Egypt and Turkey, war between, vii. . . . 429
Egyptian obelisk, arrival of the first in England, vii. 214
EINSIEDEL, General, forced to abandon Prague, iv. . 448
El Arish, Treaty of, concluded, Jan. 24, 1800, vi. . 165
ELCHO, Lord, a partisan of the young Pretender, iv. 492, 510
————, Lord, defeated by Montrose at Tippermuir, iii. 337
ELDON, John Scott, Lord, vii. . 7, 38, 93, 112, 131, 133, 160, 197, 203, 205–207, 216, 225–227, 231, 241–246, 250–254, 262–264, 269, 291, 334, 344, 447, 468, 596
ELDON, John Scott, lord chancellor; Portrait of, vii. 788
ELEANOR, queen of Edward I., i. . 680, 690, 692, 693
————, queen of Louis VII., of France— i. 438–440, 468, 475, 482, 486, 493, 494, 518
————, wife of Alfonso the Good, king of Castile, i. 480
Election of 1841, the general; its extraordinary importance, vii. 605, 606
Elections— vii. 204, 209, 277, 328, 329, 348, 450, 516, 584, 605, 649
Elections, bribery at, iv. 645
————, its vast importance, vii. . . 744
Electric telegraph; its vast importance, vii. . . 744
Electricity, experimenters on, iv. . . . 734
ELFRIC, or ÆLFRIC, archbishop of Canterbury, i. 244, 300
ELFRIDA, wife of King Edgar, i. . . 173–175
ELGIN, Lord, death of, in 1841, vi. . . . 732
Elgin marbles purchased for £35,000, vii. . . 46
ELGIVA, the Beautiful, wife of King Edwy, i. . 171, 172
ELIBANK, Lord, iv. 535

GENERAL INDEX. 113

ELIOT, Sir J., iii. 120, 121, 123, 141, 142, 144, 181, 211, 212
——, T., delivers the great seal to the king at York, iii. 286
ELLIOT, General, his brave defence of Gibraltar, v. 385, 390
ELLIOT, Admiral, vii. 616
——, Captain; his Chinese mission, vii. . 613–618
——, Sir G.; his defence of Scottish dissenters, vi. 753
Elixir of life, a supposed medicament, ii. . . 208
Elizabeth Castle, Jersey; View of, v. . . 281
ELIZABETH, czarina of Russia, iv. . . . 813
——, daughter of James I. of England, iii. 22, 25, 52, 85
—— of York, ii. 126–128, 231, 285, 287, 289, 291, 312
—— Queen, ii. 383, 395, 454, 515–519, 524, 529,
539–582, 590, 604, 612–694, 695, 737–749, 769, 803, 823
ELIZABETH, Queen, James VI. of Scotland succeeds, iii. 2–4
WOODVILLE, queen of Edward IV.—
ii. 101–103, 118–121, 125–127, 281, 285, 287, 288, 291
ELLA, or ÆLLA, founder of kingdom of Sussex, i. 142, 145
Eilandum, or Elyndome, in Wiltshire, i. . . 150
ELLENBOROUGH, Edward L., lord; Portrait, vi. 781, 782, 790
——, Lord, vii. . . 38, 93, 608, 625, &c.
ELLIS, Mr, British envoy at Persian court, vii. . 620
——, Sir Henry; his *Collection* referred to, iii. . 4
——, introduction to Domesday-book, i. . 580
ELNHAM, Thomas de, prior of Linton, ii. . . 208
ELPHINSTONE, a partisan of the young Pretender—
iv. 479, 521, 523
——, Bishop, founds university of Aberdeen, ii. 183
——, Major-general, vii. . . . 624–626
——, William, an eminent merchant, ii. . . 183
Eltham Palace, wooden roof of great hall delineated, ii. 225
ELWES, or ELVIS, Sir J., lieutenant of the Tower, iii. 53, 58
Ely, fortified camp at, i. 376–378
——, Isle of, riots in, vii. 24
—— Place, Holborn, palace of the bishop of Ely, ii. . 120
Emigrants, decree against French, v. . . . 843
Emigration in 1826, colonial, vii. . . 190, 191
—— to South Africa, North America, and
Australia, vii. 213
EMMA, queen of Ethelred, i. 177, 180, 181, 184–188, 190–192
EMMETT, one of the Association of United Irishmen, vi. 127
——, Robert, son of Dr Emmett, executed, vi. 214–217
EMPSON & DUDLEY, ministers of Henry VII., ii. 313, 314, 320
Enactment, Bill of, Lord John Russell's, vii. . 582
Enclosure Act, passed 1710, iv. . . . 680
——, passed 1800–1, vi. 781
—— riots of 1831 and 1832, vii. . . . 432
ENGELBERT of Nassau, monument of, iii. . . 575
ENGHIEN, Antoine-Henri de Bourbon, duke d', vi. 238–243
England and Austria, commercial treaty between, vii. 544
—— and Wales, map of, vii. 366
——; her relations with France, Spain, &c., vii. 539–549
English banking-system; changes in 1826, vii. . 186
—— Church, dissensions in the, vii. . . 674–681
—— in Portugal, vii. 543
Engraving, . . . iii. 577, 578; iv. 709; vi. 878–881
——, Wood, revived by Thomas Bewick, v. 527–529
Engravings, List of. See beginning of vols. i., ii., iii., &c.
ENRIQUE, Don, count of Trastamara, i. . . 776–778
Epsom race-course stand, erection of, vii. . . 304
ERASMUS, an eminent scholar, ii. 329, 338, 385, 389, 816
ERASTUS, a German divine of 16th century, iii. . 493
ERATOSTHENES, Ireland unknown to, i. . . 14
EACENWINE, founder of the kingdom of Essex, i. . 142
EREBY, Sir Antony, a parliamentarian, iii. . . 277
ERIC, founder of the kingdom of Kent, i. . . 142
ERIL, Melzi d', vice-president of Cisalpine Republic, vi. 173
ERIN, properly EIRE, pronounced *Iar*, i. . . 16
ERIZZO, Venetian ambassador at Paris, iv. . . 64
ERNEST, king of Hanover, vii. 546
Erpingham, Rutland; insurgents defeated here, ii. 104, 105
ERPINGHAM, Sir Thomas; his gallantry at Agincourt, ii. 32
ERROL, Earl of, a Jacobite, iv. 186
——, Earl of, lenity of James VI. to, iii. . 444, 452
ERSKINE, Dr John; Portrait of, vi. . . 766, 767
——, Hon. Thomas; Portrait of, vi. . . 785
——, John, the laird of Dun, iii. . . 436, 454

ERSKINE, Lord; his speech on abandonment of Bill of
Pains and Penalties, vii. 124
ERSKINE, Rev. Ebenezer, iv. 618
——, Sir H., advocates for a militia in Scotland, iv. 585
ESCALONA, Duke of, a Spanish chamberlain, iv. 322, 323
ESCOIQUIZ, the canon, vi. 406–409
ESPANA, Don Carlos de, a brave Spanish commander, vi. 655
ESPEC, Walter, present at Battle of Northallerton, i. 424
Essays, revival of periodical, in reign of Geo. III., v. 506–511
ESSE, D', D'Espanvilliers, a French general, ii. 469, 470, 488, 489
ESSEX, Arthur Capel, earl of, iii. . 731, 740, 746, 747
——, Henry Bourchier, earl of, ii. . . 323, 382
——, Henry de, hereditary standard-bearer, i. . 443
Essex House, from Hollar's view of London, ii. . 686
ESSEX, R. D., earl of, ii. 680–689; iii. 52, 53, 247, 286, 319, 515
Essex, Saxons land, and found this kingdom, i. 142, 163, 164
ESSEX, Walter Devereux, earl of, ii. . . 651
——, William Parr, earl of. See Northampton, ii.
Estaples, Peace of, ii. 299, 311
ETHELBALD, son of Ethelwulf, i. . . . 153
ETHELBERT, brother and successor of Ethelbald, i. 153
——, king of Kent, i. . 145, 203, 231, 232
ETHELFLEDA, daughter of Alfred, i. . . 162, 168
ETHELNOTH, archbishop of Canterbury, i. . 185
ETHELRED, a noble, husband of Ethelfleda, i. 162, 163, 168
—— I., succeeds his brother Ethelbert, i. . 153, 154
—— II., surnamed the Unready, i. . . 173–180
ETHELWALD, the brother of King Alfred, i. . 168
ETHELWOLD, abbot of Abingdon, i. . . . 301
ETHELWULF, king of Wessex, i. . . . 152–154
ETHERIDGE, a dramatic writer of 17th century, iv. 737
Eton College; Views of, ii. 196
Etymologies and derivations of names of places, &c.—
i. 11, 16, 17, 19, 61, 77, 92, 99, 138, 142, 144
EU, William, count of, has his eyes torn out, i. . 400
Eucharist, the, as defined by the Bloody Statute, ii. 410
Euclid, first English translation of, iv. . . 715
EUDES, of Champaign, grants of King William to, i. 374
EUGENE, Prince, iv. 33, 37, 68, 113, 149, 164, 216, 242
EUGENIUS IV., Pope, arranges a European congress, ii. 78
Europe, antagonism in, vii. 700, 701
——, interesting events in the west of, in 1830–
1834, vii. 429
Europe, portents in, vii. 535–549
——, the princes and peoples of, vii. . . 142
EUSTACE, count of Boulogne, i. . 189, 190, 365, 305
——, Prince, eldest son of Stephen, i. . 431, 437
Eutaw, Battle of, fought September 8, 1781, v. 362–364
Evangelical party of the Church, vii. . . 403, 404
EVANS, General, commander of British Legion, vii. 541, 542
——, Richard, death of, in 1832, vii. . . 443
EVELYN, quoted, iv. 6
——, Sir Ralph, iii. . . . 323, 431, 704
Evesham, View of Ruins of Monastery, &c., i. . 686
Evora, Battle of, iii. 706
EVRE, Sir Ralph, ravages the Scottish borders, ii. 441
EWART, a distinguished preacher, imprisoned, iii. 66
EWER, Colonel, made governor of Isle of Wight, iii. 386
Exchange; View of, &c., ii. . . . 787, 788
Exchequer bills, parliamentary advance of, vi. . 803
Excise-duties, alterations on the, vii. . . 720
—— scheme, the, iv. 385
Excursion-trips, with return-tickets, first appearance
of, vii. 695
Exe, river; a Danish fleet destroyed here, i. . 157
Execution of Louis XVI.; Illustration, v. . 896
Exeter, city of, i. 157, 351, 366
EXETER, Gertrude, marchioness of; imprisoned, ii. 408
——, Henry Courtnay, marquis of, ii. . 408, 505, 510
——, Henry Holland, duke of, ii. . 99, 109, 110
——, John H., duke of, inventor of the rack, iii. 519
——, Thomas Beaufort, duke of, ii. . . 49, 88
Exeter, View of, iii. 781
EXMOUTH, Lord; expedition to Algiers, vii. 34–37, 440, 441
Expenditure, reductions in the national, in 1830, vii. 289
Export-duties, proposal to abolish the, vii. . 720

114 HISTORY OF ENGLAND.

Export trade of G. Britain, vi. 795,802,804,805,808,809–815
Eynsford, William de, excommunicated by Becket, i. 448
Eyre, Mr Justice, iv. 22

Fabricius, Philip, member of the Council of Bohemia, iii. 80
Fadvan, Robert; his *Concordance of Histories*, ii. 209
Fac-similes of the signatures to the Declaration of Independence, 4th July 1776, v. 163
Factory Bill, Sir James Graham's, vii. 653–656
——— children, Lord Ashley's motions in favour of, vii. 566
———; their condition in 1833, vii. 379
Fagel, the Dutch minister, iii. 770
Fagg, Sir John, iii. 838
Fairfax, Edward, a translator of ancient poetry, iii. 602
———, Sir T., a leader in civil wars, iii. 322, 332, 366, 370
Fairly, bishop of Lismore or Argyle; deposed, iii. 484
Fairman, Colonel; connection with Orangeism, vii. 485–490
Faithorne, William, an eminent engraver, iii. 870, 883
Falaise, castle of, Prince Arthur confined here, i. 518
Falconberg, Lord, proposes Duke Edward as king, ii. 97
———, Sir John, defeated by Prince John, ii. 17
Falconbridge, Lord; beheaded at Durham, ii. 17
Falconer, Sir James, iv. 147
———, Wm., an English poet and naval writer, v. 503
Falkes, John, accused of heresy, ii. 700
Falkirk, first battle of, i. 718
———, second battle of; View of, iv. 494–497
Falkland Islands; English & Spanish dispute, iv. 895; v. 5, 6
Falkland, Lord, mortally wounded at Newbury, iii. 178, 308
Falmouth, Charles Berkely, earl of, iii. 695
Famine in Ireland, vii. 669
Fanelli, F., a sculptor in metal of 17th century, iii. 576
Faneuil Hall, Boston; View of, iv. 869
Fanshawe, Sir Richard, a poetical translator, iii. 602
Faraday and Herschel, vii. 743
Farmer, Antony, iii. 785
Farmers, proposal to afford important relief to, vii. 728
Farm-rents, great rise in, vi. 814, 819
Farnese, Alexander, prince of Parma, ii. 650, 651
Farnley Wood, insurrection at, iii. 693
Farrant, R., gentleman of chapel to Edward VI., iii. 562
Farren, Miss, the celebrated actress, death of, in 1829, vi. 318
Farringdon, Hugh, abbot; hanged and quartered, ii. 412
Fastolfe, Sir John, an English captain, ii. 54, 61, 66, 68, 276
Fasts, observance of Lent; fish-days, ii. 471
Father Mathew, the Irish temperance apostle, vii. 500–502
Fatimites, their splendid library, i. 603
Fauchet, Abbé, organises the Social Circle, v. 791
Favras, Marquis de, trial and execution of, v. 755
Fawkes, Guy or Guido, iii. 21–27, 29, 30
Fay, Sir, Godemar du, a great Norman baron, i. 764
Featherstone, William, an impostor, ii. 522
Federal union of British North-American colonies, vii. 553
Fel Ynis, a name of Britain, in the Welsh Triads, i. 8
Felo de se, abolishment of the old burial custom of, vii. 168
Felony, bill to allow counsel to prisoners on trial for, vii. 522
Felton, John; executed as a traitor, ii. 632, 633
———, John, stabs the Marquis of Buckingham, iii. 136,138
Female Reform Society, formation of a, vii. 106
——— whipping, abandoned, vi. 785
Fenwick, Sir John; beheaded on Tower-hill, iv. 65–67
Ferdinand I., emperor of Austria, vii. 546
——— II., emperor of Germany, iii. 174
——— II., king of Spain, ii. 310–323, 336
——— IV., king of Naples, vi. 616–623
——— VI., king of Spain, iv. 527, 803
——— VII., of Spain, vi. 401–413, 674–696; vii. 49–52
Ferguson, A., a Presbyterian preacher, iii. 756; iv. 141
———, Colonel, a royalist American officer, v. 322
———, Dr Adam, refused a passport by Washington; Portrait of, v. 252, 268
Ferguson, James, the great philosopher, iv. 734
Ferozshah, Battle of, vii. 714
Ferquhard, earl of Strathearn, i. 543
Ferrand, earl of Flanders, i. 525, 526

Ferrar, Robert, bishop of St David's; burnt, ii. 500, 523
Ferrars, George, M.P., arrested for debt, iv. 633, 634
Ferrers, Earl, revolts against Henry II., i. 470
———, Lord; slain at battle of Bosworth, ii. 129, 284
Ferrock, John; his letter to James I., iii. 2
Festino, a; illustration, v. 538
Festoons, iv. 695
Fête of Liberty; illustration, v. 860
——— of the Federation; illustration, v. 787
Feudal system, institution and form of, i. 563, *et seq.*
——— tenure, i. 254
———, Parliamentary inquiry into the, iii. 19
Feuillade, Duke de la, invests Turin, iv. 170
Feuillant Club, established by Lafayette and Bailly, v. 783
Field, Dr, bishop of Llandaff, impeached for bribery, iii. 82
Fielding, Henry, the novelist, v. 500
Fiennes, Colonel John, iii. 336, 423
———, Nathaniel, iii. 249, 265, 305
Fieschi, and others; their infernal machines, vii. 537
Filmer, Henry; burnt, ii. 728
Financial legislation, vi. 790–794
——— measures— vii. 100, 207, 244, 411–415, 518, 583, 639–647, 691, 719
Finch, Sir J., speaker of H. of Commons, iii. 132, 210, 226, 231
Fines, Statute of, 4 Henry VII., ii. 751
Finlaison, Mr; his annuity calculations, vii. 244
Finnit, Sir John, iii. 64
Firearms, manufacture of, vi. 837, 838
Firebrace, Sir Basil; bribed by East India Company, iv. 51
Fires of 1835–1841, destructive, vii. 590
Fish, importance of salt-water and river, in Lent, ii. 191
Fish, Simon, author of *The Supplication of Beggars*, ii. 717
Fisher, bishop of Rochester, ii. 378, 385, 386, 389
———, Captain; discloses plot against Wm. III., iv. 60, 61
Fisheries, vi. 799, 800
——— in 18th century, v. 453–455, 463
———; productiveness on coast of Britain, vii. 528, 535
Fishing, at an early period after the Conquest, i. 599, 560
Fitzalan, Thomas, son of Earl of Arundel, ii. 25, 26, 140
Fitz-Ernest, Robert, slain at Battle of Hastings, i. 215
Fitzgerald, Lord Edward, vi. 97, 123, 125, 127
Fitz-Hamon, Robert, a baron of Henry L., i. 409
Fitzherbert, Anthony, a distinguished lawyer, ii. 763
———, Mrs, death of, vii. 595
———, Mrs; her connection with the Prince of Wales, v. 650, 665, 849
Fitz-John, Eustace, slain at invasion of Wales, i. 443
Fitzmorris, a brother of the Earl of Desmond, ii. 651
Fitz-Nicholas, R., sent to the Emir al Nassir, i. 522, 523
Fitz-Osbert, William, surnamed Longbeard, i. 512
Fitz-Ralph, Richard, archbishop of Armagh, ii. 106
Fitz-Robert, William, son of Duke Robert, i. 412–417
Fitz-Stephen, captain of the *Blanche-Nef*, i. 414, 415
———, W., describes London; quoted, i. 589, 642, 668
Fitzurse, Reginald, a murderer of à Becket, i. 455, 456
Fitzwalter, Robert, general of the barons, i. 528, 531
Fitzwater, Lord, a partisan of Perkin Warbeck, ii. 300
Fitzwilliam, Earl, death of, in 1833, vii. 438
———, Sir W.; letter to high-sheriff of Surrey, ii. 541
Five-mile Act, passed October 1665, iii. 696
Flaherty, Mary, death of, in 1845, vii. 739
Flamstead, John, astronomer-royal, iv. 731
Flanders, Baldwin, earl of, i. 412, 413
———, Baldwin, first earl of Flanders, i. 153, 191
———, Guy, count of, i. 720–724
———, Philip, earl of, i. 468
———, Robert, earl of, father-in-law of Canute, i. 386
Flannels, manufacture of, vi. 844, 845
Flatman, T., a painter and poet of 17th century, iii. 882
Flax-manufactures, vi. 844
Flaxman, J., an eminent sculptor; Portrait of, vi. 876–878
———, the artist, death of, in 1826, vii. 219
Fleetwood, Sir William, iii. 117
———, William, bishop of St Asaph, iv. 247
Fleming, a Scottish pirate, warns of Spanish Armada, ii. 675

GENERAL INDEX. 115

FLEMING, Sir William, iii. . . . 263, 340
Flemish peasantry; scene on the Brussels road, v. . 686
——— troops, march of, v. . . . 794
FLETA, quoted, i. 817
FLETCHER, Andrew, lord justice-clerk of Scotland, iv. 397
——— Giles, a poet, cousin of the dramatist, iii. 600
——— John, a dramatic writer, iii. . 594, 595
——— Lord-advocate, iii. . . . 661
——— of Saltoun, iii. 736, 770–772, 793; iv. 44, 147, 173
——— Phineas, a poet, iii. . . . 600
——— Richard, bishop of London, ii. . . 885
FLEURY, Cardinal, prime-minister of France, iv. 371, 394, 438
Flodden Field, Battle of; illustration, ii. . 327–330
FLORENCE, Duke of, iii. 51
FLOWERDEW, John, of Hethersett, ii. . . 485
FLOYDE, Edward, a Catholic, iii. . . . 84
FOGGE, Captain, iii. 290
FOIX, Gaston de, seizes Beziers; enters Bayonne, ii. 59, 85, 91
Folcland, i. 248
FOLEY, Mr Paul, speaker of the House of Commons, iv. 50
FOLIOT, Gilbert, bishop of London, i. . 448, 470, 471
FOLLETT, Sir William W., death of, in 1845, vii. . 732
Folly House, Blackwall; View of, iv. . . 771
Fontainebleau, Treaty of; England and France, iv. 815, 820
Fontenoy, Battle of, fought 1745, iv. . . 451, 452
Fonthill, View of, vi. 869
Fonts, Norman-English, i. . . . 552, 553
FOOKES, Sir Henry, iii. 37
Fools, dance of; court fool and buffoon; illustration, ii. 257, 262
FORBES, Admiral, refuses to sign the death-warrant upon Admiral Byng, iv. . . . 563
FORBES, Brigadier, iv. 575
———, Duncan, lord-president, iv. 398, 473, 503, 514, 515
FORBIN; he is forced to put back to Dunkirk, iv. . 196
Ford, Colonel, defeats the Marquis de Confians, iv. 582
———, John, a dramatic writer of 17th century, iii. 594, 507
———, Thomas, a musician of 17th century, iii. . 566
Foreign trade, vi. 795
FOREST, a friar; burnt in Smithfield, ii. . . 403
———, Henry; burnt at St Andrews, ii. . . 747
Forest, New, description of, i. . . 387–389, 401
Forgery, Peel's bill to circumscribe punishment for, vii. 290
———, statutes concerning, vi. . . . 784
FOROJULIENSIS, Titus Livius, a Latin chronicler, ii. 208
Forres, ancient obelisk at, near Cruden, i. . . 221
FORSTER, Mr, raises a rebellion in Northumberland, iv. 292
———, Sir John, a warden of the English borders, ii. 594
FORTESCUE, Sir John, an adherent of James I., iii. 3, 18, 19
———, ———, chief-justice, ii. . 111, 163, 253, 517
Forth, View of the, iv. 462
Fortifications, sieges, strategy; illustrations, &c., ii. 246, 248
Forty-shilling freeholders, vii. . . . 252, 264
FOSTER, Mr Justice, iii. . . . 672, 688
———, Rev. John, death of, in 1843, vii. . . 737
FOTHERBY, Martin, bishop of Salisbury, iii. . 71
Fotheringay Castle; View of, ii. . . . 659
FOULON, M. de, executed by French revolutionists, v. 747
FOWKES, Lieutenant; royalists attempt to bribe him, iii. 282
FOWLER, Sir D., fined £5000 in reign of Charles I., iii. 525
Fox, Charles James, an eminent statesman—
iv. 876, 881; v. 8, 18, 22, 56, 63, 74, 185, 294, 303, 336, 338, 341, 377, 380, 393, 397, 399, 451, 544, 555, 584–586, 753, 848–855, 898–900; vi. 1, 174, 181, 307, 314, 315, 349, 350, 749–794
———, Commodore, captures forty French ships, iv. . 527
———, Dr Edward, bishop of Hereford, ii. . 367, 375, 725
———, George, founder of the sect of Quakers, iii. . 808
———, John, the martyrologist; his letter to Elizabeth, ii. 746
———, ———; his Portrait, iii. . 166, 433
———, Richard, a confidential minister of Henry VII.—
ii. 286, 291, 301, 305, 311, 312, 320, 323, 333
Foy or Fowey River, iii. 317
France, affairs of, vii. 271–283, 422–429, 535–541, 704–706
———, British sympathy with, in 1830, vii. . . 328
———, its territorial limits, vii. . . . 5
———, Spain invaded by, vii. . . 146–152

France, summary of its constitutional history, v. . 738
Franché-Comté, ceded to France by Spain, iii. . 717
Franchise, changes in, on passing of Reform Bill, vii. 365–369
——— in Ireland, corruption of the, vii. . 502–504
FRANCIS I., emperor of Austria, . v. 856, 859; vii. 545
——— I., emperor of Germany, iv. . . . 453
——— I., king of France, ii. 325, 332–337, 345–349, 355, 358–368, 379, 382, 383, 389, 438, 439, 442, 447, 457, 458
FRANCIS II., emperor of Germany, vi. . . 43, 280
——— II., king of France, husband of Mary Stuart, ii. 563
———, Sir Philip, v. . 627–630, 673, 674, 692, 848
———, Sir Philip, death of, vii. . . . 93
Franciscan Friars; Illustration of one, i. . 803, 804
Frankfort, Battle of, fought 1759, iv. . . 583
FRANKLIN, an apothecary, accused of selling poison, iii. 58, 59
———, Benjamin; Portrait of, v. . . 49
———, B., the American philosopher, iv. 734, 735, 828
———, Captain, the navigator; Portrait, vii. 215, 223
———'s Lodging, No. 7 Craven Street; View of, v. 94
Franks, the, of Teutonic descent, i. . . 138
FRASER, General, falls in battle against Americans, v. 208
———, Sir Simon, died as a traitor, i. . . 729, 756
FREDERIC II., king of the Two Sicilies, i. . 680
——— IV., king of Denmark, iv. . . 91, 92
——— V., Count Palatine, iii. . . 51, 89, 173
FREDERICK VI. of Denmark and Duke of Holstein, vi. 670, 691
FREDERICK WILLIAM I., king of Prussia, iv. . 414
——— II., king of Prussia—
v. 653, 677–681, 856, 857; vi. 5, 6, 81
——— III., king of Prussia. See also Bonaparte, vi. 686
FREDERICK, Prince of Wales, iv. . 380, 399, 408, 537
——— the Great, king of Prussia—
iv. 414, 415, 447, 448, 561, 575, 583, 800, 814, 815
Free Church of Scotland and its secession, vii. 673, 674
———trade and Protectionist parties, vii. . 175, 633
Freehold Land Scheme, the League's, vii. . 687
Freemen, description of, i. . . . 661
French language, early, termed the 'Romanco,' i. 188
——— Reform Bill, or new electoral law, vii. . 425
——— relations with England, &c., vii. . 539–549
——— Revolution. See Louis XVI. and N. Bonaparte.
——— Revolutions, vi. 278–283
Freyberg, Battle of, fought 1762, iv. . . 815
Friedland, Battle of, fought June 14, 1807, vi. . 393
FRIEND, Sir J.; his concern in the Invasion-plot, iv. 62, 64
FRITHRIC, abbot of St Alban's, i. . . 301
FRIZELL, William, iii. . . . 544
FROBISHER, Martin, the celebrated navigator, ii. 627, 771, 789
FROISSART, the chronicler, . i. 749, 849; ii. 7
FRONTINUS, Julius, subdued the Silures, i. . . 44
FROST, Mr; attacks Newport with 7000 followers, vii. 568, 569
Fruit, introduction of foreign, ii. . . . 806
FRY, Mr; his account of the Habeas Corpus Act, iii. 833
———, Mrs, death of, in 1845, vii. . . 739
FULK, earl of Anjou, i. . . 412, 413, 416, 417
Fullanham, now Fulham-on-the-Thames, i. . 161
FULLARTON, Colonel; his conduct in India, v. 634–636
FULTON, R.; his efforts for steam-navigation, vi. 630, 831
Funeral, monks at a; illustration, ii. . . 267
Furniture, vi. 920
——— Specimens of—
i. 634, 864; iii. 617–619, 622, 887; iv. 757
FUSELI, Henry, an eminent historical painter, vi. 872
———, the artist, death of, in 1825, vii. . 220
Fyvie Castle, Montrose nearly taken prisoner at, iii. 336

GABRIEL, a courtier of Charles I., iii. . . 94
Gael, its orthography uncertain, i. . . 18
Gaeta, city of, surrenders to the Austrians, iv. . 184
GAGE, Colonel, iii. 201, 420
———, General, governor of Boston, v. 76, 79, 106, 109–111
———, Lord, iv. 408
———, Mr G., agent of James I. to the Vatican, iii. 89
GAGES, Count de, iv. 453
GAINSBOROUGH, a celebrated English painter, v. 524

	PAGE
GALDRIC, King Henry's chaplain, i.	412
GALILEO, a celebrated philosopher, iii.	611
GALKE, secretary to Hanoverian embassy in 1713, iv.	258
GALLAS, Count, iv.	340
Galleys of the Romans, i.	30, 31, 162-165
GALLOWAY, Patrick, a fanatic preacher, iii.	13, 468
GALT, John, death of, in 1839, vii.	601
GALWAY, Lord, iv.	49, 113, 164, 171, 216
GAMA, Vasco de, a Portuguese navigator, ii.	777
GAMAIN, a locksmith of Versailles, v.	888
GAMBIER, James, lord, a British admiral, vi.	385-388, 507
GAMBLE, Mr, chaplain to the famous Monk, iii.	*430
Game-law murders, vii.	586
—— laws, bills against the, vii.	233
—— of 1829, 1830, vii.	269, 296, 688-691
GAMEL, son of Quetel of Meaux, i.	374
Games, rural and manly; illustrations, i.	259, 260
Gaming; with cards, &c.; dice-box delineated, ii.	259, 260
GARDENER, the recorder of London, iii.	163
Gardening, art of, commenced in reign of Elizabeth, iii.	557
Gardens and orchards of the Anglo-Saxons, i.	283
GARDINER, Colonel, killed at battle of Prestonpans, iv.	471
——, Mr, counsel to the Earl of Strafford, iii.	239
——, Stephen, bishop of Winchester, ii.	367, 369, 375, 380, 382, 466, 468, 493, 506, 511, 524, 526, 696
GARGRAVE, Sir Thomas; quoted, ii.	645
GARLAND, condemned as a regicide; not executed, iii.	674, 675
GARNET, Henry, superior of Jesuits in England, iii.	30-32
GARRARD, Lord-mayor, iv.	218
GARRICK, David, the great actor; Portrait of, v.	504
GARRISON, the American advocate against slavery, vii.	385, 386
GARTH, Sir Samuel, a physician, poet, and man of wit, iv.	747
Gas; London Statistics of 1823, vii.	214
GASCOIGNE, George, a poet, iii.	583, 585
——, Lord Chief-justice; his high character, ii.	17
Gascony, wars of English to retain possession of, ii.	8, 19
GASCOYNE, Sir William, Cardinal Wolsey's treasurer, ii.	372
Gaslight, introduction of, vii.	40
Gas-lighting, vi.	832
GASSION, M. de, at battle of Ramilies, 1706, iv.	169
GATES, General, a gallant American officer, v.	210, 211
——, Sir John; executed, ii.	506
GATHEREN, D. Darvel; name of crucifix in S. Wales, ii.	403
GAUDEN, John, bishop of Worcester, iii.	607
Gange question, the broad and narrow, vii.	697
Gaul, Cæsar's conquest of, i.	25
Gaulish hut, as sculptured on the Antonine column, i.	98
Gauls, the; their trade with Britain, &c., i.	25, 60, 101-104
GAULTIER, Abbé, proposes peace of Utrecht to France, iv.	233
GAUNT, Elizabeth, burned at Tyburn, iii.	782
GAVISTON, Sir Piers, a knight of Gascony, i.	730-734
GAWDY, Queen Elizabeth's serjeant, iii.	660
GAY, John, a poet and dramatist, iv.	746
GED, William, discovers art of stereotyping, iv.	684
GELL, Sir John, a parliamentarian, iii.	291
——, Sir William, death of, in 1836, vii.	600
Gomblours, Battle of; Dutch defeated here, ii.	650
GEMINUS, T., earliest English copper-plate engraver, iii.	577
General Assembly of the Church of Scotland, vii.	672, 673
—— Election of 1818, vii.	91, 92
Geneva, church of; James I. refers to its festivals, iii.	15
GENLIS, Madame, her flight from Paris, vi.	4
Genoa; siege of Naples, &c., ii.	368
Genoese carracks defeated by Duke of Bedford, ii.	35
GENTILESCHI, Artemisia, a famous painter, iii.	569
——, Horatio, an Italian painter, iii.	569
GEOFFREY, a son of Geoffrey Plantagenet, i.	442, 443
——, bishop of Contance, i.	381
——, natural son of Henry II., i.	479, 481, 485, 507
——, of Monmouth, an English chronicler, i.	8, 11
——, Prince, son of Henry II., i.	452, 468, 470-476
Geographical discoveries of 1820-1826, vii.	214, 215
Geology, iv.	736
——, science of, vii.	745
George, illustration of the, iii.	398
GEORGE I., king of Great Britain, iv.	281-374, 588, 679
GEORGE II., king of Great Britain, iv.	373-588, 679
—— III., king of Great Britain— iv. 539, 544-548, 795-898; v. 100-403, 584-738, 757-781, 797-824, 897-901; vi. 1-747; vii. 97, 113, 195
GEORGE IV., king of Great Britain— v. 15, 396, 397, 648-669, 707, 851; vi. 76-78, 565-747
GEORGE IV.; Portrait, vii.	14-125, 262-264, 293, 294
Georgia, colony of; its establishment, iv.	676
GERARD, a foreigner, persecuted for his religion, i.	557
——, a suspected Jesuit, iii.	21, 30
——, Captain, death of, in 1839, vii.	593
Gerberoy, Castle of, besieged by the Conqueror, i.	384
GERE, sheriff of Yorkshire, organises an insurrection, iii.	693
GERMAINE, Lord George; Portrait of, v.	221
Germanic tribes, their contests with the Romans, i.	26
GERMANUS, bishop of Auxerre, i.	57
Germany, formation of the Commercial League of, vii.	543
——, Protestants of, &c., ii.	141, 389
GERMINE, T., present at trial of Bishop of Lincoln, iii.	164
GERONTIUS, and other British chiefs, treachery of, i.	55
GERRARD, engages with others to murder Cromwell, iii.	416
Gheriah, taken by the English, v.	617
GHEST, Laurence; burnt, ii.	699
Ghiznee, siege and storming of, vii.	623, 628
GHIZNI, dynasty of, v.	598, 599
GIAMBELLI, F., fortifies Thames against the Armada, iii.	673
GIB, John, groom of the bed-chamber to James I., iii.	14
——, Rev. Adam, iv.	625
GIBBON, Edward, the historian, v.	89, 516, 517
GIBBONS, Grinling, a high-class sculptor, iii.	883
——, Orlando, a musician of 16th century, iii.	566
GIBBS, James, an architect of 18th century, iv.	697, 698
Gibraltar, View of the Bay and Straits of, v.	366, 396
GIFFORD, Henry, an adherent of Henry I., i.	405
——, Walter, archbishop of York, i.	408, 688
——, William, editor of the *Quarterly Review*, death of, in 1826, vii.	318
GILBERT, English, or Anglicus, a writer on medicine, i.	845
——, Sir H., step-brother of Sir W. Raleigh, iii.	538
——, Sir Humphrey, perishes at sea, ii.	791
GILDAS, an ancient British historian, i.	56, 228, 289, 347, 348
Gildhall, the German, i.	334; ii. 179, 180
GILES, Dr, rector of Chinnor, iii.	304
GILL, Thomas; his improvements in sword-cutlery, vi.	836
GILLESPIE, Rev. Thomas, a Relief minister, iv.	620
Gillyflower, introduction of, by Flemings, ii.	800
Gin Act; its passing and revision, iv.	395, 438
GINCKEL, General, at battle of Boyne, iv.	26, 33, 34, 53-55
GIOVACCHINO, a celebrated seer, i.	492
Gipsies, statute of Henry VIII. against, ii.	759
GIRALDUS CAMBRENSIS, quoted, i.	12, 586, 695
Girondists or the Gironde, v.	885
GISLEBERT, professor of theology, i.	606
GLADESDALE, Sir W., altercation between, and Joan of Arc, ii.	66
GLADSTANES, Mr G., archbishop of St Andrews, iii.	451, 466
GLADSTONE, Mr W. R.; Portrait, vii.	608-719
GLANVILLE, Ranulph de, i.	471, 484, 485, 568, 573, 574
——, Serjeant, iii.	120, 212
GLAS, Rev. John, founder of the Glasites, iv.	620
Glasgow Cathedral, View of the, vii.	515
——, foundation of the university of, ii.	199
Glass, English glass-works imitated in France, vi.	840
——, English, improved by artists from Venice, iii.	868
——, used by Anglo-Saxons, i.	310, 325
Glastonbury Abbey; execution of Whiting, &c., ii.	411, 412
——; illustration of, &c., i.	170-242
Glee Club, the, established in 1787, vi.	882
GLENCAIRN, Earl of, joins confederacy against Mary Queen of Scots, ii.	581, 603
GLENCOE, Macdonald of, iv.	45
Glencoe, View of, &c., iv.	44-46, 47
GLENDOWER, Owen, a descendant of the Welsh princes, ii.	9-18
GLENELG, Lord, retirement of, vii.	555
GLENGARRY, at battle of Dunblane, iv.	298

GENERAL INDEX.

GLENHAM, Sir Thomas, governor of Oxford, iii. . 355
GLENLYON, Campbell of, massacres Scots at Glencoe, iv. 46
Glenshiel, Battle of, fought 1719, iv. . . 334
Gloucester, from an old print, iii. . . . 306
GLOUCESTER, Gilbert de Clare, earl of, i. . 683, 686–688
———, Henry Stuart, duke of, iii. . . . 677
———, H., duke of, ii. 44, 51, 52, 54, 57–59, 79–84
———, Richard de Clare, earl of, i. . . 683
———, Robert, earl of, i. . . 416, 423–435
———, Thomas Plantagenet, duke of, i. . 791–795
———, William, duke of, iv. . . 72, 73, 96
———, William Henry, duke of, v. 21, 75, 145
Gloucestershire, jurisdiction of Wales over, iii. . 43
GLOVER, Richard, author of *Leonidas*, iv. 819; v. 102
GLYNNE, Mr, iii. 237, 261, 369
GODDARD, Colonel; his active conduct in India, v. 628–630
GODERICH, Lord, prime-minister; Portrait, vii. 236, 240–243
GODFREY, Mr, killed at the siege of Namur, iv. . 53
———, Sir Edmondbury; murdered, iii. . 718, 719
GODOLPHIN, Sydney, earl of—
    iii. 759; iv. 48, 96, 127, 148, 225, 252, 626
GODSCHALL, Sir Robert, iv. 435
GODWIN and EDMUND, sons of Harold, i. . 365–367
———, Earl, originally a cow-herd, i. . 184–194
———, William, death of, in 1836, vii. . . 604
Gold, exportation of, in 1824, vii. . . . 180
GOLDSMITH, Oliver, the eminent poet and writer, v. 502
Gomarists, a sect sprung from a Leyden professor, iii. 48
GONDOMAR, count of Monterey; his pleasantries, iii. 73, 102
GOODMAN, concerned in the Invasion-plot, iv. . 63, 67
———, John, a seminary priest, iii. . . . 232
GOODWIN, Sir Francis; his election declared void, iii. 18
GOOR, General, killed at battle of Schellenberg, iv. . 152
GORDON, Duke of, surrenders Edinburgh Castle, iv. 16, 187
———, Jane, duchess of; Portrait, v. . . 714
———, Lord George; the London riots, v. 305–312, 664
———, Lord Lewis, a partisan of young Pretender, iv. 492
——— of Earlstone, implicated in Rye-house Plot, iii. 756
———, Sir John; beheaded, ii. . . 574, 575
GORE, Sir John, arrested, iii. 431
GORGES, Brigadier, iv. 171
———, Sir Ferdinando, forsakes his friend Essex, ii. 686
GORING, Colonel, iii. . 217–267, 291, 317, 362, 383, 400
———, Sir George, a companion of James I., iii. . 64
GORTON, an Antinomian; imprisoned iii. . . 807
GORTZ, Baron, Voltaire's description of, iv. . 317, 329
GOSFORD, Lord; his Canadian commission, vii. . 551
GOSNOLD, Captain, iii. 538
Gospel, Society for Propagating in Foreign Parts, vi. 765
GOSSON, Stephen; his severe attack on music, iii. . 566
Goths, the, i. 138
GOUGE, Dr, iii. 309
GOUGH, Sir Hugh; Portrait, vii. . 617, 713–715
GOULBURN, Mr, chancellor of the Exchequer, vii.198, 608,&c.
GOURDON, Adam, a warlike baron, i. . . 687, 688
GOURNEY, T., and W. OGLE, murder Edward II., i. 745, 755
Governesses, position of, vii. . . . 657, 747
Government and Church, struggles of, vii. . . 679
——— circular issued in 1834; its reception, vii. 407
———, condition of the, in 1819, vii. . . 103
——— See Constitution, &c.
GOWAN, a Covenanter, hanged, iii. . . . 682
GOWER, John Leveson, earl, iv. . . . 436
———, John; Portrait of, i. . . 851, 852
———, Richard Hall, death of, in 1833, vii. . 439
———, Sir John, impeaches Earl of Portland, iv. 104
Gowrie Conspiracy, the, iii. 451
GOWRIE, William, earl of; beheaded, ii. . 654, 690
GOWRY, Earl of, escape of James VI. from his violence, iii. 6
GRACE DARLING, story of, vii. . . 587, 588
GRÆME, Hector, of Harlow, betrays Northumberland, iii. 630
GRAFTON, A. H. Fitzroy, duke of, iv. 839, 853, 880; v. 14, 134
———, Henry Fitzroy, duke of, iii. . . . 773
GRAHAM, George, bishop of Orkney, iii. . 206, 484
——— of Claverhouse, iii. 757; iv. 7, 15, 16, 43
———, Patrick, bishop of St Andrews, ii. . 154

GRAHAM, Sir James; Portrait, vii. . 373, 564, 608, &c.
———, Sir Richard, iii. 91
GRAMMONT, Duke of; slain at battle of Fontenoy, iv. 439,451
Grampound, Cornwall, a borough of wealth in 1621, iii. 177
GRANBY, J. M., marquis of, iv. . 800, 841, 876–878, 897
GRANDVAL, M. de, shot for conspiring against William
    III., iv. 37
GRANGE, Kirkaldy of, and Mary Stuart, ii. 601, 632, 649
Grange Park, Hants, View of, vi. . . . 893
GRANT, Colonel, mortally wounded at Carthagena, iv. 427
———, J., calculates pop. of England and Wales, iii. 654
———, John, of Norbrook, near Warwick, iii. 23, 28, 30
———, Mr Charles, colonial secretary, vii. . . 459
———, Mrs, of Laggan, death of, vii. . . 601
———, Sir Robert, death of, in 1838, vii. . . 596
———, Sir William, an eminent lawyer, vi. . 789
GRANTMESNIL, Alberic de, i. . . 383, 568
———, Hugh de, Earl of Norfolk, i. . 370, 394
———, Yvo de, i. 408
Granville, View of, vi. 217
GRATTAN, Henry, the Irish orator and statesman, vii. 126,194
———; his speech on Catholic Emancipation, vii. 771
Gravelines, Battle of; the French signally defeated, ii. 537
GRAVES, Admiral; his action with Count de Grasse, v. 354
GRAY, John de, archbishop of Canterbury, i. 521, 523, 559
———, Lord Leonard; beheaded, ii. . . 426
———, Lord R.; beheaded at Pontefract Castle, ii. !118, 121
———, Lord, severely wounded at battle of Pinkie, ii. 461, 402
———, Sir John, slain at the battle of St Albans, ii. 101
———, Sir Patrick; his mission to Douglas fails, ii. 135
———, Sir Ralph, a Yorkist; beheaded, ii. . 100, 101
———, Thomas, the distinguished English poet, v. . 502
Greece, affairs of, vii. . . . 152, 236–240, 701
———, settlement of, vii. 234, 285
Greek language; first taught in England, ii. . 815, 816
——— Testament, first edition of, in Polyglot, ii. . 816
GREENE, Robert, a dramatic writer, iii. . 578, 586
———, gold medal awarded to; illustration, v. . 363
GREENHILL, John, a painter of 17th century, iii. . 892
GREENWAY, an Englishman, killed in an affray, iii. 416
Greenwich, Treaty of, executed, ii. . . . 436
GREG, William; hanged for high treason, iv. . 194
GRÉGOIRE, Abbé, one of the revolutionary priests, v. 826, 888
Gregorian Calendar; its introduction into England, iv. 541
GREGORY, Dr Olinthus, death of, in 1838, vii. . 593
——— VII., Hildebrand, pope, i. . 206, 207, 549
——— IX., Pope, i. 803
——— XI., Pope; schism at his death, ii. . . 137
——— XIII., Pope; sends troops to assist Irish, ii.651,652
——— XVI., Pope, and the emperor of Russia, vii. 702
——— the Great, i. 145, 230
Grenada, New, Spanish revolution in, vii. . . 50
GRENVILLE, George, premier of England, iv. 816, 819, 821,
    827, 837, 849, 850, 862, 886, 888, 897; v. 51
———, J., resigns his seat at Board of Trade, iv. 556
———, Lord, vii. . . . 7, 11, 48, 135, 438
Grenville party, coalition with the, vii. . . 135
GRENVILLE, Sir R., colonises island of Roanoak, ii. 791
———, George, treasurer of the navy, iv. . 556
———, W. W. lord, v. 799; vi. 307–320, 350, 355–362
GRESHAM, Sir Richard, lord-mayor, ii. . . 403
———, Sir Thomas, builder of Royal Exchange, ii. 787, 788
———, founder of Gresham College, iv. 718
GREVILLE, Sir Fulke, chancellor of the Exchequer, iii. 55
Grey banquet at Edinburgh, vii. . . . 419
GREY DE RUTHYN, Lord, ii. . . . 9–11, 13
———, Earl, vii. 7, 59, 232, 233, 335–401, 407–420, 726, 731
———, Lady C., wife of Lord Herbert, ii. 499, 568, 569, 617
———, Lady Jane, ii. . 499–504, 509, 510, 512, 517, 518
———, Lady Mary, youngest sister of Lady Jane Grey, ii. 623
———, Lord, implicated in Rye-house Plot, iii. 740, 771, 778
Grey ministry, vii. 337–401, 407
GREY, of Wilton, Thomas, Lord, iii. . 5, 7, 8, 12–15
———, William, Lord, ii. . . 485, 495, 560
———, Sir Thomas of Heton; beheaded, ii. . . 29
GRIBELIN, engraver of first complete set of cartoons, iv. 709

HISTORY OF ENGLAND.

GRIFFIN, Charles, death of, in 1840, vii. . . 601
———, Lord, a partisan of the Pretender, iv. . 197
GRIFFITH, king of Wales, i. . . . 194, 195
———, son of Owen Glendower, ii. . . . 17
GRIG, or GREGORY, a powerful king of Scotland, i. . 219
Grignan, brigade of, iv. 157
GRIMALDI; his retirement from the stage, vii. . . 306
GRIMANI, Marco, papal legate, arrives in Scotland, ii. 437
GRIMBALD, an eminent scholar, i. . . . 305
GRIMOALD, Nicholas, a poet of 16th century, iii. . 582
GRIMSTON, H., speaker of H. of Commons, iii. 212,227, *430
GRINDAL, Edmund, archbishop of Canterbury, ii. 744, 745
Grisogono, plan of the church of, i. . . . 312
GROSTETE, Robert, a cultivator of mathematics, i. . 843
GROTIUS, Hugo, the great publicist, iii. . . 174
GROUCHY, a French marshal, vi. . . 704–709
GROVE; accused of conspiring to murder Charles II., iii. 717
———, Captain, executed, iii. 419
GRUSHILL, Sir R.; his effigy in Hoveringham church, ii. 241
GRYMBALD, abbot of St Albans, i. . . . 604
Gualior, a strong Mahratta fortress, v. . . 629, 630
GUALO, the pope's legate, i.' . . . 531, 671
Guelphs; their close alliance to the Whig party, iv. 167
GUERICKE, Otto von, inventor of the air-pump, iv. . 728
GUEST, General, governor of Edinburgh Castle, iv. 463, 478
GUIDO RENI, a celebrated painter, iii. . . 567
GUIDO's improved scale of musical notation, i. . 633
Guienne and Gascony, wars in, ii. . . 8, 19, 20, 85
GUIENNE, William, earl of Poictiers, i. . . 401
GUILDFORD, F. North, earl of; Portrait of, iv. 852, 876, 881
———, Frederic Lord, premier—
  iv. 881; v. 54, 95, 98–101, 228, 369, 374, 376, 393, 399
Guildhall, Queen Victoria at, vii. . . . 584
Guilford, Battle of, fought March 15, 1781, v. . 348, 349
GUILFORD, Lady, dismissed by Louis XII., ii. . 331
Guillotine, the adopted in France, v. . . 859
Guinea, depreciation of the, vi. . . . 807, 817
——— coin, first struck in 1662, iii. . . . 866
GUISCARD, Marquis de, stabs Mr Harley, iv. . 230, 231
GUISE, cardinal of Lorraine, brother of the duke, ii. 458
———, Duke of, ii. . . . 458, 533–535, 570–572
———, General, heads an attack on Carthagena, iv. 426
———, Mary of, queen of James V. of Scotland, iii. 644
GUIZOT, M.; Portrait, vii. . . . 704–709
———, M.; quoted, i. . . 246, 256, 355, 563, 575
———, M.; quotations from, iii. . . 497, 499, 509
GUNDULPH, bishop of Rochester, i. . . . 572, 615
Gunpowder Plot, iii. . . 8, 12, 17, 19, 20–32, 242
Guns, manufacture of, in Birmingham, vi. . . 837, 838
GUNTER, Edmund, an eminent mathematician, iii. . 717
———, Major, slain in battle of Chalgrove Field, iii. 304
GURDON, Bertrand de, shoots King Richard, i. . 514
GURTH, brother of Harold II., i. . 188, 191, 194, 212, 215
GUSTAVUS ADOLPHUS, king of Sweden, iii. . 146, 173
——— III. of Sweden, v. . 725, 729–731, 777–779, 857
GUTHRUN, a Danish king, i. . . . 157–164
GUTHRY, bishop of Moray, deposed; hanged, iii. 484, 682
GUY, count of Ponthieu, takes Harold prisoner, i. . 197
Gwalior, British intervention at, vii. . . . 630
Gwyddyl, the, settle in Scotland, i. . . . 9
GWYNN, Nell, an actress, and mistress of Charles II., iii. 706
GWYNN, John, his architectural plans, vi. . . 870
GWYNNED, Owen, king of the Welsh, i. . . 443, 451
GYLLENBORG, count, a Swedish ambassador, iv. 317, 318

HAAK, Mr T, suggests institution of Royal Society, iv. 722
Habeas Corpus Act, first suspension of, iv. . . 10
——— Suspension Bill, vii. . . 54–50, 79, 80
——— writ of, iii. 833, 834
HACKER, Colonel, a parliamentarian, iii. . 395, 678
Hackney-coaches introduced into London, iii. 543, 544
HACO, king of Norway, i. 704, 705
———, nephew of Harold, i. . . . 197, 199
Haddenrig, in Teviotdale; Douglas faction defeated
  here, ii. 433
HADDICK, General, lays Berlin under contribution, iv. 569

HADDINGTON, John Ramsay, viscount, iii. . 37, 38, 71
HADDOCK, Robert, reported to preach in his sleep, iii. 20
HADFIELD, a maniac, his attempt to shoot the king, vi. 147
HADLEY, John, inventor of the quadrant, iv. . 733
HADRIAN, a Roman emperor; Profile of, &c., i. . 47
Hague, Treaty of the, signed March 1609, iii. . 48
———, View of the, v. 594
HAILES, Lord; quoted, i. 708, 709
HAINAULT and HOLLAND, the count of, ii. . 35, 36, 57
——— Count of, entertains Queen Isabella, i. . 742
——— Jacqueline of, wife of Duke of Brabant, ii. 57–60
HALE, Lord Chief-justice, quoted, vi. . . . 776
———, Sir Matthew, iii. . 416, 431*, 654, 708, 829, 844
HALES, Judge, attorney-general, ii. . . . 371, 510
———, Mr John, a theological controversialist, iii. 178, 610
———, Sir Edward, lieutenant of the Tower, iii. 790, 799
———, Sir Robert, treasurer of England, i. . . 787
———, Sir Thomas, one of the members for Kent, iv. 106
HALFDEN, or HALFDANE, divides Northumbrian territory, i. 157
HALNED, Mr, a disciple of Richard Brothers, vi. . 757
Halidon Hill, Battle of, i. 756
HALIFAX, Charles Montague, earl of, iv. . 135, 626
———, George Montague, earl of, v. . . . 14
———, George Savile, earl of—
  iii. 733, 740, 759, 782, 829; iv. 18, 19, 56
Halifax, its population, iii. 655
HALL, Arthur, M.P.; case of, iv. . . . 636, 637
———, Joseph; his Portrait, &c., iii. . 491, 603, 802
———, Rev. Robert, an eloquent preacher, vi. . 770
———, Robert, death of, in 1834, vii. . . . 408
———, Timothy, bishop of Oxford, iv. . . . 590
HALLAM, Mr, vii. 742
———, Mr, historical observations of, i. 574, 575, 803,
  810, 811, 885; ii. 156; iii. 254, 586, 606, 613
HALLEY, Edmund, the astronomer, iv. . . 732, 733
Hamburg, great fire at, in 1842, vii. . . . 718
———, View of, vi. 345
HAMILTON, a partisan of the young Pretender, iv. . 491
———, archbishop of St Andrews, ii. . . 645, 646
———, archbishop of St Andrews, hanged, iii. . 435
———, bishop of Galloway, iii. 485
———, Captain, death of, vii. 736
———, Colonel, v. 251, 292, 301
———, Dr, his work on the National Debt, vi. 793, 794
———, Duke of, . . iii. 150, 189–199, 250, 251,
  309, 361, 352, 400; iv. 7, 43, 147, 173, 174, 187, 196, 251
HAMILTON, Duke, opposes use of torture in Scotland, iii. 756
———, Gerard, prophesies American revolt, iv. . 850
———; his advice to the Covenanters, iii. . . 730
———, James, author of the Hamiltonian system,
  death of, in 1829, vii. 318
HAMILTON, Lord Basil, iv. 90
———, Lord C., son of Duke of Chatelherault, ii. 645, 646
———, Mr John, minister at Newburn, iii. . . 184
———, of Bothwell-Haugh; shoots Regent Murray, ii. 632
———, Patrick, abbot of Ferne; burnt, ii. . . 747
———, Sir Charles, captures the island of Goree, vi. 153
———, Sir George, a Catholic, iii. . . 270, 271
———, Sir John, opposes acts of Perth Assembly, iii. 470
———, Sir Patrick, slain, ii. 352
———, Sir Patrick, iii. 647
HAMMOND, Colonel, iii. . . 333, 364, 375, 386
———, Colonel Robert, nephew of preceding, iii. 364
Hampden Clubs, vii. 29–31
HAMPDEN, concerned in Rye-house Plot, iii. . 755
———, John, iii. . 123, 177–179, 212, 291, 304
———, Mr, chairman to the House of Commons, iv. 4, 9
Hampton Court, iii. 64
———-Court Palace, iv. 122
HANCOCK, John; Portrait of, v. . . . 84, 110
Hangings, paper and leather, iii. . . . 618
HANMER, Sir Thomas, speaker of House of Commons, iv. 262
Hanover, ordinance regulating love-affairs of officers
  in army of, vii. 702
HANOVER, Sophia, electress of, iv. . . . 272

GENERAL INDEX. 119

HANSARD, Luke, the great printer, death of, in 1828, vii. 314
HANSARDS, prosecution of the, vii. . . 526, 580-583
Hanseatic League, the powerful, ii. . . . 94, 179
Hanwell Metropolitan Lunatic Asylum, vii. . . 304
HARCLAY, Sir Andrew, i. 741
HARCOURT, Jacques de; his baronial castle, &c., ii. . 49
———, Marquis d', agent of Louis XIV., iv. . 92
———, Mr, iv. 88
———, Sir Simon, Earl of, iv. . . . 237
HARDICANUTE, son of Canute, by Queen Emma, i. 184-186
HARDING, John; his *Metrical Chronicle of England*, ii. 209
HARDINGE, Sir Henry, vii. . . . 330, 629, 713-715
HARDINGTON'S mission to the Emir al Nassir, i. . 522
HARDRADA, Harold, king of Norway, i. . . 208, 209
Hardwick Hall, Derbyshire; illustration, ii. . . 849
HARDWICKE, Lord; quoted, iv. 78, 201
———, Philip York, earl of, iv. . . 550, 560
Hardwicke State-papers, iii. 14
HARDY, Thomas, death of, in 1832, vii. . . . 437
Hare Stone, Cornwall, i. 97
Harewood House, View of, vi. 864
Harfleur, town and fortress of, capitulates, &c., ii. 29, 35, 39
HARGRAVE, Mr; his parliamentary tract, iii. . . 841
HARIOT, Thomas, the traveller and algebraist, iv. . 717
Harlaw, Battle of; Lord of the Isles defeated, ii. . 132
HARLAY, a negotiator at Treaty of Ryswick, iv. . 69
HARLEY, Edward, a partisan of Sir R. Walpole, iv. . 418
———, Thomas; his mission to court of France, iv. 246
HARMAN, Sir J., wounded in a battle with the Dutch, iii. 698
HAROLD HAREFOOT, king of England, i. . . 184-186
——— II., king of England, i. . . 188, 191-215
———, son of the king of Denmark, i. . 371, 396
HARRACH, Count, an Austrian ambassador, iv. . . 94
HARRINGTON, Lord; his grant for coining brass farthings, iii. 52
HARRINGTON, Sir James, author of the *Oceana*, iii. . 612
———, Sir John; his interview with Elizabeth, ii. 684
———, Sir John, iii. 627
HARRIS, Mr George, an Invasion-plot conspirator, iv. 61
———, Mr Howel, assistant of George Whitefield, iv. 623
———, Sir Thomas, a partisan of Charles II., iii. 419
HARRISON, John, a skilful mechanic, v. . 496-498
———, Major, iii. . 332, 388, 404, 421, 427, 671, 676
HARSNET, an enemy of the archbishop of Canterbury, iii. 475
HARTLIB, Samuel, a friend of Milton, iii. 424, 557, 558
Harvests, review of successive, vii. . . . 565
HARVEY, Dr W., discoverer of circulation of the blood, ... iii. 616; iv. 718
Hasbain, Battle of, gained by Duke of Burgundy, ii. 20
HASELL, a partisan of Charles I., iii. . . . 302
HASELRIG, Hampden, iii. . . . 182, 319, 426
HASTING, a northern sea-king or viking, i. . 162-165
Hastings, Battle of, i. 213-215
———, in Sussex, View of, &c., i. . . 210, 212
HASTINGS, Lord, ii. . . 106, 112, 113, 118-121
———, Lord; beheaded at Durham, ii. . . 17
———, Marquis of, governor-general of India, vii. 65-78
———, Sir Edward, a councillor of Queen Mary, ii. 515
———, Warren, governor-general of India, v. 598, 614-657, 672-676, 693, 694, 718, 719, 770-773, 820-824
———, Warren, death of, vii. 93
Hats, notice respecting the manufacture of, ii. . 194
HATTON, Mrs, wife of Sir E. Coke; her wealth, iii. 59, 68
———, Sir C., vice-chamberlain, . ii. 660; iii. 62, 584
HATZFELDT; his conduct at the siege of Lippe, iii. 174
Havanna, View of; capitulates to English, iv. . 808, 809
HAVERSHAM, John Thompson, lord, iv. 80, 166, 178, 205
HAWES, Stephen, a poet of sixteenth century, ii. . 836
HAWKE, Sir Edward, iv. . . 554, 559, 569, 573, 578, 846
Hawking, i. 342
———; illustrations, iii. 640
HAWKINS, Captain William of Plymouth, ii. . 760
———, Sir John; Portrait of, &c., ii. 673, 680, 771, 787
HAWKSBEE, discovers production of light by friction, iv. 734
HAWKSMOOR, Nicholas, a distinguished architect, iv. 698
HAWLEY; at battle of Falkirk, iv. . 492, 494, 499, 525

HAXEY, T., incurs displeasure of Richard II., ii. 156, 157
HAY, earl of Errol, of a Norman family, i. . . 220
———, earl of Kinnoul, lord chancellor, iii. . . 477
———, Lord Charles, tried by court-martial, iv. . 585
———, Mr, a servant of the young Pretender, iv. . 501
———, Mr R. W., colonial secretary, vii. . . 190
HAYDON, the historical painter, death of, vii. . 734
HAYLS, a portrait-painter of 17th century, iii. . 882
HAYMAN, Sir Peter, reprimands Sir John Finch, iii. 141, 142
HAYTER, Thomas, bishop of Norwich, iv. . 539, 545
HAZLITT, William, death of, in 1830, vii. . . 443
HEALE, king's serjeant, iii. 9
HEALEY, Dr, the Radical leader, vii. . . 105, 108
Hearth-tax, abolished by William III., iv. . . 10
———, voted in perpetuity to the king, iii. . 685
HEATH, attorney-general, iii. . . . 119, 143
———, Nicholas, bishop of Worcester, ii. 493, 526, 539
HEATHCOTE, George, alderman, iv. . . . 475
———, Sir Gilbert, alderman, iv. . . . 217
HEBER, Bishop, death of, in 1826; Portrait, vii. 221, 222
HEBERT, a French revolutionist, vi. . . . 54-56
Hebrides; ruins of Monastery of Iona, &c., ii. 132, 133
———, the residence of sea-kings, i. . . . 170
HEDGES, Sir Charles, secretary of state, iv. . 96, 101, 127
Hedgley-Moor, Lord Montague defeats Sir R. Percy at, ii. 101
HEEMSKIRK, Dutch minister at Paris, iv. . . 96
HIGHAM, Richard, a heretic, ii. 700
HEINSIUS, a particular friend of William III., iv. 73, 149
HELIE DE ST SAEN, a Norman nobleman, i. . . 412
———, lord of La Flèche, i. 401
HEMANS, Mrs, death of, in 1835, vii. . . . 602
HEMINGFORD (properly Hemingburgh), Walter, i. . 520
HENDERSON, Alexander, minister at Leuchars, iii. 184, 357
———, Andrew, steward to Earl of Gowrie, ii. 691
———, Mr, a Scottish commissioner, iii. . . 309
Hendlip House, Worcester; View, iii. . . . 30
HENGHAM, Sir Ralph de, grand justiciary, i. . . 694
HENGIST and HORSA, Saxon pirates, i. . 57, 58, 140-142
HENLEY, Lord, on Church reform, vii. . . . 406
HENNIKER, Sir Frederick, death of, in 1825, vii. . 219
HENRIETTA MARIA, Princess, iii. 93, 106-109, 115, 117, 161, 201, 248, 272, 301, 302, 357, 361, 395, 677, 678
HENRY I., son of William I., i. . 383, 396-419, 664, 665
——— II., king of France, ii. 458
——— II., son of Geoffrey of Anjou—
 i. 434-458, 466-480, 554, 667, 668
——— III., king of France, ii. . . 649, 664, 672
——— III., the reign of, i. . . . 671-688, 837
——— IV., king of France, ii. . 640, 649, 679, 681, 682
——— IV., surnamed Bolingbroke, . . i. 791-800;
 ii. 4-23, 130, 140, 155, 165, 166, 185, 238, 239
——— V., king of England, ii. 6, 9, 15, 17, 18, 22, 24-52, 125, 130, 132, 146, 166, 185, 186, 231-235, 239-242, 255
HENRY VI., ii. 50, 52, 54-110, 114, 130, 186, 236, 242, 244
——— VI., emperor of Germany, i. . 503, 509, 510, 513
——— VII., ii. 125-130, 281-318, 381, 696-702, 771, 775, 797
——— VIII., ii. 161, 301, 312, 315, 317-456, 695, 701-729, 799
——— VIII.'s skill in music, iii. . . . 561
———, bishop of Winchester, i. 421, 427, 430-435, 442
———, count of Champagne, i. 500
———, eldest son of Henry II., i. 446, 452, 453, 467-474, 543
———, eldest son of James I., iii. . 6, 49-52, 73, 623
———, P., the Chatham of America, iv. 834; v. 77, 82, 119
———, son of David, king of Scotland, i. . 423, 425, 541
———, son of Richard, king of the Romans, i. . 688
Henry's Primer, King; or, *Tracts on the Divine Offices,* ii. 718
HENSEY, Dr Florence; he acts as a French spy, iv. 576, 577
HEPBURN, Mr, iv. 508
Heptarchy, the tributary to Egbert of Wessex, i. 150, 151
Heraldry, its rise, i. 641
Herat, Lieutenant Pottinger's skilful defence of, vii. 621
HERBERT, a manager of House of Commons, iii. . 120
———, George, a poet, author of *The Temple,* iii. 604
———, Lord, chamberlain, ii. . 320, 323, 325; 336
———, Lord Chief-justice, iii. 785
———, Sir Edward, iii. . 92, 106, 225, 226, 262, 267

	PAGE
HERBERT, Sir Henry, deputy-master of the revels, iii.	595
———, Thomas, iii.	363, 383, 396
HEREFORD, Humphrey Bohun, earl of, i.	719, 721, 722
———, Roger Fitz-Osborn, earl of, i.	380, 382
———, William Fitz-Osborn, earl of, i.	375, 380
Herefordshire Beacon; View of, i.	100
———, jurisdiction of Wales over, iii.	43
Heresy; when punished with death in England, ii.	140, 141
HEREWARD, lord of Born, in Lincolnshire, i.	376–378
HERLE, discloses plot for murdering privy-council, ii.	640
HERMAN, bishop of Winton and Shireburn, i.	604
HERODOTUS; quoted, i.	13–15, 19
HERRICK, Robert, a poet, iii.	566, 604
HERRIES, Mr, chancellor of the exchequer, vii.	236, 240
Herring-fisheries, vi.	800
———fishery; illustration, ii.	191
HERRING, Thomas, archbishop of York, iv.	476
Herrings, Battle of, fought at Rouvrai, ii.	62
HERSCHEL and FARADAY, vii.	217, 743
———, Sir William, the astronomer, vi.	890
HERTFORD, Edward Seymour, earl of, ii.	440, 445–448, 495
———, E. S., earl of, son of Protector Somerset, ii.	569
HERVEY, Captain, iv.	558
HEWET, Mr P., presents clergy's protest to the king, iii.	468
HEWIT, Dr, beheaded by Cromwell, iii.	427
HEWLET, condemned as a regicide; not executed, iii.	673, 674
HEWLEY, Lady; curious story of her bequest to the Church, vii.	680
HEWSON, Colonel, a parliamentarian, iii.	425
Hexham, Battle of, ii.	101
———, St Andrew's Church at, i.	310
———, View of, iv.	294
HEYLIN, biographer of Archbishop Laud, quoted, iii.	158, 498
HETTNER, W., establishes a music-lecture at Oxford, iii.	566
HEYWOOD, J., a dramatic writer of 16th century, iii.	579, 584
———, Peter, the rover; his death, vii.	440
———, T., a dramatic writer of 16th century, iii.	594
Hibernia, its derivation and meaning, i.	17
HIBNER, Esther; barbarous treatment of her apprentices, vii.	296
HICKES, a Presbyterian preacher; executed, iii.	779, 780
———, Dr George, the Anglo-Saxon scholar, iv.	614
HICKFORD, secretary to the Duke of Norfolk, ii.	638
HIDE, D., supposed originator of the name of Round-heads, iii.	260
HIGDEN's *Polychronicon*, with translation of Trevisa, ii.	209
HIGGINS, Francis, an Irish Protestant clergyman, iv.	217
High-commission Court, iii.	42, 694
———, origin of the, ii.	765
Highland Society of Scotland, vii.	746
Highlanders, Scottish; their descent, i.	18
Highlands of Scotland, Battle of Dunkeld, iv.	132, 133
HILL, Colonel John; his expedition to Quebec, iv.	45, 237, 248
———, executed at Tyburn, iii.	724, 725
———, General Sir Rowland, vi.	580, 588, 603, 642, 643, 657
———, Lord, death of, in 1842, vii.	731
Hill Norton, Warwickshire, assembly of Levellers at, iii.	36
HILL, Rowland, and the Post-office system; Portrait, vii.	576–580
HILL, Rowland, Rev., death of, in 1834, vii.	408
HILLIARD, N., a miniature painter of great talent, ii.	854
HILLSBOROUGH, Earl of, secretary of state, iv.	352, 871
HIMILCO, an ancient Carthaginian navigator, i.	14
HINGSTON, J., organist to the protector Cromwell, iii.	567
HIPPESLY, Sir John, iii.	137
History, evidences of genuine, i.	4
History of the World, by Sir Walter Raleigh, iii.	73
HOADLEY, Dr Benjamin; Portrait of, iv.	163, 589, 615
HOARE, Prince, death of, in 1834, vii.	443
HOBBES, T.; review of his works, &c., iii.	498, 870, 879, 880
HOBBES, T.; his controversy with Dr Wallis, iv.	724
Hochkirchen, Battle of, fought 1758, iv.	575
HOFLANDS, death of the, vii.	733
HOGARTH, Wm., the great artist, iv.	524, 589, 685, 704–706, 770
HOGG, James, the Ettrick Shepherd, death of, vii.	603, 604
Hohen Friedberg, Battle of, fought 1745, iv.	453
	PAGE
Hohenlinden, Battle of, fought December 2, 1800, vi.	152
HOLBEIN, Hans, an eminent painter—	
	ii. 318, 319, 379, 394, 413, 439, 501, 596, 750, 813, 852
HOLBORNE, R., disputes the legality of ship-money, iii.	179
HOLDER, Dr; his treatise on *Principles of Harmony*, iv.	712
HOLGATE, Robert, archbishop of York, ii.	509
HOLINSHED, Raphael, the historian; quoted, i.	8, 367, 368, 525
———, the historian, referred to, ii.	185, 687; iii. 615
HOLKAR, Jeswunt Rao, a Mahratta chief, vi.	218–225, 299–305
HOLEOT, Robert, an author of the 14th century, i.	611
Holland and Belgium, separation of, &c., vii.	428, 547
———, embassy from, to James I., &c., iii.	7, 48
HOLLAND, Henry Fox, lord, iv.	818, 819
———, Henry Rich, earl of, iii.	114, 171, 268, 383, 400
———, Lord, death of, vii.	246, 595
———, William, earl of, i.	525
HOLLAR, Winceslaus, a painter, iii.	398, 527, 545, 577, 595, 734
HOLLIS, Denzil, iii.	141, 142, 144, 261, 327, 369, 727
———, Sir Francis, statue of, iii.	576
HOLLOWAY, a Rye-house conspirator; executed, iii.	755
———, Thomas, the engraver, death of, in 1826, vii.	316
Holmby House, iii.	363
HOLMES, an old republican officer, hanged, iii.	782
———, Major, a conspirator against William III., iv.	60
———, Sir R., sent to capture the Smyrna fleet, iii.	709
———, Sir Thomas, destroys Dutch shipping, iii.	698
HOLSTEIN-BECK, Prince of, iv.	156
———, Duke of, a friend of Conrad Vorstius, iii.	48
HOLT, Lord Chief-justice, iv.	162
———, Sir Robert, his speech on Sir J. Coventry, iii.	708
Holwood House, Hayes, Kent; View of, iv.	878
Holy Alliance, vii.	2, 3, 142–146
——— days, or saints' days, suppression of many, ii.	397
Holyrood House; View of, ii.	557
Holywood, Dumfriesshire, Druidical circle, i.	61
HOME, a noble of the Scottish border, ii.	328, 329, 350–352
———, Dr, his bleaching improvements, vi.	843
———, of Wedderburn, slays De la Bastie, ii.	352
Homildon-hill, Battle of, ii.	11
HONE, William; his trials, vii.	60–63
HONEYWOOD, Colonel, wounded at Clifton Moor, iv.	490
HONTHORST, Gerard, an eminent painter, iii.	567
Hood, Samuel, Viscount, reduces Bastia, vi.	41
———, Thomas, death of, in 1845, vii.	736
HOOK, Dr, and the Chartists of Leeds; Portrait, vii.	679, 749
———, Theodore, death of, in 1841, vii.	735, 736
HOOKE, Colonel, a Jacobite agent in Scotland, iv.	185
HOOKER, R., a prose writer of 16th century, ii.	836
HOOPER, Dr, with Monmouth in his last moments, iii.	776
———, John, burnt for heresy, ii.	493, 494, 509, 529, 741
Hop-plant, introduced into England from Netherlands, ii.	806
HOPE, M., Dutch minister at Vienna, iv.	85
———, Sir John; his bravery at St Jean de Luz, vi.	657, 681
———, Sir T., a leader against royal forces at Newburn, iii.	221
———, Thomas, death of, in 1831, vii.	442
HOPETON, Sir R., petitions against church-ales, &c., iii.	161, 257
HOPKINS, Sir W., concerts plan for escape of Charles I., iii.	385
———, the master witch-hunter; his proceedings, iii.	639
HOPPE, Madame, wife of the Dutch minister in London, iv.	403
HOPSON, Admiral, present in attack upon Vigo Bay, iv.	131
HORN, Count, wounded at siege of Namur, iv.	55
HORNER, Francis, vii.	6, 9, 12, 22
HORROCKS, Samuel, a philosopher, iv.	717
Horse-racing, ii.	890
Horses, ancient British, much prized at Rome, i.	36, 106
HORSEY, Dr, chancellor of the bishop of London, ii.	704
HORSLEY, Samuel; Portrait, vi.	751–756
Horticulture: flowers, vegetables, &c., in 16th century, ii.	806
HORTON, Mrs; married to the Duke of Cumberland, v.	21
HOSIER, Rear-admiral, iv.	369
Hosiery manufactures, vi.	844, 845
HOSKINS, John, an eminent miniature-painter, iii.	569
———, Serjeant, a poet and scholar, iii.	72
Hospitallers, Knights, the, i.	491, 495
Host, representation of the passage of the, ii.	149
Hôtel de Ville, View of, v.	781

GENERAL INDEX. 121

	PAGE
HOTHAM, Sir J.; he and his son hanged, iii. 217, 267, 278, 305, 843	
———, Vice-admiral, vi.	84, 85
HOUGH, John, bishop of Lichfield, iv.	168
Hougoumont, Château of, vi.	706
House of Commons, interior of the old; View, vii.	12
——— Lords, attack on the, vii.	480
Household appointments of Queen Victoria, vii. 561, 607–609	
Houses of Parliament, exterior View of old, vii.	185
———, the new; illustration, vii.	523, 524
House-tax of 1834, vii.	413
HOVEDEN; quoted, i.	500, 583
Howard Castle, View of, iv.	696
HOWARD, Lady Catherine, queen of Henry VIII., ii. 414–423	
———, Lady Frances, wife of Earl of Essex, iii. 52–54, 60–62	
———, Lady Mary, charged with high treason, iii.	431
———, Lord, ambassador to Louis XI., ii. 113, 116, 123, 124	
———, Lord, iii.	740, 746, 747
———, Lord H., negotiates between James VI. and Cecil, ii.	692
HOWARD, Lord Thomas, lord-admiral, ii.	326, 327
———, Sir Edward, lord-admiral, ii.	321, 322
———, Thomas, Lord of Walden, iii.	4
HOWE, General Sir William, v.	109, 192, 198, 252
———, Richard, earl, an English admiral, v. 44, 76, 156, 171, 256, 385, 689, 768; vi. 8, 9, 33–37, 114	
HOWEL, author of the *Londinopolis*, published 1657, iii.	546
HOWICK, Lord; his motion to consider the distress of the country, vii.	652
Howie, Mr R., principal of College of St Andrews, iii.	472
HUBBA, a Danish king, slain with his followers, i.	159
HUBBERTHORN, Richard, an eminent Quaker, iii.	817
HUBERT, an insane Frenchman; executed, iii.	699
Hubertsburg, Treaty of, iv.	817
HUDDLESTON, a priest, confesses Charles II., iii. 761, 762, 764	
HUDSON, chaplain to Charles I., iii.	350, 352
———; his Portrait of Dryden, iii.	870
———; his Portrait of Pope, iv.	682
Hudson River, Views of the, v.	207, 208
HUGH DE MONTGOMERY, earl of Shrewsbury, i.	400
———, nephew of Aubert le Ribaud, i.	383
HUGHES, Sir Edward, assists in defence of Gibraltar, v.	389
———, Sir E.; his engagement with the French, v. 630–634	
Huguenots, the take up arms, ii.	570–573
HUGUES, Victor, the republican, vi.	86
Hull, Castle of, &c., iii.	278, 655
HUME, David, the historian and philosopher, v.	514–516
———, Joseph, vii. 173, 174, 208, 437, 480, 488–490, 534	
———, Sir George, afterwards Earl of Dunbar, iii.	64
———, Sir Patrick, nearly joins Rye-house Plot, iii.	770
HUMPHREY, Pelham, a musician of 17th century, iii.	834
Hungarians; their reform agitations in 1837, vii.	548
HUNGATE, Captain, a conspirator against William III., iv.	60
HUNGERFORD, Mr; expelled the House of Commons, iv.	50
———, Sir Thomas, i.	780
HUNNE, Richard, a merchant tailor; murdered, ii. 703–705	
HUNSDON, Lord, son of Mary Boleyn, ii.	541
HUNT; Portrait, vii. xiv, 30–32, 164, 107–112, 116, 595	
Hunting, iv.	778
——— in enclosures introduced, ii.	255
——— by Anglo-Saxons and Normans, i. 341–343, 647	
HUNTINGDON, Countess of; Portrait, v.	421
———, David, earl of, afterwards David I., i.	470
———, George Hastings, earl of, ii.	397
———, Henry Hastings, earl of, ii.	618
———, Henry of, i.	589, 590
———, John Holland, earl of, i. 791; ii. 5–7	
HUNTLEY, Earl of, a partisan of Mary Stuart, ii.	587
———, Earl of, at battle of Flodden, ii.	328
———, Earl of, taken prisoner at Pinkie, ii. 463, 574, 575	
———, Marquis of, a partisan of Charles I., iii.	203
HURRY or URRIE, a parliamentarian, joins the king, iii.	303
Husbandry implements; illustrations, iii.	558, 559
HUSK, General, iv.	494
HUSKISSON, the Right Hon. W., vii. 17, 157, 159–292, 329	
HUSS, John, and the Hussites, ii.	71
———, burned for heresy, iii.	80

	PAGE
HUTCHINSON, Colonel, condemned as a regicide, iii.	666
Huts, Gaulish, i.	98
HUTTON, Matthew, archbishop of York, iii.	19, 20
Huy; its capture and recapture, iv.	163
HYDE, Anne, daughter of Earl of Clarendon, iii.	677, 711
———, Lord-treasurer, son of Earl of Clarendon, iii.	731
———, Mr Edward. See also Clarendon, iii.	227
———, Sir Nicholas, chief-justice of King's Bench, iii.	128
HYDER ALI, an Asiatic prince, iv.	866, 888–892
———; Portrait of, v.	621
HYNDFORD, John Carmichael, earl of, iv.	423, 544
Hyperboreans, island of the, i.	15
IBERVILLE, M. de, iv.	312
Iceni, the, i.	40, 43, 44
IDA, founder of the kingdom of Bernicia, i.	142
Idel river, Nottinghamshire, Battle on its banks, i.	146
Iernis, name of Ireland in the Orphic poem, i.	14
Ignorance and fanaticism of 1835, vii.	472
ILAY, Earl of, secretary of state for Scotland, iv.	365
Illness, death and character of William IV., vii.	527–530
Illustrations, List of. See beginning of vols.	
Images, worship of, in England, ii.	145, 306
IMMYNS, John, established the Madrigal Society, iv.	712
IMOLA, Bishop of, papal legate, ii.	285
IMPEY, Sir Elijah, v.	628, 642, 691–693, 823
Import trade of Great Britain, vi. 795, 802, 804, 805, 808–815	
Incendiarism and murder at Rebecca riots, vii.	637
Inclosure Act, passed 1800–1, vi.	761
Inclosures, ii.	900
Income-tax, vii.	639, 643–645
———, carried through Parliament in 1799, vi. 138, 793	
Indemnity Bill, iv.	83, 84
Independents; their origin, ii.	745
India, iv. 802, 809, 810, 814–826, 829, 831–898; v. 591–848, 690–694, 853–855; vi. 144, 217–226, 299–305; vii. 65–76, 371, 383, 619–632, 713–715	
———, Company's Charter, renewal of, in 1833, vii. 882, 383	
———, ii. 171–195, 771–812; iii. 527–559, 851–869; iv. 654–684; v. 442–498; vi. 795–848	
———, embassy of Sighelm to, i.	266, 267
———, jurors in, vii.	207
———, route to; its importance to Britain, vii.	704
Indian cotton, attention given to growth of, vii.	589
———, mails, improvement of the, vii.	591
Indians, Group of Crow, Sioux, and Pawnee, in the costumes of their tribes, v.	202
INDULF, a Scottish king, i.	219
Indulgence, Declaration of, Dec. 26, 1662, iii.	691
Industry, general depression of, vii.	21, 22
———, history of the national, i. 91–117, 262, 584, 824; ii. 171–195, 771–812; iii. 527–559, 851–869; iv. 654–684; v. 442–498; vi. 795–848	
Infantry, main strength of the British armies, i.	36, 39
Infants' Custody Bill of 1839, vii.	574
INGLEBY, Sir William, iii.	4
INGULPHUS, quoted, i.	187, 257, 579, 609, 613
Ini, laws of, i.	203
Inner Temple, destructive fire at the, vii.	590
INNES, Father, almoner to Maria d'Este, iv.	188
INNOCENT II., Pope, i.	422
——— XII., Pope, iv.	93
Inquisition; its first establishment in Rome, &c., ii.	531
Institutions and Customs, i.	5
Insurance, fire and life, increase of, vii.	213
———, Law of, v. 432; vi. 780
———, Marine, earliest notice of, ii.	786
Insurrections in France in 1332, vii.	426
Intercursus Magnus, a mercantile treaty, ii.	774
Interest, reduced to six per cent. in 1651, iii.	859
Interregnum, 1688–9, iv.	1–5
Inverury, Battle of, gained by Bruce, i.	735
Iona; View of Monastery, &c., i. 220, 221, 229, 244, 290	
Ionian islands, captured by English in 1809–10, vi.	560
Ipswich; View of Gatehouse of Wolsey's College, ii. 814, 815	
Ireland, vii. 262–267, 339, 372, 466–465, 491–512, 536, 657–669	
———, change in Constitution of, &c., v. 434–438, 464–466	
IRELAND, Father, concerned in Popish Plot; executed, iii. 724	

HISTORY OF ENGLAND.

Ireland, its primitive Celtic population, &c.—
    i. 12–18, 217–223, 229, 459–467, 546
———, king's visit to, vii. 132
———, Lord Wellesley in, vii. . . 137, 138
———, Louis XIV. aids James II. to recover, iv. . 11
———, map of, vii. 368
———, National Congress held at Dublin, v. . 587
———, poor-law for, vii. . . . 415
———, rebellion in ; 50,000 Protestants murdered, iii. 254
———; rebellion of O'Connor & Fitzgeralds, &c., ii. 425–428
———, state of, vii. . . 251–254, 262–267
IRELAND, Robert de Vere, duke of, i. . 791, 792
———, William; his Shakspeare forgeries, vi. . 855
IRETON, Colonel; his Portrait, &c., iii. 332, 333, 364, 419, 495
Irish administration, the, vii. . . . 460
— Arms Act, vii. 660
— Brigade, the, iv. . . . 34, 156
— chieftains, charge of, ii. . . . 683
— Church and the appropriation question, vii. 461–465
———, position of the, in 1831, vii. . 387–399
— ecclesiastical commission-census, vii. . . 393
— Life Bill of 1846, vii. . . . 730
— repealers, American sympathy with the, vii. . 711
— Trade Bill, the, v. . . . 588
Iron Bridge at Colebrook Dale; View of, v. . 481
— manufactures, . . ii. 311; v. 479, 480, 482
— mining and Ironworks, vi. . . 835–837
IRVING, Rev. Edward; Portrait, vii. 306–308, 357, 409, 410
Irwell, aqueduct over the; illustration, v. . 472
ISAAC, emperor of Cyprus, i. . . . 495
ISABELLA CLARA EUGENIA, infanta of Spain, ii. 680, 685
———, queen of Charles VI., ii. 17, 20, 37–41, 44, 79
———, queen of Edward II., i. . 732, 742–755
———, queen of Richard II., ii. . 7–9, 12, 19–21
———, queen of Spain, vii. . . 541, 542
— II., queen of Spain, marriage of, vii. 707, 708
———, wife of Hugh, count de la Marche, i. 517, 674
Isle of Man, riot in 1825, vii. . . . 188
Islington cattle-market, vii. . . . 435
Ismael, storming of; 30,000 persons perished at, v. 779, 780
IVAN, czar of Russia, iv. . . . 116, 117

JACKSON, General, president of United States, vi. . 746
———, John, death of, vii. . . . 442
———, Mr, English ambassador at Sweden, iv. . 318
Jacobin Club, suppressed October 18, 1794, vi. . 61
— Club, the, v. . . . 755, 790
Jacobins; their hostility to the Girondists, v. . 885
JACQUETTA, of Luxemburg, ii. . 77, 79, 80, 101, 102
JAFFIER, Meer, nabob of Bengal, iv. 571; v. 610–612, 614–618
Jamaica, affairs of, vii. . . . 559–562
———, taken by the English, 1655, iii. . 420
JAMES, Francis, a delegate at divorce of Earl of Essex, iii. 53
— F. E., iv. 2, 121, 285, 286, 301, 303, 359, 378, 444
— FRANCIS EDWARD, prince of Wales, iii. . 792, 795
— I., king of England, iii. 2–108, 432*, 475, 550, 552
— I., king of Scotland, ii. . 19, 49, 51, 132–134, 187
— I., of Eng., ii. 588, 589, 604, 652–654, 665, 671, 691, 692
— II., iii. 279, 381, 383, 695, 711, 729, 733, 756–801, 867
— II.; effect of his voluntary exile, &c., iv. 1–26, 44
— II., king of Scotland, ii. . . 134, 135
— III., king of Scotland, ii. 114, 115, 135, 136, 301–303
— IV., king of Scotland, ii. 302–307, 311, 312, 322, 325–331
— V., king of Scotland, ii. 331, 350, 351, 430–433; iii. 644
JAMIESON, George, the Scottish Vandyke, iii. . 569
JANSEN, Alderman, iv. 537
———, Bernard, a Dutch architect, iii. . 576
———, Cornelius, a Dutch painter, iii. . 567
Japhetic or Caucasic population of Europe, i. . 10
JARDINE, Mr; quoted, iii. . . 517, 519
———, Professor, death of, in 1827, vii. . 318
Jarnac, Battle of, ii. 626
Jarrow, View of, at mouth of the river Tyne, i. . 291
Jassy, Treaty of, signed August 1791, v. . 856
JAY, John, the American revolutionist, v. 78, 85, 161, 164
— Mr, the American ambassador, vi. . . 806

JEFFERSON, Thomas, the American revolutionist, v. 109, 161
JEFFERTS, Mr, a spy in Charles XII.'s camp, iv. . 181
JEFFREY, Francis, vii. 741
———, W., affirms one Moore to be Christ, ii. . 572
JEFFREYS, Sir George—
  iii. 739, 740, 757, 758, 765, 781, 786, 790, 800, 844; iv. 22
JEKYLL, Sir Joseph, master of the Rolls, iv. 320, 336, 395
Jemappe, View of, v. 882
JENKINS, Sir Leoline, secretary of state, iii. . 741, 843
JENKINSON, A., agent for the Russia Company, ii. . 785
———, Anthony, an English engraver, iii. . 577
JENKYNS, Captain Robert, iv. . . . 405
JENNER, Baron; remodels Oxford University statutes, iii. 786
———, Dr Edward, death of, in 1823, vii. . 219
JENNINGS, Sir John; his expedition to Spain, iv. . 369
JERROLD, Douglas, and Punch, vii. . . 743
JERSEY, Lord, lord-chamberlain, iv. . . 90
Jerusalem, city of; View, i. . . . 499
———; survey of coasts of Egypt and Syria, &c., ii. 51
JERVAS, Charles, an English painter, iv. . 702
Jesuits, iii. . . . 21, 22, 30–32, 636
———, Clement XIV.'s bull against, v. . 417
Jewel House in the Tower, from an original drawing, iii. 708
Jews, baptised, admitted to the freedom of the city of
  London, vii. 308
Jews, bill in favour of admitting them to parliament, vii. 290
———; relief from municipal disabilities, vii. . 246–681
———, Russian ukase against, in 1843, vii. . . 701
———, the, in England, i. . 266, 476, 504, 505, 523, 684
JOAN, daughter of Henry II., i. . . 490, 491, 494
— OF NAVARRE, wife of Henry IV.; her Portrait, ii. 4
———, sister of King Richard, i. . . . 513
JOFFRID, abbot of Croyland, i. . . . 606
JOHN I. of France, son of Philip VI., i. . 771–776
———, king of England, i. 478, 479, 482, 486, 506–511, 514–533
— of Austria, illegitimate son of Charles V., ii. 649, 651
— VI. of Portugal, death of, vii. . . 151
JOHNSON, Dr Samuel, author of the English Dictionary—
    iii. 614; iv. 136, 819; v. 510, 511
———, Samuel, fined and whipped, iii. . . 785
———, Sir William, iv. . . . 554
JOHNSTON, Archibald, iii. . . . 485, 490
———, Sir Wm., induces Indians to join British—
    iv. 827, 864; v. 3
JOHNSTONE, Colonel Guy, v. . . . 114
———, Governor; his private correspondence with
  members of the American congress, v. . . 266
JOHNSTONE, of Warriston; tried and hanged, iii. . 683
Joint-stock Bank Acts, vii. . . . 521
——— banking-system, vii. . . . 520
——— companies and their victims, vii. 180–183
JONES, a famous architect, iii. 159, 546, 560, 571, 574, 722
———, executed as a regicide, iii. . . 676
———, John Gale, vi. . . . 526, 527, 534
———, Paul; his adventures, &c., v. . 292, 724, 786
———, Sir William, an eminent scholar, vi. 857, 860, 861
JONSON, Ben, the famous dramatic writer, iii. 582, 592, 596
JOSEPH EMANUEL, king of Portugal, iv. . . 810–812
— I., emperor of Germany, iv. . . . 235
— II., emperor of Germany—
  v. 580–591, 683–686, 721, 732–738, 774, 775
JOURDAN, Marshal, a skilful republican general, vi. 105, 642
JOYCE, a cornet in Whalley's regiment, iii. . 367
JUDITH, daughter of Charles the Bald, i. . . 153
———, niece of William I., i. . . 379, 381, 382
JULIANA, illegitimate daughter of Henry I., i. . 414
JULIUS II., Pope, ii. . . . 320, 367, 370
Junius's Letters, . iv. 871; v. 1, 14, 15, 508, 510
Juries, right of, iv. 785
Jury-box, Catholics in the, vii. . . . 494
———; remarkable trial of Sir N. Throgmorton, ii. 518
———, rights of, v. 424, 425
———, trial by, . . . iii. 838; iv. 645, 646
———, trial by, established, i. . . . 572
Justiciary, chief, office of the, i. . . . 568
JUSTUS, bishop of Rochester, i. . . 233, 234

GENERAL INDEX. 123

Jutes, the, a Saxon tribe, i. . . . 139–145
Juxon, Wm., dean of Worcester, iii. 160, 161, 243, 356, 397

Kainarji, Treaty of, v. 43
Kalb, an American officer, slain at battle of Camden, v. 321
Kater, Captain, death of, in 1835, vii. . . 592
Kays, Martin, marries Lady Mary Grey, ii. . 623
Kean, Edmund, death of, in 1833, vii. . . 441
Keane, Sir John; his Indian expedition, vii. . 623, 624
Keats, John, a distinguished poet, vi. . . 889
———, death of, in 1821 ; portrait, vii. . 222
Keene, Sir B., British consul at Madrid, iv. 379, 533, 568
Keith, ambassador of James VI. of Scotland, ii. . 665
———, Marshal, killed at battle of Hochkirchen, iv. 575
———, Sir William, governor of Berwick, i. . 756
Kelly, a nonjuring clergyman, iv. . . . 360
———, of Moriarty, assassinates Earl of Desmond, ii. 652
Kemble, Fanny; great success of her first appearance, vii. 306
Kemp, John, cardinal and archbishop of Canterbury, ii. 147
———, the chemist, death of, vii. . . . 735
Ken, Thomas, bishop of Bath and Wells, iii. . 762, 776
Kendal, iii. 656
Kenilworth, Castle of; its strength and works, ii. 289, 874
———, residence of De Montforts, i. 686, 687
Kenilworth, Dictum de, i. 687, 688
Kenmure, Lord, beheaded on Tower-hill, iv. . 309
Kennedy, Hew, undertakes to murder Auchindrane, iii. 643
Kennet, Dr, iv. 358
———, Lord-mayor; conduct at London riots, v. 308–312
Kenneth III. son of Malcolm I., i. . 218–220, 533
——— IV., called the Grim, i. . . 220, 221, 533
——— Mac Alpin, or Kenneth II., i. . 217, 218
Kent, Cantium, i. 10, 27–33, 57, 58, 77, 141, 142, 145, 150
Kent, Earl of, reads to Mary Stuart her death-warrant, ii. 668
Kent, Edmund Plantagenet, earl of, i. . 751, 752
———, Henry Grey, earl of, ii. . . . 397
Kent, insurrection of men of, under John Cade, ii. 87, 88
Kent, James, an English musician of 18th century, v. 529
Kent, Maid of; her prophecies; is put to death, ii. 717
Kent, Thomas Holland, earl of; beheaded, ii. . 5, 7
———, William, an architect, . . iii. 572 ; iv. 700
Kentish Petition, the, iv. 106
Kenyon, Lord ; his connection with Orangeism, vii. 487, 488
Keppel, Admiral, . iv. 802, 852 ; v. 242, 243, 272, 273
———, Captain, iv. 563
Ker, A., threatens to shoot Mary Queen of Scots, ii. 587
———, John, of Kersland, iv. . . . 621
Kerouaille, Mdlle, mistress of Charles II., iii. 707, 716, 761
Kerr, Lord; his charge against Marquis of Hamilton, iii. 250
———, Lord Robert, killed at battle of Culloden, iv. . 510
Kersland, Laird of, iv. 188
Kesnen, Commissioner; his policy, vii. . . 616
Ket, R.; he and his brother hanged in chains, ii. 485, 487
Kew Palace, garden front of, iv. . . . 796
Key, Alderman ; his panic, vii. . . . 336
Keyling, John, engaged in Rye-house Plot, iii. . 743
———, Josiah, a salter, iii. . . . 741, 742
Keys, executed at Tyburn, iv. . . . 63
Keys of Dover Castle ; illustration, ii. . . 810
Khelat, taken by General Willshire, vii. . . 624
Khevenhüller, drives French army out of Austria, iv. 425
Khiva, Russian allegations against people of, vii. . 624
Kildare, Gerald Fitzgerald, earl of, ii. . . 427
———, James Fitzgerald, earl of, iv. . . 477
———, T. Fitzgerald, earl of ; beheaded, ii. . 425, 426
———, Thomas Fitzgerald, earl of, ii. 289, 425–427
Kildrummie Castle ; View of the ruins, &c., i. . 727, 729
Killarney Lake, View of the, vii. . . . 501
Killikrankie, Battle of, iv. 15
Kilmarnock, Earl of ; executed, iv. . . 521, 522
Kilwarden, Lord, chief-justice of Ireland, murdered, vi. 216
Kincardine, Earl of, favours the Covenanters, iii. 694, 701
King, an eminent chemist and physician, iii. . 750
———, Captain, a servant of Sir Walter Raleigh, iii. 76
———, executed at Tyburn, iv. . . . 63
———, Gregory ; his work on condition of England, iv. 786, 787

King, John, bishop of London, iii. . . . 59
———, Sir Peter, complains of Dr Sacheverell's sermon, iv. 217
King's Bench, Chief-justice of the, i. . . 812
———, speeches, vii. . . 115, 184, 208, 224, 242,
254, 259, 271, 288, 334, 347, 348, 396, 451
Kingston, Duchess of ; her trial, v. . 148–150, 537
———, lieutenant of the Tower, ii. 373, 374, 391, 393
Kingston, St Mary's Chapel at, i. . . . 175
Kinsale, from an old drawing, iv. . . . 12
Kip, John, a Dutch engraver, iv. . . . 709
Kirby, informs of a plot to assassinate Charles II., iii. 717
Kirk, Colonel, iv. 17
———; his savage conduct, iii. . . . 778
Kirkaldy, William, laird of Grange, ii. . . 446
Kirkman, F., a publisher ; his curious advertisement, iii. 900
Kirle, Mr Anthony, iv. 634
Kirton, Mr, M.P., iii. 133, 140
Kitchen, Anthony, bishop of Llandaff, ii. . 545
Kitchener, Dr, death of, in 1827, vii. . . 313
Kits Coty House, a cromlech, near Aylesford, Kent, i. 63
Knatchbull, Sir Edward, M.P., iv. . . 265
Kneller, Sir G., a painter, iv. 128, 589, 626, 685, 701, 702
Knevett, Sir Thomas ; he surprises Fawkes, iii. . 27
Knight, Mr Payne, death of, in 1824, vii. . 220
Knighthood ; 700 persons knighted by James I., &c., iii. 4–6
Knightly, Captain, conspires against William III., iv. 60
———, Mr, searches the house of Mrs Vaux, iii. . 116
Knolles, Richard, the English historian, iii. . 614
Knollys, Sir Francis, ii. . . . 607, 610, 611
———, Sir William, ii. 687
Knowles, Sir Robert, i. 779
Knox, John, ii. . 459, 548, 554, 556, 558, 566–568, 606
———, the Scottish Reformer, iii. 186, 435, 437, 473
Knygston, an English historian of the 14th century, i. 520
Knyghton, Radnorshire, Battle of, ii. . . 11, 13
Koe, John, committed to the Tower, iii. . . 783
Konigsegg, Marshal, iv. 450
Königsmark, Count Philip Christopher, iv. . 372
Kosciuszko, Thaddeus, a Polish warrior, v. 857 ; vi. 62–67
Kuneradorf, Battle of, fought August 12, 1759, iv. . 583
Kureek, a Pindarree chief, vii. . . . 66, 67, 69
Kutusoff, a famous Russian general, vi. . 278, 279
Kyd, Captain, becomes a pirate ; hanged, iv. . 86, 105
———, Thomas, a dramatic writer of 16th century, iii. 587
Kyme, Anne, daughter of Sir W. Askew, ii. . 447, 448
Kymer, Dr Gilbert, clerk and physician to Henry VI., ii. 208
Kyriel, Sir Thomas ; beheaded, ii. . . 85, 97

Labédoyère, tried and condemned for high treason, vi. 723
Labelye, a Swiss architect, iv. . . . 701
Labour ; its condition, vii. . . . 23, 24, 651
Labourdonnais, a Frenchman, seizes Madras, v. . 600
Labnan, island of, ceded to Britain, vii. . . 632
La Chaise, Father, confessor of Louis XIV., iii. . 719
Lacy, Gilbert de, a Norman Baron, i. . 374, 424
———, Hugh de, earl of Ulster, i. . . 467, 523
———, Walter de, i. . . . 381, 400, 424
———, Walter de, earl of Meath, i. . . . 523
Ladies, admission of, to parliamentary debates, vii. 525
Lady Place, or Hurley House ; View of, iii. . 793, 794
Lafayette, v. 196, 197, 246, 265, 324, 352, 357, 740, 741,
743, 747, 749, 753–756, 782, 784–792, 825–847, 858–896
Lafayette, Marquis de ; Portrait, vii. . . 423–428
La Galissonière, Admiral, iv. . . . 558
La Hire, a celebrated French knight, ii. 49, 56, 65, 68, 69
La Hogue, Battle of, fought May 19, 1692, iv. . 38
Laing, Major, the African explorer, death of, vii. 313
Lake, Gerard, Viscount, vi. . . 217–225, 299–305
———, Sir Thomas, joint-secretary of state, iii. . 49
Lally, Count, v. 613–616
Lama, bishop of Brechin, iii. . . . 465
———, Charles ; quoted, iii. . . 581, 586, 587
———, death of, vii. 601
Lamballe, Princess of, murdered, v. . 863, 873, 878
Lambe, Dr, physician of the Duke of Buckingham, iii. 135
Lambert, a parliamentarian officer, iii. 365, 422, 432, 690

	PAGE
LAMBERT, John, a schoolmaster; burnt, ii.	406, 407, 724
LAMBERTON, William de, bishop of St Andrews, i.	723, 729
Lambeth Palace and Lombard's Tower; illustration, ii.	147
LAMPTON, Mr John George. See Lord Durham.	
LAMONT, Dr, physician to Mr Murray, M.P., iv.	536
LA MOTTE, the French envoy, slain at Flodden, ii.	323
LAMPETER, Castle of, taken by Prince of Wales, ii.	17
LAMPLUGH, Thomas, bishop of Exeter, iv.	592
LANARK, Lord, secretary of state, iii.	222, 268, 309
Lancashire, iii.	656
———, power-loom riot of 1826 in, vii.	188
LANCASTER, Captain James, iii.	529
Lancaster, county of, iii.	656
———, family colours were white and red, ii.	857
LANCASTER, Henry Plantagenet, duke of, i.	763, 769
———, earl of, i.	751, 752
———, John of Gaunt, i. 776–783, 786, 791, 794, 796	
———, duke of, ii.	52
———, Joseph, death of, in 1838, vii.	597
———, Thomas Plantagenet, earl of, i. 733, 734, 740, 741	
Landau, plan of, with its fortifications, iv.	130
Landen, Battle of, fought July 29, 1693, iv.	41
LANDER, Richard, death of, in 1834, vii.	441
Landing of George IV. at Leith, 15th August 1822, vii.	141
Landlord, O'Connell as a, vii.	665
LANDOIS, minister of Francis II. of Brittany, ii.	126, 292
LANDON, Miss L. E., death of; Portrait, vii.	602
LANDOR, Walter Savage, vii.	742
Landrecy, Siege of, iv.	249
Land-tax Act, iv.	19, 140
———title, insecurity of Irish, vii.	493
LANE, Mr, advocate for the Earl of Strafford, iii.	239
LANFRANC, abbot of Caen, i.	381, 392, 396, 547
LANGDALE, Sir M., made prisoner near Widmerpool, iii.	382
LANGHORNE, a Jesuit; executed, iii.	730
LAKOLAND, author of the *Visions of Pierce Plowman*, i.	851
LANGLEY, Sir R., foreman on trial of petitioning bishops, iii.	791
LANGNISH, Captain, iii.	263
Langside, Battle of, ii.	607
LANGTON, archbishop of Canterbury, i. 521, 522, 526, 675	
———, Walter de, Bishop of Lichfield, i.	731
Language, evidence of origin of a people, i.	6, 7
LANIER, Sir John, falls at battle of Steinkirk, iv.	37
LANNOY, viceroy of Naples for Emperor Charles V., ii.	359, 362
LANSDOWNE, Marquis of; Portrait, iii.	397, 486, 487
Lanterns of horn, invention of King Alfred, i.	166, 285
LA PLACE, a great French philosopher, assists in formation of Republican Calendar, vi.	22
LA QUADRA, signs a convention at Madrid, iv.	407
LA RABINIÈRE, a French naval commander, iv.	710
LATIMER, H., ii. 403, 410, 507, 525, 526, 696, 803, 804, 831, 832	
———, John, a Carmelite friar, i.	791
———, Lord, thrown into prison, i.	779
LA TREMOILLE, overruns Brittany, ii.	292, 294
LATTEN, Mr, a conspirator against William III., iv.	60
LAUD, Wm., archbishop of Canterbury, iii. 117, 123, 134, 138, 139, 151, 157, 159–162, 166, 177, 227, 229, 324, 326, 433	
LAUDERDALE, earl of; Portrait, iii. 362, 471, 683, 694, 713, 829	
———, Maitland, earl of, v.	338
LAURENCE, Thomas, registrar of Canterbury, ii.	385
LAURENS, Henry, American envoy to Holland, v.	333
LAURENTIUS, archbishop of Canterbury, i.	145, 233, 234
LAUTREC, a general of Francis I., in Italy, ii.	366, 368
LAUZUN, Count de, a partisan of the Pretender, iv.	24
LAVALETTE, postmaster-general under Bonaparte, vi.	724–727
LAVOISIER, the eminent chemical philosopher, vi.	56
Law, important alterations in the, vii.	290
Law in Ireland, impartiality of, vii.	495–498
LAW, James, bishop of Orkney, iii.	466
———, John, author of the South-sea scheme, iv.	353
Law reform, vii.	372
——— reforms, Lord Brougham's, vii.	420, 421
LAWES, Henry, a musician, iii.	566
LAWRENCE, archbishop of Dublin, i.	465, 466
———, Sir Thomas, an eminent painter, vi.	873, 899
———, death of, vii.	316–318

	PAGE
Laws and government of British, until Saxon conquest, i.	76–90
——— religion, evidences of truth of history, i.	5
——— of James I., king of Scotland, ii.	133
——— of the Anglo-Saxons, i.	145, 167, 203, 244
———. See Constitution, Government, and Laws.	
LAWSON, Captain, fights against Van Tromp, iii. 407, 421, *429	
LAWSON, Mr James, iii.	441
———, Vice-admiral, killed in a battle with Dutch, iii.	695
Lawyers, distinguished, of the 17th century, iii.	843
LAYER, executed at Tyburn, iv.	361
Lea, river, Hertfordshire; Danes erect a fortress here, i.	164
LEACH, Sir John, death of, in 1834, vii.	438
Leaden manufactures, vi.	837
Lead-mines of British Islands, i.	26, 92, 106, 117, 269
League, the Anti-Corn-Law—	
vii. 569–571, 583, 639, 684–688, 723–726, 730	
LEAKE, Vice-admiral, iv.	170
LEAKE; quoted,	ii. 185; iii. 552
LEAKE, Sir John, conquers island of Sardinia, iv.	201
Leather manufactures, vi.	846
Leathersellers' Hall; illustration, ii.	812
LEBRUN, the French minister for foreign affairs, v.	892, 901
———, guillotined during Reign of Terror, vi.	2, 11, 19
LECHMERE, Mr, advocates triennial parliaments, iv.	308, 310
LE CLERC, Sir W. Raleigh receives safe-conduct from, iii.	76
LE CROC; his conduct at Carberry-hill, ii.	600
Lectures, fashionable in middle of 18th century, v.	541
LEDE, Marquis of, iv.	322, 344
LEDUC, Benoît, a tailor; petitions to bury Louis XVI. v.	897
LEE, Dr Edward, archbishop of York, ii. 379, 381, 383, 399	
———, Nathaniel, a dramatic poet, iv.	737
———, Robert, lord-mayor of London, iii.	3
———, Thomas, executed at Tyburn, iii.	686
———, William, the inventor of the stocking-frame, ii.	810
LEEDS, Thomas Osborne, duke of, iv.	51, 80
Leeds, View of the Castle of, i.	740
LEEFDALE, discovers plot against William III., iv.	37
LEETH, Robert, an English engraver of 16th century, iii.	577
Legacies, imposition of stamp-duty on receipt of, vi.	780
LEGATE, Bartholomew, burnt for Arianism, iii.	48
Legate, the pope's, at no time acceptable to the English, ii.	511
LEGENDRE, a violent French revolutionist, v.	863, 884
LEGGE, chancellor of the Exchequer, iv.	555
Leghorn, French take possession of port of, vi.	805
Legion Memorial, the, iv.	108
———, Roman; cavalry, equipment, &c., i.	37, 38
Legislation, Saxon, i.	256, et seq.
Legislative or Constituent Assembly of France, v.	840
LEHWALD, Marshal, iv.	569
LEIBNITZ, Godfrey William de, a German philosopher, iii.	612
Leicester; illustration; Ruins of Abbey, &c., ii.	373, 374
LEICESTER, Robert Blanchmains, earl of, i.	498, 509
———, Robert le Bossu, earl of, i.	450
———, Robert Sydney, earl of, iii.	247, 389
———, Simon de Montfort, earl of, i.	681–687
———, Sir Robert Dudley, earl of; Portrait—	
ii. 405, 511, 575, 576, 624, 650, 656, 658, 672, 674, 750	
LEICESTER, Thomas Coke, earl of, iv.	522
LEIGHTON, Alex., a Scottish Puritanical preacher, iii.	151, 152
———, Dr R., bishop of Dunblane; Portrait, iii.	683, 802
Leipzig, Battle of, fought Oct. 16 and 18, 1813, vi.	655, 666
LELY, Sir Peter, a distinguished artist, iii.	433, 829, 832
LE MARCHAND, a sculptor of 17th century, iv.	706
LEMON, Robert, of the State-paper Office, death of, vii.	600
LENNOX, Duke of; his various patents, iii.	43
———, Earl of, falls at Flodden, ii.	328, 329
———, Earl of, ii. 436, 437, 441, 584, 592, 596, 597, 682	
———, Earl of, rebels against Regent Albany, ii.	351, 352
———, lord of Aubigny,	ii. 652; iii. 46, 439, 654
LENTHALL, a barrister, iii.	226, 429*, 526
LENTULUS, Publius; his description of Christ, iii.	811
LEO X., John de' Medici, pope, ii.	336, 345–347, 706
——— XII., Pope; his death, vii.	283
LEOFRIC, Earl, i.	184, 188, 190, 194
LEOFWINE, son of Earl Godwin, i.	185, 191 193, 215
LEOPOLD I., emperor of Germany, iv.	33, 163

GENERAL INDEX. 125

	PAGE
LEOPOLD II., v. . . 774-777, 792-797, 833,	856, 858
———, Prince, accepts the Belgian crown, vii.	428
LEPELLETIER ST FARGEAU, stabbed to the heart by one of Louis XVI.'s old body-guard, v.	396
LESLEY, Catholic bishop of Ross, ii.	564
LESLIE, General, a Covenanter, iii. 203, 205, 219-226, 252, 340
———, Sir David, iii. . . . 840, 354
———, Sir John, death of, in 1832, vii.	439
LESLY, Norman, the master of Rothes, ii.	446
LESTOCK, Admiral, iv. . . . 446, 526
L'ESTRANGE; quoted, iii.	667
LE SUEUR, Hubert, an eminent foreign artist, iii.	576
Letters, revival of, in the Western World, ii. . 200-222
LEVER, T.; his description of Cambridge University, ii.	819
LEVERSEY, Sir Michael, overcomes Earl of Holland, iii.	383
LEVI, M., a French general, iv.	586
LEVINO, Sir Richard; committed to the Tower, iv.	86, 88
LEVINGSTONE, Colonel, commander of forces in Scotland, iv.	44
Lewes Priory, View of the ruins; Battle here, i.	684, 685
LEWIS, M.P., accused by the army, iii.	369
———, Mr, gentleman of horse to Lord Feversham, iv.	62
LEWKNOR, Sir Lewis, *first* master of the ceremonies, iii. 7, 92
LEXINGTON, Lord, sent on an embassy to Madrid, iv.	250
Leyden jar, discovered by Cuneus and Lallemand, iv.	734
———, John of, a mathematician of 13th century, i.	844
LHUYD, Humphrey, a Welsh antiquary, i. . . 16, 21
Libel bill passed into a law, v. . .	852
———, cases of, . . . v. 425-428; vi. 781, 785
Library, description of a, in the 17th century, iii.	630
LICHFIELD, Earl of, captain of the king's horse-guards, iii.	343
LIGHTFOOT, Mr, counsel for the Earl of Strafford, iii.	239
Light-house, Eddystone Rock, iv.	664
———, erection of one at Plymouth, iii.	558
LIGNEVILLE, Count de, iv.	340
LIGON, his history of Barbadoes in 1647, iii.	548
LIGONIER, Colonel, present at battle of Falkirk, iv.	495
LILBURNE, J., a bookseller; his Portrait, iii. 167, 302, 303, 373
Lillo on the Scheldt, View of, v.	593
Lime, in Kent; the Roman station *Lemannæ*, i.	90
LIMERICK, Lord, iv.	434
Limerick, Treaty of, vii.	192
———, View of, &c., iv. . . . 26, 27, 34
LIN, Commissioner; his abolishment of the opium-traffic, vii	615
LINACER, Thomas, an eminent physician, iii.	819
LINCOLN, John de la Pole, earl of, ii. . . 175, 288-290
———, J., instigates tumult against foreign artisans, ii.	778
———, Major-general, an American officer, v.	282
Lincoln, state of, in 17th century, iii.	655
———, View of; ancient Roman arches, &c., i.	10, 430
Lincolnshire, insurrection of commons of, ii. 104, 397, 398
Lincoln's-inn, description of its foundation, i.	819
LINDESAY, Alexander de, a follower of Wallace, i.	715, 716
Lindisfarne, or Holy Island; View of Abbey, i. . 146, 147
LINDSAY, Alexander, a navigator and hydrographer, ii.	705
———, Lord, a royalist, iii. . . . 186, 297
———, Lord, of the Byres, ii. . . . 303, 327
———, Mr David, minister of Leith, iii. . 451, 484
———, Mr David, under-secretary to James II., iv. 141, 146
———, Sir David, a witty poet, . ii. 638; iii. 644
LINDSEY, Montague Bertie, earl of, iii.	696
———, Robert Bertie, earl of, iii.	138
———, R. B.; his bill for security of Protestantism, iii.	712
Linen manufacture in Scotland, iv. 583; v. 493; vi.	844
Lisbon, adventures of fleet of King Richard at, i.	467
———, View of, vi.	470
L'ISLE, Adam, a partisan of Duke of Burgundy, ii. 41, 45, 73, 79
LISLE, Lord, eldest son of Earl of Warwick, ii.	495
———, Mr, a Commonwealth-man, iii.	690
———, Mrs Alicia, beheaded by James II., iii.	779
———, Sir George, a royalist at battle of Naseby, iii. 333, 383
———, Sir John, a Yorkist, slain at battle of Barnet, ii.	100
Lissa, Battle of, fought December 5, 1757, iv.	570
LISTON, the comedian, death of, in 1846, vii.	734
Literary property, settlement of the law of, vii. 647-649
———, ———, subject of, v. . . . 432, 434

	PAGE
Literature, Science, and the Fine Arts—	
i. 118, 289, 603, 842; ii. 196-235, 813-854; iii. 560-616, 870-886; iv. 685-749; v. 499-532; vi. 650-905
Lithographic printing, importance of, to works of art, vii.	214
Lithotomy, first operation of, at Paris, ii.	208
LITTLETON, E. G., Irish secretary, vii. . 395-401, 418
———, Lord-keeper, iii. . . . 235, 286, 340
———, Mr, implicated in Essex-house affair, ii.	689
———, Sir Edward; his defence of ship-money, iii.	179
———, Sir T., a judge of Common Pleas, ii. 164; iii.	727
———, Sir Thomas, iv. . . .	77
LIULF, a Saxon noble, i. . . . 384, 385
Liverpool and Manchester Railway opened in 1830, vii.	329
LIVERPOOL, Charles Jenkinson, iv. . . . 798, 884
———, Earl of, vii. 7, 103, 184, 136, 184, 206, 225-228, 257
Liverpool, Litherpoole, or Lirpool, iii.	656
LIVERSEEDGE, Henry, death of, vii.	442
LIVINGSTON, Sir Alexander, a turbulent noble, ii. 184, 135
LIVINGSTONE, Lady, nurse to James I.'s oldest son, iii.	445
LIVY, the Roman historian; quoted, i.	35
LLEWELLYN, Prince; description of Welsh, &c., i. 605-698
Lloegrwys, a people of Gascony, migrated to Britain, i.	9
LLOYD, Dr, iii.	720
LLUYD, Humfrey, a Dutch engraver, iii.	577
LOBKOWITZ, Prince, iv.	448
Local Courts Bill of 1834, vii.	421
Lochgillip, Treaty of, ii.	132
Lochleven Castle, View of, &c., ii. . . 602, 604-607
LOCKE, John; his Portrait, &c., iv. . . 685, 739, 740
Locks, manufacture of, vi.	836
LODBROKE'S daughters embroider a magical banner, i.	159
LODGE, Thomas, a dramatic writer, iii.	587
LODGE'S *Illustrations of British History*; quoted, iii.	2
Lodi, Battle of, fought May 10, 1796, v.	106
LOE, Mr, counsel for Earl of Strafford, iii.	239
LOFTUS, Sir Adam, chancellor, iii.	171
LOLHARD, Walter, founder of the Lollards; burnt, ii.	141
Lollards, origin of the, &c., ii. . . 25, 38, 140-147
LOLLIUS URBICUS's expedition into Caledonia, i.	47
Lombards, or *Longobardi*; their laws, i.	145
LOMBART, Peter, a Parisian engraver, iii.	578
LOMBE, John; erected first silk-mill at Derby, iv.	682
LOMÉNIE, archbishop of Toulouse, v. . . 740, 827
London, address of the Corporation of the city of, vii. 32, 33
——— Bridge, new, foundation-stone laid in 1825, vii. 214, 435
——— Clubs, vii.	303
——— electors, Lord John Russell's letter to the, vii.	724
——— Hollar's print of the city before Great Fire, iii. 545, 699
———; illustrations, &c., ii. . 88, 89, 170, 261, 404
——— in the Roman period, i. 43, 44, 54, 86, 163, 164, 309, 435, 585, 589, 615, 684, 685, 687, 688, 743, 810
——— Monument, suicides from the, vii.	591
———, the League carries the election of the city of, vii.	686
———, Treaty of, on the affairs of Greece, vii.	238
——— University charter, vii.	455
LONDONDERRY, Lord, debate on appointment of, vii. 452, 453
———, ——— See Lord Castlereagh.	
———, Sir Charles Stewart, marquis of, vi.	665
Londonderry, View of the city, &c., iv. . . 16, 17
LONG, M.P., seized by the king, iii. . . 142, 369
———, St John, the quack-doctor, vii. . . 432, 433
LONGCHAMP, William, i. . . 485, 505, 506-508, 511
LONGLAND, John, bishop of Lincoln, ii. . . 375, 376
LONGUEVILLE, Duke of; prisoner at battle of Spurs, ii. 325, 331
LONSDALE, John Lowther, Viscount, iv.	80
LOO, v.	539
LOPEZ, Roderigo, physician to Queen Elizabeth, ii. 679, 680
Lord, Congregation of the, ii.	548
Lords, House of, position of the, vii.	365
———; View, v.	59
——— of the Articles, a Scottish committee, iv.	43
———, remarkable scene in the House of, vii. . 347, 348
LORN, Lord of, endeavours to take Bruce prisoner, i.	729
LORRAINE, Cardinal of, uncle of Mary Queen of Scots, ii.	583
Lorsch, portico at, i. . . . 312, 313
LOSINGA, Herbert, bishop of Thetford, i. . . 604, 615

LOTHIAN, Lord, protests at the proceedings instituted against Charles I., iii. . . . 352, 393
Lothians, the, i. 216, 221
LOUDON, J. C., the landscape-gardener, death of, vii. 734
———, Lord, Covenanters imprison in the Tower, iii. 207, 358
LOUGHBOROUGH, Alex. Wedderburne, Lord, v. 853; vi. 780
LOUIS, Don, king of Spain, iv. . . . 367
——— NAPOLEON and the Strasburg insurrection, vii. 537, 548
——— PHILIPPE, king of the French, vii. 422–431, 535–541
———; flies from Paris as Duke of Chartres, vi. 4
———; Portrait of, v. . . . 791, 881
——— THE DAUPHIN, son of Charles VI., ii. 26–28, 36, 37
——— IV., named D'Outremer, king of France, i. 169
——— VI. of France, receives Wm. Fitz-Robert, i. 412, 417
——— VII. of France, i. 439, 440, 442, 444–446, 452, 467–544
——— VIII., king of France, i. . 531–533, 672–675
——— IX., king of France, i. . 675, 676, 684, 689, 690
——— XI., king of France, ii. . . . 84
——— XII., king of France, ii. 292–294, 297, 311, 320, 322
——— XIII., king of France, iii. . . . 49, 88
——— XIV., king of France, iii. 706, 707, 710, 715, 717, 760, 765, 793; iv. 32, 33, 36, 47, 291
——— XV., king of France, iv. . . . 367
——— XVI., king of France— v. 739–757, 781–792, 825–847, 858–897; vi. 2–169
——— XVII., v. . . 834, 838, 863, 865, 870, 895
———, king of France, his death, vi. . 16, 93
——— XVIII., Stanislaus Xavier— v. 843; vi. 93, 689, 699, 700, 713, 714, 723, 724, 732
LOUISA OF SAVOY, mother of Francis I., ii. 356, 359–361
LOUVERTURE, Toussaint, Portrait of, vi. . . 191
LOUVET, a Girondist; his speech against Robespierre, v. 886
LOYAL, Lord, iii. 15; iv. 140–142, 146, 303, 499, 523–525
LOVE, an alderman, refuses to take the sacrament, iii. 684
LOVEL, F., Viscount, a partisan of Richard III., ii. 129, 286
———, Sir Thomas, privy-councillor, i. . 320, 323
LOVELACE, Colonel, an elegant writer of songs, &c., iii. 604
LOWE, Sir Hudson, governor of St Helena, vi. . 715–721
———, death of, vii. . . . 731
Lower Canada; suspension of its constitution in 1838, vii. 551
LOWINGER, Captain, a Dutch soldier of Fortune, iii. 282
LOWTHER, Sir James, volunteers into the army, iv. . 573
LUCAN, describes the Druids, i. . . . 61
LUCAS, Captain, a partisan of Charles II.; executed, iii. 419
LUCAS, Lord; his feelings with regard to Papists, iii. 721
———, Sir Charles, shot by Fairfax as a traitor, iii. 383
———, Sir Jervas, governor of Belvoir Castle, iii. . 344
Lucifer-matches; their utility, vii. . . 744
Lucknow, Palace of Sujah Dowla at; View of, v. . 618
LUCRETIUS, the poet, i. 105
LUCY, Richard de, a courtier of King Henry II., i. 452, 470
Luddites; their destruction of machinery, vi. . 031
Ludi, the, ii. 877–886
LUDLOW, General, a Commonwealth-man, iii. . 690
LUKIN, Lionel, death of, in 1834, vii. . . 440
LULLY, Raymond, a philosopher and alchemist, i. 844, 848
LUMLEY, General; his conduct at battle of Schellenberg, iv. 152
LUNDIE, Colonel, governor of Londonderry, iv. . 16
LUNDIN, Sir Richard, joins standard of Wallace, i. 715, 716
Lunéville, Treaty of, concluded Feb. 9, 1801, vi. . 152
LUNN, a servant of Williams, bishop of Lincoln; fined, iii. 164
LUNSFORD, Colonel, a royalist officer, iii. . 221, 267
LUPTON, Thomas, a dramatist of 16th century, iii. . 583
LUTHER, Martin, the German Reformer, ii. 376, 706–709
Lutherans of Prussia, the, vii. . . . 548
Lutzen, Birth of, Gustavus Adolphus killed at, iii. 173
LUXEMBOURG, James of, brother of Duchess of Bedford, ii. 101
Luxembourg, restored to Spain, iv. . . 70
———, View of the, v. . . . 830
LUXEMBURGH, Walleran of, count of St Pol, ii. . 10, 15
LUYNES, Duke de, minister of Louis XIII., iii. . 63, 105
LYDGATE; his ballad, *The London Lickpenny*, ii. 210, 258
LYLY, John, the Euphuist, and dramatic writer, ii. 835; iii. 586
LYNDHURST, Lord; Portrait, vii. . 361, 420, 526, 532
LYNEDOCH, Sir T. Graham, lord, vi. 581, 604, 643, 673, 690
Lynne, iii. 655

Lyon King-at-arms; Scottish herald, ii. . . 325
———, Siege of, 1793, vi. . . . 8
LYTTELTON, Sir George, chancellor of Exchequer, iv. 556, 560
LYTTLETON, Thomas, lord, v. . 89, 92, 98, 137

M'ADAM, Mr, death of, in 1836, vii. . . 593
MACADAM, his improvements in road-making, vi. 822
MACARTENEY, George, earl, governor of Madras, v. . 630
MACARTNEY, General, iv. . . . 251
MACAULAY, T. B., vii. 741
———, the historian; quoted, iv. . . 46
———, Zachary, death of, vii. . . 597
M'CARTHY, Sir Charles, a British general, vii. . 153
Macbeth, king of Scotland, i. . . 194, 221, 222
MACCHIAVELLI, principles of, ii. . . . 318
MACCLESFIELD, Lord, iv. . . . 21, 365, 366
Macclesfield, riot of 1824 in, vii. . . 174
M'DONALD, Colonel Æneas, iv. . . . 498
———, Flora; her Portrait, iv. . 515–517, 525
———, of Keppoch, killed at Culloden, iv. . 511
MACDOWAL, Duncan, defeats Bruce's brothers, i. 729
M'GINNIS, an Irish insurrectionist; he takes Newry, iii. 254
MACHADO, Antonio Alvarez, iv. . . 239
Machine breaking, act against, vii. . 24, 25, 339
MACINTOSH, Sir James; quoted, i. . . . 168
MACK, General, his surrender at Ulm, vi. . 275
MACKAY, General, iv. . . 15, 33, 36, 37
MACKENZIE, Colonel Humberstone, v. . 631, 632
———, Henry, death of, in 1831, vii. . 444
———, Sir George, iv. . . . 736
———, Sir John, a partisan of the Pretender, iv. 303
MACKEY, Mr, seizes Abbé Gaultier and Matthew Prior, iv. 236
MACKINTOSH, of Borlum, a veteran soldier, iv. . 295
———, Sir James; his *Vindiciæ Gallicæ*, v. 824
———; Portrait, vii. 101, 127, 400, 443
———; quotations from, iii. . 779
MACKWORTH, Sir Humphrey, iv. . . . 168
M'LEAN, of Drimnin, killed at battle of Culloden, iv. 511
MACLELLAN, put to death by Douglas, ii. . 135
M'LEOD, of Assin, iii. . . . 683
———, of Rasay, a partisan of young Pretender, iv. 517
M'MAHON, Hugh, iii. . . . 254
Macmillanites, another name for Cameronians, iv. 1621
M'NAGHTEN, Sir William; his death, vii. 624–627
MACPHERSON James; quoted, i. . 18, 591, 592
———; quoted, vi. 805, 807, 808, 810, 835, 840, 848
MACREADY, the tragedian, vii. . . . 740
M'VICAR, a Presbyterian preacher, iv. . . 478
Macziewicz, Battle of, fought Oct. 4, 1794, vi. . 67
MADDEN, Sir F.; account of Illuminated MS., i. 632
MADOC, a brave leader of the Welsh, i. . 711
MADOX, an English antiquary; quoted, i. 567, *et seq.*, 809
Madras, View of, &c., v. . . . 601–603
Madrid, View of, vi. . . . 608, 609
Magdalen College; dispute about a master for it, iii. 785, 786
Magdeburg, 30,000 persons perish at its capture, iii. 147
Magna Charta; Specimen of original copies, i. 528, 576, 577
MAGNUS, king of Norway and Denmark, i. . 183
MAGUIRE, Cornelius, baron of Inniskillen, iii. 252
Maheidpoor, Battle of, fought 21st December 1817, vii. 69
MAHMOUD II., Sultan, vi. . . 383, 503, 504
Mahratta wars, vii. . . . 71–78
Mail-coaches, vii. 821
———, origin of, v. . . . 466
MAILHE's report against Louis XVI., v. . 887, 893
MAILLARD, heads the mob of Paris women, v. 752, 877
MAILLEBOIS, the French marshal, iv. . 424, 453
Nails, conveyance of, vii. . . . 434
Main Plot; Raleigh, Cobham, Grey, &c., tried for, iii. 8–15, 72
Maine, ceded to Count René of Anjou, ii. . 81, 84, 86
———, people of, revolt against William, i. 379, 383, 401
MAINWARING, Colonel, iii. . . . 242
———, Dr Roger, iii. . . 123, 124, 134
MAISTER, rector of Aldington, and others, hanged, ii. 385
MAITLAND, captain of the *Bellerophon*, vi. . 714, 715
———, General, at Quatre Bras, vi. . . 704

MAITLAND, W., of Lethington, ii. 554, 559, 594, 612, 625, 649
Majesty, first addressed in England to Henry VIII., ii. 365
MALACHI, king of Ireland, death of, i. . . 429
Malayan pirates, expeditions against the, vii. . 632
MALCOLM, Alex. author of a treatise on music, iv. 713
———, Sir John; quoted, vii. . 66, 69, 70, 74-78
——— I., king of Scotland, i. . . 219, 533
——— II., king of Scotland, i. . . . 221
——— III., surnamed Caenmore, king of Scotland—
i. 194, 222, 369, 371, 372, 378, 379, 398, 399, 533-537
MALCOLM IV., king of Scotland, i. . 442, 445, 542, 543
MALESHERBES, one of the counsel of Louis XVI., v. 890-895
MALET, William, a Norman general, i. . . 370
MALIBRAN, Madame, death of, vii. . . . 599
Mallnes, View of, v. 683
MALLERY, Mr, committed to jail, iii. . . 88
MAILET-DU-PIN'S mission to Austria and Prussia, v. 864
MALLET, Robert de, a Norman baron, i. . . 408
MALMESBURY, Lord, vii. . . . . 118, &c.
Malmsbury, Abbey of, i. 615
MALMESBURY, James Harris, earl of, vi. . 98, 119
———, William of; quoted, i. . . 589, 632, 637
MALPEDIR, Earl, assassinates Duncan of Scotland, i. 538
Malplaquet, Battle of, fought Sep. 12, 1709, iv. . 216
Malta, island of ; View of, vi. . . 152, 499
MALTHUS, death of, in 1834, vii. . . . 603
———, Mr; his celebrated 'Essay,' vi. . . 862
MALTRAVERS, Lord, marries without royal consent, iii. 119
Malt-tax, debate on the, vii. . . . 414, 452
Malwood Keep, a hunting-seat in the New Forest, i. 401
Man, Isle of, royal standard hoisted in the, v. . 534
Manchester, iii. 656
——— and Liverpool Railway opened on 15th
September 1830, vii. 329
Manchester, Carlisle, Staffordshire, &c., riots at, vii. 189, 569
——— meeting, and its consequences, vii. . 107-113
MANCHESTER, Charles Montagu, earl of, iv. . 90
———, Edward Montagu, earl of, iii. . 263, 306
———, George Montagu, duke of, v. . . 89
———, Henry Montagu, earl of, iii. . . 146
MANCINI, M., nephew to Cardinal Mazarin, iii. . 427
———, Olimpia, mother of Prince Eugene, iv. . 242
MANDAT, butchered by the French revolutionists, v. 869
MANDEVILLE, Sir John, an English traveller, i. . 845
———, William de. See Albemarle, earl of, i.
MANDUBRATIUS, prince of the Trinobantes, i. . 33
MANLEON, Savaric de, leader of a foreign band, i. 530
MANLEY, John, farms the Post-office, iii. . . 552
Manners and Customs, vi. . . . 906-923
———, and Condition of the People—
ii. 236-267, 855-898 ; iii. 617-649,
887-900 ; iv. 750-792 ; v. 533-573
——— of early races, i. 5, 125, 323, 634, 864
MANNING, Thomas, death of, in 1840, vii. . . 600
MANNY, Sir Walter, a brave English general, i. 761, 762, 769
MANOURIE, bribed by Raleigh, iii. . . . 76
MANSEL, Colonel, a Presbyterian officer, iii. . 732
MANSELL, Sir R., vice-admiral of England, iii. 85, 113, 242
MANSFELDT, Count ; collects troops in England, iii. 85, 106, 126
MANSFIELD, Earl of, iv. 429, 457, 564, 852, 860, 875, 877, 887
———, Sir James, a lawyer, v. 1, 64, 143, 311, 430
Mansion House, London, View of the, v. . 9
Mantes, city of, taken and burnt by William I., i. 389
MANTEUFEL, General, a Prussian officer, iv. . 570, 583
MANTON, Mr, at Cromwell's inauguration, iii. . 423, 819
Manufactures and Arts, vi. . . . 817-848
——— and Commerce, vii. . . 20, 21
Manuscripts, illuminated, Gospel of St John, i. . 169
Map of Ireland. See Frontispiece, iv.
MAR, Earl of, a partisan of the Pretender, iv. 292, 295-299
———, third son of James II. of Scotland, ii. 132, 136
MARAT, . v. 784, 787-792, 866-896 ; vi. 3-15
MARATTI, Carlo, a painter of 17th century, iii. . 569, 820
MARBECK, John, burnt, . . . ii. 728 ; iii. 562
MARCEL, Stephen, provost of merchants of France, i. 774
MARCELLINUS, Ammianus, mention of the Scots, &c., i. 19, 63

MARCH, Earl of, a disaffected Scottish baron, ii. . 11, 49
———, Edmund, earl of, confined at Windsor, ii. 6
———, Edward, earl of. See Edward IV., ii. . 96
———, Roger, earl of, i. 791
MARCHE, Count de la, robbed of his wife, i. 517, 518, 674
———, Jaques de Bourbon, count de la, ii. . 18, 48
MARCHMONT, Earl of, iv. . . . 126, 147
MARCUS, and afterwards GRATIAN, elected emperors, i. 55
MARE, Sir Peter de la, speaker of the Commons, i. 780
Marengo, Battle of, fought June 14, 1800, vi. . 156
MARESCHAL, William, i. . . . 500, 515
MARGARET, daughter of Louis, king of France, i. 446, 470
——— OF ANJOU ; Portrait of, &c.—
ii. 81, 82, 92, 95, 97, 99-101, 105, 109, 110
——— PLANTAGENET, sister of Edward IV., ii. . 103
———, queen of James IV., ii. 307, 311, 312, 331, 349-354
———, queen of Malcolm Caenmore, i. 369, 399, 537
MARIA, infanta of Spain, iii. . . 93, 98, 100, 395
——— THERESA, queen of Louis XIV., iv. . . 84
MARIE ANTOINETTE, queen of France—
v. 739-757, 781-792, 825-847, 861-896 ; vi. 16-18
———, marriage of the Princess, vii. . . 539
Marignano, hard-contested victory of Francis I. at, ii. 334
MARJORY, queen of Robert Bruce, i. . 729, 738
Markets, opening of new London, vii. . . 301
MARKHAM, Sir Griffin, a Catholic, banished, iii. 8, 9, 13-15
———, Sir Robert, iii. 733
———, William, bishop of Chester, v. . . 15
MARLBOROUGH, Earl of, iii. . . . 538
——— John Churchill, duke of, iv. . 22, 36-39,
47, 67, 73, 126, 129-133, 152-158, 169, 180,
200, 215, 232, 239, 240, 252, 280, 284, 286, 359
———, Lady, iv. . . 19, 126, 229, 448
MARLOW, Christopher, a dramatist, iii. . . 586
MARMONT, Marshal. See also Wellington, vi. . 585, 606
———, Marshal, vii. 278-283
MARNEY, Sir H., one of Henry VIII.'s privy-council, ii. 320, 344
Marquess, the first English, was Robert de Vere, i. 882
MARR, Donald, earl of, regent of Scotland, i. . 755
———, Earl of, regent of Scotland, ii. . . 646, 647
Marriage Act, Royal, . . . ii. 80, 332 ; v. 21
——— Acts of 1822-1823, vii. . . 139, 168
———-law, improvement in the, vii. . 521, 522
Marriages, objections of Catholic clergy to mixed, vii. 548
MARRIOTT, Dr, advocate-general, examination of, v. 67-69
MARSDEN, Mr, death of, in 1837, vii. . . 600
Marseille, View of the modern city of, vi. . . 9
Marseilles, a tin emporium of the Cassiterides, i. . 26, 93
Marseillese Hymn ; origin of, v. . . . 866
MARSH, bishop of Ferns, treats acoustics methodically, iii. 886
Marshall, or Mareschall, office of the, i. . . 569
MARSTON, John, a dramatist of 16th century, iii. 592
Marston Moor, Battle of, iii. . . . 315
MARTIN, Commodore, threatens to bombard Naples, iv. 436
———, Henry ; condemned as a regicide, iii. 247, 672, 677
———, Henry, establishes the British Merchant, iv. 666
———, Sir Henry, iii. 363
——— V., Pope, ii. . . 41, 43, 71, 137, 138, 150
Martinique, surrenders to the English ; View of, iv. 810, 811
MARVELL, Andrew ; his political satires, iii. 424, 605, 666
MARY D'ESTE, of Modena, queen of James II., iii. . 711
———, second wife of James II., iv. . . 2
———, duchess of Suffolk, ii. 315, 331, 332, 338, 351, 361
———, I., daughter of Henry VIII., ii. 364, 367, 368, 384
385, 390, 394-396, 501-538, 541, 695, 734-737, 801
——— OF GUISE, queen of James V., ii. 412, 547, 551, 560, 561
———, Princess, daughter of Charles I., iii. . . 272
——— QUEEN OF SCOTS, ii. 434, 435, 469, 536, 549, 563-565
568, 574-618, 628, 629, 644, 645, 658, 660, 662-670
———, queen of William III., iv. . . 2, 5-8, 49
MASANIELLO, an Italian fisherman, iii. . . 395
MASERES, Mr, attorney-general of Quebec, v. . 66, 67
MASHAM, Mrs, bed-chamber woman to Queen Anne, iv. 192
MASON, Mr, secretary to the Duke of Buckingham, iii. 121
MASSENA, Andrew, prince of Essling, vi. 510, 511, 539-584
MASSEY, Colonel, governor of Gloucester, iii. 306, 331, 369

MASSINGER, an English dramatist, iii. . . 597
MATHEW, Father, the Irish temperance apostle, vii. 500–502
MATHEWS, Charles, death of, vii. . . . 599
MATILAS, of Austria, pledges jewels and plate, ii. 649
MATILDA, daughter of Fulk, earl of Anjou, i. 412, 413
———, eldest daughter of Henry II.; from her is
descended the present royal family of Great Britain, i. 480
MATILDA, or MAUD, queen of King Stephen, i. 421, 426, 438
———, queen of Henry I., i. . 406, 407, 413
———, Queen, married to the earl of Anjou—
i. 417, 418, 421–426, 428–435, 452
———, queen of Henry V. of Germany, i. . 412, 416
———, queen of William I., i. . 366, 370, 384, 386
MATTHEWS, Admiral; his trial by court-martial, &c., iv. 436, 446
———, Captain, iii. 771
———, General; his unworthy conduct in India, v. 833
MATUEOF, ambassador of Peter the Great, iv. . 644
MAULAO, Peter de, esquire of King John, i. . 520
MAUNSELL, Sir Robert; his mission to Algiers, iii. 537
MAURICE, a grocer, elected for Westminster, iii. . 130
———, bishop of London, i. . . . 405
———, Count; claimed to be Duke of Gueldres, iii. 46
MAUROLICO, a celebrated Italian mathematician, iv. 713
MAURY, Abbé, v. . . 743, 756, 782, 785–792, 825
Mausoleum of Burns at Dumfries; illustration, vii. . 598
MAW, Dr, a partisan of the Duke of Buckingham, iii. 121
MAXFIELD, first lay-preacher employed by Wesley, iv. 623
MAXIMILIAN, a general of Gustavus Adolphus, iii. . 146
——— I., the emperor, ii. 116, 292–298, 325, 336, 337
MAXIMUS, provincial emperor in Britain, i. . . 54
MAXWELL, James, gentleman-usher, iii. . . 216
———, John, archbishop of Tuam, iii. . 478, 484
———, Lord, escorts James V. to Caerlaverock, ii. 433
———, Lord, suspected of Papacy, iii. . . 452
———, Sir Murray, death of, in 1831, vii. . . 441
MAY, Sir Humphrey; quoted, iii. . . 134, 288, 358
MAYNARD, governor of Goritz, i. . . . 502
———, Mr; his report on ship-money, iii. 237, 320, 369, 522
Maynooth grant, great political controversy on the, vii. 667, 868
MAVO, Colonel, severely wounded, iii. . . 416
Mazanderan, pillar-temples of, i. . . . 16
MAZARIN, Cardinal, iii. . . 357, 395, 420, 427
MAZZINI, Signor; Portrait, vii. . . 699, 700
Meal-tub Plot, discovered by Dangerfield, iii. . 731, 732
Meanee, Battle of, vii. 629, 630
Meats and Caledonians, i. . . . 126
Mechanics' institutes, originated by Dr Birkbeck, vii. 211, 212
Medals, commemorating battles, iv. 18, 25, 28, 29, 157, 169,
200, 202, 223, 299; 413, 440, 579, 584; v. 96, 156, 423, 430, 520
Medical education; improvements of 1830, vii. . 432, 433
MEDICI, Mary de, mother of Louis XIII., iii. 49, 51, 247, 248
Medicine, practice of, in 15th century, ii. . . 208
———, science of, ii. 745
MEDINA CELI, Duke of, iv. 93
——— SIDONIA, Duke of, commander of the Armada, ii. 674
———, Sir Samuel de, iv. 239
Medway, Dutch fleet in the; illustration, iii. . 702
Meetings and petitions for the Reform Bill, vii. . 359
MELA, Pomponius; quoted, i. . . . 36
Melbourne administration, vii. . 418–421, 457–507
MELBOURNE, Lord; Portrait, vii. 353, 418–421, 449–807, 641
MELDRUM, Sir John; his sortie upon king's forces, iii. 293
MELFORT, secretary of state to James II., iv. 7, 14, 59, 100, 101
MELLENT, Robert de, relative of Henry I., i. . 409, 413
———, Walleran, earl of, i. . . . 538
MELLITUS, bishop of the East Saxons, i. . . 233, 234
Melun, on the Seine, taken by Henry V., ii. . 48
MELUN, Viscount de, i. 531, 532
MELVIL, Andrew, iii. . 64, 65, 438, 441, 446, 448, 463, 464
———, James, nephew of Andrew, iii. 65, 446, 463, 464
MELVILLE, Henry Dundas, viscount, vi. . 258, 815–817
———, James, assists in murder of Beaton, ii. . 446
———, Lord, his address to Charles I., iii. . 156
———, Sir J.; Queen Elizabeth as a musician, iii. 564
———, Sir James, ii. . . 298, 575–579, 588
———, Sir R., intercedes for Queen of Scots, ii. 665, 668

MÉNAGER, M., an expert diplomatist, iv. . . 285
Menai Bridge, opened in January 30, 1826, vii: . 213
Mendicant Friars, statute respecting, &c., ii. . 152, 717
Mendicity and vagrancy, vii. . . . 40
Mentz Cathedral; its style of architecture, i. . 313
MERCER, John, taken prisoner by John Philpot, i. 783
Merchant Adventurers of London; ii. . 774, 783, 784
MERCY, Count de, iv. . . . 338, 341, 392
MEREDITH, Mr, member for county of Kent, iv. . 106
MERES, Thomas, bishop of Carlisle, . i. 799; ii. 7
MERRICK, Sir John, a parliamentarian, iii. . . 291
Mersey, Isle of, Essex; blockade of, i. . . 163
MERTON, Walter de, chancellor of England, i. . 688
MESOHINES, Renouf; first earl of Cumberland, i. . 375
Messina, revolts from the Spanish viceroy, iii. . 714
Metallic currency of 1826, vii. . . . 185
——— manufactures, iv. 683
Metalline manufactures, vi. . . . 837–839
METCALFE, Sir Charles T., governor of Canada, vii. 717
Methodism, alarm of clergy at spread of, vi. . 765
———, origin of, in England, iv. . . 622–625
Methodists and their first preachers, &c., iv. . 622
METHUEN, chancellor of Ireland, iv. . . . 87
———, Sir Paul; address to George II., iv. . 377
Methuen Treaty, vii. 543
———, between Portugal and England, iv. 665
METTERNICH, Prince; Portrait, vii. . . 2, 3, 400
Mexico and Texas, American invasion of, vii. . 711
———, Spanish revolution in, vii. . . 49
Mezzotint, invention of, iii. 683
MICKLEBORNE, Sir Edward, iii. . . . 529
MICHELL, Sir Thomas; his patents from James I., iii. 524
MICKLE, the translator of Camoens, iii. . . 602
Micklebar Gate, View of, iii. . . . 287
MIDDIMAN, Samuel, a landscape line-engraver, vi. . 879
MIDDLEMORE, an agent of Elisabeth, ii. . . 610
MIDDLETON, a dramatist of 17th century, iii. . 503
———, Dr Conyers; Portrait, of, v. . . 506
———, Earl of, iii. . . . 298, 416, 681
———, Mr Hugh, knighted by King James, iii. 547
———, Mr, member for Sussex, iii. . . 242
———, Sir H.; his East Indian expedition, iii. 529, 530
MIGUEL, Don, regent of Portugal, vii. . 254–257, 271
MILAN, Duchess-dowager of; rejects Henry VIII., ii. 412
Milan, duchy and city of; its sovereigns, &c., ii: 384, 358
MILDMAY, Sir Anthony, routs a body of Levellers, iii. 36
———, Sir Henry, a parliamentarian, iii. 387, 407, 665
———, Sir Henry, his remarks on monastic and
conventual institutions, vii. . . . 759
MILES, Mr; his proposition on the sugar-duties, vii. 692
Milesians, same as Scots, a Scythian colony, i. . 15
MILCO, John; proscribed by the pope as a heretic, iii. 80
Military flogging, Mr Hume advocates abolition of, vii. 416
Militia Bill, 1642, iii. 274
MILL, James, death of, in 1836, vii. . . . 303
———, Walter, last of the Scottish martyrs, ii. . 747
MILLAR, Professor; quoted, i. . . . 250
Millenarians or Fifth Monarchy-men, iii. . 813, 817
Millenary petition; iii. 455
MILLER, Mr Patrick, an Edinburgh banker, his steam-
boat experiments, vi. 829
MILLINGATTI, Father, confessor of James II., iv. . 69
Mills; hand-mills and water-mills before the Conquest, i. 600
Milton Gallery, the, vi. 872
MILTON, J., father of the poet, a composer of music, iii. 553
———, John, the poet, iii. 399, 420, 424, 609, 666, 870–874
Milton MS., discovery of the, in State-paper Office, vii. 217
Minden, Battle of, fought July 31, 1759, iv. . 582, 583
Mines and Collieries Act of 1843, vii. . . 853
———, notices of the English, i. . 92, 117, 600–602
Mining, vi. 832–835
Minorca, Island of, taken by Duke de Crillon, v. 366, 372
Minstrels, ii. 839
Mint, arrival of Chinese treasure at the, vii. . 618
MINTO, Gilbert Eliot, earl of, vi. . . 42, 100
MINYARD, Lord, iii. 270

GENERAL INDEX. 129

	PAGE
Miquelets, riotous proceedings of, iv.	165
MIRABEAC, a French revolutionist, vi.	61
———; Portrait of, &c.—	
v. 742, 743, 751, 756, 782-792, 825-832	
MIRANDA, General, vii.	47-51
MIREPOIX, M. de, French ambassador in England, iv.	554
MIROVITCH, Vassili; executed, v.	27, 28
Miscellaneous manufactures, vi.	846-849
Mischianza Ticket; illustration, v.	251
Mistletoe, the, sacred among the Druids, i.	63
MITCHELL, James, a young Covenanter, iii.	713, 729
———, Sir Francis, a patent monopolist, iii.	82
MITFORD, Mr, his bill in favour of the Catholics, vi.	754
———, the Greek historian, death of, in 1827, vii.	318
MITTON, Colonel, a parliamentarian, iii.	356
Moderate Church party, vii.	404
MOHAMMED ALI; Portrait of, v.	643-645
———, Dost, ruler of Cabool, vii.	622-625
——— REZA KHAN, v.	623, 624
Mohawk Indians and their Canoes; illustration, v.	288
MOHUN, Lord, killed in duel with Duke of Hamilton, iv.	251
Moinmor, Battle of, fought 1115, i.	459
Mold, in Flintshire, gold breastplate found in cairn at, i.	128
MOLESWORTH, Captain, at battle of Ramilies, iv.	169
MOLINAS, Don Jose, grand inquisitor, iv.	321
Molwitz, Battle of, fought April 10, 1741, iv.	423
MOLYNEUX; his work on the government of Ireland, iv.	71
MOMPESSON, Sir Giles, a patent monopolist, iii. 82, 524, 534	
———, Sir R.; his patent from Queen Elizabeth, iii.	534
Mona, Island of, resort of Druids and Britons, i.	43, 61
Monasteries; exhibiting Norman architecture, i. 614, et seq.	
———; reformation and suppression of, &c.—	
ii. 358, 362, 381, 390, 396, 397, 402, 404, 411	
Monastic Institutions' Bill, discussions regarding, vi. 759-761	
——— orders, ii.	381, 386, 390, 396, 399, 401
MONCKTON, Robert, an English general, iv.	554, 581, 810
Moncontour, Battle of; Huguenots defeated, ii.	626
Money, form and value of, among Anglo-Saxons, i. 271, et seq.	
MONKTON, Mr, M.P., iv.	98
Monmouth, Battle of; illustration, v.	255
MONMOUTH, Charles Mordaunt, earl of, iv.	67, 345
———, Henry Carey, earl of, iii.	288
———, James Fitzroy, duke of—	
iii. 708, 730-732, 738-740, 754, 755, 768, 770-778	
Monopolies, Elizabeth revokes many, ii.	692, 693, 769
———, revocation of various by James I., iii. 5,40,151,533	
MONRO, Sir Hector, defeats the nabob of Oude, v.	618
MONROE, a leader of the Covenanters, iii.	204, 309
MONSON, Lord, a distinguished Commonwealth-man, iii.	685
———, Sir Thomas, chief-falconer, iii.	59, 60
———, Sir William; quoted, iii.	535
Monster riot in France, vii.	536, 537
MONSFRELET; historical remarks, quoted, ii. 51, 60, 62, 209	
MONTACUTE, a Norman general under William I., i.	375
———, Lord, assists Edward III., i.	753
MONTAGUE, a Catholic peer, iii.	32, 36
———, ambassador at Paris, iii.	725
———, chancellor of the Exchequer, iv.	74, 87
———, Dr James, bishop of Winchester, iii. 118, 167, 606	
———, General; his loyal reception of Charles II., iii. *432	
———, Lord, a Yorkist, ii. 99, 101, 102, 104, 106, 108, 109	
———, Mr Wortley, iv.	417
———, Sir Henry, chief-justice of King's Bench, iii. 71	
———, Walter, iii.	186
Montague House, built by Pouget, iv.	698
MONTAIGNE, George, bishop of London, iii.	121
MONTCALM, General, iv.	580, 581
MONTECUCULI, an imperialist general, iii.	714
MONTEMAR, Count of, a Spanish general, iv.	391
Montereau, Bridge of, ii.	45, 46, 48, 78
MONTESQUIOU, a French revolutionary general, v.	884
MONTFORT, family of, earls of Leicester, i.	568
———, John de, claims Brittany, i. 760-762, 768, 769	
———, Robert de, accuses earl of Essex of treason, i.	443
———, Simon de, son of great earl of Leicester, i. 686-688	
MONTGOMERY, archbishop of Glasgow, iii.	441

	PAGE
MONTGOMERY, Arnulf de, a Norman baron, i.	408
———, Philip Herbert, earl of. See Pembroke.	
———, Richard, an American officer, iv.	199, 203
———, Richard; Portrait of, v.	118
———, Roger de, i.	394, 395
MONTMORENCY, Duke of, lord-admiral of France, iii.	112
———, marshal of Rieux, ii.	18, 622
MONTREUIL, a French ambassador, iii.	346, 348, 363
———, Madame de, ii.	412
MONTROSE, Lord of, iii.	202, 380, 337-341, 354, 402
Monument, the, on Fish-street Hill, iii. 700; iv.	695
Moodkee, Battle of, vii.	713
MOORE, John, an enthusiast, ii.	572
———, Mr, iii.	151
———, Mr Arthur, M.P., iv.	87
———, Mr; quoted, i.	14, 16, 20, 23
———, Roger, attempts to make Irish help themselves, iii. 252	
———, Serjeant, originator of *Lease and Release*, iii.	517
———, Sir John, vi.	441-461
———, Sir John, lord-mayor, iii.	739
———, Thomas, a poet, vi.	858, 883, 887, 888
Moravians, in England and North America, v.	421
MORAY, Randolph, earl of, i.	729, 736, 737, 739, 749, 755
———, Sir Andrew, of Bothwell, joins Wallace, i. 715, 716	
———, Sir Robert, member of the Royal Society, iv.	725
MORDAUNT, Brigadier, iv.	512
———, Lord, a Catholic, iii.	25, 32
MORE, Hannah; Portrait, vii.	404
———, Henry, an eminent English writer, iii.	578, 610
———, Sir Antonio, a famous painter, ii.	813, 853
———, Sir George, lieutenant of the Tower, iii.	61
———, Sir T., ii. 120, 124, 354, 366, 374, 378, 384-389, 820	
———, Sir Thomas; his fondness for music, iii.	562, 605
Morea, insurrection in the, v.	36-43
MOREAU, Jean Victor, vi.	105, 152, 244-248, 666
Morella, capture of, December 17, 1707, iv.	183
MORGAN, Colonel, a partisan of Cromwell, iii.	355, 425
———, William, death of, in 1833, vii.	439
Morini, a Gallic tribe near Calais, i.	27
MORLEY, George, bishop of Winchester, iii. 178, 562, 668, 712	
———, Lord, a Roman Catholic, ii.	633
MORNINGTON, Lord, death of, in 1845, vii.	781
MORPETH, Lord; Portrait, vii.	460, 461
MORRICE, Mr, an intimate friend of General Monk, iii.	663
MORRIS, Gouverneur, an American Republican, v.	750
MORSE; his statement as to ignorance of New England, iii. 807	
MORTAIGNE, Earl of, imprisoned for life, i.	410
Mortemain, limited repeal of the statute of, iv.	144
MORTIMER, Anne, sister of Edmund, ii.	8, 89
———, Earl of, cuts off Llewellyn's head, i.	698
———, Edmund, Earl of March, ii. 6,13,14,16,24,25,29,89	
———, Hugh de, master of castle of Bridgenorth, i. 442	
———, Roger, earl of March, ii.	6
———, Roger, Lord, i.	738, 741-743, 745, 748-755
———, Roger, son of the preceding, i.	6
———, Sir Edmund; prisoner at Knyghton, ii.	11, 19
Mortimer's Cross, near Hereford, Battle of, ii.	96, 97
MORTON, Bishop; his living sequestered, iii.	491
———, Dr Nicholas, apostolical penitentiary, ii.	628, 767
———, Earl of, ii. 584, 587, 591, 606, 645-649, 652, 653	
———, John, ii.	121, 126, 286, 294, 306, 310, 771, 772
———, Mr, a laceman, iv.	210
MORVILLE, Hugh de, one of Becket's murderers, i. 455, 456	
MOSELY, Humphrey, a publisher, iii.	598
Mothers, Lord Brougham on the position of, vii. 574-576	
MOTTE, Baroness de la; the 'diamond necklace,' v.	861
———, Count de la, governor of Ghent, iv.	201
MOULIN, Peter du, iii.	609
MOUNT EDGECUMBE, George, earl of, iv.	844, 845
MOUNTAIN, Dr, dean of Westminster, iii.	54
MOUNTEAGLE, Lord, a Roman Catholic, iii.	25-30
MOUNTJOY, Charles Blount, earl of, ii.	679
———, Lord, confined in the Bastille, iv.	11
———, Lord; patent for copperas and alum mines, ii. 811	
———, Lord, successor of Essex in Ireland, ii.	693
———, William Blount, earl of, ii.	381

MOUNTNORRIS, Lord, vice-treasurer of Ireland, iii. 171
MOWBRAY, Philip de, defeated by Bruce at Inverury, i. 735–738
——, Roger de, revolts against Henry, i. 470
MOYLE, General, iv. 397
——, Mr, M.P., iii. 242
MUDIE, Robert, death of, vii. 736
Muggletonians, a sect fiercely opposed to Quakers, iii. 813
MUIR, Thomas, vi. 25–27
Mulberry-trees, James I.'s proclamation respecting, iii. 558
MULGRAVE, Lord; Portrait, vii. 460, 491, &c.
MÜLLER, John, inventor of decimal fractions, iv. 713
——, William John, death of, vii. 734
Mullingar, in Ireland, monster meeting at, vii. 658
Mummers, mummings, masqueradings, &c., called *ludi*, ii. 255
Mummy inquest in Ireland, vii. 591
MUNDEN, Admiral, iv. 145
MUNGO, St, or KENTIGERN, a bishop in Strathclyde, i. 229
Municipal institutions, rise and history of, vii. 466
—— reform, vii. 372, 465–472
——, in Ireland, vii. 505–508
Municipia, Roman division of cities, i. 85
MUNRO, Colonel, slain at battle of Edgehill, iii. 297
——, Sir Thomas, death of, in 1828, vii. 313
MUNSTER, Bishop of, an ally of King Louis, iii. 710
MURAT, Joachim, a French general, vi. 412, 493–499, 661, 681, 691–695, 701, 702, 728, 731, 732
MURDOCH, William, a Cornish engineer, vi. 825, 833
MURRAY, General, besieged in Quebec by M. Levi, iv. 586
——, J. S., earl of, ii. 470, 548, 574, 575, 580, 581, 583, 587, 597, 603–605, 612, 615–617, 625, 630, 632; iii. 649
——, John, of Broughton, a Jacobite, iv. 444, 523
——, John, the publisher, death of, vii. 738, 739
——, Lindley, the grammarian, death of, in 1826, vii. 221
——, Lord George, iv. 461, 484, 488, 490, 492–520
——, Mr Alexander, brother of Lord Elibank, iv. 535–537
——, Mungo, a confidential servant of Charles I., iii. 268
——, Sir David, a friend of Prince Henry, iii. 51, 52
——, Sir John, vi. 658–660
——, Sir Robert, a partisan of Charles I., iii. 362
——, William, iii. 273, 362
MURTACH, king of Ireland, death of, i. 459
MURTOCH O'LOCHLIN, king of Ireland, i. 459
Museum, British; illustration of its reading-room, iii. 616
MUSGRAVE, Sir Christopher, iv. 111, 133
Music, ii. 233–235; iv. 710–713; v. 529–532; vi. 881–883
——; illustrations of performers, instruments, &c., iii. 561–7
——; Mr Hullah's classes in 1842, vii. 747
Musical festivals, expansion of, in 1820–1826, vii. 216
MUSKERRY, killed in an engagement with the Dutch, iii. 695
Muslins, manufacture of, vi. 842, 848
MUSTAPHA, Sultan, of Turkey, vi. 383, 500, 502
Mutiny Act, passed 1717, iv. 324, 866; v. 403
MYAGH, Thomas, an Irishman, charged with treason, iii. 519
MYLNE, Robert, architect of Blackfriars Bridge, vi. 866
Mycenean cavalry, v. 636
Mysteries, miracles, &c., preceding regular drama, ii. 256, 257
MYTENS, Daniel, an eminent Dutch artist, iii. 567
Mythology of Scandinavia and Teutonic tribes, i. 138, 140

NAIRNE, Miss, a Jacobite lady, iv. 471
Namur, surrenders to Louis XIV., iv. 36
Nancy, Bouillé defeats the insurgents of, v. 789
Nantes, attack on, by the Vendeans, vi. 21
——, Edict of, ii. 682
——; revoked by Louis XIV., iii. 784
——, inhabitants of, offer their city to Geoffrey, i. 443
NAPIER, John, the inventor of logarithms, iv. 716
——, Lord; his death, vii. 612, 613
——, Mr D.; improvements in steam-navigation, vi. 832
——, Sir Charles; Portrait, vii. 629, 630
Naples, besieged by French and Genoese; plague here, ii. 368
——, republic of, vi. 139, 141
NAPOLEON THE GREAT; his tomb at St Helena, vii. 133, 709
NARES, James, an eminent English composer, v. 529
Naseby, Battle of, gained by the parliament, iii. 333, 334
NASH, John, an eminent architect, vii. 893, 894

NASMITH, Peter, death of, in 1831, vii. 442
NASMYTH, Alexander, death of, vii. 599
NASSAU, Frederic, prince of, iii. 7
National advancement, review of, vii. 743–749
—— and Metropolitan Unions, vii. 355, 362
—— Assembly, Paris, View of, v. 826
—— —— dissolved, v. 839
—— Convention and petition, vii. 567, 568
—— ——, French, proposed, v. 871, 884, 899
—— Debt, scheme of, first proposed in 1696, iv. 65
—— education in Ireland, scheme for, vii. 494, 495
—— ——, ministerial scheme of 1834, vii. 477
—— Guard, review of the French, vii. 273
—— industry, history of the. See Industry.
—— Manners and Habits of Scotland, iv. 780
—— registration of births, marriages, and deaths, vii. 521
—— School Society, founded 1811, vi. 765
Naturalisation Bill, vii. 563
Navarino, Battle of, fought 20th October 1827, vii. 239–242
Navarre, kingdom of, ii. 321
——, King of, mortally wounded at Rouen, ii. 570
Navigation Act, iv. 147; vi. 798
—— —— passed; consequences therefrom, iii. 496
—— Acts, vii. 165
—— in 18th century, v. 452, 453, 462, 463
——, increase of, vi. 795, 796, 799, 802, 805, 809
—— Laws, iii. 856
——; ships of war in 15th century, &c., ii.177, 339, 780
——, some tribes more addicted to, than others, i. 6, 831
Navy-office, the, established by Henry VIII., ii. 780
NAYLOR, James, an enthusiastic Quaker, iii. 811, 812
NEAL, Richard, bishop of Durham, iii. 55, 140, 475, 608
NEALE, Colonel, present at battle of Chalgrove Field, iii. 304
NECKER, James, v. 739–745, 748–750, 781, 790
Negro Emancipation Act, vii. 386
—— slavery, debates on, in 1823, vii. 168–172
NEILE, Sir Paul, iv. 723
NELSON, Horatio, viscount, vi. 41, 42, 84, 99, 100, 116, 117, 136, 137, 141, 160–164, 282, 287–296, 298
Nepaul, the mountaineer population of, vii. 619
NERO, the emperor, I. 44
NEUBURG, Marie Anne of, wife of Charles II. of Spain, iv. 92
NEVERS, Count of, killed at battle of Agincourt, ii. 33
NEVIL, George, archbishop of York, ii. 102–104, 253
——, Lord, deprived of his employments, i. 779
——, Sir Francis, committed to the Tower, iii. 264
NEVILLE, Sir Christopher, arbitrarily arrested, iii. 86
——, Sir H., his speech in answer to James I., iii. 43, 55
——, Sir Ralph, defeated by Sir James Douglas, i. 739
Newark Castle, from an original drawing, iii. 305
NEWBURG, Duke of, claims succession of Duke of Cleves, iii. 48
NEWBURGH, William of; quoted, i. 503
Newbury, Battle of, iii. 307
—— ——, Donnington Castle; illustration, iii. 307
NEWCASTLE, Duke of, his promotion of reform, vii. 293
—— ——, premier of England, iv. 560
—— ——, Earl of, defeats Lord Fairfax, iii. 305
—— ——, Thomas Holles, duke of, iv. 795, 813
Newcastle-upon-Tyne, Camden's estimation of, iii. 656
—— ——, coal-trade of, dues, &c., ii. 191
—— ——; View of, i. 383, 536
NEWCOMEN on the steam-engine, iv. 727, 728; v. 474
Newgate, View of, vii. 299
NEWPORT, Earl of, constable of the Tower, iii. 260
Newport, Chartist riot at, vii. 560
——, Rhode Island, View of, v. 257
Newspapers, English, era of, commences 1640, iii. 615
—— ——, Bulwer advocates repeal of stamp-duty on, vii. 519
—— ——, Sunday; their first appearance, vi. 759
NEWTON, Sir Isaac; Portrait, &c., iv. 635, 730
——, T., author of a translation of the *Thebais*, iii. 584
New York, great fire at, in 1845, vii. 718
——, Views of, v. 123, 166, 169
—— Zealand, British emigration to, vii. 715–717
NEY, Michael, a French marshal, vi. 700, 723, 724
NEYNOE, an Irish Catholic priest, iv. 360

GENERAL INDEX. 131

Nice, demolished by the Duke of Vendôme, iv. . 164
NICHOLAS I., of Russia; Portrait, vii. 152, 430, 544, 545
———, V., Pope, a patron of learning, ii. . . 199
NICHOLSON, Margaret, attempts George III.'s life, v. 648
———, William, bishop of Carlisle, iv. . . 520
NICOLAS, an agent or solicitor in ecclesiastical causes, i. 539
NIGEL, bishop of Ely, i. 427–429
Niger expedition, the, vii. 589
Nile, Battle of the, fought August 1, 1798, vi. . 136, 137
Nimeguen, Peace of, iii. 716
———, View of, v. 655
NIMMO, Alexander, death of, in 1832, vii. . . 439
———, Mr, an eminent engineer, vi. . . . 528
Ningpo, capture of, by the British, vii. . . . 617
NINIAN, a monk; his history of the Britons, i. . 289
———, bishop of Whithern, in Wigtonshire, i. . 229
Nisi Prius, trials by, iv. 646
NITHSDALE, Lord; his escape from the Tower, &c., iv. 308
NIVERNOIS, Duke de, a French ambassador, iv. . 515
NOAILLES, Count de, v. 785
———, Duke de, iv. 49, 439, 441
NOLLEKENS, Joseph, a celebrated sculptor, vi. . . 875
———, death of, in 1823, vii. 219
Nomenclature, its durability, &c., i. . . . 7
Nonconformists, iii. 691
Nonjurors, iv. 10
Non-residence Act of 1838, vii. 474
Non-resistance, Oath of, iii. 696
Nonsuch, Palace of; illustration, ii. . . . 844
Nootka Sound, View in, v. 763
NORBURY, Lord, shot in his own shrubbery, vii. . 497
NORFOLK, Duke of, ii. 129, 287, 296, 326–381, 344, 348, 349, 429
———, J. H., duke of, ii. 113, 116, 123, 124, 128, 129, 284
———, Ralph de Gaël, earl of, i. . . 380–383
———, Roger B., earl of, marshal of England, i. 719–722
———, Thomas Howard, duke of, ii. 360, 363, 371, 372, 374, 382, 399–401, 449, 451, 457, 510, 513, 623–626, 638–641
NORFOLK, Thomas Howard, earl of, iii. 117, 119, 169, 174
———, Thomas Mowbray, duke of, i. . 795, 796
Norfolk, town of, reduced to ashes, v. . . . 120
Norham Castle, on the Tweed; View of its ruins, i. 540, 541
NORMAN, John, introduces lord-mayor's procession, ii. 261
Normandy, wars of Henry V., ii. 29, 39, 43, 70, 72, 79, 84, 85
Normans, origin of the, i. 138
NORRIS, Baron, son of Henry, ii. 392
———, Henry, groom of the bed-chamber, ii. 379, 391–394
———, Sir H.; intrigues with Huguenots, ii. 619–622, 628
———, Sir John, an English admiral, iv. . 348, 414
———, Sir John, one of Elizabeth's generals, ii. 392, 682
North America, map of, shewing North-west Passage, vii. 594
NORTH, Francis, lord Guildford, iii. 521, 522, 780, 844, 886
———, Lord, a partisan of the Pretender, iv. . 360, 378
———, Lord, his speech against the Test Acts, vi. . 748
———, Roger, attorney-general to James II., iii. 521, 844–848
———, Sir Dudley; his Portrait, &c., iii. . 739, 851
Northallerton, *Elfer-tun*, great Battle of, i. . 424–426
Northampton, Battle of, &c., ii. . . . 95, 150
NORTHAMPTON, Henry Howard, earl of, iii. . 39, 57
———, Spencer Compton, earl of, iii. . . 288
———, William Compton, earl of, iii. . . 630
———, William Parr, marquis of, ii. 454, 487, 505
NORTHINGTON, Robert Henley, earl of, iv. . 841, 850
Northmen, or Norse tribes, the most celebrated of, i. 9, 138
NORTHUMBERLAND, Algernon Percy, earl of, iii. 174, 220
———, Earl of, ii. 112, 129
———, Earl of, murdered, ii. 296
———, H. A. Percy, earl of, ii. . 364, 373, 395
———, H. P., earl of, iii. 4–8, 21–28, 32, 33, 72, 73
———, H. P., earl of, son of Hotspur, ii. 25, 92, 132
———, Henry Percy, earl of, ii. 5, 6, 13–17, 19, 654
———, Hugh Smithson, earl of, iv. . 842, 843
———, John Dudley, duke of—
ii. 440, 442, 456, 460, 487, 491, 495–500, 502, 504–506
NORTHUMBERLAND, J. Nevill, earl of, ii. 102–104, 106, 108
———, Morcar, earl of—
i. 200, 208, 360, 361, 368, 369, 375, 378, 389, 392, 393

NORTHUMBERLAND, Robert de Mowbray, earl of, i. . 400
———, Thomas Percy, earl of, ii. . 93, 95
———, T. Percy, earl of, ii. 607, 628, 629, 630, 645
Northumbria, i. . . . 142, 146, 150, 163, 165, 176
Norway and Sweden, disputes between, vii. . . 547
Norwegians, the, of Scandinavian origin, i. . . 138
Norwich, iii. 655
NOTT, General; his victories in India, vii. . 628, 732
Nottingham Castle; View of Mortimer's Hole, i. . 754
NOTTINGHAM, Charles Howard, earl of, ii. . 675, 680
———, C. Howard, earl of, lord high admiral, iii. 3, 71
———, Countess of, insulted by Christian IV. of Denmark, iii. 33
Nottingham, Derby, and Bristol riots, vii. . 352, 353
NOTTINGHAM, Heneage Finch, earl of, iii. . . 843
———, John Mowbray, earl of, ii. . . 17
Noy, William, attorney-general, iii. . . 84, 152, 175
NUCE, Thomas, translator of the *Octavia*, iii. . . 584
Nun or Maid of Kent; prophecies, &c., ii. 384, 385, 717, 718
NUNCOMAR, an intriguing Hindoo, v. . . . 623

OAKELEY, Rev. F., deprived of his licence, vii. . 676
Oaks, grove of, i. 62
OATES, Titus; his severe sentence, &c., iii. 718, 758, 766
Oaths, act against, vi. 784
———, forms of allegiance and supremacy, iv. . 628
OBRIAN, a conspirator against Sir J. Coventry, iii. . 707
O'BRIEN, Mr; quoted, i. 15
———, Murrock, earl of Thomond, ii. . . 428
———, William Smith, vii. . . . 662–669
Observatory, Royal, at Greenwich; View, &c., iv. 731, 732
OCCAM, William, styled the Invincible, a monk, i. . 343
O'CONNELL, Daniel, the Irish liberator; Portrait—
vii. 199–203, 249–254, 265–267, 291, 330–333,
339, 388–399, 419, 479, 498–511, 657–669
———, Mr, leader of the Irish Catholics, vi. . 774
———'s tour in 1835, vii. 496
O'CONNELLY, O.; his account of Irish conspiracy, iii. 254, 255
O'CONNOR, Ambrose, an Irish Dominican, v. . 198
———, Feargus, the Chartist leader, vii. . . 567
———, the Irish antiquary; quoted, i. . . 22
———, the Irish king, ii. . . . 426, 428
Oczakoff, Siege of, v. 722, 723
ODIN, or WODIN, king of Scandinavia, i. . 138, 224–228
ODO, archbishop of Canterbury, i. . . . 172
———, bishop of Bayeux, i. 212, 214, 381, 385, 386, 392, 394, 395
———, earl of Holderness, i. . . . 400
OFFA, king of Mercia and Bretwalda, i. . 265, 266
OGDEN, Canning's remark on the case of, vii. . 83
OGILVIE, an Irishman; his defence of Prague, iv. . 424
OGILVY, a Jesuit, executed, iii. 66
OOLE, Wm., and T. GOURNEY, murder Edward II., i. 745
OGLETHORPE, General, founder of Georgia, iv. 384, 437, 490
———, Owen, bishop of Carlisle, ii. . . 542
O'HANLAN, takes Tanderage, iii. . . . 254
O'HARA, Brigadier-general, v. . . . 348, 349
———, General, iv. 10
OHTHERE, his voyage to the North Seas, i. . . 267
Oilcloth manufactured in England, iii. . . . 888
O'KEEFE, John, death of, in 1833, vii. . . . 443
Okeley, Surrey, defeat of the Danes at, i. . . 152
OKEY, Colonel, a parliamentarian officer, iii. . 429*, 690
OLAF, king of Norway, i. 356
OLAVE, king of Norway, i. 176, 177
OLDCASTLE, Sir John, ii. 25
OLDKNOW, Mr, muslin manufacturer, death of, vii. 314
Oligarchies, Roman, i. 85
Olivenza, Treaty of, June 1801, vi. . . . 169
OLIVER, Isaac, a miniature painter of 17th century, iii. 569
———, Peter, son of the preceding, iii. . . 569
———, the spy, vii. 55–58
OMFREVILLE, Robert d', a follower of the Conqueror, i. 375
OMICHUND, an intriguing Hindoo merchant, v. . 606
O'NEAL, Daniel, a royalist officer, iii. . . . 221
———, Sir Phelim, an Irish insurrectionist, iii. 252–254
O'NEIL, Hugh, Spaniards treat him as a prince, iii. 39

HISTORY OF ENGLAND.

	PAGE
O'NEIL, O'NIAL, or O'NEAL, of Ulster, ii. 428, 682–684, 693	
——, Shane, is basely assassinated, ii.	651
ONSLOW, Sir Richard, iv.	96, 204
OPDAM, Admiral, slain in a naval battle, iii.	695
Opera-house, new English, opened in 1834, vii.	441
——, Italian, vi.	882
Operatives; their state in 1830, vii.	296
Opium-eating in England, increase of, vii.	586
—— traders, question of compensation to the, vii.	615
—— war, and opium trade with China, vii.	611–619
Oporto, View of, vi.	472
OQUENDO, a Spanish admiral, iii.	208
O'QUIN, joins in the Irish insurrection of 1641, iii.	254
ORANGE, Duke of, ii.	292, 296–298
——, Prince of,	iii. 7, 105; v. 593, 676–680; vi. 669, 670, 690, 691
——, governor of the Low Countries, ii. 649, 672	
——, in service of Philip of Burgundy, ii.	74
——, William Charles Henry Frizo, Prince of, iv.	528
Orange Societies, established in England in 1813, vi.	774
——, extension of, vii.	484
—— or Brunswick Clubs, vii.	251–254
Orangeism in Great Britain and Ireland, vii. 484–490, 493	
ORDERICUS VITALIS, the historian, i. 575, 583, 584, 613, 614	
ORDOAR, earl of Devonshire, i.	173
Ordinance, the Self-denying, iii.	322
Ordnance, England famous for manufacture of, iii.	559
O'REGAN, Sir Teague; his defence of Charlemont, iv.	25
Oregon territory, dispute about the, vii. 155, 156, 712, 713	
ORKNEY, Elizabeth Villiers, countess of, iii.	103
——, Lord, at battle of Ramilies, iv.	170
Orleans, city of; narrative of siege and blockade, ii. 60–67	
ORLEANS, Bastard of, count of Dunois, ii.	62, 66
——, Charles, duke of, ii. 19–22, 26, 33–36, 51, 83, 170	
——, Duke of, brother of Charles VI., ii. 9, 12, 15, 17–21	
——, Duke of. See Louis XII., ii.	292
——, Duke of; his marriage-contract, ii.	382
——, Gaston, duke of, brother of Louis XIII., iii.	129
——, Henrietta, duchess of; poisoned, iii.	707
——, marriage and death of Duke of, vii.	539, 705
——, Philippe Egalité, duc d', v. 741, 789, 890, 893; vi. 18	
——, the Maid of, history of, &c., ii.	62–77
ORLETON, Adam, bishop of Hereford, ii.	743
ORM, or ORMIN; his Homilies, i.	301
ORMOND, Duke of, governor of Ireland, iv. 26,131,245,289,333	
——, Duke of, recalled from governing Ireland, iii. 741,759	
——, Earl of, lieutenant-general for Ireland, iii.	255
Ornaments of China-ware first brought from Italy, iii.	618
Orosius epitomised by King Alfred, i.	302
Orphans' Bill, the, iv.	50
Orpheus, story of, in Anglo-Saxon, by King Alfred, i.	296
ORRERY, Charles Boyle, earl of, iv.	741
——, Earl of, governs in Ireland after Restoration, iii.	680
ORTELIUS, A., author of *Theatrum Orbis Terrarum*, iii.	577
OSBALDESTON, master of Westminster School, iii.	165
OSBEORN, brother of the king of Denmark, i. 371, 372, 386	
OSBERNE, son of Earl Siward, slain at Dunsinane, i.	194
OSBURGHA, wife of King Ethelwulf, i.	153, 154
OSBORY, Lord; his threat to Buckingham, iii.	709
OSTORIUS, Scapula, Roman prætor in Britain, i.	40–42
Oswald, bishop of Salisbury; his church-service, i.	549
Otaheite or Tahiti, island of, vii.	706, 707
O'THOLE, joins rebellion of O'Conner and others, ii.	428
Otterbourne, Battle of; View of the Field, i.	793
OTTOBONI, the pope's legate in England, i.	688
Oude, insurrection and fighting at, vii.	619
OVERBURY, Sir Thomas; dies in a dungeon, iii. 38, 49, 53, 54	
OVERTON; his loyal attempt fails in Scotland, iii.	420
OWEN, Dr, a nonconformist; his Portrait, &c., iii. 754,802,816	
——, Nicholas, commits suicide, iii.	520
——, Robert, the Socialist, vii.	94
——, Sir John, a royalist, iii.	400
——, Thomas, condemned for high treason, iii.	57
OXFORD, Countess of; her imprisonment, ii.	16
——, Henry de Vere, earl of, iii.	68
——; his attack on Queen Victoria, vii.	572

	PAGE
OXFORD, John de Vere, earl of, ii. 109, 110, 129, 283, 306, 310	
——, Robert Harley, earl of,	iv. 40, 77, 96, 119, 145, 196, 232, 264, 279, 320, 626
Oxford and troubles in the Church, vii.	675, 676
——, Castle of; View of the Tower, i.	432, 435, 682
——, Plan of; illustrations, iii.	314, 734
——, Society, in middle of 17th century, iv.	722
——, University of; decrease of students, ii. 196, 375, 376	
——, earliest mention of, i.	306
Oxymuriatic acid, or chlorine, discovered in 1774, vi.	843

PAGE, Richard; his missions from Henry VIII., &c., ii. 336, 343	
PACHA, Ibrahim, takes possession of Syria, vii.	429
PACK, Sir C.; his suggestion about Lord-protectorship, iii.	421
Paganism, Roman and heathen temples in Britain, i.	72
Pageants, account of two royal, iii.	627, 644
PAGET, Sir William; his peace-mission to Germany, ii.	489
PAINE, James, an eminent architect, vi.	863
——, T., v. 159, 160, 289, 290, 786, 824, 885, 888; vi. 62, 862	
Pains and Penalties, bill of, vii.	122
Painting, ii. 651–854; iii. 567–569; iv. 685, 701–706; v. 518–525; vi. 871–874, 896–901	
——, early historical, i.	631
PAKENHAM, General, Sir Edward, vi.	743, 744
Palagatcherry; Fullarton crossing a mountain-stream, v.	635
Palais Bourbon, View of, v.	878
—— Royal, View of the, v.	783
Palatinate, the, iv.	209, 210
Palermo, View of, vi.	322
PALEY, William, the philosopher; Portrait of, vi.	862
PALGRAVE, Sir F.; quoted, i. 87, 248–257, 350, 351, 572, 575	
PALLADIO, Andrea, an eminent classical architect, iii.	570
PALLISER, Sir Hugh, v.	242, 243, 272, 273, 337
Pall-mall in St James's Park, iii.	641
PALM, M., a German resident at London, iv.	370
PALMER, John, first projector of mail-coaches, v.	466
——, Mr, M.P., committed to the Tower, iii.	256
——, Sir Geoffrey, an eminent English lawyer, iii. 517, 688	
——, Sir T.; executed as a traitor, ii. 469, 495, 496, 506	
PALMERSTON, Lord; Portrait, vii.	612, &c.
Palm-Sunday; its sway before the Reformation, ii. 896–898	
Pamplona, View of, vi.	645, 655
PANDULPH, the pope's legate, i.	524
Panic of 1826, and its consequences, vii.	183–188
PANTALEON SA, a Portuguese; executed for murder, iii.	416
Pantheon, View of the interior of the, vi.	868
PANZANI, Gregorio, an envoy from the Vatican, iii.	167
PAOLI, Pasquale de, iv.	857
——, the Corsican; Portrait of, vi.	39, 40
Paper dollars, specimens of American, v.	150
—— duties, reduction of the tax on the, vii.	519
——, made of cotton, in use in 12th century, i.	611
—— manufacture, vi.	847
PAPILLON, nominated a sheriff of London, iii.	739
Papists. See Catholics.	
Paradise Lost, translated into the Icelandic tongue, vii.	217
Paraguay, despotism of, vii.	51
PARIS, a Frenchman, concerned in Darnley's murder, ii.	625
——, Matthew, the English historian, i.	522, 576, 847
Paris, besieged by the Danes, i.	162
—— camp of 20,000 men formed, v.	862, 864
——, disturbance in, vii.	424
—— in reign of Charles VI., &c.,— ii. 9, 13, 20, 28, 36, 38, 42, 46, 48, 50, 72, 73, 78, 79	
—— in the autumn of 1815, vii.	4
——, Peace of, &c.,	vi. 686, 689–701; vii. 1–5
—— women entering Hall of National Assembly, View of, v.	752
PARKER, a Jacobite spy, committed to prison, iv.	59
——, Dr M., of Canterbury, ii. 486, 635, 647, 743, 744	
——, Richard, the mutineer, vi.	115, 116
——, Samuel, bishop of Oxford, iii.	786
——, Sir Hyde, at the Battle of Copenhagen, vi. 161, 164	
——, Sir Peter; Portrait of, v.	158
Parks, improvement of London, vii.	302

GENERAL INDEX. 133

Parliament ii. 86, 91-93, 96, 140, 283, 320, 321, 354, 355, 376, 635 ; iii. 18-25, 32, 42, 43 ; vii. 52, 78, 81-85, 90, 96, 102, 113, 126, 209, 224, 225, 347, 348, 455, 580-584, 606, 610, 651
———, conflict about privileges of, vii. 526, 580-583
———, forms of holding, &c., i. 780, 809, 810
———, House, Edinburgh ; View of, iv. 174
———, Houses of, burning of the, vii. 436, 437
———, statutes of, i. 675, 721, 733, 812-817, 820 ; ii. 5, 6, 25, 26, 34, 94, 95, 99, 100, 140, 141, 272, 273, 283, 284, 377, 378, 380, 395-397, 410, 467, 470, 471, 498, 633, 725, 730, 740, 759, 781 ; iii. 830-833, 857, 864-869, 900 ; iv. 19, 20, 603 ; vi. 748, 756, 775-794
Parliamentary debates, admission of ladies to, vii. 525
———, ——— inquiry on the banking system, vii. 529, 521
———, ——— leaders, vii. 7
———, ——— privileges, iv. 533-539
———, ——— reform, vii. 26-33, 65, 102, 128-131, 166, 209, 268, 291-293, 335-337, 339-348
PARMA, Duchess of, regent of the Netherlands, ii. 620
PARNELL, Sir Henry, vii. 17, 101, 411, 731
PAROTT, Sir James ; his commission to Ireland, iii. 88
PARR, Catherine, queen of Henry VIII., ii. 438, 447
———, Dr, death of, in 1825, vii. 221
———, William, earl of Essex. See Northampton.
PARRY, Dr, executed as a traitor, ii. 655, 656
———, Sir J., a commissioner at divorce of Earl of Essex, iii. 53
PARSONS, a celebrated Jesuit, iii. 33
———, Sir W., a lord-justice of Ireland, iii. 253
Parties in 1842, condition and fate of, vii. 632, 633
Partition Treaty, first and second, iv. 74-77, 85, 92-96
——— of Poland, first, v. 40
———; dismemberment, vi. 67, 68
PASCAL II., Pope, i. 551, 552
PASS, Crispin, an engraver of 17th century, iii. 577
Passaro, Cape, Battle of, fought Aug. 11, 1718, iv. 326, 327
Paston Letters ; their historical interest, &c., ii. 145, 275
PASTON, John ; death of his son, ii. 275
———, Margaret, ii. 145
———, Sir John, at the field of Stoke, ii. 275, 279
———, Sir John, a Lancastrian, at field of Barnet, ii. 109, 275
———, Sir William, justice of Common Pleas, ii. 275
Patay, Battle of ; the English defeated here, ii. 68
PATERSON ; his Isthmus of Darien scheme, iv. 51, 80-84
———, William, founds the Bank of England, iv. 657
Patna, View of, v. 612
PATON, bishop of Dunkeld, iii. 438
PATRICK, St, converted the Irish to Christianity, i. 229
PATTEN ; his description of invasion of Scotland, ii. 459-465
PAUL I., emperor of Russia, iv. 815 ; vi. 138, 163, 809
——— III., Pope, ii. 386, 399, 401
——— IV., Pope, ii. 531, 532, 543
——— V., Pope, iii. 33
PAULET, Sir Amias, some account of, ii. 333, 658, 668
Paul's School, founded by Dean Colet, ii. 815
———, Walk, illustration of, iii. 637
Pauperism, alarming increase of, in 1832, vii. 375
Pavia, sieges, battles, government, &c., ii. 358
Paving ; act passed for paving London streets, ii. 781
Peace, Treaty of, vii. 2-5
PEACHAM, Edmond ; accused of high treason, iii. 56, 57
PEACOCK or POCOCK, R., bishop of Chichester, ii. 147, 148
———, S., warrant issued for his trial by torture, iii. 518
Pearls, British, i. 26, 106, 107
PECUELL, vice-chancellor of Cambridge, iii. 785
PECKHAM, John, a mathematician of 13th century, i. 844
PEDRO, Don, Emperor of Brazil, vii. 254-257
——— IV., surnamed the Cruel, i. 776, 777
Peel administration ; first nights in parliament, vii. 609
PEEL, Sir Robert, father of the minister, death of, vii. 313
———, ——— vii. 98-100, 135, 136, 159, 199, 230, 245, 258-261, 286-294, 327-420, 448-730
PERLE, George, a dramatic writer of 16th century, iii. 585, 601
Peers, creation of thirty-six French, vii. 425
———, question about a creation of English, vii. 355, 356
———; their conduct during the Reform struggle, vii. 478

PELAGIUS, an Irish monk, i. 124
PELHAM, Mr, alderman of Hull, iii. 279
———, Mr, first lord of the treasury, iv. 441, 540, 552
PEMBROKE, Aylmer de Valence, earl of, i. 728, 729
———, Jasper Tudor, earl of, ii. 96,100,104,110,126,283
———, Philip Herbert, earl of, iii. 37, 38, 146, 358
———, R. de Clare, surnamed Strongbow, i. 461-466
———, Thomas Herbert, earl of, iii. 773 ; iv. 80, 202
———, William Herbert, earl of, iii. 146
———, William Marshall, earl of, i. 527, 671, 673-675
PEMERTON, sheriff of London, iii. 3
Penal Code, acts for mitigating the, vi. 787, 788
PENALVA, Countess of, iii. 687
PENDERGRAST, informs of plot against William III., iv. 61
PENDLETON, Dr, a Catholic, shot at, and nearly killed, ii. 519
Penitentiary House, Millbank, act for erection of, vi. 784, 785
PENN, Thomas, petition of, v. 64
———, Vice-admiral, takes the island of Jamaica, iii. 420, 696
Pennenden Heath in Kent, meeting of Protestants at, vii. 252
PENNINGTON, Vice-admiral, iii. 112
PENRUDDOCK, Captain ; executed, iii. 419
Pension Bill, iv. 382
——— list, revision of the, vii. 374
——— of £3000 a year to Mr Canning's family, vii. 244
PENTHIÈVRE, Count of, invades Guienne, &c., ii. 85, 91
Penthièvre, Fort ; View of, vi. 91
People, distress of the, in 1842, vii. 635-639
———, history of the condition of the, i. 135, 346, 658, 882 ; ii. 268-279, 899-907 ; iii. 650-660, 900-903 ; iv. 786-792 ; v. 574-583 ; vi. 924-937 ; vii., 80, 95, 104-106, 126, 586, 635-639, 651
PEPPER, General, iv. 293
PEPUSCH, Dr ; his *Treatise on Harmony,* iv. 713
PEPYS ; quoted, vii. 16
———, R., chief-justice in Ireland, iii. 596, 677, 678, 701, 704
Porceval cabinet, the, vii. 48
PERCEVAL, Lord ; his accusation against Walpole, iv. 430
PERCHE, Marie, countess of, i. 414
PERCIVAL, Right Hon. Spencer, murdered, vi. 597, 773
PERCY, Bishop ; quoted, i. 9, 10, 22
———, General, at battle of Chalgrove Field, iii. 304
———, Henry, surnamed Hotspur, i. 793 ; ii. 11, 13-15
———, Sir C.; James I.'s accession to English crown, iii. 2
———, Sir Jocelyn, a Papist, iii. 282
———, T., steward to Earl of Northumberland, iii. 21-28
PEREIRA, Sir Wm., concerned in Wm. III.'s conspiracy, iv. 59
PERRERS, Alice, a favourite of Edward III., i. 779, 783
PERRY, Mr James, of the *Morning Chronicle,* death of, vii. 521
Persia, designs of, vii. 620
———, its connection with Britain, i. 36
———, Russian interference with, vii. 545
PERSON, Anthony ; burnt, ii. 728
Personal disability introduced, vi. 778
PERTH, Duke of, a partisan of the young Pretender, iv. 484
Perth, View of, iv. 296
PESCARA, an eminent general of Charles V., ii. 358, 359
PESTALOZZI, the philanthropist, death of, in 1827, vii. 324
Pest-house, in Tothill-fields, Westminster ; illustration, iii. 695
PETER III., emperor of Russia, iv. 813-815 ; v. 28
———, of Capua, the pope's legate, i. 513
———, THE GREAT, czar of Russia, iv. 368
———, the Hermit, preaches the Crusades, i. 400, 524
PETERBOROUGH, C. Mordaunt, earl of, iv. 152, 164, 165, 171
———, Henry Mordaunt, earl of, iii. 760 ; iv. 164
Peterborough Cathedral ; new choir, vii. 435
———, questions, vii. 138, 139
PETERS, Hugh, an Independent minister, iii. 407, 675, 676
PÉTION DE VILLENEUVE, Jerome, iv. 491, 618, 619, 642, 670 ; v. 531, 835-847, 859-889 ; vi. 12, 19
Petition of Right, iii. 131, 134
PETITOT, J., carried art of enamel to highest perfection, iii. 569
PETO, a friar of the order of Observantз, ii. 381, 382
PETRE, Father, confessor of James II., iii. 782
———, Sir William, secretary of state, ii. 454
PETTY, Lord Henry, his new financial scheme, vi. 793
———, Sir Wm., author of *Political Arithmetic,* iii. 254, 854

HISTORY OF ENGLAND.

Pevensey Castle, ruins of, &c., i. . . 392-394
Petronnet, French keeper of the seals, vii. . 272, 283
Petton, Lady; her effigy in Islcham church, ii. . 245
———, Sir Thomas; his effigy, ii. . . . 247
Philadelphia, View of, v. 121
Philharmonic Society, formed 1813, vi. . . 904
Philip, Archduke, of Burgundy, ii. 116, 300, 310, 314-316
——— I., of France, i. . 383, 384, 388, 389, 397, 399
——— II., of France, i. . 476-478, 486, 490, 491, 493, 495, 497, 500, 503, 509, 511, 513, 516-527, 531
——— II., of Spain, . . ii. 511, 512, 519, 520, 531-533, 544, 547, 620, 621, 653, 672, 681
——— III., of France, surnamed le Bel, i. 711-713, 721, 723
——— III., of Spain, ii. 681
——— III., of Spain; his embassy to James I., vii. 7, 89
——— IV., of Spain, iii. 89, 93, 94
——— V., of Spain, iv. . 94, 103, 170, 250, 366, 367, 526
——— VI., of Valois, of France, i. 757, 762, 764-767, 769-771
Philippa, queen of Edward III.; her Portrait, i. 751, 768, 770
Philippe, Louis, king of the French, vii. . 422-431
Phillips, Sir Robert, iii. . . . 82, 88, 117, 139
———, the portrait-painter, death of, vii. . . 733
Philosophy, ancient, i. 62, 64
Philpot, John, an alderman of London, i. . . 783
Phœnicians, first colonisers of Britain, i. 9, 14-16, 77, 91-101
Photography, or sun-painting, vii. . . . 744
Pianoforte supersedes the harpsichord, vi. . . 883
Pichegru, Charles, a French general, vi. 92, 120, 121, 243-249
Picnic supper, nature of a. vi. 910
Picquigny, near Amiens, Treaty of, ii. . . 112, 115
Picton, Sir Thomas, killed at Waterloo, vi. . 704, 708
Picts, anciently Gwyddyl Ffichti, i. 9, 18, 19, 22, 216, 218, 229
Pic-poudre, Courts of; their regulation, ii. . . 191
Pierce, William, bishop of Bath and Wells, iii. . 218
Pietists; their windows broken by the mob, vii. . 548
Proot, Sir Christopher, committed to the Tower, iii. 35
Pigs; the Anglo-Saxons, possessed herds of swine, i. 277
Pilchards, demands for, in the Italian States, vi. . 799
Pilgrims, and pilgrimages to Rome, &c.—
    i. 182, 265, 266; ii. 145, 150, 151
Pillory, Act to abolish punishment of the, vi. . 786
Pindar, Sir Paul; his gift to St Paul's Cathedral, iii. 156
Pindarree war, vii. 65-69
Pine, John, an eminent engraver, iv. . . 709
Pinkerton, J., his views of Gothic and Celtic nations, i. 10
Pinkie, Battle of, ii. 460
Piperel, or Peverel, William, i. . . . 424
Piracy, Greek, vii. 239
Pisans, the, supporters of Guy of Lusignan, i. . 499
Pitsligo, Lord, joins standard of young Pretender, iv. 479
Pitt, William. See Chatham.
———, the British minister, . v. 333, 341, 380, 394, 395, 399, 587, 595, 657, 664, 750, 820-824, 848-855, 900; vi. 138, 154-159, 176, 177, 226-234, 267, 305-307, 749-794; vii. 47-52, 194, &c.
Pittardo, Lady of; she is charged with witchcraft, iii. 489
Pius II., Pope, proclaims a crusade against Turks, ii. 150, 656
——— VI., Pope; Portrait of, vi. . . 107, 134, 141
——— VII., Pope, vi. . 141, 185, 398, 399, 514, 515, 693
——— VIII., Pope; his accession, vii. . . . 283
Place Bill, passed December 13, 1692, iv. . . 40
——— d'Armés, Montreal, View of the, v. . . 114
——— Louis XV., View of, from an old French print, v. 865
Plague, the Great, ii. . . . 268, 310, 470, 574
———; 100,000 souls perish in 1665—
    iii. 6, 9, 18, 108, 110, 695, 697
Plans, delivery of railway, vii. 697
Plantation Trade at end of 17th century, iii. . 862
Planters of Jamaica; their conduct in 1839, vii. 559-562
Plassey, Battle of, v. 610, 611
Plata, Rio de la, proclaims its independence in 1816, vii. 51
Platen, Countess, a German mistress of George I., iv. 290
Plays, Moral, common in Scotland in 16th century, iii. 645
Pliny's *Natural History;* quoted, i. . 63, 92, 117, 127
Plots against life of Louis Philippe, vii. . . 537
Plough-Monday, ii. 893

Plough of 18th century, vi. 819
Plowden, Edmund, publishes his *Commentaries,* ii. 767
Plumer, Mr; his motion for repealing Test Act, iv. 395
Plutarch; quoted, i. 14
Plymouth, iii. 655
———, View of, iv. 260
Pococke, Admiral; his victory over Admiral d'Apché, iv. 575
Poictiers, Battle of, gained by the Black Prince, i. 772, 773
Poictiers, Richard de; quoted, i. . . . 473
———, William of, i. . . 363, 364, 584, 585, 613
Poisoning, fearful prevalence of cases of, vii. . 297
Poix, John de, nearly takes Charles VI. prisoner, ii. 37
Poland, its distracted state, &c., v. . 29-42, 855-857
——; partitions of, &c., vi. . . 5, 6, 62, 63, 66-68
——; revolt of 1830, vii. 430
Polar discovery of 1833, vii. 435
Pole, A. and E., try to liberate Mary Stuart, ii. 569, 570
——— & Co.'s Bank, failure of, vii. . . . 184
———, Henry Lord Montacute; beheaded, ii. . 408
———, John de la, brother of Duke of Suffolk, ii. 55, 56
———————— earl of Lincoln, ii. . 175, 289
———————— marries sister of Edward IV., ii. 175, 288
———, Michael de la, earl of Suffolk, lord-chancellor, ii. 175
———————— son of first earl of Suffolk, ii. 34, 175
———, Reginald, ii. 401, 407-409, 457, 510, 511, 524, 528, 538
———, William de la, chief-baron of the Exchequer, ii. 175
———————— duke of Suffolk; beheaded, ii. 54-57, 175
Police and constabulary force of Dublin, vii. . 498
———————— soldiery favourable to the reformers, vii. 363
———, medical and criminal, want of, v. . 547, 850
———, system of, vii. 39, 40
Polignac, Cardinal, ambassador in Poland, iv. 68, 226, 329
———, Prince Jules de, vii. . . 149, 274-283
Political Clubs in England in 1792, v. . . 850-852
———— Divisions, i. 76-81
———— Economy, iii. 862
———— education in Ireland, vii. . . 504, 508
———— morality, improvement in, vii. . . 743
———— unions, proclamation against, vii. . 356, 362
Pollexfen, Mr; estimates gold and silver in 1698, iii. 854
Pollok, Rev. Robert, death of, in 1827, vii. . 320
Poll-tax, causes much disturbance in England, i. 784, *et seq.*
Polo, Marco, his travels in Tatary and China, i. . 645
Poltrot, a Huguenot, assassinates the Duke of Guise, ii. 572
Polygars, group of, v. 633
Pompone, M., minister of Louis XIV., iv. . 74
Pondicherry, captured by the British, vi. . . 805
———— surrenders to Colonel Coote, v. . 616
Poniatowski, Stanislaus Augustus, of Poland, v. 34, 855-857
Ponsonby, General Sir William, vi. . . . 708
———, George, leader of the opposition, vii. . 9, 55
Pont, Robert, abbot of, his deputation to Richard, i. 509
Pontefract Castle, built by Gilbert de Lacy, i. . 374
————; death of Richard II. here; View, ii. 7, 8
Pontefract, Robert de, an adherent of Duke Robert, i. 408
Pont-y-Cysylte; View of, vi. . . . 826, 827
Poole, Mr, Speaker in the House of Commons, iv. 3
Pooley, betrays the Babington conspiracy, ii. . 657
Poor, estimate of the charges of, iv. . . . 786
———law Bill of 1834, the new, vii. . . 376-380
———, change in the, vii. 698
——— for Ireland, vii. 415
———, O'Connell on the Irish, vii. . 508-512
——— of 1832, vii. 370, 371
——— Renewal Act, debates on the, vii. . . 647
———laws, . . iv. 787; v. 581-583; vi. 592
———, considered to encourage idleness, iii. 659, 902
———, general administration of the, vii. 41-44, 85
———, projects for improving the dwellings of the, vii. 657
———rates, vi. 934, 935
———, the, laws respecting, &c., ii. 467, 468, 481, 904-907
Pope, Sir T., founder of Trinity College, Oxford, ii. 819
———, the English poet, iv. . 361, 685, 701, 743-745
Pope, the, burnt in effigy in the Palais Royal, v. 832
Popham, Andrew, a Papist, iii. . . . 785
———, Sir Home, vi. 128, 329

GENERAL INDEX. 135

Popham, Sir J., assists in proclamation of James I., iii. 3
Popish Plot, information concerning the, iii. . 717-724
Popoli, Duchess of, iv. 165
———, Duke of, recommends invasion of Naples, iv. 321
Popular action in 1831, vii. . . . 349
——— discontent in 1834, vii. . . . 416
——— ignorance of 1820-1826, vii. . . 210
Population, vi. 930, 933, 934
——— of England in 14th and 16th centuries, ii. 268, 903
———; physical characteristics of nations, i. . 5, 6
Porta, Giovanni Battista della, iv. . . 713
Portalegre, surrenders to the Duke of Berwick, iv. . 159
Porte, the, vii. 238, 242, 243
Porteous, John, hanged by Edinburgh populace, iv. 397
Porter, Anna Maria, death of, in 1832, vii. . 444
———; Endymion, iii. 91
———, Sir Robert Ker, death of, in 1842, vii. . 732
Porteus, Beilby, bishop of London; Portrait of, vi. 763, 765
Portland cabinet, the, vii. 48
Portland, Jerome Weston, earl of, iii. . 274, 291
———, Richard Weston, first earl of, iii. 141, 146, 161
———, William Bentinck, earl of, iv. 61, 69, 73, 90, 104
———, William, duke of, vi. . . . 68
Portman, Sir Wm., petitions against church-ales, &c., iii. 161
Portocarrero, Cardinal, archbishop of Toledo, iv. 93, 94
———, Don Vincente, iv. . . . 329
Ports, opening of the, in 1826, vii. . . 189
Portsmouth; Drawing of the House in which Buckingham was assassinated by Felton, iii. . 137
Portsmouth; the Romans build a fortress here, i. . 90
———; View of the Fortress and Harbour, ii. . 800
Portugal, affairs of, vii. . . 254-257, 429, 702
———, appeal from, vii. 150
———, despatch of British troops to, vii. . . 224
———, relations with, vii. . . . 269
———, the young queen of, vii. . . . 542
Port-wine; its introduction into England, iv. . 665
Post, abuses and reforms in, v. . . 466, 467, 669
———, established by James I., &c., iii. . 544, 545, 864
——— office espionage, vii. . . . 698, 699
———; growth of its revenues, vi. . . 801, 810
———— system; anecdote of Coleridge, vii. . 576-580
———— the new London, vii. . . . 303
Potato; its introduction into England, iv. . . 680
——— rot and weather in 1842, vii. . . 722-724
Potter, Dr John, archbishop of Canterbury, iv. . 193
Potteries of the Gauls and Britons, i. . . 103
Pottery, manufacture of, v. . . . 484-487
———; manufacture of crucibles and retorts, vi. . 839
Pottinger, Sir Henry, vii. . . . 617-619
Poulet, Lord, petitions against church-ales, &c., iii. 161
Pound, Mr, an aged Catholic; his petition, iii. . 22
Pound-notes, suppression of small, in 1826, vii. 184, 185
Poverty and pauperism, confusion between, vii. . 375
Powel, Mr Justice; his defence of petitioning bishops, iii. 791
Power-loom, first invented by Dr Cartwright, vi. . 842
——— riot of 1826, in Lancashire, vii. . . 188
Powis, Lady, sent to the Tower, iii. . . 732
Poynings, Sir Edward, ii. . . 320, 323, 570
———, Sir Thos.; his gallant conduct at Boulogne, ii. 442
Poyntz, commander of English forces in the north, iii. 340, 354
Præmunire, statutes of; references to them, ii. 371, 377
Pragmatic Sanction guaranteed, iv. . . 368
Prance, a Catholic silversmith, iii. . . 724
Prayer, Book of Common, review of, iii. . 820, 821
Preaching, lay, first practised by Thomas Maxfield, iv. 623
———, Whitefield's extemporaneous, iv. . 622
President steam-ship, loss of the, vii. . . 590
Press at Calcutta, vii. 909
———, freedom of the, vii. . 131, 211, 275, 287, 425
———, Louis Philippe's repression of the, vii. . 538
——— prosecutions in France, vii. . . . 425
———, the French, vii. . . 272, 273, 275, 277-279
Preston, Lord, iii. 767
———, T., a dramatic writer of 16th century, iii. 583
Preston Tower, View of, iv. . . . 470

Prestonpans, Battle of, fought September 1745, iv. 469, 470
Pretender, the Old. See James Francis Edward.
——— Young. See Charles Edward Louis.
Prevost, Sir George; his conduct in Canada, vi. 736-742
Price-current, establishment of a weekly, iii. . 544
Pride, Colonel, a parliamentarian, iii. 333, 387, 422, 425
Prideaux, Mr; his parliamentary bill, iii. . 231
Priestley, Joseph, an eminent philosopher, v. 824, 885; vi. 30
Priests, persecution of French, v. . 827-829, 842-844
Primrose, Sir Archibald, iii. . . . 683
Prince of Wales, birth of the, vii. . . 586
——— regent, outrage on the, vii. . . 52, 53
——— regent's speeches, vii. . . . 10, 79
Prince's metal, invention of, iii. . . . 869
Princess Augusta, death of, in 1840, vii. . . 594
——— royal, birth of the, vii. . . . 572
Printers, marks of early English, ii. . . 825
Printing, information about, vi. . . 847, 848
——— office, ancient Dutch; illustration, ii. . 824
———, origin of, ii. 201-206
——— type imported from Holland, iv. . . 684
Prior, M., a distinguished writer, iv. 73, 234, 249, 289, 746
Prison management, improvement in, vii. . 746
Pritchard, Dr, opinion of Celtic and Teutonic languages, i. 11
Prize-fights, iv. 775
Procession, description of a royal, iii. . . 897
Property, legislation relating to real and personal, vi. 779-782
———-tax, petitions against the, vii. . . 12-15
Prophecies and predictions of Merlin, &c., ii. . 258
Prose fiction, in 18th century, v. . . 499-506
Prosecutions for blasphemy, vii. . . . 211
Prosperity of the country in 1824, vii. . 172-174
Protectionist and Free-trade parties, vii. . . 633
Protestant Association instituted, ii. . . 656
——— worship established by law, iii. . 8, 12, 19
Protestantism, rival forms of, iii. . . 433-494
Provinces, United, intercede for King Charles's life, iii. 395
Provisions; ordinances passed for regulating price, iii. 657, 658
———, rise in prices of, vi. . . . 809
Prussia; its position with Russia in 1843, vii. . 701
———, Portraits of king and queen of, vi. . 33, 341
Prydain, lays, name of Britain, i. . . . 8
Prydain, son of Aedd the Great, i. . . 11
Prynne, W.; punished, iii. 152, 154, 166, 324, 431*, 495, 567
Ptolemy's mention of Ireland and Britain, i. 14, 20, 138
Pucelle, Girard la, an eminent English scholar, ii. 610
Puckering, Serj., counsels execution of Mary Stuart, ii. 662
Pudsey, Hugh, bishop of Durham, i. . . 485, 505
Puoin, Augustus, death of, in 1832, vii. . . 442
Puisieux, M., principal secretary of state in France, iii. 92
Pulawski, General, slain at siege of Savannah, v. . 288
Punjaub, disturbed state of the, vii. . . 625
Puppet-shows, iii. 898
Purcell, Henry, composer of music, . iii. 885; iv. 710
———, Peter, death of, in 1846, vii. . . 740
———, the rover; his death, vii. . . . 441
Purgatory, doctrine of, ii. 397
Puritans and Puritanism, . ii. 741, 743; iii. 8, 15-18
Purvay, J., forsakes tenets of Wycliffe for a benefice, ii. 144
Purveyance for the royal table, &c., iii. . . 19
Pusey, Dr; his suspension, vii. . . . 676
Putnam, General, an American officer; Portrait of, v. 108
Puttenham, Webster, a writer of the 16th century, ii. 835
Pykas, J., his deposition respecting the Scriptures, ii. 712
Pym, J., a noted parliamentarian, iii. 120, 199, 236, 310, 311
Pynsaint, Carmarthenshire, Roman mines at, i. . 117
Pyramids, Battle of the, vi. . . . 135

Quadruple Alliance, iv. 325, 450
Quakers, bill for the relief of, &c., vi. . 751, 758, 769
———, origin and tenets of, iii. . . 808-817
———, petition for total abolition of slave-trade, v. 396
———; their admission to parliament, vii. . . 407
Quarantine laws, acts passed for settlement of, vi. 787
Quatre Bras, Battle of, fought June 16, 1815, vi. . 704
Quebec Act, the, vii. 549, 550

	PAGE
Quebec, Battle of, fought September 1759, iv.	580, 581
——; View, v.	117
——, fires at, vii.	718
Queen Elizabeth's MSS., discovery of, vii.	217
—— Victoria, attacks on, vii.	571, 572
—— Victoria's accession; character; Portrait, vii.	528-533
Queen's Bench, Court of, and House of Commons, vii.	581-583
—— letter for relief of the poor, vii.	657
—— speeches, vii. 583, 606, 607, 610, 639, 727
QUEENSBERRY, James Douglas, duke of, iii.	767
Quesnoy, invested by Prince Eugene, iv.	247
Quintain, an ancient English sport; View of, i.	640
QUIROS, Don Bernardo de, iv.	92

BABY, Thomas Wentworth, Lord. See Strafford.	
Back, invented by John Holland, duke of Exeter, iii.	519
Radical, first introduction of the term, vii.	106
—— reformers in the House of Commons, vii.	533-535
Radicals, Tories, and Whigs, vii.	447
RADNOR, John Roberts, earl of, iii.	318, 705
RAEBURN, Sir Henry, the artist, death of, in 1823, vii.	220
RAFAELLE, Sanzio, an eminent painter, vii.	567
RAFFLES, Sir Stamford, death of, in 1826, vii.	219
RAIKES, Mr, a printer of Gloucester, iv.	381
Railroads, progress of, v. 471; vi.	824-826
Railway speculation; its effects, vii.	695-698
——, the first great English, vii.	304
Railways and steam, vii.	744
RAINSBOROUGH, Captain, iii. 174, 370, 371, 386
RAJAH SUITAB ROY, naib-dewan of Babar, v.	623
RALEIGH, Lady, wife of Sir Walter, iii. 72, 74, 76
——, Mr Walter, son of Sir Walter, iii.	74
——, Sir Walter, ii. 626, 652, 666, 676, 680, 681; iii. 3, 5, 7-15, 72-80, 527, 538, 614
RALPH, surnamed Le Flambard, i. 396, 406-410, 549
Ramilies, Battle of, fought May 23, 1706, iv.	169
RAMPENTON, Philip of, a learned Lollard, ii.	144
Ramsey Abbey, description of, i.	313
RANDALL, Edward, high-marshal of Havre, ii.	573, 574
Ranelagh, iv.	772
RANKLOCH, Lord, paymaster of the army, iv.	135
RANULPH, or RALPH, earl of Worcester, i.	190
Rao, Bajee, a Mahratta peishwa, vii.	72-76
Rastadt, taken by Marshal Villars, iv.	184
RASTELL, John, a law-writer and printer, ii.	703
RATCLIFFE, Egremont, a partisan of Mary Stuart, ii.	629, 630
——, Sir Richard; slain at Bosworth Field, ii.	128, 129
RAVAILLAC, Francis, a friar, stabs Henri IV., iii.	48
RAVENSWORTH, Lord, iv.	546
Raw materials, duties on, vii.	720
RAWDON, Lord; Portrait of, v. 321, 322, 351, 361
RAY, Volunteer; quoted, iv.	508
RAYMOND DE LA GUERRE; hangs Bourguignon nobles, ii.	37
——, Lord, iv.	383
RAYNALDE, T., published first book with copper-plates, iii.	577
Reading Abbey; View of the ruins of, i.	418, 419
——, View of, from Caversham Hill, iii.	301
READING, Mr; Duke of Buckingham's election, iii.	122
Reason, Festival of, celebrated in France, v.	22
REAY, Lord; accusation against Marquis of Hamilton, iii.	150
Rebecca and her children, riots of, vii.	636-639
RECALDO, Martinez de, vice-admiral of Spanish Armada, ii.	674
Reciprocity of Duties Bill, vii.	166
Recognition, Bill of, iv.	21
REDESDALE, John Freeman Mitford, vi.	753
REDEVALD, king of East Anglia, i. 145, 146, 233
REDVERS, Richard de, a powerful Norman baron, i.	409
REECE, Dr John, his pamphlet on Joanna Southcote, vi.	775
REES-AP-GRYFFITHS, king of South Wales, i.	451
REEVES, Mr; quoted, i.	818-822
Reform agitation, revival of the, vii. 95, 104, 106
—— Bill, vii. 339-348, 369
Reformation, History of the, &c., ii. 345, 696-749
Regalia of Scotland, iv.	179
Regency Bill, iv.	831
—— question; minority of Princess Victoria, vii. 327, 338

	PAGE
Regent Street, from Waterloo Place; View of, vi.	894
Regiments, names of, as they still exist, iii.	891
REGINALD, of St Augustine's, Canterbury, i.	559
Registration Bill for Ireland, Lord Stanley's, vii.	502-504
——, League, vii.	687
—— of births, marriages, and deaths, national, vii.	521
REICHSTADT, Duke de, death of, in 1832, vii.	438
Relief Synod; its founders, iv.	620
Religion—Druidism; introduction of Christianity, &c.— i. 59-75, 224-245, 547-561, 801-808
Religion, History of, ii. 187-154, 696-749; iii. 433-494, 802-827; iv. 589-625; v. 405-422; vi. 748-775
Religious crisis of 1834, vii.	401-411
—— intolerance, vii.	567
—— liberty, remarkable advance in, vii.	748
REMINGTON; remedy for James I. on his death-bed, iii.	103
Remonstrance of the State of the Kingdom; notice of, iii.	256
RENÉE, daughter of Louis XII., ii.	364
RENNELL, Major, the geographer, death of, in 1830, vii.	324
RENNIE, John; Portrait of, vii.	823
Rental of England and Wales, in 1769, v.	468
Repeal agitation, vii.	572
—— leaders, arrests and trials of the, vii.	662-665
—— monster meetings, vii.	658-662
—— of the Union, vii.	330-333
RESBY, John; burnt as a Wycliffite, ii.	153
Resumption Bill, iv.	89
Retford Bill, East, vii.	247
Revenue, account of the royal, i.	580-583
——, modern history of the public— iii. 848; iv. 650, 651; v. 439-441
—— of 1846, vii.	728
——, Sinclair's statement on the, &c., ii. 165, 166
Revolution, French. See Louis XVI., and Napoleon Bonaparte.
Revolutions in Europe, 1822, vii.	143
REYNAUD, earl of Boulogne, i.	526
REYNOLDS and SPARKS, Drs; their controversy with James I. respecting matters of religion, iii. 16, 17, 819, 820
REYNOLDS, John, a leader of the Levellers, iii.	36, 37
——, Sir John; drowned, iii.	425, 427
——, Sir Joshua, the English painter, v. 519, 520, 714
——, the United Irishman, death of, vii.	596
Rhé, island of, taken by the Huguenots, iii. 107, 128, 135
Rhode Island, Long Island, New York, &c., Map of, v.	85
——, settlement of Providence at, iii.	806
Ribbon Societies, formation of, vi.	774
Ribbonism in Ireland, vii.	493, 494
RICARDO, David, M.P., death of, in 1823; Portrait, vii.	218
RICE, Lord, chief-justice of Ireland, iv.	11
Rice, origin of the cultivation of, in Carolina, iv.	675
RICH, a merchant, an admirer of the Quaker Naylor, iii.	812
——, Colonel, iii. 387, 404, 421
——, Robert, Lord; impeached of high crimes, iii.	288
——, Sir Nathaniel; his commission to Ireland, iii. 88, 132
——, Sir Richard, solicitor-general, ii. 388, 397, 454, 456
RICHARD I., king of England, i. 452, 466, 470-514
—— II., king of England; his Portrait— i. 780-800, 838; ii. 7, 10
—— III., ii. 99, 109, 111, 114-130, 187, 283, 284
——, half-brother of Prince William, i.	414
——, natural son of Robert of Normandy, i.	401
—— of Cirencester, a Benedictine, i.	76
——, second son of William I., i.	387
RICHARDSON, Lord Chief-justice, iii. 153, 160
——, Samuel, the English novelist, v.	499
Richborough, in Kent, site of Roman station Rutupæ, i.	90
RICHELIEU, Cardinal, iii. 106, 107, 114, 125, 135, 138
——, Duke of, iii. 1-5, 93
——, his expedition to Minorca, iv. 558, 570
RICHEMONT, Arthur, count of, ii. 54-59, 68, 69, 78-80
RICHMOND, Charles Lennox, duke of, iii. 762; v. 320, 321
——, Dowager-countess of, ii. 126, 283, 287, 319, 320
——, Henry Fitzroy, duke of, ii. 364, 395
——, James Stuart, duke of, iii. 159, 249
——, John de Dreux, earl of, i. 734, 735

GENERAL INDEX.

Richmond, in Yorkshire; View of, i. . . 374
———— Palace; illustration, ii. . . 641
Rick-burning in England, in 1830, vii. . 333
RIDER, Sir Dudley, chief-justice of King's Bench, iv. 559
RIDLEY, N.; burnt, ii. 493, 503, 509, 525, 526, 696, 731
Rights, Bill of, passed 1689, iv. . . 628
Riley, John, a painter of original talent, iv. . 702
RINUCCINI, the pope's nuncio in Ireland, iii. . 357
Riots, vii. . 188, 189, 349, 352, 432, 636–639
————, the great London, v. . . 304–313
RIPPERDA, a Fleming, prime-minister of Spain, iv. . 371
RIVERS, Anthony Woodville, ii. 103, 107, 117, 118, 121, 249
————, John Savage, earl of, iii. . . 292
————, Richard Savage, earl of, iv. . 171
————, Sir Richard Woodville, earl, ii. . 80, 101–104
RIVET, John; he purchases the statue of Charles I., iii. 576
RIZZIO, David, secretary to Mary Queen of Scots, ii. 585–587
Road-making during the 18th century, v. . 470
Roads; Telford and MacAdam, vi. . . 820–823
———— in Britain, constructed by the Romans, i. . 117
ROBART, M., a servant of the Duke of Leeds, iv. . 51
ROBARTES, Richard, a merchant of Truro, iii. . 70
ROBERT, archbishop of Canterbury, i. . 189, 193, 196
————, eldest son of the Conqueror, i. 383, 384, 389, 393–411
———— II., nephew of David Bruce, i. . 774, 791, 794
———— III., king of Scotland, ii. . 9, 11, 19, 131
ROBERTS, Lewes; his work on the trade of England, iii. 540
ROBERTSON, a smuggler; his escape, iv. . 396
————, death of, aged 114, vii. . . 596
————, William, the historian, v. . 516
ROBESPIERRE, the French revolutionist—
  v. 742, 783–847, 858–890; vi. 12–18, 54–61
ROBINSON, F. J., chancellor of the exchequer, vii. 163, 207, 208
————, John, bishop of Bristol, iv. . 257
————, Sir G. B., vii. . . 613
————, Sir Thomas, secretary of state, iv. 552, 556
ROBSON, George F., death of, in 1833, vii. . 442
ROCAFERTI, inquisitor-general, iv. . 94
ROCHAMBEAU, a French general, vi. . 192
————, the French revolutionary general, v. . 860
Rochdale, iii. . . 656
ROCHE-JAQUELEIN, a leader of the Vendeans, vi. 20, 21, 90
Rochelle, city of; taken by Richelieu, iii. . 135, 138
————, La, a port in Brittany; View of, iii. . 129
Rochester Castle, View of the Keep, &c., i. . 395
———— Cathedral; View of the west front, i. 620
ROCHESTER, Lawrence Hyde, earl of, iii. 419, 759, 778, 785
————, Robert Carr, earl of, iii. 38, 49, 52, 54, 60, 62
ROCHFORD, Lady; beheaded, ii. . 423
————, Lord, son of the Earl of Wiltshire, ii. 391–394
ROCKINGHAM, C. W. Wentworth, marquis of—
  v. 59, 87, 187, 377, 380
————, Marquis of, iv. . 833, 840, 841, 879
RODERIC invests Dublin, i. . 465, 466
RODNEY, G. B., a gallant naval commander—
  iv. 578, 810; v. 313, 314, 325, 326, 364, 379, 383, 384
RODOLPHUS, Glaber; quoted, i. . 636
ROE, Sir T.; his embassy to the Indian emperor, iii. 530
ROEBUCK, Mr; investigations into election-bribery, vii. 649
ROGER, bishop of Salisbury, i. . 421, 426–428, 615
————, of Hoveden; quoted, i. . 450, 476
ROGERS, John; burnt at Smithfield, ii. . 523, 524, 735
————, the poet, vii. . . 741
ROKEBY, Sir T., defeats the Earl of Northumberland, ii. 19
ROLAND, M. and Madame, v. . 837–847, 862–896, 901
————, Madame, guillotined, vi. . 19
ROLLES, Mr; complains of his goods being seized, iii. 139
ROLLO of Powhouse, iv. . . 493
Roman and Greek writers; early history of Britain, i. 4
———— roads, the, i. . 49, 117
Romance language, the origin of the French, i. 188
Romanists, abolition of various penal acts against, vii. 666
ROMANO, Julio, a celebrated Roman painter, iii. 567
Romans, the, invade Britain, i. 26–33, 48, 51, 72, 90, 117, 658
Rome, its early connections with Britain, i. 145, 153, 165
————, schism in the papal church, &c., ii. 137, 140–142

ROMILLY, Sir Samuel; Portrait of—
  vi. 787, 790; vii. 6, 9, 11, 14, 27–30, 59, 80, 91, 93
ROMNEY, Henry Sidney, lord, iv. . 86, 90
Romney Marsh, i. . . 162, 359
RONJAT, a Frenchman, surgeon to William III., iv. 121
RONQUILLO, a Spanish ambassador, iii. . 787
Rood of Grace, the, ii. . . 722
ROOKE, Sir G., vice-admiral, iv. 42, 80, 127, 181, 160, 162, 180
ROOKWOOD, a conspirator against William III., iv. 61
————, Ambrose; executed, iii. . 24, 27–30
Rope manufactures, vi. . . 847
ROPER, Mrs, daughter of Sir Thomas More, ii. 386–388
ROQUEFEUILLE, a French admiral, iv. . 446
ROSAMOND, the Fair; her romantic history, i. 451, 482
BOSCOE, William, death of, in 1831; Portrait, vii. 443, 444
Roscommon, monster meeting at, vii. . 660
ROSE, Mr George, secretary of the Treasury, v. 850
ROSEN, General, conducts siege of Londonderry, iv. 17, 23, 24
Roses, Wars of the two, ii. . 87, 92, 94, 96, 108, 130, 105
ROSETTI, an attendant of the queen of Charles I., iii. 232
ROSNY, M. de. See also Duke of Sully, iii. . 7
Ross, Bishop of; his defence of Queen of Spots, ii. 616, 626, 639
————, Major-general, takes Washington, vi. . 740
Rossbach, Battle of, fought November 5, 1757, iv. 570
Rossi, Charles, an eminent sculptor, vi. . 901
ROSSITER, commander of English forces in the north, iii. 340
ROSSUS, John, of Warwick, a Latin chronicler, ii. 209
ROTHERHAM, archbishop of York, ii. . 119, 121, 124
ROTHES, Earl of, iv. . . 147
————, chancellor of Scotland, iii. . 156, 694
Rothesay Castle, loss of the, vii. . . 436
ROTHSAY, David, duke of, regent of Scotland, ii. 9, 11, 19, 131
ROTHSCHILD, Mr, death of, in 1836, vii. . 595
ROUBILLIAC, an eminent sculptor of French school—
  iv. 707, 712; v. 526
Rouen, city of, besieged by Henry V., &c., ii. 38–40, 43, 85
ROUEN, Walter, archbishop of, i. . 506–508
Rougemont Castle, Exeter; View of, i. . 367
ROUILLÉ, M. do; his mission to Flanders, iv. . 212
Round Table, King Arthur's, i. . . 23
———— Towers, Irish, i. . . 12–17
ROUSE, a Rye-house Plot conspirator, iii. . 740
————, Dr, chaplain to William III., iv. . 24
————, Francis, speaker of House of Commons, iii. 412
————, John, arrested, iv. . . 734
Rouvrai, Battle of Herrings fought at, ii. . 62
ROWAN, Archibald Hamilton, death of, in 1834, vii. 437
————, Hamilton, a leader of the United Irishmen, vi. 28, 124
Rowe, General, killed at Battle of Blenheim, iv. 156
ROWLEY, Admiral, bombards and burns Genoese towns, iv. 453
————, William, a dramatist of 16th century, iii. 593, 594
Rowton Heath, Battle of, gained by the Parliament, iii. 341
Roxburgh Castle, various sieges and events at, ii. 134, 185
ROXBURGH, Duke of, secretary of state for Scotland, iv. 365
————, Earl of, lord privy-seal, iii. . 183
Roy, a satirist of Wolsey, ii. . . 829, 830
————, Rammohon, the Hindoo; his death, vii. 408
Royal Academy, founded 1768, v. . 520
———— Agricultural Society; its first meeting in 1839, vii. 589
———— Exchange, burned down, vi. . 590
———— marriages, vii. . . 88, 89
———— Society of Literature, institution of, vii. 217
————, origin and history, iv. . 722–726
———— visits to King and Queen of the French, vii. 706
Royalty abolished in France, v. . . 885
———— in England, iii. . . 431
RUBENS, Peter Paul, an eminent Flemish painter, iii. 148, 568
RUDD, Anthony, bishop of St David's, iii. . 460
RUDING, Mr; quoted, i. . . 505
RUDYARD, Sir Benjamin, M.P., iii. . 212, 227
RUDYERD, erects a light-house off Plymouth, iv. 664
RUE, De la, a conspirator against William III., iv. 61
RUMBALD, Richard, a Rye-house conspirator, iii. 741, 768
RUMSEY; his depositions respecting Rye-house Plot, iii. 744
RUNDELL, Philip, the great jeweller, death of, in 1827, vii. 315
Runic Odes, admirably imitated by Gray, i. . 300

Runnymead, View of, i. 529
RUPERT, Prince, iii. 173, 174, 295, 341, 343, 344, 416, 698
Ruremond, surrenders to Marlborough, iv. . . 130
RUSHOUT, Sir John, iv. 502, 585
RUSHWORTH, John; quoted, iii. . 15, 264, 294, 517
RUSSEL, J., one of the murderers of Archbishop Sharp, iii. 730
RUSSELL, Admiral; his misconduct, iv. 34, 37, 38, 40, 68, 80
———, Lord John; Portrait—
    vii. 10, 102, 130, 244, 292, 293, 341, &c.
———, Mr J.; his gradual rise to high dignity, ii. 402, 469
———, William, Lord, iii. 62, 715, 728, 740, 745-750
Russia, affairs of, vii. 544, 545
—— and Turkey, war between, vii. . . 284
Russian influence in India, fear of, vii. . 619-621, 624
RUTH, Captain, killed at Battle of Aghrim, iv. . 11, 34
ROTHVEN, Alex., son of William, earl of Gowrie, ii. . 690
———, Lord Grey of, impeached of high crimes, iii. 288
———, one of Rizzio's murderers, ii. 586, 587, 591
Ruthven, raid of, iii. 440
RUTLAND, Duchess of; her death, in 1825, vii. . 220
———, Earl of, butchered by Clifford, ii. . 96
———, Earl of, Edward Plantagenet, ii. . 5
———, Thomas Manners, Earl of, ii. . 397
RUVIONI, a minister of Louis XIV., iii. . . 716
RYCHARDES, said to be author of the play *Misogonus*, iii. 581
Rye-house, View of, from an old print, iii. . 742
—— Plot, iii. 740-755
RYMER; quoted, iii. 582
RYSBRACH, John Michael, an eminent statuary, iv. 707
Ryswick, Treaty of, signed September 20, 1697, iv. . 69

SAARBRUCK, Prince of, iv. . . . 129, 137
Sacæ, emigrate from Scythia to Europe, i. . 138
SACHEVERELL, Dr Henry; his trial, &c., iv. . 217-222
SACKVILLE, Colonel, iv. 32, 48
———, George, Viscount, iv. 565, 576, 582, 584, 585
———————; Portrait of, v. 3, 221, 373
———, Nigellus de, rector of Harrow, i. . 454
Sacramental Test, first imported into Ireland in 1699, iv. 604
Sacraments; Henry VIII. confined them to three, ii. 397
SADLER, Sir Ralph, ii. 431, 432, 435, 443-445, 454, 529,
    550, 551, 556, 612, 629, 658
ST AIGNAN, Duke de, French ambassador at Madrid, iv. 330
ST ALBAN's, Duchess of, death of, in 1837, vii. . 595
St Alban's, *Verulamium*, i. . . . 33, 43
ST ALBANS, Henry Jermyn, earl of, iii. . 240, 342, 727
St Albans, Victory of Richard of York at, ii. . 92, 97
ST ANDREWS, Archbishop of, crowns Charles I., iii. 156, 183
St Andrews, New, iv. 82
———, See of, i. 539
———; Views, ii. . 154, 198, 199, 446, 458, 748
St Antoine, Port; View of, v. . . . 746
ST AUBYN, Sir John, iv. 437
St Bartholomew's Day, massacre of, ii. . 646, 647
St Catherine Creed, church of, consecrated by Laud, iii. 158
St Catherine's Dock, opening of the, vii. . 301
ST CLAIR, General; expedition to coast of Brittany, iv. 526
———, Hubert de, saves the life of Henry II., i. 442
St Cloud, View of, vii. . . . 280, 281
St Edmundsbury; View of, &c., i. . . 527
ST ESTEVAN, Count of, iv. . . . 92
SAINT-FOND, a French traveller, vi. 321, 324, 332, 337, 838, 844
St Germain, View of the Palace of, iv. . 180
St Giles's, Edinburgh, from an old print, iii. . 183
ST GILLES, Raymond de, earl of Toulouse, i. . 444, 445
St James's Palace; View of, iii. . . 42
———— Park, improvement of, vii. . . 302
ST JOHN,¹ Lady, speaks in favour of Mrs Lisle, iii. 779
———, Oliver; severely fined, iii. . . 56, 179
St John's, Newfoundland, fire at, vii. . . 718
——— on the Sorel, View of, v. . . 154
ST JUST, Anthony, . v. 836, 888, 892; vi. 17, 55-60
ST LEGER; beheaded, ii. 126
St Low, Sir W., one of Princess Elizabeth's officers, ii. 515, 521
St Lucie, island of, taken from the French, v. . 264
St Martin's Church, View of, iv. . . 698

St Mary Woolnoth, Lombard Street; View of, iv. . 699
St Michael, Mount of, in Normandy; View of, i. 397
St Paul's Cathedral, iii. . . . 159, 573
————, Views of, iv. . 686, 687, 693, 694
———— Cross, iii. 476, 492
ST PIERRE, Eustace de, a rich burgess of Calais, i. 769
ST POL, Walleran of Luxemburgh, ii. . 10, 15, 28
St Quintin, Battle of, ii. . . . 533
SAINTRAILLES, Poitou de, ii. . 49, 55, 56, 58, 60, 65, 69
ST RUTH, a French general, iv. . . . 33, 34
St Simonism in England, vii. . . . 410
St Stephen, Church of, at Caen; View of, i. 390, 391
St Stephen's Chapel, . . . ii. 766; iii. 783
————, Walbrook, interior of, iv. . . 690
ST VINCENT, John Jervis, earl, vi. . 116, 159
SALADIN, Sultan; his wars with the Crusaders, i. 495-501
Salads, &c., introduced from the Netherlands, ii. 806
Salamanca, View of the City of, vi. . . 606
Salaries, reduction of official, vii. . . 339
SALDANHA, General Count, Portuguese war-minister, vii. 270
SALE, General Sir Robert; Portrait, vii. . 624-628
Salerno, King Richard's visit to, i. . . 488
SALISBURY, Captain Owen; shot at a window, ii. 686
———, Countess of, Margaret Plantagenet, ii. 401, 408, 409
———, John de Montague, earl of, ii. . 6, 7
———, John of; quoted, i. . . 607-610, 633
———, Richard Nevill, earl of, ii. . 92-94, 96
———, Thomas de Montague, earl of, ii. . 54, 60, 61
———, William Longspear, earl of, i. . 525, 526
Salisbury, Cathedral of, rebuilt by Bishop Roger, i. 426, 615
————, jurisdiction of Wales over, iii. . 43
Sallee, town of, destroyed by Captain Rainsborough, iii. 174
Salt, vi. 839
———, procured by evaporation, i. . . 600
SALZ, Mr, the African explorer, death of, in 1828, vii. 313
SALTOUN, Lord; his zeal for the Pretender, iv. . 187
SAMMES, Aylett, a writer of 17th century, i. . 9
SAMOTHES, King, and the fabled giants of Britain, i. 118
SAMPSON, Dean; interview with Catherine, &c., ii. 383, 395, 406
San Roque, lines of, constructed by the Spaniards, iv. 381
—— Sebastian, taken by storm, 1813, vi. . 647, 652, 655
SANCROFT, William, archbishop of Canterbury—
    iii. 764, 765, 785; iv. 3, 9
Sanctuary at Westminster; Sketch of, ii. . 110
SANCY, Father, confessor to Marshal de Bassompierre, iii. 125
SANDERS, Mary, a Quaker, servant of Oliver Cromwell, iii. 816
SANDERSON, Sir Thomas, in favour of war with Spain, iv. 408
SANDILANDS, Sir James; his mission to France, ii. . 563
Sandown Castle, near Deal; View of, ii. . 844
SANDS, an accomplice in attack on Sir J. Coventry, iii. 707
SANDWICH, Edward Montague, earl of, iii. . 685, 696, 710
———, John Montagu, earl of, iv. 529; v. 3, 88, 308, 309, 336
Sandwich, first landing of Cæsar betwixt Walmer and, i. 28
———— Islands, ceded to Great Britain, vii. . 714
SANDYS, Colonel, falls in charging Prince Rupert, iii. 296
———, Edwin, bishop of London, ii. . . 647
———; his accusation against Sir Robert Walpole, iv. 416
———, Sir Edwin, arbitrarily arrested, iii. . 86
SANGALLO, Antonio, an eminent architect, iii. . 570
Sanitary improvement, vii. . . . 745
SANMICHELI, Michael, an Italian architect, iii. . 570
SANSUM, Rear-admiral, slain in battle, iii. . 695
SANTERRE, leader of a Parisian mob, v. . 833, 863, 897
Saragossa, city of, surrenders to Duke of Orleans, iv. 182
Saratoga Lake; View of, v. . . . 205
SARSFIELD, General, slain at battle of Landen, iv. 33, 41
Sarum, Castle of; View of the ruins, i. . 427
SAUNDERS, Chief-justice, Roger North's description of, iii. 847
———, Laurence, a powerful preacher; burnt, ii. 524
SAVAGE, Sir John; slain before Boulogne, ii. . 293
Savannah, fort and town of; View, v. . . 259
SAVARY, General; his mission to Madrid, &c., vi. 405, 408
SAVERY, Thomas; his steam-engine for draining mines, iv. 692
SAVILE, Sir Henry, provost of Eton College, iii. . 616
SAVILLE, Sir George; his inquiry into pension-list, v. 300
Savings-banks, national, vii. . . . 45, 46

GENERAL INDEX. 139

	PAGE
SAVOY, Duke of, iv.	27, 138
———, retired to a hermitage, ii.	78
Savoy, invaded by the French, v.	834
——— Palace, the; View of the ruins, i. 786, 787; iii.	820
Savoyard, Lombard, and German adventurers, ii.	37
Saw-mills first used in England about 1768, v.	496
SAWTRE, Wm., rector of Lynn; first Lollard burnt, ii.	142, 143
SAXE, Marshal, a partisan of the Pretender, iv.	443, 445, 450
Saxon language, literature, &c.—	
i. 292–301, 304, 323, 332, 333, 337, 341–346, 571, 611–614	
SAXONS, the. See also Saxon Kings—	
i. 53, 90, 138–145, 152, 153, 156–158, 165, 166, 288	
SAXTON, C.; an engraver, first publisher of county maps, iii.	577
SAY AND SELE, William Fienes, Viscount, iii. 181, 182, 204, 247	
———, Lord; beheaded by Cade's men, ii.	88
———; slain at Barnet, ii.	109
Scalds and Bards of the Scandinavians and Celts, i.	228, 229
SCALES, Thomas de, Lord, governor of the Tower, ii.	89
Scandinavia, superstitious mythology of, &c., i. 138, 224–228	
Scarcity of food, alarm of, in 1826, vii.	189, 190
SCHALKEN, Godfrey, an eminent painter, iv.	704
SCHAUB, Sir Luke, iv.	363
SCHEELE, a celebrated Swiss chemist, vi.	843
SCHEEMAKERS, an artist, designed Horse-Guards, iv. 701, 707	
Schellenberg, or Donawert, Battle of, fought 1704, iv.	152, 153
SCHEVEZ, William, archbishop of St Andrews, ii.	154
SCHILTER, his opinion of Celtic and Teutonic languages, i.	10
SCHOMBERG, Duke of, son of the following, iv.	33, 159
———, Marshal, iii. 128; iv.	18, 23, 26
Schools; foundation of Old St Paul's, &c., ii.	815–817
SCHROTTENBACH, viceroy of Naples, iv.	341
SCHULENBERG, Mademoiselle, mistress of George I., iv.	290
SCHUTZ, Baron, Hanoverian resident in England, iv. 258, 265	
SCHWARTZENBERG, Prince, vi.	684
SCHWERIN, Marshal, iv.	423, 425
SCHWICKELT, Mr, Hanoverian plenipotentiary, iv.	424
Sciacca, town of, taken by the imperialists, iv.	344
Science, progress of, i.	118, 289, 603, 842
——— See also 'Literature,' &c., ii. 196, 813;	
iii. 560, 870; iv. 695–749; v. 499–532; vi. 850–905	
Sciences, mathematical and physical, iv. 713–736; v.	518
Scilly Islands, resorted to by the Phoenicians, i.	92, 93
SCOT, a Commonwealth-man, executed as a regicide, iii.	676
———, Mr William, iii.	464
Scotch and Welsh judicature, vii.	290
———, burgh reform, vii.	85, 102
——— Church, schism in the, vii.	409
Scotland, Church of; its conflicts with the state, vii. 513, 518	
———, patronage in, vii.	669–674
———, debate concerning Royal Burghs of, v.	850
———, George IV.'s visit to; his landing at Leith, vii. 140, 141	
———, history of religion in, i.	244
———, manners and customs of, ii.	264–267
———, map of, vii.	367
———, royal arms and regalia of, iv.	viii, 179
———, sedition in, vii.	116
Scots, disputes concerning naturalisation of the, iii. 35, 646, 647	
———, the; their origin, &c., i.	18–20, 52–56
SCOTT, a Jacobite, sub-preceptor to George III., iv.	539
———, Sir Walter; bust of, vi.	883, 886–890
———, laird of Bucclench, ii.	441
———; Portrait, vii.	305, 444
SCOTTI, Marquis; his intrigues, iv.	334
Scottish banking-system in 1826, vii.	186
——— India House, View of, iv.	82
SCOTUS, Duns; destruction of copies of his works, ii.	818
Scrofula, touching for; when commenced, iii.	898
SCROGGS, Chief-justice; his partiality, iii.	724
SCROOP of Masham, Henry, Lord; beheaded, ii.	29
———, Richard, archbishop of York, ii.	13, 14, 17
SCROPE, Colonel; executed, iii.	383, 665, 672, 676
———, Lady, daughter of Lord Hunsdon, iii.	2
———, Lord; visits Mary Queen of Scots, ii.	608
SCUDAMORE and RHEES-AP-DHU, executed as rebels, ii.	18
Sculpture, ii. 851–854; iv. 706–709;	
v. 525, 526; vi. 874–878, 901, 902	

	PAGE
Sculpture of the Anglo-Saxons, i.	318
Scutage, levied by Henry II., i.	444
SEAFIELD, Earl of, secretary of state for Scotland, iv. 90, 172	
Seamen, impressment of, considered, vii.	416
Search, right of; difficulties, vii.	705, 710
Seasons, remarkable, of 1820–1826, vii.	215
Seaton House, View of, iv.	458
SEBERT, king of Essex, converted to Christianity, i.	233
Secession of the Free Church of Scotland, vii.	673, 674
SECKENDORF, Marshal, enters Bavaria, iv.	447
SECKER, bishop of Oxford, iv.	429
Secret committees, reports of, vii.	53, 81–83
Sects, impartiality to religious, in Ireland, vii.	493
Sedan-chairs; illustrations, iv.	770
———, Sir Sanders Duncomb's patent for, iii.	544
Sedgemoor, Battle of, iii.	774
Sedition, revival of, vii.	114
SEDLEY, Catherine, mistress of James II., iii.	784
———, Sir C., a poet of 17th century, iii. 875; iv.	21
Seekers, a religious sect, followers of Sir H. Vane, iii.	613
Sees, opposition to the consolidating of, vii.	679
SEGRAVE, John de, governor of Scotland, i.	725
SEGUIR, chancellor of France, iii.	554
Segura, town of, taken by Duke of Berwick, iv.	159
SELDEN, lawyer and antiquary, iii. 86, 88, 129, 133, 138, 142	
SELIM III., sultan of Turkey—	
v. 727–729; vi. 371–377, 380–383, 500	
Selsey, Isle of, i.	142
SEMPIL, Lord, iii.	452
Senassie fakeers, ravages of, in India, v.	625
Seneschal, or Dapifer Regis, office of the, i.	568
SENHOUSE, Sir Le Fleming, death of, vii.	617
Sens, city of, taken by Henry V., ii.	48
Sepoys, group of, v.	625
'September Massacre' in Paris, v.	876
Septennial Bill, passed April 26, 1716, iv.	311
Seringapatam, View of, v.	853
SERLE, persuades Ward to personate Richard II., ii.	16
Serpent, Druidical worship of the, i.	68
SERVETUS, burning of, at Geneva, iii.	806
——— controversy occasioned by his death, iv.	718
Servia, Russian despotism in, vii.	701
Sessions of 1842 and 1846, opening of the, vii.	639, 727
SETON, Christopher, a follower of Bruce, i.	729
———, Mr, commissioner for settling Union of Scotland, iv.	172
Settlement, Act of, iv.	13, 19
———, law of, iv.	41
Seven Sacraments, Defence of the, ii.	345
Seven Years' War, iv.	561
Severn, river, Victory of Alfred on banks of, &c., i. 163, 164	
SEVERUS, the emperor; his invasion of Britain, i.	49–52
Seville, View of, vi.	537
SEWARD, Miss Anna, a poetess, vi.	853
SEXBY, Colonel, iii.	66, 427
SEYMOUR, Lord Henry, blocks up ports of Spain, ii.	673
———, Mr Edward, iii.	705, 767
———, Mr Portman, iv.	233
———, Queen Jane, wife of Henry VIII., ii. 394–396, 402	
———, Sir E., a partisan of Prince of Orange, iv. 10, 77, 145	
———, Sir Francis, appointed sheriff, iii.	117, 130
———, Sir Thomas, lord high admiral, ii. 456, 471–480	
———, William, son of Lord Beauchamp, iii.	46, 47
SFORZA, Maximilian, and his Swiss allies, defeated, ii.	334
SHAFTESBURY, Earl of, iii. 413, 671, 711, 714, 728, 731–734, 740	
SHAH ALUM, governor of Allahabad and Corah, v. 618, 624	
———, SOOJAH, history of, vii.	622–628
Shakspeare Gallery, the, vi.	871
SHAKSPEARE, William, the great dramatist, iii. 560, 588–592	
Shakspeare's festival, vii.	306
SHARP, archbishop of St Andrews, iii. 683, 694, 701, 730	
———, John, archbishop of York, iv.	168
———, Richard, death of, in 1835, vii.	600
———, Wm., the line-engraver, death of, in 1824, vii.	220
SHAW, Dr, brother of the mayor, ii.	121, 122
———, Edmund, lord-mayor, ii.	119, 122
SHAXTON, Nicholas, bishop of Salisbury, ii.	410, 443

	PAGE
SHEA family, murder of, in Tipperary, vii.	210
SHEBBEARE, Dr, a reviewer and pamphleteer, iv.	576
Sheen, priory of, near Richmond, ii.	309, 329
Sheep, Anglo-Saxons valued wool more than flesh of, i.	277
SHEFFIELD, Captain, a parliamentarian officer, iii.	304
———, Edmund, baron of Butterwicke, ii.	456
Sheffield, iii.	655
———, Chartist riots at, vii.	568
———, its manufactures, vi.	635–637
———, plate, first made in 1742, iv. 634; v.	482
SHELBURNE, Earl of; Portrait, &c.— v. 96, 98, 179, 238, 297, 301, 391,	394
SHELLEY, a distinguished poet, vi.	888
———, death of, in 1822, vii.	223
———, Richard; Catholic petition to Elizabeth, ii.	656
SHEPHERD, his depositions respecting Rye-house Plot, iii.	744
———, James, executed by George I. as a traitor, iv.	324
———, presents the Agitators' manifesto, iii.	366
SHERFIELD, Mr; he is severely fined, iii.	159
SHERIDAN, the statesman, wit, and dramatist, v. 338, 339, 395, 505, 673, 694, 758, 850, 898, 890; vi. 23, 72,	756
Sheriffs; difficulties in prosecuting the Hansards, vii.	581, 582
SHIEL, Mr, vii.	251–254, 490
Ship, form of a Saxon, i.	266
———; model exhibiting a first-rate ship-of-war, iii.	863
SHIPPEN, Mr, committed to the Tower, iv.	324, 418
Ships of war of the 15th century; illustrations, ii.	177
SHIRLEY, Dr Thomas; his appeal against Sir J. Fagg, iii.	838
———, General; his attack on French fort at Niagara, iv.	554
———, James, a dramatist, iii.	592, 597, 598
Shooting-matches, iv.	774
Shop-tax, repeal of, April 1789, v.	716
Shops, early-closing movement, vii.	656
SHORE, Jane; Portrait of, &c., ii.	120, 121
SHOVELL, Sir C., an English admiral, iv.	41, 162, 183, 184
Shrewsbury, Battle of, ii.	15
SHREWSBURY, C. T., duke of, iv. 22, 66, 67, 80, 252, 280,	324
———, Countess of, iii.	46
———, Francis Talbot, earl of, ii. 470; iii.	893
———, G. T., earl of, ii. 320, 323, 353, 354, 397–	399
———, G. T., earl of, at execution of Mary Stuart, ii.	668
SIDILLA, Lady, wife of Alexander I. of Scotland, i.	538
SIBTHORPE, Robert, vicar of Brackley, iii.	124
SIBYLLA, daughter of the Count of Conversano, i.	408, 410
———, daughter of the earl of Anjou, i.	412, 413
SIDDONS, Mrs, death of, in 1831, vii.	441
SIDMOUTH, Henry Addington, viscount, vi.	159, 171–307
———, Lord, vii.	56–62, 92, 111, 114, 123, 134–136
SIDONIUS, says early Saxons delighted in a sea-life, i.	140
SIGHELM, bishop of Shireburn, i.	267
SIGISMUND, king of the Romans, and emperor-elect, ii.	34, 35
Sikh invasion, and Sikh cavalry; illustration, vii.	713
Silbury Hill, in Wiltshire, i.	67
Silk, acts of Parliament respecting, ii.	193, 775
Silk manufactures— iii. 558; v. 495; vi. 844–846; vii. 165, 174–177	
——— mill, first erected at Derby in 1719, iv.	682
——— mills in 1826, rage for building, vii.	186
——— weavers, distress among the, in 1829, vii.	268
Silures, the; Caractacus their commander, i.	6, 41, 42
SIMEON, Mr, death of, vii.	597
SIMIER, prosses suit of Duke of Anjou to Elizabeth, ii.	650
SIMNEL, Lambert. See Henry VII., ii.	287
SIMON, T., coin-maker to the Commonwealth, iii.	578
SIMPSON, a distinguished preacher, iii.	66
———, Cuthbert; tortures practised upon, ii.	735, 736
———, Mr, death of, in 1840, vii.	593
———, Thomas, an eminent mathematician, iv.	734
SINCLAIR, bishop of Dunkeld, surnamed King's Bishop, i.	739
———, Oliver, a favourite of James V., ii.	433
———, Sir J.; plan about Exchequer bills, vi. 803, 804,	819
Sinde, the Ameers of, vii.	623, 620, 630
Sinecures, abolishment of many ecclesiastical, vii.	65, 474
Sinking Fund, established in 1717— iv. 674; v. 595; vi. 791–794	
SIWARD, Earl, of Danish origin, i.	188, 190, 194, 195

	PAGE
Six Articles—Eucharist, Celibacy of Priests, &c., ii.	410, 411
SIXTUS IV., Pope, ii.	701
Skating, winter-sport of, ii.	261
SKEFFINGTON, Sir William, lord-deputy of Ireland, ii.	426
SKELTON, J., poet-laureate in reign of Henry VIII., ii.	827, 837
SKERRETT, Colonel, bravely defends Tarifa, vi.	603, 608
SKIPPON, Serjeant-major, iii.	267, 317, 333, 365
SKYRING, Mrs; enthusiastic reception of Pretender, iv.	486
SLANY, Sir Richard, iii.	292
'Slaughter of Rathcormack,' vii.	419
SLAVATTA, M., member of the council of state at Prague, iii.	80
Slave-trade, v. 306, 690, 770, 849; vi. 231, 258, 314, 315, 355–357, 767, 801; vii. 4, 10, 89, 94, 168–172, 371, 383, 647, 746	
———; English trade in, commenced by Hawkins, ii.	787
Slaves, a protector of, appointed, vii.	309
———; children of Angles sold, i.	54, 176, 230, 269, 270
Sliding-scale sanctioned by House of Commons, vii.	641
SLINGSBY, Sir Henry, beheaded by Cromwell, iii.	200, 427
SLOPER, Colonel, iv.	585
Sluys, naval victory gained here by Edward III., i.	759
SMEATON, John, a celebrated civil engineer; Portrait, v.	474
———, M., accused of having criminal conversation with Queen Anne Boleyn; confesses; executed, ii.	391–394
SMITH, Aaron, iii.	747
———, Adam, a moral and political writer, iii. 901; v.	518
———, Colonel; his services in India, v.	620
———, John Thomas, death of, vii.	442
———, Robert, the divine and mathematician, iv.	713
———, Sir Lionel, governor of Jamaica, vii.	560
———, Sir Sidney; Portrait of, vi.	10, 165
———, Sir T., death of, in 1840, vii.	594
———, Sir T., eminent as a statesman, philosopher, &c., ii.	636
———, Sir Thomas, an eminent statesman, iii.	517
———, Sydney; his criticisms; Portrait, vii.	459, 474, 667
———, the Demerara missionary, vii.	170–172
———, William, pupil of Isaac Becket, iv.	709
Smithfield, burning-place in; illustration, ii.	698
SMOLLETT; his character of William III., iv.	123, 124
———, Tobias, an author of great reputation, v.	500
Smuggling, vii.	172, 173, 210
Smyrna, English ships trading to; plundered, iii. 85; iv.	42
———, great fire at, in 1845, vii.	718
SNATT, William, a nonjuring clergyman, iv.	64
Snowdon, View of, i.	698
SOANE, Sir John, an eminent architect, vi.	865, 891, 892
SOBIESKI, John, king of Poland, iv.	68
Sobraon, Battle of, vii.	714
Social improvement, progress of, vii.	37
'Société Fraternelle,' established in 1791, v.	827
Soho, Boulton and Watt's ironworks, v.	482, 483
Soissons, Congress of, June 1728, iv.	380
Soldiery and police favourable to the reformers, vii.	363
SOLIMAN, an Arabian merchant; his mention of tea, iii.	861
Sombref, Battle of, fought June 16, 1815, vi.	704
SOMBREUIL, governor of the Invalides; saved by his daughter, v.	877–879
SOMERLED, thane of Argyle, i.	542, 543
SOMERS, John, Lord, a lawyer and statesman, iii. 790; iv. 41, 50, 68, 74, 86, 89, 90, 105, 109, 112, 202, 311, 626	
———, Sir George, captain of Virginia Company, iii.	538
SOMERSET, Charles Seymour, duke of, iv.	127
———, Edmund de Beaufort, duke of, ii.	109, 110
———, E. de Beaufort, earl of, ii. 52, 54, 84, 85, 90–92	
———, Edward Seymour, duke of— ii. 440, 441, 445, 448–451, 454–465, 471–489, 492, 495, 497	
SOMERSET, Henry de Beaufort, duke of, ii.	98–101
———, John de Beaufort, earl of, ii.	5
———, Thomas; his mission to James I., iii.	2
———, William Seymour, duke of, iii.	247, 292
Somerset House; View of, ii.	845
———; View of the Quadrangle, vi.	866
Somersetshire, Saxons of, assist King Alfred, i.	156, 158
SOMERVILLE, strangled in Newgate, ii.	654
Sombauth, gates of the temple of, restored, vii.	629
SONTAG, Mdemoiselle; her popularity, vii.	306

GENERAL INDEX. 141

	PAGE
SOPHIA DOROTHEA, of Zell, queen of Geo. I., iv.	232, 272, 273
SOABIÈRE, Samuel, a French physician, iv.	724-728
SOTHEBY, William, death of, in 1833, vii.	445
SOUBISE, a leader of the Huguenots, iii.	127, 136
SOULT, Marshal, a French general—	
vi. 579, 585, 586, 608, 641, 646-651, 655, 656, 676-680	
———, Marshal; Portrait, vii.	423-426
South American provinces, vii.	143, 149
——————— speculations and their results, vii.	181-183
—— Australia, Gawler's misgovernment of, vii.	715
—— Sea Company; its origin and fall, iv.	350-357, 668
—— Wales Turnpike Act, vii.	638
SOUTHAMPTON, Henry Wriothesley, earl of, ii. 685-689; iii. 3	
——————, T. W., earl of, ii.	451, 454-457, 491, 492
——————, Thomas Wriothesley, earl of, iii.	150, 679
SOUTHCOTE, Joanna, an extravagant fanatic, vi.	774, 775
SOUTHEY, an eminent poet, vi.	883, 885, 886
————, death of, in 1843; Portrait, vii.	738
Southwark Bridge, vi.	823
SOUTHWELL, Sir Richard, and others, arrest the Princess Elizabeth at Ashridge. See Elizabeth, ii.	515
Sovereigns, contemporary, i. 357, 670; ii. 3, 280; iii. 1, 661	
————————; lists of, iv.	vii, 793
———————— first issued in 1816, vi.	817
Spain, affairs of, vii.	146-152, 541-543, 702
——, allusions to the Cortes of, ii.	354
——, embassies to James I. from, &c., iii.	7, 706
——, high state of learning in, &c., i.	522, 604
——, the young Queen of, vi.	429
Spalatro, golden gate of Diocletian at, i.	308, 309
Spanish America, vii.	47-52
———— provincials, difficulties of the, vii.	49
———— question, vii.	707
———— revolution of 1822, vii.	143
———— troops of Charles V.; their excellence, ii.	358
SPARKES, Michael, a publisher, iii.	152
Spectacles, vi.	775
Speculation of 1824-1826, and its consequences, vii.	173-188
SPEED, John, an antiquary; quoted, i. 483, 484; iii. 615	
SPENCE, secretary to the Earl of Argyle, iii.	756
Spencean Philanthropists and their founder, vii.	31, 32
SPENCER, Earl, death of, in 1834, vii.	438
SPENSER, Edmund, the English poet, iii.	582
————, Lord. See Lord Althorp.	
Spices, commerce in, iii.	105
Spinning-mill, invented by Sir R. Arkwright, v.	401
SPINOLA, Ambrose, a celebrated general, iii.	85, 105, 106
————, Marquis; his defence of Messina, iv.	340
Spires, taking of; illustration, v.	893
Spirit in the Wall; Elizabeth Croft's imposition, ii.	519
Spitalfields Acts, vii.	165, 174
Sports, Field, rural or popular, i. 647-657, 876-881; ii. 255-267, 889-898; iii. 642; iv.	779
SPOTSWOOD, John, iii. 438, 443, 451, 453, 465, 467, 477, 484	
SPRAT, Thomas, bishop of Rochester, iii.	743, 765
SPREUL, a fanatic Scottish preacher, iii.	730, 785
Spring-guns, Lord Home's gamekeeper indicted for murder for setting, vii.	300
Spurs, Battle of the; illustration, i.	323-325
SPUNSLOW, Dr, attends Hampden in his last moments, iii.	304
Spy-system, various opinions on the, vii.	84
SQUIRES, a soldier; designs to poison Queen Elizabeth, ii.	681
STACEY, a priest; accused of magic; executed, ii.	114
STAEL, Madame de, a celebrated writer, v.	743, 858, 867
STAFFORD, E., earl of; slain in battle of Worcester, ii.	15
————, Granville L. Gower, marquis of, iv. 840; v. 2, 295	
————, Humphrey and Thomas, ii.	286, 287
————, John, archbishop of Canterbury, ii.	147
————, Sir Humphrey, defeated by Cade; slain, ii.	88
————, Thomas, a refugee of rank in France, ii.	532
————, William Howard, earl of, iii.	732
STAHL, George Ernest, a German physician, iv.	735
STAIR, Lord; draws up a Protestant faith test, iii.	736, 769
————; recommends the Union of Scotland, iv.	441
Stamford-bridge, battle between Hardrada and Harold, i.	209
STAMFORD, Henry Grey, earl of, iii.	280, 293

	PAGE
Stamp Act, the, of 1814-15, vi.	781
———— duty on newspapers, Mr Bulwer attempts to obtain repeal of, vii.	519
Stamp laws, vi.	780
————tax; its repeal, iv. 829-830, 830; v. 448-450	
Standard, Battle of the; Scots defeated, i.	424-426, 541
STANDISH, Dr; his trial, ii.	704
————, Ralph, one of the esquires of Richard II., i.	788
STANHOPE, Charles, earl, vi.	749-752, 769, 847, 848
————, Colonel William, iv.	335
————, Dean, iv.	613
————, James, earl of, iv.	165, 228, 320, 324, 355
————, Lady Hester, death of, vii.	593
————, Mr, English ambassador at Spain, iv.	85, 101
————, Sir William, called to order by Speaker, iv.	529
STANISLAUS AUGUSTUS, king of Poland, v.	855-857
STANLEY, E. G. S.; Portrait, vii.	389-395, 494, 608
————, Sir Edward, at battle of Flodden, ii.	328
————, Sir Humphrey, knight-banneret, ii.	282
————, Sir William, ii. 300; iii. 23, 24, 29	
————, T., Lord, ii. 119-121, 124, 126, 127; 120, 232, 300	
STAPLETON, Sir Philip, a parliamentarian, ii.	249, 298
Star-chamber, Westminster; origin of the name, ii.	752
————; View of, &c., iii. 17, 22, 143, 247	
Starch, art of making; imported by Mrs Dingham, ii.	884
STAREMBERG, Count, a German general, iv.	201
State, Church and, difficulties between, vii.	513-518
———— paper office, erected in 1829 by Sir John Soane, vi.	892
Statutes. See Parliament.	
STAYLEY; he is executed at Tyburn, iii.	723
Steam, iv. 680, 681; v. 474-476, 478	
——— and railways, vii.	744
———, applied to manufacturing industry, vi.	829
——— boats, invented by Livingstone and Fulton, vi. 830, 831	
——— carriage, model of, exhibited in France by John T. Cugnot, vi.	825
Steam-engine, applied to navigation, vi.	829-832
———— in the east, vii.	434
Steel, cast, Huntsman the first manufacturer of, vi.	830
——— yard Company; privileges abolished, ii.	170, 783
STEEL, Mr, attorney-general at trial of Charles I., iii.	300
STEELE, Sir Richard, iv.	262, 263, 745
Steinkirk, Battle of, fought 1692, iv.	36, 37
STERKA, Conrad; with MILICZ and JANOWA; condemned by the pope as heretics, iii.	8
STEPHEN, count of Aumale, nephew of the Conqueror, i.	400
————, nephew of Henry I., i.	416, 420-438
————, of Tours, seneschal of Anjou, i.	482
STEPHENSON, George, the engineer, vi. 824-826, 833; vii.	740
———————, Rowland, embezzlement of, vii.	208
STEPNEY, Mr, a poet and politician, iv.	96, 97
Stereotyping discovered in 1725 by William God, iv.	684
———— revived by Mr Tilloch in 1780, vi.	847
STERNE, Laurence, a divine and popular writer, v.	501
STEUBEN, Baron, a Prussian officer, v.	247, 352
STEVENS, death of, vii.	598
Stevenswært, surrenders to Marlborough, iv.	130
STEWART, Colonel, imprisoned, iii.	251
————, Dr, a royalist commissioner, iii.	329
————, Professor Dugald, death of, in 1828, vii. 318-320	
————, Sir John, constable of Scotland, ii.	61
————, Walter; executed in front of Stirling Castle, ii.	133
STIGAND, archbishop of Canterbury, i.	204, 360, 361
STILICHO, aids the Britains against Saxon incursions, i. 54, 55	
STILL, John, bishop of Bath and Wells, iii.	580
STILLINGFLEET, Edward, bishop of Worcester, iv.	580
STILLINGTON, Robert, bishop of Bath and Wells, ii. 284, 285	
Stirling Castle, View of, i.	717
Stochach, Pass of, iv.	150
Stock-jobbing, rise of, iv.	653
STOCKDALE; his prosecution of the Hansards, vii.	580-582
Stocking-frame, the, invented by William Lee, ii.	810
————— looms, exportation of, prohibited, iv.	683
————— manufacture, vi.	846
Stockings, silk knitted; first in Elizabeth's reign, ii.	867
Stocks, removal of the St Clement Danes, vii.	210

	PAGE
STODDART, Colonel, fate of, vii.	630, 631
STODTHARDT, C. A., an artist and antiquary, iii.	797
Stoke-upon-Trent; Earl of Lincoln defeated here, ii.	290
STONE, Andrew, sub-governor to Prince of Wales, iv.	539
———, Nicholas, an eminent statuary, iii.	575, 576
Stone, the Broad, Nottinghamshire, iii.	697
Stonehenge, great temple of the Druids at, i.	68, 101
Storm, of 1839, disastrous, vii.	572
STORY, Dr; executed, ii.	543, 544
STOTHARD, Thomas, death of, vii.	442
Stour, river, near Canterbury, i.	30
STOURTON, Edward, Lord, a Catholic, iii.	25, 32
STOW, John, author of *Summary of English Chronicles*, iii.	615
STOWELL, Lord, formerly Sir William Scott, vi.	789
———, Death of, vii.	596, 597
STRABO, his account of Britain and Ireland, i.	14, 93
STRAFFORD, Earl of, iii.	123, 130, 145, 168, 178, 209, 220, 230, 231, 235, 245, 495
Strasburg delivered up to the French, iv.	70
——— insurrection, the, vii.	537
STRATFORD, John, archbishop of Canterbury, i.	759
———, Nicholas, bishop of Chester, iv.	193
Strathbogie case, the, vii.	670
Strathclyde, or Reged, i.	23, 217-220
STRAW, Jack, a priest, i.	735-780
STRICKLAND, Mr, disobeys the commands of Elizabeth, ii.	635
———, Walter, captain of Cromwell's guards, iii.	424
STRODE, Mr; his speech on assault of Lambeth Palace, iii.	219
STROUD; his arrestment and imprisonment, iii.	142
STRUTT, Jedediah; Portrait of, vi.	841
STRYPE'S *Ecclesiastical Memorials*, ii.	453
STUART, Alexander, archbishop of St. Andrews, ii.	320
———, Lady A., first-cousin of James I., iii.	3, 9, 12, 46, 47
———, Sir John, vi.	351, 352
STUBBES, Philip, author of *Anatomy of Abuses*, iii.	658
STUBBS, J., condemned to lose his right hand, ii.	651
STUDLEY, J., translated the *Medea* and *Agamemnon*, iii.	584
STUKELEY; this officer slain at the Battle of Alcazar, ii.	651
STUKELY, Sir Lewis, a vice-admiral, iii.	76
STUTEVILLE, Robert de, imprisoned for life, i.	410
———, William de, a follower of King John, i.	516
STYRUM, Count, wounded at Battle of Schellenberg, iv.	153
Succession Bill, passed 1701, iv.	110, 134
SUCKLING, Sir John, a minor but graceful poet, iii.	604
SUDBURY, S., *alias* Tibold, archbishop of Canterbury, i.	787
SUDELY, Lord, a Lancastrian, wounded at St Albans, ii.	92
SUETONIUS, Paulinus; quoted, i.	26, 29, 36, 43, 44, 61
SUFFIELD, Lord, death of, vii.	586
SUFFOLK, Charles Brandon, duke of, ii.	331, 332, 351, 355-357, 360, 371, 374, 383, 393, 397-399, 416
———, Edmund de la Pole, earl of, ii.	313-315, 323
———, Frances, duchess of, ii.	499, 500
———, Henry Grey, duke of, ii.	499, 503-505, 512, 518
———, John de la Pole, duke of, ii.	175, 313-315, 323
———, Mary, duchess of, 2d daughter of Henry VII., iii.	3
———, Michael de la Pole, earl of, i.	791, 792; ii. 34, 175, 241
———, Thomas Howard, earl of, iii.	49, 71
———, William de la Pole, ii.	54, 61, 65-68, 80-87, 175, 176
Sugar-duties, debate on the, vii.	583
———, domestic and anti-slavery views of the— vii.	646, 647, 691-720
——— manufacture of the West Indies, v.	847
———, statistics of 1833, vii.	501
SUJAH DOWLA, nabob of Oude, v.	618, 625-627
SULLY, Maximilian de Bethune, duke de Rosny, iii.	7
Sulphuric acid, improvements in manufacture of, v.	495
Sumptuary laws; expense of apparel limited to rank, ii.	272
Sun, Druidical worship of the, i.	68
———painting, or photography, vii.	744
SUNDERLAND, C.S., earl of, iv.	114, 134, 180, 225, 315, 356, 358
———, Henry Spencer; his Portrait, iii.	308, 829
———, Robert Spencer, earl of, iii.	727, 759, 778, 784, 785; iv. 47, 68, 73, 115-118, 126, 134
Sunderland, its obscurity in the time of Camden, iii.	656
——— riot of the seamen in 1825-26, vii.	188

	PAGE
Supremacy, Act of, first passed in 1562, iv.	43
———; revived in full vigour by Elizabeth, ii.	545
SURAJ-U-DOWLAH, governor of Bengal, iv. 571; v.	605-611
Surat, factory established here by the English, v.	598, 599
Surgery; its low condition in 15th century, ii.	203
SURREY, earl of, succeeds his father in 1089, i.	406, 408
———, Henry Howard, earl of— ii.	449, 450, 813, 830, 838; iii. 562, 582
———, John Plantagenet, earl of, i.	686, 694, 715, 717
———, William de Warren, earl of, i.	374, 381
Suspension Bill, passed in 1794, vi.	82
———bridges, vi.	323
SUSSEX, Augustus-Frederick, duke of, vi.	75
———, Duke of; his death in 1843, vii.	731
———, Thomas Ratcliffe, earl of, ii.	622
Sussex, or kingdom of the South Saxons, i.	142
SUTHERLAND, Earl of, iii.	452
SUTTON, Sir Robert, convicted of fraud and peculation, iv.	383
SUTTON's Monument at the Chapter House, iii.	576
SUVAROFF, Alexander, a Russian general— v.	722, 723, 779, 780; vi. 66, 67, 140
Swan River settlement, state of the, vii.	371
Sweating-sickness; most severe in London, ii.	282, 363, 495
Sweden and Norway, disputes between, vii.	547
———, Revolution of 1772, v.	26
———, site of capital of the ancient chief Wodin, i.	138
SWEDENBORG, Baron Emanuel, v.	422
Swedenborgians, establishment of, in 18th century, v.	422
SWEDIAUR, Dr, his sea salt-works at Prestonpans, vi.	847
SWEYN ESTRIDSEN, king of Denmark, i.	208, 371, 372, 386
———, prince of Denmark, i.	176-180
———, second son of Earl Godwin, i.	189-193
SWIFT, a divine and politician, iv.	635, 741-743
SWINEY, Dr, death of, in 1844, vii.	740
SWINTON, a partisan of Cromwell in Scotland, iii.	683
Swiss guards, massacre of the, v.	869-871
———, the; siege of Dijon by their army, ii.	325
Switzerland, entered by the French in 1798, vi.	129
———, troubles of, vii.	547
——— warfare between aristocratic and democratic principles in, vii.	702
Swords, made anciently of a mixture of copper and tin, i.	91
———, Thomas Gill the modern improver of, vi.	836, 837
SYDENHAM, Dr Thomas, a medical writer, iv.	735
———, Lord, death of, in 1841, vii.	557-559
SYDNEY, Algernon, a martyr to liberty, iii.	727, 740, 751-754
———; his sentence reversed, iv.	11
———, Henry, brother of the preceding, iii.	793
———, Sir Philip, nephew to Leicester— ii.	656, 657, 813, 836; iii. 582, 583, 602
SYDSERF, bishop of Galloway, iii.	478, 484
SYLVESTER, Joshua; his translation of *Du Bartas*, iii.	585, 601
SYLVIUS, Bonus, or Coil the Good, a British writer, i.	124
SYMINGTON, William, his steam-boat essays, vi.	830
SYNDERCOMBE, undertakes assassination of Cromwell, iii.	420
Synod, National, meets at Westminster, iii.	311
TAAFFE, Lord; his correspondence with Charles, iii.	310
TACITUS, the historian; quoted— i.	6, 9, 16, 33, 43-47, 61, 72, 76, 106, 124, 223, 246, 352
Tahiti or Otaheite, island of, vii.	706, 707
TAILLEFER, a gigantic follower of Duke William, i.	213
TAILOR, Robert, a dramatic writer, iii.	593, 594
Talavera, Battle of, fought July 27, 1809, vi.	477-479
TALBOT, Sir Gilbert, knight-banneret, ii.	282
———, Sir John, earl of Shrewsbury, ii.	54, 68, 79, 85, 91
TALLARD, C. d'Hostun, duke de, iv.	74, 100, 136, 149, 157, 158
TALLEYRAND, Charles Maurice, v.	743, 756, 786, 827-847
———, prime-minister to Napoleon, vi.	687
———, Prince; Portrait, vii.	2-5, 540, 541
TALLIEN, John Lambert, a French republican— v.	827, 859-863, 874
TALLIS, Thomas, a famous musician, iii.	561
TAMWORTH, a dependent of the earl of Leicester, ii.	582
Tamworth manifesto, vii.	449
TANCRED, grandson of the great Ruggiero, i.	489-493

GENERAL INDEX. 143

TANFIELD, Chief-baron; his opinion on sale of land, iii. 517
TANKERVILLE, Forde Grey, earl of, iv. . . 96
TANNEGUY-DUCHATEL, chief of the Armagnacs, ii. 41, 42, 44
Tanning, ii. 812
TANUCCI, Marquis Bernardo, an Italian statesman, iv. 391
Tara, monster meeting at, vii. 658
TARBES, Bishop of; his embassy to Henry VIII., ii. 364, 365
Tariff, the new; its reception in both Houses, vii. 643–646
TARLETON, General; Portrait of, v. . . 346, 347
Tasmania, or Van Diemen's Land, vii. . . 714, 715
TATE, Nahum, an English poet, iii. . . . 878
———, Zouch, introduces the Self-denying Ordinance, iii. 322
Tax, Roman, on pasture-ground, &c., i. . . 89, 253
Taxation and debt, vii. 161–163
———, cry for the reduction of, in 1835, vii. . . 518
Taxes of the 18th century, v. 440
——— reduction of, vii. 86, 208
TAYLOR, Dr, and Sir T. Cheney, congratulate Francis I., ii. 361
———, Dr Brook, a celebrated philosopher, iv. . 731
———, Dr R., rector of Hadleigh; burnt, ii. 523, 734, 735
———, Jeremy, an eminent divine, iii. 433, 491, 578, 610
———, John, bishop of Lincoln, ii. . . 508, 509
———, Sir Robert, an eminent architect, vi. . 864, 865
Tchesmé, Battle of, fought 1770, v. . . . 36, 37
Tea, introduced into England early in 17th century, iii. 861
——— trade, duties on, vi. 790, 800
TEDDIMAN, Sir Thomas, iii. 696, 698
TEIGNMOUTH, Lord, death of, in 1834, vii. . 438
Teinds, report of commissioners on, in 1837, vii. 514–516
Telescope, great power of the, vii. . . . 744
TELFORD, the engineer, vi. . 818, 822, 823, 826, 828
———, Thomas, death of, in 1834, vii. . . 439
Telichery, View of, v. 634
Temperance movement in Ireland, vii. . . 500–502
TEMPEST; his print of Westminster Hall and Abbey, iii. 766
———, Mr, conspires against William III., iv. . 62
Templars, Knights, i. . 444, 446, 491, 495, 561, 746, 747
TEMPLE, Lord, iv. 563, 577, 583, 584
———, R. G., earl of, iv. 804, 820, 840, 862, 877; v. 218, 399
———, Sir John, Master of the Rolls, iii. . 254, 389
———, Sir William, iii. . . . 706, 712, 716
Temple, Louis XVI. conveyed prisoner to the, v. 873, 891
Temporalities Bill, passing of Irish Church, vii. . 395
Tenchebray, a strong fortress in Normandy, i. . 410
TENCIN, Cardinal de, a partisan of the Pretender, iv. 444
Ten-hour Labour Bill, debates on the, vii. . 655
TENISON, T., archbishop of Canterbury, iii. 776; iv. 50, 607
Tennis Court, iii. 640
TENNYSON, the poet, vii. 741
Tenths and First-fruits; their application, iv. . 144
Terceira, Captain Walpole sent to watch Portuguese at, vii. 270
TERMES, M., general of French forces in Scotland, ii. 489
Teronenne, laid siege to, and burnt to the ground, ii. 323–326
Territorial limits settled by the Peace, vii. . . 5
Terror, Reign of, in France, v. 876
Teschen, Treaty of, signed May 13, 1779, v. . 240
TESSÉ, René de Froulai, marshal of France, iv. . 164, 367
Test Act, passed 1673, iii. 711
TESTWOOD, Robert; burnt, ii. 728
TETZEL, John, preaches in favour of the *indulgences*, ii. 706
Teutonic language, origin of the, &c., i. . 10, 11, 138
Tewkesbury, Battle of; Queen Margaret defeated, ii. 109
Texas and Mexico, American invasion of, vii. . 711
Thames, ford of the river, at Conway Stakes, i. . 32, 142
———, grand spectacle on the, vii. . . . 590
———, Tunnel accidents, vii. 301
———, ——— commenced in 1826, vii. . 214, 744
———, ——— its projectors, &c., vi. . 827, 831
Thanet, Isle of, i. 58, 141
THARAWADDEE, the Burmese emperor, vii. . 680
Theatrical representations, iv. . . . 772, 773
Thellusson Act, passed in 39th and 40th Geo. III., vi. 779
THELWALL, John, death of, in 1834, vii. . . 437
THEOBALD, abbot of Becco, i. . 430, 435, 440, 448
———, earl of Blois, i. 413
Theobalds, View of the Great Hall at, iii. . 33, 34, 108

THEODORE, archbishop of Canterbury, i. . . 304
Theodosian Code, i. 87
THEODOSIUS, a distinguished general, i. . . 54
———, the Great, son of the preceding, i. . . 54
Theophilanthropists, society of, v. . . . 791
THEOT, Catherine, a French maniac who prophesied
  the immediate appearance of the Second Advent, vi. 58
Theowes, a lower order among the Saxons, i. . 249
Thermometer, invented at Florence, iv. . . 735
THÉROIGNE, Mademoiselle, a French revolutionist, v. 783, 871
Thistle, Order of, revived by Queen Anne, iv. . 146
THISTLEWOOD, leader of Cato-Street conspiracy, vii. 114, 115
THOMAS, John, bishop of Winchester, iv. . . 546
———, V.; says James VI. hired him to kill Elizabeth, ii. 681
———, Wm.; his *Works*; executed at Tyburn, ii. 453, 518
THOMOND, Murroch O'Brien, earl of, ii. . . 428
THOMPSON, David, death of, in 1834, vii. . . 439
THOMSON, Archibald, death of, in 1832, vii. . 440
———, Mr C. Poulett. See Lord Sydenham.
THOR, his mighty 'hammer,' i. 140
THORNHILL, Sir James, a distinguished painter, iv. 702
THORPE, a priest charged with heresy, ii. . 143, 145, 146
———, Lady de; her effigy in Ashwelthorpe church, ii. 240
Thrashing-machine; first in Great Britain about 1710, iv. 680
Three-and-a-half per cents., reduction of the, vii. 693
THROCKMORTON, Francis; tortured and executed, ii. 655
THROGMORTON, Sir N.; his trial, ii. . 518, 580, 603, 604
Thule, the *ultima* of ancient poets and geographers, i. 124
THURKHILL's host invades Ethelred's dominions, i. 179
THURLOE, John, secretary of state, iii. . 329, 416, 421
THURLOW, Edward, solicitor-general, . iv. 581; v. 4, 853
———; Portrait of, vi. . . . 752, 755, 777
THURN, Count, leader of the Calvinists, iii. . . 80
THUROT, M., a daring adventurer, iv. . . . 579
THURSTAN, abbot of Glastonbury, i. . 382, 424, 549
THYNNE, Serjeant; argues rights of Oxford University, iii. 163
TICHBORNE, Lord-mayor, iii. 423
Ticonderoga, Fort of; View of the Ruins, v. . 113
TIERNEY, George; Portrait, vii. . . 9, 97, 101, 312
Tiernsteign, View of the Castle and Town of, i. . 503
Tilbury Fort; delineation of, &c., ii. . . 673, 674
TILBURY, Gervase of; quoted, i. . . 580, 581, 583
TILDESLEY, Sir Thomas, governor of Lichfield, iii. 355
TILLEUIL, Humphrey, warden of Hastings Castle, i. 370
TILLIERS, Count de, an attendant of Henrietta Maria, iii. 126
TILLOTSON, John, archbishop of Canterbury, iv. 589, 739
———; review of his works, iii. . . . 749
TILLY, Count, compels king of Denmark to cross Elbe, iii. 129
Tilsit, Treaty of July 1807, vi. 394
Times; its opposition to the new poor-law, vii. . 378
———, testimonial to the, vii. 586
———, the, announces the repeal of the corn-laws, vii. 724
TIMUR, or TAMERLANE, a Mogul Tatar, v. . 598
Tin, vi. 834, 837
——— of the Cassiterides, i. . . 26, 91, 92, 104, 106
———, quantity of, produced in 18th century, v. . 477, 478
Tinning, art of, introduced by Yarrranton, iii. . 869
TINTORE, Giovanni, archdeacon of Naples, iii. . 560
TIPPOO SAIB, sovereign of Mysore—
  v. 632, 636, 637, 797, 853–855; vi. 144
Tithe Commutation Act of 1837, vii. . . 474, 475
Tithes, discussions on, vi. 764, 766
———, outrages on collectors of Irish, vii. 389–398, 419, 454
TITIAN, Vecelli, the great Italian painter, iii. . 567
Titles, abolishment of French hereditary, v. . 785
TITUS, Sir Silas, counsels assassination of Cromwell, iii. 427
Tobacco, extreme aversion of James I. to this article, iii. 589
Tobago, British take possession of island of, vi. . 805
Ton, Sir Thomas; conspires to seize James IV., ii. 304
TOGODUMNUS, son of Cunobelinus; slain in battle, i. 39
TOLAND, J., on the learning and religion of the Celts, iv. 111
———; quoted, i. 10
Toleration, Presbyterian opinion of, iii. . . 311
TOLLEMACHE, General, killed at Brest, iv. . 46
Tomb of Napoleon at St Helena; illustration, vii. 133
TOMKINS, brother-in-law of Waller the poet; hanged, iii. 302

	PAGE
Tonge, Dr; papers giving account of Popish Plot, iii.	717
Tonnage of Great Britain, vi.	796
Tonstain, surnamed the Fair, i.	213
Tooke, Mr; quoted, vii.	19, 87, 95, 96, 105
———, Rev. John Horne,	iv. 886; v. 13;
	vi. 69, 70, 761, 779, 810, 814–817, 861
Torch-light meetings and Chartism, vii.	567–569
Torcy, M. de, a French diplomatist, iv.	96, 102, 212
Torgau, Battle of, fought November 11, 1760, iv.	800
Tories, Whigs, and Radicals, vii.	447
Torregiano, Pietro, an eminent sculptor, ii.	853
Torrington, Arthur Herbert, earl of, iv.	12, 27
Torture, discontinued in time of Commonwealth, iii.	517, 756
Tory Chartists and factious Chartists, vii.	483
———, origin of the term, iv.	647
Tostig, son of Earl Godwin, i. 188, 191, 194, 195, 200, 208, 209	
Toulon, besieged by the Duke of Savoy, iv.	183
Toulouse, Count de, iv.	160, 170
Toulouse, earldom of, claimed by Henry II., i.	444, 445
———; View of, vi.	679
Tournaments; illustrations—the Lists, &c., ii. 250, 251, 342	
——— patronised by James IV. and James V., iii.	645
Tournay, town of; View, iv.	215, 216
Tourneur, C., a dramatic writer of some note, iii.	593, 594
Tourville, Count de, admiral of the French fleet, iv.	38, 43
Tower of London,	i. 361; iii. 9, 72, 73, 76
———, incidents connected with, ii.	107, 110,
	114, 119, 121, 125, 281, 287, 309, 313, 509, 515, 517
Towerson, Gabriel, seized by the Dutch; his fate, iii.	105
Towns, Alderman, iii.	290
Town-house, Hague, iv.	31
——— or City, British, i.	99
Townley, Mr Francis, iv.	486, 491, 520
Townshend, Charles, chancellor of Exchequer, iv. 847, 850, 852	
———, viscount, iv.	267, 316, 382
———, George, marquis of, iv.	352
———, Thomas; Portrait of, v.	60
Township, Town, derivation of the word, i.	351, 352
Towton, great victory of Edward IV. at, ii.	98, 99
Tractarians in the English Church, vii.	674–676
———; their doctrine, vii.	402, 403
Tracy, William, one of the murderers of à Becket, i. 455, 456	
Trade. See Industry.	
——— and Commerce, vi.	795–817
———, Board of, iv.	663
———, abolished, v.	299
Trades-unions; their power and tyranny, vii.	417, 566
Tradition, testimony of, i.	4, 5
Trafalgar, Battle of, fought October 21, 1805, vi.	289–296
Trafford, Sir Cecil, a partisan of King Charles, iii.	299
Trajan's Column at Rome; illustrations from, i.	38, 39
Tramroads and Railways, vi.	824–826
Traquair, Earl of, lord-treasurer of Scotland, iii. 186, 362, 480	
Trauen, Count, surrenders Capua, iv.	392
Tread-wheel, abuse of the punishment by, vii.	210
Treason,	ii. 757; iv. 637
———, amelioration of punishment of, in 1814, vi.	784
Treasurer, office of the, i.	569
Treaties, debate on foreign, vii.	11
Treating Resolution, passed 1677, vi.	779
Treby, recorder of London, iii.	748
Trelawney, Colonel, successor to Colonel Kirk, iii.	769
Tremoille, George de la, count of Guines, ii. 58, 59, 68, 69	
Trenchard, John, a Rye-house conspirator, iii.	740, 745
Tresham, Francis; dies in the Tower, iii.	24–29
———, speaker of House of Commons, assassinated, ii.	90
Tresilian, chief-justice of England, i.	792
Trevisa, John de, a chronicler of 15th century, ii.	209
Trevithick and Vivian; their steam-carriage, vi.	825, 829
Trevor, Sir John,	iii. 705, 844; iv. 20, 50
Triads; Welsh poetical histories of Britain, i.	8, 304
Tribute, Roman, imposed on a conquered people, i.	89
Trichinopoly, View of the Rock of, v.	603
Triennial Act; when passed and repealed, iii.	232, 693
——— Bill, iv.	40
Triers, Board of, appointed by Cromwell, iii.	494

	PAGE
Trim, in Ireland, monster meeting at, vii.	658
Trinity College, Cambridge, Library of, iv.	687
——— House of Deptford, Corporation of, ii.	780
Trinobantes, a people of Essex and Middlesex, i.	33, 77
Triple Alliance—England, Holland, and Sweden, iii.	706
———England, France, and Holland, iv.	317
Trojans, said to have first peopled Britain, i.	8
Tronchet, one of the counsel of Louis XVI., v.	890, 894
Troughton, Edward, death of, in 1835, vii.	593
Troyes, city of; marriage of Henry V. of France, ii. 47, 574	
Truguet, Admiral, attempts the conquest of Sardinia, vi. 8	
Trumbull, Sir William, an English statesman, iv.	61
Trussel, Sir William, speaker of parliament, i.	744
Tryon, governor of New York, v.	125, 284
Tuam, Archbishop of, slain in a skirmish near Sligo, iii.	345
Tuberville, a royalist officer, iii.	344
———, causes execution of Lord Stafford, iii.	732
Tudor, Owen; beheaded at Hereford, ii.	80, 96, 125
———; the family colours were white and green, ii.	857
Tuileries, escape of Louis XVI. from the, v.	833–836
———, remarkable scene in palace of the, vii.	281
——— View of palace of, &c., v.	755, 788, 863, 869–871
Tuke, Sir Bryan; Henry VIII.'s divorce, ii.	378
Tull; his drilling and horse-hoeing experiments, iv.	680
Tullibardine, a partisan of the young Pretender, iv.	458
Tunnelling, vi.	826
Tunstall, C., of Durham, ii. 335, 336, 359, 383, 454, 499, 505	
Turenne, Henry, de la Tour d'Auvergne, iii.	710, 714
Turgot, confessor of Queen Margaret of Scotland, i. 537–539	
———, the French Minister of finance, v.	739
Turkey and Egypt, war between, vii.	429, 703, 704
——— Russia, war between, vii.	284
Turkey Company, the; when incorporated, ii.	790
Turkish soldiers of different corps, v.	35
Turlogh O'Connor, king of Connaught, i.	459
Turner, estimates population from Domesday-book, i.	350
———, Francis, bishop of Ely, iii.	776
———, Mrs, accused of poisoning; hanged, iii.	58, 59
———, Sir James, iii.	694, 701
———, the painter, vii.	740
Turnham, Robert de, governor of Cyprus, i.	495
Turnpike-roads, vi.	821–823
———, first established in 1663, v.	469–471
Turton, Baron, iv.	22
Tweedale, Marquis of,	iii. 701; iv. 146
Twiss, Dr, prolocutor of the National Assembly, iii.	311
Tye, Christopher, an eminent composer, iii.	561
Tyler, Wat, or Walter the, i.	785–789
Tylsworth, W., burnt; daughter forced to fire the pile, ii.	599
Tyndal, Wm., prints a translation of New Testament, ii.	712
Trawley, Lord, governor of Gibraltar, iv.	559, 573
Tyrconnel, a partisan of James II., iv.	34
———, disarms the Protestants in Ireland, iii.	784, 785
Tyrone, Con O'Neil, earl of—	
	ii. 428, 682–684, 693; iii. 39, 172, 232
Tyrrel, Sir J., Rich. III.'s master of horse, ii. 125, 285, 313, 314	
———, Sir W., accidentally shot William Rufus, i. 402, 403	
Tysilio, a Welsh priest, i.	8
Tytler, James; he is outlawed, vi.	24
Ulf, Norman bishop of Dorchester, i.	189
Ulm, View of, vi.	274
Ulphus, horn of, i.	318
Ulrica Eleanora, queen of Spain, iv.	329
Ulster, Richard de Burgh, earl of, i.	739
Umfraville, Gilbert de, earl of Angus, i.	709
———, Sir Robert, ii.	182, 183
Uniformity, Act of; its articles, ii.	545
Union, repeal of the, vii.	330–333
——— with Ireland, Act of, vi.	149, 777, 778
——— with Scotland, Treaty of, 1706, iv.	172–179
——— Workhouses, vi.	929
Unions, National and Metropolitan, vii.	355, 362
Unitarians, Burke's antipathy to, v.	852
———, persecution of, vi.	755, 770
Universities of Europe; institution of, i.	605, 606, 845

GENERAL INDEX. 145

	PAGE
Universities, opening of, to Dissenters, vii.	405, 406
University charter, the London, vii.	455
Unknown tongues, the Irvingite gift of, vii.	357
Upnor Castle, iii.	701
URBAN II., Pope, i.	551
—— VI., Pope; he is excommunicated, ii.	137
URSWICK, Christopher; mission to Brittany, &c., ii. 293, 294
Useful Knowledge, Society for Promoting the Diffusion of, vii.	310-312
Uses, Statute of; it causes insurrection, ii.	397, 755
USHER, J., archbishop of Armagh, i. 22; iii. 243,433,666,819
Utrecht, Peace of; View of, iv.	233-237, 253
——, View of, v.	656
Uxbridge, View of the Treaty-house at, iii.	328
URBDA, Duke d'; his mission to Innocent XIII., iv.	93
Vagrancy and mendicity, vii.	40
Vails, abolition of the custom of, v.	536
VAL, Ambroise du, a sculptor of reputation, iii.	576
Valentine's Day, St; practices of this festival, ii.	897
Valladolid, View of, vi.	607
VALLANCEY, C., an investigator of Irish antiquities, i.	15
VALLANS, a dramatic author, iii.	583
Valley Forge, View of Washington's head-quarters at, v. 244
VALOIS, Charles de, brother of Philip III. of France, i. 712
VAN DER MEULEN, the celebrated battle-painter, iv.	704
—— GHENT, the Dutch vice-admiral, iii.	710
—— Orr, author of the equestrian statue of George I., iv. 709
—— RICHTEREN, Count, iv.	249
—— TROMP, the Dutch admiral, iii. 208, 406, 407, 415
Van Diemen's Land, or Tasmania, vii.	714, 715
VANBRUGH, Sir John, an eminent architect, iii.	573
VANDEPUT, Sir George, iv.	535
VANDERBANK, a portrait-painter, iv.	303, 685
VANDERDUSSEN, Rear-admiral, iv.	160, 212
VANDREUIL, Marquis de, a French governor, iv.	586
VANDYKE, Sir Antony, the portrait-painter— iii. 2, 110, 115, 225, 413, 433, 495, 560, 568
VANE, Sir H., supersedes Coke as secretary, iii. 209, 215, 222
——; executed, iii. 226, 238, 429*, 687, 690, 806
VANSITTART, N., chancellor of the exchequer, vii. 161, &c.
VANSOMER, Paul, an eminent portrait-painter, iii.	567
VARELST, an eminent Dutch painter of flowers, iii.	982
Varennes, detention of the king at; illustration, v.	834
VARNEY, Sir E., standard-bearer to Charles I., iii. 95, 293, 297
Vates, or Angurs, the chief poets of antiquity, i.	63-65
VAUBAN, Sebastian le Prestre, a great engineer, iv.	714
——, a marshal of France, iv. 48, 53
VAUDEMONT, Prince, of the House of Guise, iii.	34
VAUX, Lord George, committed to the Fleet prison, iii.	116
Vauxhall, as it appeared in 1751, iv.	773
VAVASOUR, Col., taken prisoner at battle of Edgehill, iii. 297
VELASCO, Don Louis de, governor of Havanna, iv.	809
——, governor of the town of Barcelona, iv.	165
VENABLES, General, a Cromwellian officer, iii.	420
Vendeans of France, vi. 20, 21, 90-92
Vendée, La; beginning of religious struggle, v. 828, 841-843
——, Peace of, February 1795, vi.	90
VENDÔME, Duke of, a general of Francis I., ii.	349, 356
——, sent to the Scottish regent, ii.	132
——, Louis Joseph, duke of, iv. 68, 136, 170
Veneti, inhabitants of Vannes, in Brittany, i.	25, 102
Venezuela, Spanish revolution in, vii.	50
Venice; carrying-trade of Venetians, &c., ii.	172, 173
Venloo, surrenders to Marlborough, iv.	130
VENNER, a wine-cooper; raises a riot in London, iii. 421, 679
VERE, Alberic, King Stephen's counsel, i.	427, 428
——, Sir Francis, a celebrated English captain, iii.	575
——, Sir Horatio, of Tilbury, iii.	81, 85
VERGNIAUD, a French revolutionist; Portrait of, v. 876-894
Verneuil, Battle of; gained by the English, ii.	56, 57
VERNON, Edward, an English admiral, iv. 404, 426, 427
——, Sir Rich., beheaded on field of Shrewsbury, ii. 15
Verona, Congress of, in 1822, vii.	142-146
VERRIO, Antonio, an eminent Neapolitan painter, iii.	881
Versailles, Views of the Palace of, v. 751, 752, 754

	PAGE
VERTUE, George, his observations on painting, i.	631
——, G., an engraver and antiquary— iii. 500, 577, 802, 851; iv. 709
Verulamium, or St Alban's, i.	33, 43
Vervins, Treaty of, ii.	681
VESPASIAN, a Roman general under Emperor Claudius, i. 40
Veto Act, passed in 1834, vi. 767; vii. 670
VETZEL, General, iv.	134
Vexin, le, a territory between rivers Epte and Oise, i. 388
Viceroyalty of Ireland, discussion on the, vii.	666
VICTOR AMADEUS II., first king of Sardinia, iv.	325
—— IV., anti-pope, i.	446
VICTORIA I., queen of England, vii. 327, 431, 498-752
VIDOMAR, viscount of Limoges, i.	514
Vienna, Congress of, vii.	2
——, View of, vi.	276
VIENNE, John de, lord-admiral of France, i.	701
VIGNOLA, or GIACOMO BAROZZIO, an Italian architect, iii. 570
VIGNOLLES, or the famous partisan La Hire, ii.	49
VILLADARIAS, General; his mission to Gibraltar, iv.	160
VILLAHERMOSA, Duke of, iii.	717
Villains, or Villeins, i. 660, 666
VILLARS, Louis Hector, duke de, iv. 136, 184, 216, 249, 385
Villeins regardant considered real property, vi.	786
VILLÈLE, the French minister; his resignation, vii.	273
Villena, siege of town of, v.	182
VILLENEUVE, admiral of the Toulon fleet, vi. 282-297
VILLEROY, a French general, iv. 53, 68, 150, 170
VILLIERS, Judith; his insanity, iii.	68, 70
——, Lord Francis, slain in a rising for the king, iii. 383
—— Mr; Portrait, vii. 570, 641, 688
Vincennes, View of, vi.	242
VINESAUF, an English historian; quoted, i. 497, 500, 502
Virgil; quoted, i.	63, 84
Virginia Association, iv.	870
Visigoths, the possessions and wars of, i.	142
VISSCHER; his print of the Great Fire of London, iii. 699
VITALIS, Ordericus, a historian of the 12th century, i. 423
VITRY, Captain; murders Concini, iii.	63
Vittoria, Battle of, fought June 21, 1813, vi. 642, 643
VIVIAN, Cardinal, his character of Henry II., i.	479
VLEIT; his print of Charles II. and ambassadors, &c., iii. 494
VOERST, Robert de, an engraver of 17th century, iii. 577
VOLTAIRE, the celebrated French philosopher, v.	838
Volunteers, the Irish, vii.	194
VOLUSENUS, Caius, first explorer of south shore of Britain, i. 27
VON ARTAVELDT, a brewer of Ghent, i.	763, 790
——, Philip, a Flemish general, i.	790
—— PARIS; burnt for denying divinity of Christ, ii. 493
—— SAVIONY, i.	564
VORSTIUS, Conrad, an Armenian, iii.	47, 48
VORTIGERN, the British king, i. 57, 58, 140-142
VORTIMER, King, son of Vortigern, i.	141
VOSTERMANS, Luke, a foreign artist of 17th century, iii. 577
VOWEL, Mr; hanged, iii.	416
VROOM, Henry Cornelius, a Dutch painter, ii.	854
WACHTENDONCK, General; takes town of Caormina, iv. 340
WACHTER, John George, a learned German antiquary, i. 10
WADE, Colonel, iii.	774
——, arrests Swedish ambassador, iv. 318, 486-490
——, Sir William, lieutenant of the Tower, iii.	53
WAGER, Sir Charles, captures a Plate fleet, iv. 202, 369
Wages, rate of, in latter part of 15th century, ii. 903, 904
——, in 16th century, iii. 658, 903
——, in 18th and 19th centuries— v. 575, 581; vi. 811, 815, 931
Wagram, Battle of, fought July 6, 1809, vi. 510, 511
WAKE, W., archbishop of Canterbury, iv. 374, 396; v. 407, 408
Wakefield, Battle of, ii.	96
WAKEFIELD, Gilbert, a scholar and critic, vi.	861
——, Priscilla, death of, in 1832, vii.	443
WAKEMAN, Sir G., physician to the queen, iii. 717, 730
Wakes, the, ii.	897
WALCHER DE LORRAINE, bishop of Durham, i. 384, 385
WALDEGRAVE, James, lord, iv. 546, 548, 567, 568, 793

HISTORY OF ENGLAND.

WALDEGRAVE, Sir Edward; committed to the Tower, ii. 545
WALDEN, Roger, dean of York, ii. . . . 140
Wales, enactment of English laws in, &c., ii. . 425
———, formerly possessed by a different race, i. 22, 216
———, Prince of, birth of the, vii. . . . 586
WALKER, a Presbyterian minister, iv. . . 16, 144
———, Adam, vi. 821
———, Henry, a writer of pamphlets, iii. . 265
———, Robert, an eminent portrait-painter, iii. . 569
———, Sir Hovenden, sent to conquer Canada, iv. 237
WALLACE, Lord, death of, in 1844, vii. . . 731
———, Wm., the Scottish champion, i. 715-719, 724-726
WALLENSTEIN, a celebrated German general, iii. 146, 173, 331
WALLER, Edmund, the poet, iii. . 302, 369, 744, 874
———, Sir Hardress, iii. 671
———, Sir Wm., an eminent military officer, iii. 291, 307, 318
WALLINGFORD, an English historian; quoted, i. . 533
Wallingford House, iii. 137
———, View of the Thames at, i. . 436, 437
WALLIS, Dr J., a learned algebraist and geometrician—
iii. 886 ; iv. 729
WALLOP, Sir Robert, confined to the Tower for life, iii. 685
WALMODEN, Countess of, mistress of George II., iv. 403
WALPOLE, Horace, earl of Orford, iii. . . 607
——— ; Portrait of, v. . . . 504, 535
———, Robert, earl of Orford—
iv. 195, 241, 286, 324, 330, 356, 374, 430, 431, 450, 626
WALSH, a Jesuit, accused of murder, iii. . . 721
———, Sir Richard, sheriff of Worcester, iii. . 28
Walsingham, Chapel of our Lady of, ii. . 145, 289, 290
WALSINGHAM, Sir Francis ; Portrait of, ii. 636, 647, 658, 750
———, Thomas of, a Benedictine, ii. . 208
——————— ; quoted, i. . . 832, 887
WALTER, Hubert, lord-chancellor, i. 502, 511, 515, 557-559
WALTHEOF, earl of Huntingdon, i. . 371, 375, 379-382
WALTON, Colonel, a parliamentarian officer, iii. . 298
———, Isaak, an ingenious and amusing writer, iii. 604, 608
WALWORTH, John, lord-mayor of London, i. . . 786
———, William, a citizen of London, i. . . 783
WANDESFORD, one of the eight managers of the Commons
in impeachment of the Duke of Buckingham, iii. 120
Wanstead House, View of, iv. . . . 700
WARBECK, Perkin, the impostor. See Henry VII., iii. 299
WARBURTON, Dr William, bishop of Gloucester, iv. . 822
WARD, the court-fool, personates Richard II., ii. . 16
———, John, a composer of music of 16th century, iii. 566
———, Mr ; his degradation, vii. . . . 676
———, R. Plumer ; quoted, vii. 103, 112, 120, 124, 130, 132
———, Sir Simon, i. 741
WARDLAW, Henry, bishop of St Andrews, ii. . . 198
Wardships, royal, diminution in the profits of, ii. 165 ; iii. 19
WARENNE, Reginald de, an adherent of William II., i. 396
WARHAM, W., of Canterbury, ii. 819, 320, 323, 334, 360, 380
Wariston, Laird of ; letter to Lord Johnston, iii. 202, 239
WARNER, lieutenant of the Tower, iii. . . 569
———, William, an English poet of 16th century, iii. 600
WARREN, Sir Peter, an English admiral, iv. . 453, 708
Warsaw, the Emperor Nicholas at, vii. . . 545
WARTON, John, fined and pilloried, iii. . . 167
———, Thomas, a poetical and prose writer, v. . 503
WARWICK, Ambrose Dudley, earl of, ii. . 570, 573
———, Ann de Beauchamp, countess of, ii. 105, 111
———, Edward Plantagenet, earl of, ii. 281, 237, 309, 310
———, John Dudley. See Northumberland.
———, R. de B., earl of, ii. 43, 44, 50, 52, 54, 80, 151, 245
———, Richard Nevil, the great earl of, ii. 92, 94-109
———, Robert Rich, earl of, iii. . 365, 367, 383, 423
———, Sir Philip, iii. . 220, 241, 245, 331, 342, 391
———, Thomas de Beauchamp, earl of, i. . 795
Warwick Castle, Guy's Tower ; View of, i. . . 734
WASHINGTON, Colonel H., governor of Worcester, iii. 355
——————— ; prisoner at battle of Eutaw, iv. 363
———, George, first president of United States—
v. 82, 122, 125, 126 ; vi. 624, 625
Wassail-bowl, the, presented by Rowena to Vortigern, i. 141
Watches, English, vi. 830

Watches, exportation of parts of, prohibited, &c., iv. 684
Watchmen, iv. 765
Water-colouring, vi. 896-898
Waterloo, Battle of, fought June 18, 1815, vi. 706-708
——— Bridge, vi. 813, 823
———, View of, vii. 315
WATSON and CLARKE, secular priests, executed, iii. 8, 9, 13
———, Bishop of Llandaff ; Portrait of, vi. . 765
———, Dr, of the Deaf and Dumb Institution, Kent
Road, London, death of, in 1829, vii. . 325
WATT, James, great improver of the steam-engine—
v. 475 ; vi. 818, 825, 828, 829
———, statue of, in Westminster Abbey, vii. 214
———, Robert, found guilty of high treason, vi. . 69, 70
WATTS, a plumber of Bristol, vi. . . . 837
Waverley novels, sale of the copyrights of the, vii. . 305
WAYNE, Brigadier-general, an American officer, v. 285
Wearmouth, Monastery of, instituted by Bishop Bene-
dict, i. 310
Wenwell, Abbey of, i. 188, 191
Weather and potato-rot in 1845, vii. . 722, 723
WEBSTER, John, a dramatic poet of 17th century, iii. 587
WEDDELL, James, death of, in 1835, vii. . . 593
Wedding, description of a, in 16th century, ii. . 887, 888
WEDGWOOD ; improvements in pottery, v. 485, 486 ; vi. 839
WEEKES, T., organist of Winchester College, iii. . 566
Weights and measures, act establishing uniformity of, vii. 178
WELDON, Colonel, a parliamentarian officer, iii. . 331
WELLESLEY, Marquis of, vi. 218-226, 299-305, 321, 400,
483, 484, 596 ; vii. 137, 138, 731
Wellington administration, vii. 241-271, 285-294, 327-337
WELLINGTON, Arthur Wellesley, duke of—
vi. 218-224, 299-305, 321, 385-388, 400, 401, 432,
433, 436, 440, 441, 470, 471, 479-487, 539-549,
576, 579, 582-586, 601-615, 641-657, 676-715 ;
vii. 1-10, 48, 93, 141-144, 226, 228, 236, 241-
271, 286-294, 327-420, 447, 485, 609, &c.
WELSH, John, a Presbyterian minister, iii. 64, 448, 462
Welsh and Scotch judicature, vii. . . . 290
———, or Cymry, i. . 19, 22, 23, 194, 195, 399, 451
WENLOCK, Lord ; slain at battle of Tewkesbury, ii. 109
WENTWORTH, Lady H. ; mistress of Duke of Monmouth, iii. 768
———, Paul, M.P., ii. 590
———, Sir G., brother of Earl of Strafford, iii. 245
———, Sir John, a friend of Earl of Somerset, iii. 50
WESLEY, Charles, death of, in 1834, vii. . . 408
———, Rev. J., founder of the Methodists, iv. 589, 622-625
———, Samuel, death of, vii. . . . 598
Wessex, kingdom of, i. . 142, 150, 152, 154, 157, 158, 160
WEST, a Rye-house conspirator, iii. . . . 741
———, Benjamin, a celebrated painter, . iii. 572 ; v. 522
———, president of the Royal Academy, death
of, in 1820, vii. 220
WEST, dean of Windsor ; his mission to James IV., ii. 322
———, Rear-admiral, iv. 558
West India Islands, map, &c., vii. . . 169-172
——— Indies, vi. 798, 799, 801
———, abolition of slavery in the, vii. . 383-387
WESTERN, Mr ; resolutions on agricultural distress, vii. 18-24
Westminster Abbey, bishopric of, suppressed, ii. . 493
———————— ; illustration of—
i. 202, 203, 314, 316, 361 ; iii. 766
———— on fire, in 1830, vii. . . 300
———— Bridge, first stone laid in 1730, iv. 701
———— election of 1834, vii. . . . 414
WESTMINSTER, Marquis of ; his death, vii. . . 740
———————, Matthew of, i. 592
WESTMORELAND, Charles Nevil, earl of, ii. . 628-630
———————, John Fane, earl of, v. . . 773
———————, Ralph Nevil, earl of, ii. . 17
WESTON, Francis ; beheaded, ii. . . 391, 392, 394
———, poisons Sir T. Overbury ; hanged, iii. . 58, 59
———, Sir R. ; his account of turnip cultivation, iii. 557
WETHERELL, Sir Charles ; his unpopularity, vii. . 354
WEYMOUTH, Thomas Thynne, viscount, . iv. 860 ; v. 3
Whale-fishery, English begin the, in reign of Elizabeth, ii. 702

GENERAL INDEX. 147

	PAGE
Whale-fishery, the, vi.	800
WHALLEY, Colonel, a parliamentarian officer, iii.	375, 432
WHARNCLIFFE, Lord, vii.	608-727
WHARTON, Philip, duke of, iv.	355, 378, 379
———, Lord, iii.	292
———, Thomas, marquis of, iv.	21, 167, 202, 203, 315
Wheat, average price of, in 17th century, iii.	657
———, price of, vi.	810, 815
———, rare use of, in 18th century, iv.	788
WHEELER, Admiral, drowned at Straits of Gibraltar, iv.	43
WHETHAMSTEDE, John de; his *Chronicon*, &c., ii.	208
Whig administration of Ireland; its effects, vii.	512
——— ministry of 1839, vii.	562
———, origin of the term,	iii. 701; iv. 647
Whigs support the government of Canning, vii.	232
———, Tories, and Radicals, vii.	447
WHITAKER, his derivation of Britannia, or Britain, i.	11, 20
WHITBREAD, Mr ; his plan of poor-law reform, &c., vii.	9, 44, 46
———; his three resolutions, v.	848
WHITE, John, and others, emigrate to Virginia, ii.	792
———, joins a conspiracy to betray the Parliament, iii.	302
———, Mr, one of the Assembly of Divines, iii.	309
———, Nicholas, master of the rolls in Ireland, ii.	618
———, William, constable of Aylesbury, iv.	143
Whiteboys of Ireland, vii.	137
———, illustration, iv.	872
WHITEFIELD, founder of Calvinistic Methodists, iv.	589, 622
Whitehall, View of, iv.	792
———, with a royal aquatic procession; illustration, iii.	759
Whitehaven, iii.	656
WHITEHEAD, Paul, a minor English poet, iv.	536
WHITELOCK, Bulstrode, a statesman and lawyer—	
iii. 120, 142, 320, 327, 429*, 665	
WHITELOCKE, Gen.; expedition to Buenos Ayres, vi.	365-369
WHITFORD, bishop of Dunblane, iii.	478
WHITGIFT, John, an English prelate,	ii. 745; iii. 17, 466
WHITING, Richard, abbot of Glastonbury, ii.	411, 412
WHITTAKER, Captain, iv.	160
WHITWORTH, C., lord, ambassador at Paris, vi.	199, 200, 207-213
WHITTINGTON, R., lord-mayor; his almshouses, &c., ii.	176
———, Sir William, father of Richard, ii.	176
WIDDERINGTON, Sir Thomas, iii.	203
WIDDRINGTON, William, lord, iv.	293
Wight, Isle of, i.	42, 153, 193
WIGHTMAN, Edward, convicted of heresy; burnt, iii.	48
———, General, gains battle of Glenshiel, iv.	334, 497
WILBERFORCE, v.	338, 393, 598, 647, 690, 770, 849, 899
———, William, vi.	33, 229-231, 314, 315, 355-357
———, the philanthropist, vii.	ii. 18, 65, 94, 98, 403
WILD, Serjeant; his impeachments against bishops, iii.	248, 325
WILDMAN, Major, a Rye-house plot conspirator, iii.	373, 419, 740
WILFRID, Bishop, glazes windows of York Cathedral, i.	310
WILKES, John, iv.	819-824, 830, 842, 854, 855, 858-862
WILKIE, Sir David, an eminent painter; Portrait of, vi.	899
———, death of, vii.	599
WILKINS; his collection of Saxon laws, i.	256
———, Sir Charles, death of, in 1836, vii.	600
———, the architect, death of, vii.	598
———, William, an eminent architect, vi.	892, 893
WILKINSON, Mr, chaplain to the Prince of Wales, iii.	51
WILLES, Lord Chief-justice, iv.	537
WILLIAM, a Norman, bishop of London, i.	189, 193
——— I., the Conqueror—	
i. 191, 196, 197, 201, 205-215, 358-391, 566	
——— I., king of Scotland—	
i. 452, 453, 468, 470, 471, 485, 543-546	
——— II., surnamed Rufus, i.	383, 389, 392-404
——— III., king of England—	
iii. 710, 715, 717, 760, 796, 798, 801; iv. 2-124, 588, 678	
WILLIAM IV., king of England; Portrait, vii.	227, 326-528
———, Prince, son of Henry I., i.	412-416
———, surnamed Longsword, i.	480, 481
———, the Good, king of Sicily, history of, i.	489
WILLIAMS, a papist, convicted of high treason, iii.	57
———, Helen Maria, death of, in 1827, vii.	321
———, J., an English divine, iii.	71, 85, 97, 101, 164, 261, 356

	PAGE
WILLIAMS, Mr; his motion on Chancery reform, vii.	205
———, Rev. Roger, iii.	806
———, Sir Charles Hanbury, iv.	541
WILLIAMSON, clerk of the crown, iii.	134
———, Sir Joseph, iv.	75, 104
WILLIS, Mr, schoolmaster to Lord-keeper Guilford, iii.	521
WILLOUGHBY DE BROKE, a general of Henry VII., ii.	295
———, Lord, of Parham, iii.	277, 369, 540, 549
———, William, first baron of Parham, ii.	456
WILLS, General, a distinguished officer, iv.	296
WILLUGHBY, Francis, a celebrated naturalist, iv.	736
WILMINGTON, Spencer Compton, earl of, iv.	374, 383, 432, 441
WILMOT, Commissary; conduct at battle of Newburn, iii.	221
———, Mr R., colonial secretary, vii.	190, 191
———, Robert, a dramatic writer of 16th century, iii.	584
WILSON, a noted smuggler; his execution, iv.	396
———, Alexander, provost of Edinburgh, iv.	398
———, Dr, chaplain to bishop of London, iii.	121
———, Professor; Portrait, vii.	741
———, Richard, a landscape painter, v.	523, 524
———, Sir Robert, vi.	480, 482, 725, 726
———, Sir Thomas; his polite style of writing, iii.	579, 831
WILTON, an eminent sculptor of the 18th century, v.	526
Wilton, Battle of, fought against the Danes, i.	157
WILTSHIRE, James Butler, earl of; beheaded, ii.	99
———, Sir T. B., earl of, ii.	363, 364, 368, 374, 376, 380
WIMBLEDON, Edward Cecil, Viscount, iii.	49, 113, 114
WIMUND, a piratical adventurer, i.	541, 542
WINCHELSEA, Daniel Finch, earl of, iv.	101, 127, 145, 358
WINCHESTER, William Paulet, marquis of, ii.	402
Winchester, View of the City of, i.	363
WINCHILSEA, Lord; his duel with Duke of Wellington, vii.	268
WINDEBANE, Colonel; he is shot, iii.	332
———, Sir Francis, iii.	160, 167, 169, 209
WINDHAM, Mr, M.P., iii.	133
———, Wm; his Portrait, vi.	174-178, 185, 307, 313, 759
Windsor Castle; captivity of James I., &c., ii.	19, 50, 52
———, preservation and improvement of, vii.	302
———, View of, vii.	1
———, Palace of; illustration, iii.	731
———, Terrace reopened, vii.	216
Winnowing-machine, introduced from Holland, iv.	680
WINSOR, a German, illuminates Pall Mall with gas, vi.	833
WINSTANLEY; erects Eddystone Light-house, iv.	664
WINSTON, Dr, iii.	287
WINTER, Robert; joins Gunpowder Plot, iii.	23, 29, 30
———, Thomas; executed, iii.	21, 24-30
WINTON, Lord, condemned for high treason, iv.	309
WINTZENRODE, Captain, iv.	482
WINWOOD, Sir R., an able statesman, iii.	47, 49, 56, 58, 73, 74
Wire-mill, the first, erected by a Dutchman at Sheen, iii.	869
WIRTEMBURG, Duke of, a suitor of Queen Elizabeth, ii.	571
WISE, Michael, an English musical composer, iii.	884
WISEMAN, Sir Richard, killed in a riot, iii.	261
WISHART, Dr, principal of University of Edinburgh, iv.	464
———, George, the Scottish martyr, ii.	445, 446
WISHEART, R., bishop of Glasgow, i.	715, 716, 728, 729, 738
WITCH OF RYE, Margery Jourdayn; burnt, ii.	83
Witchcraft, belief in, iii.	638
———, its influence, ii.	66, 68, 114, 120, 136
———, persecution of, in 18th century, v.	557
Witenagemot, manner of holding a, &c., i.	251-253, 360
WITHER, George, a Puritan poet, iii.	605
WITHERINGS, Thomas, post-office farmed out to, iii.	544
WITLAF, king of Mercia; charter to Abbey of Croyland, i.	320
Wives, Lord Brougham on the position of, vii.	574-576
Woad, *Isatis tinctoria*, used in staining skin, &c., i.	104
Wodiu, of the Scandinavians. See Odin, i.	138
WOLCOT, John, a humorist, poet, and satirist, vi.	856
WOLFE, Lieutenant-general James, iv.	579-582
WOLLASTON, Dr, death of, in 1828, vii.	321, 323, 324
———, Sir John, alderman of London, iii.	290
Wollaton, Nottinghamshire, ii.	845
WOLSELEY, Sir Charles, arrest of, vii.	105, 106, 117
WOLSEY, Thos., chief favourite of Henry VIII., ii.	323, 327, 332-336, 338, 345-348, 354-358, 360-376, 696, 705-709

	PAGE
Wolves' heads, a tribute paid by Welsh kings to Edgar, i.	173
Wood, Anthony, an eminent English antiquary, ii.	197
———; his plan of Oxford, iii.	314, 520
———, John, secretary to the earl of Murray, ii.	612, 624
———, Sir Andrew, a brave seaman of James IV., ii.	303, 304
———, Sir John; he is bribed by Lady Howard, iii.	53
———, W.; his patent for farthings and half-pence, iv.	364
Wood, Asp-wood for arrows, pattens, &c., ii.	191
Wood-engraving, vi.	880, 881
———engraving. See List prefixed to each volume.	
Woodes, Nathaniel, minister of Norwich, iii.	581
Woodhouse, a young man; hanged, ii.	639
Woodstock, presented to the Duke of Marlborough, iv.	161
———, ruins of the Royal Manor-house of, i.	481, 482
Woodville, Sir Edward, an adherent of Francis II., ii.	294
———, Sir John; he and his father beheaded, ii.	104
———, Sir Richard; beheaded, ii.	80, 101–104
Woodward, Dr, iv.	611
Wool, high price of, in reign of James I., iii.	658
Woollen cloths, manufacture of, &c.—	
i. 125, 601, 602; ii. 192, 193, 802, 807; iii. 558;	
iv. 663; v. 494, 495; vi. 844, 845; vii. 177	
Worcester, Edward Somerset, earl of, iii.	19, 20
———, marquis of, iii. 345,346; iv.726	
———, Henry Somerset, marquis of, iii.	138, 355
———, Thomas Percy, earl of; beheaded, ii.	13, 15
———, T. T., earl of; beheaded, ii. 102, 107, 206, 249	
———, William of, a Latin chronicler, ii.	208
Worcester, Battle of, iii.	405
———, Welsh resisted by Henry IV. here, ii.	18
Worcestershire, jurisdiction of Wales over, iii.	43
Worde, Wynkyn de, an early printer, iii.	630
Wordsworth, an eminent poet, vi. 858, 883–885; vii. 740	
Workhouses, iv.	787
Worms, Diet of; called to suppress Luther's doctrines, ii.	707
———, Treaty of, iv.	441
Worsley, entrance to the tunnel at, v.	473
Worsteds, manufacture of, ii.	193, 808, 809
Wotton, Dr Nicolas, ii.	454
———, Sir Edward, a guardian of Edward VI., ii.	454
Wratislaus, Count, iv.	96, 107, 151
Wren, Dr Matthew, an eminent prelate, iii. 121, 163, 230, 504	
———, Sir Christopher, an architect, iii. 522; iv. 685–695	
Wright, Christopher, joins the Gunpowder Plot, iii.	22, 28
———, John, a celebrated swordsman, iii.	21, 28
———, John, death of, vii.	737
———, Michael, a talented painter, iii.	882
———, Sir Nathan, lord-keeper, iv.	90, 145
———, Sir Robert, Chief-justice, iii.	786, 791
Wriothesley, Thomas, ii. 399, 442, 447, 448, 453–457, 492	
Wroth, Sir Thomas, iii.	380
Wulfnoth, Earl, flies with 20 of Ethelred's ships, &c., i.	179
Wulfreda, a nun, carried off by King Edgar, i.	173
Wulfstan, an ancient navigator, i.	167
———, or Lupus; his Homilies, i.	301
Wulnoth, son of Godwin, i.	188, 191, 389, 392
Wulstan, bishop of Winchester, i.	548, 549
Württemberg, Queen of; her death, vii.	312
Wyat, Sir Henry, privy-councillor, ii.	320
Wyatt, James, an eminent architect, vi. 868–870, 892, 895	
———, Sir T.; confined in Tower; executed, ii. 512–514, 518	
Wyatville, Sir Jeffry, death of, in 1840, vii.	598
Wyburd, Lieutenant, fate of, vii.	630
Wycliffe, J., a famous divine, i.	780, 807, 808
Wycliffe, John; his portrait, &c., ii.	71, 140–147, 216
Wyndham, Sir William, iv.	287, 292, 380, 388, 415
Wynton, Andrew, a Scottish author of 14th century, i.	351
Wynyard, in Durham, the seat of the Marquis of Londonderry, fire at, vii.	590
Wyoming, Vale of, from an original drawing, v.	262
Ximenes, Cardinal, an eminent Spanish minister, ii.	317
Yarmouth, iii.	655
Yarranton, Andrew, introduces art of tinning plate-iron from Germany, iii.	869
Yelverton, Sir H., an eminent lawyer, iii. 40, 55, 68, 82	
———, Sir William, a judge of King's Bench, ii.	145
Yeomans, Robert and William; hanged, iii.	302
Yeomen of the Guard instituted, ii.	283
Yniosa, a Spanish ambassador, iii.	103, 105
Yong, Sir Richard, saves the life of King James, iii.	88
Yonge, Sir William, secretary at war, iv.	437, 535
York, Duchess of, widow of Duke Richard, ii.	104
———, Duke of, vii.	202, 203, 225–227
———, Edward Augustus, duke of, iv.	795
———, Plantagenet, duke of, ii.	5, 7, 33
———, Frederick, duke of, v.	849
———, ; Portrait of— vi. 5, 6, 43, 141, 462–467, 571	
———, R. Plantagenet, duke of— ii. 79, 80, 84, 87, 89–96, 118, 121, 124, 125	
———, Sir Philip, attorney-general, iv.	386
York, House of; derivation of its title to the crown, ii. 6, 357	
———, metropolitan see and city of, i. 208, 310, 368, 369, 662	
———, Minster, Jonathan Martin sets fire to the, vii.	299
———, second fire of the, vii.	590
———, Place, a stately palace of Wolsey, ii.	372
———, Town, View of, v.	356
Yorke, Honourable Charles, iv.	877
———, Sir J., English ambassador at the Hague, v.	334
Yorkshire, rise of Yeomen in, ii.	104, 105, 397–401
Young, Arthur, vi.	819, 821, 824
———, secretary to the Board of Agriculture, death of, in 1820, vii.	218
Young, Dr, author of the *Night Thoughts*, iv.	749
———, dean of Winchester, iii.	472
———, Thomas, the philosopher, death of, vii.	322
Young England party, vii.	634
———, Germany, or Young Literature, vii.	547
Zaragoza, View of, vi.	425
Zealand, ceded to Charles I. 1630, iii.	147
Zenta, Battle of, fought 1697, iv.	68
Zillerthal Protestants; their persecution, vii.	548
Zinc, manufacture of, vi.	837
Zinzendorff, Count; Portrait of, v.	421, 422
Zinzerling, Count, iv.	171
Zisca, the celebrated commander of the Hussites, ii.	150
Zoll Verein, or Commercial League of Germany, vii.	543
Zoological Gardens, opening of the London, vii.	302
Zouch, John, Lord, fought for Richard III., ii.	284
———, Sir Edward; proclaims King Charles I., iii. 64, 108	
Zouche, Lord, assists in dispersing a popular assembly, iii.	36
Zucchero, an eminent Italian artist, ii.	549, 750
Zullichau, Battle of, fought 1759, iv.	583
Zumjungen, General, besieges Messina, iv.	340
Zuniga, commendator of Requesens, ii.	649

Edinburgh:
Printed by W. & R. Chambers.

www.ingramcontent.com/pod-product-compliance
Lightning Source LLC
Chambersburg PA
CBHW030307170426
43202CB00009B/903